ANGLO-SOVIET RELATIONS, 1917-1921

Volume III

The Anglo-Soviet Accord

PUBLISHED FOR THE CENTER OF INTERNATIONAL STUDIES

PRINCETON UNIVERSITY

A LIST OF OTHER CENTER PUBLICATIONS

APPEARS AT THE BACK OF THIS BOOK

ANGLO-SOVIET
RELATIONS, 1917-1921

The
Anglo-Soviet
Accord

BY RICHARD H. ULLMAN

PRINCETON, NEW JERSEY
PRINCETON UNIVERSITY PRESS
1972

To

Y.C.U.

who came in at the beginning

ANGLO-SOVIET
RELATIONS, 1917-1921

VOLUME I

Intervention and the War

VOLUME II

Britain and the Russian Civil War
November 1918-February 1920

VOLUME III

The Anglo-Soviet Accord

PREFACE

THE third and final volume of this study of British policy making during the initial years of Anglo-Soviet relations is an account of how the two governments went about coming to terms with each other—a process which culminated in their signature on 16 March 1921 of a trade agreement and in the *de facto* recognition by Great Britain of the Bolshevik regime in Moscow. This process was vastly complicated by the Polish offensive against Russia in the spring of 1920 and by the Soviet counteroffensive, which nearly resulted in the sovietization of Poland; it was complicated still further by the recrudescence of the old Anglo-Russian rivalry in the East, a competition made even more venomous by the ideological gulf which now divided the two governments.

Even were it not for these other issues, however, the process of reaching a *modus vivendi* would have been difficult enough. The Soviet regime, after all, was very unlike other existing political systems. Its leaders had come to power in part by virtue of their hostility to those other systems. Their hostility was directed in particular at the rulers of the United Kingdom and the British Empire who themselves symbolized the capitalist social and economic structure which the Bolsheviks sought to overturn. Needless to say, that hostility was amply returned. Within the British government (as within the Soviet government) there were important figures who firmly believed that no rapprochement of any sort was possible between two such disparate systems, and who, indeed, developed a political stake in the continuation of open conflict between them. Thus the international competition *between* the two societies became—as such competitions almost always do—an element in the competition for power and influence *within* each of the rival political structures.

Like the two preceding volumes of this study, the pages which follow focus primarily on the politics of policy making within the British government and on the relationship to this political process of the perceptions and actions of British politicians, civil servants, and military and naval officers, both in London and in the field. Once again, I have attempted to treat the course of British domestic politics and the handling of other contemporaneous problems of foreign policy only in so far as such treatment is necessary to make

vii

sense of the politics of policy toward Russia. To a greater extent than with either *Intervention and the War* or *Britain and the Russian Civil War*, however, it has been necessary to treat such matters here. Both preceding volumes were concerned primarily with the politics of military policy during and in the immediate aftermath of the First World War. This was predominantly a "closed" politics, accessible for the most part only to those whose working roles caused them to be directly involved, and also a "narrow" politics, relatively unrelated to other problems of foreign (as distinguished from military) policy. By contrast, the present volume treats a period when the British Empire was no longer engaged in a major war, when military intervention in the Russian Civil War was almost completely finished, and when the great issue of policy toward Russia, was, indeed, the whole nature of the future relationship between the two societies.

This point deserves elaboration, for it also explains why I have presumed to impose on an already overburdened readership three volumes on a subject as seemingly circumscribed as the making of British policy towards Russia during only three and one-half years. They are—in my conception, at least—three quite separate books; although they are linked chronologically and by the common topic of British policy toward Russia, each is intended to stand alone as a study of the making of foreign and military policy in a quite distinct "policy environment."

Intervention and the War dealt with strategy making during the last terrible year of the First World War, from the Bolshevik seizure of power on 7 November 1917 until the armistice of 11 November 1918. The coming to power of Lenin and his colleagues in Russia would have seized the attention of policy makers in the West almost as little as had the overthrow of Tsardom seven months earlier except for the fact that the Bolsheviks immediately set about removing Russia from the war by making peace with Germany— something the Provisional Government never could bring itself to do. Some thirty-five divisions newly transferred from the now quiet Eastern Front augmented the German forces which, in March 1918, launched the great offensive which nearly won them Paris and the war. The spearhead of the German attack was directed at the British sector; during the first week the Fifth Army suffered 120,-000 casualties, and the attrition continued at a high rate. The problem presented by Russia during this period—particularly for the British government—was how to reconstitute some countervailing weight against Germany in the East. Thus formulated, the problem was predominantly one for military specialists who (presumably) could best weigh the military benefits of various solutions against the costs of the military resources necessary to bring them about. The solution elected in London—recruitment to the Allied cause of "loyal" Russians and the transportation across Siberia to join with them of massive Japanese forces which otherwise would not have seen service against Germany—was so attractive precisely because it was seemingly so low in incremental cost. This factor made hard-pressed military planners largely oblivious to the fact that the Japanese never had any intention of allowing their forces to be so used, and to the likelihood that by training and arming "loyal" Russians to fight the Germans the Western Allies would actually be creating the conditions for a bloody and costly civil war.

If *Intervention and the War* explored the origins of Allied intervention (which was preponderantly British intervention) in Russia as an aspect of the grand strategy of the First World War, *Britain and the Russian Civil War* examined the processes by which, after the armistice of 11 November 1918, that intervention was transformed into a campaign whose avowed aim was to unseat the Bolshevik regime in Moscow, and by which during 1919 the British commitment to the anti-Bolshevik side was first enlarged and then liquidated as the perceived costs of intervention, and still more the predictable costs of success, became unpalatably large. This again was a situation where military expertise was thought to be particularly applicable. Yet at the same time, because what seemed at stake was the political future of Russia and because, with no major war simultaneously in progress, the costs of intervention were more explicitly perceived throughout British society, the issue was one that was much more likely to involve the nonmilitary as well as the military departments of the bureaucracy and also to become a part of "open" parliamentary politics. Thus *Britain and the Russian Civil War* was a study of the processes by which the government of a Great Power extricated itself from a civil war in which it was the leading foreign participant, after it had become clear that the war could not be "won" except at what was felt to be a wholly unacceptable price.

Preface

The present volume, dealing with the period commencing in February 1920, when the civil war in Russia was all but over and when there was no longer any doubt that the Bolsheviks would for the foreseeable future retain control of most, if not all, of the territory of the former Russian Empire, is therefore a study of one aspect of peacetime policy making and of the adjustment of British politicians and policy-making officials to the markedly changed conditions of the postwar world. Though its focus is on the process of coming to terms with the new regime in Russia, its context is that of British foreign policy in general. And more than was the case with either of the preceding volumes, the processes of policy making it describes were a part of the "open" politics of British society as a whole.

Something of the same may be said for Soviet policy toward Great Britain during the same period. Before 1920 the Bolshevik regime was fighting for its very existence. Foreign policy was overwhelmingly dictated by the military exigencies of the Civil War. By 1920, however, when the regime's survival was no longer in doubt, alternative policies for dealing with the external world were to a much greater extent than before an issue for discussion and debate within a fairly wide circle of the Soviet leadership. Some of this debate is described in the following pages. Because of the utilization here for the first time of a uniquely important source—the telegraphic traffic between Moscow and the Soviet mission which sat in London for much of 1920—it has often been possible to relate this debate quite directly to the actual conduct of Soviet diplomacy towards Great Britain. But lest a reader should be led to expect more than he will find here, two cautionary notes are in order: First, even given the availability of this telegraphic traffic, the materials available for the elucidation of the politics of policy making within the Soviet government are still minuscule compared to the great wealth of those at the disposal of the student of British policy. And second, the primary concern of this volume, like that of both of its predecessors, is with the politics of policy making within the *British* government.

❖

The appearance of this third volume has been delayed by a year spent in Washington as a member of the Staff of the National Security Council and of the Policy Planning Staff in the Office of the Assistant Secretary of Defense for International Security Affairs, followed by three years of fairly taxing academic administration. I have no hesitation in saying that the former experience, at any rate, was contributive of more insights into the politics of policy making, and the political processes of large organizations in general, than any academic work I have undertaken. In a number of intangible ways it has made this a better book than it otherwise would have been.

It is once again my pleasure to acknowledge my indebtedness to a number of institutions and individuals for many different sorts of assistance. The Center of International Studies, the Woodrow Wilson School of Public Affairs, and the University Research Fund —all of Princeton University—helped make possible several trips to the United Kingdom to consult archival materials, and the secretarial staff of the Center of International Studies cheerfully typed the bulk of the manuscript. The Washington Center of Foreign Policy Research of the Johns Hopkins University provided a home for the last stages of writing. Laurence H. Scott and my wife, Yoma Crosfield Ullman, gave me invaluable help with Russian translation; my wife also took on the onerous task of reading the proofs. A.J.P. Taylor, the Director of the Beaverbrook Library and a historian of twentieth-century British and European politics to whom the rest of us will ever be in debt, considerably facilitated my work in the Lloyd George Papers and, in addition, made available to me the typescript of Frances Stevenson's diaries. Captain Stephen Roskill, of Churchill College, Cambridge, similarly facilitated my access to the Hankey Papers and allowed me to use a proof copy of the second volume of his biography of Hankey. Piotr S. Wandycz, of Yale University, brought his unrivaled knowledge of the early years of Soviet-Polish diplomacy to the criticism of an early draft of the book; other parts of that version were read by Robert I. Rotberg of M.I.T., and Stephen Arbogast of the Woodrow Wilson School and Leslie H. Gelb of the Brookings Institution carefully read and commented upon the final version. To all of them I am most grateful.

Crown-copyright material in the Public Records Office, London, is published here by permission of the Controller of Her Majesty's Stationery Office.[1] Material from the Curzon Papers is published

---

[1] In citing materials from the Public Record Office I have used the standard Record Office notation system to indicate the department of origin: Cab. (Cabinet

here by permission of Viscount Scarsdale, who kindly allowed me to use them at Kedleston before their shipment to the India Office Library, where they are now housed. Similarly, the late Viscount Davidson of Little Gaddesden allowed me to use and quote from his papers before their deposit in the Beaverbrook Library. Mariott, Lady Ironside, allowed me to use and to quote from the unpublished diaries of her late husband, Field Marshal Lord Ironside, and Colonel R. Macleod gave me valuable assistance in so doing. Similarly, I wish to express my gratitude to Major Cyril J. Wilson, who allowed me to use and to quote from the unpublished diaries of his late uncle, Field Marshal Sir Henry Wilson.

I should also like to express my indebtedness to the following:

the First Beaverbrook Foundation, for permission to use and to quote from the Lloyd George and Bonar Law Papers in the Beaverbrook Library;

the Library of the University of Birmingham for permission to use and to quote from the Austen Chamberlain Papers;

the President and Fellows of Harvard College for permission to use and to quote from the Trotsky Archive and the papers of J. Pierrepont Moffat;

Baron Hankey, for permission to use and to quote from the papers and diaries of his father;

and the Librarian of Trinity College, Cambridge, for permission to use the papers of Edwin S. Montagu.[2]

Washington, D.C.   R.H.U.
November 1971

---

and Cabinet Office), F.O. (Foreign Office), and W.O. (War Office). Cabinet papers, of course, include those from all departments, which the Cabinet Office circulated (either of its own volition or at ministerial request) to members of the Cabinet. Because of the thoroughness with which the Cabinet Office went about the task of procuring and circulating departmental papers, I have not felt it necessary for the purposes of this study to make use of the files of additional departments, such as the Home Office, India Office, and Admiralty. I did attempt to locate those portions of the Home Office and Admiralty files pertaining to the intelligence activities described in Chapter VII; they were, however, untraceable, and perhaps no longer exist.

[2] The only important private collection not utilized in writing this book is that of the papers of Sir Winston S. Churchill, which remained unaccessible for general scholarly use at the time of going to press. In my view this is a loss, but not a serious one: letters *from* Churchill abound in the other collections here cited, while the authors of letters *to* Churchill often kept copies.

CONTENTS

MAPS AND ILLUSTRATIONS

Note: For photographs of Field Marshal Sir Henry Wilson, G. V.
Chicherin, and Maxim Litvinov, see Volume I. For photographs
of Major General Sir Edmund Ironside, see Volume II.

PART ONE

Coming to Terms

CHAPTER I

POLAND AND TRADE

We have failed to restore Russia to sanity by force. I believe we can save her by trade.

—David Lloyd George, 10 February 1920

In February 1920 the Great War—the "war to end war"—had been over for fifteen months. Amid great division and considerable acrimony the Allied and Associated Powers had agreed among themselves on terms of peace and then had imposed them on the defeated Germans. Almost from the outset these terms proved unenforceable. Even had the United States not withdrawn from the concert of victorious Powers and even had the war not so gravely weakened Britain and France, the principal upholders of the structure of peace, that structure—designed as it was to keep Germany in a state of military and economic inferiority to France—would have been precarious. Given the defection of the United States and the physical and psychological damage caused by the war to Britain and France, the design was hopelessly flawed.

For Britain even more than for France the fruits of victory were to prove illusory. The French sought from the peace settlement security against Germany, first and foremost. They did not get it. But they had lived with insecurity throughout the period following the unification of Germany in the mid-nineteenth century; to many Frenchmen it had become a natural, almost inevitable, condition. By contrast, the British sought from the settlement not security—not since Napoleon's day had they known insecurity—but a return to the "normal" condition of the prewar world, when the British home islands and the far-flung territories which constituted the British Empire were the most important factor in international politics, enjoying a nearly unrivaled preeminence and prestige.

The war had undermined this position, bringing changes which, while not clearly perceived, were nonetheless drastic. From an international creditor the United Kingdom became a debtor, the result of investments liquidated and foreign loans subscribed, mostly in the United States, in order to finance the war. Countries—British colonies included—which had previously been principal markets for British manufactures were forced during the war to turn to other sources of supply which then became permanent, or to develop competing industries of their own. As if this were not enough, world trade itself was hobbled by "the economic consequences of the Peace"—the pursuit of chimerical reparations from Germany and the increasing division of what had once been a world economy into competing economic blocs.

More profound in their impact upon the British Empire even than these economic effects were the political and social consequences of the war. Wartime demands for manpower and resources, abetted by the rhetoric with which a war fought to protect specific interests was converted into a universalistic crusade, accentuated working-class militancy at home and vastly accelerated the growth of nationalism and of movements for national independence among the peoples of the Empire. The peace had in fact added to the expanse of territory over which flew the Union Jack: under mandate from the League of Nations Great Britain had acquired a major share of Germany's African colonies and a protectorate over Palestine and Iraq in the Middle East. This expansion of responsibility occurred at just the moment when the task of keeping order and maintaining British rule among non-British peoples was becoming much more difficult. And it occurred at a time of explosive and costly violence closer to home, in Ireland. Thus one of the recurring *motifs* of this volume will be the warning from those who had direct charge of Britain's military resources that those resources were being dangerously overextended, a complaint that was to continue almost unabated until the decision, half a century later, to withdraw nearly all British forces from east of the Suez Canal.

If overextension will be a recurring *motif*, a central underlying theme will be that of adjustment—the adjustment of British politicians, civil servants, and military and naval officers to the changed circumstances of the postwar world and to the altered international power relationships to which those circumstances gave rise; adjustment to the accentuated forces of nationalism among the non-British peoples of the Empire and in countries like Persia, Afghan-

istan, and Egypt where Britain had previously had a predominant
influence, if not outright control; adjustment to a true mass politics
at home, the product both of a now virtually universal suffrage and
of the accretion of power given to the Labour movement by wartime demands on manpower; adjustment to a climate of opinion,
therefore, which subjected the overseas deployment of military
forces to a closer scrutiny and to greater popular constraints than,
with rare exceptions, had previously been the case.

No change was more profound in its impact both upon the international environment with which those responsible for foreign relations had to deal, or in its effect upon domestic politics—in all of
the Allied countries, of course, not only Great Britain—than the
coming to power in Russia of a movement doctrinally committed
to the overthrow of existing political arrangements in all other
countries, but particularly in the Great Powers and their overseas
territorial possessions. Britain, as the fountain and bastion of capitalism, and the British Empire, as one of capitalism's chief fruits,
occupied a special place in Bolshevik demonology. This attitude
was more than reciprocated by those whose job it was to administer
the Empire: no Power had expended more treasure or more men
in an effort to overthrow the Soviet government than had Great
Britain.

By February 1920, however, foreign intervention in the Russian
civil war was finished. If peace, of a sort, had come to most of the
lands over which the Great War had been fought following the
armistice of 11 November 1918, by February 1920 it had come to
most of the territory of the former Russian Empire. On 7 February
Admiral Aleksandr V. Kolchak, the so-called Supreme Ruler of All
Russia, whose forces—heavily supplied from abroad, mostly from
Great Britain—had less than a year before extended their sway all
the way across Siberia into European Russia, met death before a
Bolshevik firing squad. A fortnight later the last flickerings of
White resistance at Archangel and Murmansk were extinguished;
Allied forces, largely British and under British command, had with-
drawn from North Russia the previous September, before the freezing
of the rivers and seas. Only in the South—in the Crimea and along
some of the Black Sea littoral—did any sizable anti-Bolshevik force
remain in being. This was the Volunteer Army of General Anton
I. Denikin. In October 1919 it had stood, with its British advisers and

British equipment, little more than 200 miles from Moscow; but then it had begun an almost unchecked retreat which left it, by February 1920, enfeebled and demoralized. The final victory of the Bolsheviks over their internal enemies seemed only weeks away.[1]

This was a prospect scarcely viewed with enthusiasm in the West. Yet the preceding fifteen months had demonstrated conclusively that not one of the Allied governments, nor any combination of them, was willing to allocate sufficient resources to bring down the Soviet regime. Within the Allied governments there were men, such as Winston Churchill in Britain or Marshal Ferdinand Foch in France, who were anxious to do so, but only a costly campaign involving large numbers of conscript troops could have succeeded, and such was the depth of war-weariness in all the Allied countries—and, by this time, working-class distrust of governmental demands—that conscription for intervention in Russia was never a serious possibility. Never again, therefore, would Allied soldiers seek to accomplish the overthrow of Russian communism by force of arms. Churchill, Secretary of State for War and Air in the British government and the Allied statesman who had been most unceasing of all in his efforts to organize a massive campaign against the Bolsheviks, was bitterly aware that the opportunity—if ever it had actually existed—was past. On the afternoon of 14 February he gloomily told his Dundee constituents: "I take this opportunity of putting on record my sincere and profound conviction that the Great Allied Powers will, each of them and all of them, learn to rue the fact that they could not take more decided and more united action to crush the Bolshevist peril at its centre before it had grown too strong."[2]

Throughout the previous fifteen months Churchill had sought to persuade his Cabinet colleagues to commit additional British resources to the support of the anti-Bolshevik Russian armies. His efforts were in vain, however. During the first six months of 1919 he got some, but by no means all, that he requested. But when Kolchak faltered in June and none of the other White leaders seemed sufficiently likely to succeed (Denikin's sudden and dramatic drive towards Moscow had not yet really begun), those of Church-

[1] For these events, see Volume II of this study, chs. V-VII.
[2] *The Times*, 16 February 1920.

ill's colleagues who opposed intervention prevailed. In their eyes Russia had become for Churchill another Gallipoli—the ill-fated Dardanelles campaign for whose failure he was largely (and unjustly) held responsible, and for which he was dismissed from the Admiralty in 1915. He had been brought back to high office two years later as Minister of Munitions in the Coalition government of David Lloyd George, his closest political friend, in order to harness his enormous energies to the direction of British war production. At the end of 1918 Lloyd George gave Churchill the War Office so that he might cope with the difficult tasks of demobilizing the vast wartime forces and of rationalizing the deployment of the drastically reduced peacetime army across the Empire and in the occupied areas of Germany. But as Frances Stevenson, then Lloyd George's secretary, mistress, and closest confidante, and later his second wife, subsequently wrote: "L.G. had thought that the War Office, *once the war was over*, would be a safe department for Churchill, and he had not foreseen the possibilities which Russia would offer for Churchill's warlike propensities."[3] During 1919, to Lloyd George's intense dismay, Churchill devoted the bulk of his energies to the cause of the Whites in Russia.

In this enterprise he had virtually no support among his fellow Liberals in the Coalition government, and not much more from the Conservatives. Within the Conservative-dominated Coalition, the minority Liberals did not really matter: they had no alternative unless they wished to join the bulk of their party and Labour in opposition. The Conservatives did matter, however. Of those in the government only Walter Long, the First Lord of the Admiralty, seemed consistently to share Churchill's views on Russia. But Long was old and ailing, and his influence—in the government, if not in the Conservative Party—was in decline. Those who mattered most were Andrew Bonar Law, Lord Privy Seal, Leader of the House of Commons, and leader of the Conservative Party; Austen Chamberlain, the Chancellor of the Exchequer; Arthur J. Balfour, formerly Prime Minister and Foreign Secretary, now Lord President of the Council and, although even older than Long, and tired, still a power within

[3] Frances Lloyd George, *The Years that are Past*, London, 1967, p. 169 (italics in original). For a discussion of the relationship between Churchill and Lloyd George as it involved Russia, see Volume II of this study, pp. 294-304.

both the government and the party; and George Nathaniel Curzon, Earl (later, in 1921, Marquess) of Kedleston, who had replaced Balfour as Foreign Secretary in October 1919.

All of these four shared Churchill's distaste for Bolshevik methods and doctrines—a distaste which, indeed, was virtually universal among the Coalition's Parliamentary supporters—but none was prepared to go as far as he in taking active measures against the Soviet regime. Chamberlain, especially, with his eye on the gap between the government's commitments and available resources, was convinced that the country could not afford intervention in Russia. Bonar Law did not much concern himself with international affairs, but he was generally distrustful of foreign adventures and felt that they cost governments dearly in domestic popularity. Balfour *was* interested in events abroad, but he was skeptical—on philosophic as well as practical grounds—of the British government's ability decisively to influence them. Curzon, of whom we will see much in this volume, did not so much oppose intervention as wish to use the same military resources to buttress British influence elsewhere, particularly in Asia and the Middle East. For Curzon, moreover, repugnant though Bolshevism might be, the chaos and upheaval it brought to Russia at least promised to eliminate Russia for the time being as a rival to the British Empire along thousands of miles of once-contested frontier; the great defect of Churchill's policies was that by aiming at replacing Red rule with White rule, they threatened to re-create the Great Russian state that for so long had been Curzon's *bête noire.*[4]

The most important opposition to Churchill's proposals came, however, not from these Conservative ministers but from the Prime Minister, David Lloyd George. Fifty-six years old in 1919, Lloyd George was at the height of his political power. Alone among the Allied wartime leaders, his position had been resoundingly reinforced by a postwar election. In the so-called Khaki election of December 1918, of the 541 candidates who received the Coalition's endorsement signed by Lloyd George and Bonar Law, no fewer than 484 were returned: the government's supporters now outnumbered the opposition by more than five to one. By contrast, Wilson of the United States, Clemenceau of France, and Orlando of Italy were all repudiated by either their publics or their parliaments within a

[4] See Volume II, pp. 295-98.

year of the beginning of the Peace Conference. Thus in international as well as in domestic politics Lloyd George's personal position was strong: alone of the statesmen gathered around the postwar conference tables he had taken the same seat at meetings called to coordinate Allied wartime strategy, or to hammer out the terms of peace for the defeated army.

If the swollen size of the Coalition's majority was a source of strength for Lloyd George, it was by no means an unmixed blessing, for it marked a significant shift to the Right of the center of gravity in the House of Commons. Within the Coalition, Conservatives outnumbered Liberals by roughly three and one-half to one. In a sense, Lloyd George was their prisoner—and the prisoner, as well, of the inflated, jingoist rhetoric with which so many of the Coalition's followers had gone to the country in the post-armistice election campaign. Four months later, in April 1919, he found himself summoned home from the Paris Peace Conference by a cabal of 200 Coalition back-benchers alleging that he was being "soft" on the Germans and "soft" on the Bolsheviks. Thus, regarding policy toward Russia the predominent mood in the House of Commons—a mood fanned by newspapers such as *The Times* or the virulent *Morning Post* which, during the Civil War and afterwards, systematically magnified the misdeeds of the Bolsheviks while minimizing those of their White opponents—was undoubtedly far more anti-Soviet than that in the country as a whole. But the House was still the principal arena of politics. Upon outcomes in that arena, much more than on those in the country at large, depended the fortunes of the leading figures in British politics, with the exception, perhaps, only of the leaders of the Labour Party. And foremost among those whose fortunes were critically dependent on shifts and turns within the House of Commons was David Lloyd George.

Lloyd George handled the problem of Russia as he did all others: the master of compromise and temporizing, but also of ruthless (if usually less than straightforward) action, he did not commit himself until he sensed the direction and strength of the political winds, but in allowing his ministers a fairly free hand he always made certain never to close off options which in the future he might wish to pursue himself. Almost certainly he was uneasy from the outset about intervention in Russia. But provided the costs were not too great he was prepared to agree to the argument, put forward after the Armistice of November 1918 by Balfour and others, that since his government had, in effect, called into being the Russian anti-Bolshevik armies as a means of reconstituting an Eastern front against Germany after the Bolsheviks had made peace at Brest-Litovsk, Great Britain owed the White leaders sufficient assistance to enable them to hold their own—if they could attract a sufficient following—against their communist enemies.[5]

For Lloyd George the last condition—that the anti-Bolshevik cause should attract sufficient popular support—was particularly important. Like Woodrow Wilson, he viewed the civil war in Russia as somewhat akin to an especially violent election, from which would emerge victorious the party which could attract the most support: if the Whites really *deserved* to win, they would do so by virtue of the size of their popular following. Here was an argument which the Prime Minister found particularly persuasive against proposals like those of Churchill, who would have substituted Allied soldiers for the weak and undisciplined forces of the Whites. Yet though such an argument was attractive as a rationale for limiting the scale of intervention, and, eventually, for ceasing it altogether, it was nonetheless a misleading oversimplification: in conditions of civil war relative degrees of popular support may be less a determinant of success or failure than would be a military leader's ability to combine rewards and punishments in such a way as to mold together an efficient, disciplined fighting force. In Russia during 1918-19, the Bolsheviks had this ability, and their opponents did not. It is likely, also, that they did in fact have significantly greater popular support than their opponents, however that elusive concept is defined: the White generals, with their scarcely veiled plans for reinstating something like the old regime, did not offer a vision of the future particularly appealing to the peasantry on whom they counted for recruits—or forced conscripts. Lloyd George may well have been right, but for the wrong reasons.

By the autumn of 1919, in the Prime Minister's view, the Whites —and Churchill—had had their chance, and a sufficient claim on scarce British resources. On 8 November, in his annual address before the Lord Mayor's Banquet at the Guildhall, he stated: "We have given them the opportunity, if Russia wished to be liberated, of

[5] For the use of these arguments at the time of the Armistice, see Volume II, pp. 12-18, 60-61.

equipping her sons in order to free themselves. . . . We have held positions of danger in that country until the Russians were prepared to hold them themselves." And he added: "We cannot, of course, afford to continue so costly an intervention in an interminable civil war."[6] The previous August, largely in response to entreaties from Austen Chamberlain, the Cabinet had already decided to limit remaining *matériel* support to the Whites to one "final packet," all to go to Denikin, the last remaining leader with any real chance of success.[7] During the three months following his Guildhall speech, Lloyd George moved both within his own government and within the inter-Allied Supreme Council (the remaining vestige of the decision-making machinery of the Paris Peace Conference) to place relations with the Soviet regime on a new footing.

Central to his conception of a new footing was the beginning of economic relations. Here the Prime Minister was heavily influenced by the arguments of E. F. Wise, a senior official of the Ministry of Food, at the time the principal British representative on the Supreme Economic Council. Wise held that the restoration of Europe to economic health was vitally dependent upon renewed access to Russian agricultural produce—flax, timber, and, in particular, wheat, of which, in the years immediately preceding the World War, Russia had been a principal world supplier. In order to avoid delicate political questions over recognition of the Soviet government, which now controlled the means of production and distribution, Wise proposed that trade should be begun through the medium of the old Russian agricultural cooperatives, whose once-powerful central organization, known as Tsentrosoyuz, still maintained a certain precarious independence and still had its network of representatives abroad. In January 1920 Lloyd George brought Wise's proposals to a meeting of the Supreme Council in Paris; after his fulsome—and rather disingenuous—assurances that they did not imply dealings with the Soviet government itself, they were adopted on the 16th as Allied policy. This decision also implied the removal of the blockade which the Allied governments had imposed against

[6] Volume II, pp. 305-06.
[7] For the "final packet" of aid to Deniken—£11 million in "surplus non-marketable stores" and £3 million in "marketable stores," see Volume II, pp. 211-12. The last shiploads of these supplies were scheduled to reach the Black Sea ports in late March 1920. Total expenditures on intervention in Russia are tabulated in Volume II, pp. 356-68.

the Bolsheviks in 1918 and had never lifted. Here was tacit recognition that the Soviet government existed, that it was not likely to succumb to its internal opponents, and that the rest of the world would have to take at least minimal steps to come to terms with it.[8]

"Minimal" is aptly used here. During 1919 Lloyd George had had his fingers burnt on three occasions when he seemed to be inclined toward dealings with the Bolsheviks. In January, early in the Peace Conference, he and Woodrow Wilson had taken the lead in proposing a meeting, at the island of Prinkipo in the Sea of Marmora, of all the warring factions in the Russian civil war in order to make peace. Their invitation had been accepted by the Bolsheviks but indignantly rejected by the Whites. Two months later, in March, the President and Prime Minister had joined in sending to Moscow—and later in disavowing—a secret mission led by a young American, William C. Bullitt, to inquire into the terms on which Lenin might be willing to make peace. Reaction to both of these ventures in much of the British press, and especially among back-bench supporters of the Coalition in Parliament, was one of real outrage that the government should even consider having dealings with the Bolsheviks. When Lloyd George again hinted at such a notion in his November Guildhall address, the reaction was only slightly less vehement. During all this time the French government—which had reluctantly agreed that the invitation to Prinkipo could be issued in the name of the Peace Conference as a whole, while at the same time working secretly to make sure the Whites would not accept it and that therefore the proposal would fall—steadfastly maintained that entry into direct relations with the Soviet regime would constitute treason to the Entente.[9]

Thus, when the British Cabinet met on 29 January 1920 to discuss policy toward Russia, it resolved that there could be no question of

[8] See Volume II, pp. 317-21, 326, and 329-30. Wise's memorandum, "Economic Aspects of British Policy concerning Russia," 6 January 1920, is printed in E. L. Woodward and Rohan Butler, eds., *Documents on British Foreign Policy 1919-1939*, First Series, vol. II, London, 1948, no. 71, n. 2, pp. 867-70. (Hereafter volumes of this official serial publication will be referred to simply as *British Documents*. All references will be to the First Series. Woodward and Butler edited the first six volumes; for succeeding volumes Butler was joined by J.P.T. Bury; the editors of volumes referred to henceforth will not be specified.)

[9] See Volume II, pp. 99-118 (for Prinkipo), 140-57 (for the Bullitt mission), 306-08 (for reaction to the Guildhall speech), and 312-15 (for French policy).

ment—were largely in agreement with Lloyd George's policies, even if they often disapproved of his methods. The extent of this agreement can be seen in a series of memoranda and "minutes" (brief, informal intra-Departmental notes and comments) written in mid-February 1920. They are worth a fairly close examination here because they elaborated in a connected and coherent manner, as Lloyd George almost never did, many of the premises underlying British policy, and they reveal much about the assumptions and attitudes of those—politicians and civil servants alike—who set out after the failure of intervention to come to terms with the new Russia.

The first paper in the series was by R. H. Hoare, who had been Chargé d'Affaires in the British mission at Archangel during the summer of 1919 and who had returned that autumn to the Foreign Office.[14] He dealt initially with the prospects for the Bolshevik regime now that the civil war was virtually at an end. "None of the reports which have reached us recently," he began, "contain anything to support the theory that an early collapse of the Soviet Government is probable." On the other hand, there were "many indications" (he did not cite specific examples) that the Bolsheviks had modified their methods in an effort to widen their internal support, particularly among the peasantry, and the intelligentsia. Simultaneously, although the Bolshevik leaders had not abandoned the doctrine of world revolution, they nevertheless were sparing no efforts to make peace with their external enemies, and seemed at least temporarily to have laid aside any hope of spreading their doctrines abroad by force. Lenin was "above all else an opportunist," and he had evidently decided that his most urgent task was the reconstruction of Russia. For this he needed manufactured goods and railway rolling stock, which could be obtained only abroad. In payment he could offer raw materials, especially wheat.

Russian wheat, indeed, was urgently needed abroad. Hoare went on to cite "experts" (he mentioned only E. F. Wise by name) as being "convinced that unless very considerable quantities of corn can be obtained from Russia this year the outlook for Central Europe is very dark." Wheat from Russia, Hoare quoted Wise as saying, would save many in Central Europe from probable starvation. He then came to the crux of his argument, which he stated

[14] Hoare's memorandum, 16 February 1920, is in file 178568/91/38; F.O. 371/3961.

as a dilemma. On the one hand, if something such as the prolongation of the civil war or further foreign intervention, should prevent the export of Russian wheat, there would be "a grave danger of a catastrophe" in Eastern and Central Europe. On the other hand, "many observers" considered that the consolidation of the Soviet system in Russia and the diplomatic recognition of the Soviet government would be "certain to lead to disaster." Undoubtedly, he conceded, Bolshevik propaganda could work serious mischief in Central Europe and in the East. Yet propaganda was a danger which could "be met and fought against, whereas famine would inevitably mean a disaster." Here, then, was Hoare's conclusion: "Whichever course is adopted danger is involved; but the adoption of the first course [reaching an accord with the Soviet government] does not expose us to the unanswerable charge of deliberately prolonging the misery in Russia and Central Europe, simply because we are afraid of the spread of Bolshevik doctrines."

Hoare then went on to recommend specific steps. The first would be to withdraw the British military mission which was still in South Russia supervising the distribution of the final shipments of British supplies which would reach Denikin in March. Hoare also urged the removal of the British warships which were guarding the Isthmus of Perekop, the neck of the Crimea, and thus helping prevent a Bolshevik invasion of the peninsula. Yet simply cutting all connections with Denikin would not be sufficient, he said; even without British support Denikin could probably hold out long enough to disrupt the harvest and export of the year's wheat crop. Hoare also felt that on "grounds of public morality" it would be impossible so abruptly to abandon Denikin. "The conclusion is inevitable," he wrote, "that we must once again 'go to Prinkipo,' with the difference that now it is a question of endeavouring to arrange an honourable capitulation whereas a year ago or even six months ago it would have been a question of a compromise in a civil war the issue of which was doubtful." Moreover, "if the food experts are right when they say that without Russian wheat famine is almost inevitable this year," immediate action was essential.

Hoare's second recommendation was that the government should do all it could to hasten the conclusion of peace between the Soviet government and the only state to the west of Russia with which it was still conducting active hostilities, Poland. "The best means of doing that," he wrote, "would be to inform the Soviets that as soon as such a peace had been concluded (or as soon as we were satisfied that the failure of the negotiations was not the fault of the Soviets) we should be prepared to negotiate with them." On this theme he did not elaborate. Instead, he closed by emphasizing once again the urgent need for Russian wheat. Other arguments in favor of coming to terms with the Bolsheviks could be cited, he said, "such as the danger of the peaceful penetration of Russia by Germany, the instability of the Caucasian Republics and of Persia, [and] the sufferings of the Russian people," but the case as it stood seemed "overwhelmingly strong": "We have admitted that we cannot defeat Bolshevism in the field; it may be humiliating to take the course of action which is the logical result of that admission but as the welfare of Europe appears to depend on this being done, there is no room for further discussion."

Hoare's paper evoked long supporting minutes from J. D. Gregory, the head of the Russia Department, and Lord Hardinge, the Foreign Office's Permanent Under Secretary.[15] Both were in complete agreement with Hoare. As he did (and as Lloyd George did, too), they accepted without question E. F. Wise's set of linked assumptions about Russian wheat supplies—that vast surpluses were being produced, that they had been kept from the export market only by the civil war and the Allied blockade and the consequent disruption of internal transportation facilities, that with the coming of peace these supplies would rapidly be available again for export, and that they would then occupy the same prominent place in the food economy of Europe which they had before the World War, eliminating the need to depend upon more expensive North American grains. (According to Wise's analysis Central Europe faced the possibility of famine not because wheat was unavailable, but because of lack of sufficient foreign exchange to purchase it from the United States and Canada.) Indeed, as so often happens in governments (or, for that matter, in all large organizations subject to severe time constraints) "facts" such as those adduced in Wise's memorandum—almost always unverified and not infrequently inaccurate—came to dominate discussion simply by virtue of their convenience. Gregory reduced Hoare's argument to a syllogism:

[15] Both Gregory's paper, dated 19 February 1920, and Hardinge's, undated but clearly contemporaneous, are in the same file as Hoare's (cited above, n. 4).

"We are primarily interested in preventing Europe from starving. Starvation can only be prevented by the opening up of Russia. Therefore we ought to direct the whole of our diplomacy to that end."

Gregory and Hardinge also agreed with Hoare that the British government had crossed a watershed in its Russian policy. The Cabinet's resolutions of 29 January, wrote Gregory, showed that it was "evidently committed to the direction of ultimate peace with the Soviet Government." Hardinge put it more strongly: "We are already on the high road to recognition of the Soviet Govt. and the only question at issue is the rate of our progress in that direction." Hardinge concurred in the Cabinet's conclusion that the answer to this question would be largely up to Moscow. First, of course, the British government would have to extricate itself completely from its involvement with Denikin—by mediation, it was to be hoped, with the Soviet government on his behalf, in order to arrive at an arrangement whereby he and his principal officers would be allowed some sort of asylum abroad. Once that was accomplished, Hardinge wrote, "the door will be open to direct conversations with the Soviet Govt. on economic and political questions and eventually a 'modus vivendi' may be reached pending demonstration by the Soviet Govt. in its conduct of affairs of sufficient civilisation to justify full recognition." Gregory spelled out in more detail what he called the "intermediate stage of Russian policy, namely, that between armed intervention (or the support of it) and peace." He stated:

Once we have become unreservedly neutral towards the conflicting parties in Russia, there is no technical reason why there should not be some preliminary personal intercourse between Soviet Russia and this country for business purposes—subject to the necessary safeguards against propaganda. We are not technically at war with Soviet Russia and no formalities are really required for re-establishing intercourse. The arrival in this country of a technical expert sent by the Soviet Government to negotiate, say, about the renewal of rollingstock on the Russian railways, for the purposes of economic relief, need not involve or imply the establishment of diplomatic or political relations. . . .

The main object now is to get something practical done. Probably the majority of the Soviet Government are thinking the same—and are prepared to throw political doctrines to the winds so long as the revolution in general is not reversed, if only they can get their country into some sort of order and restart trade.

With these views there was no disagreement, or at least no overt expressions of dissent. No one in the Foreign Office felt it necessary to attach to these three papers a minute pointing out how tenuous were many of E. F. Wise's assumptions about the size of the current Russian wheat harvest, the ability of the Soviet government to get possession of it and to ship it abroad, and the effects that it would have on the food supply—and on the political stability—of Central Europe. No one asked whether, even if the prospective stream of Russian grain were largely chimerical, there were not still other reasons for reaching a *modus vivendi* with the Bolshevik regime or, on the contrary, whether it would not then better be left in isolation. And no one pointed out how striking it was that these three memoranda advocating an early accord with Moscow scarcely touched on the question of Bolshevik revolutionary propaganda and the problems it posed for the security of various parts of the British Empire, and that they did not touch at all on the question of European security and the problem of the future containment of Germany.

✧

Of these three expressions of views, only Hoare's referred at all to Poland, and his only briefly. He reserved his lengthier observations for, and Gregory and Hardinge devoted all of theirs to, the military situation in South Russia as the principal obstacle to the establishment of more satisfactory Anglo-Soviet relations. In February 1920 this indeed seemed to be the case, and within a few months Denikin's successor, General Baron P. N. Wrangel, was to launch an offensive against the Bolsheviks that was greatly to complicate the evolving British relationship with Soviet Russia. A still more serious campaign, however, was to be mounted by the armies under the command of General Józef Piłsudski, the Head of the Polish State. Both were to revive the hopes of those like Winston Churchill who hoped to destroy the Bolshevik regime, and they were to make much more difficult the task of others, like David Lloyd George, who hoped to come to terms with it.

The re-emergence of the independent state of Poland was one of the most important results of the World War and the chaos brought to Eastern and Central Europe by the collapse of Imperial Russia and the defeat of Germany and her allies. Since the partitions at the end of the eighteenth century, the territories inhabited by the Polish people had been divided under the rule of Russia, Austria, and Prussia. The western frontiers of the reborn Polish state were, with no little difficulty and with certain exceptions, left to be decided by subsequent plebiscites, as laid down by the Peace Conference in the treaties of peace with Germany and Austria. But because of the absence of Russia from the conference the statesmen at Paris had no means of establishing an agreed frontier between Poland and Russia in the east. Nevertheless, in the words of Jules Cambon, the Chairman of the Conference's Commission on Polish Affairs, "it had been recognized that in order to enable Poland to administer the territory occupied by her it was necessary to establish at least a provisional eastern frontier comprising territories which were indisputably Polish."[16]

The task of deciding upon this frontier was left to Cambon and his commission of experts. They were guided, so they noted in a report to the Conference on 22 April 1919, by the self-imposed principle that "the districts in which doubt arises as to the ethnographical character or wishes of the population cannot at present be assigned to the Polish State."[17] The formulation of such a principle at a time when the eventual victory of the anti-Bolshevik forces within Russia was still taken almost for granted, was not surprising; the statesmen at Paris could scarcely assign to Poland territory that would surely have been claimed by a restored Russia.

The line laid down by the Polish Commission, running from East Prussia in the north to Galicia in the south, for much of its length following the Bug River, was roughly identical to the middle section of the line which has divided Poland and the Soviet Union since 1945.[18] The Commission did not extend the line into Galicia, because the Supreme Council had been contemplating the

[16] Cambon was speaking before the Council of Heads of Delegations, Paris, 29 November 1919, 10:30 A.M.; minutes in *British Documents*, vol. II, no. 32, pp. 424-25.
[17] From Report No. 2 of the Commission on Polish Affairs, 22 April 1919; filed as Cabinet paper W.C.P. 649, Cab. 29/13. The report is summarized, and a few excerpts are printed in *British Documents*, vol. I, London, 1947, no. 64, n. 10, pp. 788-89.
[18] The recommended frontier was described in detail in Appendix I of the Polish Commission's Report No. 2, printed in *ibid.*, no. 64, n. 11, p. 790. The line ran southward from the East Prussian border approximately as follows: Grodno, Vapovka, Nemirov, and thence along the Bug River through or by such towns as Brest-Litovsk, Dorogusk, Ustilug, and Grubeshov until meeting the Galician border south of Krilov. A large-scale map showing this line from Nemirov southward is affixed between pp. 840 and 841 of *ibid.*, vol. III.

constitution of the eastern part of that area as a separate state; on 21 November 1919 the Council adopted a "Statute of Eastern Galicia" providing, instead, for a twenty-five-year Polish mandate under the League of Nations and laying down a frontier between the mandate territory and Western Galicia, which was to be incorporated outright into Poland.[19] The statute, however, lived less than a month. The idea of a mandate met with vehement opposition from the Polish government, which wanted immediate full possession of all of the territory. Warsaw proceeded simply to ignore the line, and the Council, recognizing that there was little it could do to prevent the Poles from treating Eastern Galicia as part of Poland, suspended the offending statute.[20]

Thus, in Galicia the Allies laid down no boundary between Poland and Russia. The boundary north of Galicia, however, was proclaimed in a "Declaration of the Supreme Council of the Allied and Associated Powers relative to the Provisional Eastern Frontiers of Poland" issued on 8 December 1919 and signed by Clemenceau as President of the Peace Conference. The declaration made clear that it did not imply prejudgment of any future frontier that might be established, presumably, by Polish-Russian agreement: rather, it merely stated that the Allied and Associated Powers recognized the right of the Polish government to proceed "to organize a regular administration" over the territories of the former Russian Empire situated to the west of the line.[21]

[19] Minutes, Council of Heads of Delegations, Paris, 21 November 1919, 10:30 A.M.; *ibid.*, vol. II, no. 28, pp. 377-78. The Polish Commission's Report No. 3, 17 June 1919, advocating the establishment of a separate Eastern Galicia, is printed in vol. III, pp. 829-41. The Commission's original draft "Statut de la Galicie Orientale," dated 23 August 1919, is printed in vol. I, pp. 742-52; as adopted it incorporated certain amendments proposed on 20 November and printed in vol. II, pp. 372-76. The proposed border between Poland and the mandate territory ran from the Bug River below Krilov westward to Belzec on the former frontier between Austria-Hungary and Russia and thence south-southwestward to the Czechoslovak frontier. This line left the city and province of Lwow (today, in the U.S.S.R., Lvov; its old Austrian name was Lemberg) within the mandate. Both the adopted and the rejected lines are shown on the large-scale map cited above, n. 18.

[20] Minutes, Council of Heads of Delegations, Paris, 22 December 1919, 10:30 A.M.; *ibid.*, vol. II, no. 44, p. 582.

It has been impossible in this brief space to convey even an impression of the complexities and confusions surrounding the treatment of the question of Galicia at the Peace Conference during 1919. For an authoritative account see Piotr S. Wandycz, *France and her Eastern Allies 1919-1925: French-Czechoslovak-Polish Relations from the Paris Peace Conference to Locarno*, Minneapolis, 1962, pp. 104-18.

[21] *Ibid.*, pp. 129-31. The text of the declaration is printed in *British and Foreign State Papers, 1919*, vol. CXII, London, 1922, pp. 971-72.

Nothing in this declaration, of course, stated that the Powers would *not* recognize any administration that the Poles might establish to the east of the line, and the turbulent circumstances of 1919 provided them with a clear invitation for eastward expansion. Throughout the year, taking advantage of Soviet preoccupation with the White offensives in the north, Siberia, and in the south, Piłsudski's forces pushed forward. In April they occupied Vilna, the capital of then-Soviet Lithuania. On 8 August they entered Minsk, the principal town of White Russia. Piłsudski's aim, according to his apologists, was not conquest but the erection of a federal system comprising Poland, Eastern Galicia, Lithuania, Belorussia, Ruthenia, and the Ukraine. Only as part of such a federation could these nations, formerly subjects of the Tsar, ensure their freedom from Great Russian rule. This grouping of border nationalities would later be strengthened, Piłsudski hoped, by the addition of Latvia, Estonia, and Finland.[22]

By the autumn of 1919 Polish armies controlled a wide swath of territory nearly 200 miles farther east than the line stipulated in the Allied declaration of 8 December. There, however, they paused. Sporadically, from October through December, emissaries of Piłsudski engaged in secret peace negotiations with Bolshevik representatives. For the Bolsheviks the object of these negotiations, which never reached a conclusion, was to make sure that the Poles did not aid Denikin in his drive toward Moscow. The Poles took part in these discussions while simultaneously carrying on negotiations with Denikin, who desperately needed their assistance. Denikin, however, would not unequivocally guarantee to recognize the right of the Poles—much less the right of the other border nationalities—to complete independence. So Piłsudski held his ground, and Denikin, who only later learned of the secret negotiations between Poland

[22] See, in particular, M. K. Dziewanowski, "Piłsudski's Federal Policy, 1919-1921," *Journal of Central European Affairs*, vol. X, nos. 2 and 3, July and October 1950. Opposed to Piłsudski's "federalist" views (which were shared by many politically influential elements) were the "nationalist" or "incorporationist" views of Dmowski and the National Democrats (among others), who envisioned a Poland within ethnographic limits. These two points of view have been widely discussed. See, *e.g.*, Alexander Skrzynski, *Poland and Peace*, London, 1923, pp. 36-42; Titus Komarnicki, *The Rebirth of the Polish Republic: A Study in the Diplomatic History of Europe, 1914-1920*, London, 1957, pp. 450-56; Roman Debicki, *Foreign Policy of Poland, 1919-1939*, New York, 1962, pp. 24-31; and Piotr S. Wandycz, *Soviet-Polish Relations, 1917-1921*, Cambridge, Mass., 1969, pp. 96-110, 119-24, 134-35.

and the Bolsheviks, watched as 43,000 troops of the Red Army were transferred from the Polish front to his.[23]

To the Allies, as well, Polish behavior during the autumn of 1919 was enigmatic. On 14 September the Polish premier, the pianist Ignace Paderewski, approached Lloyd George in Paris and offered to put Poland's army of over half a million men at the disposal of the Supreme Council for a march on Moscow, provided that the Allies paid £600,000 a day for these services.[24] On the other hand, he told the Council when he came before it on the following day that if the Allies instead wished Poland to make peace with the Bolsheviks they should say so: "Very advantageous terms," he said, referring obliquely to the secret Polish-Soviet discussions, had been offered.[25]

At this suggestion, both Clemenceau and Foch recoiled. Yet neither could they accept the notion of a march on Moscow: nothing would be more sure to make all Russians rally to the support of the Soviet government than an invasion by the ancient Polish enemy. Clemenceau said that "as far as he was concerned he would not make peace nor would he make war." Lloyd George did not demur. Regarding this crucial question, the Poles were given no advice.[26] But Polish support of Denikin was an altogether different matter. Early in the autumn, at the instruction of the War Office, Lieutenant General Sir Charles J. Briggs of the British military mission in South Russia journeyed to Warsaw to plead, unsuccessfully, for Piłsudski's cooperation. Sir Halford Mackinder paused in the Polish capital to make a similar appeal in December on his way to taking up his post as British High Commissioner in South Russia. Piłsudski never consented. But throughout late 1919 he maintained his troops in a warlike posture and moved them from point to point of the front in order not to lose the good will and

[23] The Polish-Soviet negotiations are authoritatively treated in Piotr S. Wandycz, "Secret Soviet-Polish Peace Talks in 1919," *Slavic Review*, vol. XXIV, no. 3, September 1965, pp. 425-49. For Poland's relations with Denikin, see Denikin's *Ocherki russkoi smuty* (Sketches of the Russian Turmoil), vol. V, Berlin, 1926, pp. 173-81, and Komarnicki, *Polish Republic*, pp. 466-69.

[24] So Lloyd George told his colleagues on the Council of Heads of Delegations, Paris, 15 September 1919, 10:30 A.M. (minutes: *British Documents*, vol. I, no. 57, p. 689).

[25] For Paderewski's remarks, see minutes, Council of Heads of Delegations, 15 September 1919, 4 P.M.; *ibid.*, no. 58, pp. 701-02.

[26] *Ibid.*, pp. 702-05.

material support of the French, who then, as later, were Poland's principal patrons.[27]

The disastrous collapse of Denikin's forces removed a major obstacle both to the recognition of Poland's independence by the government which ruled Russia, and also to the formation of the greater Poland which Piłsudski sought. Now that only the Bolsheviks stood in their way, Polish troops could resume the drive into White Russia and the Ukraine which had been suspended since the late summer. The Soviet government, of course, was fully aware of this danger, and on 22 December 1919 Chicherin addressed a wireless message to Warsaw urging the commencement of peace negotiations and stating that all differences which divided the two governments could be settled "by friendly agreement."[28]

The Polish government did not reply to this overture. But on 19 January 1920 the British Minister in Warsaw, Sir Horace Rumbold, reported to London that the Poles sought Allied guidance in choosing between the alternatives of accepting the Soviet offer and making peace on the favorable terms that could be obtained because of Poland's momentarily superior military position, or of prosecuting the war to its conclusion. Rumbold suggested that he should reply simply that the Poles should be guided by their own interests, and not by those of any of the Allies. His own opinion, he said, was that the Polish army, despite its huge size, was not strong enough to achieve Piłsudski's goals. Internally, Poland was critically weak. Hunger was widespread, owing to unemployment and rapidly rising prices. Typhus was rampant. Rumbold felt that the Poles should not resume the offensive but he warned that if they did not attack, they would themselves face the danger of a Soviet attack in the spring after the bulk of the Red Army had been transferred from the south. In order successfully to maintain a defensive posture,

---

[27] Dziewanowski, "Piłsudski's Federal Policy," pp. 124-25. For Briggs's visit, see General Sir Adrian Carton de Wiart, *Happy Odyssey*, London, 1950, p. 118. (Carton de Wiart was head of the British Military Mission in Warsaw.) For Mackinder's conversations with Piłsudski, see Rumbold (Warsaw) to Curzon, telegrams 487 and 488, 16 December 1919, and 491 of 17 December; *British Documents*, vol. III, London, 1949, no. 656, appendix A.

[28] The text of the Soviet note is printed in Ministry of Foreign Affairs of the U.S.S.R., *Dokumenty vneshnei politiki SSSR* (Documents on the Foreign Policy of the U.S.S.R.), vol. II, Moscow, 1958, pp. 312-13, and translated in Jane Degras, ed., *Soviet Documents on Foreign Policy*, vol. I, *1917-1924*, London, 1951, pp. 177-78.

Rumbold said, Poland would require considerable Allied assistance in the form of military and railway equipment.[29]

The British government's advice to the Poles, such as it was, was delivered not by Rumbold but by Lloyd George himself. In a long conversation in London on 26 January with the Polish Foreign Minister, Stanisław Patek, Lloyd George emphasized that although the Poles themselves must take full responsibility for deciding between war and peace with Soviet Russia, the British government did not wish to give Poland the slightest encouragement to make war, for by doing so it would incur responsibilities it could not discharge. In his opinion, the Prime Minister said, Bolshevism was no longer a danger outside Russia's borders; although the danger from Bolshevik propaganda was perhaps as great as ever, he thought that the Soviet leaders were afraid that if the Red Army were ever strong enough for external aggression, it would also present the communist leadership with the threat of a military *coup d'état*. Moreover, he continued, there were not sufficient foodstuffs or raw materials in Poland, Hungary, or Germany to attract an invasion by the Red Army. This last argument was one which Lloyd George seemed to find especially persuasive. He did not elaborate upon it with Patek, but the following day he told a Cabinet meeting that in his opinion "the Bolsheviks had, after all, practically nothing to gain by over-running Poland, Germany, Hungary, Persia or Roumania, or even the Caucasus, except that they might gain control of the oil fields in the latter region." All these countries, he said, "could offer nothing to the Bolshevik armies but famine and typhus." It was a lesson of history that "hordes of barbarians only over-ran foreign territories for purposes of loot."[30] Thus did Lloyd George dismiss the revolutionary challenge of the Soviet regime.

[29] Rumbold (Warsaw) to Curzon, telegram 41, 19 January 1920; *British Documents*, vol. III, no. 651.

[30] Minutes, conference of Ministers, 27 January 1920, 11:30 A.M.; Cab. 23/20. (Note: The Cabinet Secretariat distinguished between Cabinet meetings and "conferences of Ministers." The grounds upon which the distinction was made are unclear, however: though some conferences of Ministers involved only a few participants, others, of which the meeting on 27 January was an example, were attended by as many as attended an average Cabinet meeting. Nor did the conferences of Ministers lack decision-making authority. Both forms of meeting, it may be added, were also attended in many instances by persons from outside the Cabinet, such as junior or non-Cabinet Ministers, or high military officers and civil servants.)

In his conversation with Patek, the Prime Minister then turned to the question of the degree to which Great Britain would support Poland against a Soviet invasion in the future. To seek such support, of course, was the purpose of Patek's visit, and in view of the subsequent political salience of the precise nature of the government's "commitment" to come to the aid of the Poles, the British summary of Lloyd George's remarks—made by Lord Hardinge, the principal Foreign Office representative present at the meeting—should be quoted.

The Prime Minister made it clear that, in his opinion, the principal difficulty would be that the Polish armies had advanced far beyond the racial boundary into considerable territories which contained large Russian majorities. The Prime Minister said that if the Poles made a sincere attempt to make an equitable peace and the Bolsheviks either refused peace or, having made peace, proceeded to repudiate it, Great Britain would feel bound to assist Poland to the best of its power. He was sure that it would be possible both for the French and British Governments to rouse their people, exhausted as they were by five years' war, to make fresh efforts if Poland had made a sincere attempt to make peace on fair terms and the Bolsheviks rejected it and attacked Poland instead. If, on the other hand, Poland insisted on retaining within Poland areas which were indisputably Russian according to the principles generally applied by the Peace Conference, and if the Bolshevik Government refused the peace on this ground and attacked Poland in order to recover Russian districts for Russia, it would be very difficult, if not impossible, for the British Government to get public opinion to support military or financial outlay in these circumstances.[31]

This statement left unanswered two important questions. First, what specific measures—material assistance, military advisors, actual combat troops—did Lloyd George have in mind when he told Patek that the British government would "assist Poland to the best of its power" in the event of an unprovoked Soviet attack? Obviously the Prime Minister had good reasons for deliberate vagueness on this point. And, second, what response would London make in the event of a Soviet attack "in order to recover Russian districts

---

[31] Hardinge's detailed account was sent as telegram 46 to Rumbold (Warsaw); *British Documents*, vol. III, no. 664. Lloyd George himself described the interview in much the same terms (presumably speaking from Hardinge's notes) to the conference of Ministers cited above, no. 30.

for Russia" if the invading Soviet forces did not stop at the recovery of "indisputably Russian" territory, but instead went on advancing into territory indisputably Polish? Here, also, the Prime Minister was unlikely to have surrendered his freedom of action by greater specificity. Lord Hardinge, as a professional diplomat, was impressed. Lloyd George "really did it skilfully," he wrote to Curzon, who was on holiday. The Prime Minister had given Patek lots of advice, Hardinge said, but he had carefully avoided taking responsibility for it.[32]

The Polish government was also impressed. The American Minister, Hugh Gibson, telegraphed to Washington that those Poles who knew of the interview (it was not, of course, officially made public) felt that Poland had been abandoned.[33] On 9 February, at his residence in the Belweder Palace, Piłsudski told the chief of the British military mission, Brigadier General Adrian Carton de Wiart—a dashing one-eyed, one-armed winner of the Victoria Cross who was probably on better terms with the dour Polish Head of State than any other foreigner—that he thought it was just as well that Lloyd George had been so evasive. Poland had hitherto been accustomed to lean on the Western Powers. Now his countrymen would realize that they must stand alone.[34]

Along with news of the interview between Lloyd George and Patek, another Soviet peace proposal, much more specific than the one of 22 December, reached Warsaw. Signed by Lenin, Chicherin, and Trotsky, this message stated, first, that the Soviet government recognized without reservation the independence and sovereignty of Poland; second, that the Red Army would not cross the line dividing it from the Polish forces either in White Russia or in the Ukraine; and third, that the "character and spirit" of Soviet foreign policy precluded "the very possibility" that the Soviet government would enter into an agreement, with Germany or any other country, directly or indirectly aimed against the interests of Poland. The purpose of these proposals, the message stated, was to prevent the "baseless, senseless, and criminal war with Soviet Russia" into which

---

[32] Hardinge's letter, dated 27 January 1920, is in the Curzon MSS, box 22.

[33] Gibson (Warsaw) to Secretary of State, telegram 57, 2 February 1920; U.S. National Archives, State Department file 760c.61/9.

[34] Rumbold to Curzon (Warsaw), telegram 102, 10 February 1920; *British Documents*, vol. XI, London, 1961, no. 188.

Poland was being drawn by "the extreme imperialists among the Allies, the colleagues and agents of Churchill and Clemenceau."[35]

Piłsudski referred to these Bolshevik proposals during his talk on 9 February with Carton de Wiart. He had himself drawn up a statement of conditions, he said, upon which he was prepared to enter into negotiations with Moscow. They would be very stiff conditions because he felt that he had to show the Bolsheviks that Poland at present held the upper hand. Piłsudski gave the British general the impression that he had in mind not necessarily territorial aggrandizement for Poland, but the establishment of independent buffer states in the Russian-Polish borderlands. Should Moscow not accept his terms, he felt confident of being able to carry on the present war for several months. So short a time, he implied, might be sufficient for the achievement of his objectives: according to his intelligence reports the Soviet government sorely needed peace.

Piłsudski's remarks were reported to London by Rumbold, who noted that he could not help thinking that the solution Piłsudski had in mind would be only temporary, and that buffer states between Poland and Russia would be a source of future trouble.[36] Meanwhile, in Paris, Marshal Foch lent his immense prestige to Piłsudski's proposals by telling the chief of the Polish military mission that the only defensible frontier "between Europe and Bolshevism" would be the line along the Dvina River from Riga in Latvia to Vitebsk in White Russia, and then south along the Dnieper River through the eastern Ukraine to the Black Sea.[37] In effect, the line Foch suggested would separate from Russia nearly all of the territories out of which Piłsudski wished to form his federation.

The issues which divided the Polish and British governments were

[35] The text of the Soviet message, dated 28 January 1920, is in *Dokumenty vneshnei politiki*, vol. II, pp. 331-33; translation in Degras, *Soviet Documents*, pp. 179-80.

[36] Rumbold's telegram is cited above, n. 34.

[37] From a report by Major H. S. Howland, U.S. Attaché with the Polish Military and Diplomatic Mission, Paris, to the U.S. Military Attaché, 16 February 1920; National Archives, State Department file 760c.61/29. These views were Foch's own; the French government was still committed to a policy of maintaining the territorial integrity of Russia in the hopes of the eventual downfall of Bolshevism. See Wandycz, *France and her Eastern Allies*, pp. 141-42.

clearly drawn in an interview between Rumbold and Piłsudski on 17 February. The Western Powers, Piłsudski bitterly noted, could await developments in Russia. Poland, being a bordering state, could not afford such luxury. The West, he felt, did not take Poland's difficult position sufficiently into consideration. Rumbold replied by pointing out that Kolchak, Denikin, and Yudenich had failed hopelessly against the Bolsheviks, and that their failures were due to deficiencies which Britain could not remedy. The British nation was tired, he said, of helping people who could not help themselves, and it did not want to be involved in further adventures, such as encouraging the Poles to attack the Bolsheviks.[38]

✧

In all of these exchanges of views on the question of how Poland should deal with Soviet Russia, the British position had been put forward in private, as it had been when the governments of the Baltic states had sought the same advice from London the previous autumn.[39] But in mid-February, when the representatives of the Allies convened at the so-called First Conference of London primarily to discuss problems of the Turkish peace settlement and the Adriatic, Lloyd George sought the incorporation of British policy on these Russian problems into a public statement, made in the name not only of Britain but of the Allied Powers. Despite French opposition, he succeeded.

The French, represented by Alexandre Millerand, who had replaced Clemenceau as premier, and Philippe Berthelot, at the time Chief Secretary for Political Affairs at the Quai d'Orsay, later its Secretary General, put forward a wholly negative policy: the governments of all the states bordering on Russia should be told that if they engaged in any independent negotiations with the Soviet government they would be denied the protection of the Allies and thenceforth would be accorded the same treatment as Soviet Russia. As for the Bolsheviks, the Allies should declare that they would be forever ostracized from the community of civilized nations, and lines of demarcation should be laid down beyond which Soviet forces would not be allowed to pass.

[38] Rumbold described the interview in his dispatch no. 123 to Curzon, 23 February 1920; *British Documents*, vol. XI, no. 201.
[39] See Volume II, pp. 274-81, 286.

In countering these views, Lloyd George used the arguments that he had used with Patek and that the British government had put to the governments of the Baltic states five months previously—that the Allies were in no position to take responsibility for advising the border states not to make peace with the Bolsheviks. The Prime Minister also urged the necessity not only of once again securing for Europe the agricultural resources of Russia, but also of finding out precisely "what was really happening in Russia." For this purpose he proposed that a commission of investigation should be sent out—not by the Allied governments, for a governmental mission would imply recognition of the Soviet regime, but by the League of Nations. In advancing these arguments Lloyd George's task was made considerably easier by Francesco Nitti, the Italian premier, who frankly and openly said that he thought the time had come to recognize the Soviet government and thereby renew normal relations with Russia. Nitti was convinced that the Soviet regime, far from growing weaker, as the French had said, was every day growing more powerful. If the Allies were to come to terms with the Bolsheviks now, Nitti said, they would be doing so of their own free will. In the not distant future, he predicted, they would be forced to do so in order to get access to the natural resources and markets of Russia without which Europe's economy could not function.[40]

With these Italian views on one extreme and those of the French on the other, Lloyd George could play his favorite role of reasonable compromiser.[41] In order to restrain Nitti, the French reluctantly departed from their policy and gave approval to the revised draft of a public statement originally written by Lloyd George, making roughly the same points he had made to Patek, only in language somewhat less forceful. Read out in both Houses of Parliament on

[40] Russian policy was discussed at three sessions of the conference: 19 February 1920, 11 A.M.; 19 February, 4 P.M.; and 23 February, 11 A.M. Minutes in *British Documents*, vol. VII, London, 1958, nos. 16, 17, and 22. See pp. 140-43 (for Berthelot's statement), 148-52 (for Lloyd George's views), 196-97 (for Millerand's views), and 144-47, 197-98, 200-01 (for Nitti's views).

[41] See Lloyd George's remarks in the session of 23 February, 11 A.M.; *ibid.*, pp. 201-04. Millerand, speaking after Lloyd George, ruefully agreed that the British Prime Minister had not, as Nitti had done, proposed that the Allies should enter into diplomatic relations with the Soviet government, but he argued that Lloyd George's proposals would make such relations inevitable in the future. (*Ibid.*, pp. 204-05.)

24 February, the day it was approved by the conference sitting in Downing Street, the statement said:

The Allied Governments have agreed on the following conclusions:

If the communities which border on the frontiers of Soviet Russia and whose independence or *de facto* autonomy they have recognized, were to approach them and to ask for advice as to what attitude they should take with regard to Soviet Russia, the Allied Governments would reply that they cannot accept the responsibility of advising them to continue a war which may be injurious to their own interests. Still less would they advise them to adopt a policy of aggression towards Russia. If, however, Soviet Russia attacks them inside their own legitimate frontiers, the Allies will give them every possible support.

The Allies cannot enter into diplomatic relations with the Soviet Government in view of their past experiences until they have arrived at the conviction that the Bolshevist horrors have come to an end, and that the Government of Moscow is ready to conform its methods and diplomatic conduct to those of all civilised governments. . . . Commerce between Russia and Europe . . . will be encouraged to the utmost degree possible without relaxation of the attitude described above.

"Furthermore," the statement continued, "the Allies agree in the belief that it is highly desirable to obtain impartial and authoritative information regarding the conditions now prevailing in Russia." Therefore, they invited the Council of the League of Nations (upon which, of course, all three Powers were represented) to send a commission of investigation to Russia "to examine the facts."[42]

Like the decision the previous month to begin trade with the Russian cooperatives, the Allied statement of 24 February meant that Lloyd George's diplomacy had achieved all that it had sought. This achievement was measured by *The Times*'s leading article the following day, which observed, a trifle baroquely:

It is impossible not to admire the profligate art with which for over a year Mr. Lloyd George had sought for his own purpose to throw a weak, ignorant, and reluctant Europe into the venal arms of her Bolshevist se-

---

[42] 125 *H.C. Deb.*, cols. 1501-02 and 39 *H.L. Deb.* cols. 103-04. The statement was read in the Commons by Bonar Law and in the Lords by the Chancellor of the Duchy of Lancaster, the Earl of Crawford. Lloyd George's original draft is printed in *British Documents*, vol. VII, pp. 205-06. A comparison shows how few changes in substance were made by the conference. The final version was formally approved at the conference session of 24 February, 11 A.M. (minutes in *ibid.*, no. 24, pp. 217-18).

ducer. More than once she seemed about to escape the disgraceful fate. . . . More than once the degradation and the horror of such a connexion dawned upon her. She loathed it, she revolted from it, she struggled to get free. But Mr. Lloyd George knew his business. He did not hurry matters; he did not press the victim. . . . He does not compromise everything by impetuous demands for an immediate surrender. He carefully respects the remains of virtue—or the prudery—of his dupe. She might recoil even yet if matters were conducted too crudely. . . . The next step is to compromise her beyond recall. Then the path will have been opened for Lenin.[43]

✧

From Warsaw there came no marked reaction to the Allied statement. Throughout February there were discussions within the Polish government as to how to reply to the Soviet peace proposals, but of the details of these discussions Western diplomats knew little except that the resulting Polish terms would almost certainly be stringent. On 6 March Chicherin again sent a radio message to Patek, noting that the Poles had never replied to the Russian proposals, and again offering to make peace.[44] Piłsudski, meanwhile, had ordered a brief, sharp, probing attack east of Pinsk; he was amazed, he told the American Minister, at the ease with which the Poles advanced, causing the Bolsheviks to fall back abandoning their equipment.[45]

Finally, on 13 March, Patek called in the Ministers of Britain, France, Italy and the United States and handed them a note setting down the "conditions of principle" upon which the Polish government was willing to open negotiations with Moscow. These conditions were so stringent that even Rumbold, who had expected strong terms, was surprised. Russia was to renounce all rights to any territory that had been part of Poland as it existed before the first partition in 1772. In addition, Russia was to recognize the independence of all states formed on the territory of the former Russian Empire which then had *de facto* governments, and not interfere in any way in their internal affairs or their relations with other states. And the Soviet government was to cease all propaganda aimed abroad. If these, and other, less important "principles" were ac-

---

[43] *The Times*, 25 February 1920.
[44] Text in *Dokumenty vneshnei politiki*, vol. II, pp. 397-99.
[45] Gibson (Warsaw) to Secretary of State, telegram 141, 11 March 1920; U.S. National Archives, State Department file 760c.61/33.

cepted, the Polish government would be willing to enter into peace negotiations. For its part it would "determine the destiny" of the populations east of the 1772 Polish-Russian frontier "in conformity with their wishes."[46]

Although the text of this note was given to the Allied diplomats, and its substance was revealed to the Warsaw representatives of the border states, it was never officially communicated to the Soviet government.[47] Its details, however, were soon leaked to the press. *The Times* called it a *ballon d'essai*,[48] and so it surely was. The American Minister, when it was read to him by Patek, made no comments upon it; the United States had already withdrawn from the affairs of Europe.[49] But Sir Horace Rumbold did not hesitate to speak his mind. The British government would not be pleased, he told Patek, with Poland's demands that Russia should renounce all rights over territory which included most of the Ukraine and all of Lithuania. A plebiscite held under Polish military occupation, he noted, would scarcely ensure the free expression of the opinions of the inhabitants. And in accordance with instructions he had previously received from Curzon[50] Rumbold emphasized to Patek the fact that Article 87 of the Treaty of Versailles—which Poland had signed—gave the Principal Allied and Associated Powers the right to determine Poland's eastern frontiers. Poland should look to the future, he warned, and take into account the probable attitude of an eventually reconstituted non-Bolshevik Russian government toward a Polish-Soviet agreement which gave away so much Russian territory. Meanwhile, the British Minister said, if the Bolsheviks were to make peace on the basis of these Polish conditions, and then to violate their agreement by attacking Poland, the Poles would not be able to count upon receiving any assistance from Great Britain.

Later, reporting this interview to Curzon, Rumbold stated his opinion that the Polish terms were so severe that the Soviet govern-

[46] The text of the Polish note is given in Gibson's despatch of 24 March 1920 to Washington (U.S. National Archives, State Department file 760c.61/51) and is summarized in detail in Rumbold (Warsaw) to Curzon, telegram 167, 14 March (*British Documents*, vol. XI, no. 220).

[47] According to Rumbold's telegram 167 (cited n. 44). See Komarnicki, *Polish Republic*, p. 565.

[48] *The Times*, 23 March 1920.

[49] See Gibson's despatch of 24 March 1920 (cited n. 44), and Rumbold (Warsaw) to Curzon, telegram 194, 21 March, *British Documents*, vol. XI, no. 231.

[50] Curzon to Rumbold (Warsaw), telegram 134, 11 March 1920; summarized in *ibid.*, no. 221, n. 4.

ment surely would not accept them. Moscow's rejection would give the Poles an excuse to carry on the war, which they were fully prepared to do. Rumbold concluded, therefore, that the Polish government regarded the demands as a gamble from which it stood to gain no matter what decision the Bolsheviks reached. All military experts agreed, he said, that the Red Army would not for some time be strong enough to endanger the Poles.[51]

In London, the Polish terms—and, indeed, the whole Polish posture in foreign policy—were the subject of bitter criticism in a memorandum prepared by the Political Intelligence Department of the Foreign Office and circulated to the Cabinet.[52] In trying to restore the Poland of 1772, the memorandum stated, the Poles were counting on "vague, ill-formed sentimentalism" in the West to blind the Powers to the emptiness of Polish claims. In fact, the area between the line laid down by the Polish Commission of the Peace Conference as the eastern limit of territory "indisputably Polish" and the frontier of 1772 was more than three times the size of ethnic Poland, with a population of thirty million, of whom less than a tenth were Poles. "The Polish claim to these enormous areas rests exclusively on the Polish ownership of most of the big landed estates, of something like 40,000 square miles of land," the memorandum continued. "This seems hardly a valid title to dominion in these days of democracy and of agrarian reform." In order to buttress these tenuous claims, the paper maintained, peasants from Poland proper would be shipped eastward as settlers. "The position in Poland will thus be eased, the Polish landowners in White Russia and Little Russia will be provided with a White Guard of Polish settlers, and the Polish government with a conquering military garrison."

The memorandum went on to dismiss Polish proposals for the establishment of independent states between Poland and Russia as transparently fraudulent, comparable with German schemes at the time of the Treaty of Brest-Litovsk to establish a similar zone of puppet states in the East. In addition there were the pogroms. Excesses against the Jews still occurred, as in previous times. With such a record, and such tenuous claims, the memorandum con-

[51] Rumbold described his interview with Patek in telegram 169 to Curzon, 14 March 1920; *ibid.*, no. 221.
[52] "Polish Peace Terms to the Bolsheviks," Poland/003, 20 March 1920, circulated as Cabinet paper C.P. 937; Cab. 24/101.

tinued, "the Poles have truly no right to demand to be left in the [border] country 'for the sake of civilisation.' They are the most hated men in the country and hated not merely by their specially chosen victims, the Jews, but by White Russians, Little Russians and Lithuanians, alike."

Finally came policy recommendations. In such circumstances, the memorandum stated, the Allies could only reject the Polish claims. Instead, "all, but absolutely all" territory under Polish administration east of the line of 8 December 1919 should instead be placed under some kind of international control—preferably that of the League of Nations—leaving an ultimate settlement to the time when conditions within Russia were more stable. It was vitally important, however, that such control should be effective, and not simply "a cover for [the] Imperialist conquest and forcible polonisation of non-Polish territory." If international control could not be effective, it would be preferable for the British government to give Poland no assistance whatsoever, "rather than take the burden of constituting ourselves guarantors of Polish violence anywhere." Thus, London should "let the Poles and the Russians freely fight the matter out between themselves."

This memorandum is important not for the policies it recommended but as an example of the anti-Polish bias which was fairly prevalent both within the Foreign Office and the Cabinet. This is not to say that the facts it contained were incorrect or even for the most part disputable. But there were reasonable arguments which might have been advanced in favor of some of Piłsudski's ambitions, and these found no place in the paper. Throughout 1920, those who dealt with Russia and Eastern Europe within the British government were inclined, in general, to put the worst construction on any Polish policy or initiative, and in many cases to put too favorable a gloss on the motivations and behavior of Poland's enemies—of whom there were many.

As it turned out, the "conditions of principle" which were incorporated in the note from the Polish government to the Allied ministers in Warsaw, and to which the British government took such exception, were never presented to Moscow. Not until 27 March did the Poles even respond to the many Soviet proposals to make peace, and the message which Patek sent to Chicherin then stated only that Polish representatives would be ready to meet

Soviet representatives to begin peace discussions on 10 April at the town of Borisov, which was located on the front lines dividing Polish and Russian forces about fifty miles northeast of Minsk. The message proposed a cease-fire only in the immediate area of Borisov. At every other point hostilities would go on as usual.[53]

Whether or not this drastically altered message was due to Sir Horace Rumbold's warnings is unclear. A few days earlier, Piłsudski had drawn Patek aside at a diplomatic reception to ask how the arrangements for meeting the Bolsheviks were progressing. The Foreign Minister replied that all was in readiness. At this Piłsudski remarked on the anomaly that he, as Chief of State and Marshal (a title newly "offered" to him by the army), should be planning continued war while his Foreign Minister should be preparing peace. Rumbold, who heard about the conversation from Patek, wrote to Curzon that it precisely summed up the situation and added: "The Foreign Minister will do his utmost to conclude a speedy peace, while the Chief of the State will continue to hit the Bolsheviks as hard as possible."[54] In an earlier despatch, commenting on the enigmatic central figure in the complex whirl of Polish politics, Rumbold had said: "General Piłsudski is certainly a remarkable man. He keeps his own counsel, and has a definite policy in mind. He will only reveal his policy at the moment it suits him, and, in the meantime, he is very skilful in the art of suggestion."[55] By the end of March Piłsudski had revealed very little, but he had suggested much.

❖

Rumbold's description of Piłsudski might also have applied to Lloyd George in his handling of the problem of Russia. Not even his Cabinet colleagues had a clear idea of the goals of his Russian policy. Indeed, the Cabinet scarcely discussed Russian matters during the three months between January and May 1920. In his public utterances about Russia, trade was the subject Lloyd George mentioned most frequently. He developed this theme at great length on 10 February during the debate following the Address from the Throne. With further Allied intervention, war by the border states,

[53] Text in *Dokumenty vneshnei politiki*, vol. II, p. 428.
[54] Rumbold (Warsaw) to Curzon, despatch 215, 29 March 1920; *British Documents*, vol. XI, no. 239.
[55] Rumbold (Warsaw) to Curzon, despatch 194, 21 March 1920; *ibid.*, no. 231.

or—at the other extreme—formal peace negotiations all impossible, the only policy Britain might reasonably follow with regard to the Bolshevik regime, Lloyd George said, was one of commercial relations but nonrecognition. And he stated:

We have failed to restore Russia to sanity by force. I believe we can save her by trade. Commerce has a sobering influence in its operations. The simple sums in addition and subtraction which it inculcates soon dispose of wild theories. The Russian with his head in the clouds finds he is cold, and discovers that he is not clad and that he is hungry. He has no machinery for his land, and although it has been given to him, he realises that he cannot plough his land with title deeds, even if they are written by the Soviet Government. . . .[56]

Trade, in my opinion, will bring an end to the ferocity, the rapine, and the crudities of Bolshevism surer than any other method. . . . There is but one way—we must fight anarchy with abundance.[57]

These were effective debating points. (*The Times*'s lobby correspondent wrote that they constituted "the best argumentative statement of the Prime Minister's case that he has yet made.")[58] But— as Lloyd George undoubtedly intended—they served only to gloss over the political problems involved in trade with Russia. The Soviet government, however, was anxious that these problems should *not* be glossed over: Lloyd George's policies represented significant political victories for the Bolshevik leaders, and they were anxious that the world should recognize them as such. On 23 January the Soviet government gave its approval to an agreement that had been concluded in Paris three days before between the Supreme Economic Council and Tsentrosoyuz, the All-Russian Central Union of Consumers' Cooperatives.[59] An article in *Izvestiya* the same day stated that the Allies should understand that the acquisition of grain and important raw materials was a state monopoly, and that the cooperative societies were part of the governmental machinery for food distribution. It was therefore impossible, the article concluded,

[56] 125 *H.C. Deb.*, col. 44.   [57] *Ibid.*, col. 46.
[58] *The Times*, 11 February 1920.
[59] The agreement of 20 January stated that trade with the Russian cooperatives would be handled in the West by the cooperative societies of Britain, France, and Italy and that the necessary credits would be provided by the western cooperatives and by private banks and merchants; text in *Dokumenty vneshnei politiki*, vol. II, pp. 327-29. The Soviet government's approval of these arrangements, sent to the Tsentrosoyuz representatives in Paris by radio on 23 January, is printed on p. 327.

for the Allies to organize an exchange of goods with Russia in disregard of the Soviet government.[60] Another *Izvestiya* article a fortnight later attacked Lloyd George's speech of 10 February as highly hypocritical, and stated: "Mr. Lloyd George declares that the renewal of economic relations with Soviet Russia does not mean the recognition of Bolshevism. We have not asked them for this. We await such recognition from the peoples, and not from governments. Trade relations themselves will inevitably involve the formulation of political relations. We have waited long enough, but we are ready to wait still longer. History is working for us."[61]

Lloyd George, of course, was well aware of the connection which necessarily existed between "trade relations" and "political relations." He also knew that the scheme for trading through the cooperative societies, which he had so warmly advocated in Paris in mid-January, was most impractical: it would have been cripplingly inconvenient to restrict trade with Russia simply to Western cooperative societies. This was the conclusion of a special committee, composed of civil servants from all interested departments, which he ordered established shortly after his return to London. Chaired by E. F. Wise of the Ministry of Food, the so-called Inter-Departmental Russia Committee drew its other members from the Foreign Office, the Department of Overseas Trade (formally part of the Foreign Office, but in fact quite autonomous), the Treasury, the Board of Trade, the Ministry of Shipping, and the War Office and Admiralty. At its first meeting, on 24 January, the committee agreed that British firms of all kinds, and not merely cooperative societies, should be free to trade with the Russian cooperatives.[62] Therefore, when the Allied premiers met in London to draw up the policy statement that was published on 24 February, Lloyd George was quick to support Nitti's contention that although he had agreed not to enter into diplomatic relations with the Soviet regime he interpreted the statement of Allied policy to mean that each government had a free hand in the sphere of commercial relations. To Lloyd George a free hand meant that the Allied governments could also take such steps as appointing commercial agents to serve

---

[60] *Izvestiya*, 23 January 1920.   [61] *Ibid.*, 12 February 1920.

[62] Minutes, Inter-Departmental Russia Committee, 1st meeting, 24 January 1920, file 173925/142549/38; F.O. 371/4032. Hankey described the Committee's organization in "Re-opening of trading relations with the Russian people," Cabinet paper C.P. 494, 23 January; Cab. 24/94.

in Russia. In order to appease Millerand, he gave assurances that these agents, if appointed, would not be called consuls, but it must have been apparent to everyone at the conference that "commercial agents" would necessarily exercise many of the functions normally exercised by consuls.[63]

The Allied premiers entrusted the task of working out detailed arrangements for Russian trade to the Permanent Committee of the Supreme Economic Council, which had been established as part of the machinery of the Peace Conference. The British representative on the committee was Wise, and thus the formal role of the Inter-Departmental Russia Committee became one of advising Wise, its chairman, regarding the position he should adopt within the inter-Allied body and in the negotiations which it would carry on with representatives of the Russian cooperatives. Talks were already under way in London in February. They were complicated by the fact that the Russians—non-Bolshevik old-time cooperators —by no means had the confidence of the Soviet government. Obviously this situation was viewed with distaste in Moscow, and on 25 February the directorate of Tsentrosoyuz informed the representatives in London that a new delegation would be sent out to take over the negotiations. The members of this delegation, according to the message from Tsentrosoyuz, would be Maxim Litvinov, Leonid B. Krasin, Viktor P. Nogin, Solomon Z. Rozovsky, and Lev M. Khinchuk.[64]

About Litvinov, who was still in Copenhagen making arrangements for the exchange of prisoners of war following the signature of the Anglo-Soviet agreement on this subject on 12 February,[65]

[63] See the remarks of Nitti and Lloyd George at the session of 24 February 1920, 11 A.M.; minutes cited above, n. 42.

[64] The text of this message, sent by radio, is in *Dokumenty vneshnei politiki*, vol. II, pp. 391-92. For Soviet distrust of the cooperatives' representatives abroad, see the telegram from Litvinov (Copenhagen) to Chicherin, 17 February 1920, asserting that A. M. Berkenheim, chief representative of the Russian cooperatives in London, was harboring what were, in effect, very much the same intentions as those of Lloyd George—of using trade as a means of "renewing private property" in Russia and thus destroying Bolshevism (*ibid.*, p. 372). A long editorial note (*ibid.*, pp. 749-50) states that the branches abroad of the Russian cooperative societies, founded in September 1917, engaged after the Bolshevik Revolution in widespread anti-Soviet activities such as supplying goods to the various White governments. Thus, say the editors, the so-called political neutrality proclaimed by Berkenheim and his colleagues was in fact simply a cloak for "a silent underground struggle" against every aspect of Soviet economic policy.

[65] The agreement, negotiated in Copenhagen by Litvinov and James O'Grady, a

nothing more need be said here: the Deputy Commissar for Foreign Affairs appears frequently in the first two volumes of the present work. Of the other delegates, only Rozovsky and Khinchuk were active members of the cooperative organization. Khinchuk, the president of Tsentrosoyuz and an old Menshevik, was received into the Communist Party at its ninth congress in March 1920. Nogin was a Party member of long standing and a member of the Central Committee; he also held important governmental posts in economic fields. Krasin was one of the most unusual and talented figures in the Bolshevik movement. A leading member of the Party since 1904, he was also one of Russia's foremost electrical engineers and industrial managers. We shall hear more about him later; for present purposes it is sufficient to point out that in February 1920 he was both Commissar for Foreign Trade and Commissar for Transport.

This was scarcely a delegation which Moscow would send merely to work out arrangements for trade between the Russian and Western cooperatives. On 6 March, when Lloyd George was asked by his friend Lord Riddell, the newspaper publisher, "Are they representatives of the co-operative societies or the Bolshevist Government?" the Prime Minister replied: "The Soviet, undoubtedly."[66] E. F. Wise was only slightly less succinct when he wrote in a briefing paper for the government that the Russian delegates were "all trusted Communists whose claim to speak for the Co-operative movement is based on their selection for this purpose by a Central Committee to which the Soviet Government had appointed a majority of Communists."[67]

In public, however, the Prime Minister continued to insist that his government had dealt and would deal not with the Soviet government, but only with the Russian cooperatives, which, he implied, had maintained their independence. When asked in the House of Commons on 15 March what arrangements had been made by the British and Soviet governments to discuss the opening of trade relations, he replied—technically correctly—that no requests from

---

Labour member of Parliament, provided for the mutual exchange of virtually all prisoners and hostages, military and civilian, held by either side. See Volume II, pp. 340-43.

[66] Lord Riddell, *Lord Riddell's Intimate Diary of the Peace Conference and After, 1918-1923*, London, 1933, entry for 6 March 1920, p. 175.

[67] "Memorandum by Mr. E. F. Wise on Negotiations for Reopening Trade with Soviet Russia," 21 April 1920, *British Documents*, vol. XII, London, 1962, no. 687.

the Soviet government had been received, but that the "Central Board" of the Russian cooperative organizations had asked permission to send to Britain the delegation named above. The British government had consulted its Allies, Lloyd George continued, and had then replied that it was ready to receive all of the delegates named by the cooperatives except Litvinov, whom it could not admit "because on a previous occasion during 1918, when he represented the Bolshevik government in London he took advantage of diplomatic privileges to engage in political propaganda in this country."[68]

The government's ban on Litvinov's coming to Great Britain was for many weeks to be a minor but troublesome obstacle to Anglo-Soviet negotiations. Almost certainly it was due not so much to Lloyd George's fear of what the Bolshevik emissary might actually do in Britain as to his fear that the very fact of Litvinov's presence would impose too great a strain upon British relations with France and also—even more to be feared—upon the none-too-strong ties that bound together the Coalition at home. To the French, the coming to London of so prominent a Soviet representative (unlike, for example, Krasin, who was little known in the West) would imply just those "diplomatic relations" that were expressly ruled out in the Allied declaration of 24 February; at home the Tories, especially those on the back benches, could be counted upon to react even more vehemently against Litvinov than they had done when he was in London during the brief period of Anglo-Soviet cordiality in early 1918.[69] That these political factors, rather than any specific fear of Litvinov's actions, dictated the ban against his coming is indicated by the fact that the government quietly suggested that he should remain in Copenhagen, instead of returning to Russia, in order to participate in those phases of the negotiations which might usefully take place in the Danish capital. And the British govern-

[68] 126 *H.C. Deb.*, cols. 1792-93. For Litvinov's activities as representative of the Soviet government in Great Britain during 1918, see Volume I, pp. 78-81. It will be recalled that he was arrested and imprisoned *not* because of any acts that he was alleged to have committed, but as a hostage for R. H. Bruce Lockhart and other British subjects imprisoned in Russia. See Volume I, pp. 290, 293-96. These facts were quickly forgotten. In a telegram (no. 165) to the British Chargé d'Affaires in Copenhagen on 6 March 1920, the Foreign Office, explaining the government's decision on no account to allow Litvinov to enter Britain, asserted incorrectly: "He was expelled from here in September 1918 for abusing his privileges and indulging in subversive activities" (*British Documents*, vol. XII, no. 667, n. 4).

[69] For this reaction, see Volume I, pp. 79-80.

ment, which professed to fear Litvinov's conduct in London, promised to intercede with the Danish authorities to secure permission for him to remain in Copenhagen.[70] It duly interceded.[71]

In Lloyd George's view of things such a compromise was, undoubtedly, eminently reasonable. But to the Soviet government, in its curious way ever sensitive to the least diplomatic slight while at the same time maintaining that it desired recognition "from the peoples" and not from the bourgeois governments, it did not appear reasonable at all; if Litvinov were not to be allowed to enter Great Britain, then no Soviet delegation would go. Instead, the Russian delegation would join Litvinov in Copenhagen and remain there with him. If the British government wanted to proceed with the trade negotiations, British delegates would have to go to Copenhagen—and deal with Litvinov.[72]

Although Lloyd George was afraid of the domestic political consequences of allowing Litvinov to enter the United Kingdom—so much so that he did not even bother to put the decision regarding him to the Cabinet—he was also aware that there was enough support for the policy of renewed trade with Russia, both in the Commons and in the country, so that it could not be allowed to founder simply over the issue of Litvinov. Therefore, in early April, accompanied by two Foreign Office officials and his French colleague on the Permanent Committee of the Supreme Economic Council, E. F. Wise journeyed to Copenhagen for talks with the Russians. His object was to explore some of the problems involved in the restoration of trade relations and, in particular, to persuade Krasin to come to London for talks with the Prime Minister.[73] Wise could speak with no authority, however, and the Russians were after bigger game. The meetings accomplished little. Years later Litvinov com-

---

[70] So stated the London representatives of the Russian cooperatives in a radiogram to the directorate of Tsentrosoyuz, 28 February 1920; excerpts printed in *Dokumenty vneshnei politiki*, vol. II, p. 397. The same point was made more obliquely in a letter from "the British government" (which department is not specified) to the London representatives of the cooperatives on 11 March; *ibid.*, p. 408.

[71] See Curzon's telegram 186 to Grant Watson, the British Chargé in Copenhagen, 13 March 1920 (*British Documents*, vol. XII, no. 667), instructing him to urge the Danish government to allow Litvinov to remain and to grant him necessary communications facilities.

[72] Radiogram, Tsentrosoyuz to "British government," 12 March 1920, *Dokumenty vneshnei politiki*, vol. II, p. 407.

[73] Wise's long memorandum on the talks, which took place 7-9 April 1920, is cited above, n. 67.

mented sourly on the Copenhagen discussions: "Very soon it was clear that in Copenhagen, far from both governments, the talks were enmeshed in difficulties and were being uselessly dragged out."[74]

The issue of the ban on Litvinov, already inflated out of all proportion (even the King of Sweden felt constrained to appeal to Curzon to keep him out of Great Britain),[75] was raised yet once more by Lloyd George when the Supreme Council of the Allies met from 18 through 26 April—primarily to discuss the Turkish peace settlement—at the Italian resort of San Remo. The Prime Minister did so, he explained privately to Millerand on the 24th and then to the whole conference on the following day, because he wanted to be able officially to announce that the three Allied heads of government had agreed that Litvinov could not be received in their countries. To this proposal he found ready agreement.[76]

Lloyd George's primary purpose, we must suspect, was not simply to *exclude* Litvinov, but rather to bring about the *acceptance* of the other Russians, who were by this time openly acknowledged to be delegates of the Soviet government.[77] Litvinov, according to Lloyd George, "knew nothing of trade and was simply a political agitator"; when he was in London during 1918 "he had taken no interest in commercial questions, but had merely preached Bolshevism and the doctrines of Communism." This was his "sole business in life." Therefore he should not be allowed to enter any Allied country.

Krasin, on the other hand, was "a good businessman and might be useful." Indeed, explained the Prime Minister, all of the other members of the Soviet delegation were businessmen, with whom discussion would be profitable. Lloyd George was saying, in effect,

[74] From Litvinov's reminiscences as recorded by his friend, the Soviet diplomat (later Academician) I. M. Maiskii, "Anglo-sovetskoe torgovoe soglashenie 1921 goda" (The Anglo-Soviet Trade Agreement of 1921), *Voprosy Istorii* (Problems of History), 1957, no. 5 (May), p. 68.

[75] The King's appeal, made over luncheon in London on 15 April, was described by Curzon in despatch 112 to the British Minister in Stockholm the same day; *British Documents*, vol. XI, no. 250.

[76] Lloyd George met with Millerand on April, 10:30 A.M.; see Hankey's notes in *British Documents*, vol. VIII, no. 14, pp. 152-53. Minutes of the Supreme Council meeting on 25 April, 11 A.M., are in *ibid.*, no. 16, pp. 172-84.

[77] Krasin acknowledged the official status of the delegation in a telegram to the Supreme Council on 21 April 1920; French text (as transmitted from Copenhagen) in *ibid.*, pp. 184-85; Russian version in *Dokumenty vneshnei politiki*, vol. II, pp. 474-75.

that just as he knew a fanatical revolutionary when he saw one, so also could he distinguish a down-to-earth, practical trader. This was a tactic aimed particularly at overcoming the resistance of the French to anything resembling intergovernmental relations with the Bolsheviks.[78]

It was a remarkable performance, typical of the way Lloyd George operated and typical of him at his most skilful. The problem of Russia was not on the agenda for the San Remo conference. It had been settled, for the time being, at previous Allied meetings, and the settlement, such as it was, had been incorporated into the Allied statement of 24 February rejecting the possibility of anything like intergovernmental relations. Now, at San Remo, Lloyd George re-opened the subject: he wanted to warn his colleagues against that arch-Bolshevik Litvinov, and he said so in language that would have done credit to any French holder of Russian bonds. In doing so he neatly shifted the terms of debate. The question was no longer one of whether or not the Allied governments should deal with representatives of the Soviet government. Krasin and most of his colleagues were reliable, sober businessmen, according to Lloyd George; certainly they should be received. There was not even any discussion of this point, which was, in fact, the point at issue. All attention, instead, was focused on Litvinov—a Red red herring.

As almost always in the conference diplomacy of which he was a master practitioner, Lloyd George was successful: he got both what he appeared to want and what he actually wanted. From Millerand and Nitti, his Allied colleagues, he got agreement to a note stating that there would be no trade negotiations with Litvinov. But the message, addressed to Krasin, also stated that the Supreme Council had decided to authorize "representatives of the Allied Governments" to meet "the Russian Trade Delegation" (no longer would there be even the pretense that the Soviet delegates represented the cooperatives) in London as soon as possible "with a view to the immediate restarting of trade relations between Russia and other countries through the intermediary of the co-operative organisations *and otherwise*."[79] At the same session on 26 April

[78] Lloyd George's remarks quoted here are from the meetings of 24 and 25 April, cited n. 76.

[79] The Supreme Council's telegram to Krasin, drafted by the British delegation on 25 April and approved by the Council at its meeting at 5 P.M. on the 26th, is printed in *British Documents*, vol. VIII, pp. 230-31 (italics added).

at which this telegram to Krasin was approved, Lloyd George also secured the Council's assent to a draft set of instructions to guide the Permanent Committee of the Supreme Economic Council in its negotiations with the Russians. The most important section of these instructions specified that the negotiators were "to discuss with the Russian delegation, and to submit to the Allied Governments, general questions arising out of the resumption of trade." These "general questions" could not help but be political as well as commercial.

✢

On the same day that the Supreme Council approved the text of its message to Krasin, ten Polish divisions, virtually unopposed, began a surprise thrust that quickly carried them deep into the Ukraine. On 7 May they occupied Kiev, and by the 11th they had consolidated a position along much of the Dnieper River north of that principal Ukrainian city. In a proclamation to the Ukrainian people issued the day the attack began, Piłsudski declared that Polish troops would remain only until there could be established a "legitimate Ukrainian Government" in control of Ukrainian forces capable of defending the country "against a fresh invasion" by Russia, and until—presumably by the decision of an elected constituent assembly—"the free Ukrainian nation has been able to decide its own fate."[80]

The Polish attack came after a month of sporadic radio messages between Warsaw and Moscow on the subject of how and where peace talks between the two governments would commence. The Poles, it will be recalled, suggested on 27 March that delegates should meet on 10 April at Borisov, immediately behind the Polish lines in White Russia, and that there should be an armistice only in the immediate vicinity of the town. The rationale behind this proposal was first, that a general armistice would take the pressure off the Soviet forces and enable them to regroup for new attacks on Poland and, second, that Borisov's isolation and inaccessibility to the world press would deny the Bolsheviks a propaganda forum. The Soviet government, in reply, insisted that there should be a general armistice during the peace talks in order to stop the blood-

---

[80] Piłsudski's proclamation is printed in his *Errinerungen und Dokumente*, vol. IV, *Reden und Armeebefehle*, Essen, 1936, pp. 59-60. Curiously, he does not even mention the attack in his memoirs, *ibid.*, vol. II, *Das Jahr 1920*, Essen, 1935.

shed at the earliest moment, and, stipulating that the talks should be held anywhere except near the front lines, suggested that an Estonian town might provide the tranquility necessary for successful negotiations.[81] Although further notes were exchanged, neither side would make significant concessions.[82] Each appealed to the Allies for support of its position.[83] The British government, for its part, made a "friendly appeal" to the "good sense" of the Polish government to moderate its "uncompromising attitude" of insistence upon Borisov as the site for the Polish-Soviet negotiations.[84]

Shortly before the attack, on 21 April the Polish government concluded a treaty of alliance with (in the words of the treaty) "the Directory of the Independent Ukrainian People's Republic, headed by the Supreme Military Commander Semyon Petlyura."[85] Petlyura was in Warsaw at the time. Both of his colleagues in the three-man "Directory" had gone to the West during the previous autumn to try to attract Allied support for an independent, sovereign Ukraine, and they had charged him with the task of remaining on what was left of non-Bolshevik Ukrainian soil and carrying on the struggle—not only against the Bolsheviks but also against the Poles, who during 1919 had driven the already hard-pressed forces of the Directory out of Eastern Galicia. Petlyura signed the treaty with the Poles as a desperate act: he had come to the conclusion that the achievement of an independent, non-Bolshevik Ukraine

[81] For the rationale behind the Polish note of 27 March 1920 (cited above, n. 52), see the note from the Polish Minister in Washington to the Secretary of State, 19 April, *Papers Relating to the Foreign Relations of the United States,* 1920, vol. III, Washington, 1936, pp. 383-84 (hereafter this Department of State serial publication will be referred to as *Foreign Relations*), and the text of a Polish press communiqué of 20 April, printed in Komarnicki, *Polish Republic,* p. 571. The Soviet reply, sent by radio on 28 March, is in *Dokumenty Vneshnei politiki,* vol. II, pp. 427-28; translated in Degras, *Soviet Documents,* pp. 183-84.

[82] For the Polish notes, 1 and 7 April, and the Soviet notes, 2 and 8 April, and a Narkomindel statement of 23 April, see *Dokumenty vneshnei politiki,* vol. II, pp. 436-38, 447-48, 480-82.

[83] The Polish appeals are cited above, note 74. The Soviet appeal, sent by radio on 8 April 1920, is in *ibid.,* pp. 445-47. (English versions printed in *The Times,* 12 April 1920, and *British Documents,* vol. XI, no. 248.) It asserted that the Poles were behaving like the Germans at Brest-Litovsk, and stated that the influence of the Allies over the Poles was so great that if the Poles would not accept any other place than Borisov, "the *Entente* Governments will not be in a position to relieve themselves of responsibility. . . ."

[84] The appeal was made to the Polish Chargé in London and reported to Rumbold (Warsaw) by Hardinge, telegram 181, 19 April 1920; *ibid.,* no. 251.

[85] The text of the treaty is in John S. Reshetar, Jr. *The Ukrainian Revolution, 1917-1920: A Study in Nationalism,* Princeton, 1952, pp. 301-02.

would be possible only with Polish, and, in particular, Allied support, which in turn would be forthcoming only if he were to accede to Polish territorial demands and, in effect, become virtually a Polish satellite.[86] For Piłsudski, on the other hand, the agreement gave substance to the assertion that the Poles were coming not as conquerors but as liberators, and thus opened the door to his invasion of Soviet Ukraine.

To the British government the Polish offensive of 26 April virtually came as a complete surprise. Under the pretense of wishing to effect a currency reform, the Poles had closed all their frontiers for a ten-day period from the 17th and had even, to the mystification of the British Foreign Office, forbidden all telegraphic traffic.[87] Thus, although the military mission in Warsaw finally began to suspect that an attack was likely, it was unable to transmit this intelligence to London.[88] Previously, although the Cabinet had listened to a warning that it would be impossible for Piłsudski to maintain a static army in a state of readiness and that he would have to launch an offensive by late April or early May, most speculation had concerned not a Polish but a Bolshevik attack.[89]

[86] The agreement between Poland and Petlyura (signed on the Polish side not by Piłsudski, but by two officials of the Foreign Ministry) conceded to Poland all of eastern Galicia and, in effect, established for Poland a position of dominant influence over what would be the future Ukrainian state. The terms of the agreement were secret; only the fact that an alliance had been concluded was made public. Even so, it was immediately denounced as Polish imperialism by Ukrainians abroad: *ibid.*, pp. 303-07. For a Polish view, see Komarnicki, *Polish Republic*, pp. 574-80. See also E. H. Carr, *A History of Soviet Russia: The Bolshevik Revolution, 1917-1923*, vol. I, London, 1950, p. 304.

[87] See Rumbold (Warsaw) to Curzon, telegram 249, 15 April 1920, file 193402/73/55, and the minutes on it following its arrival (by post) at the Foreign Office on 22 April; F.O. 371/3901.

[88] British military mission (Warsaw) to War Office, telegram 495, 22 April 1920; W.O. 33/996, no. 4926. As late as 18 April, in his weekly report to the C.I.G.S., Lieutenant General Sir Richard Haking, commander of the Allied garrison at Danzig, reported that neither he nor the mission at Warsaw expected any "trouble"; Haking, indeed, seems to have viewed a Polish attempt to take over Danzig as more likely than a drive eastward. (File 194854/73/55; F.O. 371/3901.) War Office files do, however, contain one warning of an impending Polish attack; evidently it made no real impact on London. Major A. D. Campbell Krook of the military mission in Warsaw, stated in despatch G.1854, 12 April, to the Director of Military Intelligence: "It seems probable that a combined Polish-Ukrainian offensive is intended, as soon as possible, as a counter measure." (W.O. 106/968).

[89] The warning came from Sir Halford Mackinder, who had stopped in Warsaw on his way to taking up his brief assignment as British High Commissioner in South Russia; he was interviewed at length by the Cabinet upon his return. (Cabinet minutes 6 [20], 29 January 1920, 11:30 A.M., Appendix I; Cab. 23/20.)

Once it had come, the Polish offensive was hailed by those who had originally favored intervention in Russia. The Poles were engaged in what a later age was to call "preventive war." Had they not attacked, said a leading article in *The Times*, they would have been next—following the White armies—on the list of Soviet victims. "First and foremost," *The Times* stated, "the Poles are fighting a battle for the defence of Western civilization."[90]

Churchill, in a memorandum written on 21 May, similarly asserted that Piłsudski had moved in order to forestall a Soviet attack upon Poland which would have begun after the Red Army had completed a transfer of troops from other fronts. The Secretary of State for War was under no illusion that the Poles constituted a threat to the existence of the Soviet regime, but he did feel that they were capable of achieving Piłsudski's ambitions in the Ukraine and White Russia. And he stated that in his opinion, "there could be no greater advantage to the famine areas of Central Europe than the re-establishment of a peaceful state of the Ukraine on a basis which permitted economic and commercial transactions to take place." The outcome, Churchill said, was by no means certain. Although the Poles had taken Kiev, they might still be driven out. Nevertheless, he continued, "on the assumption that Petlyura's Government manages to set up and maintain a separate Government of a civilised type capable of liberating the corn supplies of the Ukraine, and with that territory sheltered and assisted in this task by a strong Poland, it ought not to be impossible to arrive at satisfactory conditions of a general peace in the east in the course of the present summer."[91]

Lloyd George, of course, differed with Churchill over the Polish attack as he did over everything relating to Russia. The Poles, he told Riddell on 9 May, "have gone rather mad ... and they will have to take care that they don't get their heads punched." They would be decisively defeated, he predicted a fortnight later. The invasion would reawaken Russian nationalism; Russians of all classes would join hands to defend their territory against a foreign invasion.[92]

Despite the Prime Minister's views, the Polish people initially received the impression that their attack enjoyed the support of his government. On 10 May, the day on which the Polish capture of

[90] *The Times*, 1 May 1920.
[91] Winston S. Churchill, *The Aftermath*, London, 1929, pp. 266-67.
[92] Riddell, *Diary*, entries for 9, 23, and 30 May 1920, pp. 191, 197, and 199.

Kiev was made known, the press of both Britain and Poland published an exchange of telegrams between King George V and Piłsudski. The King's message was sent on 3 May, the anniversary of the ratification of the Polish constitution of 1791, and a day celebrated as Poland's chief national holiday. The King wished, he said, to send to Piłsudski, and through him to the ancient nation which he led, "the most sincere congratulations" of himself and the British people, and their "sincere good wishes for the future of the Polish State." Great Britain had "watched with the greatest sympathy the resurrection of Poland after the long period of anguish through which she has passed." Now, "with the dawn of a new era," Poland would "enjoy unlimited prosperity and peace."[93]

The message itself was innocuous enough. But the timing of its publication, and to a certain extent its tone, gave rise to the widespread belief (which the Poles did nothing to contradict) that it was in fact intended to congratulate Piłsudski upon his victory.[94] In the House of Commons this suspicion gave rise to angry questions from Liberal and Labour members. Bonar Law, speaking in Lloyd George's absence, replied that the message had been prepared several days before the Polish attack, and had no connection with it. In fact, improbably enough, this seems to have been the case.[95] When asked whether the King had acted on the advice of ministers, Bonar Law heatedly stated: "Certainly. My hon. friend, I think, does not realize that at that time, at all events, there was no question of this War. So far as we are concerned . . . there is nothing more natural than that we should send congratulations on the National Fête Day."[96] Did this mean, a member asked, that the British government had no knowledge of the Polish attack when the telegram was sent? Lamely, Bonar Law replied once more: "So far as the British Government were aware, they had no information that this offensive was to take place."[97]

❖

The focal point of protest within Great Britain against the Polish offensive and, in particular, against any British assistance to the

---

[93] *The Times*, 10 May 1920. Piłsudski's reply, published the same day, assured the King that his words would "be echoed throughout Poland."

[94] Such was implied by *The Times* in a leading article on 10 May 1920.

[95] See the papers in file 194176/73/55 and Curzon's rueful comment following the publication of the King's message, "Not very well timed," on file 197866/—; F.O. 371/3901.

[96] 129 *H.C. Deb.*, cols. 434-35 (10 May 1920).   [97] *Ibid.*, col. 435.

Poles, came not in Parliament but outside it, in the Labour movement. In the surge of overblown patriotism which gave the Coalition its inflated majority from the "Khaki election" of December 1918, Labour won only fifty-nine seats—no indication of the movement's very real strength in the country.[98] This disparity impelled the Labour leadership to rely increasingly on extra-Parliamentary means of demonstrating disagreement with the government's policies, a practice which caused Sir Basil Thomson, the Director of Intelligence at the Home Office (*i.e.*, the head of the "Special Branch") to comment in his annual report to the Cabinet on internal security: "The worst permanent feature of the year has been a decline in the influence of Parliament."[99]

Labour had spoken out against British intervention in Russia during 1919, but despite a good deal of talk about "direct action" it had done nothing: its leadership hesitated to employ the strike—the only weapon available to it—for "political" instead of "industrial" ends.[100] By mid-1920, however, a different mood prevailed. Allied intervention to overthrow the Soviet government had failed. The passage of time had demonstrated conclusively that whatever the faults of the Soviet system (and there was much disagreement within the Labour movement on this point), the Bolsheviks had managed to gain the support of broad segments of the Russian working-class population. Now that the civil war was ending, a great era of progress could be expected in Russia. In Great Britain, however, no such progress seemed likely. The brief boom which had followed the end of the war was already ending, and unemployment, particularly in mining, was beginning to appear. In the whole pattern of relationships within industry and society, where the Labour movement had sought dramatic change, there seemed to be only stagnation.[101]

[98] Less than sixty percent of the electorate, and only one man in four in the armed forces, had voted in 1918. Nevertheless, Labour polled nearly 2.4 million votes—nearly half the vote of the Coalition. By 1920 total trades-union membership, a more reliable index of Labour's strength, reached 8,334,000. See Alan Bullock, *The Life and Times of Ernest Bevin*, vol. I, *Trade Union Leader 1881-1940*, London, 1960, pp. 99-100.

[99] "A Survey of Revolutionary Movements in Great Britain in the year 1920," Cabinet paper C.P. 2455, Cab. 24/118.

[100] For the debate over "direct action" during 1919, see *ibid.*, pp. 103-05, and Stephen R. Graubard, *British Labour and the Russian Revolution, 1917-1924*, Cambridge, Mass., 1956, pp. 74-82.

[101] Bullock, *Bevin*, pp. 163-67. Bullock notes (pp. 98-99) that the three years 1919-21 "were more disturbed by open conflict between the trade unions and the

Labour was in an angry mood, and the Polish invasion of the Ukraine provided a focus for its anger. There was no little suspicion that just as Lloyd George had given way on his assurances with regard to the postwar shape of British industrial life, so he had also given way on his assurances that the government would not encourage or support further military action against Soviet Russia. These suspicions, and Labour's new mood of angry militancy, were encapsulated in a leading article in the movement's newspaper, the *Daily Herald*, four days after Polish troops began to sweep into the Ukraine. Entitled "The Storm Bursts," the editorial stated:

> The Red Army will do its duty. But there is a duty, too, for us. . . . Without Allied approval, without Allied help in finance and in munitions, the conspirators would be powerless. The marionettes are in Warsaw, but the strings are pulled from London and from Paris.
> One word from here, and the whole mad adventure . . . must end.
> It is for British Labour to insist that that word shall be spoken, and spoken at once. . . .[102]

The first word, such as it was, came during the second week of May from stevedores at the East India Docks who were in the process of loading a Walford Lines steamship, the *Jolly George*, with a consignment of cargo for Danzig. Among the cargo the dockers found cases containing 18-pound field guns and ammunition and reportedly marked "O.H.M.S. Munitions for Poland." Immediately they sent a deputation to see Ernest Bevin, the assistant general secretary of the Dockers' Union. Without hesitation, according to his biographer, Bevin told the men that they could count on the union's backing if they refused to load or coal the ship.[103] In these circumstances the owners of the ship were forced to acquiesce; on 15 May the *Jolly George* sailed without the offending cargo.[104] Here was successful "direct action."

---

employers, or between the unions and the Government, than any other period in modern British history, with the solitary exception of 1926, the year of the General Strike."

[102] *Daily Herald*, 30 April 1920.

[103] Bullock, *Bevin*, vol. I, pp. 133-34.

[104] For the *Jolly George* incident, see (besides *ibid.*) *The Times*, 14 May 1920, and Harry Pollitt, *Serving My Time*, London, 1940, pp. 111-17. For official reactions, see Sir Basil Thomson's weekly "Report on Revolutionary Organisations in the United Kingdom," no. 54, 13 May 1920, Cabinet paper C.P. 1039, Cab. 24/103; and British Military Mission (Warsaw) to War Office, telegram 650, 10 June, W.O. 33/996, no. 5029. While there may be some doubt regarding the blatant markings of the cases, there is none about their contents.

Three days later, by a coincidence, the dockers met in Plymouth for their Triennial Conference. Bevin moved an emergency resolution congratulating the London members for "refusing to have their labour prostituted" in the service of the capitalist campaign against Russia, and calling upon the entire Labour movement to do likewise.[105] The "working people," he explained, had "a right to say where their labour and how their labour should be used." They had a right to refuse if they were "called upon either to make munitions or transport munitions for purposes which outrage our sense of justice." And Bevin went on to state the view of foreign policy which underlay his actions: "Whatever may be the merits or demerits of the theory of government of Russia, that is a matter for Russia, and we have no right to determine their form of government, any more than we would tolerate Russia determining our form of government."[106]

✧

Although the dockers gathered at Plymouth could not have known it, they were, in fact, arraying themselves against a government which was far from enthusiastic about sending arms to Poland and which, earlier in the year, had rejected proposals for sending the Poles either German or British arms.

The proposal for shipping German arms to Poland was made by the French at a meeting of the Allied council in Paris on 5 January. The Poles had asked for 300,000 Mauser rifles and a large supply of ammunition.[107] A fortnight later (no decision had been reached in Paris) Sir Horace Rumbold telegraphed from Warsaw giving the request his endorsement and that of the British military mission. The Poles, he said, had no reserve of small arms and could not manufacture any themselves; they would need them in order to resist a Soviet offensive.[108]

For the Poles to acquire any German military equipment, however—whether by purchase or by any other means—would have contravened Article 169 of the Treaty of Versailles providing for the destruction of all German armaments except for the small amounts

[105] *Daily Herald*, 19 May 1920.

[106] Bullock, *Bevin*, p. 134, from the Conference Report.

[107] Minutes, Council of Heads of Delegations, Paris, 5 January 1920, 10:30 A.M.; *British Documents*, vol. II, no. 51, pp. 691-92.

[108] Rumbold (Warsaw) to Curzon, telegram 29, 16 January 1920; summarized in an editorial note in *British Documents*, vol. XI, p. 198.

Germany was allowed to retain for maintaining internal order. This fact was pointed out to London by Lord Derby, the British Ambassador in Paris and representative on the Council, who also asserted that the reason the French and Italian governments were so anxious that the Poles should receive German weapons was so that a precedent would be established whereby they too could get their hands on some. Derby urged that the French scheme should be rejected.[109]

In London, where there was considerable uneasiness already about the harshness of the German peace treaty, Derby's advice was immediately accepted: if the Allies would not permit breaches of the treaty in favor of the Germans, they certainly could not permit any which might benefit themselves. Curzon telegraphed to Derby on 9 February: "You should maintain the attitude which you have already adopted. The full force of the Treaty should be maintained." The question was therefore settled; without British assent the Poles would receive no German rifles.[110]

Although the Treaty of Versailles prevented the Poles from obtaining German weapons, no such legal restrictions barred them from other markets. Accordingly, on 12 February they presented the Allies with requests for military supplies "necessary to put the Polish Army on a proper footing."[111] Their demands were not inconsiderable; from the British, for example, they asked five squadrons of Bristol fighters and seventy-five other aircraft, as well as tanks and artillery. Moreover, they proposed that the Allies should furnish this equipment at no charge, on the grounds that in using it, and thus arresting the spread of Bolshevism, Poland was rendering a service to the whole of Europe.[112]

The British government, of course, was scarcely more happy with this request than it had been with the request for German rifles. As Sir Horace Rumbold tartly reminded Patek, who had summoned him to present the list of Polish requirements, the Polish Foreign Minister seemed to have forgotten that Lloyd George had told him only three weeks previously that the British government did not want to give Poland the slightest encouragement to go to war.[113]

---

[109] Derby (Paris) to Curzon, telegrams 116 and 129, 31 January and 3 February 1920; *ibid.*, nos. 180 and 184.

[110] Curzon to Derby (Paris), telegram 1589 P, 9 February 1920; *ibid.*, no. 185.

[111] These were the words used by Rumbold (Warsaw) in transmitting the Polish requests to Curzon in his despatch 107, 16 February 1920; *ibid.*, no. 195.

[112] *Idem.*   [113] *Idem.*

When Rumbold's report of this interview arrived in London, Lord Hardinge commented upon it, with Curzon's initialled agreement: "The French who are responsible for providing the Poles with equipment are fairly sure not to provide what is wanted as they have absolutely failed to do so in the past. We will certainly not do so, nor the Italians either."[114]

These expressions of British policy regarding the Polish requests for German and Allied weapons were, in fact, the background to the *Jolly George* incident, a background that the angry dockers could not know. The munitions in the crates on the East India docks were not the vanguard of increasing quantities to come. Rather, they were among the last of a series of consignments which had been promised the Poles the previous October. At that time, Bonar Low explained on 17 May in answer to a Parliamentary question, when a Soviet attack on the Border States appeared likely, "a request was addressed by the Polish Government for assistance in their military commitments." And he continued:

In consequence of our commitments elsewhere the British Government were unable to give any financial assistance, but they offered to supply a certain quantity of surplus stores on condition that the cost of moving them, as well as the arrangements for transport, should be undertaken by the Polish Government. The offer was accepted. In consequence of that gift the material in question became the property of the Polish Government, and part of it is now being shipped by that Government.

Beyond that material, Bonar Law asserted, "no assistance has been or is being given to the Polish Government."[115]

For some members of the House, however, this explanation was not sufficient. As one Labour member (George Barnes) pointed out, the situation had, after all, vastly changed since the previous October. British policy, as delineated in the Allied statement of 24 February, was wholly different from what it had been in October. And Poland had attacked Russia. To these statements Bonar Law readily agreed. In reply he could only emphasize that the government regarded a bargain as a bargain. The material had been given to the Polish government, and even though some of it still remained in the United Kingdom it was nevertheless Polish property. To have refused the Poles an export permit would have broken the bargain.[116]

114 *Idem.*, n. 4.   115 129 *H.C. Deb.*, col. 1009.
116 *Ibid.*, col. 1010.

Three days later, on 20 May, in a long foreign affairs debate on the motion to adjourn the House for the Whitsuntide recess, Bonar Law explained the government's position in more detail. Poland was a creation of the Peace Conference, he said, and thus the Allies had an implied obligation to see that the Poles were able to defend themselves. Critics of the government had argued that conditions should have been put upon the use of the British weapons which had been given the Poles, but no such conditions had been made in other cases in which the British government had helped its allies, and it would have been invidious to put conditions on the Poles.[117]

These were, perhaps, *post facto* rationalizations. Bonar Law then offered a more basic explanation for the fact that shipments to the Poles were continuing: the government had not known about them. "Once a Cabinet has given a decision," he said, "it is obvious that the Head of the Government cannot follow the details." In the present case the Cabinet, including Churchill, had thought that the munitions had long before been shipped to Poland.

Now that the government was aware of the shipments, Bonar Law asked, what was it to do about them? It could, of course, suspend them in accordance with the Prime Minister's statement to Patek in January that Britain would take no steps to encourage the Poles to make war. But such a step, were it to be taken, should have come before the Polish attack: now that war was in progress, Bonar Law asserted, an embargo on munitions shipments would have a much more serious effect than simply not encouraging the Poles to make war; it would throw Britain's weight to the side of Poland's enemies.[118]

Bonar Law then reached the heart of the government's case: that influence must be based upon power, and that in Eastern Europe Britain's effective power was slight. He stated:

All this kind of criticism leaves out of account one vital fact in dealing with Eastern Europe or any one of these countries. It is no use giving advice and expressing an opinion unless you are prepared to back it. If you were to adopt the sort of attitude which has been urged upon us, we must take the responsibility of sending men to carry out our views. Is there a man in this House who will say that the British Government or the British people can be induced to throw their weight into the scale?

---

[117] *Ibid.*, col. 1698.   [118] *Ibid.*, cols. 1698-99.

The Poles, Bonar Law continued, had stated that they had launched their offensive only in order to forestall a threatened Soviet attack. The Russians, on the other hand, had stated that they had moved their troops to the Polish frontier only because they were afraid of an attack by Poland. In such a situation he was not to say who was right and who was wrong. And he added, "but I can imagine nothing that would be more discreditable to this Government or to the Supreme Council than to say to Poland, 'Even if you think it necessary for your safety, you are not to attack the Bolshevists.' Then suppose it had been found that the Poles were right, and the Bolshevists overran Poland, what would our position have been? It is obvious that you cannot have it both ways. . . . We have to leave them to work as they think best, or we have got to take the responsibility of supporting them by arms."[119]

His statement came near the close of a long debate about British policy toward the Polish-Soviet war. Much of it was devoted to a discussion of the role that the League of Nations might play in bringing about peace between Poland and Russia and, indeed, of the place of the League in British foreign policy. Although it was the first important parliamentary discussion of the League since the organization's founding, many of the attitudes displayed on that Thursday afternoon in late May 1920 were to persist throughout the period between the wars.

In this debate, which was marked by urgent appeals for League action from Sir Donald Maclean, for the Liberals, and J. R. Clynes, for Labour, the most cogent and forceful arguments in favor of League intervention came not from the Opposition benches but from Lord Robert Cecil, who sat on the Government side.[120] Cecil had been one of the principal architects of the Covenant, and he was, indeed, the leading Englishman associated with the League throughout its existence. Three days before the debate, the press

[119] *Ibid.*, cols. 1700-01.

[120] Several members, principally Lord Robert Cecil and Sir Donald Maclean, adduced the mere fact of the existence of the League as a justification for abandoning the traditional practice whereby Parliament did not discuss the internal affairs of other states. Article II of the Covenant, they pointed out, declared "any war or threat of war, whether immediately affecting any of the Members of the League or not . . . a matter of concern to the whole League." The bellicosity of the Poles, they said, gave rise to a threat of war, and therefore made it perfectly proper for the House of Commons to criticize the policies of the Polish government. This doctrine was, however, rejected by the Speaker. (*Ibid.*, cols. 1653-58.)

had published an exchange of letters between Cecil, as Chairman of the Executive Committee of the League of Nations Union, and Curzon.[121] Cecil had written on 3 May stating that "for months past" Poland had been "notoriously preparing to attack Russia"; no matter who won, he said, the situation contained dangerous implications for the future peace of Europe, and he therefore hoped that the League Council would be summoned at the instance of the British government to deal with it.

Curzon's letter in reply on 11 May asserted that until quite recently the government had had no evidence that the Poles were planning an attack. In any case the "episode" did not "constitute an outbreak of war," but was "merely a phase of a war which has been going on for some time." Curzon wrote that he did not see how the British government could "invoke the intervention of the League of Nations to check an offensive by the Poles in the course of their conflict with the Bolshevists." The government had told the Poles that it could offer them no advice and that they must "choose peace or war on their own responsibility." Having left the Poles free to choose, the Foreign Secretary continued, "I hardly think it is open to us to attempt to repress their action when they have made their choice. Such an attempt would certainly be regarded as intervention in favor of the Bolshevists and against our Allies—a result which it would be difficult to defend." Even if such intervention were desirable, Curzon concluded, the League would find itself in a very difficult position if it were to try to mediate between Poland and a Russian government which did not recognize the League's authority.[122]

---

[121] *The Times*, 17 May 1920. As a copy of a letter of 14 May from Curzon to Cecil (Curzon MSS, box 65) indicates, Cecil insisted that the correspondence be published—and released it to the press—against Curzon's wishes.

[122] On 7 May, four days previous to Curzon's reply to Cecil, the Soviet government for all practical purposes rejected the League's request that it be allowed to send to Russia a commission of investigation to obtain "impartial and reliable information regarding the conditions now prevailing in Russia." The League Council had made the request in accordance with the wishes of the Allied Supreme Council expressed, it will be remembered, in its statement of 24 February (cited above, n. 42).

The Soviet statement welcomed the League's proposal in principle, while observing that the organization had previously not "made the smallest effort officially to communicate the fact of its existence to the Russian people." But it noted that Poland, a member of the League, was engaged in making war upon Russia with the active support of certain other members. Therefore, "for military reasons," the Soviet government did not wish at the present time to admit "representatives of

It was to arguments like Curzon's that Cecil addressed himself on the floor of the House of Commons. Both the Poles and the Bolsheviks, he thought, would respond to pressure from the League. It did not matter that the Russians were not members: they anxiously sought trade relations with the principal Powers, and would surely do nothing to jeopardize their prospects of achieving them. As for the Poles, Cecil said, there was no doubt whatever that for economic reasons they could not afford to defy the wishes of the League Council. He admitted that the present moment, with Polish forces deep in Russian territory, was not propitious for League intervention: it might appear to be an effort on behalf of the Bolsheviks. But the League of Nations Union, he said, had written to the British government as early as 4 February—when a Soviet attack upon Poland, rather than the reverse, had seemed likely—urging that the League should take action.

The question, Cecil asserted, was whether the League was a reality or not. He sought, he said, definite proof that the government really did intend "to make the League the essential organ of international relations," instead, as he feared, of allowing it "to rust away in inutility." For him this was "the question . . . of all questions in politics." If he were forced to conclude that the government "were not in earnest in this matter" he would have no choice but to cross the floor and vote with the Opposition.[123]

Bonar Law's reply to Cecil's entreaties was brief, somewhat beside the point, and heavily edged with sarcasm. "My Noble Friend seems to think that whenever he thinks the League should take action, that ought to be enough," he said. "That is not our view. Our view is that it should only take action if it can be effective." He appreciated Cecil's enthusiasm, he said. However, he added, "There must be wisdom as well." Bonar Law scarcely attempted to argue with Cecil, but simply asserted; "I know that there are others who take as keen an interest as my Noble Friend does, but take a different view, and think that, if you were to try to get the League of Nations mixed up with the settlement of this War, neutrals would

---

nations which have, in fact, renounced their neutrality in the war on Soviet Russia." After peace had been achieved, the commissions would be received. (The Soviet statement is in *Dokumenty vneshnei politiki*, vol. II, pp. 506-07; translation in Degras, *Soviet Documents*, pp. 186-87.)

[123] 126 *H.C. Deb.*, cols. 1682-91.

not come into it, and you would damn it as an effective instrument."[124]

As debating point, this was only a little better than the remark of the Conservative backbencher who rose while Cecil was speaking and interjected: "I am a believer, in a sense, in the League of Nations in the future, but I want security first."[125] Security, presumably, would be heightened by a Polish victory over the Bolsheviks. The League would be ill-advised to interfere. Scarcely two months later, however, the same Coalition back benches would be the scene of appeals of a different sort: for the League to take action to stem the advance of an invading Red Army upon the gates of Warsaw.

[124] *Ibid.*, cols. 1701-03.
[125] *Ibid.*, col. 1691. The backbencher was Lt. Col. Sir J. Norton-Griffiths.

CHAPTER II

WRANGEL

I am entirely in favour of getting out of this tangle in which the War Office have involved us by the worship of their battered fetish, Denikin.

—*Curzon, 15 March 1920*

THE efforts of the British government to avoid involvement in the deepening crisis of the Polish-Soviet war and at the same time to move toward the establishment of trade relations with the Soviet regime by no means represented the limits of the "Russian problem" in 1920 so far as London was concerned. In South Russia the civil war still smoldered; when the remnants of Denikin's armies retreated to the Crimea in March, there to fight again, a sizable part of the British military mission of 2,000 men went with them. Two British battalions continued to occupy the port of Batum on the Black Sea coast of Transcaucasia. In mid-May a British force at Enzeli, on the Caspian coast of Persia, was forced to withdraw in the face of a Bolshevik landing. And at various points throughout Soviet-controlled territory a number of British subjects—military personnel and civilians—remained imprisoned. Each of these situations placed difficulties in the way of the normalization of relations that leading members of both the British and Soviet governments considered to be in their immediate interest, and therefore each must find a place in this account. The present chapter will deal only with events in South Russia. The other problems will fill subsequent niches. But the reader must not forget that they existed; those who at the time had to face them, both in London and in the field, certainly did not.

✧

By early January 1920, Denikin's Volunteer Army had retreated southeast of the Don. Disease, desertion, and the cold of the most terrible winter in forty years had halved their numbers from the

100,000 that in October had penetrated to within nearly 200 miles of Moscow. On 10 January, just after Rostov had fallen and the White forces had entrenched themselves on the heights around Bataisk across the river, Major General H. C. Holman, the head of the British military mission, and Sir Halford Mackinder, the geographer and Unionist M.P. who only a few days previously had arrived as British High Commissioner in South Russia, had guaranteed to Denikin that if the worst came Great Britain would evacuate the wives and families of Russian officers. They made this guarantee on their own authority to help restore the shattered morale of the White officers, who presumably would be better able to hold their ground if they had assurances that their families were safe. (The families of other ranks, they assumed, would not be subject to Bolshevik reprisals, and therefore could remain.)[1]

In London, Field Marshal Sir Henry Wilson, the Chief of the Imperial General Staff, and Winston Churchill, the Secretary of State at the War Office, felt that Mackinder and Holman had left them with no alternative, and Wilson telegraphed their agreement to Holman.[2] A fortnight later, on 27 January, Wilson brought to the Cabinet the problem of precisely how the guarantee would be fulfilled. At that meeting, and at another on the 29th, he found that his own reservations were fully shared. Mackinder and Holman had pledged British assistance, but they had not specified a place where the refugees would be taken. The Cabinet decided that they could not be removed from Russia. Because of the likely incidence of typhus and other diseases, few countries would receive them. In addition, it would be impossible to find the money which would be required to settle a large number of Russian refugees abroad: certainly the British government could not provide it, and the record of the other Powers held out little hope that they could be induced to take part in a sustained combined effort. Therefore, the Cabinet decided, the refugees could be taken only to the Crimea, which was still in anti-Bolshevik hands and whose approaches across the narrow Isthmus of Perekop could be defended by the guns of British warships. Although the formal British guarantee applied only to the families of White officers, the Cabinet decided that if Denikin lacked

---

[1] For Mackinder's mission, and the circumstances of his guarantee, see Volume II, pp. 217-18, 325.
[2] See Volume II, p. 325.

sufficient shipping of his own to transport to the Crimea all the troops he considered necessary for its defense, any otherwise unused British shipping could be employed for that purpose. The Cabinet also reached another decision, although it was not incorporated in any official resolution: since it would be impossible for the Whites to hold out indefinitely in the Crimea, especially as they would receive little material assistance from abroad, the "only practical alternative" would be for them to negotiate with the Bolsheviks a capitulation by which—perhaps with the exception of their highest officers —they could be "reabsorbed" into Russia.[3]

The Cabinet discussed the possibility of negotiations between the Whites and the Bolsheviks only in general terms. It reached no conclusions, for example, as to how negotiations between the two sides might be brought about. In any case, the military situation itself no longer seemed so urgent. Behind the natural barrier of the Don and its tributary, the Manych, the retreat of the Volunteer Army halted; for a brief period, at least, it seemed as if the British guarantee might not, after all, have to be effected, and that the Whites might be able to fight their enemies to some kind of standstill. General Holman thought so. On 3 February he delivered a stern *aide-mémoire* to Denikin's headquarters at the railway junction of Tikhoretskaya. In his opinion, he wrote, Denikin was "now for the first time in a position to achieve success," because he could consolidate his control over a limited area and build up a solid base for operations. Even if the White forces had reached Moscow the previous autumn, Holman said, they would ultimately have failed because they would not have been able to control the area behind them. And, he continued, "The establishment of order in the restricted area now held by you is within the scope of practical politics, provided you receive the support which I am sure Great Britain will afford you on the conditions which Mr. Mackinder has doubtless laid before you."[4]

In holding out to Denikin the hope of continued British support Holman was, apparently, once again acting on his own, as he and

[3] These two Cabinet sessions were: Conference of Ministers, 27 January 1920, 11:30 A.M., minutes appended to those of Cabinet 8 (20); and Cabinet 7 (20), 29 January, 4:30 P.M.; both in Cab. 23/20.

[4] "Major-General Sir H. C. Holman's Final Report of the British Military Mission, South Russia" (undated, but prepared in April 1920), para. 135; file N 3724/3724/38, F.O. 371/5448.

Mackinder had done in guaranteeing British assistance in evacuating Russian families: Churchill had told the House of Commons in late October that no more aid would be sent to Denikin once the supplies already allocated had been shipped out.[5] Nor, it seems, had Mackinder offered further support to Denikin. The British High Commission had left South Russia to return to England on 16 January, after perhaps the briefest High Commission on record, and neither his reports on his mission nor his private papers mention any promises of continued British assistance or any conditions under which such assistance might have been rendered.[6]

Holman, however, set down his own conditions in his *aide-mémoire*. Throughout their service in South Russia, he said, British officers had been amazed to find thousands of Russian officers idle in the streets and cafés of cities far behind the front, despite the desperate military situation. Unless these officers made a determined effort, Holman said, the White cause was doomed. Moreover, he wrote, Denikin had consistently disregarded the counsel of British military and naval advisers; unless he paid them more heed in the future, Holman would withdraw the missions, and Denikin could expect "no patch of help from any other countries." Holman did not confine his conditions to military matters; he extended them to the sphere of politics as well. Bluntly he wrote:

Up to the present the material help which we have given you has been unconditional. But the British people expected that you would recognize the principle of free government for which they themselves were prepared to fight to the last man during the world war.

It would, of course, be idle to pretend that we have no personal interest in your struggle. All those who see clearly fully understand that Bolshevism is just as dangerous to our Empire as it is to Russia. I have always insisted in my reports to my Government that your troops are in effect outposts of the British Empire against Bolshevism in the East and that it is our duty to support them.

[5] See Volume II, p. 304, n. 18. The final shipments of supplies for Denikin were scheduled to arrive at Novorossiisk in late March 1920. After those shipments the Whites would be permitted to *buy* additional materials, but would be given no more.

[6] Mackinder's final report on his mission, dated 21 January 1920, together with interim reports and other related documents (all circulated to the Cabinet), is printed in *British Documents*, vol. III, no. 656, pp. 768-98. The "Private Papers of Sir H. J. Mackinder relating to his Mission to South Russia" are collected in F.O. 800/251. On his return to London Mackinder gave the Cabinet a lengthy briefing on his mission: Cabinet 6 (20), 29 January, 11:30 A.M., Appendix I; Cab. 23/20.

But the British people are not wholly convinced that you are fighting for freedom of the people of Russia, and neglecting as is their wont a danger whose imminence they do not realize, do not consider it incumbent upon them to interfere in what they regard as a Russian civil war. Those who do understand the true state of affairs want you to help them in their two-fold struggle against the Bolsheviks and against those who disbelieve in your aims.

I must see clearly where my duty lies. I have my duty towards you, but I have also my duty towards my Government. It is therefore necessary for me to know why Your Excellency is unable to listen to the advice of those who earnestly desire to help you, and are reluctant to avail yourself of their knowledge and efforts.[7]

Here, it should be noted, Holman was arguing that in his view the dangers of Bolshevism to the British Empire were so great that Britain should support Denikin without regard to his politics. But the mass of the British people were not so far-sighted and did not realize the menace that Bolshevism held for them. They would support Denikin only if he upheld "the principle of free government." Therefore, as a matter of political necessity, he should do so. Coming as it did at the end of Denikin's long retreat and at a time of near desperation this was not an argument likely to impress the White commander. Denikin told Holman that he felt that the disintegration of his forces was due not to any question of style of government, but to a growing belief that the Allies were inclining toward an understanding with the Bolsheviks at the expense of the White cause. Denikin said that he believed Holman to be a sincere well-wisher of Russia, but he also believed that the British general had little power to induce London to take the steps necessary to avoid disaster.[8]

[7] From Holman's *aide-mémoire* to Denikin, 3 February 1920, cited above, n. 4.

[8] This conversation took place immediately following Holman's presentation of his *aide-mémoire* on 3 February 1920. Holman summarized it in paragraphs 136-40 of his Final Report. A fortnight later, with Denikin continuing to disregard the advice of the British Mission, Holman directed an even stronger *aide-mémoire* to the White general, asserting:

"It has become clear to me that you do not consider my opinions or representations as worthy of your support.

"The same thing happened in Siberia until my Government was forced to suspend substantial aid to Admiral Kolchak.

"Admiral Kolchak is now a prisoner and opposition to the Bolsheviks has practically ceased throughout Siberia. . . .

"Will you follow his example, or will you listen to those who, having no personal interests to satisfy, see the game more clearly than the sorely tried players, and see also those who are not playing for the side?" (Final Report, paragraph 145.)

In this supposition Denikin was correct. Neither Holman nor Mackinder had any real influence on British policy. Back in London Mackinder advocated a program of financial assistance and trade credits to bring some semblance of order out of the economic chaos in the White-controlled territories. He also urged that the British government use its influence in bringing about an anti-Bolshevik combination between Denikin and the Poles.[9] Both of these suggestions were rejected by the government. As Curzon explained on 9 February in a telegram to Brigadier General Terence Keyes, who became Acting High Commissioner when Mackinder returned to England, Britain would neither encourage nor support a Polish attack against the Bolsheviks, and the government felt that any form of economic assistance to Denikin would be useless until his military and political position was "stabilised." The conclusion of Curzon's telegram was virtually an epitaph upon Britain's involvement in South Russia:

I fully realise how difficult your position is, after so many months of loyal and active co-operation with General Denikin. It has, however, been impossible to control the course of events, and I am now firmly convinced that, in view of the failure of his administration to gain the good-will and loyal support of the population, no support which we could have given him in either men, money or materials would have sufficed to bring about the overthrow of the Bolsheviks, and the establishment of a stable Government in Russia.[10]

Curzon's estimate was accurate. By February 1920 the "course of events" in South Russia had nearly run to the *dénouement* which had been made virtually inevitable by Denikin's failure to win local support. Only at the eleventh hour did he act to grant concessions to the Kuban Cossacks, whose assistance he sorely needed, but his efforts did not succeed in rallying them to his side.[11] Nor did

[9] In his final report, 21 January 1920, and in his appearance before the Cabinet, 29 January; both cited above, n. 6.

[10] Curzon to Keyes (Novorossiisk), telegram 81, 9 February 1920; *British Documents*, vol. III, no. 676.

[11] These concessions—made, perhaps, with an eye to Holman's warnings as well—included the establishment in early February of a "Government of South Russia" with N. M. Melnikov, one of the leading figures in the Cossack Krug (which had recently reasserted itself as a deliberative assembly) as premier. Improbably enough, N. V. Chaikovsky, the first head of the Archangel government, was named minister for propaganda. The new "government" was never anything more than a slight gesture in the direction of liberalization, however, because Denikin retained in his own hands the supreme military authority—which, in the circumstances, meant

those of General Holman, who—unknown to the British government—sent a manifesto to the Cossacks in the name of the King, and who had British planes fly over parts of the Kuban dropping proclamations signed by himself in his capacity as "honorary Cossack."[12]

The collapse, when it came, was abrupt. During the first days of March Soviet cavalry under the command of Semen Budenny—a former sergeant in the Tsar's army who as a Bolshevik commander gave vivid meaning to Trotsky's famous (and audacious) cry, "Proletarians to horse!"—crossed the Don and outflanked the White stronghold of Bataisk. Threatened with an attack from the rear, the defenders withdrew. After 9 March, when Budenny occupied Tikhoretskaya, all thought of serious resistance was abandoned; now there was only a race to reach the sea at Novorossiisk before the Red Army could get there. Fighting sporadic rearguard actions, often more a rabble than a disciplined military force, the remnants of the Volunteer Army and the Don Cossacks (who had mostly remained loyal to Denikin) made their way, together with hordes of civilian fugitives, towards the fuelless, typhus-ridden, already jammed port. The twentieth century has witnessed many such scenes of refugee masses fleeing towards the sea to escape an oncoming army; the evacuation of Novorossiisk was one of the first and one of the most terrible.[13]

As in every such evacuation, there were innumerably more refugees than there were places on the ships, both foreign and Russian, in Novorossiisk harbor. That some semblance of order was preserved was due in large measure to the presence of the nearly 2,000 officers and men of the British military mission. Many of them had been stationed in Novorossiisk itself, which had been the port of entry for

---

virtually dictatorial control. See G. N. Rakovskii, *V stane Belykh (ot Orla do Novorossiiska)* (In the Camp of the Whites [From Orel to Novorossiisk]), Constantinople, 1920, pp. 270-77; Denikin, *Ocherki russkoi smuty*, vol. V, pp. 306-10; and George A. Brinkley, *The Volunteer Army and Allied Intervention in South Russia, 1917-1921*, Notre Dame, Indiana, 1966, p. 224.

[12] See Churchill's reply to Colonel Malone's question in the House of Commons on 23 March 1920 (127 *H.C. Deb.* cols. 221-22); also William Henry Chamberlin, *The Russian Revolution, 1917-1921*, New York, 1935, vol. II, p. 286.

[13] For Denikin's last campaigns and the retreat to Novorossiisk see his *Ocherki russkoi smuty*, vol. V, pp. 315-29; C. E. Bechhofer-Roberts, *In Denikin's Russia and the Caucasus, 1919-1920*, London, 1921, pp. 199-224; and William Henry Chamberlin, *The Russian Revolution, 1917-1921*, New York, 1935, vol. II, pp. 286-87.

nearly all of the British military supplies sent to Denikin's forces. The greater number, however, including R.A.F. and tank contingents and liaison officers and instructors of every sort, had shared in the victories and defeats of the White armies throughout South Russia. As they converged upon Novorossiisk along the choked railway lines they joined in the rearguard fighting. Once in the town, they patrolled the streets around the waterfront.[14]

They also worked to destroy the vast quantities of British military supplies that had been discharged—some of it months previously— and left standing on the quays because of the chaos and lack of organization that prevailed in the rear of the White forces. New De Havilland 9 bombing aircraft, still in their packing cases, were pushed to the end of a pier to be pulverized by tanks. When their duties of destruction were completed the tanks were sent waddling off the docks into the bay, there to be joined by rows of field guns stripped of their breech-blocks. In all, something like £10,000,000 worth of supplies was either destroyed or left to the invading Bolsheviks.[15]

The troops of the military mission were augmented in these tasks by a battalion sent from Constantinople by General Sir George Milne, the commander of the British Army of the Black Sea, as the occupying forces in Turkey were called. The employment both of the mission troops and of the reinforcing battalion had been the subject of anxious exchanges between Milne and the War Office. Under the letter of Mackinder's guarantee to Denikin, Milne pointed out, Britain's role should have been limited simply to the evacuation of officers' families, followed by the withdrawal of the British mission. That would mean, he said, "abandoning to the Bolsheviks 6,000 wounded, the intelligentsia of non-Bolsheviks, the Volunteer

[14] The U.S. representative in South Russia, Rear Admiral N. A. McCully, reported that the British military mission made the "only organized effort" to maintain order during the evacuation. (Unnumbered report from McCully [Feodosiya] to Secretary of State Colby, 30 March 1920; U.S. National Archives, State Department file 861.00/6857.)

The strength of the British mission was given by Churchill in the House of Commons on 2 March 1920 as 394 officers and 1,529 other ranks, including 93 officers and 291 other ranks of the Royal Air Force. (126 *H.C. Deb.* col. 221.) One of these R.A.F. officers, Captain Marion Aten, has written (with Arthur Orrmont) a graphic account of these events: *Last Train over Rostov Bridge*, New York, 1961, pp. 234-328.

[15] Aten and Orrmont, *Rostov Bridge*, p. 320, and McCully's report, cited above, n. 14. Lists of the most important stores abandoned at Taganrog and Novorossiisk are in appendices D and O to Holman's Final Report, cited above, n. 4.

Army, and Denikin himself"; the British departure in those circumstances would be the signal for a general rising in which "Denikin's army would be cut up and the intelligentsia massacred." In Milne's view, it was essential for the future of Russia that the Volunteer Army and the "intelligentsia" be evacuated to the Crimea from where they could enter into negotiations with the Bolsheviks to assure their safety. Therefore, he faced a choice between adhering to the letter of Mackinder's pledge and using British troops to "hold on" until all those loyal to Denikin had been evacuated. The latter alternative would undoubtedly expose British forces to some dangers, Milne admitted, but their actions "would always redound to the honour and prestige of Great Britain." From London came ambiguous instructions essentially leaving the decision up to Milne. Urgent on the list of the War Office's priorities, however, was the safety of Denikin himself. Churchill was determined that the Russian leader of "indomitable patriotism and fighting spirit" should not fall "victim to the vengeance of his enemies" and be brutally slaughtered, as had been Kolchak's fate in Siberia.[16]

The evacuation was completed in the early hours of 27 March. During the previous month some 10,000 refugees and 3,000 ill and wounded soldiers had been removed, largely on British transports. In the forty-eight hours following 25 March Russian ships, using coal brought by the British from Constantinople, evacuated over 60,000 people, and on the night of 26-27 March another 10,000 troops of Denikin's army, together with the British military mission, were removed on British warships. On the 26th, as Novorossiisk came under sporadic fire from the guns of advancing Soviet forces in the encircling hills, the harbor echoed throughout the day with the deeper roar of the much larger guns of the British battleship *Emperor of India* and the cruiser *Calypso*, and those of the French cruiser *Waldeck Rousseau*. Along the waterfront, in the biting wind of the notorious Black Sea *bora*, massed troops and refugees extended for over three miles, awaiting the impossible. Most of the remaining soldiers of the Volunteer Army found their way onto the ships, but many Don Cossacks were perforce left behind. An American observer, describing the scene in a telegram to the State Department, concluded tersely: "Customary wretchedness and suffering have oc-

[16] Milne (Constantinople) to War Office, telegram G.C. 359, 20 March 1920; War Office to Milne, telegram 84216; W.O. 33/1000, nos. 5836, 5838.

curred."[17] Denikin himself, writing in his memoirs, was more eloquent: "Novorossiisk, crammed full beyond all measure, literally impossible to get through, overflowing with waves of humanity, buzzed like a devastated hive. A struggle went on for 'a place on the steamer'—a struggle for salvation. Many a human drama was played out in the confines of the town during those terrible days. In the face of great danger many a bestial feeling poured forth into the light, when bared terrors stifled the conscience and man became a ferocious enemy to man."[18]

In London, Sir Henry Wilson studied reports of the evacuation, and noted in his diary on the evening of 29 March: "So ends in practical disaster another of Winston's military attempts. Antwerp, Dardanelles, Denikin. His judgment is always at fault, and he is hopeless when in power."[19]

❖

At the Foreign Office, the British involvement in the evacuation was looked upon with no little anxiety and some annoyance. Curzon expressed the annoyance in a petulant minute on 15 March: "I am entirely in favour of getting out of this tangle in which the War Office have involved us by the worship of their battered fetish, Denikin."[20] R. H. Hoare neatly summarized the anxiety in another minute ten days later. "The situation in South Russia at the present time is a case of running a really grave risk with no possibly good result," he wrote. If British forces participated in the operations of evacuation, there was a real danger that, no matter how earnestly officers on the spot endeavored to carry out instructions from London not to get their troops involved in combat, a situation might arise in which no soldier could refuse to fight. In running such a risk the British government would be doing "absolutely nothing" to promote Denikin's cause, which everyone agreed was "utterly and hopelessly lost" even if he did succeed in escaping to the Crimea. Moreover, if serious fighting did take place between British and Soviet forces,

---

[17] McCully (Novorossiisk) to Secretary of State, telegram 33, 26 March 1920; *Foreign Relations*, 1920, vol. III, Washington, 1936, p. 589. See the extensive collection of reports from British naval officers at Novorossiisk in file 201209/1089/38; F.O. 371/3982. Also General Sir George Milne's undated despatch published as the 4th Supplement to *The London Gazette* of 4 January 1921, p. 173, and Aten and Orrmont, *Rostov Bridge*, pp. 328-82.

[18] Denikin, *Ocherki russkoi smuty*, vol. V, p. 349.

[19] Wilson MS diary, entry for 29 March 1920.

[20] On file 184448/1089/38; F.O. 371/3980.

it would seriously jeopardize the Anglo-Soviet trade negotiations which were about to begin. Those negotiations would be difficult and delicate enough in any case; they would be very much more difficult if the Soviet government "had the least justification for thinking that we are still trying to hold Denikin's Government up."[21]

Views such as Hoare's seem to have been widespread in the Foreign Office and, indeed, throughout the British government. The Crimea was a redoubt which could be fairly easily defended, but Denikin must not be allowed to use it as a base for renewing his struggle against the Bolsheviks. Thus Walter Long, First Lord of the Admiralty, wrote in a paper to the Cabinet on 22 March: "I recommend that Denikin should be urged to come to terms with the Soviet authorities, and informed that the support of the British Navy is solely to enable him to exact satisfactory conditions whilst still in possession of the Crimea. These terms would, I presume, include guarantees for the personal safety of women and children, and the remnants of the Volunteer Army."[22] There was general agreement, as well, that a further evacuation was out of the question. The Crimea was Russian territory; another evacuation would take the many thousands of refugees abroad and raise very difficult social and financial problems. Even so strong a partisan of Denikin as General Keyes felt that no other solution was possible.[23] And on 30 March, with the operation of evacuation complete, General Milne telegraphed to London:

> I trust it may be possible now . . . for the Allies to intervene and insist that some arrangement is come to between the contending parties in South Russia. It appears to me that Denikin realizes his cause is lost, but he is a brave man and refuses to give in; his army is now a mob of armed men without horses, guns or equipment. Discontent is rife. . . . In the Crimea disease is rampant and there may soon be a very serious shortage of food. Many inhabitants desire neither Denikin nor his army. I am very doubtful whether he will be able to hold Crimea for any length of time, and an evacuation such as took place at Novorossiisk is out of the question in case of its falling.[24]

[21] Hoare's minute, 25 March 1920, is on file 187165/1089/38; F.O. 371/3980.

[22] "South Russia. Admiralty Memorandum to the Cabinet," 22 March 1920, Cabinet paper C.P. 933; Cab. 24/101.

[23] See Keyes's telegram 64 (Novorossiisk) to Curzon, 13 March 1920, file 185237/1089/38; F.O. 371/3980. For Keyes's background and views, see Volume II, p. 223.

[24] Milne (Constantinople) to War Office, telegram G.C. 448, 30 March 1920; W.O. 33/1000.

In order that Denikin should entertain no possible doubt as to the attitude of the British government, Curzon telegraphed instructions to Vice Admiral Sir John de Robeck, the British High Commissioner at Constantinople and therefore the senior British diplomatic officer in the area (as well as senior naval officer—he also commanded the Black Sea Squadron), laying down the basis of a note to Denikin designed to counteract any hopes he might have "that all is not really and finally over." Because of its importance, the Foreign Secretary cleared the text of his telegram with the Cabinet before transmitting it to de Robeck.[25] The resulting note could hardly have been more stern. It stated:

The British High Commissioner at Constantinople has been ordered by his Government to make a communication to General Denikin in the following sense:

The Supreme Council is of the opinion that the prolongation of the civil war in Russia is, on the whole, the most disquieting element in the present European situation.

His Britannic Majesty's Government wishes to submit to General Denikin's attention that it would be of advantage, in the present situation, to make a *démarche* to the Soviet Government with a view towards requesting an amnesty for the population of the Crimea in general, and for the personnel of the Volunteer Army in particular. Absolutely convinced that the abandonment of the unequal struggle would be the most advantageous thing for Russia, the British Government will take upon itself the responsibility of making this *démarche*, once it has obtained General Denikin's consent, and will place at the disposal of himself and his principal adherents a hospitable refuge in Great Britain.

The British Government, which in the past furnished him with a large measure of assistance, thanks only to which the struggle has been possible up until now, believes itself justified in hoping that this proposition will be accepted. If, however, General Denikin should judge it his duty to refuse, in order to prolong a manifestly hopeless struggle, the British Government will find itself obligated to renounce all responsibility for this action and to cease to furnish him with assistance or subvention of any kind from that time forward.[26]

[25] Cabinet minutes 17 (20), 31 March 1920, 6 P.M.; Cab. 23/20. Curzon to de Robeck (Constantinople), telegram 273, 31 March; *British Documents*, vol. XII, no. 673.

[26] The note to Denikin, given by de Robeck to Wrangel (see below), is in Wrangel's memoirs, "Zapiski (Noyabr 1916 g.–Noyabr 1920 g.)" (Notes [November 1916–November 1920]), printed as two complete issues, nos. V and VI, of the

As it turned out, de Robeck handed this note not to Denikin but to his successor, General Baron Pyotr Nikolaevich Wrangel. Once the evacuation to the Crimea was complete, Denikin announced his intention to resign and a Military Council requested him to name Wrangel to his place. A brilliant leader of cavalry forces during the War, Wrangel was later the architect of some of the White Army's greatest victories. He was also its most able strategist: in vain he had pleaded with Denikin during the summer of 1919 to stop after his first successes and organize his rear instead of dissipating his forces in the wild, pell-mell drive upon Moscow.[27] Wrangel was well known to the British in South Russia. Mackinder, in his final report on his mission, left a vivid description of him.

He is a striking and distinguished figure. Tall, slim and erect, he would look almost gaunt in civilian clothes, but wears a most becoming Cossack General's uniform. His head is shaven and his look direct. He speaks with a loud voice, and is said at times to drink, and I should think he could be tactless, but he is an intelligent man, with a wider range of ideas than Denikin. He is, however, vain and ambitious, and allows his ambition to appear. Undoubtedly he is the best organiser among Denikin's generals; the Caucasian army is the only group in the Volunteer army whose discipline has risen to the Western level. He is admired by the younger officers.[28]

Mackinder did not comment on Wrangel's political views. A British military intelligence report of the previous year did, however. Wrangel was much more reactionary than Denikin, it said, with even less understanding of, and sympathy for, the aspirations of the border peoples who wanted independence from Russian rule. "From every point of view," it stated, "his accession to Denikin's position would be almost a calamity."[29]

Wrangel came to the Military Council which selected him as commander from a brief period of exile. He had long been a rival of Denikin, and in mid-February 1920 their quarrel reached a breaking point. Denikin first deprived him of all real responsibility and then

journal *Beloe delo* (The White Cause), Berlin, 1928. The note in its original French text and in Russian translation is in no. V, pp. 304-05.

[27] *Ibid.*, pp. 160-93. Properly transliterated from Russian, Wrangel should be spelled Vrangel. However, as a Baltic nobleman he himself used the German form, and later writers have always done the same.

[28] From Mackinder's report of 21 January 1920, cited above, n. 6.

[29] General Staff Intelligence, G.H.Q. Constantinople, report 4063 "I," "Conditions in Ekaterinodar, April 1919," undated, file 612/2/2/11552; F.O. 608/207.

ordered him to leave Russian territory. Wrangel joined his family in Constantinople.[30] There, his reputation for being a reactionary did not prevent him from entering into close relations with British diplomatic and military authorities, particularly Admiral de Robeck, who arranged for him to go to the Military Council at Sebastopol on board the British battleship *Emperor of India*. Before his departure, at breakfast on 2 April, de Robeck handed him the note which Curzon had instructed him to present to Denikin. It was a sharp reminder that no matter how sympathetic to the White cause the British representatives on the spot might be—and de Robeck made plain his own sympathies in handing Wrangel the note—their government in London, preparing to enter into trade relations with the Bolsheviks, was considerably more aloof.[31]

The note seemed to accomplish its purpose. At the Sebastopol council Wrangel agreed to assume the Supreme Command only in order to negotiate with the Allies to secure a safe asylum for *all* who had fought against the Bolsheviks and who did not wish to trust to any amnesty which they might grant. He took command on 4 April.[32] Denikin left immediately for Constantinople and soon went on to England. Virtually the first action which Wrangel took as Supreme Commander was to reply to the British note. In a telegram to de Robeck, he stated:

The British government's categorical demand to cease the struggle makes it impossible for my army to continue it. In placing upon the British government all the moral responsibility for the decision it has made, and in absolutely refusing to admit the possibility of direct negotiations with the enemy, I leave the fate of the army, of the fleet, and of the population of the territories occupied by us . . . to the just estimation of the British government.

I consider that those who at the most critical moment have denied their support to the South Russian armies which have remained invariably loyal to the common cause of the Allies are honor bound to take measures aimed at guaranteeing the inviolability of all members of the armed forces,

[30] Keyes (Novorossiisk) to Curzon, telegram 54, 4 March 1920, file 183538/1089/38; F.O. 371/3980. Bristol (U.S. High Commissioner, Constantinople) to Colby, telegram 212, 16 March; U.S. National Archives, State Department file 861.00/6596.

[31] Wrangel, "Zapiski," *Beloe delo*, no. V, pp. 301-04. De Robeck (Constantinople) to Curzon, despatch 360, 16 March 1920, and to Admiralty, despatch Z. 432/6589/50, 2 April; files 188385/1089/38 and 192812/—, F.O. 371/3981.

[32] Keyes (Constantinople) to Curzon, telegram 73, 5 April 1920; *British Documents*, vol. XII, no. 679. See Wrangel, "Zapiski," *Beloe delo*, no. VI, pp. 8-12.

of the population of the regions they occupy, of the refugees who wish to return to Russia, and of all those who have fought the Bolsheviks and are now in the prisons of Soviet Russia.

I have the right to ask my subordinates to sacrifice their lives for the safety of the country, but I cannot demand that those who consider it a dishonor should accept an amnesty from the hands of the enemy and profit by it.

Therefore I find it absolutely necessary that the possibility that the British government has offered to the Commander in Chief and his principal collaborators of finding a refuge outside of Russia should be extended in the same measure to all those who prefer expatriation to the clemency of the enemy.

For them I am ready to accept the hardest of living conditions abroad, which should constitute a sufficient guarantee that such an opportunity will be used only by those whose sentiments will not permit the acceptance of clemency from the enemy.

It is well understood that I count myself first among the above.

The question of the armistice should be settled as rapidly as possible so that the representatives of the English command attached to my general staff might take charge of its execution.

In order to accomplish calmly all the work connected with the cessation of military operations and the liquidation of the civil and military administrative organs, it is indispensable that I should have at least two months after the completion of peace negotiations before the Crimea is remitted to Soviet control.

During that period it is necessary that the Allies should continue to furnish the Army and the population of the occupied region with all that they need.[33]

Here, it should be noted, Wrangel made very far-reaching demands upon the British government. It was to "guarantee the inviolability" of his forces and the population of the Crimea, to find all who wanted it a refuge outside of Russia, and to furnish all necessary supplies to both the Army and the civilian population for a period extending until two months *after* the completion of peace negotiations—which themselves would be conducted not by Wrangel but by the British. All these were obligations which the British government would not have assumed readily. Yet it never made a direct reply to Wrangel's note, and an indirect reply, when it was made, unaccountably came only three weeks later. Thus Wrangel was only

[33] Wrangel's reply, dated 4 April 1920, is printed in Russian and French versions in *ibid.*, pp. 13-14.

belatedly disabused of the opinion that his exchange of notes with de Robeck constituted a contractual relationship between himself and London. With disillusionment came great bitterness.

The indirect reply was a telegram from Curzon to de Robeck on 24 April.[34] In the intervening period Curzon had begun his negotiations with Chicherin for an armistice in the Crimea, but thus far they were not auspicious. As the Foreign Secretary told de Robeck, Chicherin was "endeavouring to make an agreement hinging upon political concessions elsewhere which we are unable to make." Therefore, he said, since it appeared that Britain would not be able to make terms for Wrangel, there was no alternative but that he should make them for himself. In the meantime, Curzon's telegram stated, the War Office felt that Britain's military obligations to the White forces in the South had been discharged with the evacuation of Novorossiisk. The government did not contemplate leaving its military mission in the Crimea, and thought that it should be withdrawn with the least possible delay. Finally, the government could not "by grant of either . . . military equipment or supplies" encourage Wrangel "to continue a struggle that can have but one result." Wrangel's demands were thus almost entirely rejected. Yet, as de Robeck stated in reply to Curzon, Wrangel could scarcely enter into negotiations

---

[34] The facts of this situation are very confusing. On 5 April General Keyes telegraphed to Curzon a summary of Wrangel's note to de Robeck, and added his own opinion: "In view of communication [*i.e.*, de Robeck's original note to Wrangel] being in nature of ultimatum, General Vrangel's [*sic*] acceptance of the responsibility for initiating negotiations for peace unconditionally lays on us the obligation to ensure intervention being accepted and effectively carried out." (Telegram 73, Constantinople, *British Documents*, vol. XII, no. 679.)

Curzon seems not to have replied directly to Keyes's message, which reached the Foreign Office on 6 April. On the 7th there arrived a badly mutilated telegram from de Robeck conveying the text of Wrangel's note (telegram 344, sent on the 6th from Constantinople). To it Curzon responded: "From such parts as we decypher, I gather that Wrangel wishes to lay down conditions before any negotiations are begun. He does not seem to realise the situation, and you should inform him that if he wishes us to conduct negotiations for him he must place himself unreservedly in our hands." (Telegram 311, file 190427/1089/38; F.O. 371/3981.) To this message de Robeck replied on 14 April: "Wrangel communication outlined in my 344 did not lay down conditions, but rather asked for information." (Telegram 383, file 191837/—) This was clearly a misreading of Wrangel's note, which certainly *had* laid down conditions.

Presumably Curzon felt that Wrangel's note to de Robeck did not need a direct reply. Only thus can one explain his delay until 24 April and the nature of his reply at that time: Curzon (San Remo) to de Robeck (Constantinople), telegram 24, *British Documents*, vol. XII, no. 688. Curzon was in San Remo at the inter-Allied conference. Undoubtedly another reason for his delay was preoccupation with the conference.

with Moscow himself; his more militant followers would look upon such direct negotiations as treason.[35]

Thus left on his own, Wrangel was to plan once more to renew the battle, rather than to initiate contacts with Moscow. In the first week of June, as we shall see, these plans ripened into a great and ultimately disastrous offensive. At just that time, ironically enough, Curzon's negotiations with Chicherin, begun so inauspiciously, were themselves to ripen into a solution which Wrangel's followers might well have found acceptable. These negotiations must be summarized here. They began with a message from Curzon on 11 April.[36] He had agreed, he said, to use his "best efforts" to make peace between the two warring sides; therefore he urged the Soviet government, "in the interests both of Russia and of humanity, to issue orders for the termination of hostilities, and to grant a general amnesty upon the disbandment of the Volunteer Army." Postponement of such a solution would only result in needless bloodshed: Wrangel was perhaps incapable of a major offensive northward, but he was certainly capable of offering stubborn resistance for some months to come in the Crimea.

Curzon went on to explain why his government had a "special interest" in the fate of the Volunteer Army: "That army represented the Russian elements that stood by us in the Great War, in which Russia originally participated as an ally, and we have been in honour bound to stand by them to the end. Now that they have failed we must equally use our best endeavours to save them from destruction as well as disaster." Soviet Russia and Great Britain, the Foreign Secretary continued, were about to embark upon trade negotiations. Yet trade would scarcely be possible with a Russia whose economy was still burdened by civil war. Moreover, if these Anglo-Soviet trade negotiations were to coincide with renewed carnage in South Russia, or with Soviet reprisals upon White prisoners of war, British public opinion would demand that they should cease. Here was the only threat implied in Curzon's message. But six days later, having received no reply from Chicherin, he added another:

I explained to you in my telegram that I cannot permit the South Russian forces to suffer disaster as well as defeat, and failing a prompt reply from

---

[35] De Robeck (Constantinople) to Curzon (San Remo), unnumbered telegram, 27 April 1920; *British Documents*, vol. XII, no. 690.
[36] Curzon to Chicherin (as telegram 112 to Reval), 11 April 1920; *ibid.*, no. 681.

you that you are prepared to accept my mediation and to suspend any further Southern offensive that may be in contemplation, His Majesty's Government will have no alternative but to issue orders to His Majesty's ships in the Black Sea to give all the protection in their power to the army in the Crimea, and preserve for them the asylum which they have found there by preventing its invasion by the Soviet forces.[37]

For Wrangel, to whom copies of the Anglo-Soviet correspondence were shown by the British liaison officers with his forces, these were comforting words.[38]

They were perhaps unnecessarily belligerent, however: Chicherin's reply to Curzon's first telegram was already in the process of transmission through the British consulate at Reval.[39] The Soviet government, Chicherin said, preferred not to enter into a discussion regarding the validity of the arguments adduced by Curzon to justify British support of the Volunteer Army. "We will only state that your note makes clear that you will consider your obligations towards these Russian elements fulfilled once their security against reprisals has been assured, and that a new page will then be opened in Anglo-Russian relations." Like the British government, Chicherin continued, the Soviet government also felt that the questions which divided them were interdependent. Trade between the two countries clearly depended on peaceful conditions in Russia. But the peace of Russia was more menaced by the hostile activities of the Poles (it should be noted that Chicherin made this statement twelve days *previous* to the launching of the great Polish offensive of 26 April) than by those of "the remnants of Denikin's forces." Finally, just as the British government was concerned regarding the fate of its former allies, so the Soviet government feared for the safety of *its* earlier allies, the former members of Bela Kun's Hungarian Soviet Government, now held prisoner in Austria. Chicherin requested that Curzon use his influence to ensure their free passage to Russia. And he added that this, and every other question which divided Russia and Britain, could best be settled by allowing Litvinov to come to London for direct political discussions.

[37] Curzon to Chicherin (telegram 119 to Reval), 17 April 1920; *ibid.*, no. 684.
[38] Wrangel, *Beloe delo*, no. VI, pp. 46-47. Similar promises of support were conveyed to Wrangel by the French military mission.
[39] Chicherin to Curzon, 14 April 1920; *Dokumenty vneshnei politiki*, vol. II, pp. 453-54; English translation in Degras, *Soviet Documents*, vol. I, pp. 184-85. For the circumstances of delay, see *British Documents*, vol. XII, no. 684, n. 2.

For Curzon these conditions—repeated in a subsequent Soviet message on 20 April[40]—were unacceptable. They were the "political concessions elsewhere" to which he alluded in his telegram to de Robeck on 24 April instructing the Admiral to advise Wrangel to make his own terms with Moscow.[41] In a message sent to Chicherin the same day Curzon said that he was unable to recognize any connection between the situation in the Crimea and that of Bela Kun and his colleagues in an Austrian jail over which the British government had no control. Nor, he said, for reasons with which Chicherin was familiar could he negotiate with Litvinov in London.[42]

The arrival of Curzon's telegram in Moscow coincided with the beginning of the powerful Polish offensive which within a few days carried Piłsudski's forces all the way to Kiev. Now peace in the Crimea became a matter of even higher priority for the Soviet government: Budenny's cavalry would be needed elsewhere. On 28 April Chicherin sent another message to Curzon, this time withdrawing his previous conditions and proposing to make peace with Wrangel on the same terms Moscow had offered to the White forces in Archangel the previous February—in essence, a guarantee that their lives would be safe if they should decide to remain in Soviet Russia, or of their safe departure if they should elect to leave, in exchange for their total surrender.[43] And in a speech to a workers' congress in Moscow

---

[40] Chicherin to Curzon, 20 April 1920; *Dokumenty vneshnei politiki*, vol. II, pp. 470-71.

[41] Cited above, n. 34.

[42] Curzon (San Remo) to Hardinge (London) for radio to Chicherin, telegram 25, 24 April 1920; *British Documents*, vol. XII, no. 689.
Why Bela Kun and his colleagues continued to languish in an Austrian jail is unclear. When the Austrian government learned of the Soviet request for their release it informed the British Legation in Vienna that so far as it was concerned the prisoners (who were held, allegedly, for their own protection) were an embarrassment, and that it was anxious to have them transferred to Russia if the Great Powers would allow it (Vienna telegram 228, 30 April 1920; *ibid.*, no. 148). Meanwhile Bonar Law had already stated in the House of Commons that the British government "obviously" had no objection to their being sent to Russia (128 *H.C. Deb.* col. 838; 26 April 1920), and on 15 May Curzon telegraphed to the British minister at Vienna that the matter was one entirely between the Austrian and Russian governments, in which Great Britain could not intervene (telegram 168; *ibid.*, no. 154). Soon afterward they were released.

[43] Chicherin to Curzon, 28 April 1920, *Dokumenty vneshnei politiki*, vol. II, pp. 490-91; English translation in *British Documents*, vol. XII, no. 692 (Reval telegram 88, 29 April). Chicherin set forth the terms his government was prepared to offer the White forces at Archangel in a radio message to Curzon on 21 February 1920, *Dokumenty vneshnei politiki*, vol. II, pp. 384-85; English version in *British Documents*, vol. III, no. 696.

the following day, Lenin bitterly remarked that "in the last stage of the negotiations with us about the Crimea the British government has considerably changed its originally favorable attitude," a change which could only have been due to the Polish attack.[44]

In an immediate sense, Lenin was incorrect. Curzon's note of which he complained had in fact been drafted before London had any inkling of the forthcoming Polish offensive, and it actually represented no "hardening" of the British position. The Foreign Office's attitude to Chicherin's negotiating tactics was encapsulated in a brief minute by J. D. Gregory, the head of the Russia Department, two weeks previously. Gregory wrote: "I don't think we ought to tolerate for a moment being manoeuvred by the Soviet Govt. It is undignified and we gain nothing. I do not see why we should sacrifice everything to the success of the Krassin negotiations. And I certainly do not think we should permit the Soviet Govt. to befog every issue by 'linking it up' with another one."[45]

By the time Chicherin's note of 28 April had reached London, however, the Polish offensive was well under way. As R. H. Hoare noted in a minute which initiated an intensive discussion within the Foreign Office, the situation had "radically changed."[46] Not only had the Polish attack placed heavy demands upon the Red Army, but Wrangel himself had achieved an "important little victory" over Soviet forces opposing his in the Isthmus of Perekop. There was no doubt, Hoare wrote, that Chicherin's " 'gracious' " new offer was probably "a measure of panic" in Moscow. ("The Bolsheviks are liable to panic, but they recover fairly rapidly," he commented.) It was very difficult to know what to do next. In Great Britain there was a considerable body of public opinion, including the entire Labour Party, which not only would condemn the Polish offensive, and do so with increasing vigor the longer it lasted, but would also insist that the British government bring the South Russian negotiations to a rapid conclusion. Hoare continued:

If we do this it will naturally release a very considerable force, which the Soviet Govt. will be able to turn against the Poles, as to whose intentions we know nothing. They talk vaguely of setting up buffer states between themselves and Soviet Russia. This is really quite meaningless,

[44] V. I. Lenin, *Collected Works*, vol. 31, Moscow, 1966, p. 119.
[45] Minute on file 191025/1089/38, 15 April 1920; F.O. 371/3981.
[46] Minute on file 195172/1089/38, 1 May 1920; F.O. 371/3981.

as the moment the Polish armies were withdrawn, they would be re-absorbed by Russia. We can only assume that the Poles hope by their offensive to extract from the Soviet Govt. acceptance in principle of their peace terms, and to do so within the course of the next week or two. Unless the Soviet Govt. lose their heads, which is, I think, unlikely, the Poles will probably not be successful, and they will find themselves exactly where they were before the offensive, except that they will be occupying rather more Russian territory than they were before. From the point of view of the Bolsheviks the only thing which is vital is a prompt solution in South Russia, either by negotiation or force of arms, as a junction between the Poles and the Volunteer Army would create a dangerous situation for them. They are sure to realize this and will undoubtedly attack in force unless the negotiations look promising.

Hoare accurately described the complexities of the situation, but he had no very specific recommendation for British policy. First, he said, it was necessary to "obtain from the Poles, for our own information, a definite statement of their military objective, and their political objects." Second, Curzon should reply to Chicherin that the situation of the Volunteer Army had been completely changed by the Polish offensive and its own recent successes in the Perekop, and that it would be unlikely to accept terms which amounted to complete surrender. In the circumstances the only practicable course would be the initiation of direct negotiations between representatives of Wrangel and the Soviet government, attended by a British officer. If Moscow accepted such a notion in principle, it should communicate directly with Wrangel.

Hoare did not spell out the sort of outcome he thought might be achieved by means of such direct negotiations. Nor did his colleagues, who in general agreed with his proposed procedure. Regarding the Polish offensive, however, they urged even greater British aloofness. J. D. Gregory wrote:

I should be inclined to make no communication to the Poles or to refer to the Polish offensive in our reply to Tchicherine. The Polish offensive is the Poles' own affair. We have taken no responsibility for it and it would, I think, be a pity to intervene. It might conceivably lead to something—either a detaching of the Ukraine from Soviet Russia or even to upsetting of the Soviet Govt.—although I fear we can hardly count on that. In any case, it appears wiser to watch events for the moment.[47]

[47] Gregory's minute, also on 1 May 1920, was on the same file.

To these remarks Lord Hardinge, the Permanent Under Secretary, added: "We should do our utmost to prolong negotiations which will become easier if the Poles get to Kieff as seems likely in the next day or two, and at the same time maintain our attitude of defending the Crimea with our warships until an armistice has been concluded." And Curzon wrote:

"Let us keep clear of the Polish business. If it succeeds we shall get better terms.
"If it fails ours will not be the blame."[48]

Accordingly, the note Curzon sent to Chicherin on 3 May did not mention Poland, and it did propose direct negotiations between the two warring sides in South Russia. The arrangements that had been proposed for North Russia, it said, involving virtual unconditional surrender, would be scarcely appropriate. The note concluded with a general statement clearly reflecting the Foreign Office's assessment of the straitened circumstances in which the Soviet government now found itself. Referring by implication to the Baltic states and to Georgia and Armenia (Azerbaijan had already succumbed to a combined internal uprising and invasion by the Red Army),[49] and also to Wrangel, Curzon stated:

In reply to your enquiry as to further conditions I have indicated that negotiations are doomed to failure whether in Europe or in Asia as long as Soviet forces are engaged in open hostilities with those whom we are actually defending with our arms or in whose political independence we are closely concerned. The only method by which peace can be successfully re-established is by an assurance to desist from these attacks. If this be given and adhered to the first of the necessary conditions will have been fulfilled, and negotiations can be pursued in a friendly spirit.[50]

Here, undoubtedly, was a "hardening" of the British position, but the last thing that Curzon or anyone else in the Foreign Office wanted was a renewal of Russian civil war and the concomitant prospect of new British involvement. Throughout the spring the Foreign Office had felt real discomfort over the fact that the Admiralty's orders governing the use of gunfire from British ships in

[48] Hardinge's minute, undated but clearly written either on 1 or 2 May 1920, and Curzon's, dated 2 May, were also on file 195172/—.
[49] For these events in Azerbaijan, see below, chap. VIII.
[50] Curzon to Chicherin (telegram 130 to Reval), 3 May 1920; *British Documents*, vol. XII, no. 693.

support first of Denikin and then of Wrangel were not as restrictive as the Cabinet had intended they should be.[51] Now, in late April, in his capacity as Commander in Chief of the Mediterranean Fleet, Admiral de Robeck sent to the Admiralty a series of telegrams stating that British naval assistance could enable Wrangel to move forward to stronger defensive positions and that British coal, meat, and flour could help sustain the morale of his forces. When these telegrams arrived with a covering letter from the Admiralty asking for the Foreign Office's views, Gregory minuted, with full agreement from Hardinge and Curzon: "Our decision has been, not to supply General Wrangel with the means of continuing hostilities, but merely to use our fleet to protect his forces from annihilation. It would, I feel, be retrograde policy to start again supplying him with coal and foodstuffs to enable him to hold out a little longer against an attack which is almost bound to succeed if made in force. It would be the thin end of the wedge and we should virtually have revived the policy of intervention which, we thought, had been closed once and for all." Gregory's minute, almost unchanged, went as a formal note from the Foreign Office to the Admiralty.[52]

[51] There were no formal Cabinet decisions governing the use of British naval forces in the Black Sea, but throughout all the meetings which dealt with Russian problems during the first half of 1920 ran the assumption that the British Empire was not at war with the Soviet government, and that, therefore, as the Foreign Office put it in a formal note to the Admiralty on 19 March, "no further Naval action should be undertaken by His Majesty's ships, which is not absolutely necessary in order to safeguard the withdrawal of the British Mission" from Novorossiisk. (File 184448/1089/38; F.O. 371/3980.)

In response to this note, the Admiralty on 25 March sent the following orders to de Robeck in his capacity as Commander in Chief, Mediterranean: "The Cabinet has decided that British Navy is not to take offensive action against the Soviet Government. This decision does not apply to any measures necessary to ensure the safety of mission and evacuation of refugees under Mackinder guarantee." (File 188263/—; F.O. 371/3981.) The trouble with this formulation, of course, was that the determination of the meaning of "any measures necessary" was left to naval officers on the spot. On 26 April, after the British government had begun its intercession with Moscow on behalf of Wrangel, the Admiralty sent new orders to de Robeck. "You are authorised to give such assistance as possible to protect Crimea from being invaded. No men should be landed. Operations should continue until Soviet commences to negotiate with Wrangel." (File 194251/—; *ibid.*) These orders allowed for even more widely ranging actions of "protection." Wrangel could argue that both his probing actions in May and his full-scale offensive in June were aimed merely at protecting the Crimea.

[52] These materials—de Robeck's telegrams 76Z, 77Z, and 78Z to the Admiralty, all dated 27 April 1920; the Admiralty's note to the Foreign Office, 30 April; Gregory's minute, 7 May; undated agreeing minutes by Hardinge and Curzon; and the Foreign Office's note to the Admiralty, 12 May—are all in file 195210/1089/38; F.O. 371/3981.

Wrangel

The Foreign Office's desire to forestall a new flaring up of the civil war was matched by that of the Soviet government to bring about a South Russian settlement that could free needed troops for the Polish front. Chicherin replied immediately to what he called Curzon's "conciliatory" note and stated that Moscow was ready "in the largest measure" to meet the wishes of the British government in order to bring about "the bloodless liquidation of the Crimean front" on the basis of a general amnesty for Wrangel's forces. The "earnest desire" of the Soviet government, he said, was "to celebrate the conclusion of a general agreement with Great Britain about all questions concerning both Governments." To Curzon this was entirely satisfactory. On 17 May he telegraphed to Chicherin that everything at last seemed ready for the immediate opening of negotiations on the spot in South Russia.[53] And in a memorandum to his Cabinet colleagues on 27 May, summarizing the issues outstanding between the British and Soviet governments preparatory to the beginning of talks with Krasin four days later, the Foreign Secretary noted, with reference to Wrangel:

Here we have more nearly come to an agreement with the Soviet Government than in any other quarter. In spite of the fact that we have been strongly pressed to lend assistance to [Wrangel's] force in its threatened advance outside the Crimea—an assistance which would easily convert it into a very powerful weapon of offence against the Soviet in Southern Russia—we have adhered to our resolve to bring hostilities in that region to a close as soon as possible. Chicherin has accepted our proposals for negotiations on the basis of a general amnesty, British military and political officers to take part in these proceedings; and we are now only awaiting information as to time and place.[54]

The negotiations in South Russia were never to occur. Instead, on the night of 6-7 June Wrangel's forces emerged by land and sea from positions astride the narrow neck of the Isthmus of Perekop connecting the Crimea with the mainland and launched a carefully prepared offensive against their Bolshevik enemies. He had decided to attack, Wrangel told British liaison officers, "not with any

[53] Chicherin to Curzon, 5 May 1920; *Dokumenty vneshnei politiki*, vol. II, pp. 502-03; English version in *British Documents*, vol. XII, no. 694. Curzon to Chicherin (telegram 147 to Reval), 17 May; *ibid.*, no. 700.
[54] Curzon's memorandum (Cabinet paper C.P. 1350) is printed in *ibid.*, no. 708.

aggressive intention but solely to obtain food."[55] With the population of the Crimea swollen not only by the influx of White soldiers but also by countless civilian refugees there was insufficient locally produced food; therefore, Wrangel said, he had given orders to move into the rich agricultural region north of the peninsula. Despite fierce opposition, by the end of June his forces succeeded in establishing a broad front extending in an arc in the west from the Black Sea up the Dnieper River to Nikopol and then southeastward to a point near Berdyansk (now Oskpenko) on the Sea of Azov.[56] There they paused; Wrangel would not repeat Denikin's error of failing to secure his rear.

There is no doubt that the shortage of food was one of the chief reasons impelling Wrangel to advance out of his Crimean refuge. But it was far from the only reason. With quite surprising speed he had transformed the collection of tired, ragged, demoralized soldiers he had inherited from Denikin into what expert observers generally conceded to be a fine fighting force.[57] If he had once thought simply of holding on until the British government could negotiate with the Bolsheviks an honorable amnesty for his men, he soon grew more ambitious. There are indications, however, that Wrangel never thought simply of holding on while the British negotiated an amnesty for his men. According to his chief of staff, General P. S. Makhrov, on the very day he took command following the Military Council at Sebastopol in April, Wrangel told his closest associates that he intended to continue the war, but that until he could build up his forces he would agree to the British proposals for negotiations "to avoid giving England an opportunity to leave us in the lurch." The protection of British naval guns and the continued flow of sup-

---

[55] De Robeck (Constantinople) to Curzon, telegram 657, 5 June 1920; *ibid.*, no. 716.

[56] Wrangel, "Zapiski," *Beloe delo*, no. VI, pp. 104-36. George Stewart, *The White Armies of Russia: A Chronicle of Counter-Revolution and Allied Intervention*, New York, 1933, pp. 369-70, and esp. the excellent map between pp. 360-61.

[57] Thus General Milne reported to the War Office (telegram I. 8623) on 19 May 1920 after returning to Constantinople after a visit to the Crimea: "Wrangel has brought about an extraordinary change in his army. . . . Morale is high. . . . Generally I consider the situation satisfactory and the Crimea should be strong in another fortnight. The general opinion is that owing to local risings against its power Bolshevism is breaking up internally. [Wrangel's army] seems to merit our support." (W.O. 33/1000, no. 6035.) See also Admiral McCully (Sebastopol) to Colby, telegram 52, 16 May; *Foreign Relations, 1920*, vol. III, pp. 599-600.

plies were essential while the reorganization went forward.[58] On 1 June, when Wrangel's design was increasingly apparent, Lord Hardinge minuted: "Gen. Wrangel seems to be engaged in a crooked game and to be hoodwinking us in order to gain time."[59]

Wrangel's initial objective was control of the mainland immediately north of the Crimea. There not only would his followers be able to feed themselves, and thus vastly increase their ability to defend their Crimean redoubt, but they would also be able to establish a base from which the future salvation of all Russia might be accomplished. From the newly captured territories would come both food and additional men and horses. Early in June, just before the beginning of his offensive, Wrangel published a *prikaz* establishing what he termed district "agrarian soviets" and providing for certain limited measures of land redistribution under their direction. In doing so he aimed at depriving the Bolsheviks of their chief propaganda weapon; by such means he would gain the support of the populations of the regions his troops would soon occupy. In fact his whole domestic program was deliberately aimed at producing a maximum propaganda effect, both at home and abroad. Its tone was liberal, but Wrangel, who took for himself the title of "regent" as well as Supreme Commander, proved much sterner and more authoritarian than Denikin.[60]

In mid-May Curzon had instructed Admiral de Robeck to make clear to Wrangel that there would be no change in British policy as a result of the Polish offensive, and that the British government aimed at ending hostilities in South Russia as soon as possible. On 1 June, disquieted by rumors that Wrangel would shortly launch an attack, Curzon telegraphed a stern warning that if he did so the British government would be "unable to concern themselves any further with the fate of his army."[61] Messages of this kind, however, had to be conveyed to Wrangel through Brigadier General J.S.J.

---

[58] Brinkley, *Volunteer Army*, p. 242, citing a manuscript account by Makhrov in the Columbia University Russian Archive.

[59] On file 201010/1089/38; F.O. 371/3982.

[60] For the argument regarding food (and an apology for Wrangel), see de Robeck (Constantinople) to Curzon, telegram 657, 5 June 1920; *British Documents*, vol. XII, no. 716. For Wrangel's civil programs, see his "Zapiski," *Beloe delo*, no. VI, pp. 55-76, and Brinkley, *Volunteer Army*, pp. 243-47.

[61] Curzon to de Robeck (Constantinople), telegram 488, 1 June 1920; *British Documents*, vol. XII, no. 710.

Percy, who in April had succeeded Holman as head of the British military mission. He was hardly a satisfactory medium. In his memoirs Wrangel noted that Percy, like Holman before him, freely and openly expressed his disapproval of the policies he was called upon to implement.[62] His disapproval, if not his open expression of it, was shared by Admiral de Robeck at Constantinople. In a telegram to Curzon on 7 June, the day Wrangel began his attack, de Robeck stated that should it succeed, as he thought probable, the Soviet government would be forced to negotiate with London on much less favorable terms. Given the open hostility of the Bolsheviks to British interests throughout the East, de Robeck said, he could only regret that British policy should now be "to withhold support from disciplined, organised and efficient force that is opposing Soviet in South Russia." Loyally, however, the High Commissioner added: "Whilst permitting myself this expression of personal views policy of His Majesty's Government will of course be carried out fully to my best ability."[63]

Both Curzon and Hardinge felt that Wrangel's actions had left the British government no alternative but the immediate withdrawal of the military mission and the cessation of every shred of British support. "We have to keep faith with the Soviet Govt.," Hardinge noted on 7 June in a minute that was initialled by Curzon as well, "though Wrangel has not kept faith with us & will place us . . . in an entirely false position."[64] The War Office's reaction, however—surely (although available records give no indication) that of Churchill personally—was to try to make the blow to Wrangel as soft as possible while still not completely departing from the policy laid down by Curzon. To General Milne at Constantinople on 9 June went a telegram: "Now there is so much improvement in position of Wrangel's forces in Crimea, it is desirable to take advantage of the opportunity so offered to effect withdrawal of British mission. Please, therefore, take steps to withdraw the personnel as unobtrusively as circumstances permit in order that the stability of Wrangel's position may not be adversely affected."[65]

[62] For Percy's attitude, see Wrangel, "Zapiski," *Beloe delo*, no. VI, pp. 110-11; for Holman's, see Denikin, *Ocherki russkoi smuty*, vol. V, pp. 346-47, 354.
[63] De Robeck (Constantinople) to Curzon, telegram 663, 7 June 1920; *British Documents*, vol. XII, no. 718.
[64] On file 202088/1089/38; F.O. 371/3982.
[65] C.I.G.S. to Milne (Constantinople), telegram 85137, 9 June 1920; W.O. 33/1000, no. 6122.

Curzon's incredulity at this "unaccountable War Office telegram," with its implications that the British government actually approved of Wrangel's offensive, was matched only by his outrage. He took his case to Lloyd George and Bonar Law, who agreed with him, and Churchill was asked to submit a new draft telegram for Cabinet approval.[66] The Cabinet met on the afternoon of 11 June. Immediately afterwards, telegrams went out to Milne and de Robeck ordering the military mission's prompt withdrawal. "British Naval forces," the Admiralty told de Robeck, "are to afford no, repeat no, support to Wrangel in offence or defence." Nor would Wrangel receive any British diplomatic assistance. He would have to make his own terms with his Bolshevik enemies.[67] The specified measures quickly went into effect. On 27 June the military mission of some 175 officers and 450 other ranks (in itself a considerable reduction from the nearly 2,000 British officers and men who had served with Denikin on the mainland) was evacuated, leaving only one colonel and three other officers, who thenceforth functioned essentially as observers.[68] At the same time the ships of the Royal Navy, which until the beginning of Wrangel's offensive (and even to a certain extent afterwards) had given him active fire support, now disengaged and withdrew to Turkish waters. So completely was Wrangel deprived of British supplies that the government even refused a request by a retired officer, then in business, that he be allowed to sell the Whites 50,000 surplus cavalry saddles, bridles, and swords.[69]

Wrangel was alone. Britain had been his only substantial source of outside support. The French government, despite its repeated advice to him that he should not negotiate with the Bolsheviks but instead should continue the struggle against them, never had a large

[66] So Curzon stated in a minute on file 203264/1089/38, 11 June 1920; F.O. 371/3982. The same file contained other Foreign Office minutes on the War Office telegram, all expressing outrage.

[67] Conference of Ministers, 11 June 1920, 5:30 P.M.; minutes filed as Appendix I to Cabinet 37 (20), Cab. 23/21. The text of the approved telegram to General Milne is included with these minutes. The Foreign Office and Admiralty telegrams to Admiral de Robeck, also on 11 June, are in *British Documents*, vol. XII, no. 721.

[68] From a general report by Admiral McCully (Sebastopol) to Colby, 15 July 1920, pp. 40-41; U.S. National Archives, State Department file 861.00/7281. Regarding the composition of the British military mission before its evacuation see Churchill's statements of 23 March and 20 and 22 April; 127 *H.C. Deb.*, col. 268, and 128 *ibid.*, cols. 195 and 593. See also Wrangel's remarks, *Beloe delo*, no. VI, p. 110.

[69] See de Robeck (Constantinople) to Curzon, telegram 772, 2 July 1920, and Curzon's reply, telegram 640, 9 July; *British Documents*, vol. XII, nos. 736 and 740.

military mission in the Crimea, nor did it furnish the White forces
there with any but token amounts of supplies. Once Wrangel had
begun his offensive the advice he received from Paris did not change.
But for some inexplicable reason the French also withdrew their
military mission, leaving only four junior officers.[70]

Throughout the summer of 1920 Wrangel was able to cling to
the territories he had taken in his June offensive, although an attempt
at a seaborne invasion of the Kuban proved a costly failure. He was
able to hold his positions, however, not because of superior force or
superior generalship, but because the Red Army was occupied with
the Poles. Winston Churchill crisply summarized Wrangel's situation in a memorandum to the Cabinet on 26 June. "As soon as the
Bolsheviks are able to divert their main strength from Poland,"
Churchill wrote, "they will crush him."[71]

[70] From McCully's report of 15 July 1920 cited above, n. 68. McCully wrote that
the French mission had only been a fraction of the size of the British, and that
throughout the Crimean episode it "never took a very active part in South Russian
affairs and was rather skeptical of any success by Wrangel."

[71] Cabinet paper C.P. 1540, "British Attitude towards the Poles and Wrangel,"
Cab. 24/108.

CHAPTER III

~~~~~~

KRASIN

The British government from the first did not dare to lead the negotiations officially. Comrade Krasin was obliged to arrive in London
in a Trojan horse named the Tsentrosoyuz.

—*Karl Radek in* Izvestiya, *9 July 1920*

The blow has fallen. A Bolshevist, a real live representative of Lenin,
has spoken with the British Prime Minister face to face. A being, as
Serjeant Buzfuz would say, erect upon two legs and bearing the
outward form and semblance of a man, was seen to approach 10
Downing Street, yesterday, to ring at the door and gain admission.
To add verisimilitude, we are informed that Mr. Krassin and his colleagues "walked from Downing Street by way of the Foreign Office
steps into the Horse Guards Parade." The Bolshevist pretends to go
downstairs like any ordinary mortal, but without doubt in doing so
he conceals some dark design. Probably if scrutinised his method of
locomotion would be found to depend on some inhuman device.
Meanwhile, Mr. Lloyd George has seen him and lives.

—*Manchester Guardian, 1 June 1920*

~~~~~~

LEONID BORISOVICH KRASIN[1] was one of the most remarkable figures in the early history of the Soviet regime. To a greater degree
than anyone else during the two decades preceding 1917 he succeeded in leading a double life: to the world he was one of Russia's
leading engineers and industrialists; to the Bolsheviks and their
allies he was one of the handful of men around Lenin who most
decisively contributed to the growth and development of the revolutionary movement.[2] His success in both of these spheres—and in

---

[1] Krasin is the correct transliteration from the Russian; he himself, however,
signed his name Krassin when writing in German or English, and it often appears
as such in Western works.

[2] During the period 1904-09 Krasin, A. A. Bogdanov, and Lenin made up a
secret finance and military affairs committee of the Central Committee of the Russian Social Democratic Labor Party, controlling all the party's funds and assuring
the dominance of the Bolshevik faction. Overall policy was in Lenin's hands, and

[89]

keeping his associates and patrons in the former from discovering his activities in the latter—was due to a great genius for organization and to a manner which was at once persuasive, imperturbable, gentle, and urbane. Another contradiction in his life was almost as great: although the outbreak of World War I found him the managing director of the Russian subsidiaries of the vast German electrical complex of Siemens Shückert, he threw his heart and soul into the war against Germany, and was largely instrumental in setting up a powerful committee to control Russian war production. His support of the war effort also sharply divided him from his Bolshevik colleagues, but the roots of the division lay in a dispute over a matter of party tactics several years earlier.[3]

Despite his break with his former comrades of the underground, Krasin's enormous ability and his wide experience in industry and commerce made it inevitable that after the Bolshevik seizure of power the new regime should seek his services in the highest levels of its economic apparatus. In late 1918 he was made president of a newly founded "extraordinary commission for the supply of the Red Army" and Commissar both for Foreign Trade and for Transport. A British intelligence report in June 1920 called him "practically the economic dictator of the country."[4] This was something of an exaggeration; his role was that of the master technocrat, responsive always to political direction.

With his experience in business abroad it was natural that Krasin should also be called upon for diplomatic assignments. After the Treaty of Brest-Litovsk he accompanied Adolf Joffe to Berlin, where

---

technical direction fell to Krasin. He supervised the collection of funds by legal and illegal means (including counterfeiting and robberies), established a huge underground printing plant in Baku which produced most of the party's propaganda, organized the smuggling of literature and of arms, and established secret laboratories (including one where he himself worked) to develop and produce terrorist bombs. See B. L. Mogilevskii, *Nikitich* (*Leonid Borisovich Krasin*), Moscow, 1963, pp. 6-78, and R. F. Karpovna, *L. B. Krasin—sovetskii diplomat*, Moscow, 1962, pp. 9-41.

[3] The two Soviet biographies cited above gloss over both Krasin's support of the war effort and his earlier differences with the Party. For the former, see the biography by his wife, Lubov Krassin, *Leonid Krassin: His Life and Work*, London, n.d. [1929], pp. 40-41, and Leonard Schapiro, *The Communist Party of the Soviet Union*, New York, 1960, p. 143; for the latter, see *ibid.*, pp. 107-10.

[4] Directorate of Intelligence (Home Office), "Economic Conditions and Trade Prospects in Soviet Russia," Special Report no. 18, June 1920, circulated as Cabinet Paper C.P. 1586; Cab. 24/108. The report asserted that Krasin was "credited with strong pro-German leanings."

his previous acquaintance with a number of the magnates of German industry proved very useful. During the winter of 1919-20 he led the Soviet delegation which negotiated the peace treaty with Estonia. And in the spring of 1920, as the most important Soviet official in the field of foreign trade, he journeyed to Scandinavia. On 18 May Curzon instructed the British Chargé d'Affaires in Copenhagen to tell Krasin that Lloyd George would be glad to receive him in London.[5]

The invitation to Krasin was in accordance with the resolution approved by the Allied Supreme Council at San Remo on 26 April which, it will be remembered, authorized the beginning of negotiations between "representatives of the Allied governments" and "the Russian Trade Delegation." On 19 May, in a note to the Supreme Council, Krasin agreed to come to London. His note implicitly resolved the minor but vexing problem that had been created during the preceding two months by the British government's refusal to allow Litvinov to come to England. Litvinov would remain in Copenhagen, Krasin said, but the Russian delegation would continue to regard him as one of its members and would seek his advice whenever it was needed. To this end Krasin asked that the Russians should be allowed to communicate freely in cipher not only with their government in Moscow but also with Litvinov.[6] Here was a compromise acceptable to both sides: Lloyd George could tell the House of Commons that the British government had stood firm (although Bonar Law somewhat disarmingly admitted that the government had no objections to negotiating with Litvinov; it merely insisted that the negotiations should not take place within the United Kingdom),[7] while the Russians could save a certain amount of face by pointing to their right to consult Litvinov when they wished.

Krasin arrived in London on 27 May. He had been preceded some ten days earlier by three subordinate officials of the Soviet trade delegation who, along with some Russian clerks and typists, had come to set up the mission's headquarters in the First Avenue Hotel in

---

[5] Curzon to Grant Watson (Copenhagen), telegram 320, 18 May 1920; *British Documents*, vol. XII, no. 703.

[6] Krasin's note, conveyed in a letter to William Peters of the Foreign Office's Department of Overseas Trade, is printed in *Dokumenty vneshnei politiki*, vol. II, pp. 532-34.

[7] Bonar Law was replying to a question in the House on 10 May 1920; 129 *H.C. Deb.*, col. 55.

High Holborn and to work out various other arrangements.[8] From the British government they secured four privileges: they and their fellow members of the delegation would be allowed to enter and leave the United Kingdom freely; they would be able to communicate—in cipher if necessary—by post, telegraph, and wireless with Moscow and with Soviet representatives elsewhere, such as Litvinov in Copenhagen; they would be allowed to send and receive couriers; and they would be able to send and receive despatch bags under seal. In exchange for these privileges the government required all of them except Krasin to sign the following declaration: "While in the United Kingdom I will not interfere in any way in the politics or internal affairs of the country. I also undertake not to grant interviews to representatives of the Press without the approval of the British Government." Krasin refused to sign the declaration on the grounds that it was derogatory to his dignity. But he gave his word that he would adhere to its terms.[9]

The government's agreement to such a distinction's being drawn between Krasin and his colleagues reflected its thinking that the elegant, courtly Krasin was somehow a "good Bolshevik," or, indeed, not a Bolshevik at all. A report prepared the preceding month by Sir Basil Thomson's Directorate of Intelligence declared:

Krassin's real desire is to deal Bolshevism into the ways of normal democracy. What restrains him from embarking on such a policy or from publicly avowing what he knows perfectly well to be true, that the existing Soviet *regime* is the antithesis of genuine communism, is his fear of the extremists.

"Indeed," the report continued, showing just how unreliable was

[8] The three were Nogin and Rozovsky, who had been named in February to the original Tsentrosoyuz mission (see above, chap. I), and N. K. Klishko, an official of the Commissariat for Foreign Trade, who had replaced Khinchuk, the most prominent cooperator among the original delegation.

[9] Foreign Office memorandum for the Attorney General, "Status and privileges of Monsieur L. B. Krassin, Russian Delegate in the United Kingdom," 26 November 1920, file N 2852/2852/38; F.O. 371/5447. The terms of the declaration signed by members of the Soviet delegation were worked out by Edward Shortt, the Home Secretary, and conveyed by him to Lloyd George (with Bonar Law's endorsement) on 24 March; Lloyd George MSS, file F/45/6/26. It is worth noting that despite the controversy which later developed over the sojourn in the United Kingdom of the Soviet mission, and despite the apparently central role of the Home Office in such matters, this was the *only* communication on the subject between the Prime Minister and the Home Secretary during the entire period covered by this volume that I have been able to find.

the information upon which the analysis was based, "his contempt for the official creed has been visibly modified since Peters, the famous organiser of the Terror, imprisoned him, along with Lenin, for a few hours."[10] That the British government took seriously characterizations of this sort is shown by the fact that in mid-May it was decided not to press Krasin to come to London, lest Moscow should become suspicious and his "value to the Allies" be jeopardized.[11]

Although Krasin's political views might have been the subject of debate (he himself was most discreet about them), the charm and attraction of his personality were undeniable. Although the Bolshevik leaders in Moscow (and later, when he came to England, Kamenev) were subjected to repeated personal abuse in the British press, Krasin was never attacked personally. Beatrice Webb, predisposed toward sympathy but far from uncritical, left a vivid impression of her first meeting with him. In her diary she wrote:

Krassin, with his tall lithe figure, his head perfectly set on his shoulders, with his finely chiselled features, simple manner and direct glance, looks, every inch of him, the highly bred and highly trained human being, a veritable aristocrat of intellect and bearing. So far as one can gather from listening to him [he spoke, Mrs. Webb noted, in flawless German] he is a curious combination of the practical expert and the convinced adherent of a dogmatic creed. But one is tempted to wonder whether this creed does not consist almost entirely in an insistent demand for the subordination of each individual to the working plan of the scientifically trained mind; though, of course, the plan is assumed to be devised in the interests of the community as a whole.[12]

Krasin's first meeting with Lloyd George and other members of the Cabinet took place on 31 May, the Monday following his arrival in England. On the previous Friday, the 28th, Lloyd George called together his colleagues to discuss the government's general strategy toward the negotiations. Before them they had a paper prepared by

[10] Directorate of Intelligence (Home Office), "A Monthly Review of Revolutionary Movements in British Dominions Overseas and Foreign Countries," No. 18, April 1920, circulated as Cabinet Paper C.P. 1130; Cab. 24/104.

[11] Reported by U.S. Ambassador Davis to Secretary of State, telegram 795, 15 May 1920; U.S. National Archives, State Department file 661.4116/27.

[12] Margaret I. Cole, ed. *Beatrice Webb's Diaries, 1912-1924*, London, 1952, p. 191 (entry for 4 September 1920).

Curzon.[13] Now that Krasin had at last arrived and it was possible "to deal with a member of the Soviet Executive," Curzon wrote, "it seems desirable that we should seize the opportunity of coming to some understanding concerning the many points on which the Soviet Government and ourselves are at issue in different parts of Europe and the East." Trade, the ostensible purpose of the negotiations, he dismissed as of secondary importance. It was known from a great variety of sources, he said, that the Soviet government was faced with "complete economic disaster" and that it was ready to "pay almost any price" for the assistance which Great Britain, more than any other country, could give. "We can hardly come to its rescue without exacting our own price for it," he continued, "and it seems to me that price can far better be paid in a cessation of Bolshevik hostility in parts of the world of importance to us, than in the ostensible interchange of commodities, the existence of which on any considerable scale in Russia there is grave reason to doubt."

The Foreign Secretary went on to single out two sets of questions on which he sought Soviet agreement. First was the continued detention of British civil and military prisoners in Russia; the Soviet government seemed to be throwing up unnecessary obstacles to the speedy release envisioned in the accord the two governments had signed in Copenhagen in February. Second were all those cases "in which the Bolsheviks are either openly at war with peoples or States in whom we are concerned, or are engaged in propaganda, plots, and alliances directed against British interests or the British Empire in the East." Here he referred to Soviet efforts to sign a treaty with Afghanistan, which would give Moscow a base from which to foment disorder among the tribes along the northwest frontier of India, and to Bolshevik armed incursions into Persia and the states of the Caucasus, culminating in the invasion and takeover of Azerbaijan in late April and the landing of a force at Enzeli on the Caspian coast of Persia in mid-May. In addition, Curzon said, there was Wrangel. Here, however, the two governments were nearer accord than over any other question. (Scarcely a week later, of course, Wrangel was to launch the offensive which caused the British government to abandon him entirely and, ironically, for which Moscow was to blame Britain.)

---

[13] Curzon's memorandum of 27 May 1920 (Cabinet Paper C.P. 1350; Cab. 94/106) is in *British Documents*, vol. XII, no. 708.

Curzon's paper did not mention the Polish-Soviet war, but his colleagues at the Cabinet meeting of 28 May did.[14] At that time the Poles were deep in Soviet territory, holding Kiev. This fact, it was suggested—unfortunately, the Cabinet minutes, like most for the period, do not indicate by whom—provided the British government with an opportunity for "driving a good bargain." It should offer the Soviet government its wholehearted cooperation in arranging a peace with both Wrangel and the Poles. In return, it should insist upon a "comprehensive arrangement" on all the matters Curzon mentioned in his paper, and also one providing for the curbing of communist propaganda in the United Kingdom, the Allied countries, and Central Europe. This proposal won general agreement from the ministers present. So did the contention that little good would come merely from the exchange of British products for Russian gold. Although the early stages of revived trade, until Russia's transportation system could be repaired, would necessarily consist primarily of an exchange of Western goods for Russian gold, it was nevertheless important to begin the flow of Russian raw materials to Europe as soon as possible. The West had need for them. And outsiders would be brought into close contact "with the peasants and others who were actually producing in Russia"; thus trade would exert a moderating effect on Soviet politics. Finally, the meeting touched briefly on the large and complicated problem of Soviet debts to British creditors. The Cabinet agreed that it would be desirable to get Krasin to come to a general understanding, perhaps recognizing the debts in principle, even if he were unprepared to discuss specific issues.

Another conclusion reached at the meeting on 28 May was that participation of representatives of the other Allied governments in the talks with Krasin would be particularly desirable, especially in view of the Cabinet's hope of reaching a "comprehensive arrangement" with Moscow. Allied participation had been contemplated at San Remo; in any case the British government did not wish to appear guilty of dealings behind the backs of its allies in order to advance purely British interests. Accordingly, that same day Curzon saw Paul Cambon, the French Ambassador, and urged that his government should take part in the talks. The French refused. In

[14] Conference of Ministers, 28 May 1920, noon; minutes appended to those of Cabinet 33 (20), Cab. 23/21.

Paris the San Remo agreement was interpreted as meaning that only lower-level officials—technicians, in the eyes of the French—should take part in negotiations with the Russians: discussions involving members of governments, or even ambassadors, would imply recognition of the Soviet regime. Moreover, Cambon told Curzon (showing, perhaps, the extent to which the wish was father to the thought), the French government's information was that Krasin was "an extreme Bolshevist, imbued with their worst and most dangerous theories."[15] Because of the French refusal, the British did not extend an invitation to the Italians: isolation would only make the French government more intransigent.

❖

In a very real sense the meeting between Krasin and Lloyd George on 31 May was a dramatic occasion—the first on which an emissary of the Soviet government had been officially received by the head of the government of a Great Power. Lloyd George himself keenly appreciated the significance of the encounter; at dinner the previous evening he talked at length about it.[16] The press, too, was well aware of it. Nearly every day of the preceding week *The Times* carried leading articles decrying the iniquities of trading with the Bolsheviks (who were not, it insisted yet once again, for the most part real Russians at all, but Jews) and accusing Lloyd George of deliberately deceiving the British people by his repeated assertions that the Soviet delegation represented merely the Russian cooperative societies. On 28 May, in an editorial entitled "The Bolshevist Triumph," *The Times* reminded Bonar Law and Curzon—the leading Conservative members of the Coalition—that unless the principle of ministerial responsibility had been abandoned, they would have to share in the responsibility of the rest of the Cabinet. "If they stand by," the leader stated, "and suffer the Prime Minister to see this representative of a blood-stained despot, for whom they have consistently professed their horror and contempt, there is no reason why they should not shake hands with him themselves."[17]

[15] Curzon described his interview with Cambon in a letter to Lloyd George, 28 May 1920; *British Documents*, vol. XII, no. 709. The French government's response is described in an editorial note, *ibid.*, vol. VIII, pp. 280-81. Because of the French refusal, it was decided not to extend an invitation to the Italians.

[16] Riddell, *Diary*, p. 198 (entry for 30 May 1920).

[17] *The Times*, 24, 26, 28 May 1920.

Krasin

With N. K. Klishko, his principal assistant,[18] Krasin arrived at 10 Downing Street by taxi in the middle of the afternoon. They were ushered into the Prime Minister's office. Lloyd George greeted them, and then proceeded to introduce Krasin to his colleagues, one by one. First was Bonar Law, next Sir Robert Horne, President of the Board of Trade, then Cecil Harmsworth, Parliamentary Under Secretary for Foreign Affairs. Krasin shook hands with each. Only Curzon was left. Krasin held out his hand to the Foreign Secretary. Despite his expressed desire to negotiate with the Soviet government, Curzon remained motionless, staring into the fireplace, his hands clasped behind him. Immediately the room filled with tension. "Curzon!" Lloyd George exclaimed, "Be a gentleman!" Unwillingly, George Nathaniel Curzon, Baron Ravensdale of Ravensdale, Viscount Scarsdale of Scarsdale, Earl Curzon of Kedleston, turned and shook Krasin's still outstretched hand. The meeting had begun.[19]

[18] Klishko was an interesting figure, with a cosmopolitan background somewhat similar to that of Krasin or Litvinov. Born at Vilna in 1880 and educated as an engineer at Petrograd University, he arrived in England in 1907 as a political refugee and found employment with Vickers, the large engineering and armaments firm. According to a Scotland Yard report of June 1920 he was for some years an advisor to Sir Francis Barker, the Vice-Chairman of Vickers concerned with the firm's Eastern operations; the same report also states that there was evidence that he was simultaneously engaged in exporting arms to Russia for the use of revolutionary organizations. He lived in England until September 1918, returning to Russia with Litvinov when the latter was deported. Before his departure his London house had been something of a center for revolutionary Russians, and Kamenev made it his first destination during his brief visit in February 1918. (A subsequent police search, however, revealed nothing but some correspondence with Chicherin over the provisions of funds for political refugees in the United Kingdom.) On his return to Russia in 1918 Klishko set to work with Krasin reorganizing the railway system. His appointment as secretary to Krasin's mission to London was a result of his knowledge of English and of England. Scotland Yard's assessment of him was that he was more an opportunist than an ideologue. It noted, however, that immediately upon his arrival in London in May 1920 he got in touch with "Communist elements," presumably Feodor Rothstein. (Directorate of Intelligence report, 19 June 1920, file 205275/205275/38; F.O. 271/4058.)

[19] This magnificent scene was described by Krasin to I. M. Maiskii who relates it in his "Anglo-sovetskoe torgovoe soglashenie" (cited chap. I, n. 74), pp. 69-70. The minutes of the meeting are printed as "Secretary's Notes of a Conference of British Ministers with the Head of the Russian Trade Delegation, held at 10, Downing Street, London, S.W.1., on Monday, 31 May 1920, at 2:45 P.M." in *British Documents*, vol. VIII, no. 24, pp. 281-90, and are amplified by two segments of the Russian delegation's own minutes printed as appendices, pp. 290-92. Hankey, present as secretary, noted that *he*, alone among the British participants, successfully avoided shaking hands with the Russians (MS diary, Churchill College, Cambridge, entry for 31 May 1920).

At the outset, Lloyd George suggested that each side should state what it considered the principal obstacles in the way of the resumption of trade between Britain and Russia. Krasin agreed, and with Klishko serving as interpreter he quickly proceeded to present a Soviet bill of particulars. Most important, he said, was the question of whether the two governments were at war or at peace. At that moment Polish forces were deep within Russian territory, yet there was not a single munitions factory within Poland: the Poles could not possibly make war on Russia without support from one or more of the *Entente* Powers. Until the war ended, Krasin said, and Russia's transportation systems were available for nonmilitary traffic, export would be almost impossible, despite the fact that in the Kuban and in western Siberia some fifteen million tons of grain were awaiting shipment and elsewhere there were similarly stranded large stocks of other resources, such as timber, flax, and oil.

The Polish war, and the *de facto* state of hostilities which existed between Soviet Russia and the Allies, obviously worked to prevent any resumption of trade relations. Yet at the same time, Krasin said, it would be unnecessary and undesirable to postpone the resumption of trade until all the controversial questions which divided the Bolsheviks and the Allies had been definitely and formally settled. There were, however, certain specific issues whose resolution was necessary before trade could take place. First was the blockade. The Scandinavian governments were actually ignorant as to whether or not the Allies had lifted the blockade;[20] it was essential, Krasin said, that they should do so and definitely declare it done. Next was the legal basis of trade. Soviet goods, currencies, and documents would have to be legally protected against attachment in Great Britain by creditors of previous Russian governments. All debts arising from current trade, Krasin assured his listeners, would be settled normally, but the whole question of previous debts must be deferred until "the time of the official negotiations on the complete restoration of peace relations."[21]

Another problem, Krasin pointed out, was commercial representa-

---

[20] It will be remembered that the blockade had been formally lifted with the coming into effect of the Treaty of Versailles in July 1919. The Allied governments, however, had made no announcement to that effect, and had continued to enforce a moderately effective *de facto* embargo on shipments to Soviet Russia. See vol. II, pp. 290-91.

[21] *British Documents*, vol. VIII, p. 292 (from the Soviet delegation's minutes).

tion. Trade representatives would have to be exchanged on a mutual and reciprocal basis; they would have to be guaranteed freedom of movement, freedom of communication with their home government, and certain diplomatic privileges. Krasin concluded by asserting that he and his colleagues in Moscow had no illusions regarding the immediate restoration of pre-war commercial relations. The Soviet regime had somehow managed to carry on for nearly three years, and if necessary Russia could continue to live as a "closed state." Russia was a vast country, rich in raw material, foodstuffs, and manpower; the last three years had taught the Soviet leaders how to get along without external help. If the Allies wished to resume trading, they would have to meet Russia's terms. And the conditions which he had laid down, Krasin asserted, were the minimum his government was prepared to accept.

Krasin presented his case, Hankey noted later in his diary, "in a masterly manner." Lloyd George was much impressed—as, indeed, he had expected to be.[22] Now it was his turn. He did not wish, the Prime Minister said, to comment on Krasin's statement without consulting his colleagues. But he did state that Great Britain was giving no support or assistance of any kind to the Poles in their attack on Russia, and that the British government had warned the Poles that if they attacked Russia they would do so entirely on their own responsibility and would have to take the consequences. Moreover, Lloyd George said, he did not believe that any other *Entente* government was actively assisting Poland—a questionable opinion.

The Prime Minister then turned to British grievances. Primary among them was the whole question of Soviet propaganda and agitation. Propaganda conducted by one government against the institutions of another, Lloyd George asserted, was in reality an act of war. Trade relations and hostile propaganda were obviously incompatible. For that reason the British government would not allow Litvinov back into Great Britain; how could it be sure that the trade representatives whom Krasin held to be so necessary would confine themselves to their legitimate duties and not engage in propaganda?

Soviet propaganda in Britain, Lloyd George said, was only one

[22] Hankey MS diary, entry for 31 May 1920. See Stephen Roskill, *Hankey: Man of Secrets*, vol. II, *1919-1931*, London, 1972, p. 170. Hankey noted that Krasin's "hands moved nervously all the time, but his voice was firm and rather sympathetic."

aspect of the larger problem of Soviet agitation and revolutionary activity in the British Empire and, indeed, throughout the East. Bolshevik agents were reportedly stirring up trouble in Asia Minor, in Persia, in Afghanistan, and among the tribes on the northwest frontier of India. Red Army troops, moreover, were now threatening Georgia and the Allied garrison at Batum. All these hostile activities, the Prime Minister insisted, must cease before trade between Britain and Russia could be reopened.

In rapid succession, he then briefly listed additional British demands. The Soviet government must grant an amnesty to Wrangel and his forces; Britain would continue to "lend a friendly hand" to the Whites providing they did not decide to continue the struggle. The 150 or so British military and civilian prisoners still in Russia should, without exception, be freed immediately. The Soviet fleet must desist from hostile acts in the Baltic, Black, and Caspian seas. In the Caspian, Lloyd George said, Russian ships must not visit Persian ports without the Persian government's permission; oddly enough, this was his only recorded reference to the landing of Soviet troops, and the consequent forced evacuation of the British garrison, which had occurred just two weeks before at the Persian port of Enzeli.[23]

With the exception of a quickly reached agreement that the Anglo-Soviet discussions should be absolutely secret, with only agreed communiques given to the press, Lloyd George's remarks concluded the initial session. The Prime Minister, in fact, had done almost all the talking for the British side. This was a pattern which would be duplicated at subsequent meetings. Curzon, despite his stated wish to negotiate "a cessation of Bolshevik hostility in parts of the world of importance to us," generally left the task to Lloyd George.

On 7 June the two sides met for a second session. During the intervening week Lloyd George called his Cabinet colleagues together twice to consider the negotiations. Most of the first meeting, on 3 June, was devoted to a discussion of a Treasury memorandum, submitted with a covering note by Austen Chamberlain, dealing

---

[23] For the events at Enzeli, see below, chap. IX. Wrangel, it will be remembered, had not yet made his move to break out of the Crimea and launch his offensive northward. That move was to come only a week later, but the British government had little advance notice; see above, chap. II.

with the status in the United Kingdom of any gold which the Soviet government might use to finance its purchases of British goods.[24] It is best to postpone discussion of the more technical aspects of the trade negotiations for a later place in this account, just as the two sides themselves postponed their own detailed discussions until the autumn of 1920. But here it should be noted that the Treasury, echoing the predominant opinion of the City of London, regarded Soviet gold as (in the words of Chamberlain's note) "stolen property." The Soviet government had come to power by illegal means and had sequestered the property, including the gold, of previous legally recognized Russian governments and of Russian and foreign citizens and business organizations. If the Soviet government were to be recognized by the British government, its property would then be immune from attachment in the courts of Great Britain by creditors of former Russian governments or of Russian firms or individuals. But until such recognition it would not have immunity. Therefore, Chamberlain wrote, it seemed to him "both wrong and impracticable to make this gold the basis of trade with Russia."

At the meeting on the 3rd, however, the Treasury's position was sharply disputed by both of the Law Officers of the Crown, Sir Gordon Hewart, the Attorney General, and Sir Ernest Pollock, the Solicitor General. They argued that although the British government had not officially recognized the Soviet government, the mere fact of its dealings with Krasin implied that it regarded the Moscow regime as a *de facto* government; as such, its property would be safe from attachment in British courts. Therefore, despite the fact that the Soviet government had undoubtedly requisitioned its holdings of gold, and even if it did not have a secure title to it, the Law Officers did not see how litigation could be initiated to lay hands upon it.

The argument was not pursued to a definite resolution. In any case, the legal question would have to be resolved by bringing a test case before a British court; the Cabinet could only deal with the political question of whether or not to go ahead with trade negotiations, keeping in mind that in the absence of full *de jure* recognition

---

[24] Conference of Ministers, 3 June 1920, 5:30 P.M.; minutes appended to those of Cabinet 33 (20), Cab. 23/21. The Treasury memorandum, by B. P. Blackett, the Controller of Finance, was circulated as Cabinet paper C.P. 1394, 3 June; Cab. 24/106.

of the Soviet government there might be future legal complications over the security of Soviet gold in the United Kingdom. Regarding this political question there was a strong disposition to proceed. Even Chamberlain seems to have shared it, despite his qualms about Soviet gold. "I think that the opening up of trade is right & indeed necessary," he had written to his sister earlier in the year.[25] Thus, with no dissenting voices—perhaps because Churchill was absent—the Cabinet on 3 June reached a series of linked conclusions:

1. It was highly important for the British Empire to resume trade with Russia as soon as possible.

2. Gold would necessarily form the basis of this trade until Russian capacities for the production and shipment of materials for export were regenerated. The Board of Trade was asked to take up with the Treasury the possible problems involved in dealing with Soviet gold.

3. It was desirable that private traders should take the lead, with as little a role for the British government as possible.

4. Every effort should be made to induce the other Allies to participate in the trade negotiations.

Regarding Allied participation, it was contended that the combination of commercial and imperial interests gave the British government a stronger interest than any of the other Allies in the early conduct of trade negotiations. The Italians came next, because of the food shortage in Italy and the prospect of Russian grain. France, on the other hand, stood to gain least from a mere resumption of trade, and, indeed, if Western trade were resumed before the French could reach a satisfactory debt settlement with Moscow they would lose one of their few bargaining counters. From the point of view of the British government, however, it was less urgent a matter to induce the Bolsheviks to pay Russia's debts than to induce them to cease their agitation and propaganda in the Empire.

Thus, London and Paris had divergent goals and divergent priorities. They disagreed not only on the desirability of holding negotiations but also on the objectives of the negotiations once they took place. This divergence was tacitly recognized by the Cabinet's abandonment of its earlier reluctance to allow the Italians to take part in the conversations with Krasin unless the French also were

---

[25] Chamberlain's letter to his sister Ida, 28 February 1920, is in his papers in the Library of the University of Birmingham.

present. It was decided to hold the next session four days later, on 7 June, and to invite the Italian Embassy to send a representative.

The Cabinet meeting on 3 June did not consider any of the more strictly political issues at stake between the British and Soviet governments. On the afternoon of the 7th, however, just an hour before his second talk with Krasin, Lloyd George called another meeting[26] in order to concert his government's position on three such issues—Wrangel, Poland, and "propaganda" (as the whole complex of Soviet revolutionary activities came to be called). Regarding Wrangel, it was agreed that Krasin should be told that the British government was willing to mediate between him and the Bolsheviks; that it would not support him if he attempted to break out of the Crimea and, indeed, that in such an eventuality it would feel relieved of all responsibility towards him; but that if he remained within the Crimea and if Soviet forces attacked him, the British government would reserve the right to act as it saw fit. Lloyd George duly made such a statement to Krasin at their meeting which followed.[27] Yet as they talked the British position was being overtaken by events: on that very day Wrangel began the thrust out of the Crimea that would soon result in London's total break with him.

Regarding Poland, the conference of Ministers and civil servants decided not to suggest to the Poles—who at that moment were at the point of their maximum penetration into Soviet territory—that they should negotiate peace with Moscow, "since the British Government would in that case be held to have incurred a certain responsibility in the event of the failure of these negotiations." As it happened, and to Lloyd George's undoubted relief, Krasin did not request such a British overture. Later, when the tide of battle had turned, London would make one without any prodding from Moscow.

Regarding the issue of "propaganda," the group had before it a memorandum submitted by Krasin two days previously in response to some of the questions which Lloyd George had raised at their initial meeting. Krasin claimed that his statement was provisional, subject to amplification from Moscow. But its most important part,

[26] Conference of Ministers, 7 June 1920, 4:45 P.M.; minutes appended to those of Cabinet 35 (20), Cab. 23/21.
[27] Minutes: "Secretary's Notes of a Conference of British Ministers with the Head of the Russian Trade Delegation . . . June 7, 1920, at 5:45 P.M." in *British Documents*, vol. VIII, no. 25, pp. 292-306.

an explanation of his government's use of propaganda, was scarcely tentative in its wording. It stated:

On the question of anti-English propaganda by the Soviet Government I have the honour to state:—

Following several open acts of war by the British land and sea forces who attacked Soviet Russia, inflicting losses on Russian peasants and workmen, the Soviet Government was obliged from motives of self-protection to safeguard itself from these attacks, for which neither the Soviet Government nor the Russian people had given any cause, by employing all means in their power which would help them to combat the aggressive policy of the British Government as regards Soviet Russia. The complete cessation of whatever means and methods are at present being employed in the East against the British Government entirely depends on the future line of action of the British Government.

If Great Britain is prepared to give actual guarantees of her peaceful intentions as regards Soviet Russia, and if the British Government is prepared to refuse all further help to the enemies of Soviet Russia, she, in turn, is prepared to furnish full guarantees from participation in or connivance at any kind of hostile action, not only in the East but elsewhere.[28]

The conference of Ministers at Downing Street concluded that the guarantees proposed in this latter paragraph were sufficiently wide. At the meeting with Krasin which followed, the Soviet representative reiterated them in much the same language. The minutes record him as saying, in response to questioning by Curzon, that "if Great Britain showed that she was ready not to engage in hostilities against Soviet Russia, then Soviet Russia would be prepared to consider and revise her policy in the Far [*sic*] East, and to cease the support of movements and forces which were hostile to the British Government." And he added: "Not only in the East, but everywhere." Under the heading of hostile activities he explicitly included propaganda. "The Government of the Russian Soviet Republic," he said, would "give an undertaking, if an agreement was reached, not to carry on propaganda against the British Empire, which would completely satisfy the wishes of the British Government." For the benefit of the Italian Chargé d'Affaires, Lloyd George asked if these promises would extend to Britain's allies. Krasin replied that they would.[29]

[28] Krasin's memorandum, dated 5 June 1920 (circulated as Cabinet paper C.P. 1421) is printed as n. 1 to *idem* (pp. 293-94).

[29] *Ibid.*, pp. 303-04.

Krasin

The meeting with Krasin on 7 June was an even larger gathering than the first such session a week earlier. Lloyd George had with him not only Bonar Law, Curzon, and Horne, along with Wise and assorted officials from his own secretariat and from the Board of Trade (none, it should be noted, from the Foreign Office), but also Chamberlain, Balfour, and Walter Long. It was not surprising, therefore, that Krasin should afterwards have requested from Lloyd George an altogether different and much smaller format where they could hold a "frank conversation" away from "extremists." (There were, he told Lloyd George, "extremists on both sides." Those in Russia "preferred world revolution to world peace," but they were in a minority; "the Allied extremists preferred war with Russia to peace with the Soviet Government.")[30]

The Prime Minister consented to the small meeting, and therefore late on the afternoon of 16 June, this time without Klishko, Krasin once again came to 10 Downing Street, to find only Lloyd George, Horne, and Philip Kerr—and, oddly enough, Dr. Fridtjof Nansen, the Norwegian explorer and relief administrator, who said nothing but duly certified Kerr's minutes as "a fair summary of the proceedings." Yet, small meeting or large, the striking thing about the sessions on 7 and 16 June is that they covered virtually the same ground. Whatever magic that Krasin expected from relative intimacy did not come forth.

At both meetings, the British side (with Curzon taking the lead on 7 June) raised the issue of "propaganda," and at both meetings—somewhat more strongly on the 16th—Krasin stated that his government would abandon its "propaganda" in Asia provided there were "a general peace." Krasin did not, it should be noted, distinguish between the Soviet government and "nongovernmental" sources of propaganda and revolutionary activities, such as the Communist International or the communist parties of Great Britain and the various countries of the East. Nor did Lloyd George press him regarding such a distinction. During neither this nor any of the subsequent Anglo-Soviet conversations before the signature of the

[30] Minutes: "Interview between M. Krassin and the Prime Minister, held at 10, Downing Street on Wednesday, June 16th at 5:30 P.M."; Lloyd George MSS, file F/202/3/19. Foreign Office files contain no record of this meeting. Thus, as is not the case for other meetings between the Prime Minister and the Soviet delegates, minutes do not appear in the series of *British Documents*. Minutes of the 7 June meeting are cited above, n. 27.

trade agreement the following March did the British negotiators ever attempt to make the Soviet government admit—or deny—responsibility for actions and statements by these organizations. In subsequent years the Soviet government would solemnly and piously declare that it was scrupulously obeying its obligations not to make hostile propaganda, while allowing the Comintern—in the name of free speech—to pursue its campaign of agitation and vilification.

"Propaganda" was one of the two principal issues which was to arouse more heat and controversy during the coming months and years than any of the other matters which divided Russia and the West.[31] The other issue was the Russian debts. At the first Anglo-Soviet meeting, on 31 May, Krasin had asserted that the question of previous debts must be deferred until "the complete restoration of peace relations" between Russia and the Allies. Then Lloyd George had said nothing. At the meetings on both 7 and 16 June, however, he replied at length. No one suggested, he said, that the resumption of trade should wait until Russia's obligations had been completely discharged. But *recognition* of these obligations could not be postponed until some later stage. Trade with Russia, when revived, would be conducted by the same group of firms which had done so before the war—"by firms which knew about Russia, who could speak Russian and who had in their employment men who were familiar with the conditions of Russian trade." These were, the Prime Minister said, "the very firms to whom Russia owed money for goods actually given to Russia." Unless the Russian government acknowledged those debts, "these traders would certainly refuse to go into the business." Krasin, "as a business man," would surely understand that. He hoped, therefore, that Krasin would be able to assure him that the Soviet regime "accepted in principle the obligations contracted by the Russian Government towards private Allied subjects . . . whether in the shape of prerevolution debts or guarantees, or claims arising out of the seizure or nationalization of property belonging to or controlled by such subjects." Lloyd George emphasized that he was not referring to "the debt owing to the British or other foreign Governments"; this debt, he said, "must be treated on an entirely separate footing"—there was no necessity to settle it before the resumption of normal trade.

[31] See the discussion of "propaganda" in George F. Kennan, *Russia and the West under Lenin and Stalin*, Boston, 1960, pp. 198-99.

Krasin

Here, it should be noted, in the separation of private and state debts and the insistence that the former should be recognized by the Soviet government immediately, the British committed a serious tactical blunder. Although Britain was Russia's leading creditor (the pre-war Russian debt to Britain was £50 million, the war debt £579 million; for France the same figures were £330 million and £159 million),[32] virtually all the Russian debt to Britain was owed to the British *government*, and not to private individuals. British private loans amounted to only £17.5 million, and in January 1918 nearly all these debts, even, were taken over by the British government.[33] The Russian debt to France, however, was owed largely to private citizens. French investors financed much of the pre-war Russian railway and industrial construction boom. During the war Russian government bonds were sold on the Paris Bourse.[34] These debts, moreover, were not concentrated in the hands of a few large firms or individuals, but were held by scores of thousands of *petits gens* scattered over the length and breadth of France. The British government's insistence upon Soviet recognition of these private debts was, naturally, quite cheering to the French government and to French public opinion, but it was a gesture that could bring few concrete rewards to Great Britain, and it was certain to complicate vastly the task of reaching an Anglo-Soviet accord.

Nor was this picture changed much when the values of nationalized and confiscated properties were taken into account, because compared with the size of the debt these values were small. And here again the largest share—£76 million—of properties nationalized by the Soviet government without compensation was French. Nationalized British holdings (largely mines, petroleum resources, and forest lands) amounted to £52 million, and the Germans and

---

[32] The Russian war debt figures are known with some degree of accuracy. Those cited here are from the Carnegie Endowment study by Alexander M. Michelson, Paul N. Apostol, and Michael W. Bernatzky, *Russian Public Finance during the War*, New Haven, Conn., 1928, p. 320. The British and French shares of the debt were by far the greatest. Next came the United States, with £46 million, and Japan, with £31 million. It is much more difficult to find figures for the amount of the pre-war debt held by creditors of individual foreign states; those cited here for Britain and France are from A. I. Gukovsky, *Antanta i Oktiabrskaya Revolyutsiya* (The Entente and the October Revolution), Moscow, 1931, p. 108.

[33] See Volume I, pp. 69-70.

[34] For a table of the various French loans to and investments in Russia, see *Le Temps*, 6 July 1922.

Belgians came next with smaller amounts.[35] These sums were not sizable, but in Britain, at least, the firms whose Russian holdings had been nationalized constituted the only organized interest which opposed the resumption of trade with Russia until the debts had been recognized. Yet even here there was not unanimity: some firms were anxious temporarily to forget the past in order to resume trade with Russia. Therefore, in insisting upon the payment of private debts Lloyd George was making a demand which would have little real economic or political impact within Great Britain and which, because of the great size of the Russian private debt to France, could never have been agreed to by the Soviet government.

On both 7 and 16 June the Prime Minister's remarks about the Russian debt were perhaps the most important by the British side in long sessions devoted to the clarification of positions, rather than to bargaining. But the British also asserted themselves on a number of other issues. On 7 June Curzon sharply accused the Soviet government of not adhering to the O'Grady-Litvinov agreement regarding repatriation of prisoners, and then went on to charge it with "direct aggression against Persia" in the form of the landings at Enzeli. To Krasin's request for the reciprocal exchange of trade representatives, Lloyd George replied that because of the Soviet governmental monopoly of foreign trade, the Russians would need only a very small delegation in Great Britain; on the other hand, many British private firms would wish representation in Russia. Each government, moreover, must have the power to veto any representative selected by the other. In addition, Lloyd George said, the British government considered it essential that any agreement or contact between British subjects and Russian trading organizations should be interpreted and dealt with exclusively by British courts: at least for the time being British traders did not understand or have confidence in the Soviet judicial system. Regarding the fear, expressed by Krasin, that Russian goods might be attached by British claimants

---

[35] These figures are from P. V. Ol, *Innostrannie kapitaly v Rossii* (Foreign Capital in Russia), Petrograd, 1922. Leo Pasvolsky and Harold G. Moulton in their *Russian Debts and Russian Reconstruction*, New York, 1924, p. 182, cite Ol's figures and term his work "the only reasonably authoritative study of foreign investments in Russian private corporations and enterprises." German holdings, £45 million, were only slightly smaller than British, while the figures for Belgium and the United States were £33 million and £12 million. For a recent work confirming these figures see John P. Sontag, "Tsarist Debts and Tsarist Foreign Policy," *Slavic Review*, vol. XXVII, no. 4, December 1968, pp. 529-41.

before peace was formally established between the two countries, the Prime Minister confidently implied that the Russians would have nothing to fear so long as they recognized the private Allied debts.

Like Lloyd George and his colleagues, Krasin used both the 7 and 16 June meetings to touch upon a number of issues other than "propaganda" and the debts: the Polish offensive (again he implied that Britain was supporting Poland; after all, he said, were they not both members of the League of Nations?), Persia (Persian-Soviet relations were entirely friendly; he had word from Moscow that Soviet forces were already leaving Enzeli), Georgia (any threat to Georgia's independence came not from Moscow but from the Allied garrison at Batum), Wrangel (if he would capitulate he would certainly get reasonable terms), and the question of the Baltic, Black, and Caspian Seas (the best way to bring about their "complete disarmament" would be for warships of non-littoral states to withdraw). These were not issues of crucial importance, and the two sides were not far apart on them. Nor did they have serious differences regarding what might be called the "modalities" of trade, assuming it were restored. As Lloyd George remarked at the close of the meeting on 16 June, he thought that they were near agreement on every point but two—debts and "propaganda." Yet unless they could agree on them the negotiations would come to nothing. His own view, he said, was that it was very important to come to terms quickly. If the negotiations failed, "things might drift on indefinitely." Those people in both countries who were opposed to a negotiated settlement might gain the upper hand, just as in Britain and France after the French Revolution. "The consequences had been twenty years of bloodshed ending in a Napoleonic despotism in Europe"—an experience he would not like to see repeated.

After his meeting with Krasin on the 7th, Lloyd George went to put the case for negotiations to the House of Commons. The debate that evening—on a routine adjournment motion—was not distinguished. One after another half a dozen Conservatives on the Government back benches rose to attack Bolshevism as abhorrent and to assert that there were, in fact, no goods in Russia to be traded, and that therefore the Bolsheviks would have to use confiscated gold which, in France at least, would be regarded as "stolen goods." Of the Prime Minister's critics, only Sir Samuel Hoare was both cogent and moderate. He pointed to the fact that negotiations were underway between two governments each of which wished the destruction of the other. "I want to put it no higher than this," he said, "but it seems to me unlikely that any stable arrangement can be made when the Governments hold such an opinion of each other."[36]

Lloyd George spoke following Hoare and quickly dismissed the latter's argument. It was absurd, he said, to argue that Britain should not trade with Russia because she abhorred the Russian government. She had, after all, traded with the Tsar's government, "with its corruption, its misgovernment, its pogroms, its scores of thousands of innocent people massacred." Britain had, indeed, "opened up most of the cannibal trade of the world, whether in the South Seas or in Kumassie." The atrocities of the Turks had been much worse than those of the Bolsheviks, "yet it never entered our heads not to trade with them." And Lloyd George continued: "It would be very pleasant if there were no trading relations except with people just like ourselves—those who had a sane government, and who show the same wisdom and judgement. But we cannot indulge in these things; they are a luxury. . . . We must take such governments as we find them, and thank God how very happy we ourselves are here."[37]

Lloyd George's argument sounded very sensible and very English, and he received the enthusiastic support of the Labour Opposition. But the Prime Minister had dismissed Hoare's argument too easily. It was true, as he had said, that Britain had been able to carry on lucrative commercial relations with a number of countries whose political systems were viewed with distaste by the British people. But Lloyd George failed to point out that neither the Tsar nor the Sultan nor the Ashanti were committed, as was the new regime in Russia, to the revolutionary dissolution of the British Empire. And, as the *New Statesman* tartly observed, the Prime Minister's speech would furnish the Bolsheviks with seemingly conclusive proof of their deeply held belief that *bourgeois* governments would do anything for gold and for concessions.[38]

❖

The criticism of Lloyd George's Russian policy by back-bench Conservatives in the House of Commons was matched in content

---

[36] 130 *H.C. Deb.* col. 162. [37] *Ibid.*, col. 169.
[38] *New Statesman*, vol. XV, no. 374, 12 June 1920, p. 268.

and in tone by a series of vituperative editorials in *The Times* which ran every day for nearly a week.[39] But the harshest criticism came from France. Commenting on Lloyd George's remarks in the House, the *Echo de Paris* wrote: "It would be impossible to state more brutally that political interest must be subordinated to commercialism and that the chief desire of the Foreign Office is to sell cotton goods." And the *République Française* spoke for the French government and much of the French public when it stated: "An alliance of which at least one member is thinking almost entirely of its own self-interest ceases to be an alliance."[40]

It was inevitable that this heated French reaction to the British negotiations should color the inter-Allied conference held at Boulogne on 21 and 22 June. The conference met to attempt to reconcile Allied differences on the questions of German disarmament and reparations. On these questions, too, British and French policies diverged widely, and on Sunday, 20 June, Millerand crossed the Channel to meet Lloyd George at Sir Philip Sassoon's estate at Lympne for a day of frank discussion before the conference opened. Both premiers were accompanied by their financial and military advisers; for most of the day all the participants met together to discuss German problems and the rapidly worsening military situation in Turkey which had resulted from Mustafa Kemal's establishment of a provisional government at Ankara in April. Late in the afternoon, however, Lloyd George said that he wished to have a private word with Millerand about his negotiations with Krasin.

As the others filed out, leaving only the two premiers and their secretaries,[41] Lloyd George explained that the British had felt that because of the need to secure guarantees against hostile Soviet activities in the East, negotiations with Krasin could not be left to economic experts, but had to be handled by Cabinet Ministers. This, of course, was precisely what the French most disliked, and Millerand sharply criticized Lloyd George for departing from the agreement reached at San Remo and engaging in political discussions with the

[39] *The Times*, 3, 4, 5, 7, and 8 June 1920 (6 June was a Sunday).

[40] *The Times*, 9 June 1920, printed a long series of quotations from French editorials of the previous day. See also telegram 651 from Sir George Grahame (Paris) to Curzon, 2 June; *British Documents*, vol. XII, no. 712.

[41] "British Secretary's Notes of a Conversation at Lympne, on Sunday, June 20, 1920, at 5:45 P.M.," *ibid.*, vol. VIII, no. 29, pp. 323-28. The British secretary was Sir Maurice Hankey.

Russians.[42] But the Prime Minister denied that political negotiations had taken place. They would come, he said, only with full peace discussions, and he had thus far declined to discuss peace with the Bolsheviks. Nevertheless, the British government had "overwhelming reasons" for insisting that the Russians should "call off their hounds in the East," and therefore he felt constrained to press for an agreement on the question. But he emphasized that in his opinion such an agreement was not necessarily a part of a general peace; it could come merely as a part of trade negotiations, and therefore he did not feel that by carrying on such discussions with Krasin he was in any way departing from the policy agreed upon by the Allies at San Remo.

Lloyd George then put forward an argument which underlined the differences between British and French policy. He regarded the Soviet government, he said, much as he regarded the regime of Mustafa Kemal in Turkey, "not as a regular Government, but as being in *de facto* control." (By this time, it should be noted, Kemal controlled virtually all Turkey beyond Constantinople.) He did not mind entering into negotiations with the Soviet government "as the *de facto* controller" over such issues as propaganda and prisoners of war, but this was quite different from recognizing the Moscow authorities as a *de jure* government.

With this position Millerand heatedly disagreed. He had never refused to enter into *commercial* relations with Russia, he said. Indeed, he had even encouraged French traders and manufacturers to send representatives to Russia, and he had sent technical experts to London to talk with Krasin.[43] But all this depended upon Krasin's being a commercial representative, and not a governmental delegate. The French government, Millerand said, adamantly opposed any *political* discussions with the Russians—and discussions about propaganda and Bolshevik hostility in the East were patently political—

[42] For the San Remo conference, see above, chap. I.

[43] Millerand was here referring to a series of discussions, originating on 17 May 1920, between members of the Russian trade delegation and the Permanent Committee of the Supreme Economic Council, with E. F. Wise as chairman, and participation by French, Belgian, and Italian officials. The sporadic discussions were concerned mostly with trading details. "No minutes of these conversations have been traced in Foreign Office archives," say the editors of *British Documents*, vol. VIII (p. 326, n. 6). This is not surprising; the Foreign Office was bypassed throughout the Russian trade negotiations. Minutes (given to the U.S. Embassy) are to be found, however, in U.S. National Archives, State Department file 661.4116/—.

because they would confer upon the Soviet government "the prestige and authority" of recognition as a *de facto* government.

If the Soviet government insisted upon some kind of political settlement before they would begin trading, Millerand continued, he would ask them whether they acknowledged their responsibility for the debts of the Russian governments which preceded them. If so, then France would gladly accord them recognition. If not, and if they continued to insist upon a political settlement, France could not agree to commercial relations. Millerand did leave one door ajar: if Moscow wanted simply commercial relations, "without any change in the [political] position, and without any *de facto* recognition," that might be possible.

Thus the British and French positions were poles apart. Yet Lloyd George, who concluded the conversation, once again attempted to span them with a verbal bridge, and once again demonstrated the fundamentally unsatisfactory nature of his type of informal conference diplomacy. He did not, the minutes record him as saying, "disagree in the least with M. Millerand's statement." Indeed, the conversation "had shown the importance of discussing the matter face to face. If only he and M. Millerand had lived within 'cab call' of one another, he believed that none of the difficulties would have arisen."[44]

Such assurances did nothing to blunt the edge of Millerand's attack two days later in the closing session of the Boulogne conference when the Allied statesmen, having discussed German and Turkish problems, turned to the question of Russia.[45] Even more vehemently than at Lympne the French premier asserted that only when the Soviet government gave evidence—by acknowledging responsibility for the Russian debts—that its good behavior could be relied upon, would he allow French representatives to take part in political negotiations with the Bolsheviks. In response Lloyd George could only repeat that there was no question of recognizing the Soviet regime *de jure*; the British government simply considered that British interests in the East made it imperative to secure the end of Bolshevik propaganda and agitation.

Throughout the discussion the Italian, Belgian, and Japanese rep-

[44] *British Documents*, vol. VIII, p. 328.
[45] "British Secretary's Draft Notes of an Inter-Allied Conference held at the Villa Belle, Boulogne, on Tuesday, June 22, 1920, at 11:15 A.M."; *ibid.*, no. 36, pp. 375-78.

resentatives sat almost entirely silent. On this occasion Lloyd George was not so optimistic about the extent of Anglo-French agreement. To Millerand's gloomy warning that the negotiations between the British and Soviet governments would only add to the prestige and authority of the Bolsheviks and thus make them even more dangerous in the future, he replied that he doubted whether there was any use in continuing the discussion. Accordingly, it was adjourned *sine die*. The mood was set for the much more serious Anglo-French disagreements over Russia which the following months would bring.

❖

Lloyd George must have expected obstinacy from Millerand, and he must have known that he could not carry the French government with him in his efforts to come to terms with the Soviet regime. He must surely have been dismayed, however, to encounter similar obduracy from Krasin, who, he felt, represented a force for moderation within the Soviet system.[46] At their next meeting, on 29 June, the Soviet Commissar for Foreign Trade was blunt and unyielding. For Lloyd George the experience cannot have been pleasant.

On the other hand, it cannot have been wholly unexpected. During the two weeks preceding this meeting Krasin had received a stream of remonstrative telegrams from Chicherin insisting that he stiffen his whole approach to his negotiations with the British government. Most, if not all, of these telegrams were intercepted and deciphered at the Royal Navy's Code and Cypher School, and then sent to the Prime Minister. The task of breaking the Soviet code was a formidable one: by comparison with the codes used by other governments at the time, it was one of great complexity; its key was changed at least daily; sometimes, presumably when the subject was highly sensitive, there would be as many as three key changes within a single message.[47]

---

[46] On several occasions in June Lloyd George told Riddell that he felt that Krasin was an able man who earnestly wanted to reach an agreement with Great Britain, but that his efforts were being opposed by Chicherin and others in Moscow. See Riddell, *Diary*, pp. 204, 206, 207.

[47] I have found these intercepted Soviet telegrams in two places, the Lloyd George papers and those of J.C.C. Davidson (later Lord Davidson of Little Gaddesden), who, as Bonar Law's private secretary, managed all his chief's "secret service" work and retained in his own possession many of the papers which passed through his hands. (There is, however, no mention of the Soviet telegrams in Robert Rhodes James's *Memoirs of a Conservative: J.C.C. Davidson's Memoirs and Papers 1910-1937*, London, 1969.) There is much duplication of the intercepted traffic between the Lloyd George and Davidson collections; on the other hand, each contains a num-

Distribution within the British government of the deciphered intercepted telegrams ("intercepts," as they were called) was narrowly restricted. No copies may be found in the files of the Foreign Office, and although Foreign Office officials concerned with Russia knew of their contents, they made only the most oblique references to them in intra-office minutes.[48] Copies were, it seems, distributed to

---

ber of items not present in the other. Both contain only the deciphered, translated versions; I have seen neither the cipher originals nor the Russian versions. As is noted below, there seem to be no copies in the Foreign Office archives, nor elsewhere in the available collections at the Public Record Office. This is scarcely surprising, given the sensitive nature of the source.

Those who distributed the deciphered and translated telegrams assigned each a serial number, referred to in subsequent references here as the "intercept number." Nearly all the copies in both the Lloyd George and Davidson MSS bear such numbers. Although there are hundreds of such telegrams in the two collections combined, they do not contain the entire series, if these numbers are a guide. This may be due to difficulties in reception or deciphering, or because the deciphering authorities did not consider the missing messages important enough to circulate to the Prime Minister and Bonar Law. Similarly, nearly all of them also carried Soviet serial numbers, assigned by the respective senders in Moscow, London, and elsewhere. These series, of course, are also incomplete in the two collections; it is unlikely that the British were able to intercept and decipher *every* Soviet message to and from the United Kingdom.

In August and September 1920 the intercepted messages were to become a source of very considerable controversy within the higher reaches of the British government. Chapter VII is devoted to this controversy, and the special characteristics of the "intercepts" are there treated in more detail. (The complexity of the Soviet ciphers, including key changes, was described in a memorandum from Hankey to Lloyd George, 8 September 1920, Davidson MSS.) Both from internal evidence and from the circumstances of this controversy I conclude that the telegrams were, indeed, genuine, and not a "black" fabrication. I have also found two instances where the texts were later published by the Soviet government in Lenin's collected works (cited below, n. 51, and chap. VII, n. 8).

The Royal Navy's Code and Cypher School (which on 1 April 1922 was transferred from the administrative responsibility of the Admiralty to that of the Foreign Office) also figures in chap. VII. I have been able to discover relatively little about it, however, except the fact that its existence was threatened by the intense controversy over the intercepts. During the period of our concern it had an "establishment" of some ninety persons. It is not mentioned in David Kahn's *The Codebreakers: The Story of Secret Writing*, New York, 1967, the generally acknowledged authoritative work on the subject. Kahn does, however, extensively treat the Admiralty's famous "Room 40," the scene of critically important wartime codebreaking activities (pp. 266-350). Nor is the Code and Cypher School mentioned in Admiral Sir William James, *The Code Breakers of Room 40: The Story of Admiral Sir William R. Hall, Genius of British Counter-Espionage*, New York, 1956, or in Alfred W. Ewing, *The Man of Room 40: The Life of Sir Alfred Ewing*, London, n.d. [1939].

[48] Sometimes these references were less than oblique, however. Thus, when it appeared that there was sentiment within the Foreign Office to deny the Soviet trade mission the requested privilege of sending and receiving sealed diplomatic bags, Owen St. C. O'Malley, of the Northern Department, minuted: "If the Bolsheviks are told that they can send cypher telegrams but not letters by bag, they will draw the obvious conclusion that we can read their cypher. This seems to me in itself a

the Prime Minister, to Bonar Law, to Curzon, to Winston Churchill and Walter Long, the political heads of the fighting services (Churchill combined the Army and the Air Force; Long was First Lord of the Admiralty), and also to the Chiefs of Staff. Whether or not they ever reached civil servants such as E. F. Wise of the Ministry of Food, who was charged with interdepartmental coordination relating to the trade negotiations, is impossible to determine from available materials; given the prevailing distrust of Wise, however, it is most unlikely that any did reach him.[49] As we will see, during the late summer of 1920 the intercepts were to provide the basis for a heated political controversy which threatened the existence of the Coalition government and, therefore, Lloyd George's political career. For our present purposes, because we do not have at our disposal all of the traffic between London and Moscow (whether because the missing telegrams were not intercepted or deciphered, or because they simply never made their way into available collections, is unclear), they provide an invaluable but not comprehensive insight into the substance, the methods, and the style of early Soviet diplomacy.

For the initial phase of the Anglo-Soviet negotiations (Krasin returned to Moscow on 1 July, thus ending what might be called the first phase), we have Chicherin's explosive reactions to the reports Krasin was sending him from London, but not the reports themselves. Chicherin's reactions, however, are sufficient to point up the nature of these reports and the profound differences, both on substance and on style, between Krasin and those in Moscow responsible for the formulation of Soviet foreign policy. "Lloyd George apparently wishes that we should give everything, bind ourselves, put down the revolution in the East and release every British subject, all this for the sake of the problematic benefit of the renewal of trade relations, which is not yet a matter for discussion," Chicherin

---

sufficient reason for allowing bags of limited size to pass to and fro." Lord Hardinge commented, with Curzon's initialled endorsement: "I agree as to this condition being made and a limit placed on the weight of the bags. The more they are encouraged to send cypher tels. the better for us." (26 May 1920, file 200748/200748/38; F.O. 371/4056.) But direct references of this sort were very infrequent.

[49] Wise enjoyed the favor of Lloyd George and the suspicious resentment of most of the rest of the Cabinet, who regarded him as much too pro-Soviet; see Volume II, p. 327.

telegraphed on 12 June in response to Krasin's reports of his first two meetings with Lloyd George. He continued:

However necessary locomotives may be we must not sacrifice everything for the doubtful possibility of perhaps getting a few of them. To show firmness does not imply the renouncing of results. You must in no wise yield to British blackmailing. The situation that has been created in the East is a difficult one for England. In Persia they are almost helpless in the face of the revolution. Disloyalty is increasing amongst the Indian troops. . . . By a policy of capitulation we shall attain nothing . . . and if we do nothing else but make concessions, we shall not even get loco-motives. The French demand for an embargo being placed on our gold is preparing the way for roguery on a large scale. You must believe abso-lutely nothing and show the greatest firmness.[50]

And Chicherin passed on the following message from Lenin: "This is my advice to Krassin: that swine Lloyd George has no scruples or shame in the way he deceives: don't believe a word he says and gull him three times as much."[51]

Five days later, Chicherin summarized the London discussions in a long report to a closed meeting of the All-Russian Central Execu-tive Committee (the 200-man "executive committee" of the Congress of Soviets; in fact it wielded little more real power than its parent body, the locus of decision making having long since passed to the Council of Peoples' Commissars, or Sovnarkom).[52] He depicted a bourgeois coalition, led by Great Britain, trying by every means to undermine the Soviet regime, and a Soviet diplomacy fully capable of holding its own. We will have cause to consider some of Chicherin's arguments in detail in the following chapter. Here it is sufficient to note that militant though his speech was, to Krasin he telegraphed a

[50] Chicherin to Krasin, 12 June 1920. Copies of these intercepted telegrams bore both a Soviet transmission number and a number assigned by the British decipherers; thus this was Moscow's telegram 55 and intercept 002930; Lloyd George MSS, file F/12/3/50 (also Davidson MSS).

[51] Chicherin to Krasin, telegram 56, 12 June 1920; intercept 002966, Davidson MSS. Lenin's original version is also available. In a note to Chicherin on 11 July he wrote: "I advise you: 1) To Krasin in cipher: 'That scoundrel [*merzavets*] Lloyd George deceives you godlessly [*bezbozhno*] and shamelessly [*besstydno*], don't believe one word he says and deceive him three times as much.'" (Lenin, *Polnoe sobranie sochinenii*, 5th ed., vol. 51, Moscow, 1965, p. 215.) Whether the slight but picturesque discrepancies are due to Chicherin's editing or to the British transla-tion is, of course, impossible to determine.

[52] A somewhat abridged version of Chicherin's speech of 17 June 1920 is in *Dokumenty vneshnei politiki*, vol. II, pp. 638-61; see especially pp. 641-46.

summary implying that it was not sufficiently militant for his audience:

Osinsky, the president of the Voronezh Executive Committee, Koganovich and especially Sosnovsky spoke against taking up too peaceful and conciliatory an attitude in favour of a more pronounced revolutionary policy.... All the appeals of the opposition speakers for adopting a more bellicose policy were met with rousing applause. This shows that a pacific and conciliatory policy is not very popular. . . . Great indignation is caused in particular by Britain's policy, which strives to deceive us by alleged negotiations, eggs on Wrangel and Poland, at the same time declaring that she has nothing to do with them, strives to get everything out of us without giving us anything in return, strives to bind us in the West and in the East, to deprive us of all freedom of action, to feed us on empty promises, to control our foreign trade and, while holding us in their power, to play the part of a benefactor.

Chicherin summarized for Krasin the implications of the meeting. "All appeals for firmness against this policy of deception and hypocrisy find an echo in the masses." And he continued: "I repeat that it is absolutely inadmissible to adopt before Lloyd George the tone of the accused."[53]

By implication, Chicherin had belabored Krasin for not being sufficiently sensitive to Soviet domestic politics. He then went on, a week later, to charge him directly with insensitivity to British domestic politics. Krasin had apparently telegraphed urging that Moscow agree to Lloyd George's demand that the Soviet government should recognize its indebtedness to British private creditors. The fact that such a demand had been made, however, had become known to the Labour Party, which was meeting in its annual conference at Scarborough on 22-25 June. Ben Turner, of the Textile Workers, just back from a six-week visit to Russia as chairman of a joint Labour Party–Trades Union Congress "fact-finding" delegation, reported that he had learned that the negotiations were in danger of breaking down "because the commercial classes were squeezing and trying to get their last drop of blood." The Soviet government, he said, was willing to recognize the debts of previous Russian governments going back to 1905. (The Soviet government, in fact, had never made such a statement, nor would it.) But "the

---

[53] Chicherin to Krasin, telegrams 72-74, 18 June 1920; intercept 003049, Lloyd George MSS, file F/12/3/50.

commercial classes of the other countries insisted on obtaining more, and demanded that all the private debts of the capitalists must also be recognized and paid by the Russian Government as a preliminary to negotiations. Trade relations and peace were being delayed at the bidding of commercial investors."[54] Two days later, the conference duly resolved that "No private or financial interests should be allowed to stand in the way of an immediate resumption of trade with Russia."[55]

Turner's statement and the resolution were each but one of many addressed by the conference to perceived injustices of all sorts. Not surprisingly, however, they assumed in the eyes of the Soviet government an importance out of all deserved proportion. Thus Chicherin indignantly telegraphed Krasin on 25 June that from reports reaching Moscow of the Labour Party Conference, "We found out for the first time something of which you had not informed us, namely, that the question of creditors had become a matter which was being used for wide popular agitation, one of the points in the struggle of labour organisations against the Government. This essential point was not brought to our knowledge by you and yet the part played in our general policy by our relations to labour organisations and by the value we place on agitation is so great that it changes the situation profoundly." Therefore, Chicherin continued,

Before we can come to a final decision with reference to British creditors we must receive from you detailed data of the agitation which is being carried on in connection with this subject, details of the struggle, how wide it is and to what extent the masses are interested; we must know what took place besides the debates at Scarborough. We are awaiting a detailed report from you. Write "very urgent" at the top of your cyphered message on this subject. This information is necessary in order to enable us to investigate the question of creditors here.[56]

Unfortunately, we do not have Krasin's "very urgent" reply to this request—if, indeed, he ever sent one. We do not know, therefore,

---

[54] Labour Party, *Report of the Twentieth Annual Conference held in the Olympia, Scarborough, on June 22nd, 23rd, 24th and 25th, 1920*, London, 1920, p. 136. For an account of the Labour Party–T.U.C. mission to Russia, see Graubard, *British Labour and the Russian Revolution*, pp. 214-17.

[55] Labour Party, *Twentieth Annual Conference*, p. 176.

[56] Chicherin to Krasin, telegrams 189-97, 25 June 1920; intercept 003178, Davidson MSS.

whether, like Chicherin, he exaggerated the political importance of Turner's statement, the conference resolution, and other signs, such as militant editorials in the *Daily Herald*, of "agitation" on the issue of private creditors. On the other hand, he may have been sufficiently sensitive to the British political situation to perceive that the Labour movement would be most unlikely to be roused to more than rhetoric over such an issue (unlike, for example, the issue which arose later in the summer of possible British military intervention in the Polish-Soviet war). And he may have sensed that Lloyd George was so little dependent upon Labour support, or even Labour good will, that over such an issue Labour's voice would be insignificant compared to that of the "commercial classes." In any case, whatever Krasin may have replied, Chicherin had other sources—principally Feodor Rothstein, a Bolshevik who had lived many years in England (he was a British citizen) and who in 1921-22 would be Soviet Minister at Teheran—more doctrinaire, and therefore more likely than Krasin to reinforce the predispositions of Chicherin and his colleagues in Moscow.[57]

In his telegram of 25 June, and in another the following day,[58] Chicherin went on to argue at length against Krasin's explicit and implied positions on a number of questions that had arisen in his discussions with Lloyd George. First was that of the recognition of debts to private creditors, which Krasin evidently had recommended to Moscow. Aside from the fact that the Labour Party opposed the British government's insistence on such recognition, Chicherin commented, more basic points were involved. "It is not at all clear from your messages," he said, "what exactly we are going to receive in return for this vast concession in principle." The mere fact that the British government had agreed "on paper" to enter into trade relations with Soviet Russia was "absolutely insufficient"; London would have to agree to concrete measures—removing every vestige of the blockade, and consenting to the admission of any representative, such as Litvinov, whom Moscow might appoint. In any case, a Soviet concession, if it were to come, would be in principle only. Krasin was

[57] The British government regarded Rothstein as the principal Bolshevik agent resident in the United Kingdom. Almost certainly he was. See Walter Kendall, *The Revolutionary Movement in Great Britain, 1900-21*, London, 1969, pp. 241-46.

[58] Chicherin to Krasin, telegram 175-80, 26 June 1920; intercept 03177, Davidson MSS. (Why this message should bear lower Soviet transmission and British intercept numbers than that of the previous day—cited n. 56—is unclear.)

ordered not to make any binding statements without first communicating the full text to Moscow. Statements regarding the debts were to be "as vague as possible," in a form "which would bind us as little as possible." Concrete terms would await future formal peace negotiations between the two governments.

Nevertheless, Chicherin conceded by telegram to Krasin that even the principle of recognizing Soviet responsibility for the debts of previous Russian governments to private British traders would be "an enormous step." And he insisted: "We must not sell it too cheap." The British would, of course, have to lift the blockade and admit all Soviet representatives. "But first of all," Chicherin stated, "we must make the greatest use of this concession for purposes of agitation." He explained: "May all the French Rentiers tear their hair because their ministers are Clemenceau and Millerand, and not Lloyd George, and because the idiotic policy of the French Government has deprived them of what their English confrères have received! You must drum that into every Frenchman."

Despite these implications that Krasin might make the "colossal concession," permission to do so was not actually given. Two issues intervened. The first was Wrangel's offensive from the confines of the Crimea. Chicherin could not believe that London had ceased its support of the White forces. The British were "playing a most perfidious and base double-faced game" which, he said, "arouses here the greatest indignation, and at such a moment the recognition of British creditors would provoke in our masses the strongest opposition." The second issue was Japan's activity in Siberia. Additional Japanese forces had arrived, indicating an intention to occupy territory as far west as Irkutsk. Japan was "closely bound in alliance to England," Chicherin stated; the question of Japanese policy would be on the Soviet agenda for formal peace negotiations with London. In the meantime, Krasin was to raise both issues with Lloyd George. Moscow would postpone its decision on whether or not to make a concession on debts until he had reported back.

A second major topic of contention between the two governments on which Krasin seems to have recommended some sort of concession was Soviet policy regarding the East. "You speak also in your telegrams of the cessation of hostile activities in the East, etc.," Chicherin telegraphed to Krasin. "Political obligations like this, however, must certainly be put aside. They will be raised only in the course of regular and formal peace negotiations." While this may have disposed of the issue, Chicherin then added:

You write that we exaggerate the influence of the East upon British policy, for Curzon knows that we shall "do the dirty" all the same. That is not so. In unofficial conversations you must make it clear that we are able to cause them serious damage in the East if we so wish. Picture to them what will happen if we send a Red Army to Persia, Mesopotamia and Afghanistan. We are awaited and yearned for there and it is only the moderation of our policy which causes a slow development [of the revolutionary situation] in that country. They are under an obligation to us for our carefulness in this connection but we should only have to change our tactics in the East in order to bring a catastrophe upon England. You must point by unofficial conversations to the enormous part played by an agreement with us and to the fact that we have up till now been careful there, with a view to preparing for the possibility of peace in the West. Both in the East and in the West the British have short arms.[59]

Finally, Chicherin dealt with the possibility that if the Soviet side refused to make concessions regarding either debts or Soviet activities in the East until actually engaged in formal peace negotiations with London, the British might simply break off altogether the "informal" trade negotiations with Krasin and pursue, instead, a more actively anti-Soviet course of action. "You speak of a new advance against us of fourteen nations," he told Krasin, and continued:

This is impossible. The feeling of the masses in the Baltic States is such that such an eventuality is precluded. Even the Finnish Government shows striking evidence of its desire for peace. . . . Only a temporary cessation of negotiations is possible, but no active measures against us are possible. . . . Even Roumania has shown no signs of wishing to join up with Poland even in the hour of the latter's victory and now each day sees an improvement in our military situation.

Despite his seeming confidence in his own judgment of the situation, however, Chicherin sought further corroboration. Besides asking Krasin for his opinion, he instructed him: "Report what competent students of international politics amongst our London comrades think about possible danger in the event of negotiations breaking down. We consider that such a rupture would be temporary and that England herself would soon begin to curry favor with us. It is, how-

[59] From the message of 25 June 1920, cited n. 56.

ever, important for us to know the opinion of competent London experts."[60]

We do not, unfortunately, have Krasin's reply to this request. We do not, therefore, know which "experts" he consulted—if any. Later in the summer of 1920, as we will see, the Soviet delegation was to develop extensive contacts within the British Left. Undoubtedly Krasin had already begun quietly to cultivate sympathetic Britons— not only those members of splinter parties such as the British Socialist Party, the Socialist Labour Party, and the Workers' Socialist Federation, who were to come together in August to form the British Communist Party, but also those in the main stream of the Labour Party. An "expert" who was invariably consulted was Feodor Rothstein. So, also, was Litvinov—still restively perching in Copenhagen—to whom all of the telegraphic traffic between Moscow and the London delegation was duly repeated.[61] To Krasin on 26 June Litvinov telegraphed:

I recommend to Moscow to agree on a platonic promise of recognition of private claims but that should be done in the most careful manner, and, if possible, for the present only as regards the English so as to excite French jealousy. We can give a promise only against a guarantee that all obstacles in the way of beginning trade and the free sale of gold be immediately removed, and that no new conditions be laid upon us.[62]

Litvinov, of course, during his days in London in 1918 and his negotiations in Copenhagen of the Anglo-Soviet agreement on prisoner exchanges, had had extensive experience of British diplomacy; he was at least as expert upon it as were any of his colleagues. To the British he ascribed what a later era would term "salami tactics": "The English [his telegram continued] are in the habit, when they obtain concessions in one question, of immediately bringing less important demands and of stating: 'Once you have given way on the big question don't be obstinate about trifles.'"

Chicherin's scolding telegrams must inevitably have made Krasin well aware that Moscow looked upon him only as a technician, and not in any sense as a political operator with discretionary authority. It was this awareness, perhaps, which caused Krasin to suggest that the Commissar for Foreign Affairs himself should come to London

[60] *Idem.* [61] Each telegram is so marked.
[62] Litvinov (Copenhagen) to Krasin (London) and Chicherin (Moscow), telegrams 252 and 1038 (respectively); intercept 003161, Davidson MSS.

to carry on the discussions with the British. Chicherin sharply refused, telling Krasin: "My coming to London now, when there are no formal peace negotiations, would be the greatest folly and humiliation, would indicate that we are ready to agree to anything, and would completely ruin our policy of gradually extorting concessions from England. We do not believe in a new, sharp change of attitude on the part of England, because she is too deeply committed, but she will continue as long as possible her two-faced policy, which we must meet by firmness."[63]

The essence of firmness, for Chicherin, was to be unwavering in enforcing the distinction between trade discussion and formal peace negotiations. "You must resolutely refuse any political promises as long as there are no real peace negotiations, and agreements about the East or in general about the cessation of a hostile policy must be left absolutely to the formal peace negotiations," he told Krasin in his telegram of 26 June. And as if Krasin had not already grasped his point, he added: "It is necessary to repeat unceasingly and to emphasize in every possible way that we shall willingly agree to all such transactions, but shall agree only in the case of formal peace negotiations. Then, of course, we shall not permit any objection to our representatives and experts."

These telegrams formed the background to Krasin's next meeting with Lloyd George, late on the afternoon of 29 June.[64] The meeting came at the Prime Minister's request. He was about to return to the Continent for yet another set of conferences—this time a preliminary inter-Allied conference at Brussels and then the long-heralded first meeting on "normal" terms between the Allies and the Germans, at the Belgian resort of Spa. When Krasin arrived at 10 Downing Street, he found virtually the same small group (without "extremists") as at his last visit—Lloyd George, Horne, Kerr, Wise, and an interpreter. Lloyd George opened the meeting by observing, quite erroneously, that their "negotiations had been brought to a point that only one or two important questions remained to be settled"; he was therefore anxious, before meeting his Allied colleagues at Brussels, to know whether or not the Soviet government would agree to

[63] Chicherin's message of 26 June 1920, cited n. 58.
[64] "Secretary's Notes of a Conference with the Russian Trade Delegation . . . ," London, 29 June 1920, 5:30 P.M.; *British Documents*, vol. VIII, no. 37, pp. 380-88.

Britain's terms. He had to know without further delay whether or not trading relations were to be resumed.

In response, Krasin said that he found himself in a difficult position. Although he had come as the head of a trading delegation he had immediately found himself involved in political negotiations, while Litvinov, who had been appointed by Moscow to handle political questions, had been denied permission to enter Great Britain. Moreover, Krasin said, nearly one-third of his cable communications with Moscow had been lost entirely and the rest badly garbled.[65] And because of the difficulties of obtaining visas for transit through other countries, not a single Soviet courier had yet arrived. Therefore, he had had to rely on his previous instructions from Moscow in preparing a formal answer to the questions raised by the British government. He then had read out (either by Klishko, his assistant, or Peters, the British interpreter—the minutes do not indicate which one) the text of a long note which, as Lloyd George interjected before the reading was finished, "appeared more in the nature of a lecture than of a business reply."[66]

The note considered first the British demand for the cessation of Soviet propaganda and hostile acts. It drew a distinction between the two: on the one hand there was "the propaganda of communistic ideas amongst the labouring masses of Western European States and the organisation of the working classes of these countries for the final struggle with the capitalist regime"; on the other there was "the general direction of the foreign policy of Soviet Russia, against the Powers of the *Entente*, in particular, of Great Britain, and also participation in, or cognisance of, hostile actions and undertakings directed against Great Britain in various countries of the Near and Middle East, including India." Here, indeed, was a frank admission of both the goals and the tactics of Soviet policy. The Soviet government, the note declared, was prepared to cease *both* of these activities. It would "give a formal undertaking not to carry on such propaganda in Great Britain, either openly or secretly, and not to interfere with the internal political life of Great Britain"; it would also "readily agree to revise the foundations of its foreign policy, and,

[65] The available "intercepts" provide no positive substantiation of this contention, although the lacunae suggest that it might have been correct.
[66] *British Documents*, vol. VIII, p. 385. The translated version of Krasin's note is on pp. 381-85. The original Russian version is printed in *Dokumenty vneshnei politiki*, vol. II, pp. 593-98.

in particular, not to take part in any hostile actions or undertakings directed against Great Britain." In return, the British government must make similar undertakings, the whole arrangement to be "confirmed in a special agreement between the two Governments . . . worked out at a special conference, consisting of an equal number of representatives of the two Governments . . . without the right on the part of either side to set aside persons participating in such a conference." Even this arrangement, the note continued, would not be fully satisfactory, because such undertakings on the part of Great Britain would be largely vitiated by the fact that Britain's allies would be free to attack Soviet Russia and to support her enemies. Therefore, the only really satisfactory solution would be a general peace conference in which all of the Powers which had made war on Russia would participate.

The note then turned to the question of debts, and flatly rejected the British demand for Soviet recognition of an obligation to pay the Russian debts to private individuals. Giving priority to these debts would only increase the wealth of British "capitalist circles" which had already utilized the war for personal profit. "Debts of private persons," the note said, were "only a part of the mutual obligations of the two countries." A matter "of incomparably greater urgency" was the recognition of claims against the Allied governments by "hundreds of thousands of the widows and orphans of the workers and peasants of Soviet Russia, the Ukraine, the Caucasus and Siberia, whose relatives have died through British and French bullets and shells during the so-called intervention—i.e., during the entirely unprovoked military interference of the *Entente* in the internal affairs of Russia." Moreover, all Russian obligations to British subjects had "been annulled by actions of the British Government itself, from the moment when that Government began war and intervention against Soviet Russia and declared the blockade . . . in order to compel the Russian people, through hunger and privations, to deny those forms of State life which that people chose for itself." Therefore, there could be "no question of recognition of agreements which do not exist." Instead, it would be necessary to reach new agreements for the settlement of claims on a mutual basis, which would be possible "only on recognition of the Soviet Government and on re-establishment of peaceful relations between the countries after peace negotiations and the signing of a peace treaty."

Thus, as Chicherin had instructed, Krasin's note linked both cessation of propaganda and settlement of the debt to a formal peace conference after which Soviet Russia would be a full-fledged member of the family of nations. If the British did not wish to take such a step, the note continued, trading relations between Britain and Russia could nonetheless be resumed on condition that 1) all such questions as the cessation of hostile activities and the settlement of mutual claims should be postponed until an eventual peace conference; 2) each government should announce the immediate resumption of trade and a temporary moratorium on all property claims; 3) they would immediately agree upon the main bases on which trade could be carried on, such as the mutual exchange of trade representatives with immunity from arrest and other quasi-diplomatic privileges and agreement on the mutual acceptance of legal and commercial documents. Elaborating on this last condition, the note specifically rejected Lloyd George's previous insistence that each government be given the right to refuse in advance any trade representative assigned by the other; the bourgeois governments of Europe might well regard any Soviet representative as *persona non grata*. Instead, each government should be able to demand the recall only of those trade representatives *proved* to have infringed the law or interfered in the internal affairs of the country.

With these remarks—and with a closing appeal to "the British Government and the whole British people, and its labouring masses in particular" for a "complete unconditional and general peace" between Russia and the states which had made war upon her—the long and (for the British listeners) tedious reading of Krasin's note was finished. For his part, Lloyd George said, it had filled him with despair. He had done his best to put an end to the conflict between Russia and the Western Powers. He had hoped that the resumption of trade relations would be a first step that would lead "ultimately, perhaps sooner" to permanent peace. He had, indeed, taken political risks even to initiate trade negotiations. And now the Soviet note constituted a refusal to accept the only conditions under which the resumption of trade relations would have been possible; Krasin, the Prime Minister said, should have no delusions about that. Trade would clearly be impossible so long as active hostilities or hostile propaganda continued. Concerning debts, he required only that the Soviet government "should make such an acknowledgement of its liability to pay those who had supplied Russia with goods" in order to "create confidence among Western traders and merchants necessary to the restarting of trade on a considerable scale." (This was, in fact, nothing but the "platonic promise" which Litvinov had recommended.) Yet Krasin rejected these proposals. Finally, Krasin had said nothing about the release of prisoners, which was also an essential prerequisite to trade.

In reply, Krasin tried his best to minimize the effects of the note which had been read in his name. He was, he said, merely the head of a commercial delegation. His staff comprised only commercial experts, not men versed in military and diplomatic affairs. He had stated that his government would, in principle, agree to a mutual cessation of hostile activities, but he was not empowered to deal finally with the matter. He asked, therefore, for a written statement which he could send to Moscow listing exactly what the British government required in regard both to propaganda and to foreign debts.

These remarks did nothing to hearten Lloyd George. It was not really a matter of consulting experts, he said. (And besides, he added, the British government had no objection to Krasin's bringing with him anyone except Litvinov.) The fundamental question was simply whether the British Empire and Soviet Russia were going to abandon hostile activities against one another or not. Once again Lloyd George stated the central tenet of his policy: the "first and necessary step" towards peace was the resumption of trade relations, and for that purpose an agreement to end hostilities was essential. And once again Krasin asserted that the Soviet government insisted upon general peace negotiations. The impasse—between a policy of cautious, piecemeal measures politically acceptable in a liberal democracy and one of sweeping, dramatic gestures with great propaganda value—was one that would often becloud Soviet-Western negotiations during succeeding decades.

At this point Lloyd George stopped the conversation. Negotiations could be prolonged no longer, he said. He was about to meet his Allied colleagues in Belgium, and therefore he would need an answer within a week as to whether the Soviet government proposed to continue hostilities or to make an agreement upon the grounds he had indicated—in short, "whether it was to be agreement or rupture." If the Russians chose the latter, he wished to know it in order that he might take counsel with his allies.

Faced with this ultimatum, Krasin asked to be allowed to return to Moscow before the Soviet reply was sent. Lloyd George consented, and said he would have the Navy convey him to Reval immediately. If the Russians agreed to the British conditions, which he would forward to Krasin in writing on the following day, they could send to London any experts they wanted except Litvinov. As he ushered his visitor out of his office, the Prime Minister commented that ever since the Prinkipo proposals he had done his best to bring about peace between Russia and the West. If the current negotiations broke down, he said, the chances for peace would be worse than they would have been had the talks never taken place. But in any case, he wanted to know definitely where he stood.[67]

Two days later Krasin was steaming toward the Baltic Sea aboard the flagship of a British destroyer flotilla. In his luggage was a memorandum for transmission to his colleagues in the Soviet government, formally putting into writing the conditions put to him by Lloyd George in their meetings which the British government held must be fulfilled before Anglo-Soviet trade might begin.[68] Krasin was

[67] *British Documents*, vol. VIII, p. 388.

[68] The British memorandum, dated 30 June 1920 and circulated to the House of Commons on 14 July (131 *H.C. Deb.*, cols. 2369-71) asked for "categorical replies, yes or no" as to whether the Soviet government was willing to enter into a trade agreement on the following conditions:

1. A mutual undertaking to refrain from hostile action against each other, and from conducting "any official propaganda, direct or indirect, against the institutions of the other party." In particular, the Soviet government was to refrain from "any attempt by military action or propaganda to encourage any of the peoples of Asia in any form of hostile action against the interests of the British Empire." This was "the fundamental condition of any trading agreement between Russia and any Western Power. Trade is only possible under conditions of peace or armistice. *The British Government propose what is tantamount to a general armistice, as the condition of the resumption of trade relations, in the hope that this armistice may lead ere long to a general peace.*" (Italics added.)

2. ". . . all British subjects in Russia should immediately be permitted to return home, all Russian subjects in Great Britain or other parts of the British Empire who desire to return to Russia being similarly released."

3. The Soviet government must "recognise in principle that it is liable to pay compensation to private citizens who have supplied goods or services to Russia for which they have not been paid. . . . The British government does not ask that these debts should be settled now. It is prepared to leave the determination of Russia's liabilities under this head, as well as other questions relating to debts or claims by Great Britain on Russia or by Russia on Great Britain, to be mutually settled at the negotiations of peace. But it considers it necessary that the Soviet Government should

welcomed aboard the destroyer by all the ship's officers, and was given the captain's cabin. Behind the flagship the other ships of the flotilla ran in a tight formation clearly intended as a demonstration of Britain's naval efficiency. Lloyd George had spared no effort.[69]

❖

Krasin's journey to Russia marked the end of the first phase of Anglo-Soviet negotiations. When he returned to England four weeks later the dramatic and sweeping Soviet military success against Poland had vastly complicated the task of reaching an agreement. The June negotiations, however, had highlighted the basic weaknesses of the personal diplomacy of David Lloyd George.

The Prime Minister had invited Krasin to England because he

---

make a declaration on this point in order to give the necessary confidence to Western merchants, manufacturers and workers to embark upon manufacturing and trading operations."

4. The British government agrees to the conditions laid down by the Soviet government regarding reciprocal trade facilities, except that it cannot give up the right (which it freely accords to Russia) to exclude the entry of any person who is *non grata* to itself. "It asserts, however, that it has no intention of debarring any Russian on the ground of his Communist opinions, provided the agents of the Russian Government comply with the normal conditions for friendly international intercourse."

In closing, the memorandum laid down the same ultimatum which Lloyd George gave to Krasin at their last meeting. If the Soviet government agreed to the conditions, trade discussions could be continued with any Russian representatives except those already refused admission to Britain (*i.e.*, Litvinov). "Should, however, no affirmative reply be obtained within one week, . . . the British Government will regard the negotiations at an end, and, in view of the declared unwillingness of the Soviet Government to cease its attacks upon the British Empire, will take counsel with its Allies as to the measures required to deal with the situation."

Although the memorandum did not mince words, the version finally presented was considerably more moderate in tone than earlier drafts. It was evidently prepared entirely in the Prime Minister's secretariat. Successive drafts, all dated 30 June 1920, some bearing extensive corrections in Lloyd George's hand, are in Lloyd George MSS, file F/202/3/20.

[69] See Krasin's letters to his wife written on shipboard, 2 and 3 July 1920, printed in Krassin, *Krassin*, pp. 126-28. It need scarcely be added that the Navy's hospitality was not a product of Admiralty generosity. On 25 June 1920 Walter Long, the First Lord, wrote to Curzon urging in the name of the Admiralty that Krasin and his fellow Soviet delegates should be detained in Great Britain until all British prisoners in Soviet hands were freed. The Foreign Office did not agree. Hardinge wrote to Curzon two days later noting that he knew of no precedent for such an action, and that "to detain Krassin and his rascally crew because we have failed to come to terms with him for the reopening of trade with Russia and to obtain the acceptance of one of the most important of our conditions [*i.e.*, that relating to prisoners], would, I venture to think, be a dastardly act on our part." (Curzon MSS, Box 22).

was a "good Bolshevik," a sober businessman as compared with the "dangerous revolutionary," Litvinov. Both in Parliament and in the councils of the Allies Lloyd George had made much of his forth-right and principled refusal to treat with Litvinov. Thus Krasin had come, and Lloyd George had offered him the whole loaf of peace in the guise of a mere trade agreement. But Krasin, despite his impressive background (perhaps, indeed, because of it), was primarily a specialist in commercial matters. With considerable justification he could plead his lack of authority when confronted with Lloyd George's political proposals. Had the Prime Minister been dealing with Litvinov, however, he might have succeeded in reaching the political agreement he sought.

By excluding Litvinov, Lloyd George was paying what he felt to be necessary obeisance to the dictates of domestic politics. For that reason he felt constrained to state publicly that he had no intention of entering into full-scale diplomatic negotiations for peace with Soviet Russia, although at the same time he was aiming at just such a political goal under the guise of a trade agreement. Yet excluding Litvinov made the agreement Lloyd George wanted much more difficult to achieve. The Prime Minister was too subtle by half.

Moreover, his subtlety was largely ineffective. To his Conservative critics, both in Parliament and in the press, there was no such thing as a "good Bolshevik"; one was as bad as the next. And the same critics constantly alleged that behind the façade of trade negotiations with the Russian delegation, the Prime Minister was in fact carrying on political discussions. Had the discussions been openly political, and had they been carried on with Litvinov instead of with Krasin (after all, as one member reminded the House of Commons, a British representative—O'Grady—had spent months negotiating with Litvinov in Copenhagen over the prisoner of war agreement),[70] Lloyd George's room for maneuver would not have been notably more circumscribed.

If the Prime Minister's subtlety did his cause little good at home, it was appreciated even less in Moscow. In his surreptitious way he had, in fact, gone a long way toward meeting the substance of the Soviet government's demands, and in doing so he had run serious political risks and had greatly angered the French. But the Soviet

[70] 129 *H.C. Deb.*, col. 55 (10 May 1920).

leaders, despite their desire to appeal to "the whole British people, and its labouring masses in particular," were equally anxious for recognition and acceptance in the community of sovereign states. To them a trade agreement which carried with it the substance of a peace treaty was scarcely a substitute for a formal peace accord. Without the form the substance was insufficient despite the efforts that Lloyd George had made and the risks he had run.

PART TWO

The Polish-Soviet War

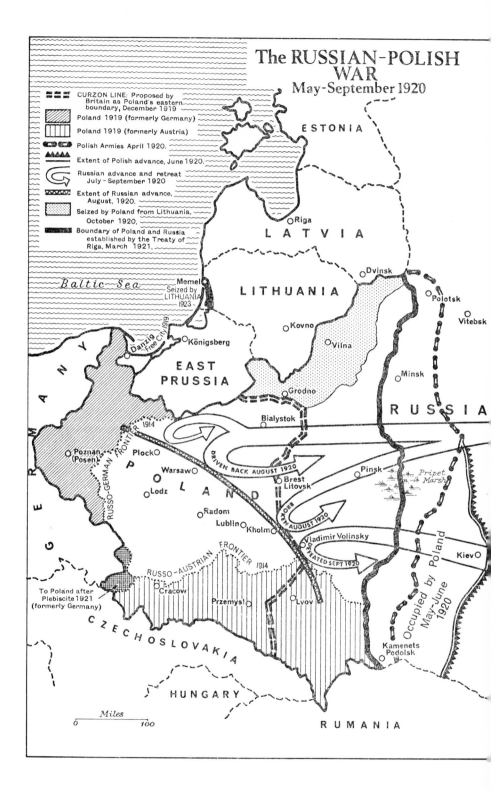

The RUSSIAN-POLISH WAR
May–September 1920

CURZON LINE: Proposed by Britain as Poland's eastern boundary, December 1919

Poland 1919 (formerly Germany)

Poland 1919 (formerly Austria)

Polish Armies April 1920.

Extent of Polish advance, June 1920.

Russian advance and retreat July – September 1920

Extent of Russian advance, August, 1920.

Seized by Poland from Lithuania, October 1920,

Boundary of Poland and Russia established by the Treaty of Riga, March 1921,

Baltic Sea

ESTONIA

LATVIA

Riga

Dvinsk

Polotsk

Vitebsk

LITHUANIA

Kovno

Vilna

Minsk

Memel
Seized by LITHUANIA 1923

Danzig Free City 1919

Königsberg

EAST PRUSSIA

Grodno

RUSSIA

Bialystok

G E R M A N Y

Poznan (Posen)

Plock

Warsaw

Lodz

P O L A N D

DRIVEN BACK AUGUST 1920

Pinsk

Pripet Marsh

FRONTIER 1914

RUSSO-GERMAN

Radom

Lublin

Kholm

Brest Litovsk

ROSA KEN AUGUST 1920

Vladimir Volinsky

DEFEATED SEPT 1920

Kiev

To Poland after Plebiscite 1921 (formerly Germany)

RUSSO-AUSTRIAN

FRONTIER 1914

Cracow

Przemysl

Lvov

Occupied by Poland May-June 1920

Kamenets Podolsk

C Z E C H O S L O V A K I A

HUNGARY

RUMANIA

Miles

0   100

CHAPTER IV

SPA

It looks as though the Poles will in the end be beaten. It will be very serious if they are.

H.

But not undeserved.

C.

—*Minutes by Lords Hardinge and Curzon, 14 June 1920*[1]

I do not believe for a moment that the Soviet Government fear armed intervention by the Allies.

CMP

There is nothing to fear.

H.

C.

—*Minutes by C. M. Palairet and Lord Hardinge, with Lord Curzon's agreement, 20 July 1920*[2]

ON 11 June 1920 Polish forces evacuated Kiev after holding the city for just thirty-five days. The evacuation was intended only as a tactical regroupment to enable the Poles to meet a threatened Russian counterattack from the north, but it marked the beginning of a steadily accelerating retreat which two months later was to find the Red Army at the gates of Warsaw. Although the full weight of the Soviet offensive did not fall until the beginning of July, constant pressure throughout June nevertheless forced the Poles to fall back to the line they had occupied in April before their invasion of the Ukraine. Then, on 28 June, a Soviet cavalry army under the command of Budenny, who had been transferred from the southern front, crossed the Sluch River and began to sweep west towards Lvov. And during the first week of July, Soviet infantry under the twenty-seven-year-old Mikhail N. Tukhachevsky, who had led the Red

[1] File 203409/73/55; F.O. 371/3902.
[2] File 208677/207846/38; F.O. 371/4058. Palairet was a member of the Foreign Office's Northern Department.

Army against Kolchak in Siberia, decisively defeated a large Polish army on the Berezina River, east of Minsk, and began a drive toward Warsaw at a steady rate of thirteen miles per day—nearly as fast as the men could march. Of these events one of the Polish commanders later wrote: "It was generally felt that a period of tragic helplessness had set in, during which the major part of the Polish army was in its retreat not unlike a rudderless boat on stormy seas."[3]

In Warsaw, public and government alike reacted to the news from the front with a mood of dark depression, made worse, so foreign observers reported, by the fact that while Soviet armies were advancing toward Poland Soviet representatives were negotiating in London with the British Prime Minister. The Polish government, as so often, was of two minds regarding the Soviet offensive. Piłsudski and the generals, according to Sir Horace Rumbold, were inclined to gamble that the campaign was the last effort of which the Red Army was capable, and that a subsequent Polish counteroffensive would bring about the collapse of the Soviet regime and thus spare Poland the necessity of coming to terms with the Bolsheviks. On the other hand Rumbold reported that Prince Eustachy Sapieha, the former Polish ambassador in London who in late June became Minister for Foreign Affairs when a prolonged cabinet crisis brought Władysław Grabski to the premiership, hoped that the Allies would bluntly tell both sides to make peace; the Polish government would find it easier to approach the Bolsheviks if ordered to do so by the Allies. Rumbold himself strongly favored such a course of action. The Allies, he urged Curzon, should "tell Poland categorically that she must try to come to terms with Bolsheviks at once" before the Polish army was completely destroyed.[4]

The first two weeks of the Bolshevik offensive coincided with the most important thus far of the postwar international conferences— the talks between the Allies and the Germans at the Belgian watering place of Spa, preceded on 2 and 3 July by inter-Allied discussions

---

[3] Quoted from General L. Sikorski's *Nad Wisla i Wkra* (On the Vistula and Wkra), Lvov, 1928, in Marjan Kukiel, "The Polish-Soviet Campaign of 1920," *Slavonic Review*, vol. VIII, no. 22, London, June 1929, p. 56.

[4] U.S. Chargé d'Affaires (Warsaw) to Secretary of State, telegram 323, 12 June 1920 (*Foreign Relations*, 1920, vol. III, p. 384), and Rumbold (Warsaw) to Curzon, telegrams 392, 438, and 449 of 7, 25, and 28 June and unnumbered telegram of 3 July (*British Documents*, vol. XI, nos. 288, 302, 304, and 308).

at Brussels. Both of these gatherings were preoccupied with the problem of Germany's obligations, in the form of disarmament and reparations, under the Treaty of Versailles. To these concerns the military situation in Poland, threatening as it did the whole structure of the peace, formed a somber backdrop. A week before the conference Winston Churchill posed some of the questions which had to be faced by the Allies when he asked, in a memorandum to his Cabinet colleagues:

Are we looking ahead at all and making up our minds what we shall do if there is a complete Polish collapse and if Poland is over-run by the Bolshevik armies or its government overturned by an internal Bolshevik rising? Would it be the policy of the British Government to remain impassive in the face of such an event, which may be conceivably near? If so, what would be the policy of the French Government? In the event of the collapse of Poland, what reaction would this situation entail upon the German position? It would clearly not be possible to disarm Germany if her eastern frontiers were in contact with a Bolshevised area. . . . We ought at any rate to consider in advance what our line of action should be.[5]

Churchill wrote on 26 June. During the intervening five days before the departure of Lloyd George and Curzon for the conferences in Belgium, the Cabinet did not discuss the Polish situation. Nor would there be any Cabinet discussion of it for the next month, despite its steadily growing seriousness. Moreover, the Prime Minister's behavior at Spa makes it clear that he crossed the Channel on 1 July without himself having resolved upon any definite course of action.[6]

To Lloyd George, Poland's invasion of the Ukraine and the subsequent Soviet counteroffensive were, together, only one aspect (although admittedly the most urgent) of the "Polish problem." He was also concerned about Poland's relations with her other neighbors, as was the Foreign Office. E. H. Carr, then a junior member of the Northern Department, concluded after a lengthy tour of Poland and its border areas in May and June 1920: "Poland has by her foreign policy brought things to such a pass that her downfall is now the dearest wish of every one of her neighbors, great or small." And

---

[5] Cabinet paper C.P. 1540, 26 June 1920; Cab. 24/108. (Excerpts in Churchill, *Aftermath*, p. 267.)

[6] Nor was the Soviet advance upon Poland mentioned during the discussion between Lloyd George and Krasin on 29 June 1920 (see above, chap. III).

this, Carr noted, "without in one single case gaining the smallest practical advantage in exchange for the hate she has provoked."[7] To the south, Poland and Czechoslovakia were verging upon armed conflict over possession of the duchy of Teschen, and Polish-German relations were nearly as inflamed over Upper Silesia. To the west, in the Polish Corridor, there was similar acrimony between Poland and Germany over forthcoming plebiscites in the contested provinces of Allenstein and Marienwerder, an acrimony scarcely lessened by frequent Polish interference with German rail traffic across the Corridor. Farther north, the Poles steadily and repeatedly tried to extend their control over the commercial and social life of the Free City of Danzig; in doing so they aroused enormous bitterness among the Danzigers.[8]

All these disputes had future implications which were enormous and disastrous. Yet in the summer of 1920, in the context of the Soviet counterattack, they seemed less urgently threatening to Poland's security than did her conflict with Lithuania. One of Piłsudski's strongest ambitions was the revival of the federal union which had existed between the two states during the two centuries preceding the partitions of Poland. Failing a union—and the three million Lithuanians had few illusions that a union with twenty million Poles would offer them any real national autonomy—Piłsudski hoped to whittle independent Lithuania down to the narrowest possible ethnographical limits. The focus of dispute was the city of Vilna. The capital of the Grand Duchy of Lithuania until its union with Poland in 1569, Vilna was also the scene of Piłsudski's childhood. After the war it was claimed by both Poland and Lithuania, and each produced statistics to show that its nationals were locally predominant. (In fact, Poles and Jews in roughly equal numbers seem to have made up the bulk of the city's population, while Belorussians were

---

[7] "Notes on a Tour to Danzig, Warsaw and the Eastern Plebiscite Areas," 11 May–8 June 1920, file F.O. 371/3902 (entered 15 June); F.O. 205318/73/55.

[8] Aside from the above report, see: for Teschen, Carr's memorandum of 12 June 1920, *British Documents*, vol. X, London, 1960, no. 505; for the plebiscite areas, the report by H. D. Beaumont, British representative on the Marienwerder Plebiscite Commission, 25 February 1920, *ibid.*, no. 553; for Danzig, the report by Sir Reginald Tower, Allied Administrator in Danzig, to the President of the Conference of Ambassadors (Paris), 17 March 1920, *ibid.*, no. 226. In partial justification of Polish conduct regarding Danzig, it should be noted that the precise nature of the relationship between Poland and the Free City had not yet been determined. See below, chap. VI.

the leading ethnic group in the surrounding countryside.) Following the withdrawal of occupying German forces in late 1918, Vilna
was proclaimed capital of independent Lithuania. In January 1919,
however, the city was taken by the Red Army. The Bolsheviks, in
their turn, were driven out by combined Polish and Lithuanian
forces in April, but the Poles entered Vilna first, and there they
remained, despite the fact that the city was east of the line drawn
by the Allies on 8 December 1919. They were, moreover, not satisfied with their position, and (in the words of a British Foreign
Office analysis) kept "continually nibbling further and further into
Lithuanian territory" until, by the spring of 1920, the two nations
were close to war.[9] In such circumstances, although little love was
lost between the Lithuanians and the Bolsheviks, the Lithuanians
were not predisposed to render Poland any assistance against the
Soviet offensive which began in June.

These, then, were the most important matters in dispute between
Poland and her neighbors other than Soviet Russia. All of them,
it should be noted, had their origins in the fact that Poland's frontiers were hastily drawn and, in places, ill defined; in dealing with
them the Poles behaved tactlessly and aggressively, but their behavior cannot be dismissed as mere rapacity. With the possible exception of the Polish-Lithuanian dispute, which had a direct bearing
upon Polish-Soviet relations, these matters would not concern us
here but for their accumulation in the mind of David Lloyd George
as a kind of bill of grievances against the Poles. At the Peace Conference in Paris the Prime Minister had shown himself to be no great
friend of Poland; a year later he dismissed Polish territorial claims
as "preposterous" and "arrogant." On 30 May 1920, with Polish
troops occupying Kiev, he told Lord Riddell: "The Poles have
quarrelled with all their neighbours, and they are a menace to the
peace of Europe."[10]

[9] Memorandum on Polish-Lithuanian relations, 10 February 1920, by O. C. Harvey; *British Documents*, vol. XI, no. 189. For these events see Alfred Erich Senn,
The Emergence of Modern Lithuania, New York, 1959, pp. 47-217; Senn discusses
census statistics for Vilna and the surrounding region on pp. 42-43. For the line of
8 December 1919, see above, chap. I, n. 21.

[10] At the Peace Conference Lloyd George was the least sympathetic of all the
Allied leaders to Poland's territorial claims. See his remarks when Paderewski was
interviewed by the Council of Four, 5 June 1919, 11:30 A.M.; *Foreign Relations, Paris
Peace Conference*, vol. VI, pp. 197-99. For the later remarks see Riddell, *Diary*,

Lloyd George carried these attitudes to the conferences in Belgium in July. At Spa, and at the brief interlude in Brussels which preceded that major conference, consideration of the Polish-Soviet conflict was largely informal. On only one occasion was there a full-scale inter-Allied meeting on the subject. But there were repeated private conversations during which Lloyd George tried to work out a policy. In nearly every instance—as at all of the conferences thus far during 1920—his will prevailed: as the only leader of the war years and of the Peace Conference who was still a member of the Council of the Allies, he spoke with great authority.

A dinner at the Belgian premier's house on 3 July was typical. Marshal Foch drew Lloyd George and Henry Wilson off into a corner where they were later joined by Millerand. Foch expressed great apprehension about the plight of the Poles and urged strongly—without, apparently, suggesting specific steps—that the Allies take some sort of action. To this Lloyd George replied (as Wilson recorded in his diary) that he "would not budge in the matter until Patek came to him cap in hand." Before the subject could even be discussed, he insisted, the Poles should comply with three conditions. First, they should take the initiative and ask the Allies for assistance and also propose to the Russians that peace should be made. Second, they should come to terms with Lithuania and with their other neighbors. Third, they should adopt a reasonable and conciliatory attitude regarding Danzig.[11]

During this conversation Lloyd George did not attempt to suggest what actions the Allies might take if the Poles complied with his conditions. But the military advisers could not help but concern themselves with such considerations. Wilson, Foch, and Weygand, Foch's chief of staff, had already met during the afternoon, and Foch—who the previous day had told Wilson that he was afraid the whole Polish army might break under the Soviet attack[12]—had presented a paper which made four proposals: 1) The Allies should

---

entries for 9 and 30 May 1920, pp. 191, 198. Hankey (MS diary, entry for 23 May) noted similar remarks by Lloyd George. For a discussion of Lloyd George's attitudes, see Norman Davies, "Lloyd George and Poland," *Journal of Contemporary History*, vol. 6, no. 3, 1971, pp. 132-55.

[11] Wilson MS diary, entry for 3 July 1920. Minutes, "Note of a Conversation between the Prime Minister and Marshal Foch in regard to Poland," S-15, Cab. 23/35. Summary telegram from Curzon (Brussels) to Hardinge (London), 4 July; *British Documents*, vol. XI, no. 310.

[12] Wilson MS diary, entry for 2 July 1920.

find out what the Poles wanted. 2) If their wishes were reasonable then the Allies should guarantee them support. 3) The Allies should give the Poles arms. 4) The Polish forces should be ordered to stand where they were, for a further retreat would ruin their morale. These were scarcely helpful suggestions, and Wilson easily pointed out their drawbacks. Though retreating, the Poles were still 200 kilometers beyond Poland's ethnographic frontiers, he said. To ask them to stand where they were would run the risk of consolidating all Russia against them—in his view a much greater risk than the loss of morale entailed in a continued retreat. More important, however, he did not know what support the Allies could give other than moral support, and he saw no use in promising what could not be performed. And in his diary he commented:

There is no way of aiding the Poles with our troops. I think the Frocks [Wilson's term for politicians—they wore frock coats], in view of all their speeches about Poland, ought at once to define the Russian frontiers of Poland & tell the Poles to get behind it, & tell the Bolsheviks not to cross it. If however, the Bolsheviks do cross it, saying of course, it is only a temporary measure the Frocks are helpless. From my point of view I don't mind either the Boches or the Bolsheviks over-running Poland as I want Russia & Germany to be touching & thus to ensure constant friction & enmity. I never believed in Poland being able to stand alone between those great countries & all the Frocks' schemes for a Polish Danzig & a Corridor etc have always appeared to me to be childish.[13]

In effect, Wilson was willing to write off Poland; as he told Foch and Weygand, he had "always opposed these cursed small States."[14] Whether or not Lloyd George was also willing to do so is a much more difficult question. His whole handling of the Polish problem was characterized by indirectness. No aspect of the Prime Minister's role in these events is more puzzling than a conversation he had with Foch over dinner at Spa on 8 July.[15] Once again the Marshal

[13] *Ibid.*, entry for 3 July 1920.   [14] *Idem.*
[15] Lloyd George himself wrote a detailed summary of this conversation with Foch and his subsequent one with Millerand on the evening of 8 July 1920; *British Documents*, vol. VIII, no. 51A. Lloyd George did not indicate who else was present—presumably the two conversations were *tête-à-tête*—but Henry Wilson notes the presence that evening of himself, Sir Laming Worthington-Evans (a junior minister), Kerr, Hankey, and Sassoon, in addition to Foch, Millerand, and the Prime Minister; Wilson MS. diary, entry for 8 July. Hankey did not mention the conversations either in his diary or in the letters to his wife which he wrote almost daily from Spa (Hankey MSS).

took a gloomy view of Poland's prospects: the army was disintegrating; panic and demoralization were spreading throughout the country; if the Bolsheviks wanted to get to Warsaw, Foch said, there was nothing to prevent them. In his view the collapse was due mainly to weakness of government. At Lloyd George's mention of the name of Władysław Grabski, who had recently become premier, Foch simply threw up his hands in a gesture of contempt.

The Prime Minister then asked (in the words of the memorandum on the conversation which he wrote himself) "whether, if England were prepared to send men and material to assist the Poles to defend or to recover their independence against the Bolsheviks, France would give the same assistance." With great emphasis Foch replied: "No. No men." In his opinion, he said, the only assistance France would give would be to supply officers and to help the Poles create a strong government. As to the latter, he was not hopeful: he did not know where the material for a strong government would come from.

For Lloyd George, an offer simply to send officers was insufficient. They would be of very little use, he told Foch, "unless there was some stiffening of troops for the Polish Army." The Prime Minister then became more specific. The Polish collapse, he said, seemed to have been the result of Soviet cavalry attacks. Would France send cavalry to help the Poles if England were prepared to do so as well? Again Foch was quite clear, Lloyd George wrote, that France would not.

This ended the conversation. After dinner Lloyd George had a long talk with Millerand. The latter informed him that he planned to see Grabski, who was coming to Spa from Warsaw, the following afternoon. When Lloyd George asked what Millerand proposed to tell Grabski, the French premier merely shrugged his shoulders: clearly he had no idea how to cope with the Polish situation either. Lloyd George then told Millerand what Foch had said about the impossibility of sending French troops (as opposed to officers) to Poland. Millerand concurred. The next exchange, according to Lloyd George's notes, went as follows: "I told him that placed us in rather a humiliating position—that we had undertaken by the Peace Treaty to defend the independence of Poland, and that if we allowed the Bolsheviks to trample the national independence of Poland out of existence under the hoofs of Buddennie's cavalry, we would be eternally dishonoured. He agreed also with that. I told him that although England was very exhausted and tired, and bending under he[r] burdens, still if the Englishman's sense of fair play were roused Britain would in my opinion be prepared to make considerable further sacrifices for the independence of Poland." To this, Lloyd George wrote, Millerand did not respond.[16]

Of all Lloyd George's remarks on policy towards Soviet Russia which we have any record, these to Foch and Millerand are the most inexplicable. Previously he had warned the Poles that if they persisted in making war upon Russia they would face the consequences of their actions alone. On the very next day, as we shall see, he was to take a similarly stern line with the Polish Premier, Grabski. Yet to Foch and Millerand on the evening of 8 July he spoke not only of sending to Poland British advisers and equipment, but of sending British troops as well. How incongruous it all was: here was Foch, who so often had spoken of raising large anti-Bolshevik armies, now admitting that France could do nothing, and Lloyd George, heretofore the resolute opponent of all Foch's grandiose schemes, now speaking of stiffening Poland's resistance with British infantry and cavalry!

In the past, as we have seen, the Prime Minister would secure the consent of his Allied colleagues to his Russian policies by going around the table and asking each man how many troops he would be willing to send to fight the Bolsheviks. The answer, invariably, was none. And now, when he put the same question to Foch and Millerand, their answer was the same. This time, however—if his own notes were accurate—it was he, rather than they, who seemed eager to intervene. Perhaps this tactic was merely an especially elaborate effort by Lloyd George again to drive home to the French the fact that, despite their ostentatious anti-Bolshevism, they were not prepared to support their sentiments with armed action, and that such was the case even when the British, for once, seemed willing to offer their own troops for the job. Perhaps this is too ingenious an explanation, yet it is no less convincing than its alternative: that Lloyd George was, in fact, willing to commit British soldiers to fight for Poland. In 1920, given the extent of working-class unrest in Britain and the turbulence which prevailed in Ireland and throughout the Empire, it was no easy matter for the Prime Minister to draw a

[16] From Lloyd George's memorandum cited in n. 15.

line across Eastern Europe and to say to the Red Army, "thus far but no farther."

Lloyd George's remarks are even more inexplicable when considered in the light of the rest of his after-dinner conversation with Millerand. Earlier in the day a telegram had come from Chicherin containing the Soviet reply to the statement of conditions which the British had given Krasin to take back to Moscow.[17] Lloyd George handed copies of both documents to Millerand and asked the latter's opinion of them.

Chicherin's telegram was very short. The Soviet government, it stated, accepted the "principles" laid down in the British *aide-mémoire* as the basis for an agreement between the two countries, the agreement to be the subject of negotiations which the two governments must begin without delay. Furthermore, the telegram said, the Soviet government agreed to consider the British proposals as a state of armistice between the two countries and as a first step towards a definite peace. At the same time, the Soviet government protested against the British allegations regarding Soviet activities against the British Empire in the East; the absence of peace between Britain and Russia had been due only to a lack of a disposition toward peace on the part of the British government.[18]

The Soviet telegram was skilfully worded. It seemed to accept the British proposals, and therefore gave the British government no ground to carry out its threat to break off the negotiations. Lloyd George was well aware of this fact; to Bonar Law in London he cabled that Chicherin's message was "complete acceptance of our terms and we had better take it as such."[19] Yet the Soviet note also linked acceptance of the British terms to the immediate beginning of formal peace negotiations. This implication, of course, embarrassed Lloyd George and displeased Millerand. The French premier was satisfied with the original British ultimatum. But in Chicherin's

[17] For the British conditions, see above, chap. III, n. 68.

[18] Chicherin's telegram to Curzon, dated 7 July 1920, is printed in *Dokumenty vneshnei politiki*, vol. III, pp. 16-17. A translation was given to the House of Commons on 14 July by Bonar Law (131 *H.C. Deb.*, cols. 2371-72).

[19] Lloyd George (Spa) to Bonar Law (London), in telegram 26 to Foreign Office, drafted 8 July 1920 but sent 9 July; *British Documents*, vol. XII, no. 739, n. 2. The Prime Minister instructed Bonar Law to lay the texts of both the British ultimatum and the Soviet reply before the House of Commons. Hankey wrote to his wife that Lloyd George was "very excited" by the Soviet note, and added: "It means peace with Russia—a very great factor in the peace of the world" (8 July; Hankey MSS, file 3/28).

reply, he told Lloyd George, he saw an attempt to widen commercial talks into political discussions. He then asked the Prime Minister what he proposed to do about the situation. "I told him [Lloyd George recorded] that I had always been very frank with him and that I would give him a frank answer. I said 'My object is peace.' He seemed to my surprise to be rather pleased and said 'oui—oui.' I said the world wanted an end to all this bloodshed and conflict, and to settle down to business, and that our information was that these attacks upon Bolshevik Russia were simply strengthening not merely the Communist Government but the Communist elements in the Government, and that as soon as Russia was at peace Russia would disintegrate."[20]

Millerand then asked how France could be brought into the negotiations with Moscow, adding that he himself thought that France could come in if the Soviet government acknowledged its responsibility for Russia's state debts—presumably debts both to other states and to private persons. Lloyd George replied that he thought that Krasin's position on state debts was sound: that commercial negotiations could discuss only commercial debts, and that consideration of state debts must take place only in discussions of a formal peace. The best way to bring France in, Lloyd George said, would be for Britain to reply to Chicherin by proposing peace between Poland and Russia; if the Soviet government accepted, France would inevitably be brought into the negotiations as one of the protectors of Poland's independence. According to the Prime Minister's notes, Millerand agreed.

Peace between Poland and Russia would, of course, require the agreement of the Poles as well as that of the Bolsheviks; Lloyd George set himself the task of securing Polish agreement in several extremely blunt sessions at Spa with Polish representatives who had come ostensibly to state their opinions informally on the German issues before the conference, but in fact to ask for Allied assistance.

On 6 July, with Curzon and Philip Kerr, the Prime Minister met with Stanisław Patek, formerly Poland's Foreign Minister, now a minister without portfolio in the reconstituted Warsaw government. It had been Patek whom Lloyd George had warned the previous

---

[20] From Lloyd George's memorandum cited above, n. 15.

January that unless Poland made peace she would have to face the consequences alone. In the very different military situation which prevailed in July, Lloyd George again asked if the Poles had made any recent approaches to the Soviet government. Patek replied that the moment was inopportune; if they were to propose peace while their army was still retreating, it would look like weakness, or even surrender. In that case, Lloyd George said, there was nothing the Allies could do for Poland, nor would there be so long as the Poles pursued a policy of imperialism instead of "true nationalism" towards their neighbors. "Let Poland accept true nationalism and not imperialism as the basis for its policy," Lloyd George said, "and she would find that Great Britain would stick by her loyally just as she stuck by her other Allies."[21]

During the next several days, as the Soviet advance toward Poland continued, the attitude of the Polish negotiators at Spa changed radically. On 7 July the Polish government telegraphed to the Spa conference formally requesting Allied aid. The appeal was sent, Prince Sapieha told Sir Horace Rumbold, after a review of the "bankrupt situation" of the nation. It contained the usual declarations to the effect that in fighting the Russians the Poles were not simply protecting themselves, but were forming a "living rampart" which defended the "households of civilization" against the "Bolshevik flood." But it also stated that Poland would accept whatever measures the Supreme Council might think necessary in order to secure Allied assistance.[22]

These appeals by Patek and Sapieha were dramatically reinforced by Grabski, the Polish premier, who suddenly (and apparently against the advice of Piłsudski) journeyed to Spa. Grabski virtually prostrated himself before Lloyd George and Millerand, along with Curzon, Foch, and Weygand, at a meeting on the afternoon of 9 July.[23] The Polish government recognized, he said, that it was to blame for the desperate situation, and that it would have to change

[21] "Notes of a Meeting held at the Hotel Britannique, Spa, Tuesday, 6th July, 1920," *British Documents*, vol. VIII, no. 46, pp. 441-42.

[22] A translation of the appeal, telegraphed to Curzon at Spa by Rumbold on 7 July 1920, is printed in *ibid.*, vol. VIII, no. 55, n. 3, pp. 505-06. The official text, from the Polish Minister of Foreign Affairs to the President of the Supreme Council, was transmitted by the French Minister. See Rumbold (Warsaw) to Curzon (Spa), telegram 3, 7 July 1920; *ibid.*, vol. XI, no. 313.

[23] "Notes of a Meeting held at the Villa Neubois, Spa," 9 July 1920, 3 P.M.; *ibid.*, no. 55, pp. 502-06. Weygand took his own notes; they are printed in his *Mémoires*, vol. II, *Mirages et réalité*, Paris, 1957, pp. 89-91.

its policies both toward Poland's neighbors and toward the Allies. It recognized that it would have to leave decisions regarding Poland's vital interests—even the determination of frontiers—to the Allied Powers. Poland had been carried away by strong men with great visions, but the visions did not correspond with the reality. Even Piłsudski acknowledged his mistake, Grabski stated. Now the generals wished only to defend the nation, but they had no reserves and lacked equipment of all sorts, which they hoped the Allies would send. The government had decided to ask the Allies to help Poland make peace in any way that seemed best, and his colleagues had given him authority to accept the Allies' conditions. One thing, however, he asked: if the Bolsheviks refused a fair peace and invaded Polish territory, could Poland count upon Allied support?

Lloyd George replied by reciting a long list of Poland's alleged offenses against her neighbors. He was not sure, he said, whether the Allies—overburdened as they were with taxation and war debt, and weakened by millions of casualties—could do very much to help Poland. Still, he thought it might be possible "to do something" if Poland's independence were imperiled. But he could not approach Parliament for assistance unless he could say that Poland had abandoned annexationist ambitions and sought only independence within its own ethnographic frontiers. "If Poland was ready to give assurances to this effect," the Prime Minister said, "then Great Britain was prepared to *consider* what steps it could take to press Russia to make peace, and if Russia refused, what steps she could give Poland to preserve her independence."[24]

Grabski was grasping at straws, and he could scarcely object even to so tenuous a promise. The following morning, 10 July, Lloyd George, Curzon, Kerr, and Millerand, along with Count Carlo Sforza, the Italian Foreign Minister, Viscount Chinda, the Japanese Ambassador in London, and Philippe Berthelot of the Quai d'Orsay, met to consider drafts of conditions to which the Russians and the Poles would be asked to agree.[25] As in nearly every instance in which the Allies met to discuss policy toward Soviet Russia, only the British had taken the trouble to prepare drafts; invariably British policy prevailed.

[24] *British Documents*, vol. VIII, p. 505 (italics added).
[25] "British Secretary's Notes of a Conversation held at the Villa Fraineuse, Spa," 10 July 1920, 10:30 A.M.; *ibid.*, no. 57, pp. 513-16.

To the meeting on the 10th Lloyd George brought the draft of an agreement which Grabski would be "invited" to sign, and the draft of a British reply, in the name of the Allies, to Chicherin's recently received telegram accepting the terms of the *aide-mémoire* which the British had handed to Krasin.[26] The Poles were asked to agree: first, to sign an immediate armistice on the basis that Polish forces should retire to the line fixed by the Supreme Council on 8 December 1919 as the provisional boundary of Polish administration and that Soviet forces should halt twenty kilometers east of the line; second, to send plenipotentiaries to a conference in London to be attended by delegates from Soviet Russia, Finland, the Baltic States, and Eastern Galicia for the purpose of making peace between Russia and her neighbors; and third, to accept the decision of the Supreme Council as to the boundaries of Lithuania, the future of Eastern Galicia, the Teschen question, and the Danzig-Poland Treaty.

These were the terms to be put to the Poles. In return the Allies were to make two promises. First, they would immediately make a similar proposal to Soviet Russia. Second—and here, after all, was the object for which Grabski had come to Spa—if the Russians refused the armistice and passed the line laid down by the Supreme Council, the Allies would "give Poland all the assistance, especially in war material, which is possible, consistent with their own exhaustion and the heavy liabilities they are carrying elsewhere, to enable the Polish people to defend their independence and national existence." This was scant assurance. The Allies bound themselves scarcely at all—so slightly, in fact, that at the meeting on the morning of the 10th there was virtually no discussion of the agreement which Grabski would be asked to sign that afternoon.[27] All discussion focussed on the note that would be sent to Moscow.

The British draft note (which had been circulated the previous afternoon) asked the Soviet government to accept the first two conditions proposed to the Poles. If the Russians agreed to the London conference, they could send any delegates they wished, even

[26] The two drafts are appended to *idem*, pp. 518 and 517 respectively. For the *aide-mémoire* handed to Krasin on 1 July, see above, chap. III, n. 68.

[27] Millerand, however, remarked that so much did he agree with the British draft that "so long as Poland did not accept an armistice he meant to stand by her." No one bothered to point out that his statement was contrary to the whole spirit of the British proposal.

Litvinov. The note further proposed that the Soviet government should also sign an armistice with Wrangel on the condition that his forces should immediately retire to the Crimea, and that he should be invited to London while the conference was in session. (This, it should be noted, was a month after Wrangel had broken out of the Crimea, and after the British had washed their hands of him.) Finally, the draft note requested a Soviet reply within a week. The Polish government, it stated, had requested Allied intervention. Although the British government had bound itself not to assist the Poles in their attack on Russia, and would take no action hostile to Russia, it was also "bound under the Treaty of Peace to defend the integrity and independence of Poland within its legitimate ethnographic frontiers."

When Lloyd George placed this draft note before his Allied colleagues, Millerand immediately proposed that Soviet participation in the London conference should be made contingent upon Soviet assumption of the debts of the previous Russian governments. Otherwise, he said, France could not join Britain in proposing a Polish-Soviet armistice. If he signed the note along with Lloyd George, his signature would constitute a first French *démarche* towards the Soviet government. He would be recognizing the Moscow regime, but otherwise the situation would remain the same. However, if the British note included "some formula in regard to debts," then he could sign it. To Lloyd George's heated retort that *his* object was to save Poland, Millerand blandly stated that the problem for him was "to reconcile the conflicting interests of saving Poland and guaranteeing French interests."[28]

Lloyd George was well aware that at a time of sweeping military success the Bolsheviks would never agree to recognize their predecessors' debts; Allied insistence on such a prerequisite to an East European peace conference would simply ensure that a conference would never take place. Therefore, since the French would not sign the British draft, and since inclusion of the Italians—who approved of the note—would only emphasize the absence of the French, it was agreed that the *démarche* would come from the British alone.[29]

It now remained to secure Grabski's signature to the terms which

[28] *British Documents*, vol. VIII, no. 57, p. 515.
[29] *Ibid.*, pp. 515-16.

had been drawn up for Poland. The morning discussions had taken only half an hour, after which the Allied representatives had returned to the real business of the Spa conference: talking reparations with the Germans. During the afternoon there were two sessions with Grabski, wedged between talks with the Germans which lasted well into the evening.[30] Contemporary accounts indicate that the Polish premier found himself closeted with Lloyd George alone, and that the Prime Minister "cowed" Grabski with a virtual ultimatum delivered in "curt, peremptory tones."[31] This is not quite true: with the exception of Viscount Chinda, the Japanese delegate, who had assured himself during the morning that none of Japan's vital interests were at stake,[32] Lloyd George was accompanied by all those with whom he had earlier thrashed out the draft notes. Yet even the muted language of Sir Maurice Hankey's minutes[33] does not disguise the fact that the Prime Minister was curt and peremptory.

Presented with the British draft note which he was asked to sign, Grabski balked at three points: first, that the line behind which the Poles were asked to retire was west of Vilna and thus would exclude that city from "Polish administration"; second, that Soviet forces would be allowed to approach within twenty kilometers of the line (Grabski proposed 100 kilometers); and third, that the

[30] The Allied statesmen met with Grabski from 3 to 4 P.M. on July 1920 and gave him the draft agreement to consider. They then went back to their talks with the Germans and adjourned for ten minutes at 5:45 P.M., when Grabski signed the agreement. The minutes of both sessions were recorded by Sir Maurice Hankey as "British Secretary's Notes of a Conversation at the Villa Fraineuse, Spa"; *British Documents*, vol. VIII, no. 59, pp. 524-30.

[31] A. L. Kennedy, *Old Diplomacy and New*, London, 1923, p. 322. The author, *The Times*'s Warsaw correspondent, on 15 July 1920 received an account of Grabski's mission from Prince Sapieha. Nicolson, *Curzon*, p. 207, says "Lord Curzon was not present at the crucial interview between Mr. Lloyd George and M. Grabski."

[32] At the meeting on 9 July Chinda gave his approval to both of the British draft notes "on the clear and distinct understanding . . . that Siberia was altogether excluded" from any arrangements which might be reached between the Allies and the Soviet government (*British Documents*, vol. VIII, p. 516).

[33] The Polish minutes of this meeting have been published in the collection, *Dokumenty i materialy do historii stosunków polskorazieckich* (Documents and Materials on the History of Polish-Soviet Relations), vol. III, Warsaw, 1964, no. 84, pp. 155-62. Their substance follows so closely that of Hankey's minutes (cited above, n. 30) as to indicate that they are, in fact, simply a translation. Regrettably, Hankey does not seem to have described the meeting in his diary or letters. It was standard British practice to circulate draft minutes of all international conversations for approval and, if necessary, correction, by the other participants (see the preface to *British Documents*, vol. VIII, p. vii).

populations east of the line would not be consulted as to whether or not they wanted to be "surrendered to the Bolsheviks." Grabski also pointed out that the Supreme Council's line of 8 December 1919 did not extend into Galicia. What, he asked, would happen to the Polish troops then in Eastern Galicia?

To this question Lloyd George replied that the opposing armies might stand where they stood at the moment of the armistice. And to Grabski's three objections the Prime Minister bluntly remarked: first, that the inability of the Poles to come to terms with the Lithuanians was "the whole trouble throughout the recent history of Poland," and that when the Poles were prepared to abandon their claim to Vilna they "should again approach the Powers"; second, that it was useless making proposals which the Bolsheviks would not possibly accept, such as halting their forces 100 kilometers east of the dividing line, and that until the Polish government was willing "to recognise facts," there was "no basis for discussion"; and third, that if Grabski felt that Poland was sufficiently powerful not only to preserve its own independence "but also the rights of Polish peoples beyond the frontier," he had no reason to appeal to the Powers. Elaborating on the issue of Vilna, the matter about which Grabski showed the most concern, Lloyd George declared that it was "really a question between Lithuania and Russia, and not a Polish question at all." And Curzon, who had sat silent throughout most of the discussion, interjected that as the object of both the Poles and the Allies, he assumed, was to keep Vilna out of the hands of the Bolsheviks, the Lithuanians might be allowed to occupy the city.[34]

This suggestion hardly aroused Grabski's enthusiasm, but as he had earlier insisted that the problem of Vilna could be settled between the Poles and the Lithuanians, he had no choice but to accept it. The agreement he eventually signed contained three modifications designed to meet his objections: the Soviet armies would be asked to halt not twenty but fifty kilometers east of the line fixed by the Supreme Council on 8 December 1919; Vilna, however, was to be excluded from the zone to be occupied by the Bolsheviks and was to be handed over immediately to the Lithuanians; and in Eastern Galicia the Polish and Soviet armies were to stand on the line they had reached by the date of the prospective armistice,

[34] *Ibid.*, pp. 526-27.

and then to retire ten kilometers on each side so as to create a neutral zone.[35]

From the Polish point of view, these were not very significant concessions. Faced with such unpalatable prospects, and not having received a word of support from Millerand, Berthelot, or Sforza,[36] Grabski could only ask what assistance Poland would receive if the Soviet government rejected the Allied proposals and proceeded to invade Poland. Lloyd George replied that the Allies would have to discuss the question with their military advisers; he could not say at the moment, but aid might take the form of *matériel* or officers. When Grabski asked if the Allies could send troops as well as officers, both Lloyd George and Millerand stated that they could not. Poland had "hundreds of thousands of able-bodied men," Lloyd George said, and should therefore supply all the troops. But the Allies might be able to send aircraft and even pilots.[37]

Despite the tenuous nature of this promise of Allied assistance, Grabski had no choice but to sign the agreement which the Allies put before him: the military situation was critical. Only if the Poles agreed would the British proposals of peace be sent to the Soviet government. If the Russians accepted, the Poles would never know whether or not the territorial price exacted by the Allies was too high, but at least Poland would remain independent; on the other hand, if the Russians refused, it seemed likely that only large-scale Allied assistance could stem the advance of the Red Army, and that assistance would be worth nearly any price.

Grabski affixed his signature to the agreement a few minutes before 6 P.M. on 10 July. The conference at Spa droned on until the 16th, but for the Polish premier it was over; nervous and crestfallen, he left Belgium immediately to return to Warsaw.[38] A few days after his return a young diplomat in the American Legation there reported on the proceedings in a letter to his Chief of Mission, on leave in the United States, and commented: "Knowing Grabski, can you imagine him as a worthy antagonist for Lloyd George?

[35] The final text of the agreement signed by Grabski is in *ibid.*, p. 530.

[36] Sforza later wrote that he "tried to obtain more favorable terms for the Poles" and "tried to soften for Poland" the measures proposed by Lloyd George. The published records, however, belie him. (Count Carlo Sforza, *Diplomatic Europe since the Treaty of Versailles*, New Haven, Conn., 1928, p. 21.)

[37] *British Documents*, vol. VIII, p. 528.

[38] Kennedy, *Old Diplomacy*, p. 322.

The result must have been so pitiful that it could scarcely have amused Lloyd George to play with him."[39]

✧

The day following Grabski's departure the British government telegraphed to Chicherin a revised version of the note which had been discussed in draft by the Allied representatives on the morning of 10 July.[40] It will be remembered that the purpose of this note was to propose to Moscow a settlement of the war with Poland based upon the same terms to which Grabski had agreed. Unfortunately, the terms offered to Chicherin differed from those offered to Grabski in one important respect: the designation of the line that was to divide Polish and Soviet-held territory in Eastern Galicia.

The agreement signed by Grabski stipulated that Polish forces would retire to "the line fixed by the Peace Conference on the 8th December, 1919, as the provisional boundary of Polish administration." This line, it will be recalled, ran from East Prussia in the north to Galicia in the south. There, at the town of Krilov, it stopped, owing to the fact that the status of Eastern Galicia had not yet been determined.[41] Therefore, because of this unspecified southern boundary, the document signed by Grabski further stipulated that in Eastern Galicia the opposing armies would "stand on the line which they have reached on the date of the armistice," and then each would back off ten kilometers to create a neutral zone.

The note telegraphed to Chicherin contained a similar stipulation regarding Eastern Galicia. And it likewise referred to "the line previously laid down by the Peace Conference as the eastern ethnographic boundary of Poland." However it then proceeded to describe a line which did *not* stop at Krilov, but went on *also* to include the line laid down by the Supreme Council in the short-lived "Statute of Eastern Galicia" of November 1919 as the boundary between Poland proper and the proposed Polish mandate territory of Eastern Galicia.[42]

Thus the line which the British government, in the name of the

[39] Letter, J. Pierrepont Moffat (Warsaw) to Hugh Gibson (Washington), 20 July 1920; Moffat MSS, Harvard University Library.

[40] The text as sent was given to the House of Commons by Bonar Law on 14 July 1920, and is printed in 131 *H.C. Deb.*, cols. 2372-74. A Russian translation is in *Dokumenty vneshnei politiki*, vol. III, Moscow, 1959, pp. 54-55.

[41] See above, chap. I, n. 18.

[42] See above, chap. I, n. 19.

Allies, proposed on 11 July 1920 as the future boundary between Poland and Russia was one whose northern segment had been delineated a year earlier at a time when it was universally expected that Poland's neighbor would be a White, and not a Red, Russia, and whose southern segment had been intended to separate territory *wholly* Polish and territory which, because of a Polish mandate over it, would to all intents be Polish. The entire line almost immediately became known in the British press as the Curzon Line—not because the Foreign Secretary had had anything to do with its definition, but because the telegram to Chicherin delineating it bore his signature. As events turned out, the Polish military successes of the late summer of 1920 seemed to deprive it of any but academic interest. But during the Second World War, as early as December 1941, when Hitler's armies were deep in Russian territory, Stalin insisted to his Allied partners that the proper frontier between Russia and Poland should be the Curzon Line, and he went on so insisting throughout the war. With minor modifications his wish was fulfilled.[43]

The Foreign Office and Cabinet archives contain no clue as to the cause of the discrepancy between the agreement signed by Grabski and the note sent to Moscow. It has been suggested, with no proof whatsoever, that "bad faith on the part of some members of Lloyd George's staff" is to blame.[44] Simple carelessness, however, seems a more probable explanation than bad faith: anyone seeking to extend Soviet control over Eastern Galicia (or to exclude that territory from Polish control) would have omitted the contradictory clause in the note to Moscow stipulating that the opposing armies would stand on the armistice line, wherever that might happen to be.

Carelessness, if that is the explanation, might well have stemmed from the fact that the Prime Minister was conducting his Russian policy himself, with very little reference to the Foreign Office. Although Foreign Office officials took part in the negotiations with the Germans at Spa, they did not attend the discussions which dealt

[43] For the significance of the Curzon Line during World War II, see Herbert Feis, *Churchill, Roosevelt, Stalin: The War They Waged and the Peace They Sought*, Princeton, 1957, pp. 31, 285-87, 293 n. 14, 294, 300, 374, 382, 454-60, 522-25. See also Feis's appendix, "Note about Origins and Nature of the So-called Curzon Line," pp. 657-60.

[44] See, for example, Komarnicki, *Polish Republic*, pp. 612. See also Witold Sworakowski, "An Error Regarding Eastern Galicia in Curzon's Note to the Soviet Government," *Journal of Central European Affairs*, vol. IV (1944-45), pp. 1-26.

with Poland, Curzon was there—probably because Lloyd George could not in decency exclude him—but the bulk of the work was left to Philip Kerr, the Prime Minister's private secretary, who certainly was not expert in the geography and ethnography of the Polish-Russian borderlands. If the "Curzon Line" should bear any man's name it surely should be Kerr's. On the day following the despatch of the telegram to Moscow, Kerr told Riddell that the Foreign Office "had no conception of policy in its wider sense" and "did not in the least understand" what Lloyd George was driving at; in particular, he said, the officials "did not understand the necessity for achieving a Russian settlement" before European recovery could take place.[45] Kerr's solution—and Lloyd George's—of by-passing the Foreign Office was scarcely more satisfactory. Talking with Riddell on 22 July 1920, Winston Churchill gave voice to a feeling of uneasiness shared by many people. Riddell recorded Churchill's words in his diary:

At present the P.M. is conducting the business of the Foreign Office with Kerr's assistance. I don't think that any man who does not hold a leading position in the State should be permitted to exercise so much influence on important questions of policy as Kerr does. I told him so the other night. I said to him, "You have no real responsibility. If things go wrong, others have to take the consequences. All you have to do is to walk out of Downing Street." They are formulating schemes which affect the lives of millions and the destinies of the world, and all this is done behind the scenes.[46]

Undoubtedly Kerr grasped the subtle interrelationships among the broad policies Lloyd George was pursuing; less easy to master, however, were the endless details which underlay each problem. In dealing with the Polish-Soviet conflict at Spa, Kerr was unencumbered by expert assistance. It is not unlikely that he was entirely unaware that in describing to Moscow what came to be called the Curzon Line he was joining together two lines whose origins, both in circumstance and in purpose, were widely different.

❖

So far removed from the hands of the Foreign Office was the handling of the problem of Russia that three days after the Warsaw

[45] Riddell, *Diary*, p. 219, entry for 12 July 1920.
[46] *Ibid.*, p. 223, entry for 22 July 1920.

press reported what had happened at Spa Sir Horace Rumbold had yet to hear from his own government on the subject—and this despite the fact that he had previously been asked to delay home leave and to remain at Warsaw precisely in order to be available in case London should attempt to mediate between the Poles and the Russians.[47] Twice he was driven to telegraph pleas for information. His second and particularly plaintive telegram stated:

> It would have been very useful to me to have received telegraphic communication of Prime Minister's message to Soviet Government with regard to an armistice etc. As it is I am dependent for information about this and about communications to Polish delegates on reports in the Press and on what my Italian Colleague or Poles tell me.

"This," the British Minister added, "puts me at a disadvantage."[48]

Rumbold's position was made all the more embarrassing by the extreme distaste with which the Polish government and public viewed the agreement which Grabski had signed at Spa. Indeed, after his return to Warsaw on 12 July the premier refused to make the agreement public, because he felt that it would only undermine national morale and damage his political position. Later in the week, after the terms of the agreement were given to the House of Commons by Bonar Law and published in the Warsaw press, the Polish government still refused to make any statement as to whether or not the press reports were accurate. In private, however, Grabski was extremely bitter. He blamed Lloyd George most of all, but he also complained that neither Millerand nor Sforza had raised a voice in Poland's behalf during the crucial sessions at Spa; instead they had acquiesced in terms that "put an end to Poland's dreams of greatness."[49]

Both within the government and among the Polish public the hope prevailed that the Soviet government would reject the terms offered in the British note so that Poland, in its turn, would no longer be bound by them. There were many who wanted to repudi-

[47] U.S. Chargé d'Affaires (Warsaw), to Secretary of State, telegram 345, 30 June 1920; U.S. National Archives, State Department file 760c.61/363.

[48] Rumbold (Warsaw) to Curzon (Spa), telegram 12 (514 to London), 14 July 1920; *British Documents*, vol. XI, no. 329. Rumbold's first telegram on the subject, 511 of 12 July, is no. 322.

[49] U.S. Chargé (Warsaw) to Secretary of State, despatch 531, 17 July 1920; U.S. National Archives, State Department file 760c.61/161.

ate Grabski altogether and announce that he had not been empowered to sign the agreement without the consent of the Diet or of the Council of National Defence. Nevertheless the combination of Grabski's humiliation and the continuing desperateness of the military situation did give rise to a great burst of patriotic sentiment; the government floated a large internal loan, and in Warsaw and throughout the country men of all ages queued at recruiting booths to join the army.[50]

❖

The Polish-Soviet war was not, of course, the main business of the Spa Conference. The talks with Grabski had been hastily arranged because of the alarming transformation in the military situation in the East, and they had been sandwiched between sessions which dealt with the question for which the conference had been convened, the endorsement of the reparations and disarmament clauses of the Versailles Treaty. During most of the conference the two sets of problems—German and Polish-Soviet—had been treated separately, as if they existed in watertight compartments, but on 13 and 14 July (after Grabski had returned to Poland) they suddenly came together as one large problem when Lloyd George asked his colleagues to speculate upon the possibility that Soviet forces, rejecting all appeals for an armistice, might overrun Poland and extend Moscow's domination to the frontiers of Germany.

This was, it scarcely needs stating, no novel speculation. Throughout the first six months of 1920, within both the Foreign Office and the British Embassy in Berlin, there had been rumors and reports on the one hand of overtures by German militarist elements for an anti-Bolshevik alliance of Western resources and German arms, and on the other of the possible growth of a German-Soviet combination to undermine the foundations of the peace. As time passed, and as the Red Army's drive towards Poland gathered momentum, a third possibility was added to these two: the sovietization of Germany through Russian conquest and internal revolution. On 1 July, before the start of the Spa Conference, the British Chargé d'Affaires in Berlin reported that "German circles" were discussing three possible plans of action: to form a new army to fight the Bolsheviks; to join

[50] *Idem.*

with the Bolsheviks; or to split the country, abandoning Prussia and Saxony and forming a fighting front in Bavaria, Württemberg, and the Rhineland.[51]

At Spa the crisis in the Polish-Soviet war coincided with a crisis in the relations between the Allies and the Germans when it became apparent that the Germans could not—or would not—meet Allied demands of reparation, particularly regarding coal deliveries which had been promised to France in reparation for German wartime destruction of French mines. The crisis was compounded by the fact that the German army stood at 200,000 men, instead of the 100,000 established as a maximum limit in the Versailles Treaty, and that no fewer than two million rifles which should have been handed over to the Allies for destruction were still unaccounted for—either lost or in the hands of the German civilian population. For these violations of the treaty—especially for the nondelivery of the promised coal—the French urged that unless the Germans rapidly proceeded to show their good faith Allied troops should occupy the rich industrial and mining region of the Ruhr valley. To the French proposal, which was supported by the Belgians and the Italians, Lloyd George reluctantly and with certain reservations consented.[52]

This policy was already agreed upon by 10 July, when the conversations with Grabski finished and the Polish premier left Spa. During the next few days Lloyd George grew increasingly concerned about the connection between the two problems, Russian and German, which the conference faced. On 12 July he remarked to his colleagues that if he were the German government he would prefer a temporary period of Bolshevik rule to humiliation before the Allies. On the following day, at a meeting hastily convened when it was learned that the Germans were about to reject the Allied demands on coal deliveries, he urged that the Allies should not break off the talks with the Germans until the Soviet government had replied to the British note of the 11th. If the Russians refused to make peace,

---

[51] Kilmarnock (Berlin) to Hardinge, telegram 392, 1 July 1920; *British Documents*, vol. IX, London, 1960, no. 552. See also Kilmarnock's despatch 52, 20 February, and the accompanying report by General Malcolm, Chief of the British Military Mission in Berlin, 11 February (*ibid.*, no. 51, pp. 78-83), and Kilmarnock's despatch 102, 6 March (*ibid.*, no. 81).

[52] See minutes of meetings between the Allied and German delegations, Spa, 7 July, 3:30 P.M., and 10 July, 4:30 P.M., *ibid.*, vol. VIII, nos. 48 and 61; and of meetings of Allied representatives, 8 July, 11:15 A.M., and 14 July, 10:30 A.M., *ibid.*, nos. 50 and 71.

he said, the Allies would have to give what support they could to the Poles. In that case the Bolsheviks would probably make overtures to Germany which the Germans would be much more likely to reject if the Allies had not yet brought things to a rupture with them. On the other hand, if the Russians did agree to an armistice, the Allies would be more free to treat Germany as they saw fit.[53]

The Prime Minister emphasized his opinion that the Allies were facing a dangerous situation in which the risk of a Soviet-German combination was great. His view was echoed by Sforza. Italy was even more hungry for coal than France, he said, yet if the Powers acted too hastily they might within a few weeks find themselves the vanquished, instead of the victorious. Lloyd George agreed: they might be "confronted with millions of Russians." To Millerand, however, the greatest danger was to show "any sign of weakness towards Germany." If the Allies "gave way at all before Germany," he said, "the situation was lost."[54]

Lloyd George's urgings prevailed: the Allies did play for time. A few minutes later, when they filed into the adjoining conference room to hear the German foreign minister formally state that his country was unable to deliver the requested amount of coal, the Belgian premier, Delacroix, who was chairman of the conference, merely stated that the Allied Powers would reply in due course.[55]

On the following morning, therefore, the Allied statesmen called in Marshal Foch and the Belgian chief of staff for a military opinion on (as the question was set by Delacroix) "in what way pressure could be exerted on Germany to compel her to carry out the coal deliveries provided for in the treaty."[56] Lloyd George immediately objected, saying that the question was larger. Assuming, he said, that the Bolsheviks refused an armistice and made up their minds to crush Poland and march to the German frontier, he had two questions to put to Foch: first, what was to be done in Poland, and, second, should the Allies occupy the Ruhr before "clearing up" the Polish situation?

---

[53] Minutes, meetings of Allied representatives, Spa, 12 July, 10:30 A.M., and 13 July, 5:15 P.M.; *ibid.*, no. 64 (esp. p. 565) and no. 67 (esp. pp. 582-83).

[54] *Ibid.*, pp. 583-84.

[55] Minutes, Allied-German meeting, Spa, 13 July 1920, 5:30 P.M.; *ibid.*, no. 70, pp. 594-96.

[56] Minutes, meeting of Allied representatives, Spa, 14 July 1920, 11:30 A.M.; *ibid.*, no. 71, pp. 597-605.

To the first, Foch replied simply that in his opinion the Poles could check the Soviet offensive if they would establish a national government which would not waver and would act with firmness and decision in cooperation with the Allies. Just as the Italians had been able to check the enemy after Caporetto once they had a government "determined to resist foot by foot," so, Foch said, the Poles could do the same. But he did not specify what the Allies might do to help.

If the Poles failed, Foch continued, turning to Lloyd George's second question, the best line of conduct would still be to seize the Ruhr basin, because occupation of the Ruhr would make it impossible for Germany to carry on a war. Foch's reply led Curzon to ask whether the real danger was not a complete collapse of Germany and an internal revolution assisted by Soviet arms, rather than a military combination of Germany and Russia. But Foch rejoined that nothing was to be gained by postponing the occupation of the Ruhr: whether the Russians came to terms with the Poles or not, the Allies would still find themselves opposing the Germans; if the Russians refused to make peace the Allies would have to fight them as well.

Foch did not really meet the objection, raised by Lloyd George the previous day, that in the event of a Russian refusal it might pay the Allies to avoid a rupture with Germany. But Lloyd George did not raise the objection again; he felt, he told the gathering, that the time had come when the Allies had to choose between abandoning the Treaty of Versailles or taking definite steps to enforce it. That being the case, he said, his chief concern was that the occupation of the Ruhr should be carried out so as to avoid conflicts with the German workers which would have the effect of antagonizing the workers in Allied countries.

In the end, the Prime Minister's concern was unnecessary: there was no occupation of the Ruhr. After the meeting Lloyd George met privately with the German foreign minister, Walter Simons, and persuaded him that the Allied threat to occupy the Ruhr was deadly serious.[57] On the following day the German delegation agreed in large part to the Allied demands, and on 16 July, at the final

[57] "Notes of a Conversation held at the Hôtel Britannique, Spa . . . , July 14, 1920," *ibid.*, no. 74. The notes were by Philip Kerr, the only other person present.

session of the conference, a protocol to that effect was duly signed.[58]

Before this final session Lloyd George, Millerand, Marshal Foch, and Sir Henry Wilson met to consider the Polish situation, which was no less critical because of the eleventh-hour solution—or postponement—of the German problems facing the Allies at Spa. Lloyd George was very pessimistic; the Red Army, he predicted, would completely overrun Poland. Despite this gloomy outlook, however, both of the marshals rejected the solution of simply pouring more arms into Poland; with Wilson agreeing, Foch repeated what he had said two days previously—that such a measure would do no good unless and until the Poles formed "a good national government, fully representative of a united people determined to stand against invasion."[59] Lloyd George at once asked if Foch would go to Poland as a symbol of Allied interest and authority to steady the situation. Both Millerand and Wilson rejected this proposal, Wilson saying that "it would never do to risk the priceless asset of Foch's name in a wild scheme of this sort," but Millerand did agree that an Anglo-French mission of some sort should be sent, and that among its French members would be General Maxime Weygand, Foch's chief of staff.[60]

✧

Meanwhile, in Moscow, the receipt of the British note of 11 July, which *Izvestiya* likened to the Austrian ultimatum to Serbia of July 1914,[61] forced to a climax several months of debate within the Soviet government as to the nature and ends of British policy toward Russia. Broadly speaking, the debate was over whether the British Cabinet was wholly committed to the destruction of the Soviet system by renewed intervention in support of the Poles and Wrangel, or whether the Cabinet did not include a significant faction which sought to come to terms with the Bolshevik regime. Those who felt that there were two conflicting strands of policy within the British government identified Churchill and Curzon with the "policy of

[58] Minutes, meeting of Allied representatives, Spa, 15 July 1920, 11 A.M. (*ibid.*, no. 75), and Allied-German meeting, 16 July, 5 P.M. (*ibid.*, no. 77).

[59] The words are those of Wilson, who described the scene in his MS diary, entry for 16 July 1920 (see Callwell, *Henry Wilson*, vol. II, p. 253).

[60] Curzon to Derby (Paris), telegram 802, 20 July 1920; *British Documents*, vol. XI, no. 336.

[61] *Izvestiya*, 21 July 1920.

the cudgel," while Lloyd George and Sir Robert Horne, the President of the Board of Trade, were held to be the leading "realists."[62]

This was a debate filled with practical consequences for Soviet policy. If the British were held to be acting in good faith when they proposed a trading agreement and peace in Eastern Europe, then at least for the present it was advantageous to the Bolsheviks to come to a *modus vivendi* with London; on the other hand, if British policy was looked upon as entirely interventionist and anti-Soviet, then any concessions from the Soviet side would be wasted. Until that day when Soviet archives are fully open to Western scholars (assuming that the relevant papers still exist), we will have only limited knowledge about the extent of this debate within the Soviet government. It seems clear, however, that Chicherin was the most outspoken member of the circle, including Lenin, which viewed British policy as more or less monolithic in its interventionist policies, while Trotsky, with the support of Krasin, was the leading proponent of the position that there were two conflicting strands of policy emanating from London.[63]

Trotsky's point of view was clearly stated in a memorandum to Chicherin (with copies to Lenin, Kamenev, Krestinskii, and Bukharin)[64] on 4 June 1920, at a time when Polish troops still occupied Kiev and only four days following the first conversation between Lloyd George and Krasin. There was, he asserted, "by no means absolutely only one line" of British policy, and it would be possible, and obviously to the advantage of the Soviet government, to prevent

[62] The most elaborate exposition written from this latter point of view was not contemporaneous, but is found in I. M. Maiskii's article, "Anglo-sovetskoe torgovoe soglashenie 1921 goda" (cited above, Chapter I, n. 74), published in 1957. Maiskii was Ambassador in Britain from 1932 to 1943; his article was based upon the recollections of Krasin and Litvinov. Although extremely pro-British himself, he nevertheless felt constrained to make clear that the difference between the "die-hards" (as he called Churchill and Curzon) and the "realists" was one not of principle but of tactics (p. 61).

[63] Karl Radek also held this latter view. In a long article in *Izvestiya* on 9 July 1920 he expressed cautious enthusiasm over the degree of accord that had been reached between Krasin and Lloyd George, as evidenced in the British terms Krasin had brought back to Russia. Radek warned against undue optimism, however, saying: "If the Poles or Wrangel are successful in their efforts to defeat us, it is certain that England would at once join our enemies. We are furthermore not safe from the secret hostility of the British military party, which remains opposed to every agreement with Soviet Russia."

[64] Trotsky's memorandum of 4 June 1920 is in the Trotsky Archive, Houghton Library, Harvard University, folder T-533. With Stalin and Zinoviev these four constituted (with Trotsky) the Politburo.

the consolidation of British policy into one anti-Soviet line. It was rapidly becoming apparent that London feared most of all the influence of Bolshevism in the East. These fears, Trotsky implied, were at least for the moment largely groundless: all the facts about the situation in Khiva, Persia, Bukhara, and Afghanistan indicated that the "Soviet transformation" of those countries would be long and difficult in coming. From this, he said, it followed "that the potential Soviet revolution in the East is now advantageous for us chiefly as a most important element of the diplomatic barter with England." In other words, by calling a halt—temporarily, at least— to Soviet military pressure in the East, and also to the more blatant forms of agitation (but not, Trotsky made clear, to "political education" or to party organizational work), Moscow could strengthen the hand of those members of the British Cabinet who sought a *rapprochement* with the Soviet regime.

Trotsky offered no evidence to support his assertion that there was "by no means absolutely only one line" of British policy. His opponents, however, offered little in the way of evidence to support their counterassertions. Lenin's reaction was immediate: appended to the copy of Trotsky's memorandum which is with his papers in the Harvard University Library is a heavily underlined urgent note handwritten by Lenin on the same day. In total opposition to Trotsky's view the note stated: "Krasin is doing this, but it is *hopeless*. Krasin is the most 'good natured' of men, a more *good natured* does not exist. The talks of Lloyd George with Krasin have shown *with full clarity* that England is helping and *will help* both the Poles and Wrangel. *There is absolutely only one line.*"[65] And on this same day, as we have seen, Chicherin telegraphed to Krasin in London relaying Lenin's admonition not to "believe a word" Lloyd George said, and to "gull him three times as much."[66]

Chicherin gave full exposition to this interpretation of British policy in his long report to the Central Executive Committee on 17 June.[67] His report was intended as a general survey of Soviet Russia's relations with the outside world; much of it, however, was devoted to what Chicherin obviously viewed as the single most important event of Russia's foreign relations during the first half of 1920—

[65] Trotsky Archive, folder T-533.
[66] Lenin's message is cited above, chap. III, n. 51.
[67] Chicherin's report, is cited above, chap. III, n. 52.

the negotiations between Lloyd George and Krasin in London. Chicherin was filled with anger at the political terms which Lloyd George had laid down as necessary preconditions for the beginning of trade. The British, he said, sought to tie the hands of the Soviet government regarding the Polish war, Wrangel, and especially Soviet activities in the East, while holding out "only the problematical promise of trade negotiations." They sought to "skim off the cream" while offering nothing substantial in return. They themselves had not even ceased supplying arms to Wrangel and to the Poles. And Chicherin went on to mock Bonar Law's assurances in the House of Commons that in continuing to support Moscow's enemies Britain was merely an honorable trader making good on past contracts upon which she could not, in good faith, renege. In describing British policy Chicherin evinced a mixture of admiration and contempt and even hatred, attitudes no doubt at least partly attributable to the fact that he, like his father and his maternal grandfather before him, had served in the Tsar's Foreign Office. The essence of his description was the following:

Against us, as in earlier times, is a tightly knit coalition of imperialist governments, and as in earlier times the basic and leading force is the English government. If we examine the policy of England, we shall see in it an extraordinary complexity. In it there are manifold currents, seeming fluctuations, perpetual zigzags and, so it seems, internal contradictions, but at the same time, if one looks at it as a whole, it presents an astonishing unity. The ruling classes of England with their traditions of diplomatic skill present a deep unity of policy amid manifold apparent contradictions. And its many voices turn out to be notes of one melody, of a basic line which has the aim, as it appears at the present moment, on the one hand of endeavoring to suffocate us and on the other hand to deprive us of freedom of action, to bind us and at the same time to dull us, to endeavor to deprive us of the vigilance which is vital to us. The fundamentals of the policy of England are clear to us. Her goal is to cause us to pour forth blood, to incite one enemy after another, so that we should perpetually be occupied on the fronts and never be at rest and should never devote all our forces to internal construction. . . . This policy takes many forms. On the one hand, arms are given to Poland and protection is shown to Wrangel, on the other hand peaceful assurances are made to us with an amiable expression—the selfsame government promises us an agreement at the very moment when it is inciting our enemies against us and arming them against us. We will make an agreement with

England, we are ready for it, but let it be a real agreement, binding both sides, let there be genuine negotiations. We do not wish to be the victims of deceit.[68]

Chicherin's observations of 17 June, like Trotsky's remarks in his memorandum of the 4th, were intended not as specific prescriptions but as general reflections upon British policy. But with the arrival of Curzon's note of 11 July laying down a provisional frontier between Russia and Poland, summoning a conference in London to make peace in Eastern Europe, and threatening British intervention if the Russians did not comply, the debate within the Soviet government necessarily shifted its focus from the tentative and the general to the immediate and the specific: how should Moscow reply to this virtual ultimatum?

Trotsky was at the front when the British message arrived. As soon as he learned of it, on 13 July, he telegraphed his Politburo colleagues in Moscow urging the acceptance of British mediation to bring about peace with Poland; after all, he asserted, Poland was an independent state "on whose inviolability we have never made an attempt." And in a supplementary telegram sent the same day Trotsky suggested that Soviet agreement to a truce and peace negotiations with Poland should be made contingent upon a similar truce being reached between Russia and the Powers which had incited and sustained the Poles in their attack.[69] In both telegrams he advised his colleagues to study carefully, through the British press and through the reports of Soviet representatives whom Krasin left behind him in London when he departed for Russia on 1 July, the reaction of British "governing and opposition circles" to Curzon's ultimatum.[70]

[68] *Dokumenty vneshnei politiki*, vol. II, pp. 641-42.

[69] Trotsky to Chicherin, Lenin, Krestinskii, Stalin, and Kalinin, telegrams 702 and 703 (the latter added Kamenev to the addressees) 13 July 1920; Trotsky Archive, folders T-544 and T-545. (As is the case with all messages from the Trotsky Archive here cited, the place of sending is not specified.)

[70] The Soviet representatives remaining in London—Klishko, Rothstein, and Rozovsky—telegraphed their views on the 14th. Their conclusions largely matched Trotsky's, but their attention was not so much on "governing and opposition circles" as on the masses, and their arguments were predominantly tactical in nature. "We consider," they said, "that a point blank refusal will be less intelligible to the masses than the rejection of some of the points and the conditional acceptance of others supplemented by conditions and demands put forward by us. We must show the masses that we are not threatening Polish independence and integrity but that we ourselves are obliged to look for guarantees against the machinations of the enemy. . . . Complete agreement will disappoint the masses, lower our prestige in their eyes and will in itself prepare a second Versailles peace for us." (Klishko to Chicherin, telegrams 261 and 262, 14 July 1920; Lloyd George MSS, file F/203/1/11.)

Although Trotsky advocated a conciliatory attitude towards the British offer of mediation between Russia and Poland, he counselled rejection of any such outside intervention in the Bolsheviks' dispute with Wrangel. The latter was a Russian internal matter; Lloyd George refused to permit Soviet interference in Britain's internal affairs, Trotsky noted. Moreover, he thought that such a policy did not involve any great risks: the Allies would scarcely be willing to make an issue out of Wrangel's fate especially if the Soviet government simultaneously agreed to accept British mediation with regard to Poland. Trotsky also urged that the Soviet reply to Curzon's note should make clear that Moscow was accepting only the mediation of Great Britain, and not that of the League of Nations, and that Soviet delegates to London peace talks would expect the same rights as the delegates of any free and independent country.

These were Trotsky's views. Except for a brief message from Lenin to Stalin (who was in Kharkov superintending operations on the southern front) summarizing Curzon's note and asserting that "all this is a piece of knavery aimed at the annexation of the Crimea . . . to snatch victory out of our hands with the aid of false promises"—and not commenting at all upon the much more important Polish part of the note[71]—we do not know the views of any other member of the Politburo.[72] But whatever their individual views, the reply to the British note that was sent collectively in their names represented a decisive repudiation of Trotsky's position.

In bitter and sarcastic language the Soviet note, sent by radio on

[71] Lenin's own notes on his "telephonogram" (*i.e.*, a message—not a conversation—transmitted over telephone lines) to Stalin are printed in his *Sochineniya*, 4th ed., vol. 31 (Moscow, 1955), p. 179; the editors date it as either 12 or 13 July 1920. The message is not included in previous editions of Lenin's works.

[72] We do, perhaps, know something of Stalin's views. The editors of his *Sochineniya* write: "Stalin's telegram in reply was sent to Lenin on 13 July 1920 from Kharkov. In the telegram Stalin, entirely agreeing with Lenin's estimate of Curzon's note of 12 July (the date of its receipt in Moscow), gave his proposals for the answer of the Soviet government to Curzon's note." (p. 511, n. 39) And: ". . . Lenin's proposals coincided with Stalin's, contained in the telegram of 13 July 1920 addressed to Lenin. On the basis of Lenin's proposals . . . adopted by the Plenum of the Ts[entral] K[ommittee of the Communist Party] on 16 July 1920 . . . there was drawn up the radiotelegram of the People's Commissar for Foreign Affairs to the English Government of 17 July 1920." (p. 511, n. 40) Stalin's telegram is not included in his own *Sochineniya*.

It is interesting that there was no discussion of the British note in the Soviet press preceding the Soviet government's reply. The readers of *Pravda* and *Izvestiya* first learned of the "Curzon ultimatum" (as it was called) when both papers printed it, together with the Soviet reply, on 18 July.

17 July,[73] rejected British or any other outside mediation in the war between Russia and Poland. The British government's desire to assist in the establishment of peace in Eastern Europe, it said, although welcome, was rather late in coming: there had been no evidence of a similar desire two months before when Polish armies were deep in Russian territory. Outside mediation was unacceptable to Moscow because of the likelihood that the mediating Power would put its own interests ahead of those of both Russia and Poland. "In regard to peace with Poland," said the note, "the Soviet Government considers it necessary to take into account, besides the interests and aspirations of the Russian working masses, only the interests and aspirations of the Polish working masses, and consequently it considers it possible to reach peace with Poland solely by direct negotiation."[74] Should the Poles propose the opening of peace negotiations, they would not be rebuffed by Moscow. Moreover, the Soviet government would agree to a frontier more favorable to Poland than the line laid down in the British note (*i.e.*, the "Curzon Line") which had been originally determined by the Supreme Council "under the influence of counterrevolutionary Russian elements" and which clearly reflected "the anti-Polish policy of Tsarism and of the imperialist White Russian bourgeoisie." And in a scarcely veiled hint of Soviet ambitions regarding Poland, the note added: "Soviet

[73] The text of the Soviet note of 17 July 1920, addressed to Curzon and signed by Chicherin, is printed in *Dokumenty vneshnei politiki*, vol. III, pp. 47-53. An abridged translation is in Degras, *Soviet Documents*, pp. 194-97.

[74] Curiously, the Soviet note reserved its strongest condemnation for the League of Nations, which was mentioned only once in the British note of 11 July, and then as an afterthought. The draft discussed by the Allied representatives at Spa on 10 July stated that Britain was "bound under the Treaty of Peace to defend the integrity of independence of Poland within its legitimate ethnographic frontiers." In the final version, the reference was made more specific by the replacement of the words "Treaty of Peace" with "Covenant of the League of Nations" (which was, of course, a part of the peace treaty with Germany).

The Soviet reply, however, gave the impression that the British had proposed League mediation of the Polish-Soviet dispute, although they had not. The reply stated:

"Even less tolerable to the Soviet government is the intervention in this matter of the group of governments called the League of Nations, to the Covenant of which the British government makes reference in justifying its ultimatum of 12 July. The so-called League of Nations has never informed the Russian government of its establishment and its existence, and the Soviet government has never had occasion to take any decision on its recognition or non-recognition of this association. . . .

"The Soviet government cannot in any circumstances agree to a group of Powers taking on themselves the functions of a supreme court over all States on the earth. . . . Therefore it categorically rejects any interference whatever by this association in the matter of peace between Russia and Poland."

Russia is the more ready to meet the interests and wishes of the Polish people in regard to the terms of peace the farther the Polish people go in their internal life along the road which will create a firm foundation for truly fraternal relations between the working masses of Poland, Russia, and the Ukraine, White Russia, and Lithuania and will provide a guarantee that Poland will cease to serve as an instrument of aggression and intrigue against the workers and peasants of Soviet Russia and other nations."

Turning to Wrangel (and here Trotsky and his Politburo colleagues were evidently in agreement) the Russian note sharply rejected the British proposal that the White forces should retire from the mainland to the Crimea[75] and that during the ensuing armistice the connecting isthmus should be a neutral zone, pending the peace conference in London to which Wrangel would be invited. Wrangel's campaign, the note asserted, was "indissolubly connected" with the Polish offensive, and both were dependent upon the Allies—indeed, were it not for continued Allied shipments of military supplies, mostly in British ships, Wrangel would long since have been liquidated. The Soviet government could not "remain indifferent" to the British government's "repeated attempts to transform the Crimean peninsula into an inviolable asylum for the mutinous general and for other mutineers" and thus make the Crimea a "British territory" as Murmansk and Archangel had been less than a year previously. Yet "in its anxiety to reach an armistice with the British government and to meet its wishes" the Soviet government was ready, the note stated, once again to offer to guarantee the personal safety of Wrangel, his army, and all refugees to whom he had given protection, on condition that they should surrender immediately all territory they occupied, and all their weapons and military supplies.

Finally, the note rejected the British proposal for an Eastern European peace conference in London. The Soviet government had already concluded peace with Estonia and Lithuania, and negotiations were proceeding with Finland and Latvia: since Moscow intended to negotiate with the Poles independently, there would be no need for a conference. On the other hand, the Soviet government was most anxious "to put an end to the struggle" between Russia

---

[75] At this time, it will be remembered, Wrangel's forces had broken out of the Crimea and successfully occupied sizeable territory on the mainland. (See above, chap. II.)

and Great Britain and to reach a "final peace" with the British government. Therefore, it was sending to London an "enlarged" delegation which would conduct negotiations whose basis would be the already given Soviet agreement to the conditions which Lloyd George laid down to Krasin before the latter left Britain early in July.[76]

Here, then, was the Soviet reply. Its meaning for the most part was straightforward enough—a flat repudiation of the policies which Lloyd George had pressed upon his colleagues and upon the Poles at Spa. Only in its reference to the "internal life" of the Polish people was it in any way unclear. Moreover, if Trotsky had had his way, there would have been no ambiguities on this point either. Despite his disagreement with the policies embodied in the note, he was apparently asked by his Politburo colleagues to justify these policies in an appeal to the peoples of Russia and the Ukraine (and by implication to the people of Poland as well). The draft of this appeal printed in his collected works is Trotsky at his most vitriolic. Britain, especially, he singled out for scornful abuse. Concerning Soviet aims in Poland, where his colleagues' note was ambiguous Trotsky's draft was crystal clear. It stated:

In order that the Polish people should receive an honorable peace, a just frontier and—in the person of Russia—a brotherly neighbor, ready to come to its aid and share its all, it is necessary that the Polish working people should fling off from its neck those eternally discredited ones who are in power over it, who have called into being this dishonorable war and who ought to pay for it. It is necessary that the Polish working people should cease to be the weapon in the hands of their bourgeois-aristocratic government and parliament, who are themselves a weapon in the hands of Anglo-French capital. It is necessary that the Polish workers and peasants should drive away their capitalists, their landowners, their ravishers and oppressors and should set up for themselves the power of the soviets—the power of the workers and the peasants. Such is the shortest and most direct way to the most honorable and just peace. Before the peoples of the whole world, at this present fatal hour of history, we point out this path to the Polish people—and we bind ourselves to show the Polish people our full support on that path.[77]

[76] For the British conditions see above, chap. III, n. 51.

[77] Trotsky's draft of the appeal is printed in his *Sochineniya*, vol. XVII, *Sovetskaya respublika i kapitalisticheskii mir* (The Soviet Republic and the Capitalist World), part II, *Grazhdanskaya voina* (The Civil War), Moscow-Leningrad, 1926, pp. 424-30

There are times, however—particularly in dealings with war aims —when ambiguity has its advantages, and Trotsky's colleagues evidently felt that his frank admission that Moscow aimed at nothing less than a communist Poland was, to say the least, untactful. Thus the version of the appeal which appeared in *Izvestiya* and *Pravda* on 21 July over the signatures of Lenin, Trotsky, Chicherin, Kurskii (Commissar for Justice), and Fotieva (Secretary of the Sovnarkom) omitted this paragraph altogether; its replacement was quite innocuous: "In order that the Polish people should receive an honorable peace, a just frontier and, in the person of Russia, a brotherly neighbor ready to come to its aid and share its all, it is necessary that the Polish people itself should want this. We would long ago have come to an honorable peace agreement with the Polish workers and peasants. The cause of peace now depends above all on the pressure of the Polish workers and peasants on their bourgeoisie and landowners."[78]

The published version of the long appeal incorporated one other change from Trotsky's draft: two particularly anti-British remarks were discreetly omitted—the statement "England called forth the Polish war, and England is answerable for it," and a reference to London as "that center where are laid out all the snares against the Soviet Republic and where was issued the order to begin the Polish attack on the Ukraine and Russia."[79] Trotsky was nothing if not thorough.

On the evening of Sunday, 18 July 1920, when the Russian reply to the British note of the 11th reached London, Lloyd George had as his guest for dinner at Cobham, his country house, the ubiquitous Riddell. Except for the newspaper publisher, the dinner was a family

---

(the quoted passage is pp. 428-29). The editors of the volume do not indicate that the document is a draft, and they incorrectly cite *Izvestiya*, no. 159, 21 July 1920, as its source. In fact, as is shown here, there were significant differences between Trotsky's version and that which appeared in *Izvestiya* (and also on the same day in *Pravda*). Presumably the editors were not aware that it had been altered before publication. There is no trace of the document among the papers in the Trotsky Archive at Harvard.

[78] The text of the appeal (dated 20 July 1920) as it was published in *Izvestiya*, no. 159, and *Pravda*, no. 159, on 21 July 1920 is printed in *Dokumenty vneshnei politiki*, vol. III, pp. 55-60 (the quoted paragraph is on p. 59). An abridged English translation of the published version, broadcast by Moscow Radio, was printed in *The Times*, 22 July 1920.

[79] Both are in Trotsky, *Sochineniya*, vol. XVII, part II, p. 425.

affair: there was only Lloyd George, his daughter Megan, and his secretary (later his second wife), Frances Stevenson. During the meal, according to the entry Riddell made that evening in his diary, the Prime Minister was preoccupied, and small things irritated him. The week which the Russians had been given in which to reply had expired, and no message had come.

After dinner the two men sat talking in the summer house in the garden. Riddell described what then took place as follows:

> Several times during the evening, as we sat there in the dusk, L.G. alluded to the expected reply from the Soviet Government. . . . He was evidently very excited and telephoned two or three times to ascertain if the Russian cable had arrived. The conduct of international affairs is a great game. L.G. was just as eager about this message as a lover awaiting a telegram. He said, "Much depends on the Soviet reply."
>
> At about 9.30 a telephone message arrived saying that the Russian telegram, 2,400 words, had come. L.G. dashed into the house to hear it and shortly returned saying that the message was too long to read over the telephone, but the gist of it was that, while the Russians did not admit the right of any nation or group of nations to intervene in the dispute between Russia and Poland, they would grant an armistice if the Poles asked for one, as there was nothing they desired more than peace.
>
> "I don't call that unreasonable, do you?" enquired L.G. I replied that I thought the condition was quite reasonable, and asked whether Krassin was returning.
>
> L.G.: "Yes, but I must stop him. I cannot see him while the Russians are fighting the Poles. I must telegraph to stop the destroyer in which Krassin is to travel."
>
> (He at once telephoned to that effect and gave instructions for the Russian despatch to be sent to him by messenger).[80]

The British government's response to the Soviet note was twofold. First, on the following day, 19 July, a telegram—apparently drafted in the Prime Minister's office, not in the Foreign Office—went out to Sir Horace Rumbold in Warsaw, commenting that although the meaning of the Russian note was "doubtful on certain points," it

[80] Riddell, *Diary*, entry for 18 July 1920, pp. 220-21. The version of the Soviet note which reached Lloyd George at Cobham was evidently one furnished by Klishko, in Krasin's absence chief of the trade mission in London. It was marked "subject to correction." Another version—similar, however, in all important respects—was transmitted by the British mission in Reval as Leslie to Curzon, telegram 154, 18 July (received on the 19th); file 208602/207846/38; F.O. 371/4058. Both are appended to minutes, Cabinet 41 (20), 20 July, 11:30 A.M.; Cab. 23/22.

nevertheless indicated that Moscow would not reject a proposal from Warsaw for peace negotiations, and would "also consider in the most friendly spirit any subsidiary proposal for armistice." Moreover, the Soviet government would agree to a boundary more favorable to Poland than the line drawn by the Supreme Council in December 1919. "Please, therefore," the telegram instructed Rumbold, "immediately call upon the Polish Government and ask them in view of the Soviet's reply to send immediately formal message to Moscow and Soviet army headquarters proposing peace and asking for an immediate armistice."[81]

Second, on 20 July Lloyd George called together the Cabinet to give *post facto* approval to these instructions to Rumbold, and to consider a draft British reply to Moscow. The meeting's minutes are typical of those taken when nothing, in fact, is decided. Poland's army was outweighed and demoralized; only an armistice could prevent the Russians from overrunning the country; although she "had probably brought upon herself her present desperate situation by ill-advised attacks directly contrary to the advice of the Allies," the fact remained that if nothing were done Polish independence might well be extinguished; and if Poland "disappeared and were absorbed into Soviet Russia, this might be a prelude to the union of the latter with the Bolshevist elements in Germany and the postponement of European peace."[82]

In the face of this dire prognosis the Cabinet approved Lloyd George's draft reply to the Soviet note. It was despatched later that day. Curzon described it accurately in a telegram to Lord Derby in Paris: it "avoids controversial issues," he said.[83] The Soviet note, it began, had raised questions on which there were "profound differences" between the British and Soviet governments. These would be left for future discussion; for the present the British government objected to the proposed Eastern European peace conference in London, the British government did not have "the least desire" to insist upon it. "They only proposed that the Conference should meet in

[81] Curzon to Rumbold (Warsaw), telegram 318, 19 July 1920, *British Documents*, vol. XI, no. 335. That the telegram came from 10 Downing Street is implied in the Cabinet minutes cited below, no. 82.

[82] Minutes, Cabinet 41 (20), 20 July 1920, 11:30 A.M.; Cab. 23/22.

[83] Curzon to Derby (Paris), telegram 802, 20 July 1920 (repeated to Rumbold in Warsaw on 21 July); *British Documents*, vol. XI, no. 336. The text of the reply to Moscow, sent as telegram 198 to the British consul at Reval, 20 July 1920, is in *ibid.*, vol. VIII, pp. 649-50; it was published by *The Times* on 26 July.

London because they thought it would bring Russia into relations with the Peace Conference and so pave the way to a better understanding between Russia and the outer world."

All that mattered, the reply continued, was that negotiations between the Russians and the Poles should begin immediately and be carried out in good faith, and that they should lead to a permanent peace which would secure "the abstention on the part of either nation from any interference in the internal policy of the other." The Allies had already urged the Poles immediately to initiate negotiations for an armistice and for peace. If the Soviet armies continued to advance despite a Polish request for an armistice, "the British Government and its Allies must necessarily assume that it is the intention of the Soviet Government to make war on the Polish people and will in conjunction with their Allies give to Poland the assistance and support they have promised in that event." Finally, the note concluded, because negotiations for the resumption of trade between Britain and Russia could not be usefully pursued if Soviet forces invaded Poland, the British government had telegraphed to Krasin and his colleagues, who were waiting at Reval, telling them to delay their departure until a Soviet-Polish armistice had been agreed to.

The British reply referred to "assistance and support" promised by the Allies to Poland. Yet there had been no such promises, a fact which surely must have been surmised by the Soviet government. A week previously, following the despatch of the "ultimatum" from Spa which bore Curzon's signature, Klishko reported to Moscow from London that the Foreign Office had telephoned the editors of the principal newspapers asking them to play down the implied threat in the British note: it was a diplomatic bluff which the Allies had no material means to support.[84] After the Cabinet meeting of the 20th, Henry Wilson commented angrily in his diary: "A Cabinet this morning, LG presiding, of some 20 *fools*. We spent three whole hours discussing what last night's telegram from the Bolshevists meant, when it is as plain as a pikestaff—an impudent refusal of all Frock demands. The Gadarene swine never galloped as fast as these Frocks."[85]

Wilson himself had no concrete recommendations, however. On

[84] Klishko to Chicherin, telegrams 3-4, 13 July 1920; intercept 03679, Davidson MSS.
[85] Wilson MS diary, entry for 20 July 1920. (Callwell, *Henry Wilson*, vol. II, p. 253, omits "*fools*.")

27 July he distributed a General Staff paper, "Military Liabilities of the Empire," which, after describing how thinly stretched Britain's military resources were, commented about Poland in language whose vagueness matched that of the Cabinet's minutes:

> Another possible commitment which cannot be altogether ignored is that of intervention on behalf of Poland should that State be in danger of being overwhelmed by Russia. The provision of actual troops would be a matter for very grave consideration, given our heavy commitments elsewhere, but the destruction of Poland, followed by chaos all over Central Europe might be the alternative. The complete abrogation of the Versailles Peace Treaty would inevitably follow, and with it would vanish any hope of effecting the disarmament of Germany.[86]

Conspicuously absent was any estimate of what kind of intervention in Poland might be effective—or possible.

Moreover, Wilson's caustic comment on the Cabinet's response to the Soviet note did not take into account two significant assumptions on the part of Lloyd George. First was his supposition that once the Soviet forces entered territory that really was Polish, and therefore had to encounter a hostile local population, their advance would slow down.[87] Second, and more important, was that Moscow did not intend to install a communist government in Warsaw. He made explicit this latter assumption in a meeting with a deputation from the Parliamentary Committee of the Trades Union Congress on 22 July. The Soviet note was ambiguous, he told the deputation. Its statement rejecting a general peace conference in London in favor of "peace with Poland solely by direct negotiation" could also be read to imply that Moscow would negotiate only with the "Polish working masses," which would mean a "proletariat Government." The British reply to this note, Lloyd George said, deliberately assumed that such was *not* Moscow's meaning, "and that the Polish people are to choose their Government, whether a good or bad one."[88] For the time being, therefore, Moscow would get the benefit of the doubt. Given the existing obstacles to effective British intervention on the side of the Poles, such a tactic was scarcely surprising.

The only concrete (as opposed to rhetorical) result of the Cabinet

---

[86] This paper may be found in W.O. 33/1004 or in Cab. 4/7/3.

[87] See Hankey's letter to Lloyd George disputing this assumption, from Paris, 22 July 1920; copy in Curzon MSS, box 22.

[88] *The Times*, 26 July 1920.

meeting of 20 July was a decision to implement Lloyd George's tentative agreement with Millerand that a high-level Anglo-French diplomatic and military mission should go to Warsaw to survey the situation and to give advice to the Polish government. As British diplomatic representative the Cabinet selected Lord D'Abernon, a banker and financier who because of his ability to deal with the complex problems of reparations (and also because of Lloyd George's distrust of professional diplomats) had just become British Ambassador in Berlin. Chosen to accompany him were General Sir Percy de B. Radcliffe, the Director of Military Operations at the War Office, and—at D'Abernon's urgent request—Sir Maurice Hankey, secretary to the Cabinet. The three British representatives left for Paris that same evening and on the following morning they met with Millerand. When D'Abernon read out the text of the British note which had just been sent to Moscow, the French premier offered no comments or criticisms. But he immediately agreed that the French mission should also include a political as well as a military representative and later that day he appointed J. J. Jusserand, the French Ambassador in Washington (then on leave in Paris), to accompany General Weygand.[89]

The Anglo-French mission set out on its long journey the following evening, travelling in a special train that would serve as its quarters in the Polish capital and also, if the need arose, as a ready means of escaping the Red Army. That same night Curzon gave Sir Horace Rumbold his first indication that the "small temporary Mission" was on its way. Lest the British Minister should feel that he was being elbowed aside (he did) the Foreign Secretary sent soothing words: "Lord D'Abernon will in no sense supersede you or assume any of your functions, your manner of performing which has given complete satisfaction to His Majesty's Government. You will, I am sure, render the Mission every assistance in your power."[90]

To D'Abernon Curzon gave instructions as brief as they were vague, stating merely that he and his colleagues were to advise the British government concerning measures that might be taken in

[89] Derby (Paris) to Curzon, telegram 838, 21 July 1920; *British Documents*, vol. X (London, 1960), no. 261. See Viscount D'Abernon, *The Eighteenth Decisive Battle of the World*, Warsaw, 1920, London, 1931, p. 16.
[90] Curzon to Rumbold (Warsaw), telegram 326, 21 July 1920; *British Documents*, vol. XI, no. 338. Rumbold offered to go on leave while D'Abernon was in Warsaw: Rumbold to Curzon, telegram 548, 22 July; *ibid.*, no. 340.

conjunction with the Polish and other governments regarding "all questions raised by the negotiations tending towards the conclusion of an armistice between Poland and Soviet Russia." These instructions were in marked contrast to those Millerand gave to the French representatives. The latter implied that the attempt to negotiate a peace with the Bolsheviks would fail, and that therefore the French mission should determine how France and her allies might give the Poles (provided that they themselves did not abandon the struggle) the moral and material support that would enable them to complete the construction of their republic within "frontiers encircling lands indisputably Polish."[91]

✧

Meanwhile, on 21 July, Lloyd George went before the House of Commons with a long-awaited statement of policy. He professed to give the House a general survey of what had happened at Spa, but most of his speech, and nearly all those which came afterward, dealt with only the Polish-Russian war. As he had done at Spa he drew a gloomy picture of a Soviet Poland extending the sphere of communist control up to the frontiers of Germany, and he evoked the specter of a reactionary Germany joining forces with a revolutionary Russia to deprive the Allies of their victory. Undoubtedly, he said, the Poles had made mistakes. Their offensive against Russia was both foolish and reckless; their only excuse—and one which had to be taken into account—was the threat of Soviet interference in Poland's internal affairs. And he added: "Let us assume that it was a mistake for the Poles to have pursued that policy of trying to set up a buffer community between Soviet land and themselves. If it was a mistake, a mistake of that kind does not justify a nation in being wiped out. Poland—independent Poland—is essential to the whole fabric of peace."[92]

Lloyd George repeatedly emphasized the importance to British policy of a genuinely independent Poland. His principal criticism of the Soviet note of 17 July was that it was ambiguous on this point. He did not give the House its text (his only explanation for not

[91] The text of D'Abernon's instructions is given (in French translation) in Weygand, *Mirages et réalité*, p. 97. They were closely paraphrased in Curzon's telegram 326 to Rumbold, cited above, n. 90. See also D'Abernon, *Eighteenth Battle*, pp. 16-17. The text of the instructions to the French mission, 21 July 1920, is in Weygand, pp. 95-97.

[92] 132 *H.C. Deb.*, col. 482.

doing so was its excessive length and repetitiveness) but instead summarized its main points. Some phrases, he said, seemed to indicate that the Soviet government was prepared to discuss peace terms only with a Polish "proletariat government." If such were the correct interpretation, he continued, it was "an intolerable one." The Bolsheviks had no right to dictate the sort of government the Poles should have.[93]

So long as the Bolsheviks respected Poland's independence, the Prime Minister said, it was a matter of no great consequence to the British government that they had rejected the idea of a general Eastern European peace conference in London, although he himself felt that such a conference, bringing "all elements" together, would be the surest way to get real peace in Europe. He then came to the crux of his speech: what would happen if the Poles sued for an armistice and the Red Army nevertheless continued its advance. In that case, he said, "we shall have to give such assistance as is in our power to the Polish Government. The Poles have a very considerable number of troops. They have no lack of brave men. . . . What they lack is equipment, and especially organisation. . . . France and ourselves could supply that. I think France and ourselves could supply them with the means for organising their forces. . . . It is to the British interest, it is to the European interest, that Poland should not be wiped out. It would be fatal to the peace of Europe, and the consequences would be disastrous beyond measure."[94]

Lloyd George was, of course, deliberately vague concerning what steps the government might take if the Russian advance persisted, saying merely that D'Abernon and Radcliffe had been sent to Poland "to investigate the conditions and to report as to what steps can be taken in order to assist the Polish people to defend their own territory." Surprisingly, although several members of the House spoke as if the country were once again on the brink of war,[95] and *The Times*'s political correspondent observed that it had become evident for the first time that British assistance to Poland "might not be confined to munitions and advice,"[96] no one pressed the Prime

[93] *Ibid.*, col. 484. Lloyd George was not aware, as most other members were not, that the text of the Soviet note of 17 July had been leaked to the *Daily Herald* by the Soviet trade delegation in London, and printed in that very morning's edition.
[94] 132 *H.C. Deb.*, col. 484.
[95] See especially the speech by J. H. Thomas, general secretary of the National Union of Railwaymen; *ibid.*, cols. 542-43.
[96] *The Times*, 22 July 1920.

Minister to state more specifically what Britain's role in Poland's defense might be, and not a single member went so far as to argue that British officers, much less British troops, should be sent. For the most part the issue was shrouded in generalities or avoided entirely, and members from both sides of the House chose the much easier course of reexamining the events of the recent past.

Of these interventions, the most trenchant came from Lord Robert Cecil, who sharply criticized the "unfortunate and disastrous" futility of the government's position, taken during the preceding January and February and adhered to throughout the Polish invasion of Russia, that it could give the Poles no advice as to whether or not they should make peace with the Bolsheviks, on the grounds that giving the Poles advice would mean that if Poland were then invaded Britain would have to stand by her. "What was so plain to everybody else, and apparently was not plain to the Government," Cecil said, "was that it would be very difficult, if not impossible, for those who had signed the Treaty of Versailles to submit to the extinction of Poland by Russian troops whether we had given any promise or not."[97]

Two months previously, when the House of Commons had last discussed the Polish-Soviet war, there had been much attention to the role that the League of Nations might play in the conflict. Then, with Polish troops in Kiev, Bonar Law (speaking in Lloyd George's absence) had summarily rejected the proposal, put forward by Cecil and others, that the British government should invoke the Covenant of the League of Nations to force the Poles to withdraw from Russia. Now, however, with the Red Army nearly at the Curzon Line, Lloyd George invoked the Covenant to justify British assistance to the Poles against the Russians. If Soviet forces invaded ethnographic Poland, he said, Great Britain would be "bound by the covenants she has entered into . . . to give every assistance in her power to the party which is assailed."[98]

This was the Prime Minister's only reference to the League, but it aroused a stream of comments from others. Herbert Asquith, who had been returned to the House and to the leadership of the Liberal Party in a by-election the previous February, urged that *all* action

[97] 132 *H.C. Deb.*, col. 519.
[98] *Ibid.*, col. 486. For Cecil's earlier proposal, see above, chap. I.

in defense of Poland should be taken "under the authority and, if possible, on the initiative of the League," so as to add vital impetus to the international organization.[99] Cecil, as the Englishman most closely identified with the League and as one who invariably spoke out on League matters, warned that the government could not simply go to war to help Poland and justify its actions by reference to the Covenant. Instead, it would have to abide by decisions of the League Council, which had not yet even considered the matter. The Covenant did not give each Power a hunting license, he said. Its purpose was to restrain independent action, not to encourage it. Tom Shaw, of the Weavers' Union, pushed these arguments further. He recalled that at the time of the Polish attack on Russia two months before, the government had not been willing to invoke Article 11 (which made any war or threat of war, whether immediately affecting League members or not, a "matter of concern" to the whole League) in order to restrain the Poles. The Covenant was too valuable a document, Shaw said, to have one clause lifted out when it seemed to fit a Power's purposes and another clause left carefully concealed. "It inflicts the obligation to defend your ally from attack, but it also inflicts the obligation to see that your ally does not unjustly attack others."[100]

The most widely noted criticism of Lloyd George's reference to the Covenant as justification for possible British intervention in the Polish-Soviet war came not from the House of Commons but, because of the eminence of its author, in a letter from Viscount Grey of Fallodon to Lord Robert Cecil, written four days following the debate and published in *The Times* on 28 July. The former Foreign Secretary urged Cecil, as head of the League of Nations Union, and all others who cared about the League to protest against the Prime Minister's implication that Britain had a "League obligation" to go to war in defense of Poland. Such an untruth did deadly injury to the League, he said, by giving the impression Britain might be involved in the Russo-Polish war by virtue of the mere fact of

---

[99] 132 *H.C. Deb.*, col. 498. Although Russia did not figure much in Asquith's election speeches, on the night before polling day he stated in his closing address: "I say resume trade relations by all means with Russia, get rid of the blockade, which is doing injury to us and to the world more than it is to Russia. I go farther; I say make peace with Russia." (*The Times*, 12 February 1920.)

[100] 132 *H.C. Deb.*, col. 520 (Cecil) and col. 510 (Shaw).

League membership. This was not so. "Membership in the League of Nations," Grey said, "is essentially only membership in a co-operative association of Governments to work for international friendship; to bring peace by discussion, based upon justice, not force." Not Britain's membership of the League but the government's ignoring of it had now brought the country once more to the threshold of war. And he continued, making the same point Shaw had made, but in language more sharply drawn:

> The League was not invoked to restrain Poland, one of its own members, from aggression . . . as it should have been. To invoke the League now to support Poland by arms against the consequences of her action is not merely illogical; it is, in fact, a great misuse of the League, for it perverts it into an instrument for carrying on war after having prevented it from exercising its first and greatest function of making peace.
>
> This perversion of the League, unless repudiated, will impair its future usefulness and imperil its very existence. . . .

✧

During the debate in the House of Commons on 21 July it was taken for granted that, as Grabski had promised the Allies at Spa, the Poles would immediately ask the Soviet government for an armistice. In Warsaw, however, Sir Horace Rumbold was discovering that this assumption was by no means warranted.

From the moment he received instructions from Curzon to press the Polish government to propose peace negotiations to Moscow, the British Minister devoted himself to that end. Curzon's telegram of instructions arrived at night on 20 July. As soon as it was decoded Rumbold drove to the Belweder Palace, where Piłsudski was conducting a meeting of the National Defense Council, and told Sapieha, the foreign minister, what Curzon had said. Early the following morning he returned to ask Sapieha whether the appeal for an armistice had been sent. It had not. Instead, the Poles were busying themselves with the formation of a new government, apparently because late in the previous night's session the Defense Council had received a telegram from Paris purporting to convey a portion of the Soviet note to the British government of 17 July, according to which Moscow would be more willing to negotiate with a Polish government reformed on a wide and democratic basis. So Piłsudski allowed the civilian politicians the amusement of their politics (from which, on 24 July, the leader of the Peasant Party, Witos—"a stage peasant," as Hankey described him to Lloyd George[101]—emerged as premier, with the leader of the Socialist Party, Dszszynski, as vice-premier) while he and the generals took advantage of the delay to attempt to bring about a change in the military situation that would help secure better terms from the Russians.

When Rumbold learned from Sapieha on the morning of the 21st that the armistice appeal had not been sent, he was filled with despair. He could not understand, he told the foreign minister, how a chance telegram from Paris could have affected the Defense Council's formal request to appeal for an armistice. The generals were sadly deluded, he said, if they thought that there was anything between Grodno and Warsaw but a disorganized mass of soldiery. Once again they were flaunting civilian authority; this time, Rumbold told Sapieha, they were gambling with the very existence of the nation.[102]

After these remarks, and with a promise from Sapieha that the necessary messages—one to the Soviet government in Moscow and another to the Red Army's field command—would be sent within twenty-four hours whether or not a new government had been formed, the British Minister returned to his Legation to await developments. But no word came, and early on the following morning, 22 July, he went again to the Foreign Ministry, and again he met with excuses and delays. The messages had not been sent because Piłsudski wished to approve the texts himself; the Marshal, who had been up all night working, would not rise until late morning, and Sapieha did not dare disturb him.

Rumbold was still to receive a telegram from London, instructing him to inform the Poles that unless they immediately applied for an armistice they would receive no further support from Great Britain.[103] He scarcely needed such instructions, however. In measured but angry words he told Sapieha that his failure to have the

---

[101] In a letter to Lloyd George from Warsaw, 25 July 1920; copy in Curzon MSS, box 22. Lord D'Abernon provided a fuller description of Witos: "The new Prime Minister, a genuine peasant, prides himself on never having worn a tie; wears high boots like peasants in the Ballet Russe; speaks no known tongue. But is rather attractive." (Letter to Curzon from Warsaw, 26 July, Curzon MSS, box 22.)

[102] Rumbold described these events in telegram 546 to Curzon, 21 July 1920; *British Documents*, vol. XI, no. 339.

[103] The telegram—Curzon to Rumbold, no. 329, 22 July 1920—was drafted by Philip Kerr and sent without change by the Foreign Office; file 209206/40430/55, F.O. 371/3915.

messages sent within the twenty-four-hour period constituted a breach of a formal engagement. The British government had approached the Bolsheviks, he said, on the assumption that the Poles would immediately give effect to its "imperative advice." The messages were to be despatched at once: if Piłsudski attempted to block their despatch he would see the Marshal himself, enter a formal protest against his dilatory action, and throw all responsibility for the consequences upon him.[104]

Later that day, at noon, when he learned that the messages still had not been sent, Rumbold arranged that he and General Carton de Wiart, the head of the British Military Mission, should go to Piłsudski. But the trip was not necessary: in the meantime Rumbold so "harried" (the word he used in describing his action to Curzon) the Poles that the messages were broadcast by Warsaw radio in the early afternoon. "I left no doubt in mind of Polish Government," Rumbold said in his telegram to London, "that I considered that they had been guilty of criminal folly in delaying despatch of their messages and that they had not acted honourably towards us." And he added: "In fact I literally had to force them under threats to send out messages."[105]

The messages sent were short and simple. One, from the Polish to the Soviet government, took note of the Soviet willingness, as expressed in Chicherin's note of 17 July to Curzon, to "accept peace proposals provided they are sent from the Polish Government," and it therefore requested the immediate cessation of hostilities and the opening of peace negotiations. A second, from the Polish to the Soviet military high command, asked the Russians to name a place where negotiators could meet, and requested a timely reply.[106]

Thus, with the knowledge that its armies were in headlong retreat and the realization that its capital would soon be menaced, the

[104] Reported by Rumbold to Curzon in telegram 556, 23 July 1920; *ibid.*, no. 345.

[105] *Idem.* Rumbold described the events of 20-23 July 1920 in great detail in despatch 482 to Curzon, 23 July; file 209868/40430/55, F.O. 371/3916.

[106] The former note, from Sapieha to Chicherin, is printed in its original Polish in *Dokumenty i materiały do historii stosunków polsko-radzieckich*, vol. III, no. 106 (English version in Rumbold [Warsaw] to Curzon, 23 July 1920; *British Documents*, vol. XI, no. 344). The latter note, from the Polish to the Soviet high commands, is printed in its original French—first as *sent* by Warsaw, then as *received* by Moscow radio, in *Dokumenty i materiały . . . polsko-radzieckich*, vol. III, no. 107. There are important differences—the principal one being that as sent from Warsaw it requested a reply by 3 A.M. on 25 July, while as received in Moscow this became 3 A.M. on 30 July.

Polish government took a first step of compliance with the demands Lloyd George had made at Spa. Now, by the terms of the implicit contract, it was the turn of the Allies—particularly the British—to act. Help of a sort was already on its way in the form of the Anglo-French special mission, but there was no indication that anything more than advice and supplies would be sent, and only the former in quantity. For Sir Horace Rumbold, in a moment of cautious optimism on the day preceding the arrival of General Weygand and his British and French colleagues, these seemed perhaps sufficient, given the fact that the Poles had at last moved to open negotiations for peace. He felt, he telegraphed to Curzon on 24 July, that the Poles at last realized fully "that if they are saved from disaster they will owe their salvation to action of His Majesty's Government."[107] The following weeks would prove the irony of these words.

[107] Rumbold (Warsaw) to Curzon, telegram 573, 24 July; *ibid.*, no. 352.

CHAPTER V

KAMENEV'S NOTE

It has become . . . clear that the Soviet Government intend delaying the armistice negotiations indefinitely and it is highly probable that they mean to dictate terms in Warsaw which is well within their power to do.

— *General Percy de B. Radcliffe, Warsaw, 3 August 1920*[1]

Our mistake is that we are artificially delaying negotiations with the Poles instead of beginning them by putting forward armistice negotiations of such a nature that their fulfillment would require long enough time to enable us to occupy Lemberg, Mlava, and even Warsaw.

— *Maxim Litvinov, Copenhagen, 5 August 1920*[2]

THE Polish government might just as well have spared itself the agonies of reaching a decision to sue the Bolsheviks for peace. Its overtures to Moscow, when finally they came, were too late. Units of the Red Army had already crossed the line specified in Curzon's note to Chicherin a fortnight previously, and they showed no signs of halting in their pursuit of the retreating Poles. Their commander, Tukhachevsky, had solid military reasons for continuing the advance: the Poles would stand to gain far more from a breathing spell than would the Russians, especially as the stream of supplies from the West might thicken to a flood. More important, there was no disposition in Moscow to call a halt. Trotsky had argued for stopping at the Curzon line—roughly the ethnographic frontier of Poland—and there making a public offer of peace: a precipitate invasion, he thought, would only unite the Poles around Piłsudski in a fierce defense of their homeland. But Lenin disagreed. Here was a sudden, unexpected opportunity to carry the Revolution to

[1] Radcliffe to C.I.G.S., telegram 851, 3 August 1920; W.O. 33/966.
[2] Litvinov to Kamenev (London) and Chicherin (Moscow), telegram 303, 5 August 1920; intercept 003686, Davidson MSS.

the borders of Germany, and perhaps even across them. The Polish proletariat would welcome the Red Army as liberators. For Lenin this was unusually wishful thinking, made more so, perhaps, by the boisterous enthusiasm of the delegates to the Second Congress of the Communist International in Moscow in late July, who followed the army's progress on large display maps. Lenin's ardor was decisive: the Politburo rejected Trotsky's counsels of moderation. In the wake of Budenny's cavalry and Tukhachevsky's infantry as they swept across the Curzon line came a "provisional Polish revolutionary committee," cadres for a communist government—and forerunners of another group who made the same crossing a quarter of a century later.[3]

The Soviet decision to impose a communist government on Poland was, of course, unknown in the West. For Moscow it involved considerable risks: once the limits of "national" Poland had been crossed it was no longer so easy to play the innocent victim of aggression, the upholder of the principle of national self-determination, who wished only to be left in undisturbed peace. This was the role which had won so many adherents for non-intervention in Russia among groups, such as the British Labour Party, which abhorred Moscow's totalitarian methods. Thus the *New Statesman* could warn on 17 July 1920:

As we write there is a report that Moscow will refuse the British terms and will order the Red armies to march on Warsaw and establish there a communist government. We shall not believe that until we are forced; but if we are forced we shall certainly not oppose—and we hope that British Liberals and Labourists will not oppose—any measures which the British Government may decide to take in support of Poland.[4]

And a week later, in even stronger terms:

If the Soviet government decided to march on Warsaw in face of our protest, then we shall have no alternative but to break off the negotiations for a resumption of trade, reopen formal hostilities, and give the Poles all the assistance we can. . . . It is one thing to tolerate the maintenance of the tyranny which the Russian Bolsheviks have established in their own country; it would be quite another thing to tolerate an attempt to establish

---

[3] Carr, *Bolshevik Revolution*, vol. III, pp. 209-13; Deutscher, *Prophet Armed*, pp. 463-68; James W. Hulse, *The Forming of the Communist International*, Stanford, 1964, pp. 188-92.

[4] *New Statesman*, vol. XV, no. 379, 17 July 1920, p. 405.

a similar tyranny by force of arms in another land. In such a case our moral obligation to the Poles—however richly they may have deserved their fate—would be scarcely less clear than was our obligation to support the Belgians in 1914.[5]

These were blunt words. Yet in the weeks following their publication the *New Statesman*, along with nearly all of the rest of the Labour movement, was to take a very different line, advocating "direct action" to prevent the British government from aiding the Poles as they faced the Red Army at the gates of Warsaw. That it could do so was a tribute to the skill by which Soviet diplomacy succeeded in obscuring the issues, and in once again throwing the onus for continued warfare on Warsaw, not on Moscow.

This Soviet diplomatic effort took two forms. The first was to delay the actual commencement of negotiations with the Poles, and then, once they had begun, to prolong them as long as possible in the hope that while they were proceeding the Red Army could overrun Warsaw and, in effect, make negotiations irrelevant. Here the Russians were nearly successful. Through a series of "misunderstandings" about dates, place, credentials, receipt or lack of receipt of radio messages, and whether or not the negotiators were simply to arrange an armistice or to discuss preliminary terms of peace as well, the start of serious conversations was delayed until 17 August, at Minsk, when the Red Army had nearly reached the gates of Warsaw.[6] The second aspect of Moscow's diplomatic effort was an attempt to mislead the West, particularly the British government, regarding the seriousness of Soviet desires to come to terms with the Poles, and then, once negotiations had started, regarding the nature of the terms the Soviet government was prepared to offer. Here, too, the Russians were largely successful.

The measure of their success, moreover, was also a measure of the failure of the personal diplomacy of David Lloyd George. During late July and August 1920 the Prime Minister turned his diplomatic talents towards reaching an accommodation with the Bolsheviks, the French government, and the British Labour movement. In the

---

[5] *Ibid.*, no. 380, 24 July 1920, p. 436.

[6] For these delays and evasions, see Wandycz, *Soviet-Polish Relations*, pp. 223-24, 232-35; Komarnicki, *Polish Republic*, pp. 644-50; also Prince Sapieha's note to Rumbold (Warsaw), 6 August 1920, *British Documents*, vol. XI, no. 448, and Rumbold's despatch 514 to Curzon, 8 August, *ibid.*, no. 405. For an example, see above, chap. IV, n. 106.

interests of bringing clarity to these tangled events, this chapter and the one that follows will examine each of these relationships.

❖

"Letters," Lloyd George told a group of cronies after one of the many international conferences of the summer of 1920, "are the very devil." He was speaking of diplomatic notes between governments, and he continued: "If you want to settle a thing, you see your opponent and talk it over with him. The last thing you do is write him a letter."[7] There had been many a "letter" between the British and the Soviet governments in the few weeks following Krasin's departure on 1 July. Now, at the end of that month, the Soviet Commissar for Foreign Trade was returning, his return made possible by a conciliatory telegram from Chicherin on the 23rd asserting that the Soviet government would, after all, agree to participate in a London conference and stating that Moscow had issued orders to the Red Army's high command to meet Polish representatives for the beginning of talks relating to an armistice and peace.[8] Although the telegram went on to demand that before any conference could take place Wrangel must have surrendered, Lloyd George was not troubled—the British government, after all, had washed its hands of Wrangel—and he regarded it as a welcome change from the bitter, sarcastic note of the 17th which had been the initial Soviet response to Britain's effort to draw a line between the Russian and Polish forces. The Prime Minister received this latest message just as he was leaving his country home for a game of golf. Riddell, his golf partner, records his reaction: "L.G. was in a high state of glee. When we arrived at the golf club he sat down in the dressing-room and wrote out a message to his secretary in Downing Street, instructing him what documents to issue to the Press. A very precise little document." And on the following day Riddell noted in his diary: "L.G. told me that the Bolsheviks had agreed to attend a conference in London. He said, 'This is a great occasion. The Russians wish the leading Allies to attend, and, if necessary, the small nations whose territories abut on Russia, so that a generous discussion on peace may take place. I am very pleased.'"[9]

[7] Riddell, *Diary*, p. 206, entry for 21 June 1920.
[8] The text, sent by radio from Moscow, is in *Dokumenty vneshnei politiki*, vol. III, pp. 61-62. It was received on 24 July 1920, read to the House of Commons on the 26th (132 *H.C. Deb.*, cols. 974-75), and printed in *The Times* on the 27th.
[9] Riddell, *Diary*, pp. 225-26, entries for 24 and 25 July 1920.

There is no wonder that Lloyd George was pleased. Ever since the end of 1918 he had felt that the most effective way to make peace between the Allies and the Bolshevik regime was by means of a general conference. His proposal as it developed in the summer of 1920 bore a strong resemblance to the Prinkipo idea of eighteen months before. Then, it will be remembered, Lloyd George and Wilson hoped to convene a conference of all of the warring parties to the Russian civil war. Its principal purpose would have been to bring peace to Russia. But an important by-product, so far as Lloyd George was concerned, would have been to bring together the Bolsheviks and representatives of the Great Powers to resolve the questions outstanding between them. Now, in 1920, the Prime Minister had proposed at Spa in July that there should gather at London a conference not of warring Russian factions—the outcome of the civil war (even with Wrangel still in the field) had effectively been decided—but of representatives of Soviet Russia and of all the states on her western borders. Yet here again the purpose of such a conference, in Lloyd George's eyes, quickly grew.

It grew despite the rebuff Chicherin administered in his note of 17 July replying to the invitation from Spa. The Soviet government was already in the process of bilaterally negotiating peace with its neighbors, Chicherin had said; since Moscow intended to negotiate bilaterally with the Poles as well, there would be no need for an Eastern European conference.[10] The British government's response to this rebuff had been to say that they had proposed such a conference "because they thought it would bring Russia into relations with the Peace Conference"[11]—not at all the same thing as a mere gathering of Eastern Europeans. Here was an idea from which Moscow stood to gain much more. Given the extent of Russia's power in comparison with that of her neighbors, it was clearly to Soviet advantage to negotiate bilaterally with the border states. But if an Eastern European conference could be converted into a means of bringing about a settlement between the Bolsheviks and the Allies, its advantages would far outweigh its drawbacks. So Chicherin's telegram of 23 July, the one which so much pleased Lloyd George, stated that the Soviet government was "willing to meet the desire of the British Government to convene a Conference with the pur-

[10] Chicherin's note is cited above, chap. IV, n. 73.
[11] The British note of 20 July 1920 is cited above, chap. IV, n. 83.

pose of establishing a definite agreement between Russia and the Powers which participate in hostile actions against her or support such, and is of the belief that the said Conference should be composed of representatives of Russia and of the leading Powers of the Entente."[12]

The British government, of course, had never *publicly* expressed a desire for a conference of general settlement with the Bolsheviks. That such a conference now came into the range of distinct possibilities was, perhaps, an important accomplishment of Soviet diplomacy. But it also well suited the purposes of David Lloyd George. "After all," he was later to tell the Soviet mission in London, "it was only a point of procedure, of getting a conference of the Powers round the same table. That was the thing that matters—was to get them meeting for the first time round the same table."[13]

To get them meeting, however, required more than agreement on the part of the British and the Russians. French hostility had been the principal factor responsible for the failure of the Prinkipo proposal. Now, a year and a half later, the government of Alexandre Millerand was scarcely more receptive to a meeting between the Allies and the Bolsheviks than the government of Clemenceau had been. Yet the French were anxious enough for British support—or acquiescence—in their efforts to extract reparations payments from the Germans so as to temper their opposition to Lloyd George's moves toward Moscow. Thus at Spa Millerand had not objected to the British proposals for an Eastern European conference in London; French presence at such a conference would not have been required —or expected. But it would obviously be necessary at the sort of gathering which began to take shape in the Anglo-Soviet note exchanges. Lloyd George therefore set himself the task of converting Millerand's acquiescence to one type of conference into agreement actually to participate in a conference of a very different type.

To do so the Prime Minister, with Curzon, crossed the Channel to Boulogne, where they met Millerand for talks lasting the afternoon of 27 July. The task was not easy. The two premiers did not get on well together, and Millerand's dislike and distrust of Lloyd George had recently been heightened by what he considered to have

---

[12] Chicherin's telegram is cited above, n. 8.
[13] From "Draft Notes of a Conference held at 10, Downing Street, on Friday, August 6, 1920, at 3:30 P.M.," *British Documents*, vol. VIII, no. 82, p. 695.

been an insult at Spa.[14] The Boulogne meeting came at Lloyd George's request. Immediately upon his arrival he proceeded to put the British case for a conference with the Bolsheviks. Although it still was not clear whether or not the Red Army had crossed the line laid down in Curzon's note of 11 July, the military news was generally so bad that the British government had felt, the Prime Minister said, "that something should be telegraphed at once which would be an inducement to the Soviets to offer fairly good terms to Poland." This "something" was confirmation of the British government's willingness to participate in the sort of conference to which Chicherin referred in his message of 23 July. Such a message, indeed, had been sent to Moscow on the 26th, the day before Lloyd George's trip to Boulogne.[15]

The Prime Minister emphasized to Millerand that he had been acting in the name of a united Cabinet. Usually when Russian questions were discussed, he said, two or three different views were expressed. But now the Cabinet was unanimous that the Allies must either fight or make peace; since "neither Britain nor France would stand any more fighting" the first alternative was ruled out, leaving only the second. The previous week he had told the House of Commons that if Poland were invaded Britain would in the last resort be prepared to fight; his statement had been received with uneasiness even among the Conservatives, Lloyd George said, and it had aroused the apprehensions of the public, who felt that "the Poles had made a mess of it, and had only themselves to blame." Although he might succeed in getting the House to agree to send munitions to Poland, and perhaps a little money, that would be all. Even

---

[14] The incident occurred on 12 July. Millerand was eager to return to Paris to review the Bastille Day parade on the 14th, and even threatened to break off negotiations with the Germans if a conclusion were not reached by then. Lloyd George tried to dissuade him, saying that he would have to tell Parliament "that all was going well, but that the 14th July had spoilt everything." The Prime Minister begged Millerand "to find some presentable gentleman to take his place in the sun. He would thereby save a headache for himself and perhaps, if his choice were discreet, rid himself of an undesirable colleague!" ("British Secretary's Notes of an Inter-Allied Conference . . . July 12, 1920, at 10:30 A.M.," *ibid.*, no. 64, pp. 564-65 and 568.) Millerand told a close friend (who told Riddell) that he felt that Lloyd George had publicly made fun of him, and that he had mistrusted Lloyd George ever since. (Riddell, *Diary*, p. 243, entry for 26 October 1920.)

[15] "British Secretary's Draft Notes of a Conference between M. Millerand and Mr. Lloyd George . . . ," Boulogne, 27 July 1920, 12 noon; *British Documents*, vol. VIII, no. 79, pp. 650-61. All subsequent quotations are from these minutes. The British telegram to Chicherin of 26 July is printed as Appendix 1, p. 662.

Winston Churchill concurred in this judgment, which had been unanimous in the Cabinet.[16]

If the Bolsheviks nevertheless insisted on imposing "impossible" terms on Poland, Lloyd George continued, the British and French governments would have to face the situation and make the best of it. But the general feeling in Great Britain was that the Bolsheviks could not be quashed by force of arms. When Chicherin's telegram was read to the House of Commons, there had been universal relief at the opportunity it seemed to present to make peace. However, the Cabinet was extremely anxious that France should participate in the proposed London conference. The Italians, and probably the Japanese, would also be invited, but "the most important thing was that France and Great Britain should take common action." The Prime Minister concluded by citing two inducements to Millerand: first, joint action would strengthen Poland if the Soviet terms were excessively severe; second, when it came to holding out for Soviet payment of the pre-war Russian debts, it would be greatly to their common advantage if the French as well as the British took part in the negotiations.

Lloyd George did not explain just what "joint action" he had in mind which could possibly strengthen the Poles, but he had already excluded from the range of possibilities any other than material and financial support. Millerand, of course, also hoped for "joint action" of the British and the French governments, but action of a very different sort. Just as direct negotiations between the Allies and the Bolsheviks had long been one of Lloyd George's aims, so French policy had striven to avoid them. Thus, in the eyes of the French the Anglo-Soviet correspondence regarding a conference was just one more unilateral British move whose effect, if not its purpose, would be further to undermine the Entente. Millerand therefore laid down a series of conditions which, he said, would have to be met before France would participate in a conference with the Bolsheviks. Three were important. First, the Polish question must be discussed and Polish representatives must be present; if the Russians insisted on conducting direct negotiations between themselves

---

[16] Presumably, Lloyd George was referring to the Cabinet's meeting of 20 July 1920 (cited above, chap. IV, n. 82) and a "Conference of Ministers" the day preceding his talk with Millerand (26 July, 11:30 A.M., minutes as Appendix IV to Cabinet 51 (20); Cab. 23/22).

and the Poles, the conference would serve no immediate purpose. Second, the Soviet government must acknowledge its responsibility for the financial obligations of previous Russian governments. And third, it "must agree to set up a popular Constitution for the people of Russia." (Pressed by Lloyd George to explain what he meant, Millerand said that he "envisaged a Constituent Assembly popularly elected.")

Millerand was not a skillful negotiator—much less skillful, Lloyd George must surely have reflected, than were the representatives of the Soviet regime. The latter two of Millerand's three conditions were obviously put forward in order to give France grounds not to participate, but they were so clearly certain to be rejected by Moscow that Lloyd George could easily separate them from the first—Polish participation—to which he heartily agreed. Then he was able to imply that if the French were truly interested in saving Poland, and not simply in preserving their own purity in an imperfect world, they would participate in a conference whose first business would be the settlement of the Polish-Soviet war. Afterward, "when the Polish question had been disposed of," the French could decide whether or not to stay on. "But the first thing was to get France to come to the conference in order to save Poland." To this proposal Millerand could only grudgingly agree, "out of deference to the British Government, and on account of France's interest on Poland's behalf." Thus, once again Lloyd George was able to secure the stated agreement of the French government to a Russian policy with which it was wholly out of sympathy. We shall shortly have cause to examine the utility of such "agreement."

Since French assent had been obtained only on condition that Poland should be the subject of discussion, Lloyd George now turned to securing Soviet compliance. Even before going to Boulogne he had issued orders for the British destroyer waiting at Reval to bring immediately to the United Kingdom the "enlarged delegation" of which Chicherin had spoken in his telegram of 17 July. Previously Lloyd George had refused to allow Krasin and his colleagues to return, holding (in the words of Curzon's note to Chicherin of the 20th) that trade negotiations could not usefully be pursued if the Red Army invaded Poland, and that the Soviet delegation should not come to London until an armistice had been reached. As we have seen, Chicherin's conciliatory telegram of the

23rd caused the Prime Minister to change his mind. The British reply on the 26th (the telegram which so displeased Millerand) had urged that the embarking Russian delegates "should be authorized by the Soviet Government not merely to conclude the trade agreement between Russia and the Allied Governments [*sic*], but also to discuss preliminary arrangements for the proposed peace conference, because communications by cable will involve delay and possible misunderstanding."[17] Here was Lloyd George's dislike of "letters."

Krasin was accompanied on his trip back to England by Lev Borisovich Kamenev, the president of the Moscow Soviet and the head of the Moscow Communist Party organization. He was the principal "enlargement" to the Russian delegation which had been agreed upon between the Soviet and British governments. His presence, however, signified much more than simply the addition of another negotiator. Unlike Krasin—or, for that matter, Litvinov—Kamenev was a member of the highest councils of the Communist Party, the Central Committee and its guiding Politburo. As such he was close to Lenin. And as such he had participated in the Politburo's decision to carry the war against Poland through to the sovietization of the country.[18] According to the letter of credentials which he addressed to Curzon on 3 August, he was chairman (with Krasin now vice-chairman) of "a special peace delegation" which the Soviet Government had appointed in order "to enter into negotiations with the British Government and also with the Governments of its Allies for the complete restoration of peaceful relations between the above-mentioned countries and to sign to this effect a peace treaty as well as any other political and economic agreement."[19]

The visit was Kamenev's second diplomatic mission to the West.

---

[17] The British telegram of 26 July is cited above, n. 15.

[18] Whether or not Kamenev should go to London was a subject of controversy within the Soviet government. Chicherin and Kamenev both strongly favored it, presumably because they lacked confidence in Krasin's ability to conduct political negotiations. Lenin at first strongly opposed Kamenev's going—the negotiations, he wrote in a note to Chicherin and Kamenev on 10 July, concerned "*only* trade"; they should therefore send "*only* 'merchants.'" A day later, however, he changed his mind (we do not know why) and agreed that Kamenev should take charge of the mission, with Krasin as his deputy. (Lenin, *Polnoe sobranie sochinenii*, 5th ed., vol. 51, no. 419, and n. 268, p. 438. Italics in original.)

[19] Kamenev's "letter of credentials" is printed in *British Documents*, vol. VIII, p. 669.

Two and one-half years previously, at the end of February 1918, he had come to Great Britain on his way to establishing himself as Soviet Plenipotentiary in France. On his landing in Aberdeen, as readers of the first volume of this work will remember, police searched him and stripped him of most of his possessions, including his diplomatic bag and a check for £5,000. Allowed to proceed to London, he found when he arrived that the French government had revoked its previously given permission for him to enter France. Thereupon he was interrogated by British officials and told to leave the United Kingdom without delay.[20] His 1920 mission was to be of longer duration, but of similar outcome.

Kamenev (born Rozenfeld) was thirty-seven years old in 1920. Of those who met him on his visits to England, Beatrice Webb has left the most complete description. In early September 1920, when he came with Krasin to a session of the Fabian Summer School, she noted in her diary:

Kameneff, a short, thick-set man with blunt features and a shifty eye, has changed considerably in appearance and manner since the evening, three years ago, when he was brought to Grosvenor Road by Litvinoff to complain of the insulting behaviour of Scotland Yard in its seizure of his "diplomatic valise" and to threaten us with reprisals on the English in Petrograd. He has grown stouter and far more self-important. Instead of the disagreeable combination of whines and threats of three years ago, he has developed the self-assured manner and easy address of one accustomed to exercise power over masses of men; moreover, it was clear from his private talk and clever speech that he had trained himself in the arts of diplomacy as these arts would be conceived by a common but shrewd journalist. Without intellectual distinction, moral refinement or personal charm, he is still a somewhat unpleasant personage.[21]

We have already had occasion to note Mrs. Webb's fascination with Krasin; perhaps Kamenev lacked the charm of his colleague (by comparison most men did), but Mrs. Webb's description nevertheless seems to have been hard on him. Others have been more generous. According to E. H. Carr, there is general agreement that Kamenev was "a highly intelligent and cultivated man of amiable manners." Amiability, indeed, was a weakness as well as a strength: he was a moderate, a conciliator, a man for whom compromise came

[20] See Volume I, p. 81.
[21] Cole, *Beatrice Webb's Diaries*, p. 191, entry for 4 September 1920.

easily, one who distrusted dogma and who was always ready to hear, and perhaps heed, the opinions of others.[22] Like many of his colleagues, he had lived in exile abroad. Indeed, as he wryly told Lloyd George, while in Paris he had once even been a pupil of Millerand.[23] By nearly as great a margin as Krasin did Kamenev fail to fit the contemporary Western stereotype of the "Bolshevik revolutionary." Like Krasin, he was a formidable negotiating opponent for the British Prime Minister.

At Lloyd George's request, the two Soviet emissaries came to 10 Downing Street on the afternoon of 4 August, almost immediately after their arrival in London. They were accompanied by Klishko; the Prime Minister was joined by Bonar Law, E. F. Wise, Philip Kerr, and Sir Maurice Hankey, Secretary to the Cabinet, who himself had just returned from service with the D'Abernon mission in Warsaw. During the week which separated this meeting and that of the two premiers at Boulogne, the Red Army had given incontrovertible evidence that it was not disposed to stop on the line laid down at Spa. On 30 July Lord D'Abernon telegraphed from Warsaw that Soviet troops were advancing deep within "what is unquestionably ethnographical Poland."[24] Neither had the Russians shown any serious interest in negotiating with the Poles. The Polish delegates who met with Soviet representatives at the isolated town of Baranowicze (now, in the U.S.S.R., Baranovichi) on the 30th, as had been arranged, were sent back to Warsaw after three days of fruitless discussions and told to appear at Minsk on 4 August and to bring with them authority to negotiate not only an armistice, but preliminary terms of peace as well.[25] To Lloyd George these events were bitterly disappointing, for they undermined his whole position. If the Soviet government really did intend to negotiate peace terms with the Poles at Minsk, he told Kamenev and Krasin, there

---

[22] See Carr's sharply drawn sketch of Kamenev in *Socialism in One Country 1924-26*, vol. I, London, 1958, pp. 158-62. The quotation here is from pp. 161-62.

[23] In their conversation of 6 August 1920, cited below, n. 41.

[24] In Rumbold (Warsaw) to Curzon, telegram 615, 30 July 1920; *British Documents*, vol. XI, no. 371.

[25] For these events see Rumbold (Warsaw) to Curzon, despatch 514, 8 August 1920; *ibid.*, no. 405. The Polish version is given in a note from Prince Sapieha, the minister of foreign affairs, to Rumbold on 6 August; *ibid.*, no. 448. For the Soviet version see Kamenev's letter of 5 August to Lloyd George, printed in *The Times*, 7 August (Russian text in *Dokumenty vneshnei politiki*, vol. III, pp. 83-86). This in turn drew a reply from the Polish Chargé d'Affaires in London on 6 August (*The Times*, 7 August).

could be no London conference, for the French would not partic-ipate unless Poland were discussed. Even more important, however, the invasion of Poland and the treatment of the Polish negotiators seemed to demonstrate that the Soviet government's loudly expressed anxiety for peace was "utterly false," and that they had only been trifling with the British government in order to gain time to enter Warsaw and establish a communist regime. The fact that the Red Army was continuing its invasion despite the Polish appeal for an armistice, Lloyd George said, ended the existing understanding between the British and Soviet governments, and freed the British for any action they wished. Accordingly, they would once again take steps to supply arms to the Poles. That morning he had issued orders for British naval units to go to the Baltic in order to reimpose the blockade on Russia; it would take three days to ready the fleet, but unless an armistice were signed within that time the ships would sail.[26]

Kamenev's reply to these allegations, as recorded in the British minutes, sounds highly disingenuous. The Soviet government could not risk stopping its offensive until it could exact "military guar-antees" against future Polish attack. The conclusion of an armistice did not, therefore, simply mean drawing a line between the op-posing armies, nor could it be confined to purely military questions: it would have to include such measures on the part of the Poles as partial demobilization, an end to recruitment and munitions manu-facture, and limitations on supplies for the front. Negotiations for an armistice had been held up because the Polish delegates had no powers to deal with these questions. Nevertheless, Kamenev added, "if the necessity of obtaining these guarantees delayed the armistice, and the Soviet armies were unable to stop their advance because of this, it did not mean that Soviet Russia was in any way attacking the independence of Poland."[27]

[26] For this interview see "Draft Notes of a Conference held at 10, Downing Street, S.W., on Wednesday, August 4, 1920, at 4:15 P.M.," *British Documents*, vol. VIII, no. 81, pp. 670-80.

[27] That the British minutes of this meeting do not unduly compress Kamenev's words, and thus make them appear too disingenuous, is seen in the fact that he gave a similar assurance to Lloyd George in his letter of 5 August (cited above, n. 25). The Soviet advance, he said, was "purely a military operation," and "does not in the least prejudge the nature of the peace treaty, and does not constitute an attempt against the independence and integrity of the Polish State in its ethnographical frontiers. The Russian Soviet Government have more than once pledged themselves fully to respect the independence of Poland and the right of her people to political

The meeting was a curious one; it scarcely should have increased Lloyd George's predilection for personal diplomacy rather than "letters." Throughout its ninety inconclusive minutes the Prime Minister continued to assert that the Soviet advance left his government no choice but to honor its obligations to the Poles, and the Russians continued to insist that their side had been acting in good faith, with no intent to delay or deceive. In the end Kamenev promised to learn from Moscow exactly what terms the Soviet government had in store for the Poles.[28] Lloyd George, for his part, promised to delay for the time being any public announcement of the forthcoming British measures, such as ordering out the Baltic fleet, in order not to give the Poles new grounds for optimism and therefore for refusing to accept satisfactory Soviet terms. True to his word, the Prime Minister went before the House of Commons on the following afternoon to declare just how grave a view the government took of the Soviet invasion of Poland, but he said almost nothing about possible British measures. The situation was so critical, he said, that he would say nothing more until the following Monday (it was then Thursday); in the interval, he would again see both the Russians and Millerand.[29] In fact, Lloyd George seems to have expected the worst. In a talk with the American Ambassador after his statement in the House, he admitted that he felt that the Red Army would push on to Warsaw without delay and there install a communist government.[30]

❖

Lloyd George's gloomy prediction of Soviet success coincided with—and probably owed much to—the views with which Sir Maurice Hankey had just returned after four days in Warsaw. Hankey had returned in order to report to the Cabinet. As its long-time Secretary he carried enormous and well-merited prestige, and

---

self-determination, and the intended terms of armistice and peace in no way include any restriction of the Polish people in this respect."

[28] See Kamenev's telegram sent following this meeting to Chicherin, with instructions that it should be given urgently to Lenin, *Dokumenty vneshnei politiki*, vol. III, p. 81. Although Kamenev described Lloyd George's threats, he did not explicitly ask his government about armistice terms.

[29] 132 *H.C. Deb.*, col. 2629.

[30] Davis (London) to Secretary of State, telegram 1184, 6 August 1920, 5 P.M.; U.S. National Archives, State Department file 760c.61/143. Also Davis' telegram 1177, 5 August, 2 P.M., State Department file 661.4116/78.

in addition he was a personal confidant of the Prime Minister. Regarding the Polish crisis his advice was not novel—it reinforced, rather than contradicted, what Lord D'Abernon and Sir Horace Rumbold were telegraphing from Warsaw—but it was important because Hankey himself was a participant at the very heart of the policy-making process. And as an eyewitness of the situation in Poland, he could speak within the councils of the government with irrefutable authority. This was particularly the case because the essence of his advice—that Great Britain should make no military commitment to the Poles and, indeed, should look ahead to the problems for British foreign policy that would be posed by a communist Poland—clearly fit well with the Prime Minister's predilections.

Hankey was scarcely an unbiased observer, however. On the day of his departure for Poland, 20 July, he entered in his diary that he had vainly protested to Lloyd George against sending him "on this ridiculous and vague mission." The Prime Minister knew, he wrote, "that I have both a dislike and contempt for the Poles, and that I don't believe, in the long run, anything can be done to save them, and finally that I am doubtful if they are worth saving." On his return journey to London from Warsaw, Hankey wrote a long report on his mission.[31] Its essence was encapsulated in the following summary paragraph:

> Having regard to the shattered condition of the Polish Army, due to the ceaseless retreat over more than 200 miles, the state of its armament, the weakness of the High Military Command, Staff, and Administration, the vain and feckless character of the nation, the weakness due to the three nationalities of which the Polish race consists, the detestation of Poland by all its neighbours, and the precarious nature of its communications with the outside world, I do not think it is possible for the Allies, in the time available, to place Poland in a condition to resist for long a continued attack by the Bolshevists.

Given this conclusion, he continued, the best that could be hoped for would be that the "final crash" would somehow be postponed "until other forms of influence can be brought to bear on the Bolshevists." Principal among these would be "a refusal of trading relations with

---

[31] "Personal Report by Sir Maurice Hankey on his visit to Warsaw, July 1920," 3 August 1920; Cabinet paper C.P. 1724; Cab. 24/110. Its introductory "summary of conclusions" is printed in British Documents, vol. XI, no. 381, pp. 429-34. See Roskill, *Hankey*, vol. II, p. 181.

Soviet Russia"; such a lever would be "far more powerful than any military assistance which the Allies can give to Poland."

Hankey nevertheless went on to make a series of recommendations for British policy in the event that diplomatic leverage were to prove insufficient to secure Poland's independence, and the Allies were to decide to support the Poles in continuing the war in the hope of securing better terms from Moscow. In particular, he advised that no British troops should be sent to Poland, and that for the present —until the Polish Higher Military Command showed some signs of capacity—no officers should be sent either. "I would not," Hankey wrote, "take the responsibility of exposing the lives of British officers in the present chaos of confusion and incapacity." Instead, the Poles should make maximum use of the 600 officers of the French Military Mission already on the spot. British active support should be confined to controlling the port of Danzig in order to make sure that there were no stoppages in the flow of material assistance to the Poles.[32] Not only should the British government limit its own assistance, Hankey continued, but it should also be wary of seeking the cooperation of other more vulnerable nations, such as Lithuania, Finland, and Rumania—as the French and, of course, the Poles wanted to do. Their aid should not be sought without careful investigation of their actual military capacity, and unless it were made certain that their own needs of military assistance and of war materials of all kinds could be met. Hankey wrote: "It would be criminal to engulf these States unless there is a reasonable prospect of a good result."

Hankey's own view, of course, was that such a prospect was very slight. "If Soviet Russia persists in the offensive our efforts to save Poland will probably fail," he reiterated at the close of his statement. He then proceeded to sketch out the consequences of such a failure: "The Russian boundary will then march with that of Germany, who is anxiously watching the situation. An understanding between the two countries will ensue. Germany will seek to obtain Upper Silesia, the corridor, Danzig, and the wheat of the Ukraine, estimated at 10 million tons. Russia will obtain locomotives and rolling-stock, agricultural implements, and in course of time, other manufactures worked up from her own raw materials." Until this point, Hankey's projection sounded like many others, especially those made during

---

[32] For the situation at Danzig, see below, chap. VI.

the War, of the dangers of a Russo-German combination.[33] But his prescriptions for British policy were radically different. Should these predicted events occur, he wrote, the French would undoubtedly want the British to join them in occupying the Ruhr in order to deprive Germany of the power to re-arm. Such a step, however, would serve only to cement the two outcast Powers more tightly; it would be a drastic mistake. Instead, Hankey proposed an alternative vision of the future:

> It is suggested that a more far-sighted policy would be to recognise that Poland has by her own folly precipitated a fate that could only have been avoided by the display of greater wisdom on her part; while doing what we can to secure tolerable conditions for Poland to *cultivate good relations with Germany; and to use Germany as the bridge by which in the course of years British capital may be introduced to Russia and normal relations may be restored.* We should trust for the moment to exhaustion and later to the innate dislike between Germany and Russia, and to the gradual improvement of our relations with both parties to avoid a military alliance against us. In the meantime, as soon as our obligations of honour are fulfilled, *we should pull out of all military responsibilities in Poland and leave Central and East Europe to work out its own fate without our intervention.* For our own future we should depend as in the past mainly on our overseas connections.[34]

Hankey's advice that the British government should improve its relations with *both* Germany and Soviet Russia came during what inevitably was a period of intense speculation, in all the capitals of Europe, regarding the role that Germany might play in the approaching crisis of the Polish-Soviet campaign. The German government itself on 20 July declared its absolute neutrality, and issued decrees forbidding the transit across Germany of supplies for either of the contending armies.[35] Within Germany it was generally

---

[33] See Volume I, pp. 24, 169, 305, and Volume II, pp. 54-55, 222-23, 248-50, 300, 345.

[34] Italics added.

[35] See Günter Rosenfeld, *Sowjetrussland und Deutschland 1917-1922*, Berlin, 1960, p. 281. At this time both Soviet and German leaders employed the image of Poland as a bridge between Russia and Germany—but with different implications. On 24 July Trotsky told an audience of railwaymen that Poland would shortly cease to be a defensive barrier against Russia, and would instead become "a Red Bridge of social revolution for the whole of Western Europe." (*The Times*, 26 July 1920.) Two days later the German minister for foreign affairs, Simons, told the Reichstag: "I believe that Poland must look forward to a very troubled future if she aims at acting as a barrier between Russia and Germany. She should rather

agreed that this was the only safe course of action. Cooperation
with the Russians might succeed in revising the Treaty of Versailles by, in effect, repartitioning Poland, but such a policy would
bring Bolshevism to Germany's eastern frontiers while at the same
time exposing her in the west to the likelihood of French retaliation
in the form of occupation of the Ruhr. On the other hand, there
were few Germans who could easily contemplate assisting the hated
Poles.

To some Germans, however, "assisting" the Poles (in fact, taking
over the Polish war effort) presented great opportunities. Field
Marshal Erich von Ludendorff, the wartime master of the German
military machine, and Major General Max Hoffmann, who had
commanded German forces on the Eastern Front at the time of
Brest-Litovsk, approached British officers on the inter-Allied control commission in Berlin and proposed that, in view of the dangers
which the spread of Bolshevism had for all Europe, Germany should
be allowed to raise an army under Ludendorff's command to invade Russia. In exchange for these services, Germany would revert
to her old territorial boundaries in the East, and would participate
equally with Britain and France in the economic "reconstruction"
of Russia. Ludendorff felt that he would have an ally in Winston
Churchill; he even sent word that he wanted Churchill to come to
Germany *incognito* to discuss these proposals with him.[36]

Within the Foreign Office, where there was acute awareness both
of the degree to which the Anglo-French *Entente* had already
been strained and of how much greater the rift would become if
the British government were to give any encouragement to German
revisionist ambitions, schemes such as Ludendorff's were given scarcely even cursory consideration.[37] The German marshal was correct,

---

aim at acting as a bridge between these two countries." (A translation of Simons'
speech was sent to Curzon as despatch 621 from Kilmarnock in Berlin 27 July;
British Documents, vol. X, no. 186.)

[36] Reports of interviews with Ludendorff and Hoffmann by Lt. Col. W. Stewart
Roddie of the British mission in Berlin were circulated to the Cabinet by Churchill
on 9 March 1920 as Cabinet paper C.P. 831; Cab. 24/100. For later contacts see
Kilmarnock (Berlin) to Curzon, telegram 439, 24 July 1920; *British Documents*,
vol. X, no. 183. For a discussion of Germany's possible use of the Polish-Soviet
conflict to regain its 1914 frontiers, see Christian Höltje, *Die Weimarer Republik
und das Ostlocarno-Problem, 1919-1934*, Wurzberg, 1958, pp. 26-30, and Carroll,
Western Opinion, pp. 148-52.

[37] See Hardinge's minute on Kilmarnock's telegram of 24 July, cited above, n. 36.

however, in sensing a kindred spirit in Churchill. On 28 July, in a signed article in *The Evening News*, Churchill publicly proclaimed that the Allies might well have to call upon the Germans for assistance against the Bolsheviks. Should Poland collapse, he argued, and Russia and Germany be brought into direct contact, "it is necessary to realise that an awful, yet in some ways wonderful, choice will be presented to Germany." Churchill went on to define the choice. Despite their defeat in the War, he wrote, the German people would nevertheless "have it in their hands either to renew and redouble the miseries of Europe, or to render a service to civilisation of the very highest order . . . either to sink their own civilisation in the general Bolshevist welter and spread the reign of chaos far and wide throughout the Continent; or on the other hand, by a supreme effort of sobriety, of firmness, of self-restraint and courage . . . to build a dyke of peaceful, lawful, patient strength and virtue against the flood of red barbarism flowing from the East, and thus safeguard her own interests and the interests of her principal antagonists in the West." And he concluded: "If the Germans were able to render such a service, not by reckless military adventure or with ulterior motives, they would unquestionably have taken a giant step upon the path of self-redemption which would lead them surely and swiftly as the years pass by to their own great place in the councils of Christendom, and would have rendered easier the sincere co-operation between Britain, France and Germany on which the very salvation of Europe depends."

Churchill's article was scarcely explicit in its recommendations for action. But certainly his image of "a dyke of peaceful, lawful, patient strength" cannot easily be read to imply the anti-Bolshevik crusade for which Ludendorff, and Churchill himself only a year previously, had appealed. On 6 August, nine days after Churchill's *Evening News* article, the General Staff produced a paper, "The German Situation from a Military Aspect,"[38] undoubtedly influenced by the views of the Secretary of State. Existing Allied policy, the memorandum stated, left Germany with only two possibilities: either "to continue in her present state of subjection to the Entente, under the iron heel of French militarism" (a parenthetical note added, "Whether she has deserved this fate or not does not enter into the problem") or "to ally herself with Bolshevik Russia, or Nation-

---

[38] Cabinet paper 1782, Cab. 24/4, circulated by Churchill on 16 August 1920.

alist Russia, as the case may be, and to break the Versailles Treaty by force of arms." Of these alternatives, the second would surely prove more attractive in the long run. As a third course of action, however, the memorandum proposed:

We should treat Germany, as long as she has a moderate Government like the present one, which moreover appears to be making an honest effort to carry out the Peace Treaty, as a Sovereign Great Power, though as a debtor to the Entente. We should abandon all idea of hatred and vengeance, and cease treating the German people as outcasts and pariahs. We should help her economically and, in fact, re-admit her to the European family of nations. We must leave her with sufficient armed strength to keep order in her own country, and to meet the Red danger, which has overthrown Poland and is threatening the world.

Although the authors of the General Staff memorandum could speak of a "Red danger . . . threatening the world" and could assume that its conquest of Poland was a foregone conclusion, nevertheless their policy recommendations corresponded with Churchill's notion of a dyke. "We should not deny to the Germans reasonable facilities for self defence, and should allow the German Government to call a temporary halt in its measures for disarmament," the paper stated. "On the other hand, there is no necessity for us to show undue alarm at the Red military menace, nor to constitute Germany as our barrier against Bolshevism, with a free hand as regards military measures."

The key to a peaceful Europe, the memorandum concluded, lay not so much in the East as in the West—in defusing the vindictive anti-German hostility of France and Belgium which drove Germans, in despair, to think of Eastern adventures or Eastern alliances. In turn, French and Belgian attitudes could be changed only by meeting the understandable concerns of those peoples for their security. And: "The only way to do this is for Great Britain to enter upon a defensive alliance or agreement with France and Belgium, with a view to assuring these countries of our support against German aggression." Thus not an alliance against Bolshevism with the Germany of Ludendorff, but a renewal of the *Entente* with France combined with a policy of lifting from Germany the more unjust and discriminatory burdens of Versailles, was the path to conciliation in Europe. "Great Britain cannot afford to be involved in a renewal of hostilities on the Continent of Europe; our commitments [elsewhere] are too great." Underlying this whole edifice, but never explicitly stated, was the assumption that although Soviet Russia might well succeed in imposing communism on Poland, it could not do so on a Germany which had a stake, and a role, in the West.

The General Staff's memorandum, of course, was much more detailed than Churchill's rather suggestive newspaper article in its statement of these arguments. It is only natural that there were many, in England and on the Continent, who chose to regard Churchill's article as a plea for a German campaign against Russia, and who regarded it—coming as it did from the Secretary of State for War and Air in Lloyd George's government—as a British *ballon d'essai*. Not surprisingly, reactions were almost universally hostile, not least of all from the German government, whose Foreign Minister told the British Chargé d'Affaires that Germany would not allow herself to be used as a "valet" to further the military ambitions of other nations.[39] In London, Lloyd George was clearly embarrassed —as he so often was—by his colleague's latest solution to the Russian problem. Replying to questions in the House of Commons on 2 August, the Prime Minister stated lamely that Churchill's article did "not bear the interpretation sought to be placed on it"; that he was not aware of anything in it which "cuts across any declaration of policy" by the government; and that he thought the article to be not "so much an expression of policy as of a hankering." When his questioners persisted, Lloyd George exploded: "I really cannot control my colleagues' desires," and added: "I am not aware of any rule that precludes a Cabinet Minister from contributing articles to newspapers, even to newspapers that are opposing His Majesty's Government."[40]

❖

Lloyd George's second meeting with Kamenev[41]—on Friday, 6 August, two days after their first encounter—was a tiring five-hour session which by dint of its length and repetitiveness perhaps served to steel the Prime Minister for an even more arduous two days of

[39] Kilmarnock (Berlin) to Curzon, telegram 462, 3 August 1920; *British Documents*, vol. X, no. 189.

[40] 132 *H.C. Deb.*, cols. 1995-97. British and French press reaction to Churchill's article was almost entirely hostile; for a good survey see Carroll, *Western Opinion*, pp. 154-56.

[41] "Draft Notes of a Conference held . . . August 6, 1920, at 3:30 P.M." *British Documents*, vol. VIII, no. 82, pp. 681-707.

talks with Millerand at Lympne the following Sunday and Monday. Although the participants could not know it, these were the final negotiations before the crisis in the Polish-Soviet war which culminated in the rout of the Red Army before Warsaw little more than a week later. Both sets of talks served only to underline the fact that despite the great victory Britain and France had won over the Germans, their postwar role in Eastern Europe would be essentially that of spectators.

There was no reason, in fact, why the meeting with the Soviet representatives on the 6th should even have taken place: Kamenev had not yet received a reply from Moscow to his request for information as to the precise terms the Soviet government would offer the Poles, and therefore he could only put forward the same general conditions he had outlined on the 4th. These were not peace terms, but Kamenev's own notion of the sort of military guarantees which would be necessary for an armistice *prior* to a peace conference: measures for partial disarmament and demobilization, cessation of Allied assistance both to the Poles and to Wrangel (who was still in the mainland positions seized by his June thrust out of the Crimea), and the establishment of control commissions within Poland to ensure the carrying out of these measures. Lloyd George responded with the assertion that although he could understand why the Russians, after being attacked by the Poles, might want such military guarantees, he doubted whether he could secure Millerand's agreement to them. But in any case, he said, they were unnecessary. Instead the Soviet government should be content with written pledges from the British and the French that they would take no steps to rebuild the battered Polish armed forces during an armistice: without such external support the Poles could scarcely be a serious threat. "To have on paper a guarantee for the demobilisation of the Polish army was not worth imperilling European peace for," Lloyd George said. "It was worth Soviet Russia demanding a guarantee that we should not use the interval to re-equip either Poland or Wrangel." He went on to request an "authoritative statement" on behalf of the Soviet government by Sunday morning, when he would meet Millerand at Lympne. He had no doubt, he said, that Soviet forces could destroy Poland if they wished. But then they would not have peace with the Western Powers, who were bound by the Covenant of the League of Nations to support Poland. Therefore, the Soviet government would have to choose between punishing the Poles—admittedly an attractive alternative, since in many respects perhaps they "deserved to be 'spanked'"—and "peace all round." The Russians would have to make this decision within forty-eight hours, after which time the British and French governments would have to make their own decisions.

Most important, Lloyd George continued, was that fighting in Poland should stop before public opinion—especially in France, but also in Britain—reacted so violently that a normalization of relations between Russia and the West became altogether impossible. "Unless there was a stoppage within the next forty-eight hours," he said, "the conference, trade, and everything else" would be out of the question.[42] Yet it was clearly impossible for the Soviet and Polish negotiators to arrange even an *armistice* within that short time. Therefore the Prime Minister called in Sir Henry Wilson, who laid down conditions for a *truce* under which the opposing armies would cease fire and stand on their present positions until an armistice could be negotiated.[43] For the Red Army, because of its extended lines of communication and superior military position, these were the only conditions required; neither the Poles nor the Allies, however, would be allowed to take any steps to build up the Polish side. These terms met with approval from Kamenev and Krasin, who promised to telegraph them immediately to Moscow. If the Soviet government accepted them, Lloyd George said, they would have no war with Great Britain, regardless of what the French thought. Meanwhile, however, units of the fleet were already under way for Copenhagen. If the Russians refused to make peace he would order the blockade reimposed. And he would also begin once again to send supplies to Wrangel, and to assist him with the British Black Sea fleet.

[42] At this session, as at the meeting with the Russians two days before, Lloyd George reiterated that France would not participate in the proposed London conference unless the question of the Polish-Soviet peace were discussed. However, on this occasion he added: "but once she is in she is willing to remain there to discuss all the rest"—a statement for which, on the basis of Millerand's past assertions, there was no justification (*British Documents*, vol. VIII, p. 691).

[43] The text of the truce proposal drawn up at this session and given to Kamenev for transmission to Moscow is printed as appendix 2 (pp. 707-08) to *ibid.*, no. 82. On account of Field Marshal Wilson's opinion that forty-eight hours was too short a period in which to arrange a truce, the note extended it a day, and set midnight on 9-10 August as the time the truce would take effect.

Lord Curzon (l.), Sir Robert Horne (center), and David Lloyd George (r.)
(photographed at the Cannes Conference, January 1922).

Trotsky (marked with "X") reviewing Soviet troops in Red Square. The banner (right) indicates that it is May Day. The year is not specified; probably it was 1921.

Polish soldiers marching in Warsaw, 1920.

Piłsudski conferring with one of his field commanders, General Edward Smigly-Rydz, 1920.

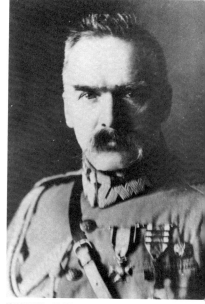

Józef Piłsudski, Marshal of Poland, Chief of State, 1920.

Polish soldiers guarding Soviet prisoners of war, 1920.

General Baron Pyotr N. Wrangel,
June 1920.

General Anton I. Denikin in his private
railroad car at Novorossiisk a few hours
before his army's evacuation to the
Crimea, March 1920.

Quayside scene during the evacuation
of Novorossiisk, March 1920.

Wrangel reviewing troops before his headquarters at Sebastopol, June 1920.

A shipload of Wrangel's troops fleeing Sebastopol for Constantinople, November 1920.

Krassin   Lloyd George   Bonar Law   Curzon
RUSSIAN JAZZ

Cartoon by David Low in the London *Star* on 31 May 1920, the day of the first meeting between Lloyd George and Krasin.

Leonid B. Krasin arriving at 10 Downing Street for his second meeting with Lloyd George, 7 June 1920. Paying off the taxi is, presumably, his principal assistant, N. K. Klishko.

Lev B. Kamenev (photographed in June 1922).

'inston S. Churchill (at Inverness, Septem-
r 1921).

Krasin outside the Board of Trade on the day
he signed the Anglo-Soviet trade agreement,
16 March 1921.

Reza Khan (later, Reza Shah Pahlevi) with his son, the present Shah of Iran.

Kamenev's Note

The preceding paragraphs give some notion of the outcome of the long discussion between Lloyd George and the Soviet representatives on that Friday afternoon in early August 1920, but they convey no sense of the tediousness (each side repeated its few points countless times, with only minor variations) or the atmosphere of unreality which are so striking to one who, half a century later, bothers to read through the many pages of minutes. Yet here they were trying to settle a conflict thousands of miles away on the basis of incomplete information and inadequate communications facilities, and with only one of the warring parties represented.[44] Thus Kamenev was able to tell Lloyd George nothing on Friday which he had not been able to tell him at their first meeting two days previously. Moreover, there was one fact which Kamenev could not disclose—that so far as it was in Moscow's power to effect it, the outcome of the Soviet-Polish conflict had already been decided: as we have seen, the Politburo had voted to press on to a complete victory and a Soviet Poland. To the extent that the Soviet regime's commitment to this decision was single-minded—and that is a question which we can scarcely answer[45]—the tedious negotiations in London were a gigantic deception.

The existence of this deception, and the degree to which responsibility for its perpetration was divided between Kamenev on the one hand and the Soviet government in Moscow on the other were later to become issues of considerable moment in Anglo-Soviet rela-

[44] Telegraphic communication between London and Moscow (by way of Reval) sometimes still required as much as several days; radio was faster but less certain. Radio was the only means of communication between Moscow and Warsaw. The failure of the Russians to receive Polish radio transmissions, or their garbling of Polish messages, was at the heart of one of the controversies between the two sides. The Russians blamed atmospheric conditions; the Poles alleged that the Russians were simply procrastinating in order not to reach an agreement which would halt their advance. (See the exchanges cited above, n. 25.) Communication between Moscow and the front was also poor. Lenin complained in a telegram to Kamenev on 14 August that there was an almost complete absence of news from Poland. (Letter, Lenin to Chicherin, enclosing telegram for Kamenev, 14 August 1920; *Leninskii sbornik*, vol. 36, Moscow, 1959, p. 119.)

[45] It is difficult to say to what extent there was hesitation within the Soviet government over whether or not the military subjugation of Poland should be carried to a conclusion. On 2 August Lenin telegraphed Stalin that there was a growing feeling within the Central Committee that peace should be made with Poland in order to free resources for coping with Wrangel. (Lenin, *Sochineniya*, 4th ed., vol. 31, p. 239.) For other evidence of lack of accord on this question see Korbel, *Poland between East and West*, pp. 51-54. Korbel concludes that Lenin, at least, did not waver in his determination.

tions, in the relationship between Lloyd George and the Soviet mission in London, and in the politics of the Coalition government. It should be noted here, therefore, that the intercepted telegraphic traffic makes clear that Kamenev was a witting party to it, as was Litvinov, who was still in Copenhagen. Yet each disagreed with Moscow regarding tactics. On 4 August, the day of his first meeting with Lloyd George, Kamenev telegraphed Chicherin, assuring him that he was "absolutely convinced of the necessity, without paying any attention to the distracted condition of England, of firmly carrying out the policy of the Central Committee," but recommending: "At the present moment a solemn manifesto is very desirable from the Central Executive Committee and the Soviet of People's Commissaries about the independence of Poland in wide ethnographic boundaries."[46] The purpose of this declaration, Kamenev would make clear in subsequent telegrams, was to deprive the British government of any pretext for intervention. Meanwhile, *within* the ethnographic boundaries of Poland, there would be established a communist government. The manifesto would buy for Moscow the necessary time.

Litvinov, more outspoken, more waspish than Kamenev, said as much in a message to Kamenev and Chicherin the following day. The Soviet government was erring, Litvinov complained, in thus far leaving to Lloyd George the initiative in stipulating armistice conditions. He explained:

Our mistake is, that we are artificially delaying negotiations with the Poles instead of beginning them by putting forward armistice conditions of such a nature that their fulfilment would require long enough to enable us to occupy Lemberg [Lwow], Mlava, and even Warsaw.

In particular the demand which I advised, that we should have the right to send out control missions to Danzig and the most important points on the Western frontier of Poland, would necessitate prolonged discussion with the Allies and would not be considered by anyone as an exaggerated demand. . . . I recommend that, without even waiting for the return of the Polish Delegation, you should announce our armistice conditions publicly and inform the British Government of them. I am glad that the suggestions given by our representatives in London coincide with those previously given by me. . . . It is extremely important to give evi-

---

[46] Kamenev (London) to Chicherin, unnumbered telegram, 4 August 1920; no intercept number given, Davidson MSS.

dence of our readiness for an armistice under certain conditions and for recognising the inviolability of the ethnographic boundaries. By delays we even put a weapon into the hands of our enemies.[47]

From London, on 6 August, the day of his second meeting with Lloyd George, Kamenev telegraphed that orders had been given that morning for the departure of the British fleet toward the Baltic. And he reiterated his earlier demand: "Telegraph urgently the proposed conditions of armistice, and also the guarantees from the Entente upon which we should consent to the immediate cessation of the advance of our armies. The publication of these conditions would be of the most serious importance for England. We have reason to believe that England is seeking a way out, and will support the most rigorous guarantees within reason, even in spite of France."[48] Indeed, for Kamenev a primary objective of Soviet diplomacy was the exacerbation of differences between Britain and France. In his message of the 4th he had stated: "Only that policy is right which aims at that rupture."[49]

In the days which followed, Soviet diplomacy was eminently successful at exacerbating—and exploiting—Anglo-French differences. If the negotiations between Kamenev and Lloyd George in London involved a deception, so, in a sense, did the discussions between Lloyd George and Millerand which took place on Sunday and Monday, 8 and 9 August, at Sir Philip Sassoon's house at Lympne. So, indeed, had all Anglo-French dealings over the problem of Russia since the end of the War. The basis of this deception was that Lloyd George was unwilling to state frankly just how far he intended to go toward coming to terms with the Soviet regime, and the French, of course, could not easily state the degree to which they were prepared actually to sabotage the developing Anglo-Russian accord.

The underlying division between the two governments was well

[47] Litvinov (Copenhagen) to Kamenev (London), telegrams 303-04, 5 August 1920; intercept 003686, Davidson MSS. Although nowhere is there explicit indication, the context of this message indicates that it was addressed to Moscow as well.

[48] Kamenev (London) to Chicherin, telegram 360, 6 August 1920; intercept 003687, Davidson MSS. None of the intercepts indicate times of sending. Therefore we cannot tell whether this message was sent before or after Kamenev's meeting with Lloyd George; the same is true of his message of 4 August, cited above, n. 46. Nor do any of these indicate the dates on which the intercepts were circulated within the British government.

[49] Cited above, n. 46.

delineated by Millerand at the first session of the Lympne conference on Sunday morning. The conference itself had been conceived
as a means by which the two governments could make a final survey
of the Polish-Soviet crisis and then decide upon joint action. For
that reason Lloyd George had insisted that he needed a definite
reply from Moscow within forty-eight hours—by Sunday morning.
This reply did not arrive until noon, however, and therefore the two
premiers and their assistants—Lloyd George was accompanied by
Curzon, Balfour, Henry Wilson, Hankey, and Admiral Lord Beatty,
the First Sea Lord, while Millerand brought only Berthelot and
Foch—had perforce to devote their first hour and a quarter together
to general speculations.[50] Gloomily (Lloyd George said the situation
was the "most dangerous one that had arisen since 1914"—a sentiment shared not only by Millerand, but also by *The Times* and the
Daily Herald)[51] they discussed the various elements, and found
themselves in agreement upon them. The Poles were much to
blame; moreover, they were led by an intriguer—Piłsudski—whose
reluctance to take advice might even be a sign of darker purposes,
such as a desire to betray his allies and throw in his lot with their
enemies.[52] Indeed, the Poles were scarcely attempting to fight. Warsaw would certainly fall; the only question was whether the Bolsheviks would keep Poland for themselves or divide the carcass with
the Germans. As for the Western Allies, they could do very little.
Public opinion in neither Britain nor France would tolerate sending
troops to fight in Poland. On all these points the two governments
were agreed. Yet, as Millerand pointed out, there was a "great
fundamental difference" between himself and Lloyd George: despite
the similarity in their assessments of the situation, the British Prime
Minister nevertheless "anticipated satisfactory results" from his negotiations with the Soviet government.[53]

In drawing this conclusion Millerand was genuinely puzzled, as

[50] "British Secretary's Notes of an Anglo-French Conference, held at Lympne on
Sunday, August 8, 1920, at 10:45 A.M.," *British Documents*, vol. VIII, no. 83, pp.
709-16.

[51] *Idem.*, p. 709. See the leading articles in *The Times*, 6 and 7 August 1920,
and the *Daily Herald*, 8 (a special Sunday edition) and 9 August.

[52] Especially Lloyd George, but also Millerand, gave free vent to feelings that the
Poles themselves were largely responsible for the situation in which they found
themselves. Although Millerand was more reluctant to cast blanket blame on Poland,
his distrust of Piłsudski was equal to that felt by Lloyd George. See *British Documents*, vol. VIII, pp. 709, 711, 713, 733, 734.

[53] *Ibid.*, p. 715.

anyone is puzzled when he reaches a conclusion contrary to that reached by another apparently reasonable man confronted by the same evidence. Here is where Lloyd George's deception became of crucial importance: he could not let Millerand (or, indeed, the great majority of his own supporters in Parliament) know the extent to which he could with equanimity contemplate a fundamental revision in the shape of the Europe of Versailles. For Millerand, as for Clemenceau, the Soviet conquest of Poland would be an unmitigated disaster, whether the Russians incorporated Poland's territory themselves (or, as was more likely, set it up as a nominally independent satellite) or whether they and the Germans combined in a new partition. Either way the whole structure of the postwar settlement—on which French security, as the French saw it, vitally depended—would be undermined.

The conception of security shared by Lloyd George and his successors was fundamentally different, however. Where the French sought to avoid future war with Germany by confronting her with overwhelming strength artificially preserved through the Versailles Treaty and alliances with client states (themselves a product of the Paris Peace), the British sought the same end through accommodations.[54] Lloyd George was more of a "realist" than his French opposite numbers; more easily than they could he afford to be one. Thus he could forecast the destruction of Poland and still hope for "satisfactory results" from negotiations with the Soviet government. This was the policy Hankey had urged: after doing its best to get decent terms for the Poles, the British government would then strive for a gradual improvement in its relations with both Germany and Russia.[55] Here was appeasement, or accommodation, in the best sense of the word.

Commitment to a policy of this kind by no means implied that Lloyd George was prepared simply to abandon the Poles without taking any steps to help them to resist the Soviet invasion. Even had he wanted to do so, the domestic political costs of such a disengagement would have been too great, and Lloyd George was never one to fail to take domestic political costs into account. But there is no

[54] The best treatment of British and French conceptions of security during these years remains Arnold Wolfers, *Britain and France between Two Wars*, New York, 1940.

[55] Throughout the two days of the Lympne conference Lloyd George repeatedly referred to the views Hankey had brought back from his mission to Warsaw.

reason to think that he wanted to do so. On the contrary, all of his statements during these critical weeks for which we have any record —statements in Parliament, in diplomatic negotiations, to domestic groups who called on him in Downing Street—indicate that he felt a strong sense of sympathy for the Poles in their plight, and an equally strong sense of outrage at the prospect that the Soviet government might be deliberately misleading him as to its willingness to make an equitable peace with Poland. Thus he was prepared to take measures, within limits that would impose no strain on British capabilities, to help the Poles. But he was also prepared, once these measures were seen to fail, as he expected them to, to resume his trade negotiations with Moscow at the point at which they had been broken off. Therefore, throughout the Polish crisis Lloyd George's behavior was somewhat ambiguous. This ambiguity puzzled and angered the French; as we shall see, it also made some of Lloyd George's own countrymen suspect him even of deliberately aiding the Communist cause.

Millerand's ruminations about the differences in outlook between the British Prime Minister and himself were interrupted by the arrival of two Soviet messages, their texts telephoned down from London. The first was a brief note from Kamenev saying that although he had not yet heard from Moscow regarding the proposal for a cease-fire and truce which Henry Wilson and Lloyd George had drawn up at their Friday conference, he had received a reply to the inquiry he had made after his first meeting (Wednesday, 4 August) with the British. Chicherin had stated that the Soviet government would begin withdrawing its forces to the Curzon line "immediately on the acceptance by Poland of armistice terms, which will deal principally with the reduction of her armed strength."[56] This was scarcely a new position, and the subsequent British proposal for an immediate truce had been made precisely in order to avoid a situation in which the Red Army would take Warsaw while protracted armistice negotiations were still under way. It was to the truce proposal that the second Soviet message replied. In a radio-telegram to Kamenev (sent, apparently, *en clair* through commercial channels and "unofficially supplied to Downing Street" by the

---

[56] Kamenev's note is printed as Appendix 2 (pp. 722-23) to *British Documents*, vol. VIII, no. 83; Russian version in *Dokumenty vneshnei politiki*, vol. III, p. 97.

Marconi Company)[57] Chicherin instructed him to inform the British government that half an hour before the truce proposal arrived in Moscow the Russians had finally heard that the Poles were willing to send delegates to Minsk to negotiate both an armistice and preliminary conditions of peace. That being the case, Chicherin said, the Soviet government was convinced that proceeding with those arrangements—the two delegations would meet at Minsk on the 11th—was the quickest and simplest way to achieve the object to which the British truce proposal was addressed, "the cessation of hostilities and the establishment of peaceful relations between Russia and Poland on the basis of full independence of Poland." In other words, the British proposal was flatly rejected.

A third Soviet message also arrived at Lympne that August Sunday noon, but we know much less about it than we do about the other two. This was a communication from Chicherin to Kamenev in which, according to Field Marshal Wilson's entry in his diary that evening, "the Armistice terms to the Poles was [*sic*] fully set out."[58] Unlike the other two messages, the third was an "intercept" (Wilson's term). In the course of this work we have noted other such "intercepts," but no copy of this one seems to have found its way into the available collections of records and papers, and Wilson's diary remains our only source regarding it. Although the texts of the first two messages were circulated to the statesmen at Lympne and appended to the British minutes of the conference, these minutes contain only one veiled hint that the third message even existed: at the afternoon session on Sunday Lloyd George remarked that the Polish delegates at Minsk "would possibly be given the terms of which the conference had seen that day a forecast which might or might not prove a correct one; that is to say, they would have to have an army under Russian proletariat control."[59] The minutes contain no clue as to the form this "forecast" took, nor when it was "seen" by the members of the conference. We can only conjecture

[57] So states the contemporary introductory heading printed along with the radio-telegram as Appendix 3 (p. 723) to *British Documents*, vol. VIII, no. 83; Russian version in *Dokumenty vneshnei politiki*, vol. III, pp. 95-96. For a discussion of the government's ability to acquire such commercial cable traffic, see below, chap. VII, n. 49.

[58] Wilson MS diary, entry for 8 August 1920.

[59] "British Secretary's Notes of an Anglo-French Conference held . . . August 8, 1920, at 4:45 P.M.," *British Documents*, vol. VIII, no. 84, pp. 726-27.

that the British did not want to reveal the extent to which they had access to Soviet communications, and that therefore they gave the French only the vaguest sort of information, and did so presumably during the informal conversations which took place between the formal sessions of the Lympne gathering.

Whatever Lloyd George might have meant by "forecast," Henry Wilson's diary implies that the information at the British government's disposal was far from vague. He wrote that the terms "included Soviet Government, Demobilisation, Disarmament, Workmen's Army, etc." Allowing for the compression of a diarist who was writing only for himself, and for Wilson's lack of interest in the details of the Soviet armistice terms, his capsule headings are, as we shall see, not inaccurate. Nor is his description of what followed: "This settled the matter, so all the afternoon was devoted to consideration of what we can do & it amounts, of course, to very little."[60]

In fact, not only the afternoon but all the following day was given over to a discussion of what response the two Powers might make now that the Soviet government had so clearly indicated its intention to disregard the British efforts at mediation.[61] The argument took forms which were all too familiar: with Foch doing most of the talking, the French once again proposed that the border states should be organized into making a great anti-Soviet effort, while the British kept pointing out how impossible such a scheme actually was. They themselves, Lloyd George said, could do nothing more than give naval support and contribute a certain number of uniforms, pack saddles, and similar equipment. He warned that whatever the Allies might do would "certainly fall far short" of what would really be necessary to secure Poland against a Soviet victory; therefore, he said, they should be wary of making "too high-flown pronouncements" which in retrospect would only emphasize their powerlessness.[62]

The conference decided that such Allied support for Poland as could be brought to bear (the formal conference resolutions explicitly excluded the possibility that troops would be sent) would also be given to Wrangel, who was still entrenched in the Crimea

[60] Wilson MS diary, entry for 8 August 1920.
[61] Minutes of the sessions on Monday, 9 August 1920, at 10:30 A.M. and 2:45 P.M., are in *British Documents*, vol. VIII, nos. 85 and 86, pp. 731-55.
[62] *Ibid.*, no. 84, p. 726.

and in the mainland positions he had seized as a result of his June offensive. This was not a decision which greatly satisfied Lloyd George, for it meant re-creating an involvement from which the British had extricated themselves only with difficulty. But Admiral Beatty, for the Royal Navy, insisted that the Crimea and its approaches were a theater of operations in which seapower could decisively affect land warfare.[63] Unless the Allies did give active assistance to Wrangel, he said, he could see no reason for reimposing the blockade in the Baltic, the only type of naval support which could be given the landlocked Poles. Beatty was dubious as to the actual effects a blockade would have; moreover, it meant participation in a highly unpalatable form of war. Blockade duty, he continued, "was a most unpopular service, involving all the risks of war and none of the glamour and glory. The hardships involved were very considerable, and on their return the seamen were always met with reproaches, such as that the navy was the weapon of the capitalist against the labouring classes. This . . . had had a certain effect on British sailors, and might be expected to have more."[64] Only a week previously Beatty had received a deputation of seamen bearing bitter complaints about the service. At Lympne he confided to Henry Wilson how worried he was. "He told me," Wilson wrote in his diary, "that these men were out for Soviets at every port, & although he thought the immediate danger was over he was most nervous & anxious about the future."[65]

Lloyd George seized upon Beatty's statement to reiterate a point he had already repeatedly made: it showed why, he said, that before taking any action he wanted "to make overwhelmingly clear to

[63] Beatty outlined the actions he recommended in support of Wrangel in a memorandum to the conference:

"As regards naval operations in the Black Sea, the first step is to re-establish the Naval Mission at General Wrangel's headquarters. The following operations could be undertaken:–

(a) To convey General Wrangel's forces to any point in the Black Sea and Sea of Azov, and to cover their disembarkation.
(b) To support the flanks of General Wrangel's army where they rest on the Sea.
(c) To harass the Bolshevik forces on the coast roads wherever they are to be found.
(d) To blockade the Russian coast in occupation of the Bolsheviks.
(e) To carry out any operations on the sea which General Wrangel may require." ("Annex" to "Draft Note by Military and Naval Advisers," 8 August 1920; *ibid.*, no. 85, Appendix I, p. 746.)

[64] *Ibid.*, no. 85, p. 741.

[65] Wilson MS diary, entry for 7 August 1920; Wilson noted on 9 August that Beatty again expressed these concerns to him.

British public opinion, both to the men of the navy and to the working classes" that he was doing everything possible to achieve peace. If it could be said that he had missed any opportunity to make peace, "it would rot the navy, and it would rot the working classes and lead to the triumph of Bolshevism in England."[66] Therefore the Prime Minister insisted that the Allies should make clear that they were contemplating military action not in order to interfere in the internal affairs of Russia—as an anti-Bolshevik campaign—but solely to help the Poles defend their independence within their ethnographic frontiers. For that reason, he said, if the Poles accepted Soviet armistice or peace terms, the Allies could not intervene even if they might themselves disapprove of the terms.

Millerand objected to this formulation, which implied that France and Britain would have to stand by while Piłsudski might turn his country over to Bolshevism, but he could not overcome Lloyd George's insistence. He objected much more to Lloyd George's subsequent suggestion that the blockade be undertaken as a League of Nations action to assist a fellow member to maintain its independence, and that the United States and Germany should be invited to join the League's members in participating. For Millerand the notion of *inviting* the Germans to cooperate was intolerable; the French people, he said, would construe it as complete surrender, and it would stir up the same resentments that had been roused by Churchill's *Evening News* article. The Allies should *forbid* the Germans from trading with Soviet Russia, he said, not invite their cooperation on terms of equality.[67]

Lloyd George's mild observation that there was no way by which the Germans could legally be forbidden to trade with Russia only served to make Millerand angrier. His greatest anger, however, came over the Prime Minister's reluctance to expel Kamenev and Krasin from Great Britain. Here was a matter which lay at the very heart of the bitter disagreements which characterized both days of the Lympne conference, for it concerned the fundamental question of long-range policy toward the Soviet government. Any actions the Allies might take to assist Poland, Millerand said, would be undermined if the two Soviet representatives were allowed to remain in London: in diplomacy, form was as important as substance. If Lloyd

[66] *British Documents*, vol. VIII, no. 85, p. 741.
[67] *Idem*, p. 742.

George would only see the facts as they were he would realize that the Soviet government had been laughing at the Allies ever since the Spa conference. Kamenev and Krasin had for long enough made a "laughingstock" of the British government; they should be required to leave immediately.[68]

Lloyd George refused, and justified his refusal with two arguments. First, though "it was no use suggesting that to turn out MM. Kamenev and Krassin would save Warsaw," the threat of their expulsion and the consequent rupture of relations between London and Moscow was one of the last remaining means of applying pressure on the Soviet regime. It should not be wasted. This was an argument strong only by comparison with Lloyd George's second. Although he had not consulted his Cabinet colleagues, he said, his "own very hasty conclusion" was that they would be in favor of continuing the trade negotiations with Russia, regardless of the Polish events, "because there was so much raw material in that country which was sorely needed by the whole world, and because the British Government believed that the resumption of trading would have the effect of disintegrating Bolshevism." The risks involved in resuming trade would be greater for the Bolsheviks than for the Allies: "when in a position to compare the two forms of government side by side, society, as generally organized, would prefer democracy to Sovietism."[69] In the end, however, Lloyd George at least partly gave way. The formal resolutions of the Lympne conference stated that the British would inform the Soviet government that unless it reached an agreement with the Poles by the following Sunday evening (it was then Monday), Kamenev and Krasin would be required to leave England immediately.[70]

The last act of the conference was the approval of a "Declaration to Poland," drafted by Berthelot and Philip Kerr, which reflected Lloyd George's aversion to "high-flown pronouncements." The French and British governments, it stated, considered that at the forthcoming negotiations at Minsk the Polish government should do its utmost to conclude an armistice and, if necessary, preliminary conditions of peace, on terms which would secure Poland's independence within its ethnographic frontiers. However, if the Soviet

---

[68] *Idem*, pp. 737-39.   [69] *Idem*, p. 736.
[70] The conference resolutions are printed as Appendix 3 to *idem*, pp. 747-48, modified by *ibid.*, no. 86, n. 2.

government insisted on terms which infringed Poland's "legitimate independence," and if the Poles rejected them, the two Allied governments would:

(i) Take all the steps they can to interrupt contact between Russia and the outside world and to put pressure on Russia by other means to respect the independence of Poland.

(ii) Supply the Polish armies with military material for twenty-two divisions and military advice; but they cannot in any circumstances send Allied troops over and above the missions already there.

(iii) Do their utmost to keep open the communications between Poland and the Allies.

These measures, the declaration continued, would be taken provided the Polish government took certain actions of its own. All of the actions requested reflected the great distrust of Piłsudski felt by both the British and the French, and their anger at the fact that thus far he had kept the military command as well as the national leadership in his own hands and had refused either to give General Weygand effective scope to plan operations or to make what Paris considered to be effective use of the 600-man French military mission on the scene.[71] The stipulated actions were that the Polish government:

(a) Makes a public declaration that it is their intention to fight to the end for their independence against the Soviet attack.

(b) Appoints a Commander-in-chief, who shall have no other functions and will accept the effective assistance of Allied officers.

(c) Will accept and act upon the military advice tendered to them by the Allies.

(d) Maintains the Polish army at a strength of twenty-two divisions completed so far as possible to their normal effectives.

(e) Defends at all costs the line of the Vistula in case the line held at this moment by the Polish armies cannot be maintained.[72]

With the approval of the declaration to the Polish government the two days of meetings at Lympne were concluded. On the whole they had gone the way Lloyd George had wanted: the agreed verbal formulae were more in accord with his wishes than with those of the French. As a result, according to Henry Wilson's diary, Millerand

---

[71] See Marshal Foch's remarks, *ibid.*, no. 86, pp. 749-50, and Sir Maurice Hankey's report cited above, n. 30.

[72] "Declaration to Poland," 9 August 1920; *ibid.*, no. 86, Appendix 4, pp. 754-55.

and Foch left Lympne very angry. Foch remarked bitterly to his old friend Wilson that if the British did not get rid of Lloyd George they would lose their empire.[73] Moreover, the verbal formulae were just that and nothing more. Riddell, who was at Lympne handling press relations for Lloyd George, noted in his diary: "The Conference broke up with a strangely unreal air. One felt that the real feelings of those who had taken part in it were not openly expressed."[74] As in every other instance we have seen of Anglo-French discussions involving Soviet Russia, agreed formulae masked profound disagreements concerning not only Russia but the whole shape of postwar Europe. In this instance, as we shall see, the French were quick to make their disagreement known.

While the British and French premiers were concluding their discussions at Lympne, a meeting of a very different sort was under way in a large room within the Palace of Westminster. The leaders of the Labour movement had gathered in order to plan measures to prevent the government from making war against Russia. They included the Parliamentary Labour Party (*i.e.*, the Labour M.P.'s), the Parliamentary Committee of the Trades Union Council, and the Labour Party Executive. Their choice of meeting-place was singularly ironic, because their meeting resulted in the creation of a Council of Action whose whole purpose for existing was to organize action against the government for political purposes *outside* the Parliamentary arena. Soon, under the guidance of the Central Council of Action, some 350 local Councils, scattered throughout the country, came into being. Whether or not these Councils marked, as A.J.P. Taylor has said, "the nearest point to revolution ever reached in this country,"[75] they certainly represented one of the most significant attempts in this century by an organized interest group within a democratic society to impose a foreign policy on a government. As such they have been much noted[76]—so much so that in this account of the making of the British government's policies they need only brief description.

---

[73] Wilson MS diary, entry for 9 August 1920.

[74] Riddell, *Diary*, p. 231, entry for 9 August 1920.

[75] A.J.P. Taylor, *The Trouble Makers: Dissent over Foreign Policy, 1792-1939*, London, 1957, p. 164.

[76] The best accounts are Graubard, *British Labour*, pp. 97-114; Bullock, *Bevin*, pp. 135-42; and Carroll, *Western Opinion*, pp. 166-80.

Labour's concern over the Russo-Polish war had been steadily mounting. During the time of the Polish offensive into the Ukraine in May, as we have seen, London dockworkers, supported by their union, refused to load cases which they suspected to contain munitions for Poland.[77] A movement to generalize this boycott by extending it to the railways collapsed, however, when the Great Northern Railway threatened to fire any men who hindered the company in the discharge of its contracts; in existing conditions of unemployment, the National Union of Railwaymen felt that it could not jeopardize its members' jobs unless they were overwhelmingly in favor of a national strike, which they were not.[78] This decision by the union's leadership would have created a much greater storm within the Labour movement than it did were it not for the fact that the Polish offensive was so short-lived. By early June, when this decision was reached, the tide of battle had almost turned. Moreover, Labour really had little to complain about. There is no reason to disbelieve the government's statements that the munitions then being shipped to Poland were the last of a surplus lot the Poles had purchased and paid for in October 1919.[79]

Paradoxically, it was not until the Red Army had broken the Polish advance and had pushed the Polish forces back to the frontiers of ethnographic Poland that the "Hands Off Russia" movement (as it was called) gathered the momentum which gave rise to the Councils of Action. Only then did it seem that British resources, and perhaps British armed forces as well, would be committed on a large scale to another anti-Soviet campaign. Faced with the prospect of British intervention on the side of the Poles, the Labour movement began to make plans to nullify it by "direct action"—industrial action for political, not industrial, goals.[80] Thus on Sunday, 8 August, the first day of the Lympne conference, resolutions to "down tools" in the event of a war were passed by local

---

[77] See above, chap. I. [78] *Daily Herald*, 5 June 1920.

[79] These statements are cited above, chap. I, n. 115 and n. 117.

[80] The issue of the propriety of "direct action," as opposed to parliamentary action, for political goals was one of the most emotion-laden disputes within the Labour movement. The strike was obviously Labour's principal weapon in achieving industrial goals, but many (although by no means all) of the Party's leadership shrank from using it for "political" objectives. At the Party's Annual Conference in June 1920 a resolution favoring a general strike to compel the government to make peace with Russia was decisively defeated (Labour Party, *Report of the Twentieth Annual Conference*, pp. 138-44). See William Mellor, *Direct Action*, London, 1920, for a sententious but useful statement of the arguments involved.

Labour Party and trade union branch meetings all over the country.[81] A special Sunday edition of the *Daily Herald* proclaimed in a banner headline: "NOT A MAN, NOT A GUN, NOT A SOU!" Under it an editorial urged: "If Lloyd George declares for war today —STOP THE WHOLE WORK OF THE COUNTRY TO-MORROW." And on the following day the same paper declared:

WORKERS! YOU WILL NOT BE DECEIVED!

You know it is the same old gang at the same old game: seeking to shed your blood in capitalism's filthy quarrels: lying, intriguing, ruining the world.

WAR IS UPON US! DOWN TOOLS TO STOP IT!

Meanwhile, in slightly more measured tones, the special joint meeting of the executive bodies of the Labour movement at the House of Commons on the 9th, when the Council of Action was formed, also passed a resolution warning the government that "the whole industrial power of the organized workers would be used to defeat this war" which was being "engineered" by the Allies.[82]

For the first time, even Sir Basil Thomson, the Director of Intelligence at the Home Office (*i.e.*, the chief of domestic intelligence and counterintelligence activities), was impressed by the scale of the demonstrations. Previous numbers of his weekly "Report on Revolutionary Organisations in the United Kingdom" had belittled the efforts of the "Hands Off Russia" movement.[83] The British worker, in Thomson's view, was sensible, pragmatic, isolationist, scornful of foreign ideologies and doctrines, unlikely to be moved to action by political (as opposed to economic) appeals. Of the weekend of 7-8 August 1920, however, he wrote:

There were remarkable demonstrations against war in practically every part of the country and in spite of the holiday season audiences which generally number a hundred or so grew to thousands. . . . Some fifty reports received on this subject may be summed up in the words of my Lancashire correspondent, who writes: "Never have we known such

[81] See *The Times* and the *Daily Herald*, 9 August 1920.

[82] *The Times*, 10 August 1920, carried both the text of the resolution and a complete account of the meeting.

[83] Thus, in his report for 3 June 1920, Thomson wrote: "The little band of extremists in London have been holding demonstrations in Grosvenor Square against the Polish offensive. The worst part of these demonstrations is that the speakers are able to point out to the East End Jews, who form the greater part of their audience, the difference between the conditions in which they live and those in the West End." (Report 57, Cabinet paper C.P. 1400; Cab. 24/106.)

excitement and antagonism to be aroused against any project as has been aroused amongst the workers by the possibility of war with Russia. On every hand ex-Service men are saying they will never take part in any war again. The workers are dead set against a war with Russia."

Thomson's own conclusion was blunt: "It is a new departure for the Labour Party to force the hand of the Government in a matter of foreign policy, and it is a precedent that will not easily be forgotten."[84]

In nearly all the statements and resolutions which sprang from these meetings, the common thread was a strongly held feeling that Labour, in particular, had been hoodwinked into supporting the government's entry into war in 1914, and that the movement would not be so blind again. Disillusionment with the war brought disillusionment with the peace. Thus the annual Labour Party Conference, meeting at Scarborough in late June 1920, had resolved that the treaties of peace violated not only Britain's war aims but also the pledges made to the enemy at the time of the Armistice, and had called for their immediate revision.[85] Poland—for so many the symbol of a righted wrong—became for Labour a symbol of the injustices of the treaties. Any vestige of sympathy for the Poles as underdogs evaporated at the time of the Polish offensive into the Ukraine. Not only did Labour feel that the Polish imperialists deserved to be defeated at the hands of the Red Army, but this attitude was accompanied by a naive faith in Moscow's pronouncements that it was only Polish militarism, and not Polish independence, which Soviet forces would destroy.

All these views were reflected in an interview between Lloyd George (with Bonar Law present but silent) and a delegation from the Council of Action on 10 August. The Prime Minister refused to make a statement, he said at the outset—he would do so in the House of Commons that afternoon, since "we have not had a Soviet established in this country yet"—but he would comment on statements and answer questions put to him. The delegation's spokesman was Ernest Bevin who, indeed, had been the instigator of the joint meeting which gave birth to the Council. Bevin emphasized that the threat of "direct action" was a real one, and that Labour would invoke it in opposition not only to direct British military action, but

---

[84] Report 67, 12 August 1920, Cabinet paper C.P. 1772; Cab. 24/110.
[85] Labour Party, *Report of the Twentieth Annual Conference*, pp. 132-40.

also to "indirect war, either by blockade or by the supply of munitions or by assisting the forces that are now at war with Russia."[86] To Lloyd George's puzzled question as to what Labour would do if Poland's independence were endangered, Bevin replied: "Our answer is this—that the hypothesis does not hold good, that the independence of Poland is not at stake." Pressed again by the Prime Minister, Bevin could only state: "The public declarations of Russia up to now, in Kameneff's letter and in all the declarations we have seen, is [*sic*] that they are not challenging the independence of Poland." And the conversation continued:

THE PRIME MINISTER: Let us assume everything you are putting, and let us assume that the French have interfered, and we have interfered, and the Poles have interfered. I ask you again: If Soviet Russia does what Tsarist Russia did and says "We mean to destroy your independence" (they will not put it like that but it will substantially mean the destruction of her independence), do you mean to say that then Labour in this country will not permit the Government to send a single pair of boots to people who are fighting for their liberty as we understand liberty in this country?

MR. BEVIN: Labour will consider its position when that occasion arises.

THE PRIME MINISTER: Very well. That is quite good enough for me.

MR. BEVIN: But I want to make this perfectly clear—that that condition has not arisen.

THE PRIME MINISTER: No. You need not make that clear to me, because I agree with you. I do not think it has arisen, but it will arise one way or the other when the terms are known.

MR. BEVIN: But supposing the Polish people themselves agreed upon a Constitution which did not suit the Allied Powers?

THE PRIME MINISTER: What have we to do with that? That is their business, not ours.

MR. BEVIN: It is their business?

THE PRIME MINISTER: Certainly. What have we to say to that? I do not care what the Constitution is. If they like to have a Mikado there, that is their business.

MR. BEVIN: That is what we wanted to know.

THE PRIME MINISTER: Not if it is done by force, you understand; only if it is done by their choice.

MR. BEVIN: I quite understand.

[86] A transcript of the conversation, made by a stenographer brought along by the Labour delegation, was printed in the *Daily Herald*, 11 August 1920. Much of it is also printed in Bullock, *Bevin*, pp. 136-38.

The difficulty, however, was that Bevin did not understand. Lloyd George could not make the Labour delegation comprehend just how reluctant he was to take action in support of the Poles. Such was the Prime Minister's reputation for deviousness, especially on the Russian question, that few of his statements were accepted at face value. Neither did Lloyd George understand his Labour visitors. Poland, a small state, was in the process of being invaded by a large one; where was Labour's traditional support of the weak? The failure of communication between the two sides was almost total.

In departing, Bevin inquired whether Lloyd George would object if the Council of Action were to interview Kamenev and Krasin, and also Polish representatives in London. The Prime Minister replied that he would object to the Council's seeing the Russians. An exchange of written communications would be acceptable, but once the Soviet delegation got in touch with "political parties," its pledge not to interfere in British domestic politics would become blurred and impossible to enforce. Bevin denied that the Council was a "mere political party," but Lloyd George insisted that it was, and added: "It is a very dangerous precedent for diplomatic agents to begin trafficking with political parties in a country." It did not help the cause of peace, he said, echoing annoyed heads of governments before and after him confronted by private citizens seeking contact with their adversaries, when "there is a party in this country rather supporting the view taken by the other country and they go and meet that party and begin intriguing." Labour's behavior had already "stiffened the backs" of the Bolsheviks. "Quite unconsciously you stood in the way of peace."

Regardless of Lloyd George's injunction, a delegation from the Council of Action called on Kamenev and Krasin that same day. The Soviet representatives had naturally followed the growth of the "Hands Off Russia" movement with excitement and, as we will see, with financial support. "The labouring organisations of England are countering war with Soviet Russia with their own war against the Government which is forcing the British people to the support of British and especially French imperialists," Kamenev had telegraphed to Chicherin on 7 August.[87] And on the 10th, after meeting with the Council of Action, he exclaimed: "The most astonishing

---

[87] Kamenev (London) to Chicherin, telegrams 370-72, 7 August 1920; intercept 003705, Davidson MSS.

feature in the current agitation is that the workers are coming forward on our side, not because we are right or wrong, but because they must be with Russia at all costs, and on any terms."[88] But on the previous day, perhaps because he was in a less ebullient mood, he had cautioned: "I do not wish, however, to hide the fact that the artificial establishment of a Soviet regime in Poland may cause this feeling to cool."[89] Litvinov, from Copenhagen, was more cautious. There was a danger, he telegraphed to Chicherin on the 7th, "in the possibility that the British workers may not keep up till the bitter end their fight against the war, and if they lost a general engagement in England, a situation would be produced analogous to that which exists in France, and Churchill's hands would finally be left free."[90]

One of Kamenev's principal reasons, therefore, for urging Moscow to publish its armistice terms, including a statement guaranteeing the inviolability of Poland's ethnographic frontiers, was (as he put it in his telegram of the 10th) "to confirm the favourable turn of events" and to strengthen Soviet efforts to win support among "pacifists of the working classes and the lower middle-class." Thus, he said, the Soviet delegation at the Minsk talks should immediately publish a declaration "of the independence and sovereignty of Poland" within wide boundaries. "Plan out the course of the Minsk Conference as well as possible," he urged. "It is really a negotiation with England. In return for the independence of Poland you can obtain, and ought to obtain, compensation not only in Poland but also from the Entente (Wrangel)." For his own part, Kamenev added somewhat cryptically, he would not publish the armistice conditions until after Lloyd George's statement in the House of Commons.

✣

In his statement made that same afternoon, the Prime Minister returned to many of the points he had earlier made to the delegation

---

[88] Kamenev (London) to Chicherin, telegrams 387-88, 10 August 1920; intercept 003748, circulated 13 August, Davidson MSS. There are no available records as to what transpired on this occasion between the Soviet mission and the Council of Action.

[89] Kamenev (London) to Chicherin, telegrams 384-86, 9 August 1920; no intercept number given, Davidson MSS.

[90] Litvinov (Copenhagen) to Kamenev (London) and Chicherin, telegrams 307 and 1167, 7 August 1920; intercept 003701, Davidson MSS.

from the Council of Action.[91] "I appeal to a party which is organised and claims to be organised to protect the weak," he said. Before a packed House, with Kamenev and Krasin, as well as the American Ambassador and the Duke of York (later King George VI) looking down from the galleries, the Prime Minister reviewed the whole course of the Polish-Soviet war, blaming the Poles for their spring offensive and stating that the Russians were entitled to terms of peace which guaranteed them against future attacks, but then going on sharply to criticize the Soviet side for its "very suspicious delays" of the armistice negotiations and its seeming insistence on pressing the pursuit of the Polish forces until all Poland was overrun. Now, he said, the Allied governments would look carefully at the talks scheduled to begin the following day at Minsk. They might possibly fail because of a Polish refusal to accept conditions which a "fair-minded man" would consider that the Soviet side was only just to exact. In that case, "then the Allies [here Lloyd George was on shaky ground in speaking for the French government as well as for his own] could not support Poland."

On the other hand, if the Russians should insist on conditions inconsistent with Poland's existence as a free nation, and the Poles should therefore decide to go on fighting, the Allies—who were responsible for Poland's resurrection—could not be indifferent. The basis of the League of Nations was that the nations who had signed the Covenant bound themselves together to defend those who could not defend themselves. But the Prime Minister added an important qualification: "That covenant, as I understand it, does not contemplate, necessarily, military action in support of the imperilled nation. It contemplates economic pressure." The contention that support of Poland necessarily would mean war was inconsistent with the whole theory of the covenant Britain had entered into. "We contemplate other methods of bringing pressure upon the recalcitrant nations who are guilty of acts of aggression," Lloyd George said. He then went on briefly to detail the various measures which the Lympne conference had decided might be taken in support not only of the Poles but also of Wrangel. Assisting Wrangel, he emphasized, would be no small step for the British government, for it would mean a return to the old interventionist policy of attacking Soviet Russia

[91] For Lloyd George's statement, see 133 *H.C. Deb.*, cols. 254-72.

inside her own territory. Such a change in policy would perforce mean the end of the Anglo-Soviet trade negotiations.

Lloyd George then turned to his visit that morning from the representatives of the Council of Action—"a very influential body of men representing very powerful opinion in this country," he called them. "I gather from them," he continued, "as I have gathered from the Press, that we are supposed to be engaged in a reactionary conspiracy to destroy a democratic Government representing peasants and workmen." Briefly he ran through a series of quotations from various statements by members of the Labour Party delegation (some of whose members were also members of the Council of Action) just returned from its journey of investigation to Moscow, all criticizing the Soviet regime for being nondemocratic and authoritarian.[92] This was perhaps irrelevant, but effective as a debating tactic. Labour had accused his government of trying to crush the Soviet government simply because it was revolutionary, he continued. That was untrue: in 1917 he had supported the Russian Provisional Government, which was also revolutionary; "if we did break with this one, it was not because it was a revolutionary Government. It was because it broke the bond it entered into, which was to pursue the war to the end." Here was a bit of history. Lloyd George followed it with some political theory:

I say now that if they want peace they can get it. The London Conference proposal was intended to establish peace. Sovietism we are quite prepared to fight with the same weapons with which we fight every political creed with which we do not agree. In the end, one or other will triumph, or something else will emerge that will better suit the times. . . .

This is their test. I do not believe that a mere revenge on Poland, mere punishment of Poland, mere destruction of Poland, is enough in itself, unless there is some other motive, to induce the Soviet Government to decline peace with the world. The point is this. Are they for peace, or have they something else on their minds? Frankly, I think they them-

[92] *Ibid.*, cols. 267-69. The Labour delegation left for Russia in late April. Some of its members returned in June, in time for the annual Party conference; others returned in early August. For an account of their journey see Graubard, *British Labour*, pp. 214-22. In his speech Lloyd George quoted principally from informal statements by members of the delegation on their return. Their remarks were echoed, however, in their formal report (Labour Party and Trades Union Congress, *The Report of the British Labour Delegation to Russia*, London, 1920), which was not published until the autumn.

selves are divided. In every land you get men who urge wild, extravagant, irrational views . . . who are merely out to destroy and to shatter, and who dance only to the music of smashing furniture. . . .

The West would soon know, Lloyd George concluded, whether these or "the saner elements" were in control in Moscow.[93]

As it turned out, "soon" meant almost immediately. Kamenev subsequently described the ensuing scene:

> When Lloyd George spoke in Parliament we sat upstairs in a box. Below us were the Members of Parliament among whom were a few of our friends, representatives of the working people. To one of these I handed a sealed envelope and said "If, after Lloyd George's speech, I bow my head to you, then please hand him this packet, if I do not, then do not hand him the packet."
>
> Lloyd George made a speech full of antipathy for Soviet Russia. After his speech I gave the sign agreed upon and he was handed the packet, which contained our conditions for peace.[94]

Kamenev's letter, released simultaneously to the *Daily Herald*, conveyed to Lloyd George "the terms of the Armistice and Preliminaries for Peace which will be submitted at Minsk by the Russian Delegates."[95] In the circumstances they did not seem ungenerous—an indication, perhaps, that the Soviet government was in fact prepared to pursue a "saner" approach. Naturally enough, the Poles had a number of obligations thrust upon them. Within one month they were to demobilize their army to a professional cadre of 10,000 men supplemented by annual drafts of 50,000 one-year trainees. Polish forces were immediately to withdraw to a line fifty versts (roughly thirty-three miles) behind the armistice line, which would be the line dividing the two sides at the moment the armistice took effect; on the other hand, the final Polish-Russian frontier would in the main follow the Curzon line, with modifications in Poland's favor. The Poles were to hand over to the Russians all arms over and above those needed by the 60,000-man Polish army and by "the Civic Militia"—an organization not described or even mentioned elsewhere in Kamenev's letter. They were also to demobilize their war

---

[93] 133 *H.C. Deb.*, cols. 271-72.

[94] From a speech Kamenev made on his return to Russia, reported in *Petrogradskaya Pravda*, 25 September 1920; translation in Lloyd George MSS, file F/202/3/25.

[95] The text of Kamenev's letter is in 133 *H.C. Deb.*, cols. 351-53.

industries and to receive no military assistance, of either personnel or matériel, from abroad. Finally, they were to place a railway line to the Baltic at the disposal of Soviet commercial traffic, and the Polish state was to give free gifts of land to the families of all Polish citizens killed, wounded, or otherwise incapacitated in the course of the war with Russia. (This last requirement was particularly misconceived: nothing could better ensure the *embourgeoisement* of the Polish peasantry than allowing them small-holdings, as Soviet leaders were to learn in their own country.) For their part the Russians —again reflecting the realities of the existing military situation—took very few obligations on themselves, promising simply to withdraw their own forces from the Polish front as soon as the Poles had demobilized, and to reduce their numbers to a figure that would be mutually agreed upon.

These, according to Kamenev's letter, were the Soviet terms, subject only to the reservation that they might later "be supplemented by details of secondary moment." As we shall see, it was possible to disagree over the definition of "secondary." Lloyd George brought the letter to the House of Commons that night at 10 P.M., at the close of the long debate which he had opened with his own statement some six hours earlier. As he entered the chamber he found that several members already possessed copies of the letter because of its publication in a special early edition of the following morning's *Daily Herald*. He then read its text to the House, but refrained from expressing his opinion of it. "We have given our preliminary impression to the Polish Government," he said. Any comment in the House would have the effect of removing the negotiations from the hands of the Poles.[96]

The Prime Minister had, however, reached his own conclusions regarding the Soviet terms. He presented them to a hurriedly called meeting of all the Cabinet members he could assemble, in Bonar Law's room at the House of Commons at 7 P.M. that evening, immediately after receiving Kamenev's note.[97] The terms, he told his

[96] *Ibid.*, col. 353.
[97] Minutes, conference of Ministers, 10 August 1920, 7 P.M.; filed as Appendix II to Cabinet 49 (20), Cab. 23/22. Aside from Lloyd George and Bonar Law, those present were Balfour, Curzon, Chamberlain, Churchill, Long, Milner (Secretary of State for Colonies), Fisher (Education), Addison (Health), Worthington-Evans (Minister without portfolio), and Philip Kerr.

colleagues, "were not nearly so severe as had been imposed by the Allies upon Germany and Austria." Certainly he did not think that Great Britain could make war to secure better conditions than Moscow had offered. The minutes of the meeting attribute views to no other participant, and give little indication as to the nature of the discussion. They do, however, make clear that Lloyd George's opinion was the predominant one. The minutes state:

> As regards the terms themselves it was generally agreed that they were as reasonable as could be expected, but that certain terms, vis. the future strength of the Polish Army and the final frontiers might require further examination. A great cause of satisfaction was that the conditions secured the independence of Poland and—assuming the bona-fides of the Soviet Government and its delegates in London—the British Government could not, it was felt, without a serious breach of faith, now proceed with the hostile measures contemplated at the Lympne Conference, in the event of affairs taking a sinister turn.

Crucial to this optimistic assessment, of course, was the stated assumption that the Soviet side was proceeding in good faith. Not all of the ministers gathered in Bonar Law's room that August evening shared this assumption. The minutes continue: "On the other hand it was strongly urged that it was essential for the Allies to contemplate the possibility of bad faith on the part of the Soviets, and attention was drawn to the condition which laid down that all arms over and above such as may be required for the needs of the reduced Army, as well as of the Civic Militia, shall be handed over to Soviet Russia and the Ukraine, and it was suggested that this might mean that the arms were required for a Red Army in Poland."

Given their general interpretation of the Soviet terms, Lloyd George told his colleagues, they therefore had to make two decisions. In transmitting the terms to the Polish government, should the British government express its opinion of them? And if so, should it consult the French government in advance? The answer to the first question was clearly affirmative: the Poles should be told where London stood. But the Cabinet decided not to consult Paris in advance. "The French almost invariably adopted the negative attitude in the first instance," the minutes of the meeting stated. Their representatives had come to Lympne with the intention of issuing a "violent and impossible" anti-Bolshevik proclamation; they were "passionately anti-communist," but the present case had "nothing to do with communism."[98]

With these decisions made, Curzon took sheets of House of Commons note paper and, in his large, loopy hand, scrawled out in pencil, with many crossings-out, the texts of "very urgent" telegrams to Paris and Warsaw.[99] To Sir George Grahame, the Chargé d'Affaires in Paris, he stated that the Cabinet was unanimous in thinking—particularly after the day's debate—that public sentiment both in Parliament and in the country would not justify the government in undertaking hostilities against the Soviet government to secure better terms than those offered; he hoped, Curzon said, that the French government would agree, and would so advise its minister at Warsaw. The second message, to Sir Horace Rumbold, instructed the British minister to inform the Polish government of the Cabinet's opinion that "provided these terms are *bona fide* offered at Minsk, and that no substantial addition is made to them they would appear to leave the independence of Poland within her ethnographic frontiers unimpaired." The Polish government would of course be at liberty to try to negotiate better terms, Curzon continued, but the British government "could not assume responsibility of taking hostile action against Russia if conditions now offered, in their general substance, were refused."

Thus the Soviet government, through Kamenev's note, had won for itself a respite. Not for the moment would the British destroyer

[98] Ironically, the assertion that the present case had "nothing to do with communism" precisely echoed remarks made during the afternoon's House of Commons debate by Herbert Asquith, the leader of the Opposition Liberals. Commenting on the rather anti-Soviet tone of Lloyd George's statement, Asquith said:

"When we are told, as we are told constantly, that the army with which Poland now has to deal is a Bolshevist Army and a Red Army, and a propagandist army, composed of missionaries of the creed which the Prime Minister has just been denouncing, I venture to say that that is a complete mis-statement. In all probability a very small proportion either of the officers or of the men . . . now invading Poland from Russia are Bolshevists in creed or have anything to do with Bolshevism. . . . [T]he effect of the Polish invasion, wantonly undertaken, and connived at by the tacit acquiescence of Europe, was to unite Russia, and to fuse into one body that which has proved a most powerful and effective military force including men of the old as well as the new regime. The army which is now advancing through Poland and threatening Warsaw are not Bolshevists exclusively, or mainly. . . . [T]hey are the flower of the military rule and experience of Russia, and that is the serious situation with which we have to deal." (133 *H.C. Deb.*, col. 275.)

[99] Curzon to Grahame (Paris), telegram 509, 10 August 1920, 10 P.M., file 211435/40430/55; F.O. 371/3917. Curzon to Rumbold (Warsaw), telegram 377, 10 August 1920, 10 P.M., *British Documents*, vol. XI, no. 411.

squadron then pausing at Copenhagen proceed into Baltic waters to initiate the measures of blockade planned at Lympne. Nor for the moment would the guns of the Black Sea Fleet fire in support of Wrangel. A week later, when the Polish negotiators at Minsk finally received the actual Soviet terms, they were found to differ in vital respects from those Kamenev had given Lloyd George. Then, as we will see, it could scarcely be said that they left Poland's independence unimpaired.

CHAPTER VI

PIŁSUDSKI'S VICTORY AND
KAMENEV'S DECEPTION

All necessary explanations have been given and swallowed, but in any case we have gained two weeks.
—*Kamenev to Chicherin, 26 August 1920*[1]

THE cadres for a communist Polish government who followed in the wake of the Red Army as it swept toward Warsaw in August 1920 actually came within sight of the capital's rooftops, but they came no farther. There, on the 16th, Polish forces not only blocked the advancing Russians but set them on a retreat as rapid as had been their advance. The Poles owed their victory to many factors: Soviet errors—Tukhachevsky's advance had been too rapid, and he made the mistake of dividing his forces, in an effort to encircle Warsaw, rather than concentrating them all directly against the capital; Polish tenacity and courage—once within territory inhabited by their own people the Poles began to fight with a vigor and discipline they had not displayed since they had begun to retreat at Kiev in June; and, not least, Piłsudski's generalship—he himself formulated the maneuver which saved Warsaw, and it was he who inspired both officers and men. Poland's victory, moreover, was due almost entirely to Polish efforts, and owed very little to Allied assistance: in the critical moments before Warsaw Piłsudski largely disregarded the advice of Weygand and the large French military mission, and kept his own counsel. The Polish victory was unexpected. It came just in time to prevent the imposition on Poland of a communist regime. And it ended the gravest international crisis since the World War.

If the plot of nearly every comic opera hinges upon a tangle of misunderstandings, the record of the Polish-Soviet crisis from Lloyd

---

[1] Kamenev (London) to Chicherin, telegram 529, 26 August 1920; intercept 003946, Lloyd George MSS, file F/203/1/11.

George's receipt of Kamenev's note on 10 August until the time, later in the month, when the Polish success was unmistakably apparent, reads like the scenario of a gigantic, if macabre, *opera buffa*. In their richness and elaboration the misunderstandings of these weeks had few parallels. Communication between the British and French governments, scarcely effective during the preceding months, now seemed to fail completely. Indeed, the width of the gulf between them was exceeded during the 1920's only at the time of the French invasion of the Ruhr in January 1923. This lack of understanding between the Allied capitals was matched, however, by that between the British government and its domestic critics, both Left and Right. Meanwhile, in the battle zone itself, Polish and Soviet delegates finally began to negotiate. Here too, however, there were overtones of comic opera. For some time Moscow Radio was unable—or unwilling—to receive Polish messages. And when negotiations actually began, communications between Minsk and the front were so poor that for several days the delegates of both sides talked on in complete ignorance of the dramatic reversal in the fortunes of war which followed the Battle of Warsaw.

Even the armies in the field seemed to cooperate in giving the August crisis its odd aspect of macabre comedy. "It would be a profound mistake," Lord D'Abernon, the head of the British special political-diplomatic mission, wrote from Warsaw on 28 August, "to regard the war which is now being carried on in Poland as being similar, in any essential particular, to the great war which has just come to an end." The whole Polish-Soviet war was one of swift movement, totally unlike the bloody pitched battles on the Western Front (for which the French military advisers urged the Poles to prepare) and at the same time marked by relatively little of the fierce brutality which had characterized the equally swift-moving warfare of the Russian civil war. There was "no particular animosity or rancour between the mass of the combatants on each side," D'Abernon observed. He continued: "There are no savage attacks, there is no question of heroic resistance. It is a war of manoeuvre and not of position. The game of war is conducted on lines similar to chess between high-class players—directly one side has a serious advantage the other resigns and withdraws to another table or another field. When they are considerably out-numbered, or out-manoeuvered, or out-flanked, the troops either retire or surrender: no authority among their officers is sufficient to induce them to take any other course."[2] Sir Horace Rumbold's summation was apposite. "It may truly be said," he wrote to Curzon on 24 August, "that the political consequences of the Polish victory are as incalculable as the military operations are in many ways grotesque."[3]

✧

In telling the Poles on 10 August that the terms conveyed by Kamenev "would appear to leave the independence of Poland within her ethnographic frontiers unimpaired," and therefore seemed sufficiently acceptable—provided they were *bona fide*—as not to justify Britain's undertaking hostilities in the event that Warsaw refused them, the British government acted unilaterally, without consulting the French. Within the government there was no little discomfort that this should be so. In a long despatch to Lord Derby in Paris, Curzon attempted to explain why the Cabinet had acted so precipitately. His arguments deserve extensive exposition here.[4]

The debate in the House of Commons on 10 August, Curzon said, showed conclusively that every section of Parliamentary opinion, and not Labour alone, strongly opposed actual British participation in the Polish-Soviet war. Parliamentary consent even for the limited measures of assistance to Poland which had been formulated at Lympne would be obtained "only in case the terms proposed to the Polish Government were absolutely impossible." Curzon then came to the crux of his argument. The fundamental principle laid down at Lympne, he said, was that the Allies must secure Poland's legitimate independence within ethnographic frontiers. And he continued:

As soon, therefore, as it appeared to the British Government that this condition was broadly conceded by the proposed terms, and as it was clear to the Cabinet that, if they were rejected *in limine* it would be impossible to secure the assent of the British Parliament to the contemplated operations, His Majesty's Government, knowing that the Polish delegates were to meet the Russian delegates the next day, and feeling

---

[2] D'Abernon (Warsaw) to Curzon, despatch 55, 28 August 1920; file 213597/73/55, F.O. 371/3919.
[3] Rumbold (Warsaw) to Curzon, despatch 535, 24 August 1920; file 213154/73/55, F.O. 371/3919.
[4] Curzon to Derby (Paris), despatch 2758, 13 August 1920; *British Documents*, vol. XI, no. 431.

apprehensive that, relying upon the support of Great Britain and France, they might reject the proposals *in toto*, felt it only fair to acquaint the Polish Government with the British view of the facts of the case.

This advice . . . did not presume the acceptance of the whole of the terms by ourselves, still less a suggestion to the Polish Government that they should accept them *en bloc*. Several of them were of a character that would demand the closest scrutiny, and probably substantial amendment; but we did not think that, as a basis of negotiation, they should be rejected without qualification at the start. This was the advice that we considered ourselves entitled to give to the Polish Government on our own account.

Of course, Curzon added, the French government was "equally entitled" to give advice to the Poles, so long as it was consistent with the decisions reached at Lympne.

Here, at first glance, was an eminently reasonable argument. Yet it was made less reasonable by the fact that under the arrangements agreed upon at Lympne, the principal anti-Soviet measures contemplated were naval, and therefore the responsibility of the British. Thus a unilateral British decision not to implement the Lympne plans would mean in effect that the Poles would receive no significant additional Allied support no matter what position the French government might take. Moreover, the British decision seemed rather different when spelled out at length in Curzon's despatch than when conveyed to the Poles by means of a brief telegram which arrived in Warsaw only one day following the arrival of the Lympne conference's declaration on Poland.[5] Although the Lympne declaration had stated that the Allies could provide only limited support, its effect had been reassuring. The news of the later British decision, therefore, was received with shocked dismay: the Polish government understandably overlooked all of the qualifications which are apparent in Curzon's despatch to Derby, and chose to regard Sir Horace Rumbold's *démarche* as British advice to make peace on the Soviet terms as given. In an interview which Rumbold described as "very painful" Prince Sapieha, the Polish Minister for Foreign Affairs, asserted that he could not believe the Allies would ask Poland to accept terms amounting to a shameful capitulation.[6]

---

[5] The Lympne declaration was sent as Curzon's telegram 375 to Rumbold (Warsaw), 9 August 1920; see *ibid.*, no. 407, n. 1. The advice regarding the Soviet terms was sent as telegram 377, 10 August; cited above, chapter V, n. 99.

[6] Rumbold (Warsaw) to Curzon, telegram 684, 11 August 1920; *British Docu-*

Warsaw's interpretation of the British advice was well described by Jusserand, the French member of the special Anglo-French diplomatic mission in the Polish capital. To Millerand he telegraphed: "In other words, if Poland today follows instructions received yesterday from Great Britain [i.e., the Lympne declaration urging the Poles to revitalize their military establishment] and safeguards thereby her future, Great Britain will abandon her. The demand is both inadmissible and monstrous. Kamenev's conditions represent the maximum of what would be demanded, and the fact that Mr. Lloyd George accepts them means that Poland cannot even bargain."[7]

Such an interpretation, it should be noted, assumed that the British advice to the Polish government was public, when in fact it was intended to be strictly confidential precisely in order to allow the Poles to retain their freedom to bargain. The assumption was warranted, however, because the British advice—or, rather, a distorted version of it which implied the complete abandonment of Poland—was leaked to the press by the Quai d'Orsay, along with the French government's opinion that, contrary to what London might think, the Soviet terms were totally unacceptable.[8] From Warsaw Lord D'Abernon commented dryly: "The result has been to make the position, both for Rumbold and myself, extremely difficult."[9]

✣

At the time of all these recriminations, however, the dispute over advice to the Poles had been relegated to second place behind an even more acrimonious Anglo-French controversy. On the afternoon of 11 August the French government announced that it had decided to recognize General Wrangel's government at Sebastopol in the Crimea as the *de facto* government of South Russia. This news came as a stunning surprise, but it should not have done so. On 20 July, in the midst of a speech to the Chamber of Deputies principally devoted to a summary of the Spa conference's decisions regarding

---

ments, vol. XI, no. 418. See also Prince Sapieha's telegram to the Polish mission in London (and handed to the Foreign Office), 13 August; *ibid.*, no. 430.

[7] André Géraud ("Pertinax"), "British Policy as Seen by a Frenchman," *Journal of the Royal Institute of International Affairs*, vol. IX, no. 2, March 1930, p. 170. Géraud quotes the entire text of this telegram without stating how he obtained it. The date is not given, but its context places it as 11 August 1920.

[8] See *The Times*, 12, 13, and 14 August 1920.

[9] In a letter to Sir Maurice Hankey, 12 August 1920; registered file 18/Z/13, Cab. 21/180.

Germany, Millerand observed that Wrangel's government had succeeded in winning the support of the local population. Should that government request recognition from France, he said, and should it accompany its request with a declaration acknowledging its responsibility for "all the obligations contracted by previous Russian governments with foreign states," French recognition would be forthcoming.[10]

Incredibly enough, although Millerand's remarks were reported in *The Times*, they seem to have gone unnoticed by both the British government and the informed public—including the editors of *The Times*, who described the announcement on 11 August of French recognition as a "bombshell," an accurate assessment of its impact upon London.[11] Both Government and Opposition learned of it from the same sources, the evening papers of the 11th. "I read it," Lloyd George told a questioner in the House of Commons, "with very great surprise and anxiety." Indeed, he said, he could scarcely believe it. After all, he had just returned from spending two days with Millerand at Lympne. Nothing had been said regarding the recognition of Wrangel; surely Millerand would have mentioned such an intention had he had it in mind. For that reason, Lloyd George said, he could only conclude that the reports were in error.[12]

The Prime Minister had left a Cabinet meeting in order to reply to this questioner in the House. By the time he returned, the news of the French *démarche* had been confirmed by a telephone conversation with the British Embassy in Paris. ("Even yet," Curzon tele-

[10] *Journal officiel, Chambre des Députés*, 1920, p. 2976. Wrangel made the required declaration of debts and request for recognition from France on 8 August. For an account of his negotiations with Paris see his memoirs in *Beloe delo*, vol. VI, pp. 127-29, 144-47.

[11] *The Times*, 12 August 1920. *The Times*'s reference to Millerand's mention of Wrangel on 20 July was buried in the middle of a long column (21 July) devoted to the speech. Apparently it was unnoticed in the Foreign Office.

[12] 133 *H.C. Deb.*, cols. 495-97. Millerand's mention of Wrangel, and probable French recognition, seems not to have been reported by the British Embassy in Paris, nor called to the attention of the British government by the French Embassy in London. On 15 August the counsellor of the French Embassy, de Fleuriau, left an apologetic note at the Foreign Office stating that at the end of July he had, indeed, received instructions to raise with the British "the conditions under which [Wrangel] might be recognized by the French government," but that he did not do so with "plainness comporting with M. Millerand's instructions." Therefore, he said, Lloyd George and Curzon were insufficiently informed of Millerand's intentions, while the latter, "for his part, believed them to be fully informed. That explains why the question of Wrangel was not discussed at Lympne." (*British Documents*, vol. XI, no. 441, p. 493, n. 1.)

graphed afterward to Paris, "we entertain the hope that some mistake has been made and in view of what happened at Lympne that the announcement has been made without the authority of the French Government.")[13] Not surprisingly, the Cabinet concluded that there was little it could do: the British government had already backed off from the Lympne decision to furnish naval support to Wrangel. There remained only a store of rifles at Constantinople which the Anglo-French conferees at Lympne had also earmarked for Wrangel; instructions now went out from London that these, too, would be denied him.[14]

Inevitably, the French action was interpreted in London as a direct retaliation for the British government's failure to consult Paris before advising the Poles that the Soviet terms seemed acceptable. Moreover, as Professor Seton-Watson's *New Europe* pointed out in a mordant editorial, the French were aiming not simply at expressing their annoyance, but at "deliberate sabotage" of the British attempt to bring about a Russo-Polish peace: the Poles would take heart at the prospect of greater assistance from Wrangel, and have greater reason to reject the Soviet terms.[15] Maurice Paléologue, the Secretary General of the Quai d'Orsay, implied as much to Neville Henderson in an interview on the afternoon of the 11th, saying (according to Henderson's report) that "there was no other course open" to the French government after the British *démarche* at Warsaw.[16] In subsequent private statements, and to the press, both Millerand and Paléologue attempted to deny these implications by calling attention to their previously expressed intentions regarding Wrangel, and asserting that the decision to accord him recognition had been taken at a *morning* cabinet meeting on the 11th which had already been adjourned by noon, when the participants first received word of the

---

[13] Curzon to Henderson (Paris), telegram 904, 11 August 1920; *ibid.*, no. 422.

[14] Minutes, Cabinet 47 (20), 11 August 1920, 6 P.M.; Cab. 23/22. Henry Wilson's description of this Cabinet meeting is worth noting: "I found the Frocks in a great state of excitement, abusing the French, rushing off into the House to answer Labour Members about this Wrangel affair and in short a Cabinet of perfectly useless querulous feeble old men. . . . It seems to me the French have a perfect right to repudiate our idea of the independence of Poland but they are unwise in acknowledging Wrangel. I am afraid all this will lead to serious trouble." (MS diary, entry for 11 August 1920.)

[15] *The New Europe*, vol. XVI, no. 201, 19 August 1920, p. 122.

[16] Henderson (Paris) to Curzon, telegram 960, 11 August 1920; *British Documents*, vol. XI, no. 417. Henderson was then First Secretary and acting Chargé d'Affaires of the Paris Embassy.

British advice to the Poles.[17] Lord Derby, the British Ambassador and a man with extremely good connections in French political circles, was convinced that this assertion was truthful.[18] Curzon, for his part, was willing to accept it. In a personal letter to Derby on the 13th he wrote: "The whole thing as I see it was the French reply, not to Warsaw (because they did not know what we had done there), but to Lympne. Millerand had tried to get us to repudiate Kameneff and all his work at Lympne; and having failed, went back to Paris and sought to queer our pitch there."[19] Curzon went on to emphasize the extent of the rift which had been opened between the two governments. "This is the second splash of the French in 4-5 months,"[20] he wrote. "Could the Alliance survive a third?"

✧

The French recognition of Wrangel was a quixotic gesture made at least as much with a domestic political purpose in view as with any real hope for ultimate success in itself. As Derby explained in a private letter to Curzon:

They will whittle, indeed have already whittled the recognition down to a very small compass. It is not to mean material help. It is only moral support for what it is worth. There is no doubt the lure in it was the recognition of pre-War debts. The pre-War debts of Russia to France lie very heavy on them. It affects all sorts and conditions of men from the highest to the lowest and for the first time they have got a Government, however feeble it may be, to recognise this Debt and that in itself with the French Public will to a great extent outweigh the dangers but even that has not succeeded and I do not myself think that there can be any Military agreement.[21]

[17] See Henderson's report of a conversation with Paléologue on the morning of 12 August (Paris telegram 965; *ibid.*, no. 426) and, in particular, the long telegram from Millerand to de Fleuriau in London, 14 August, a copy of which was given Lord Derby by Paléologue and forwarded to Curzon with his despatch 2623, 15 August; *ibid.*, no. 441. See also *The Times* 13 August, whose Paris correspondent reported similarly.
[18] Derby (Paris) to Curzon, private letter, 16 August 1920; Curzon MSS, box 22. Derby had just returned to Paris from a period of leave.
[19] Curzon to Derby (Paris), 13 August 1920; *British Documents*, vol. XI, no. 432.
[20] The first "splash" occurred in early April, when French and Belgian forces extended their occupation of the Rhineland in reply to the German government's moving of troops into the demilitarized zone in order to suppress a workers' riot in the wake of the abortive rightist Kapp putsch. The British government disassociated itself from this French response.
[21] From Derby's letter to Curzon cited above, n. 18.

This was one explanation; the recognition can also be viewed, as it was by the French Embassy in London, simply as a gaffe.[22] Like so many acts of French diplomacy during these years following World War I, it served only to emphasize how completely France was dependent upon Great Britain for the continuation of her status as a great power. Without British support, Wrangel would—and did—receive virtually nothing. The only real measures contemplated at Lympne for helping him were operations by the Royal Navy. As the French government made clear in the course of its protracted efforts following 11 August to heal the breach with Britain, no French troops would be sent to the Crimea.[23] Thus, failing British participation, Wrangel would be sent little besides a French high commissioner and a minor amount of munitions. Viewed in the light of these facts the French recognition of Wrangel seems an act of political cynicism. With Soviet armies advancing rapidly upon Warsaw, even in Paris it must have seemed likely that they would finish with the Poles and then turn on Wrangel. What would be his prospects then, no matter how much local support he could command? And who if not the one European power which recognized him would bear the responsibility of protecting his forces from annihilation?

The British, it was clear, would wait for definite news from Minsk.

[22] So de Fleuriau told Curzon in their interview on 13 August. See Curzon's despatch 2758 to Derby, cited above, n. 4.

[23] In an effort to reconcile the divergent British and French policies, Millerand offered to state publicly that recognition of Wrangel did not mean that any French troops would be sent to Russia (telegram, Millerand to Fleuriau, 16 August 1920, sent by latter to Curzon on same day, *British Documents*, vol. XI, no. 447; see also Derby's telegram 986 to Curzon, 17 August; *ibid.*, no. 449).

These and other French efforts to close the breach between the two governments received little sympathy from London. As Curzon told Derby on 17 August, an "attempt to find a form of words that would bridge over a gap that has a real existence is not likely to lead to satisfactory results" (telegram 919; *ibid.*, no. 450). The French government's efforts were made no easier by its response to the so-called "Colby Note" of 10 August, a statement by the American Secretary of State of Washington's attitude towards the Soviet government. Millerand's reply, on the 14th (like the American note, released to the press), stated that his government completely agreed with the American government that the Soviet regime was a pariah it could not recognize, and that in this spirit it had taken steps to recognize an alternative Russian government (Wrangel's). For the Colby Note see *Foreign Relations, 1920*, vol. III, pp. 463-68; for the French reply, *ibid.*, pp. 469-70. The latter was characterized by Curzon as "a very strange method of repairing the breach . . . in language calculated to cause the maximum of offence to us" (Curzon to Derby, telegram 913, 15 August; *British Documents*, vol. XI, no. 438). For an account of the origins and effects of the Colby Note, see Carroll, *Western Opinion*, pp. 188-202.

London's interpretation of the Lympne agreements was that the measures contemplated would not be put into effect until it had been demonstrated that the Soviet government did not intend to offer acceptable armistice terms to the Poles. Here was the importance of Kamenev's letter conveying terms which the British government considered to be broadly acceptable: it gave Moscow a great psychological advantage. Previous to its arrival the British would have to be shown that the Bolsheviks did not intend to offer reasonable terms to the Poles, but the demonstration could not be long delayed. Although Lloyd George had said at Lympne that the British government would not go to war for the sake of the forty-eight hours' difference between 9 August, the date of the original British truce proposal, and 11 August, when (according to Chicherin's note) the armistice discussions were supposed actually to begin, he was in no mood for longer delay. Kamenev's letter of the 10th, however, made it seem much more likely that the Soviet terms would be acceptable.

This expectation, in turn, made the prospect of further delays in the start of the Minsk negotiations more tolerable than it would otherwise have been, especially when circumstances made the delays seem the fault as much of the Poles as of the Russians. Thus a Soviet truce team appeared at the front at the stipulated place and time on 9 August, ostensibly ready to escort the Polish delegation to Minsk. But no Polish delegation appeared—and not surprisingly, because although the Soviet government had informed London of all these arrangements, it had evidently neglected to make sure that Warsaw was informed.[24] Kamenev's letter, therefore, bought Moscow valuable time in which the military conquest of Poland might be completed without undue risk of British intervention. This is not to say that the Poles, for their part, were eager to begin negotiations. Lord D'Abernon noted in his diary in Warsaw on 12 August that he could not criticize the Polish government for having drawn the conclusion "that any negotiation with Moscow before the coming battle is mere trifling and can by no possibility lead to serious re-

[24] Apparently the Polish government first learned that their delegates were expected on the 9th at the front from a news agency despatch from Lympne. See *The Times*, 12 August 1920, for despatches from Warsaw and statements by the Polish Legation in London. It is curious that the recent massive joint Polish-Soviet production, *Dokumenty i materiały do historii stosunków polsko-radzieckich*, vol. III, does not print the text of the radio message from Chicherin to Sapieha allegedly sent on 7 August; this message is printed in the earlier *Dokumenty vneshnei politiki*, vol. III, p. 91.

sult."[25] Not until the 14th, with Soviet armies converging upon Warsaw, did the Polish delegation cross the front lines. And not until the 17th did the discussions at Minsk actually begin. By then, although it was too early for the negotiators at Minsk to know it, Piłsudski had driven home the first blows of his brilliant counter-attack.

✧

In Great Britain the period between the Lympne conference and the astounding Polish victory on the Vistula was one of anxious waiting—anxious for the government, which wondered whether it would be called upon to redeem the promises it had made at Spa and Lympne; anxious for the Labour movement, which feared (and hoped?) that if the government acted to aid the Poles, the Council of Action would be forced to match its militant declarations with deeds; and anxious, also, for a section of what can only be called the military Establishment, which laid plans to meet "direct action" from the Left with direct action of a more familar sort.[26] Had the nightmares—or fantasies—of all these groups come true, the United Kingdom would have been plunged simultaneously into foreign war abroad and civil war at home.

An index of Parliamentary concern was the special arrangements the government made to assure that the two chambers, once disbanded for the long summer recess, might quickly be reconvened. On 16 August, when the House of Commons finally rose for the vacation, Bonar Law introduced into the adjournment motion a provision whereby the Speaker, on the advice of the government, might recall the body at any time. A similar motion was passed in the Lords.[27] The sitting on the 16th was itself unusual; the government had originally intended to adjourn the House on the 12th, but the news of the French recognition of Wrangel on the 11th caused it to postpone the following day's sitting until the following Monday, the 16th. By then, it was hoped, there would be news from Minsk, and the meaning of the French action would have become clearer, so that the government would be able to declare its intentions.[28]

[25] D'Abernon, *Eighteenth Decisive Battle*, p. 74.
[26] For these plans, see the following chapter.
[27] 133 *H.C. Deb.*, cols. 663-65; 41 *H.L. Deb.*, col. 1240.
[28] 133 *H.C. Deb.*, cols. 406-07 (11 August 1920).

As we have seen, these hopes were not fulfilled. The government knew little more on the 16th than it did on the 11th regarding the Russo-Polish negotiations, or lack of them, and regarding Wrangel it knew simply that the news of French recognition was true. The intervening weekend, however, did bring an impressive demonstration by the Council of Action, and it was this which most preoccupied those who spoke in the House on Monday.

The occasion was a Special Conference of representatives of the entire Labour movement at the Central Hall, Westminster, on the morning of Friday, 13 August, to listen to reports by the Council of Action, and to give it national endorsement. In attendance were 689 delegates from the trades unions and 355 from the Parliamentary Labour Party and local constituency organizations. For the first time a body representing all of the many elements in the movement gave approval to the principle of using industrial action for political ends. The conference's main resolution, which passed unanimously, stated:

That this Conference of Trade Union and Labour representatives hails with satisfaction the Russian Government's declaration in favour of the complete independence of Poland as set forth in their Peace Terms to Poland, and, realizing the gravity of the international situation, pledges itself to resist any and every form of military and naval intervention against the Soviet Government of Russia.

It accordingly instructs the Council of Action to remain in being until they have secured:

(1) An absolute guarantee that the armed forces of Great Britain shall not be used in support of Poland, Baron Wrangel, or any other military or naval effort against the Soviet Government.

(2) The withdrawal of all British naval forces operating directly or indirectly as a blockading influence against Russia.

(3) The recognition of the Russian Soviet Government and the establishment of unrestricted trading and commercial relationships between Great Britain and Russia.

This Conference further refuses to be associated with any Alliance between Great Britain and France or any other country which commits us to any support of Wrangel, Poland, or the supply of munitions or other war material for any form of attack upon Soviet Russia.

The Conference authorizes the Council of Action to call for any and every form of withdrawal of labour which circumstances may require to give effect to the foregoing policy, and calls upon every Trade Union official, Executive Committee, Local Council of Action, and the membership in general to act swiftly, loyally and courageously in order to sweep away secret bargaining and diplomacy and to insure that the foreign policy of Great Britain may be in accord with the well-known desires of the people for an end to war and the interminable threats of war.[29]

The implications of this resolution were spelled out by J. H. Thomas, one of Labour's most distinguished parliamentarians and trade-union leaders, who always before had been resolutely opposed to the principle of direct action. To stormy applause he stated: "I do not want you to be under any misapprehension that giving effect to this resolution means a mere strike. When you vote for this resolution do not do so on the assumption that you are merely voting for a simple down-tools policy. It is nothing of the kind. . . . It means a challenge to the whole Constitution of the country."[30]

Lloyd George agreed with this appraisal. On the following Monday, 16 August, he told the House of Commons that Labour's apparent willingness to bypass constitutional forms was "one of the most formidable challenges ever given to democracy, and without hesitation every Government must accept that challenge."[31] Yet although he was willing to concede that the principle of direct action offered a basic challenge to the Constitution he chose to belittle the challenge actually offered by the Council of Action: it was, he said, like "the swinging of a sledge hammer against an open door . . . merely for purposes of display."[32] Labour had tried to convince the public that "had it not been for this dire threat, this country would have been plunged into war." Eyeing the Opposition across the chamber, the Prime Minister stated: "There is not a responsible man on those Benches who does not know that is not true."[33]

Earlier in the afternoon's debate Bonar Law had made the same point with even more emphasis. "It has been suggested that this outburst of public opinion has dictated our attitude," he said. "On the contrary, the outburst of public opinion, which has been very remarkable, was an outburst not antagonistic to, but in support of

---

[29] Council of Action, *Labour and the Russian-Polish War*, London, 1920, pp. 20-21. (This pamphlet is a verbatim account of the 13 August Special Conference.)

[30] *Ibid.*, p. 16.   [31] 133 *H.C. Deb.*, col. 687.

[32] *Ibid.*, col. 595. (Lloyd George made this comparison not during the debate itself, but in a reply during Question Hour.)

[33] *Ibid.*, col. 688.

our policy." He was glad to be able to say, he continued, that the government's policy, reaffirmed at the Lympne conference, had been "enthusiastically adopted by the Country." Bonar Law finished his speech, which was on the recess adjournment motion providing for the quick recall of Parliament, by assuring the House: "If we cannot succeed in securing a general peace . . . this Government will not land this country in any warlike operations unless on grounds so plain and obvious that the whole country will be behind us." Speaking at almost the same moment in the House of Lords, Curzon gave the same assurances.[34]

These were, perhaps, good debating tactics, appealing as they did to the sense of realism and pragmatism so deeply ingrained in the British Labour movement. There was undoubtedly a certain degree of bluff behind the impressive unanimity of the Labour Conference the previous Friday, and a politician as sensitive as Lloyd George was surely well aware of it. They were good tactics provided that the government was certain it would not have to intervene to help the Poles. Yet on 16 August there was no way Lloyd George or Bonar Law could know that they would not be driven to do so; if they *had* been, ridicule would not have made the Labour opposition more tractable. Here, of course, is the great unanswerable question of the summer of 1920. Had the Poles not saved themselves, would the Allies—especially the British—have stepped in to help them?

---

[34] *Ibid.*, cols. 665-68, and 41 *H.L. Deb.*, cols. 1241-42.
It should be noted that the government gave even these assurances to Parliament with considerable reluctance. They had originally been requested by Asquith, on behalf of the Opposition Liberals, and J. R. Clynes, for Labour, in the course of debate on the afternoon of 10 August (133 *H.C. Deb.*, cols. 279 and 287). In the Cabinet meeting which followed in order to consider Kamenev's letter, Lloyd George expressed concern that a promise by the government to consult Parliament *before* carrying out the anti-Soviet measures agreed upon at Lympne would weaken the credibility of the threat of these measures in the eyes of the Soviet government, which knew full well the strength of antiwar sentiment in Great Britain. On the other hand, it was argued that the government could not "ask for a blank cheque"—although it had every right to prepare for the contingency of hostilities, it was "not justified in going beyond those preparations without consulting Parliament." In the end Lloyd George's view prevailed: it was agreed that the government could *not* undertake not to act in an emergency without first consulting Parliament, and that in such circumstances it would summon Parliament immediately and ask for *post facto* approval of its actions. Parliament could, of course, disapprove, and thus bring down the government, but not unless a substantial number of government supporters were to vote with the Opposition—a much less likely eventuality than would have been the expression of serious reservations from the Government benches *before* the initiation of military measures. (Minutes, Conference of Ministers, 10 August 1920, 7 P.M.; cited above, chap. V., n. 97.)

And had the British government done so, would the Labour movement have made good its threat of "a challenge to the whole Constitution of the country?"

If Lloyd George was confident that he would not be forced into intervening, he was depending upon a very weak reed—Kamenev's letter conveying the terms Moscow proposed to offer the Poles. In his speech in the House on 16 August Bonar Law made much of the fact that only the previous day Lloyd George had received another letter from Kamenev stating in the most categorical way that, despite the provocative behavior of the French, the Soviet government would not alter those terms.[35] Yet we have seen that at Lympne there had been at least an inkling, by way of an intercepted Russian message, that some of the Soviet terms would be incompatible with the continued existence of an independent Poland.[36]

There is, of course, the possibility that Lloyd George had already made up his mind that the military situation in Poland was so hopeless, and the resources at the disposal of his government for changing it so slight, that any intervention would be useless, and that therefore he would sanction none no matter what the circumstances. In that case the taunt that Labour was battering at an open door becomes a truism—although one known only to Lloyd George, the doorkeeper. This possibility obviously cannot be dismissed, but it does not seem likely. It would have been politically as difficult for Lloyd George not to have intervened at all in Poland's behalf, once it had been demonstrated that the Soviet demands would not allow real Polish independence, as it would have been for him to have ordered massive intervention. The latter would have been made impossible by the Labour movement, despite the lip service paid to the independence of Poland in the Special Conference resolution.

It is more difficult to conclude that complete non-intervention would have been impossible, but Lloyd George had committed himself to such an extent at Lympne that both the domestic and the international political price of blatant non-fulfillment would have been very high. Given the Prime Minister's past performance and his political style, it is reasonable to suppose that had his hand been called he would have chosen a typical Lloyd-Georgian compromise:

[35] 133 *H.C. Deb.*, col. 667. For the text of Kamenev's note of 15 August, see *Dokumenty vneshnei politiki*, vol. III, p. 136; English version published in *The Daily Herald*, 16 August 1920.

[36] See above, chap. V.

intervention to a degree sufficient to allow him to tell the French (and his few interventionist domestic critics) that he had met his commitments, but slight enough to allow him to evade, if not entirely to avoid, the blows—both verbal and actual—of his Labour opposition.[37] This is, after all, how he had dealt with the Russian problem since mid-1919. In the Polish situation it might well have been true that such a fine line of compromise did not exist. But if any man could have found it, that man was Lloyd George.

❖

Two rather minor aspects of the British involvement in the Polish-Soviet crisis offer some insight into the government's approach to the larger problem. The first is the fact that although it sent a naval squadron to Helsingfors as a warning to Moscow, the British government nevertheless continued during these weeks to refuse to supply arms requested by the Finnish government, and at the same time continued to encourage the Finns to abandon their irredentist claims on Eastern Karelia and to put an end to their three years of on-again, off-again warfare with the Soviet government.[38] Similarly, London also worked to discourage the conclusion of an anti-Soviet defensive alliance among the three Baltic states, Finland, and Poland—despite the fact that such a union, if it could have been formed, might have done much to eliminate the destructive hostility between Poland and Lithuania—on the grounds that it would have been needlessly provocative to Moscow.[39]

The common thread running through these actions and expressions of views is the recognition that the eastern Baltic would in-

[37] Apparently the Council of Action made plans to cope with such an eventuality. On 18 August 1920 *The Times* carried a report from Bradford that the Council in all probability would not order a general strike, which it felt could quickly be broken, but rather a strike only of those engaged in the manufacture or transport of munitions.

[38] For the purpose and effects of sending units of the Royal Navy to Helsingfors see Curzon to Kidston (Helsingfors), telegram 199, 11 August 1920, and Kidston to Curzon, telegram 572, 14 August; *British Documents*, vol. XI, nos. 419 and 435. For the British refusal to sell arms to the Finns or to aid them in purchasing them elsewhere see Curzon to Kilmarnock (Berlin), telegram 195, 13 June 1920, *ibid.*, vol. X, no. 98; and minutes by Hardinge and Curzon on Kidston (Helsingfors) to Curzon, telegram 574, 16 August, *ibid.*, vol. XI, no. 445, n. 1. For Finnish claims on Eastern Karelia, and British reactions to them, see Hardinge to Acton (Helsingfors), despatch 89, 21 April 1920, *ibid.*, no. 256; Curzon to Hicks-Beach (Helsingfors), telegram 142, 5 May, *ibid.*, no. 255, n. 5; and Curzon to Kidston (Helsingfors), telegram 210, 2 September, *ibid.*, no. 510.

[39] Curzon to Tallents (Riga), telegram 237, 11 August 1920; *ibid.*, no. 420.

evitably be a Russian sphere of influence, and that no foreseeable combination of power—including within it British power—could change this fact. A British naval squadron based at Helsingfors could prevent the Russian fleet from emerging from Kronstadt and thereby perhaps secure better terms for Finland in the Finnish-Soviet peace negotiations which were then in progress, but in London's view it could have little effect on the ultimate outcome of the Russo-Polish war. The Poles would have to save themselves.

This dictum applied also to the second of the two minor aspects of the British involvement which we should consider here: the problems created by the refusal of the German dockworkers of Danzig to handle munitions passing through that port. During a period in early August, as the war approached its final crisis, this recalcitrance threatened to cut off Poland's supply of munitions completely, because Danzig at this time was the only channel through which such supplies could flow: Germany's declaration of neutrality on 20 July was followed by a similar declaration from the government of Czechoslovakia on 10 August, but even before that Czech railroad workers made clear that they would not handle munitions destined for Poland.[40] Danzig, moreover, was completely under the authority of the Allies at this time. Although the Treaty of Versailles provided that it should be established as a Free City under the protection of the League of Nations, it also provided for Allied control of it as an occupied territory until a constitution for the Free City had been drawn up and a treaty negotiated to regulate its relations with Poland.[41] This did not occur until November 1920. Thus, during the summer of 1920 Danzig was governed by an Allied Administrator responsible to the Conference of Ambassadors (the successor to the Supreme Council) in Paris. The Administrator was a British diplomat, Sir Reginald Tower, and at his disposal as occupying forces were two British battalions and a smaller French force, all under the command of General Sir Richard Haking.

[40] For the holding up of munitions shipments by Czech workers, see Crane (Prague) to Secretary of State, telegrams 157 and 162, 26 June and 3 July 1920; U.S. National Archives, State Department file nos. 760c.61/74 and—/83. For the Czech declaration of neutrality: Clerk (Prague) to Curzon, telegram 138, 10 August; *British Documents*, vol. XI, no. 410.

[41] See John Brown Mason, *The Danzig Dilemma: A Study in Peacemaking by Compromise*, Stanford, 1946, pp. 61-63. Under paragraph 2, article 104 of the Treaty of Versailles Poland was guaranteed "without any restriction the free use of service of all waterways, docks, basins, wharves and other works within the territory of the Free City necessary for Polish imports and exports."

As his despatches and telegrams make clear, Tower was more sympathetic towards the Danzigers than to the Poles.[42] There was nothing malicious or conspiratorial about this: one generally has fellow-feelings toward the people with whom one works, and Tower's duties made it necessary for him to work closely with the Danzigers. Although he tried to be impartial, his sympathies made him receptive to the arguments of the Danzig dockworkers against unloading ships carrying munitions for Poland, and more mindful of the consequences of trying to force the issue with the dockworkers than fearful of a Soviet victory over the Poles.

Tower's was the nearsightedness of the man on the spot. General Haking was better able to see the large situation, but he was also blunt in his warnings that any attempt to introduce Polish labor into the port, or even to use British military labor on a large scale (British troops had unloaded one vessel in late July)[43] might result in widespread violence containable only by a garrison much larger than his. Early in August he telegraphed that in order to make it possible to unload munitions he would need at least four additional battalions, and would have to impose "complete military domination" on the city.[44]

Faced with these problems the British government initially equivocated. Lloyd George and Millerand discussed Danzig at Boulogne on 27 July and seem to have decided (the conference minutes are unclear) that Tower should spare no effort to get the munitions cargoes unloaded by "other than military" labor.[45] On 5 August Curzon telegraphed Tower that, in particular, the employment of British labor, military or civilian, was not considered feasible—not an unwise conclusion considering the views of the British Labour movement. Curzon suggested instead the use of Polish labor, ac-

---

[42] See, *e.g.*, Tower's despatches 43, 85, and 120 to the Conference of Ambassadors (Paris), 17 March, 19 April, and 12 August 1920; *British Documents*, vol. XI, nos. 226, 252, and 427. Rumbold in Warsaw took it upon himself to reply, giving the Polish side, to the first of these; see Rumbold to Curzon, despatch 218, 29 March, *ibid.*, no. 240. For a recent pro-Polish view, see Komarnicki, *Polish Republic*, pp. 651-55.

[43] Tower allowed British troops to unload the vessel at the strong urging of the special Anglo-French diplomatic-military mission in Warsaw. See Tower (Danzig) to Curzon, telegram 21, 28 July 1920; *ibid.*, no. 359.

[44] Haking's message was sent as Tower's telegram 26 to Curzon, 6 August 1920; *ibid.*, no. 393.

[45] Reported by Curzon to Tower (Danzig), telegram 29, 28 July 1920; *ibid.*, no. 358. For the relevant minutes of the Boulogne conference, 27 July, see *ibid.*, vol. VIII, no. 79, p. 661.

companied "in the last resort" by an increase in the size of the Allied garrison. Tower responded that Polish labor was completely out of the question.[46] This stalemate continued—punctuated by appeals from the Polish government, justifiably outraged over its loss of rights guaranteed by the Treaty of Versailles—until after the Polish victory on the Vistula.

In the end the French forced the issue. On 22 August a French cruiser arrived and its crew began to unload rifles and ammunition into Polish barges which would be guarded during their trip out of Danzig by French soldiers drawn from the occupation garrison.[47] On the following day, at Lucerne, where he had gone for a holiday, Lloyd George told Giovanni Giolitti, Nitti's successor as Italian premier, that he had concluded that if the British and Italian governments did not join the French in supporting the Poles over Danzig, it would appear that they were not upholding the Treaty of Versailles when Poland was clearly in the right. The Prime Minister had been much influenced in this view by Hankey, who, while passing through Danzig on his mission to Warsaw, had concluded (as he wrote in his diary) "that the Danzigers wanted to be more firmly handled." Accordingly, Hankey drafted for Lloyd George a telegram to Paris saying that he and Giolitti had agreed that the Conference of Ambassadors should instruct Tower that if the Danzig dockworkers refused to unload and convey munitions, then any available labor should be used, under the protection of whatever Allied military force appeared necessary.[48] In Danzig itself the news of this decision had what Tower described as "instant effect": the Danzigers, who had been thought to be so fierce that the War Office's Director of Military Operations (General Radcliffe, who, it will be remembered, was the military representative on Lord D'Abernon's special mission to Warsaw) had estimated only three days previously that no fewer than sixteen Allied battalions would be necessary to keep order if munitions were unloaded, gave in completely. Both the dockworkers and the railwaymen an-

[46] Curzon to Tower (Danzig), telegram 32, 5 August 1920; *ibid.*, vol. XI, no. 385. Tower to Curzon, telegram 31, 8 August; *ibid.*, no. 404.

[47] Tower (Danzig) to Curzon, telegram 42, 23 August 1920; *ibid.*, no. 471.

[48] "Notes of a Conversation held at the Villa Haslihorn, Lucerne, on Monday, August 23, 1920, at 10.30 A.M.;" *ibid.*, vol. VIII, no. 89, pp. 780-81. Lloyd George's unnumbered *en clair* telegram to Derby (Paris), 23 August, is printed as appendix 2, pp. 781-82. Hankey MS diary, entry for 18 September, 1920.

nounced that henceforth they would handle any and all cargoes to and from Poland.[49]

By then, of course, the magnitude of the Polish victory over the Bolsheviks had become known. The blockage of Danzig could no longer affect the outcome of the struggle to the East, which was obviously the principal motivation behind the threatened general strike from the beginning. To defy the Allies now would bring Danzig only new hardships, with no conceivable reward. Would the Danzigers have given in so easily to the threat of force while a Soviet victory over Poland still seemed likely? Obviously we cannot know, but we can suspect that they would have. Why did the British government take so long to make the response it finally made? Here it seems likely that the delay was due to bureaucratic rather than policy considerations. Tower, on the scene, was clearly reluctant to force the issue. Curzon—rather abstractly, perhaps—was fully aware of the injustice of the situation, but he could not imagine where, under normal procedures, the government could find the troops necessary to correct it.[50] It was clear, however, that normal procedures could not be followed, and that troops, if sent, would have to be drawn from other equally demanding commitments. Only Lloyd George could cut through the bureaucratic fog. Yet it is possible that the matter did not really seize his attention until after mid-August, by which time the barrage of telegrams from Warsaw and Paris—and Hankey's confirming observations—had undoubtedly made something of an impression.[51] Before then he was absorbed in his dealings with Kamenev and the Council of Action. In any case—and here, perhaps, is the most important factor—the issue of more munitions for Poland became rather academic for Lloyd George during the crucial week of 10-17 August. Then he felt that the Russo-Polish conflict would be settled not by Polish

---

[49] Tower (Danzig) to Curzon, telegram 49, 26 August 1920; *ibid.*, vol. XI, no. 489. For the actual orders to Tower from the Conference of Ambassadors, see Henderson (Paris) to Curzon, telegram 1022, 24 August; *ibid.*, no. 480. For General Radcliffe's estimate of sixteen battalions see Tower to Curzon, telegram 40, 20 August; *ibid.*, no. 467.

[50] See Curzon's typically Curzonesque minute of 18 August 1920; *ibid.*, no. 451, n. 1.

[51] Thus, on 5 August Lloyd George confidently told the House of Commons: "We have taken effective steps to remove the obstacles in the way of the transmission to Poland from Danzig of military supplies which were detained at that port" (132 *H.C. Deb.*, col. 2629). If Lloyd George had been paying close attention to the problem he would surely have known that no such steps had been taken.

arms but by Polish disarmament. This, after all, had been the purport of Kamenev's letter of the 10th.

❖

If the intercepted telegram which arrived at Lympne on 8 August might have been read by Lloyd George and his colleagues as an indication that the note they received from Kamenev two days later did not accurately convey the conditions of peace which Moscow intended to impose on Warsaw, subsequent "intercepts"—virtually all of them, however, not circulated within the British government until after 16 August, when the tide of battle began to flow in Poland's favor[52]—made this fact absolutely clear. They also made clear, moreover, that Kamenev was well aware of the discrepancy and that between him and the rest of the Politburo in Moscow there was sharp disagreement as to how its existence should be presented to the world.

There was, in fact, only one point at contention—what came to be called the "militia clause" of the Soviet conditions. Kamenev's note of 10 August to Lloyd George, it will be recalled, had stated without elaboration that "All arms, over and above such as may be required for the needs of the Army as reduced [to 50,000 men] above *as well as of the Civic Militia*, shall be handed over to Soviet Russia and the Ukraine."[53] This was the only mention of the "civic militia" in Kamenev's note. There was no indication as to either its composition or its size. The term "civic militia" itself apparently originated either with Kamenev or with another member of the delegation more familiar with the usages of the English language and the images of sturdy independent yeomen guarding their village gates which those words conjure up. Certainly they did not imply what Chicherin and the Politburo had in mind: armed Polish workers more powerful than the weakened Polish army, serving under the most propitious circumstances—after the Red Army had occupied the country—as the instrument for the imposition of Communist rule, or, if things did not work out so well, serving at least to prevent a rebirth of Polish militarism.

[52] Available evidence does not indicate what factors controlled the amount of elapsed time between transmission of the telegrams in Moscow or London and their circulation of deciphered translated copies within the British government. It should be remembered, as well, that not all the copies within the Lloyd George and Davidson MSS bear circulation dates.
[53] Italics added.

The Polish-Soviet War

As the dialogue of telegrams between London and Moscow made increasingly clear, Chicherin had no wish to disguise these intentions, evidently supposing that they would serve to galvanize revolutionary sentiment among Western workers. Thus, to Kamenev on 12 August he telegraphed: "Have you explained in the press the idea of arming the workmen as a new type of guarantee of peace? To the Imperialist land proprietors we oppose the class which does not want war. Is it not possible to boom this point by agitators so as to bring it home to a wide public?"[54] This message crossed two from Kamenev sent that same day, one saying "I again point out that the point about the arming of trade unions should be presented at Minsk as the creation of a Citizens' Militia,"[55] the other stating:

I have just no[w] had a conversation with the Council of Action in full force; the attitude even of the most "right" members is magnificent. Two thousand delegates are expected at to-morrow's special congress. A resolution in favour of general peace with Russia and against France, with a genuine threat of a strike, is assured. . . . The English Committee asserts that its action will be decisive, since it holds in its hands the supply of coal to France, and *advises no change in the published conditions for armistice*, which the workmen of England have decided to use as their own basis. It would be fine to receive, for tomorrow's congress, news that the Minsk Conference has met, *and that the terms presented by us strictly correspond with the published terms.*[56]

Kamenev reiterated these arguments in a telegram to Moscow the following morning, before the opening of the congress. The preceding evening, he said, three leading members of the Council of Action came to him.

They said [he related] that the interests of the solidarity and decisiveness of the action of the British workmen demand that (the conditions published by us) remain unchanged. They said "The whole movement is in our hands. We will not let George move a finger. We will squeeze France. We will stop the supply of coal if the published conditions remain unchanged. If they are changed the movement will be upset and feeling

[54] Chicherin to Kamenev (London), telegram 326, 12 August 1920; intercept 003792, circulated 17 August, Lloyd George MSS, file F/203/1/9, also Davidson MSS.
[55] Kamenev (London) to Chicherin, telegrams 404-05, 12 August 1920; intercept 003790, circulated 17 August, Lloyd George MSS, file F/203/1/9, also Davidson MSS.
[56] Kamenev (London) to Chicherin, telegrams 413-14, 12 August 1920; intercept 003776, circulated 14 August, Lloyd George MSS, file F/203/1/1, also Davidson MSS. (Emphasis added. Note the early circulation date of this intercept.)

shaken. If the Russian delegates at Minsk keep to these conditions then British labour will not let George escape, otherwise he will slip away, taking advantage of the first pretext to join up with France."[57]

All these circumstances, together with the rapidly growing rift between Britain and France, Kamenev continued, "change our initial position." Here, it should be noted, was an implication that Kamenev's "original position" may have been that one version of the Soviet conditions should be presented to the British government, and another to the Poles. "The letter to Lloyd George about the possible change of conditions (see my telegrams) I of course did not send," he continued, and he explained:

We suggest that Minsk should adhere strictly to the published conditions for the following reasons:—

First: the undivided sympathy and understanding of the workers of England is more important than the most thorough-going reduction of the Polish army, even from the point of view of war with France.

Second: Unless we abide by our first conditions, we shall not be able to add fuel to the conflict between England and France, which at present is more important for us than anything else.

Third: and most important: The Poles will refuse our first conditions in any case.

An interview with Sapieha which took place on the 11th, is published to-day. He says: "Kameneff's terms are inacceptable. No disarmament is admissible." That settles the question in my opinion. If we keep to our first conditions, we shall return from Minsk, having shown our moderation and sincerity, won over the British workers completely and kept our hands free.[58]

Not only Lloyd George, but also Parliament and the press, Kamenev said, had acknowledged the "justice" of the peace conditions he had conveyed. Desire for peace with Russia was "taking possession of the whole of England from top to bottom." And Lloyd George, too, would be "compelled to follow this path unless by our behaviour at Minsk we sow distrust among the workers and the Asquithians, and give Millerand and Churchill an opportunity of proving their sagacity."

In another message to Chicherin that same day, Kamenev took

[57] Kamenev (London) to Litvinov (Copenhagen), copies to Chicherin and Lenin, telegrams 266-68, 13 August 1920; intercept 003793, circulated 17 August, Lloyd George MSS, file F/203/1/1, also Davidson MSS.
[58] *Idem.* For the interview with Sapieha see *The Times*, 13 August 1920.

sharp issue with Moscow's instructions for him to make propaganda out of the Soviet wish to arm the Polish workers. "To boom the arming of the workmen at the present moment here is absolutely disadvantageous, and only likely to spoil the situation described in our preceding telegrams," he said. "Instead of booming this in London it would be better to get all weapons over and above those that are required for the army of 50,000 and distribute them to the workmen."[59]

Not surprisingly, Kamenev grew even more insistent after the Special Conference of the Labour movement on the 13th. The meeting, he reported, had made the Council of Action "the greatest factor in world policy."[60] Once again, he said, the Council's leaders had come to him to declare that if Russia stood by its peace terms as published, the Council would prevent any anti-Soviet action by Great Britain. Because the increasingly vigorous Labour movement represented a real threat to Lloyd George, "his immediate object will be to stop this movement by proving our insincerity or our willingness to make peace with Poland and it would be the greatest blunder if we should in any way help Lloyd George." Thus far, Kamenev indicated, the achievements of Soviet (and his own) diplomacy had been "both unexpected and wide by means of calculated manoeuvres"; here he presumably meant the manner in which he had employed his note to Lloyd George. These achievements, he said, could be destroyed "by obstinately insisting on the wording of one point which was put forward by me under quite different conditions and calculated to produce a different effect and which, to judge from your telegram, has now assumed the form of some sort of new doctrine."

In Kamenev's view, Soviet diplomacy could in the circumstances achieve much more through a display of magnanimity than through duplicity. In exchange for its willingness to conclude peace with Poland, the Soviet government should demand immediate opening of peace (and not merely "trade") negotiations with Great Britain. He continued:

[59] Kamenev (London) to Chicherin, telegram 427, 13 August 1920; intercept 003809, circulated 18 August, Lloyd George MSS, file F/31/1/39.

[60] Kamenev (London) to Litvinov (Copenhagen), copies to Lenin and Chicherin, telegrams 282-83, 285-87 (a note on the file copy says 284 was garbled and therefore indecipherable), 14 August 1920; intercept 003813, circulated 18 August, Lloyd George MSS file F/31/1/39, also Davidson MSS.

We must not allow the ferment created among the workmen to subside. I should consider it extremely useful if in the course of the Minsk negotiations we could indulge in some act of magnanimity over and above our programme and calculated to influence British labour. Send as often as possible reports to the Council for publication on the progress of the negotiations in Minsk. I am almost sure that under the influence of France the Poles will nevertheless reject our modest terms, which have already been recognised by the whole of England except Churchill.

Here, then, was one of the principal assumptions underlying Kamenev's choice of tactics: that Moscow would have no need to expose its real conditions of peace because the Poles would in any case reject even the more moderate ones already made public, thus allowing the Red Army to complete its occupation of the country. Whether or not these arguments had any effect on his colleagues Kamenev did not know. His telegram went on sharply to rebuke Lenin: "You have not fulfilled a single one of my requests, you have not expressed your gratitude to the workmen of England, you do not inform me of the plans and of the attitude of the Central Executive Committee. It is difficult to work under conditions like this, particularly when we have to deal with an organisation like the Council of Action which demands information daily."[61]

Kamenev's message coincided with an equally sharp rebuke addressed to himself. On 14 August Chicherin, also worried about appearances of duplicity, telegraphed: "It is not understood why, in the laying down of your written conditions, no mention is made of the arming of workmen, and this has placed us in a very awkward position as the later publication of this very radical condition will give an impression of perfidy."[62] The same message went on to say that Karol Daniszewski, the Polish communist at the head of the Soviet delegation to the Minsk talks, was "somewhat strengthening the original draft of the terms," defining some more sharply, and stipulating "that the functions of police and gendarmerie be handed over to the armed workmen." For Kamenev, this news must have recalled a warning from Litvinov in Copenhagen nine days previously. "I am afraid," said Litvinov, who shared Kamenev's view of the necessity to be constantly mindful of Western opinion, "that

[61] *Idem.*
[62] Chicherin to Kamenev (London), telegrams 335-36, 14 August 1920; intercept 003814, circulated 18 August, Lloyd George MSS, file F/31/1/39.

the excessive activity of the Polish Communists in Moscow or of Stalin may deprive us of our present winning position."[63]

It should be emphasized that the issue in contention between Kamenev and Lenin, whose views dominated the Politburo in this instance as in so many others, was one of tactics rather than objectives. Kamenev made this plain in a telegram on the 15th, when he again urged that Daniszewski should present the same terms at Minsk as had been given Lloyd George in London.[64] He continued:

It is the business of our delegates . . . to make clear what we mean by a civil militia, to guarantee themselves against this being transformed into a regular army and especially under cover of this guarantee to carry out in actual fact the points of the arming of the workmen. . . . [T]he workman element of this militia will of itself alone be able to give us a guarantee that arms left by us . . . will not be again turned to the use of imperialistic aims. The English . . . will easily consent to this, but if we openly make a declaration about the arming of the workmen this might easily be considered as interference and direct "Sovietisation."

I trust that you understand the importance I attach to the procedure of the negotiations which is dictated to me by the desire to preserve the strength and unity of the working anti-militarist movement in England. As far as we understand the following and no more are to be our chief proposals at Minsk: "The handing over to Russia and the Ukraine of all arms over and above those necessary for the army reduced according to point one and for the arming of a civil militia."

The rest can be brought in under the guise of definition of the extent and control of this militia.[65]

On the copy of this "intercept" which can be found in the Lloyd George Papers, the quoted passage is singled out with a heavy vertical pencil line, while the last sentence is underscored. And in the margin there appears, in Winston Churchill's characteristic handwriting: "This is an unmistakable avowal of mala fides."

---

[63] Litvinov (Copenhagen) to Kamenev (London), telegrams 303-04, 5 August 1920; intercept 003686, Davidson MSS. Litvinov's reference to Stalin is unclear. Although Stalin was a cautious advocate of the march on Warsaw, he was occupied at this time with the campaign on the southern front near Lvov. See Deutscher, *Prophet Armed*, pp. 465-66.

[64] Kamenev (London) to Litvinov (Copenhagen), copies to Chicherin and Lenin, telegrams 290-92, 15 August 1920; intercept 003816, circulated 18 August; Lloyd George MSS, file F/31/1/39, also Davidson MSS.

[65] The quoted passage, of course, was (with due allowances for translation from English to Russian and back again) from Kamenev's letter to Lloyd George of 10 August. Italics in the last paragraph added.

Whether because of the force of Kamenev's arguments or not, Chicherin telegraphed two days later that Moscow would follow the course he recommended. "Only the day before yesterday," the Commissar for Foreign Affairs stated, "on the publication of news of the Extraordinary London Congress, we changed our line of action, adapting it to the internal state of affairs in England, so as not to allow Lloyd George to break up the English movement." Chicherin was never one to accept advice gracefully, however; now he found another reason for taking issue with Kamenev. "Therefore," he said, "the arming of the workmen according to your modified suggestion would be, we think, a great mistake, since it was not published in the conditions in London."[66]

Surely close to despair at the tone of these messages from Moscow, Kamenev patiently replied with a long explanation of what he had in mind. He saw no difficulties with regard to Moscow's change in course, he said. His "sole point of departure" from Chicherin's conditions was his preference for "a more veiled formulation of the point about the arming of the workmen." His colleagues should understand that his formulation had been based on the fact that he had had to present it on 10 August, when it still looked as if Lloyd George and Millerand might be able to come to an agreement, and at the very moment of the formation of the Council of Action, whose approval was in the circumstances vitally necessary. Rothstein had at the time asserted that, more than anything else, a bald statement of Soviet intention to arm the Polish workers would "upset" the Council of Action and facilitate an Anglo-French accord. Given these objectives, Kamenev continued, he had achieved them: Lloyd George and Millerand had been unable to find common ground, and the Council of Action stood firmly behind the Soviet position.

But he would insist once again, he said, that contrary to what Chicherin's message implied, his own statement in London had in no way hamstrung either the Soviet government in Moscow or its delegation at Minsk. In his letter to Lloyd George, after all, "the creation and arming of a civil militia is exactly and clearly stated." Kamenev's implication was that therefore he (and Moscow) could not be accused of "perfidy." He continued:

[66] Chicherin to Kamenev (London), telegrams 351-52, 17 August 1920; no intercept number or circulation date on file copy, Lloyd George MSS, file F/203/1/10, also Davidson MSS.

It is the business of the Minsk delegates to develop this point further. Not only this point but all other points need to be further developed and made concrete, e.g. decision as to the form of control, etc. However far you may go in direct negotiations with the Poles concerning disarmament, the reduction of the army or the civil militia—these are questions of one and the same kind, and they should be decided after consideration of the present situation. The most important point is that to-day the labour movement both in France and in England is considerably stronger and more determined than it was ten days ago—that to-day Lloyd George and even Millerand are considerably more tied in their possible actions than they were ten days ago, and you can act considerably more firmly than at the moment when we published the terms.

And in an admonitory tone indicative, perhaps, of his higher position within the councils of the Communist Party than that occupied by Chicherin, Kamenev added: "I hope that you and I will not have to return to this point again, that the Executive Committee will recognize that in changing the formulation there was no mistake but simply a manoeuvre required by the local situation here ten days ago."[67]

Chicherin did, however, return to the point one last time, and he did so in a way which made himself appear as merely the neutral transmitter of information. On 26 August he telegraphed to Kamenev "the text of an extract from the minutes of the meeting of the political bureau on August 20th." The relevant portion read: "The political bureau expresses regret that the Delegation omitted the clause concerning the arming of the workers and requests that no omissions be made in the future."[68]

These telegrams between the Soviet government and its representatives in London were all available within the highest reaches of the British government, but with only a few exceptions they were not circulated until late August, after the Polish crisis was resolved: decipherment and translation evidently took nearly a week, sometimes longer. The actual presentation of the Soviet terms to the Poles took place on 19 August at the second meeting between the two delegations at Minsk. They stated that the small Polish army would be "supplemented by a civil militia, to be organized among

[67] Kamenev (London) to Chicherin, telegrams 481-85, 19 August 1920; intercept 003877, circulated 24 August 1920, Davidson MSS.

[68] Chicherin to Kamenev (London), telegrams 411-13, 26 August 1920; intercept 003957, circulated 31 August, Lloyd George MSS, file F/9/2/42.

the workers, to maintain order and safeguard the security of the population."[69] Chicherin had, in fact, already described the civil militia and its role in a set of answers written on 11 August to questions put to him by a correspondent of the International News Service. The Polish workers, he said, would be armed for the maintenance of public order, and he explained:

> The workers' militia will be a counterpoise to Polish Imperialist landlords. Thus the Soviet Government seeks the best guarantee in arming the Polish workers, trusting to find in them a bulwark for peace. This is quite a new idea in international affairs. The Polish people is deserving of the greatest attention.
>
> . . . Instead of Russian occupation, the Soviet Government relies on arming the Polish workers to maintain peace.

Chicherin's explanation was published in the *Berliner Tageblatt* on 15 August; that same day it was also broadcast by Moscow Radio, and it was printed in *The Times* on the 17th. The *Tageblatt's* version, however, was noticed and immediately telegraphed to London by the British mission in Berlin. On the incoming telegram (it arrived at the Foreign Office on the 16th), J. D. Gregory minuted, with the initialled agreement of Lords Hardinge and Curzon: "This would be nothing less than the establishment of armed Bolshevism in Poland—which would signify a radical modification of the Soviet terms as presented to us."[70]

Soviet statements subsequent to the Polish victory, when the whole matter had become merely academic, were equally frank in implying that in the eyes of the Soviet leadership the civic militia was the instrument by which the communist rule would have been imposed upon Poland in the unlikely event that the Red Army, by its very presence, did not succeed in doing so.[71] Whether or not such a militia—even a large one, such as Moscow evidently in-

[69] The text of the Soviet terms given the Poles at Minsk on 19 August 1920 is in *Dokumenty i materiały do historii stosunków polsko-radzieckich*, vol. III, no. 189, along with the protocol of that day's session of the Minsk conference (document no. 188). The Soviet terms are also in *Dokumenty vneshnei politiki*, vol. III, pp. 137-39, where they are incorrectly dated 17 August, as is the English translation in Degras, *Soviet Documents*, vol. I, pp. 201-02.

[70] Gregory's minute was on Kilmarnock (Berlin) to Curzon, telegram 483, 15 August 1920; file 211722/40430/55, F.O. 371/3917.

[71] See, *e.g.*, Lenin's speech of 2 October 1920 before the Third All-Russia Congress of Leather Industry Workers in Moscow, in his *Polnoe sobranie sochinenii*, vol. 41, pp. 322 and 325.

tended—would have been sufficient to serve such a purpose in the absence of a clear-cut Soviet military victory, is quite another question. During these early years of their rule the Soviet leaders were repeatedly to express their faith in the working classes of other nations. Thus the terms handed to the Poles at Minsk also went on to stipulate that during the armistice the fifty-verst (thirty-one miles) neutral zone to be created by the withdrawal of Polish forces would be under Polish civilian administration, supervised by mixed Polish-Russian commissions and a "special trade union commission" of Poles. Here was evidence of yet additional faith in the Polish worker. We can only conjecture that had the Soviet leaders succeeded in imposing terms of this sort on Poland they would have found the Polish working class as nationalistic, unadventurous, and opportunistic as the workers of the rest of the world turned out time after time to be, to Moscow's bitter disappointment.

News of the Soviet terms—and of the Polish victory—reached Lloyd George on his holiday at Lucerne. He had left London early on the morning of 18 August, by which time word had come that the Poles had launched a counterattack in defense of Warsaw, but when the outcome of the battle was still completely in doubt. According to a government press release, he hoped to remain away at least three weeks.[72] The very fact that he could leave at such a time is strong indication that the measures he had contemplated taking in the event that the Russians refused to cease their attack, or failed to come to satisfactory terms, were scarcely more than perfunctory ones which could be executed in his absence. Not only had Lloyd George not known of the Polish victory when he left London, but it seems also that, somehow, he had not heard of the "revised" Soviet terms either—a surprising fact considering the wide publicity given to Chicherin's statement concerning them. Thus when he met Giolitti at Lucerne on 22 August, he presented the Italian premier with a draft press communiqué which stated that their two governments were "gratified" that "the Soviet's official terms of peace to be submitted at Minsk, as communicated to the British Government," contained no conditions which might be said to infringe upon Poland's independence! From his remarks to Giolitti, it seems clear that although Lloyd George had heard something about the Russian demand for a Polish workers' militia, he

[72] *The Times*, 18 August 1920.

nonetheless regarded it only as a rumor, or as a policy merely under consideration in Moscow and not yet adopted. It was very important, he said, "for Russia to stand by the conditions which Kamenev had communicated to the British Government."[73]

On the following morning, however, at his second (and last) session with Giolitti, Lloyd George had copies of both *The Times* and the *Daily Herald* of the 21st containing the text of the Minsk terms as released by the Soviet delegation in London the previous evening. Now there could be no doubt that Kamenev's previously transmitted version was less than complete. But neither could there any longer be fears for Poland's safety. The same newspapers carried reports that the Poles had driven back Soviet forces over 100 miles from Warsaw. Lloyd George told Giolitti in opening their conversation that he had telegrams from D'Abernon in Warsaw stating it was likely that the Red Army would be almost entirely destroyed.[74] Therefore, in the light of this new information, a new communiqué was drafted—again by the British. To ask that Poland should create a militia "drawn from one class of its citizens to the exclusion of all others," it said, "is only an indirect method of organizing a force to overthrow this democratic constitution." The British and Italian governments, which had been "taking steps in the face of much misrepresentation to restore communication between Russia and the world outside," could view this development only with profound regret. And the statement continued: "To have added such a condition after M. Kameneff's pledges to the British Government that nothing which was not of a secondary nature was omitted from his summary of the terms is a gross breach of faith, and negotiations of any kind with a Government which so lightly treats its word become difficult, if not impossible."[75]

Although the communiqué as a whole constituted a strong condemnation of Soviet aims and methods, so far as Lloyd George was concerned the operative word was "difficult," not "impossible." As Riddell had noted in his diary *en route* with the Prime Minister: "No doubt he is fond of mountains, but I think his real reason is

---

[73] "Notes of a Conversation held at the Villa Haslihorn, Lucerne, on Sunday, August 22, 1920, at 10 A.M.;" *British Documents*, vol. VIII, no. 87, p. 765. The British draft press communiqué is appended, pp. 774-75.
[74] "Notes of a Conversation . . . Monday, August 23, 1920, at 10.30 A.M.;" *ibid.*, no. 89, p. 777.
[75] *The Times*, 24 August 1920.

that he is anxious to meet Giolitti . . . in order to make a combination with him on the Russian and Polish questions. L.G.'s antipathy to the French very marked." And after the two-day conference was over and the communiqué issued, Riddell found Lloyd George "still keen on making peace" with the Soviet regime, despite his disappointment at its evident duplicity.[76] The conference minutes bear him out. Notwithstanding the telegram of "cordial salute" which Lloyd George and Giolitti sent to Millerand at the conclusion of their talks, their conversations bristled with remarks hostile to the French government and its policies. Moreover, Lloyd George got Giolitti's explicit agreement that a London conference for the purpose of establishing "normal relations" between Russia and "the rest of the world" was still desirable; that if trade negotiations with Kamenev and Krasin were resumed in London the Italian government would send a representative to join them; and that, in the meantime, the Italian government (like the British government) would not recognize Wrangel.[77]

Giolitti was the only foreign statesman Lloyd George saw during his holiday, which lasted precisely three weeks. While he was resting in Switzerland a small group of high-ranking military and naval officers in London—as we shall see in the next chapter—were plotting against him. Their aim was to frustrate his Russian policy, but they would not have been disappointed if their efforts resulted in his being driven from office as well. All this was unknown to the Prime Minister, however, as he enjoyed his holiday. We can imagine, indeed, that the victory which enabled the Poles to make peace eventually on their own terms rather than on Moscow's enabled him to enjoy the Swiss mountains even more than he had expected. For in sweeping the remnants of Tukhachevsky's forces before them, Piłsudski's armies also swept away what Lloyd George undoubtedly regarded as the last political barrier to an Anglo-Soviet *détente*.

[76] Riddell, *Diary*, pp. 232-33, entries for 18 and 23 August 1920.

[77] See the memorandum, "Conclusions of a Conversation between Mr. Lloyd George and Signor Giolitti . . . August 22, 1920, at 10 A.M.;" *British Documents*, vol. VIII, no. 88.

CHAPTER VII

THE "INTERCEPTS"

Is L. G. a traitor?—*Henry Wilson's diary, 23 July 1920*

By defeating the Red Army on the approaches to Warsaw the Poles lifted from Lloyd George and his colleagues the burden of deciding whether or not to expend British resources—and perhaps even British lives—in Poland's defense. Equally important, the Polish victory enabled the British government to avoid a head-on confrontation with a Labour movement that was united, under the banner of "Hands Off Russia," as it had been on few previous issues. Within two weeks of the formation of the National Council of Action in London, local councils had been formed in nearly all the industrial centers of Great Britain. As Sir Basil Thomson, the Director of Intelligence at the Home Office, noted in his weekly report to the Cabinet on "Revolutionary Organisations in the United Kingdom" for 26 August, "just as the formation of the National Council united, for the first time, Left and Right leaders, so the local councils are permeating the great mass of the workers which is usually apathetic."[1]

By then Thomson no longer feared that the councils would employ industrial action—a general strike—to prevent British intervention to save Poland: the Poles had rendered that particular issue moot. Instead, he had begun to fear revolutionary upheaval in the British Isles themselves. Ireland, of course, was already in flames. The passage earlier in August of the Restoration of Order in Ireland Act marked the British government's decision to attempt to reimpose Westminster's authority by force of arms. In Brixton jail near London, Terence McSwiney, the Lord Mayor of Cork, a schoolteacher turned I.R.A. brigade commander, had begun the much-publicized hunger strike that would lead to his death in October. More serious a danger to public order in Britain was the prospect

[1] Report 69, Cabinet paper C.P. 1805; Cab. 24/111.

of a mining strike that would lead to more widespread labor turmoil. On 12 August a special conference of the Miners' Federation —the most militant and class-conscious of British trade unions— voted to poll its entire million-man membership on the advisability of a strike for higher wages. The results, announced on the 30th, were nearly three to one in favor of a strike, which was set for 25 September. Because the government still retained its wartime control over the mines (and therefore over miners' pay), the strike loomed as more than a simple industrial dispute. On 31 August the railwaymen and the transport workers announced that they would support their partners in the so-called Triple Industrial Alliance.[2]

The fact that this support was very lukewarm did not prevent Thomson and others in the government—in particular, the highest-ranking officers of the armed services—from fearing the worst: a general strike coordinated and fanned by the National Council of Action and its local branches, ending in revolutionary violence. The diary of Field Marshal Sir Henry Wilson makes clear just how seriously this threat was taken. On 17 and 18 August he met in long conferences, first with his own staff and then with the chiefs of staff of all home Army commands, planning what he called "a possible war with the 'Council of Action.'" On the 24th he received an intelligence estimate stating that the ranks of "revolutionaries" contained some 100,000 ex-soldiers, and that although they probably did not yet contemplate "shooting," the extremists among them nevertheless "meant business." Two days later Wilson called a meeting of commanding generals and their staffs; they decided to stockpile rifles, machine guns, and other equipment—later including tanks—at infantry depots throughout Britain in order, according to Wilson's diary, "to start off Loyalists when they join up." Here, indeed, was the rhetoric of full-blown civil war.[3]

Behind the working-class unrest, it was generally agreed, lay real grievances. "The tension over the Polish situation is largely artificial and is really due only to the fear of conscription," Thomson wrote in his report for 19 August, "but there are genuine grievances in the increase in rents, railway fares, bread and coal, and behind

---

[2] For these events see, *inter alia*, Bullock, *Bevin*, pp. 150-51, R. Page Arnot, *The Miners: Years of Struggle*, London, 1953, pp. 226-275, and, of course, the daily newspapers of the period.

[3] Wilson MS diary, entries for 17, 18, 19, 24, and 26 August 1920.

all hangs the dark shadow of unemployment." Yet, Thomson and others maintained, none of these factors would have been sufficient to endanger civic order had it not been for the presence in Great Britain of Kamenev, Krasin, and the other members of the Soviet delegation, who had set about—in contravention of their pledge not to interfere in British domestic politics—to foment revolution. "It is not too much to say," Thomson reported to the Cabinet on 2 September, "that the Russian Trading Delegation has become a greater menace to the stability of this country than anything that has happened since the Armistice."[4]

Thomson, we have had other occasions to note, was not an alarmist—unlike, for instance, Sir Henry Wilson. Previously he had tended to belittle the strength of revolutionary sentiments among the British people and the influence of foreign movements upon them.[5] Yet in August and September 1920 he and many other occupants of high places in British public life, including a number of Cabinet ministers, adopted a wildly exaggerated view of the power to work mischief of the small Soviet mission that had sat uneasily in London since late May. These politicians and officials all agreed that one step before all others was necessary if the government was to preserve order at home: the Soviet mission must be expelled from Britain forthwith.

✧

Judged by the standards of an age which takes for granted swollen apparatus for the infiltration of other societies and the subversion of their political processes, the deeds (or misdeeds) of the members of the Soviet trade mission in London during 1920 seem almost routine. Although the bills of particulars drawn up within the British government detailing their activities filled many pages with outraged prose, the list of their "crimes" may with dispassion be reduced to three—one general, two particular.

The "general" misdeed was that of interfering, with the ultimate purpose of fomenting revolution, in the domestic politics of Great Britain. To support its contention that the Soviet mission *intended*

---

[4] Directorate of Intelligence (Home Office), Report on Revolutionary Organisations in the United Kingdom, reports 68 and 70, 19 August and 2 September 1920, Cabinet papers C.P. 1793 and 1830; Cab. 24/110 and 24/111.

[5] See above, chap. V, n. 83, and Volume II, pp. 132-33.

such interference, the British government had an impressive collection of intercepted and decyphered telegrams between the mission and Moscow. Yet even the most incriminating among them were oddly abstract and almost academic in nature. Thus Lenin instructed Kamenev on 15 August, when it still appeared likely that Warsaw would fall to the Red Army:

I advise you to make use of the question put by the Council of Action concerning the freedom of the Polish nation to determine its own fate, by making a detailed written statement of the most popular character explaining the meaning of freedom from the landowners and capitalists. Compare the attitude in the districts through which the Red Army has passed with that of the rest of Poland. Let this letter be signed by some British Communist; for your own part add merely that you recognise the freedom of the Polish nation to determine its own fate and ask for a reply as to which of the members of the Council of Action share the opinions of the British Communist and which of the members reject them. This Communist must not call himself a communist in the letter. Perhaps [Robert] Williams would be this Communist? Bear in mind that we reckon to take Warsaw on the 16th instant.[6]

A week later, after the magnitude of the military reversal before Warsaw had become apparent, Chicherin passed on to Kamenev instructions from the Politburo that he should change his approach:

The movement of British labour has reached an impasse. Lloyd George has declared that he too is striving for peace with Russia and is holding England back from war with her; this is made easier by the present phase of the military operations. Thus the British labour movement has nothing to feed on. The hour has struck when it is time to pass from defensive pacifist watchwords to offensive ones. It would be well if the workers were to demand now no longer merely peace with Russia, but assistance for Soviet Russia against Poland and Wrangel. The workers themselves could form volunteer detachments for fighting on the Polish front, but more important still they could conduct a wide campaign demanding the rendering of direct assistance to Soviet Russia for this struggle. Speaking generally the pacifist watchwords are not suited to the times. It is desirable that they should pass to more definite watchwords,

[6] Lenin (through Chicherin) to Kamenev (London), telegram, 15 August 1920; intercept 003829, from Appendix C to Directorate of Intelligence memorandum, headed "Breaches on the part of the Russian Soviet Government's Delegation . . ." undated but *circa* 1 September, Lloyd George MSS, file F/203/1/5, also in Davidson MSS. Henceforward this compilation will be cited as "Appendix C"; telegrams within it are not numbered, but intercept numbers are given.

watchwords more akin to us. The political bureau finds a change like this desirable.[7]

These two messages have been quoted here at such length because they formed a major part of what the British government considered to be its most damning evidence that Moscow was ordering the delegation in London to interfere in British domestic politics by making propaganda among British workers. A third message, generally regarded, as we will see, as the last straw, came from Lenin to Kamenev on 20 August. Lenin stated:

It is hardly likely that we will take Warsaw soon. The enemy has concentrated his forces there and is advancing. It is quite clear that Lloyd George and Churchill have apportioned the rôles and that Lloyd George, under cover of pacifist phrases, supports the actual policy of the French and of Churchill and makes fools of idiots like Henderson and company. Use all your forces to explain this to the British workers. Write articles for them yourself and develop this idea, teaching them the theories of Marx; give them practical demonstrations how to make use of the vacillations towards the left of people like Henderson and teach them how to agitate among the masses. In this lies your chief task. But of course all this must be done absolutely unofficially and confidentially and the most prudent diplomacy must be maintained.[8]

To Kamenev, in London, the reality of the British labor movement seemed rather more intractable than did the somewhat idealized image held by his colleagues in Moscow. Despite a number of meetings with the leaders of the Council of Action, he could not prevent them from sending a telegram to the Soviet government urging the abandonment of the so-called militia clause of its peace terms for the Poles as seeming to impinge upon Poland's independence and thus playing into the hands of Russia's enemies in the West.[9] And on 25 August Kamenev reported that the strength of the Right within

[7] Chicherin to Kamenev (London), telegram, 22 August 1920; intercept 003908, "Appendix C," cited above.

[8] Lenin (through Chicherin) to Kamenev (London), telegram 375, 20 August 1920; intercept 003934, Lloyd George MSS, file F/203/1/11. This message is printed in Lenin's *Polnoe sobranie sochinenii* (5th ed.), vol. 51, no. 473. Lenin sent it to Chicherin with a note saying that unless Chicherin objected, it should be sent to Kamenev. The texts are the same except for the last sentence here quoted, which does not appear in Lenin's original version. Chicherin, as the regime's chief diplomat, presumably added this cautionary note himself.

[9] Kamenev (London) to Chicherin and Lenin, telegrams 315-16 (through Litvinov, Copenhagen), 25 August 1920; intercept 003956, circulated 31 August, Lloyd George MSS, file F/9/2/42, also Davidson MSS.

the Council was such that even a resolution calling for the immediate opening of peace negotiations between London and Moscow and the recall of British warships from Russian waters was adopted only after a fierce internal struggle. Experiences such as these had convinced him, he commented ruefully, "that it is no use cherishing too optimistic hopes of the strength of the [labor] movement."[10]

When the Soviet trade delegation arrived in May, its members had each pledged that they would "not interfere in any way in the politics or internal affairs" of the United Kingdom; Kamenev, also, had agreed to abide by these terms when he arrived at the beginning of August. He—and Krasin as well—had had frequent contact with the members of the Council of Action. These relationships, together with their efforts (and intentions) at making propaganda, and a comical attempt by Rothstein and Milyutin to subvert the crew of a British destroyer which carried them from the United Kingdom to Reval in early August, constituted the "general" misdeeds of which the mission was guilty.[11]

The particular misdeeds must be regarded as more serious offenses. One was Kamenev's calculated attempt to mislead the British government regarding the nature of the "militia clause" which Moscow intended to present to the Poles in order to preserve a climate of domestic opinion which made British intervention on the side of the Poles nearly unthinkable. The second was the giving of financial subsidies to pro-Soviet organizations within British society, including especially lavish support of the *Daily Herald*, but also significant assistance to other, more parochial journals, and to the infant Communist Party of Great Britain.

The *Daily Herald* occupied a unique and important place within the Labour movement. Founded in 1908 as a weekly, becoming a daily in 1912, reverting to weekly appearance during the War, and then resuming publication as a daily in March 1919, it remained

[10] Kamenev (London) to Chicherin, telegram 528, 25 August 1920; intercept 003937, Davidson MSS.
[11] The Davidson MSS contain a number of papers by military and civilian departments summing up the British government's case against the Soviet delegation; perhaps the most comprehensive was the Directorate of Intelligence memorandum cited above, n. 6. The episode at sea was described in a note from V. W. Baddeley, Assistant Secretary of the Admiralty, to the Foreign Office, 24 August 1920; Davidson MSS.

independent, with close but far from binding connections to both the Labour Party and the trades unions. It had been edited from its outset by George Lansbury, a pacifist intellectual and one of the great moral forces within the Labour movement; its contributors included the leading socialist intellectuals of the era. At the same time, because the trades unions came to its rescue with financial support when it was facing insolvency in late 1919, the unions won and retained the right to name three of the six members of the newspaper's board of directors.[12]

Despite its union support, however, the *Herald* remained near the brink of insolvency. Lansbury was one of the staunchest of British sympathizers with the Bolshevik regime, and he therefore sought assistance from it during a visit to Moscow during February and March 1920. As messages from Chicherin to Litvinov, in Copenhagen, made clear, Lansbury was especially anxious for Soviet help in arranging for credits, presumably secured by Soviet gold, whereby the *Herald* could purchase newsprint in Sweden and Finland. "Lansbury does not wish to depend on us financially, but wishes that purely commercial relations should be established between us," Chicherin said. The requested credits were arranged, although the available intercepted messages do not indicate their amount or their terms.[13]

They were not, in any case, sufficient: shortly after the Soviet trade delegation arrived in London in the late spring Krasin, Klishko, and Nogin met with Lansbury and a few of his senior colleagues. According to Sir Basil Thomson's reports, on that occasion Krasin apparently rejected or at least referred elsewhere an overture from Lansbury for some sort of direct Soviet subsidy, perhaps because he was mindful of the delegation's promises not to interfere in British domestic politics. In any case, a few days after the meeting Francis Meynell—then, at twenty-nine, the *Herald*'s youngest director, in 1921 editor of the short-lived journal *The Communist*, and subse-

[12] Bullock, *Bevin*, 111-13. For the history of the *Herald*, see George Lansbury, *The Miracle of Fleet Street: The Story of the Daily Herald*, London, 1925, and Raymond Postgate, *The Life of George Lansbury*, London, 1951.

[13] These wireless exchanges in February and March 1920 between Litvinov and Chicherin were not found in the collections of papers used in writing this book. Eight such messages, however, were released by the government and published in *The Times* and other newspapers on 19 August 1920. See below, n. 46. The quoted message was dated 23 February.

quently distinguished as a book designer, publisher, and advertising executive—went to Copenhagen to plead the newspaper's cause with Litvinov.[14]

The available intercepted telegrams between Krasin and his superiors in Moscow do not contain recommendations of support for the *Herald*. Litvinov was apparently less reticent. "If we do not support the 'Daily Herald' which is now passing through a fresh crisis paper will have to turn 'Right' trade union," he reported to Chicherin in mid-June. Since Lansbury's journey to Moscow earlier in the year, he said, the *Herald* had moved considerably leftward, and now had come to advocate direct action in support of the Soviet regime. "In Russian questions it acts as if it were our organ." It needed, Litvinov said, £50,000 for six months, after which it once again hoped to be on firm ground. "I beg for early and favorable answer," he concluded, "especially because there is no hope of establishment of a purely Communist paper."[15]

Litvinov's appeal, backed up with reminders from the delegation in London that Meynell needed an urgent reply, proved effective. When Kamenev and Krasin arrived in England at the beginning of August (Krasin, it will be remembered, had returned to Russia for consultations after his initial round of talks with Lloyd George) they brought with them over £40,000 worth of cut precious stones, mostly diamonds, and a considerable quantity of platinum. During the third week of August they sold most of their stones on the London market ("rumour of these large disposals has brought Jew dealers from all parts of Europe to London," stated a report by Sir Basil Thomson).[16] On 20 August Kamenev telegraphed to Chicherin that

---

[14] Of several reports of these transactions, the fullest is the memorandum cited above, n. 6. Sir Francis (as he now is) Meynell has recently described his role in his autobiography: *My Lives*, London, 1971, pp. 117-25.

[15] This message, from Litvinov (Copenhagen) to Chicherin, is the only one in the various compilations of evidence against the Soviet mission that was not either a wireless or cable telegram intercepted in "normal" ways. Instead, it was transmitted in a telegram from Lord Kilmarnock, the British Minister in Berlin, to Curzon, on 11 July 1920; Kilmarnock stated it came during the latter half of June from "an absolutely sure source" which he was "not at liberty to reveal." (Kilmarnock's message was reproduced in Appendix "A" to the memorandum cited above, n. 6. Litvinov's was part of the selection released to the press on 18 August. In the published version Litvinov's message was incorrectly dated 11 July. In both versions the sum 50,000 is listed as francs, rather than pounds, but a note in the memorandum states that the latter was definitely intended.)

[16] Letter, Thomson to J.C.C. Davidson, 31 August 1920; Davidson MSS. See Meynell, *My Lives*, pp. 119-22.

"£40,000 of the money realised was paid over to the newspaper as decided by the Central Executive Committee of the Russian Communist Party." These proceeds, in the form of banknotes, were then taken by Francis Meynell and Edgar Lansbury (George Lansbury's son) and invested in Exchequer Bonds. The details of all these transactions, down to the numbers of the banknotes used, were carefully followed by the British government.[17]

Within the next few weeks the total amount placed at the disposal of the *Herald* came to something like £75,000.[18] Subsequent publicity, as we will see, caused the newspaper's board of directors to return the money to the Soviet delegation; however, the fact of its payment in the first place represented the mission's largest and most flagrant act of interference in British domestic politics. There were, of course, other subsidies at least partly attributable to the presence in the United Kingdom of the Soviet delegation. But in those cases the delegation simply served as a convenient conduit for funds that would in any case have been transferred. Walter Kendall devotes much of his imposing work, *The Revolutionary Movement in Britain 1900-1921*, to describing the processes by which the various radical parties (or factions) which came together in August 1920 to form the Communist Party of Great Britain received financial support from Soviet sources, and therefore incentives to adhere to the directives of the Communist International. These processes existed before the arrival of the trade delegation. They involved a network of clandestine couriers bringing to the United Kingdom funds (or precious goods realizable as funds) that were for the most part distributed to their financial recipients by Feodor Rothstein. These funds amounted to much less than those given to the *Daily Herald*, but they were not inconsiderable.[19] Unquestionably the presence of the delegation made their provision and distribution somewhat easier. But in such activities the delegation was only useful, not essential.

[17] Of several reports in the Davidson MSS on these transactions, the most detailed is one headed "Report on the Disposal of Gems . . ." 8 September 1920 (copy also in Lloyd George MSS, file F/203/1/12). Kamenev reported on sales of some of the gems, and plans for selling platinum, in telegram 491 to Chicherin, 20 August; intercept 003878, circulated 24 August, Davidson MSS. This telegram was headed, "For Lezhava: to be decyphered personally." (A. M. Lezhava, a Bolshevik since 1904, was a senior official in the Commissariat for Foreign Trade.)

[18] As we will see below, the *Herald* itself admitted to this figure.

[19] Kendall, *Revolutionary Movement in Britain*, pp. 236-56.

Here, then, stripped of the more sensational language used in many of the official papers that set forward its details, is the outline of the British government's case against the Soviet trade delegation. From the perspective of half a century, it does not seem worthy of much alarm. Even in 1920, however, such attempts to interfere in domestic politics were not so infrequent as to warrant the outcry within the upper reaches of the British government that was prompted by the revelations of the Soviet delegation's activities. And one is tempted to conclude that even in 1920 the outcry would not have been so loud had not a number of those who reacted most strongly not felt that in expelling the Russian delegates from England they would also succeed in blocking, once and for all, the Russian policy of David Lloyd George—and perhaps even in driving the Prime Minister from office.

Because the campaign to expel the Soviet delegation masked political purposes in some instances so much more far-reaching, it had about it some aspects of a conspiracy. Especially did this seem the case because Lloyd George was abroad on holiday. With most of his Cabinet colleagues also away from London, the processes of government continued simply by momentum, without direction. The absence of decision, and of a decision-making procedure, magnified the anxieties and the frustrations of those within the government who wanted decisions made. Foremost among these—the term "leading conspirator" is melodramatic, but not too strong—was Field Marshal Sir Henry Wilson, Chief of the Imperial General Staff and one of the most "political" officers to wear a British uniform in the present century.

In the course of this study we have often noted Wilson's acrimonious comments on men and events. Presumably they were confined to his diary and to a very few of his most intimate friends. Wilson was surely too skilful in his relationships to allow these feelings to be widely vented; he would not for so long have retained his high position had he not behaved with discretion. His diary entries, however, make plain that he neither liked nor respected the Prime Minister. We have seen Wilson's contempt for "Frocks"—the politicians; he was especially suspicious of Lloyd George, the consummate politician, particularly on the issues of Ireland and Russia, upon which they disagreed most. Frequently he referred to Lloyd

George as a "fool." In some diary entries he made more serious allegations. Thus on 15 January 1920, *en route* to Paris where he had suddenly been summoned by the Prime Minister because of the apparent crisis in the Near East and the Caucasus which concluded the second volume of this account,[20] Wilson wrote: "We are undoubtedly coming to a very, very critical time. I keep wondering if L.G. is a traitor & a Bolshevist, & I will watch him very carefully."[21]

This was not the first instance in which Wilson, in his diary, had called Lloyd George a Bolshevist. Precisely a year before, at the time of the Prinkipo proposals, he had done so, remarking also that the Prime Minister's "tacit agreement to Bolshevism is a most dangerous thing."[22] But he had not previously speculated that Lloyd George might be a traitor. "Bolshevist" can be (and has been) used in several different senses, ranging from its literal meaning to simply an implication of dissatisfaction with an established order. "Traitor," when used seriously, has but one meaning; it is clear and unambiguous. Repeatedly, as 1920 wore on, Wilson raised in his dairy the possibility that the Prime Minister he served (and who had appointed him C.I.G.S. in early 1918) might be guilty of treason. Thus, on 27 May, commenting on Lloyd George's decision not to use force against Avonmouth dockers who had refused to load Army trucks on ships bound for Ireland, he wrote: "I wonder, is L.G. allowing England to drift into Bolshevism on purpose? I always wonder this when he funks."[23] And on 23 July, regarding the government's failure to take measures sufficient to repress new outbreaks of violence in Ireland: "Is L.G. a traitor? I have often put this query in my Diary."[24]

Wilson's suspicions were to reach their greatest intensity during the August crisis in the Polish-Russian struggle. On the 6th, it will be remembered, he was summoned in to the second meeting between Lloyd George and Kamenev and Krasin in order to draw up the proposal for a truce which was subsequently sent to Moscow in the name of the British government. He was, in fact, present for most of the meeting (as was also Bonar Law, whom Wilson mentions only in recording the mere fact of his presence). In his diary Wilson

---

[20] See Volume II, pp. 327-39.
[21] Wilson MS diary, entry for 15 January 1920.
[22] *Ibid.*, entries for 12, 13, and 19 January 1919 (for 12 January see Callwell, *Henry Wilson*, vol. II, p. 163).
[23] Wilson MS diary, entry for 27 May 1920.   [24] *Ibid.*, entry for 23 July 1920.

described the two Soviet emissaries as "a villainous pair of scoun-drels," and he went on to note: "I was horrified at the way L.G. spoke of & referred to the French in front of these cut-throats. And also in [*sic*] the almost servile way in which he looked after Russian inter-ests & was hostile to the Poles. . . . The whole tone of LG shocked me very much. He was with <u>friends</u> in Kamenev & Krassin & to-gether they discussed the French & the Poles." Wilson at one point suggested that the truce proposal should specify that orders for a cease-fire be issued not from Moscow and Warsaw, but from the field headquarters of the opposing armies, because Warsaw might well already have fallen to the Red Army. In his diary he described the reaction of his listeners: "The 2 Bolsheviks and LG burst out laugh-ing, Kamenev having to stuff his handkerchief into his mouth. It was quite clear to me that all three knew, & that LG approved of the occupation of Warsaw by the Bolsheviks. It was an amazing 5 hours meeting. It left me, as I say, with a clear sense that L.G. is in com-pany with friends & kindred spirits when with the Bolsheviks, & it raised more acutely than ever <u>whether he is deliberately shepherding England into chaos & destruction</u>."[25] And at Lympne, three days later, regarding Lloyd George's refusal to expel Kamenev and Krasin from the country, Wilson wrote: "LG[s] attitude is incompre-hensible unless he is terrified of the Bolsheviks or unless he himself is Bolshevik."[26]

Thus far we have seen only comments in a diary—the means, perhaps, by which Wilson gave fullest vent to his frustrations and anxieties. It required the Council of Action to bring him to consider taking action himself. His diary makes clear that he regarded the Council as a revolutionary threat to the whole fabric of British so-ciety. On 17 August, the day he began making plans with his staff for (as he put it) "crushing" the Council of Action, he received a file of intercepted Soviet telegrams that indicated more clearly than had previous ones the connection between the Council and the dele-gation in London. He read them that night, and wrote in his diary: "They are the most scandalous productions. They discuss openly the best method of fomenting discord between France & ourselves, the best way of trapping LG & the Cabinet, the best way for arming

[25] *Ibid.*, entry for 6 August 1920 (underscored in original); cf. Callwell, *Wilson*, vol. II, pp. 256-57.
[26] Wilson MS diary, entry for 9 August 1920.

the British 'proletariat,' the meetings which Kameneff had with the 'Council of action' and what 'Bob' Williams had promised. A most terrifying set of telegrams & the most terrifying part of it all is the fact that L.G. & his Cabinet read all of this & <u>are afraid</u> to fling Kameneff & Krassin out of England."[27]

The following morning—18 August, the day of Lloyd George's departure—Wilson discussed the telegrams with his deputy, General Sir Charles Harington, and the Director of Military Intelligence, Lieutenant General Sir William Thwaites. "It seemed to me," Wilson wrote, "& they agreed, that we could not pass them over in silence thereby tacitly agreeing to the Bolsheviks plotting our destruction in our very midst." Their next move was to call in Sir Basil Thomson.[28]

Thomson knew, as they did not, that the Soviet delegation's behavior had been discussed the previous day by the Cabinet. Although the Cabinet agreed that the Russians had violated the pledges under which they had been allowed to enter the United Kingdom, it nevertheless decided that the government should take no action against them for the present and, instead, should wait (in the words of the minutes of the meeting) "until the situation in Poland had further developed, when the *bona fide* or other of the Bolshevist Government would be fully established." At the same time it decided to release to the press, without attribution, a selection of intercepted messages demonstrating that Moscow had been subsidizing the *Daily Herald,* and that Curzon should write to Kamenev demanding an explanation for the delegation's breach of its undertakings.[29]

Thomson related all this to Wilson and his colleagues. He also said that after the meeting Lloyd George had placed so many conditions on Curzon's sending his draft note to Kamenev that the Foreign Secretary had determined he could not send it. Similarly, Thomson said, the Cabinet had withdrawn from the selection of telegrams relating to the *Daily Herald* one referring to Kamenev, because Lloyd George had felt that if it were published there would be a general outcry for Kamenev's expulsion. Finally, Thomson told his military listeners, he was himself perturbed that E. F. Wise, despite his markedly pro-Bolshevik leanings, still had easy access to 10 Downing Street. "Thomson made no bones about the matter,"

---

[27] *Ibid.,* entry for 17 August 1920.   [28] *Ibid.,* entry for 18 August 1920.
[29] Minutes, Cabinet 49 (20); Cab. 23/22. For publication of the selected messages, see below, n. 46.

Wilson wrote in his diary after describing their meeting, "& said that he was seriously beginning to think L.G. was a traitor."[30]

Following his talk with Basil Thomson on 18 August, Wilson sought out Winston Churchill who, as Secretary of State for War, was his immediate superior. He described their conversation in his diary:

I told him that these intercepts had gravely disturbed me and that I found it difficult to understand the attitude of L.G. & of the Cabinet, that telegrams of this sort put a severe strain on our (Soldiers) loyalty to the Cabinet as though we wished to be loyal to the Government we had a higher loyalty still to our King & to England. Winston was much excited. He said it was quite true that L.G. was dragging the Cabinet step by step towards Bolshevism and he enumerated the different steps from Prinkipo to to-day when although pretending to uphold the integrity of Poland we did <u>nothing</u> to insure it & we prevented arms & stores passing through Danzig. He asked me to write a note on the subject & I said I would. The whole thing is most perplexing & worse and my often recurring suspicions of LG[S] loyalty crowd in on me tonight.[31]

Here, it may be noted, Wilson was using the time-honored language of the military revolutionary—doubting the "loyalty" of the established authorities and proclaiming a "higher loyalty" of his own. In many countries these words would be a preface to a *coup d'état*; in Great Britain they preceded the drafting of a paper. Its content was pure melodrama. Wilson wrote:

The authority of Government, its right and its power to govern, has been rudely challenged by the "Council of Action" a body of men which claims to represent English Labour and Democracy. On receipt of the challenge the Government thought the situation so serious that it instantly called into action all the machinery it possessed for combatting this threat against the life of the nation and I was ordered to make military plans to meet the danger. . . .

Whilst engaged on this work I am suddenly confronted by a series of telegrams which are passing between Kameneff and Krassin in London, Litvinoff in Copenhagen and Tchitcherin and Lenin in Moscow. These telegrams establish beyond all possibility of dispute three amazing and disturbing facts:—

[30] Wilson MS diary, entry for 18 August 1920; cf. Callwell, *Wilson*, vol. II, p. 259, where the quoted sentence is omitted.

[31] Wilson MS diary, entry for 18 August 1920; for this passage Callwell's version (*Wilson*, p. 259) bears virtually no relationship to the original.

1. That Kameneff and Krassin while enjoying the hospitality of England are engaged, with the Soviet Government, in a plot to create red revolution and ruin in this country.
2. That Kameneff and the Soviet Government are engaged in a plot to split the Alliance and the Friendship between England and France.
3. That the "Council of Action" is in the closest touch and collaboration with the Russian Soviet for the downfall and ruin of England.

In view of the dispersion of our Forces, in view of the dangerous weakness to which we are reduced in every theatre but more particularly in Great Britain, and in view of the insidious and disloyal propaganda to which all of His Majesty's Forces are being subjected it is a military necessity to expose the whole of this traitorous combination, to explain to the troops what it is they may be called upon to fight and to make clear to them by drastic action against both the "Council of Action" and the Russian delegates in England what attitude His Majesty's Government is going to adopt in this matter. Without such action I cannot say what may happen in the event of a Revolutionary attempt by the "Council of Action" in Great Britain and by affiliated societies in Ireland, Egypt, Mesopotamia, India and other theatres.

I await the decision of the Government.[32]

Wilson's memorandum did not, of course, state what he proposed to do if his wait for a decision from his political superiors proved disappointing: they were, presumably, to draw their own conclusions. But with his Army colleagues, Generals Harington and Thwaites (who, he noted in his diary, were in complete agreement with all his paper had said), he left no doubts. In his diary for 19 August he wrote:

I would not be surprised if my note to Winston led to my resignation & I said this to Tim [Harington] and Bill [Thwaites]. I said I did not in any way wish to compromise their position but they both said that if I went they also would go & Bill said that P de B [Major General Sir Percy de Blaquiere Radcliffe, Director of Military Operations, then in Warsaw with the special Anglo-French mission] would also go. This would be a severe business for the Government and indeed I don't think that they could stand it on this particular point.[33]

Wilson knew that his chances of bringing down Lloyd George's government would be significantly increased if he could enlist the

---

[32] Wilson to Churchill, 18 August 1920; a copy of this paper, like many of the others exchanged among those who "plotted" against Lloyd George, is in the Davidson MSS—presumably because it was furnished to Bonar Law.
[33] Wilson MS diary, entry for 19 August 1920.

support of the leading officers of the Navy and Air Force as well. So—also on 19 August—in the absence on holiday of the First Sea Lord, Admiral Earl Beatty, he called in the Second Sea Lord, Admiral Sir Montague Browning, and the deputy chief of the Naval Staff, Vice Admiral Sir Osmond de B. Brock, and showed them the intercepted telegrams and his note to Churchill. To his surprise, both thought the note too strong. They did not, he wrote in his diary, appear to share the apprehension Beatty had expressed to him at Lympne about revolutionary unrest in the Fleet. Wilson was, however, able to enlist to his cause Rear Admiral Hugh F. P. Sinclair, the Director of Naval Intelligence; later in the month Sinclair told him that Earl Beatty would join them. He also got a favorable response from Air Marshal Sir Hugh Trenchard, the Chief of the Air Staff. After an interview with Trenchard on 24 August, Wilson wrote: "Trenchard . . . thinks, like Basil Thomson, that LG is a traitor."[34] Thus by the end of August the C.I.G.S. had succeeded in putting together a formidable combination: the ranking officers of the fighting services—himself, Beatty, and Trenchard—and the heads of the military, naval, and civilian intelligence services—Thwaites, Sinclair, and Basil Thomson.

Meanwhile, Wilson worked to make sure that he had Churchill's unwavering support. On 23 August he received from Churchill (who was in the country) a draft of a covering minute that the Secretary of State proposed to send to Lloyd George and the senior members of the Cabinet along with Wilson's note. Churchill reviewed the evidence against the Russian delegation and recalled the Prime Minister's pledge to Millerand at Lympne that "if Kameneff and Krasin engaged in propaganda they would be turned out at once." He then made his principal point:

I feel bound to bring to the notice of my colleagues the perturbation which is caused to the British officers who are concerned with this intelligence work when they see what they cannot help but regard as a deliberate and dangerous conspiracy aimed at the main security of the State unfolding itself before the eyes of the executive Government without any steps being taken to interfere with it. In these circumstances the Government might at any time find itself confronted with disclosures and resignations which would be deeply injurious. I therefore ask specifically, What is the service which Kameneff and Krassin are expected to render

[34] Wilson MS diary, entries for 19 August, 1 September and 24 August 1920.

this country which justifies us in delaying their expulsion? Their presence here is a source of continued and increasing danger. It is an encouragement to every revolutionary enterprise. The miners' strike, with all its indefinite possibilities, is drawing steadily nearer. Are we really going to sit still until we see the combination of the money from Moscow, the Kameneff-Krassin propaganda, the Council of Action, and something very like a general strike, all acting and reacting on one another, while at the same time our military forces are at their very weakest?[35]

Wilson obviously applauded Churchill's statement, but he noted bitterly that the Secretary of State did not identify himself with the perturbed officers. "He does not mention that he had thought of resigning!" the C.I.G.S. wrote in his diary.[36] When the two then met on the following day, Wilson found Churchill (who had come up to London) unsure as to whether or not he would in fact disseminate their notes to his Cabinet colleagues. He therefore worked at persuading him.

I told Winston [Wilson wrote in his diary] it was the chance of his life to come out as an Englishman & that in one bound he would recover his lost position & be hailed as saviour by all that is best in England. I think we have got him pretty well fixed. I warned him that we Soldiers might have to take action if he did not & that in that case his position would be impossible. He agreed. He said he was "much worried" about LG[S] attitude and so am I, and it will take some explaining to ease my mind of the suspicion that LG is a traitor.[37]

Despite Churchill's agreement, however, he still did not act. Not until the following day (25 August) and yet another effort by the Field Marshal[38] did he finally send out the two papers. The seven addressees were Lloyd George, Bonar Law, Balfour, Austen Chamberlain, Curzon, Milner, who was then Secretary of State for the Colonies, and Edward Shortt, the Home Secretary.

To Lloyd George, Churchill sent also a much more conciliatory personal letter. He was quite certain, he wrote, "that Kameneff and Krassin ought to be given their passports," and he begged the Prime Minister carefully to consider his memorandum. No purpose would be served by allowing the Russians to remain. Their cynical mis-

---

[35] The paper Churchill actually circulated on 25 August 1920 (dated the previous day) is in the Davidson MSS. Presumably the draft Wilson saw on the 23rd (Wilson MS diary) varied not significantly, if at all.

[36] Wilson MS diary 23 August 1920.

[37] *Ibid.*, entry for 24 August 1920.   [38] *Ibid.*, entry for 25 August 1920.

representation of the Soviet peace terms to Poland demonstrated that they could contribute nothing to the process of peacemaking. "Secondly," Churchill said, "as to trade with Russia, why is it necessary to do more than lift the Blockade and authorise British subjects to trade freely if they choose and if they can? Why have we, a monarchical country with a large Conservative majority in the House of Commons, got to undertake the role of being the official bear-leaders to these ruffianly conspirators and revolutionaries?"[39]

The "Conservative majority" loomed large in Churchill's thinking. Of all the ties that bound him to Lloyd George, perhaps the strongest was their shared position as Liberals with, for different reasons, only a tenuous connection to the Liberal establishment and membership in a Coalition government which existed only by sufferance of the Conservative majority. Earlier in 1920 they had collaborated in an abortive attempt to form a fusion Centre Party of Coalition Liberals and Conservatives, and by so doing to make more secure their own political positions.[40] From his perspective, then, Churchill saw the continued presence of Kamenev and Krasin as having only baleful consequences. "They have done much to render the Labour situation more dangerous," he wrote, "while so far as the Tory Party is concerned the harm done to our political and party interests is progressive and continuous." He continued: "From a national point of view their presence is most dangerous. From a party point of view it is simply estranging day after day the strong and dominant forces in our national life which you were so proud to lead in the war and which gave you their confidence at its close. I am very deeply distressed about the position because it is ever my desire to be a help and not a hindrance to you."[41]

❖

Henry Wilson did not see Churchill's letter to Lloyd George. Had he done so he would have had even more reason to feel that Churchill was not to be relied upon to take action against the Prime Minister. During the last days of August he was to learn that this

---

[39] Churchill to Lloyd George (Lucerne), 26 August 1920; Lloyd George MSS, file F/9/2/41.

[40] For this effort, see Trevor Wilson, *The Downfall of the Liberal Party 1914-1935*, London, 1966, pp. 193-98, and Kenneth O. Morgan, "Lloyd George's Stage Army: the Coalition Liberals, 1918-22," in A.J.P. Taylor, ed., *Lloyd George: Twelve Essays*, London, 1971, pp. 246-48.

[41] From Churchill's letter to Lloyd George, cited above, n. 39.

was true of all the "Frocks." Churchill told him that Austen Chamberlain, Milner, and Curzon had all written him in favor of "qualified action" (the term used in Wilson's diary), and that Balfour had sent a telegram to Lloyd George urging him to consider Wilson's and Churchill's memoranda carefully, but that none, apparently, was willing to press the issue to the point of breaking with the Prime Minister.[42]

The Field Marshal was not wholly discouraged, however. "Not one of these knaves would have moved if I had not written my note," he commented in his diary.[43] Meanwhile, he worked at strengthening his case. To his own paper he added others by Basil Thomson ("showing the connection between Kameneff and our Labour, etc.") and Admiral Sinclair ("on the Bolshevik danger to the Navy, of the establishment of Soviets in the Ports, etc."). This trilogy was duly circulated, while the three authors met almost daily to fulminate against the Prime Minister and to consider leaking to the press the intercepted Soviet telegrams—a decision they could never quite reach.[44]

One reason they did not do so was an uneasiness over the possible consequences of making public the fact that the British government had succeeded in breaking the Soviet codes and was reading the Soviet mission's telegraphic traffic. During late August and early September 1920 there took place within the British intelligence community and among the politicians with access to that community a veiled but nonetheless intense debate over the advantages and disadvantages of publication. Although some of the details of that debate have been lost to the historian (or else are unavailable), much can be stated with certainty.

It should be noted, incidentally, that this debate took place after, and not before, the publication on 19 August (as we have seen, by Cabinet decision) of eight messages relating to the Soviet subsidy

---

[42] Wilson MS diary, entries for 26 and 31 August 1920. The letters from Milner, Chamberlain, and Curzon are not to be found in Lloyd George's papers or in their own. Balfour's telegram to Lloyd George, 28 August, is in the Lloyd George MSS, file F/58/1/51, and Davidson MSS. Churchill did not characterize it accurately. It urged the Prime Minister to consider asking Moscow to recall Kamenev; it did not mention either Churchill's or Wilson's memoranda.

[43] Wilson MS diary, entry for 26 August 1920.

[44] The characterizations are by Wilson (MS diary, entry for 1 September 1920). The Davidson MSS contain several papers written at about this time by Thomson and Sinclair; Wilson's characterizations (MS diary, entry for 1 September 1920) apply to them all, and it is not clear exactly which two he had in mind.

of the *Daily Herald*. These were all wireless messages—available, presumably, unlike cable traffic, to anyone with an adequate receiving set. All, moreover, were in a cipher that differed from that in which many, probably most, of the cable messages were sent.[45] For these reasons (although I have found no record of its being thus explicitly argued), publication of the *Herald* messages was evidently regarded by the British intelligence community as not having *seriously* compromised its interception operations.[46]

Neither, as it happened, did publication of these messages compromise the Soviet delegation in London. They were all messages between Chicherin and Litvinov, who was in Copenhagen. Five of the eight dated from before the delegation had even arrived in London. Of the remaining three the last was dated 22 July, before there had been any inkling regarding the diamonds carried into England by Kamenev and Krasin in August. Even the *Herald* was not seriously compromised by these messages: although they conveyed George Lansbury's desire for Soviet support, they also made clear that he desired it on commercial terms.

Despite the publication of these wireless messages, therefore, the issue remained fully alive. Winston Churchill summed it up precisely when he wrote to Curzon on 28 August that he had asked Henry Wilson "to convene a meeting with Basil Thomson and the Directors of Military and Naval Intelligence to report to what extent the incriminating telegrams can be published without undue damage to the permanent interests of the cipher school."[47] The Code and Cypher School, it will be remembered, was the agency within the Directorate of Naval Intelligence which performed the operation of

[45] See, *e.g.*, Churchill's letter to Lloyd George of 26 August 1920 (cited above, n. 39): "The Bolsheviks know, through the publications about the 'Daily Herald,' that the cipher 'Marta' in which the wireless telegrams were sent is compromised and has been decoded. They would therefore learn no secrets as to this cipher if the rest of the telegrams in it, or such of them as are relevant, were made public."

[46] The Admiralty released a statement containing the texts of the eight messages and explanatory notes to all British national daily newspapers except the *Herald* on 18 August 1920. They were published the following day. It had been intended that newspapers should state that they had obtained the messages from sources in "a neutral country" (obviously Denmark, where Litvinov was). But *The Times* erred and introduced the compilation with the bald statement: "The following wireless messages have been intercepted by the British Government." This infuriated Lloyd George, who feared that such treatment would jeopardize the interception and decoding operations; see Hankey's letter to the Home Secretary, 21 August (registered file 18/Q/362, Cab. 21/179).

[47] Churchill to Curzon, 28 August 1920; Curzon MSS, box 65.

deciphering the intercepted Soviet messages—and, apparently, the messages of all other governments it could get its hands on. Its "permanent interests" were both substantive and bureaucratic—substantive in the "national interest" and "security" senses which motivate any foreign affairs agency, and bureaucratic in the sense that its members inevitably felt that they had a personal stake in the School's ability to enlarge the scope and importance of its organizational responsibilities.

An initial response to Churchill's request was put forward by Admiral Sinclair. On 27 August, after consultation with Basil Thomson, he drew up what he called "a statement setting out the 'pros and cons' for the publication of the telegrams."[48] Under the heading "arguments against" he listed: Publication would reveal "that the British Government has a definite system whereby the messages of other Governments are decoded and read." Such knowledge would cause other governments to employ new ciphers of such a nature as to render their breaking either impossible or so time-consuming as largely to negate the value of the information obtained. Such knowledge might also make it much more difficult, if not impossible, for the government to obtain copies of cablegrams to and from England; the existing system of obtaining them by the warrant of the Home Secretary from the cable companies, some of them foreign owned, would "inevitably be attacked," and the chances for passage by Parliament of the new Official Secrets Act, under which the government would be empowered in the future to obtain copies of foreign cablegrams, would be very seriously diminished.[49]

[48] Sinclair to Wilson, letter with attached minute, 27 August 1920; Davidson MSS.

[49] During the autumn of 1920 the government introduced and secured passage of "An Act to Amend the Official Secrets Act, 1911," giving itself very drastic powers in a number of areas. Clause 4 provided that "where it appears to a Secretary of State [*n.b., any* Secretary of State] that such a course is expedient in the public interest" he may request from cable or wireless companies the texts of any telegrams sent to or from any place outside of the United Kingdom. Sir Gordon Hewart, the Attorney General, stated during the second-reading debate on 2 December that the purpose of the clause was "to enable the authorities to detect and deal with attempts at spying by foreign agents" and that it was needed in order to replace similar powers which the government had had during the war but which had lapsed shortly after the Armistice. (135 *H.C. Deb.*, col. 1539.) Several Liberal members spoke strongly against this and other aspects of the bill as serious infringements on liberty; the Soviet mission and its communications were not mentioned, however. (For the second-reading debate, see *ibid.*, cols. 1537-82; for third reading, and passage, on 16 December, see 136 *H.C. Deb.*, cols. 938-79; the House of Lords gave the bill only cursory consideration.)

Under the heading "arguments for" Sinclair listed: Publication "would convict the Russian Delegation of carrying on propaganda and of association with the Council of Action"; it "would complete the chain of the 'Daily Herald' revelations"; it "would furnish further grounds for expelling the Russian Delegates" from the United Kingdom; and it "might lead to the break up of Soviet influence" in Britain "by detaching the modern elements from the extremists." These arguments for publication, it should be noted, were very different from those Sinclair adduced against it. The benefits of publication would be general and political; the government would be able to accomplish perhaps more easily something—the expulsion of the Soviet mission—which it presumably would be able to accomplish anyway, while the real benefits—the break-up of Soviet influence within the Labour movement and the detachment of moderates from extremists—were far less certain of achievement. On the other hand, the costs were operational and specific: publication of the intercepted telegrams would run a substantial risk of curtailing both the Code and Cypher School's supply of ciphered cables and its ability to decipher the cables it received. Thus it posed a real threat to the school's continued existence as an important element of the British intelligence community.

To the school, needless to say, the benefits of publication did not outweigh the costs. But the school seems to have been alone in this view. On 26 August, in his private letter to Lloyd George, Churchill wrote that he had "reason to believe that the military and naval personnel engaged in the secret telegrams, including the Directors of Military and Naval Intelligence, consider that the advantages of publishing the telegrams far exceed the disadvantages. . . . No more deadly propaganda has ever come before me than this publication will make."[50] Churchill had reached this conclusion, it may be noted, *before* he received the report he had asked Henry Wilson to obtain from General Thwaites, Admiral Sinclair, and Sir Basil Thomson, but he could have had no doubt that they would agree that the interests of the Code and Cypher School—and, therefore, future British access to the communications of other governments—were of secondary importance by comparison with the seeming revolutionary danger to Great Britain. On 1 September Wilson, Sinclair, and Thomson submitted to Churchill a paper which stated:

[50] From Churchill's letter to Lloyd George cited above, n. 39.

The presence of the Russian Trading Delegation has become in our opinion the gravest danger which this country has had to face since the Armistice.

This being so, we think that the publication of the de-cyphered cables has become so imperative that we must face the risks that will be entailed.[51]

The paper did not, however, specify what these "risks" might be. Nor did it even mention the Code and Cypher School. Instead, in the next sentence, it turned to tactics. Selected cables should be published in installments over several days. "Not knowing what is to come next, the extremists will hesitate to reply to them and when all have been published it will be too late for them to minimise the effect." In order to meet implicitly the argument that reading the Russian delegation's cables was a breach of diplomatic etiquette, the government should explain that the misconduct revealed in the intercepted *wireless* messages about the *Daily Herald* (apparently radio messages were regarded as fair game but cable messages were not) seemed so serious that it had "thought it necessary to examine cables that had been handed in [to cable company offices] by the Trading Delegation." It had done so to see if the Russians had broken their pledges not to interfere in British politics; now, "finding what had been going on, the Government thought it necessary, in the public interest, to publish the text of the cables." The paper concluded: "If this has the effect we anticipate it is quite possible that the movement for establishing Councils of Action all over the country may break up."

Although this paper did not contain the assessment Churchill had requested of possible "damage to the permanent interests of the Code and Cypher School," he nevertheless circulated it with enthusiasm to Cabinet members in range of London. His accompanying note stated:

I trust my colleagues after studying these papers will find themselves able to agree to the unanimous proposals of the War Office, the Admiralty, and the Home Office, both in regard to the expulsion of the Bolshevik

[51] There are two papers dated 1 September 1920 in the Davidson MSS and Lloyd George MSS (file F/203/1/2) which are relevant here. One is a short (half-page) minute to Churchill bearing the signatures of Wilson (who signed for General Thwaites as his superior), Sinclair, and Thomson. The second, transmitted under cover of the first, is a much longer (five-page) unsigned memorandum for which, it is clear, the same three shared responsibility. It is to this second paper that the references here and below refer.

delegation and in regard to the immediate disclosure of the perfidy and treachery of which we have been the object. I have carefully weighed the pros and cons of this question, and I am convinced that the danger to the State which has been wrought by the intrigues of these revolutionaries and the disastrous effect which will be produced on their plans by the exposure of their methods outweighs all other considerations. I am in entire agreement with the Chief of the Imperial General Staff on this subject, and I beg that action may be taken as soon as the Prime Minister has been consulted.[52]

Churchill's note, like the memorandum it transmitted, was not so much argument as exhortation. This is not surprising. For the defense and preservation of its "permanent interests" the Code and Cypher School had no access, either formal or informal, to the politicians who made decisions which affected its welfare, and scarcely even any access to the wider intelligence community, other than through Admiral Sinclair, the Director of Naval Intelligence. On at least one occasion Sinclair did convey to the Cabinet that the school was "still very concerned as to what may be the result of publishing the Russian telegrams in full,"[53] but there is no evidence that any papers by anyone operationally connected with intelligence collection, either within the school or elsewhere within the British intelligence community, ever made their way up to the Cabinet. There is no evidence, moreover, that the Foreign Office ever got involved at all in the question as to whether or not the telegrams should be published—although the repercussions of making public the fact that the British government was reading secret cable traffic would be felt first of all by the Foreign Office. The files contain a strong memorandum from Curzon to Lloyd George urging the expulsion of Kamenev and Krasin,[54] but no scrap from him nor from anyone else at the Foreign Office on the wisdom or unwisdom of publication.

Although Sinclair, as Director of Naval Intelligence, was the titular (but not operational) head of the Code and Cypher School, his interests and its were by no means identical. An ordnance officer who had become D.N.I. from a Fleet command in 1919 and who would return to the Fleet as Chief of the Submarine Service in 1921—just as

[52] Churchill's note, 2 September 1920, is in the Davidson MSS.

[53] Letter, Sinclair to Davidson, 5 September 1920; Davidson MSS.

[54] Curzon to Lloyd George, 2 September 1920; Lloyd George MSS, file F/203/1/3, copy also in Balfour MSS, vol. 49734.

The Intercepts

General Thwaites had left a divisional command to become Director of Military Intelligence in 1918 and would assume another field command in 1922[55]—Sinclair undoubtedly attributed less value to future collection of intelligence than did those for whom such collection, or, indeed, intelligence work in general, was a principal part of their careers. Sinclair's position was epitomized in a note he wrote on 9 September:

> From a Naval point of view I consider the expulsion of these persons to be absolutely essential. I am perfectly convinced that they are at the bottom of all the endeavours to promote unrest in H.M. Navy. The extent of the strenuous efforts that are being made to spread Bolshevism amongst officers and men does not appear to be realised. . . .
>
> Apart, however, from the purely Naval point of view, as Head of the Code and Cypher School, I am most strongly of opinion that publication of the telegrams offers such an opportunity of dealing a death blow to the revolutionary movement in this country as may never occur again. I will go so far as to say that *even if the publication of the telegrams was to result in not another message being decoded, then the present situation would fully justify it.*[56]

[55] *After* Sinclair's tour as Chief of the Submarine Service, he returned to intelligence work as Head of the Secret Intelligence Service and Controller of M.I.6, the two agencies—one predominantly civilian, the other its military branch—charged with the conduct of British espionage activities abroad, a position he then held for nearly two decades. But of course he did not know of this future role in 1920.
It should also be noted that Sir Basil Thomson did not fit this pattern of sometime intelligence service. Since 1913 he had been Assistant Commissioner of the Metropolitan Police and Head of the so-called Special Branch, and therefore in charge of all non-military counter-espionage activities. In 1919 he was also made head of the Home Office's Directorate of Special Intelligence, a title which added nothing to his duties but which gave him direct access to the Prime Minister and the Cabinet, enabling him to by-pass the Commissioner of Metropolitan Police. He would retain these positions until November 1922, when he was forced to resign both over a dispute with a newly installed Commissioner, who insisted that Thomson's activities should be subject to his control. See the heated Commons discussion of this issue, 3 November 1922 (147 *H.C. Deb.*, cols. 2041-86). Not surprisingly, there is very little published (or unpublished) information available about the structure and organization of the British Intelligence services. The most informative works are Richard Deacon, *A History of the British Secret Service*, London 1969, and a German handbook published during World War II, *Secret Service: Bedrohung der Welt. Beiträge zur Geschichte und Praxis des englischen Geheimdienstes*, Hannes Schneider, ed., Nürnberg, 1940. But even these books are relatively unspecific (neither, it should be noted, mentions the Code and Cypher School). I am grateful to Mr. Donald McCormick ("Richard Deacon") for further information.
[56] Letter, Sinclair to J. T. Davies, 9 September 1920; Lloyd George MSS, file F/34/1/43 (italics added).

Absolutist arguments like this are put forward, of course, precisely in order to neutralize arguments which weigh costs and benefits at the margin; Sinclair (like, indeed, Thwaites, Thomson, Wilson, and Churchill) was, in effect, dismissing all cost-benefit calculations by the flat assertion that any conceivable price was worth paying for the benefits that would accrue to the publication of the intercepted telegrams. Such arguments occur within all bureaucracies, in all eras. Other, less committed bureaucrats counter them by emphasizing just those marginal calculations which their advocate colleagues dismiss. Within the British government, the official who could least afford to play an advocate's role—and who was temperamentally among those least inclined to do so—was Sir Maurice Hankey, Secretary to the Cabinet and one of Lloyd George's closest advisers on matters of policy. Hankey had been with the Prime Minister on his holiday at Lucerne, and on the receiving end of the flow of communications coming out from London. On 8 September, just after their return and after talks with both Sinclair and Thomson, Hankey addressed to Lloyd George a long memorandum on "how far we shall lose by publishing the de-coded messages."[57]

At the outset he stated a basic premise: "I do not think it is possible if the messages are published to conceal permanently how they came into our hands." He continued: "This particular cypher is a very ingenious one which was discovered by great cleverness and hard work. The key of the cypher is changed daily and sometimes as often as three times in one message. Hence if it becomes known that we de-coded the messages all the Governments of the world will probably soon discover that no messages are safe."

Yet, Hankey asserted, "to a great extent" that fact was already known. He reminded Lloyd George that Clemenceau, at the Council of Four during the Peace Conference, had "never made any secret that the Quai d'Orsay de-coded every message that reached Paris." It was, moreover, "practically certain that the Americans suspect us of de-coding messages." That the Germans were also aware of these British activities, and that they deciphered whatever messages they could obtain, had been revealed in the memoirs of Count von Bernstorff, the German ambassador in Washington at the time of American entry into the war.[58] Finally, Hankey said, the Prime

---

[57] Memorandum, Hankey to Lloyd George, 8 September 1920; Davidson MSS.
[58] Hankey quoted two paragraphs from Bernstorff's book, *My Three Years in*

Minister would "recall that the Russians were the first to introduce us to this system of de-coding, and I believe one of our most skilful experts was and is of Russian origin." Therefore, it must be presumed that the Soviet government, which retained many officials of the old regime, "knows something of our efforts in this direction."

Why, then, should the British government hesitate to make known that it was reading the Soviet mission's telegraphic traffic? Hankey could adduce only two reasons. First was the difficulty of the task of breaking this particular Soviet code. "It is worth bearing in mind," he said, "that continental nations are apt to consider us as lacking in astuteness and to underrate us in this respect. It is a pity to remove this amiable weakness of theirs." Second was the possible domestic repercussion: "public opinion may experience a shock if it realises what has been going on."

If it were decided not to publish the telegrams, Hankey said, the government could nevertheless make "a perfectly good case" for expelling Kamenev and Krasin. He cited four grounds. First was Kamenev's deliberate misleading of the British government regarding the Soviet terms for peace with Poland; this was a matter of public record. Second was Kamenev's relations with the Council of Action; that he had attended its first meeting could be demonstrated from sources other than the cables. Third was the Soviet subsidy to the *Daily Herald*; Scotland Yard had traced the passage of both the jewels and the bank notes. Fourth was propaganda; while the cables revealed that Moscow had instructed the delegation in London to regard propaganda as its principal purpose, the *Herald* subsidies alone were sufficient to prove this the case. Indeed, Hankey wrote, "the fact is self-evident. Almost every note that Kameneff sends to you is obvious propaganda." Thus the government had sufficient evidence to expel the Russians without compromising the decipher-ing of the telegrams, which would "merely dot the *i*s and cross the *t*s." Yet, Hankey conceded, "it is true that the decoded messages convey an atmosphere that should deal a crushing blow at all revo-lutionary organisations, which it would be difficult to achieve by other methods." Firmly astride the bureaucratic fence, he concluded:

America, New York, 1920, p. 324 and p. 342, stating that the British had read "all" German cypher telegrams during the war, and asserting that "nowadays there is no cypher which is absolutely safe" from the experts all major governments em-ployed.

"The whole problem is one of balancing the pro's and con's set forth above."

❖

The problem was, of course, the Prime Minister's. But for him the question of whether or not to publish the Soviet telegrams was less urgent than that of whether or not to expel the Russian mission. On this point, as August wore on into September his advisers, both official and political, and his Cabinet colleagues all seemed to agree: the Russians must go. Even Philip Kerr, who in late August scrawled a note to the Prime Minister urging him "not to be in too precipitate a hurry" to expel the Russians, wrote again on 2 September that "I think we must ask K & K to leave." In his earlier note Kerr had stated: "No doubt Lenin & Kameneff are doing all they can to upset Western capitalist society. But they are not having much success." The swelling stridency of the Council of Action, he surmised, was due not to the presence of the Soviet delegation ("I cannot trace any real trouble to K & K, which is immediately & seriously dangerous, except the Daily Herald subsidy") but to real fears that the British government, which had "interfered in Russia in the past," would risk war to save the Poles from the defeat they had brought on themselves. "If we are to break with K & K it must be because we have definitely made up our minds that we cannot come to terms with Soviet Russia & are prepared to abide by the consequences, eg, propaganda in India etc," Kerr wrote in his August note. Yet by 2 September, he was prepared to urge their expulsion—"because there is simple and absolute proof that they have broken their pledges & are interfering in our internal politics for revolutionary ends." Kerr had joined the club.[59]

Lloyd George was more constant. His instincts told him not to expel the Soviet mission, and from his holiday retreat, against a drumfire of minatory messages from London, he persisted. On 27 August, in reply to a strong telegram from Edward Shortt, the Home Secretary, who feared "serious revolutionary disturbances" if the threatened miners' strike were to take place and who regarded the Soviet delegation as the "focus and inspiration" of agitation, the Prime Minister requested detailed evidence of the Russians' mis-

[59] Kerr's notes are in the Lloyd George MSS, files F/90/1/16 and F/24/3/9. The first is undated but is clearly from mid-August 1920. The second was addressed to Hankey, whom Kerr asked to relay its message to Lloyd George.

deeds; meanwhile Shortt was to take no action against them.[60] Two days later, in a telegram to Bonar Law and Balfour, he put forward what he called a "few considerations before irreparable action" were taken.[61] And on 2 September he dictated to Hankey a long memorandum, intended for Bonar Law and "any one Minister whom he would like to consult in regard to it,"[62] raising these and other considerations.

He began his memorandum by conceding that his critics were factually correct. "On the merits there is no doubt that there is a case for expulsion," he said. "The Soviet delegates have been guilty of a flagrant breach of the conditions under which they were permitted to enter England. They have been guilty of perfidy and of trickery which would disgrace any government except the Soviet Government of Russia." Yet he asked: "Would the British Empire gain more by their expulsion or by their retention?"

There might well be circumstances, Lloyd George continued, in which such a question could not even be asked—if, for instance, Kamenev and Krasin had so flagrantly violated their pledges that their retention might damage the British government's prestige internationally or domestically, they clearly would have to go regardless of any benefits that might accrue from their presence. "But the mere fact that there has been no general demand for their expulsion, even from papers of a generally anti-Bolshevic [*sic*] character, shows clearly that the character of the evidence is so far hidden from the public," and largely confined to the deciphered messages. Therefore the decision could still be treated "as a profit and loss account" one of whose elements must be the effect of disclosing the source of information. So long as the Soviet delegation remained, its communications would give the British government "a real insight into Bolshevist intentions and policy." If they left, the flow of communications would perforce stop, whether or not Moscow took steps to protect its ciphers.

[60] Telegrams, Shortt to Lloyd George, 26 August 1920, and Lloyd George to Ernest Evans (one of his private secretaries) with instructions for Shortt, 27 August; Davidson MSS.

[61] Telegram, Lloyd George (Lucerne) to Bonar Law and Balfour, 29 August 1920 (date received); Lloyd George MSS, file F/31/1/41, and Davidson MSS.

[62] So Hankey indicated in a covering note to Ernest Evans on 2 September 1920; Davidson MSS. "Memorandum on the Proposal to Expel Messrs. Kameneff and Krassin," 2 September; Davidson MSS, and file 18/E/194, Cab. 21/173. It should be noted that Hankey's own diary and letters are almost entirely unrevealing regarding the events discussed in this chapter.

Expulsion would also have to be examined for its effect upon "real *bona fide* working class opinion," Lloyd George said. "The workmen are not Bolshevist, in fact, the vast majority of the workmen of Great Britain are opposed to Communist theories." Yet, he continued, "there is a real suspicion amongst them that our objection to the Soviet Government is due not to the misconduct of the Bolshevists, but to the fact that the Russian Government is revolutionary; that it is a Government of peasants and workmen; and that all the governing classes of Europe dislike it for that reason." In the long run, these misapprehensions could be corrected by intelligent counter-propaganda. But in the short run, the only convincing evidence of misconduct on the part of the Soviet delegation—that contained in the intercepted telegrams—was in itself "a little repugnant to British methods. It looks like inviting men into your home and then opening their letters. It is perfectly justifiable where you suspect that your guests mean to steal the plate, but it is unpleasant to be compelled to reveal the steps which you have been driven to take, and unless the most overwhelming necessity drove us into it we would naturally feel reluctant to do so, and it is certainly not the best evidence to go to the public upon."

If the Soviet delegates were not expelled, they would undoubtedly continue their propaganda, which, Lloyd George said, in turn raised two questions: First, was it dangerous? Second, could it be stopped, or even mitigated, by their expulsion? His answer to each was negative. Bolshevik propaganda was crude, displaying not only an ignorance of the facts but, more important, of British working-class psychology.

It does more to discredit Bolshevism than any amount of general abuse directed against it. The more the working classes get to know about its doctrines the less they will like it. It is only formidable at a distance when seen through impenetrable mists. Fortunately, the Bolshevists have such a complete belief in themselves and their policy that they do not conceal even the most obnoxious, impracticable, and crazy parts of their proposals. . . . The real dangers to England do not emanate from Bolshevism. Bolshevism is almost a safeguard to society, for it infects all classes with a horror of what may happen if the present organisation of society is overthrown. There is a dread that the alternative is Russian Sovietism.

Yet even supposing Bolshevik propaganda were really dangerous,

Lloyd George continued, there was nothing Moscow could accomplish through the Soviet delegates in England that could not be done just as effectively if they left. Only their subsidizing of the *Daily Herald* had really been a "formidable contribution." But "much more obscure agents" than Kamenev and Krasin could have brought precious stones or currency into England and accomplished the same end.

Given the fact that Soviet activities directed against the British Empire would continue whether or not the Russian delegates remained, Lloyd George said, their very presence in England made it easier to exert a restraining influence. The threat of expulsion, and of breaking off trade relations, would "have some influence upon [Soviet] action in the East." He agreed, he said, "that you cannot trust to their word or to their honour, but you can rely up to a certain point upon their fear that if they carry things too far, or if they operate too openly, trading relations will be broken off." Given existing unrest in the Empire, such restraints were "worth a good deal." And in any case, so long as the delegation remained, Soviet communications would be susceptible to interception that would facilitate for the police the task of monitoring revolutionary activities.

The Prime Minister concluded his memorandum with a long passage reviewing the arguments he had often put forward in favor of trade with Russia and against the use of political criteria as grounds for refusing to trade. As for Kamenev and Krasin, he would warn them that the government had evidence that their mission was violating the conditions under which it was permitted entry into the United Kingdom, and that if these infringements continued the trade negotiations would be terminated. Meanwhile, depending on the replies the Russians gave, "trading relations should be prosecuted" in order that Britain should not lose Soviet trade by default to others. If the Cabinet disagreed, Lloyd George said, he hoped a decision could be put off until he returned a week or so hence.

Unknown to Lloyd George, however, at virtually the same moment he was at work on his memorandum the Cabinet—or what can best be described as a rump session of it—was meeting in order to reach a decision. Ministerial participants were Bonar Law, Balfour, and Sir Robert Horne who, as President of the Board of Trade, had responsibility not only for the trade negotiations but also (with the

Minister of Labour) for the preservation of tranquility in British industry.[63] Bonar Law had called them together at least in part in response to a note from Churchill—drafted the previous day after a meeting with Horne, Sir Eric Geddes, the Minister of Transport, and Henry Wilson—asking him to convene those ministers within range of London to discuss expelling the Soviet representatives.[64] In the absence of other ministers (not even Churchill himself could attend) Bonar Law included Lord Hardinge for the Foreign Office, Sir James Craig for the Admiralty, Sir Basil Thomson, Philip Kerr, and J.C.C. Davidson, his own private secretary, who handled his contacts with the intelligence departments.

If Churchill's request was the catalyst for the 2 September meeting, the root cause was the newly circulated text of Lenin's telegram of 20 August telling Kamenev that since an early Soviet victory over the Poles seemed unlikely, the delegation in London should regard as its "chief task" the spread of agitation among the British masses.[65] Those who saw this telegram seem to have regarded it as the last straw. Balfour told the others that until then he had thought a warning to Kamenev (along the lines Lloyd George was at that moment proposing from Lucerne) might be sufficient. But that course was now impossible. "There could be no doubt as to what the Russian delegates were doing," the summary of the meeting records him as saying, "and simply to make a polite communication warning them would be like warning a man whom we knew to be a murderer that the evidence about his intentions was arousing grave suspicion." It was generally agreed, the summary continued,

(1) That in view of our knowledge of the activities of the Russian delegates it was impossible to allow them to remain in the country. So many people now knew the facts that they would be bound to come out

---

[63] There are four sources for this meeting: 1) Conference of Ministers, 2 September 1920, 11 A.M., 10 Downing Street; minutes appended to those of Cabinet 53 (20), Cab. 23/22. 2) A more elaborate, informal summary in the Davidson MSS. 3) A letter from Thomas Jones, of the Cabinet Secretariat, to Hankey at Lucerne, 2 September 1920; Lloyd George MSS, file F/24/3/8. 4) A letter from J.C.C. Davidson to Lord Stamfordham, the King's private secretary, 2 September 1920; Bonar Law MSS, file 101/4/85.

[64] Churchill to Bonar Law, 1 September 1920; Davidson MSS. Wilson MS diary, entry for 1 September 1920. Neither Churchill nor Geddes attended the conference of ministers on the 2nd; the former had departed for a brief holiday (as he told Bonar Law) to "have a few days sunshine before the strike issue comes to a head."

[65] Lenin's telegram is cited above, n. 8.

and the Government would then be in the position of having allowed them to remain during an industrial crisis though it was fully informed about their actions.

(2) That merely to expel the trade delegates without giving our full case would make the labour situation in this country worse. If they were to be expelled, it would be necessary to publish all the documents upon which the decision was taken. On the other hand, if the documents were published it would undoubtedly have a great effect on the labour world and would probably discredit the extreme strike movement.

Along with the intercepted telegrams, the meeting concluded, the government should also release an explanatory statement "making it clear that the expulsion of the Russian Trade Delegation did not mean war with Russia or any change in our general policy of peace and appeasement." A draft of this statement, by Philip Kerr, went even further: the expulsion of the delegation, it said, signalled no alteration in the desire of the British government "for the resumption of trade between the citizens of the two countries." But "normal relations between the two Governments" would be possible "only when the Government of Moscow have abandoned their attempt to interfere in the affairs of their neighbours and to subvert the democratic institutions of friendly peoples."[66]

Kerr's draft statement, the minutes of the rump Cabinet session, and the latest intercepted telegrams were despatched by courier to Lloyd George along with a letter from Bonar Law. He too had changed his mind after seeing Lenin's telegram to Kamenev. Like Balfour, he had been proceeding on the assumption that no action need be taken regarding the Russians at least until Lloyd George's return. But now, he said, "I have definitely come to the conclusion that we ought to send them away." Accordingly, he asked the Prime Minister to telegraph by Saturday (it was then Thursday) whether he agreed; if so, Bonar Law would write to Kamenev requesting the delegation to leave.[67]

Lloyd George did not receive these materials until, at the earliest, late on Friday, 3 September—perhaps not even until the following day, when he sent Bonar Law a reply that was, as he put it, "dictated

[66] Kerr's draft, 2 September 1920, is in the Davidson MSS. It is unsigned, but Bonar Law, in the letter cited in n. 67, identified him as its author.
[67] Bonar Law to Lloyd George (Lucerne), 2 September 1920; Lloyd George MSS, file F/31/1/43 (original) and Bonar Law MSS, file 101/4/86 (copy).

. . . straight on the machine."[68] It was an impassioned appeal; some of its passages, indeed, were almost incoherent, so great was Lloyd George's evident urgency. He had no closer political friend than the man, five years his senior, who led the Conservative majority upon which the Coalition government rested; Frances Stevenson, referring to their relationship, called Bonar Law "an ideal companion with whom [Lloyd George] could laugh and joke and enjoy himself"— an opinion shared by less privileged observers.[69] On the basis of this relationship, Lloyd George could write as bluntly as he did. His letter began: "I have hardly had time to read the whole of the voluminous correspondence and appendices, but I have read quite enough to grasp the situation as it seems to be developing in England. The difference between the proposal you invite my assent to and the one which I put forward is only material as a question of practice, but when the carrying of the whole of the moderate opinion of England with us is involved, practical consequences count." His own proposal, he said, was to write to Kamenev and Krasin charging, without indicating the nature of the evidence, that the Soviet delegation had violated its pledges on four specific counts: subsidizing the *Daily Herald*, collaborating with the Council of Action, engaging in active propaganda, and deceiving the British public regarding the Soviet peace terms for Poland. "An explanation could be demanded from them within 48 hours," he continued. "There is nothing to communicate with Moscow about. It is a question entirely of their own action."

Whether the Russians denied or affirmed and attempted to excuse these allegations, the Prime Minister went on, "we could act with effect." If they denied them, the government could publish the telegrams; if they confirmed them, the telegrams might still be published "if necessary." Here, it should be noted, in contemplating publication, Lloyd George departed from his position of only two

[68] Lloyd George (Lucerne) to Bonar Law, 4 September 1920; Davidson MSS (original) and Lloyd George MSS, file F/31/1/44 (copy).

[69] Entry for 12 May 1921, in Frances Stevenson, *Lloyd George: A Diary*, A.J.P. Taylor, ed., London, 1971, p. 215. It is much to be regretted that among the many lacunae in this invaluable diary was the entire summer and early autumn of 1920; presumably Miss Stevenson was too busy to make entries. Regarding the Lloyd George–Bonar Law relationship, see also Thomas Jones, *Whitehall Diary* (Keith Middlemas, ed.), vol. I, *1916-1925*, London, 1969, entry for 22 October 1922, p. 215, and Robert Blake, *The Unknown Prime Minister: The Life and Times of Andrew Bonar Law 1858-1923*, London, 1955, pp. 342-43.

days before and moved closer to that of his colleagues. But their difference, he asserted, was that he would proceed much more cautiously. He explained:

I attach so much importance to the very great perils which are coming for mastery between the forces of veiled anarchy which are challenging governments everywhere, and the constitution of the country upon carrying the whole moderate opinion with us [*sic*]. It would be a mistake, and it may turn out to be a fatal mistake, if we rely merely upon the opinion of one section or class. I should like to carry not only Conservative opinion in England but moderate Liberal opinion and moderate Labour opinion. I believe you can do so provided we are not too precipitate, and provided also we give these people every opportunity to explain. I agree with you that on the face of it explanation seems impossible. I cannot see how they can get over these intercepts. The difference in time cannot be so important as to risk the failure to carry the kind of Liberalism which is represented with such distinction by our colleague [H.A.L.] Fisher and the kind of labour represented by [Arthur] Henderson, [Tom] Shaw, the Lancashire M.P. [?] and a few others whom I could name. If the working classes are united against that the lookout is grave, and the gravity would be intensified if what I call intellectual liberalism unites with Labour against us. The great struggle which is coming must not be partisan. I have been thinking a good deal about the situation here, and I have become more and more convinced that the time has arrived for coming to grips with the conspiracy which is seeking to utilise Labour for the purpose of overthrowing the existing organisation of the time. This opportunity will show itself over the miners demand. . . . Now is the acceptable moment for putting everything to the test. We must show Labour that the Government mean to be masters, I need hardly say this Government, but government of the land; but we must carry with us every phase of rational sane well-ordered opinion. To use the old phrase "we must have every man of goodwill" without distinction of Party on our side. There must be no suspicion that we are utilising conditions in order to carry out or to return to a reactionary *regime*. Hence my plea for avoiding anything in the nature of precipitancy. I again entreat you to consider the proposal I put forward that we should demand an explanation before we take action.

"One other point," the Prime Minister continued. He had decided to return to England by Tuesday night (it was then Saturday). It would be a "misfortune" if action were taken before then, without general Cabinet consultation, especially "when it might leak out that I had given different advice." He urged: "The difference between Monday and Wednesday cannot be vital. I would like therefore if we could get together a fairly representative gathering of Ministers including if possible Fisher, Gordon Hewart, and Addison, as well as those who are already in town. Chamberlain I should very much like to be present. His attitude has been pre-eminently sane and wise throughout this unfortunate Russian business."

❖

It was not Wednesday, but Friday, 10 September, when the Cabinet finally met to confront the issue. Of the four members whose presence Lloyd George specifically requested, two—Fisher and Addison—came, along with Bonar Law, Horne, Thomas J. Macnamara, Minister of Labour, Sir Laming Worthington-Evans, Minister without portfolio, Sir Hamar Greenwood, Chief Secretary for Ireland, and Lord Hardinge, representing the Foreign Office. Strikingly absent were those members—Churchill, Curzon, Shortt, Walter Long—whom Lloyd George would not have characterized as "pre-eminently sane and wise" on Russian business.[70]

An even smaller group (Lloyd George, Bonar Law, Horne, Greenwood, Fisher, and Hardinge) *had* gathered on the previous Wednesday, but had taken no decisions. Possibly Lloyd George, just back the previous evening, wanted to gather more of his colleagues for so important a matter: the minutes of the meeting merely state that discussion was "postponed until the issue of the threatened miners' strike became clearer."[71] The strike became no more clear during the intervening two days, but one fact did: on Thursday, 9 September, the Prime Minister received a letter from Kamenev formally announcing that he had been called home to Moscow "for consultations."[72]

Actually, and as those within the British government with access to the intercepted Russian telegrams well knew, Kamenev had been wanting to go home for some time. He first expressed such a wish in a telegram on 19 August.[73] In a message on 30 August he explained why he wished to leave. Until the results of peace negotia-

---

[70] Conference of Ministers, 10 September 1920, noon; minutes appended to those of Cabinet 51 (20), Cab. 23/22.

[71] Conference of Ministers, 8 September 1920, 3 P.M.; minutes appended to those of Cabinet 53 (20), Cab. 23/22.

[72] Cabinet paper C.P. 1840, Cab. 24/111.

[73] Kamenev (London) to Chicherin, telegrams 481-83, 19 August 1920, intercept 003877; Davidson MSS.

tions between the Russians and the Poles became evident, he said, "a dead period" in Anglo-Soviet relations would be inevitable. Moreover, "all the intelligence work which it was possible to do has been done." Therefore, he continued,

I think that there is no longer any object in remaining in London. If we commence advancing into ethnographic Poland it would be better if I were temporarily absent from here. Krassin offers no objections. I therefore beg to remind the Central Executive Committee that I was only appointed temporarily and ask the Committee to permit me to return. In order to deprive my departure of any political significance I will say that I am leaving in order to consult . . . as the situation is now changed. Personally I urgently insist on receiving permission to leave for Moscow. I am languishing here for lack of something to do.[74]

Kamenev's appeal was granted reluctant assent. On 6 September Chicherin told him that the Politburo had agreed to allow him to come to Moscow "for not more than one week to report and for information purposes subject, however, absolutely to the possibility for you to return to England being guaranteed." Chicherin recalled that Rothstein had left England without such a guarantee, and was now vainly awaiting a visa in Reval. Therefore, he said, "an indispensable condition" of Kamenev's departure was his obtaining a return visa and a definite promise from the British government that he would be allowed to return.[75]

Thus, in his note of 9 September informing Lloyd George of his departure, Kamenev duly stated that his consultations in Moscow would last only one week. He also asked for an interview with the Prime Minister in order to receive any suggestions the British government might wish to make toward "the speedy establishment of a general peace" between the two countries. This interview was scheduled for 4:30 P.M. on the 10th. At noon Lloyd George put the matter before the Cabinet. The minutes indicate, somewhat surprisingly, that he was given a fairly free hand. Although there was strong sentiment that Kamenev should be told he was *persona non grata*, there was also expressed the fear that if he were not allowed to return it would be difficult not to apply the same treatment to other "equally culpable" members of the Soviet mission, including

[74] Kamenev (London) to Chicherin, telegram 568, 30 August 1920, intercept 003981; Davidson MSS.
[75] Chicherin to Kamenev (London), telegrams 475-76, 6 September 1920, intercept 004056, circulated 9 September; Davidson MSS.

Klishko, and that in such an event Moscow might withdraw Krasin "and the more honourable members," with the result that "the door would be closed to the trade negotiations which at present held out some prospects of useful results." It was agreed, therefore, that the Prime Minister should warn Kamenev that he had violated the conditions upon which he had been granted entry to Great Britain; the Cabinet also agreed that Lloyd George should not specify to Kamenev the nature of the evidence against him, and that the decision whether or not to publish the telegrams should be postponed pending the outcome of their interview.[76]

Kamenev undoubtedly knew that the interview would not be an easy one. Two weeks before, he had reported to Chicherin: "The Churchillites have today started a campaign about my intrigues with the Council of Action."[77] Three days before, he commented that the absence of Parliament on summer recess had left the government's hands free. "Its attitude is one of hostile expectancy," he said. "The campaign against us is gathering force."[78] And on the very morning of his meeting with Lloyd George the *Daily Herald* published an article admitting that it had received Russian gems. These were, it said, a gift from the Communist International, made without conditions in order to help the *Herald* out of a critical financial position caused by rising production costs and the nearly universal refusal of advertisers to purchase space in a socialist publication. According to the article Francis Meynell (and not the Russian mission) had brought the gems into the country, and had gone about selling them without informing his co-directors on the newspaper's board. Now the others had discovered his misguided but generous act. Should the paper accept the money, it asked its readers, or raise its newsstand price from one penny to two?[79] (Confronted publicly with such a choice, the paper's directors, if not its readers, could only choose the latter alternative—and accept Meynell's resignation.)[80]

While Kamenev may therefore have feared that his meeting with

---

[76] Conference of Ministers, 10 September 1920; minutes cited above, n. 70.

[77] Kamenev (London) to Chicherin, telegrams 541-43, 29 August 1920, intercept 003964, circulated 31 August; Lloyd George MSS, file F/9/2/42, and Davidson MSS.

[78] Kamenev (London) to Chicherin, telegram 625, 7 September 1920, intercept 004065, circulated 9 September; Davidson MSS.

[79] *Daily Herald*, 10 September 1920.

[80] *Daily Herald*, 15 September 1920, reporting on a meeting of the paper's directors the previous day. See Meynell, *My Lives*, pp. 122-23.

Lloyd George would not be easy, he surely was unprepared for the onslaught loosed upon him. Contrary to the wild surmises of Henry Wilson and his co-conspirators, Lloyd George had no reason to spare Kamenev so long as expelling him did not also destroy the chances for the trade agreement and the Anglo-Soviet accord which the Prime Minister so earnestly sought. The Cabinet's free hand gave him the leeway he needed. Clearly he had to take *some* action against the Soviet mission: the political pressures from within his government (augmented by a strongly worded message from the King)[81] were enormous. He chose, therefore, to aim all his allegations at Kamenev, undoubtedly hoping that vigorous action against Kamenev would enable him to allow Krasin and the rest of the mission to remain, and that Moscow, similarly interested in the conclusion of a trade agreement, would not withdraw them in protest.

The two men were not alone. Lloyd George had with him Bonar Law, Hankey, and Thomas Jones, deputy secretary to the Cabinet, and Kamenev was accompanied by Krasin and Klishko. William Peters, of the Foreign Office's Department of Overseas Trade, served as interpreter, as he had done for all the previous Anglo-Soviet conversations. Lloyd George began by reviewing the conditions under which the Soviet mission had been allowed entry. They were not

[81] King George V, personally deeply anti-Bolshevik, took a strong interest in the question of whether or not the Soviet mission would be expelled. On 4 September 1920, after receiving a letter from J.C.C. Davidson rather too optimistically implying, on the basis of the rump Cabinet session two days before, that the Russians would be banished and the intercepted telegrams published, Lord Stamfordham, the King's private secretary, replied from Balmoral Castle: "The King is delighted to hear of the probable 'eviction' of the Russian Soviet delegation from the country and only hopes that it may have the further good results which you anticipate in putting an end both to the Coal Strike and to the McSwiney agitation." (Bonar Law MSS, files 101/4/85 and 99/5/2.)

When nearly a week passed and nothing happened, Stamfordham wrote to Lloyd George on 10 September that the King had read Basil Thomson's report of 2 September (cited above, n. 4) "with much concern," and had noted that on the 8th the Cabinet had postponed consideration of whether or not to expel the Russians. "The King," Stamfordham wrote, "of course, at this distance and not having a Minister in attendance, is unaware of the reasons for this decision, or why the Delegation is not immediately expelled from the country." (Lloyd George MSS, file F/29/4/25.)

Six days later, having heard nothing, Stamfordham wrote angrily to J. T. Davies of Lloyd George's secretariat, saying that the King expected a reply of some sort. (Lloyd George MSS, file F/29/4/27.) His letter crossed one sent the previous day by Bonar Law, attempting to justify the government's policy; Stamfordham's letter of the 10th, Bonar Law said, "has now been given to me" to handle—surely a minor masterstroke on Lloyd George's part. (Bonar Law MSS, file 101/4/88.)

exceptional conditions: no government, least of all the Soviet government, would allow foreign emissaries to interfere in its internal affairs. Now, he said, he would have "to speak things which are very disagreeable" about Kamenev. He made clear that in doing so he did not include Krasin, who, so far as he knew, had remained "faithful to the honourable pledge which he gave."[82]

Kamenev, however, had been guilty of "gross breach of faith." Insofar as he had acted in accord with instructions from Moscow, the Soviet government was also implicated. Lloyd George made three principal allegations against Kamenev. The first was subsidizing the *Daily Herald*. The *Herald* had admitted as much—but only because its editors had feared exposure. Second, Kamenev had "co-operated with an active political section which is carrying on a campaign to force the Government of the country to take a particular line of action"—the Council of Action. For these two misdeeds alone, had Kamenev not been leaving the next day, he would have been asked to leave. Yet more serious than either, Lloyd George made clear, was the fact that Kamenev had misled him regarding the Soviet peace terms for Poland. Kamenev's note of 10 August, conveying the proposed terms, stated "distinctly" that there would be no changes "except changes of a secondary nature." But, Lloyd George went on, Kamenev knew at the time that there was "at least one other condition" beyond the ones he conveyed to him. "He knew that the Soviet Government meant to insist on that condition, and he knew that that condition was quite incompatible with the independence of Poland." Yet on the basis of Kamenev's note the British government had informed the Poles that the Soviet terms seemed not to justify asking the British public to make the sacrifices that would have been entailed in rendering active assistance to Poland. Then Kamenev had written him a second letter, in which he said that he was authorized to say that the terms he had conveyed accurately represented the terms which the Soviet government intended to impose on the Poles. "At that time, not only was that not true," Lloyd George said, "but M. Kamenev knew it was untrue." And he added:

I can demonstrate this if challenged. I can make no more serious charge

---

[82] "Secretary's Notes of a Conference with the Russian Trade Delegation, held at 10, Downing Street . . . September 10, 1920, at 4:30 P.M."; *British Documents*, vol. VIII, pp. 783-91.

against any public person than that. We get our information even about Russia, and we know that M. Kamenev sent that to us without the authority of his Government, that he withheld that condition in spite of the protests of his Government, that his Government has censured him for withholding that condition and that his only answer has been to boast that the withholding of that fact had served its purpose. What was that purpose? To mislead the British Government, and to deceive the working men of this country until, as he thought, the hour of danger had passed.[83]

These were Lloyd George's three allegations. He spoke longer, but only to add emphasis to his basic points. The minutes of the meeting, taken apparently in verbatim form, leave no doubt that the Prime Minister was genuinely deeply angered. For his part, Kamenev did not speak until Lloyd George had finished. Then he denied the first two allegations and attempted to explain away the third. "I did not give, had no powers to give and have no powers to give any subsidy or support to any newspaper whatever," he said, to Lloyd George's expressed incredulity, adding: "We would be mad if, carrying on this policy of peace, we tried secretly to buy up newspapers and persons in Great Britain; and, by the way, we consider these quite impossible to be bought." Regarding the Council of Action, Kamenev said, he had "several times been visited by Members of Parliament who are also members of the Council of Action, and I consider that I have no right to refuse to receive Members of Parliament who come to me." At the outset of each of these conversations, he said, he had reminded his callers of his pledge not to interfere in British politics. Never once did they ask him for advice, nor did he render any. "It was only a case of giving information."

On the question of Poland, "I consider that here, too, the agents of the British Government who have informed and are informing the Prime Minister on these matters have been misled in just the same way as the agents who informed them on the matter of the newspaper," Kamenev said. The intercepted telegrams, he clearly implied, did not tell the whole story:

I do not wish to conceal that anxiety, and say it quite frankly, that inside the Soviet Government a certain struggle went on regarding the exact formulation of the terms of peace or armistice to be offered to Poland. I took part in that struggle, and I doubt whether anyone could bring

[83] *Ibid.*, p. 786.

against me the accusation that my share in this struggle is anything other than smoothed [*sic*] the way to peace. To understand the dispute and correspondence on the subject inside the Government it is not enough to have merely access to telegrams; it is necessary to take into account the internal co-relation of forces inside the Government. I consider that after the Russian Government gave up the condition regarding the Workers' Militia, a condition the giving up of which I myself urged from the beginning, when this point was given up the matter ended. That was three weeks ago.[84]

Thus, Kamenev's statement makes evident that there were two possible explanations of his conduct in conveying false information to the British government. In either case he was trying to buy time— either, as Lloyd George implied, to forestall British intervention while the Red Army imposed a soviet-style regime on the Poles, or, as he himself implied, in order to allow time for him to convince his Politburo colleagues that *their* terms should be modified to accord with the ones he gave Lloyd George. Either interpretation is plausible. We will not know which is correct until we know much more about the alignment of forces at that time within the Soviet leadership.

Lloyd George made clear after Kamenev had finished that regardless of his explanations he could not be allowed to remain in Great Britain: although he may have disagreed with his own government's decision, he was nevertheless still guilty of keeping that decision from the British government and people. In addition, the Prime Minister flatly refused to accept his denials of interference in British internal affairs; "in view of the irrefutable evidence which we have in our possession," he said, "the denials of M. Kamenev are startling and make it more difficult than ever for us to conduct negotiations through him."

There were, as well, certain other members of the Soviet delegation "about whom we may have to make a communication later on," Lloyd George said. But he rejected Kamenev's contention that the mission was "one single unit" among whose members individual responsibilities could not be distinguished. Krasin, he made clear, was welcome to stay, and trade negotiations could be resumed: the actions to which the British government objected had been com-

[84] *Ibid.*, p. 789.

mitted by the "political," not the "trading," side of the Soviet delegation. In June and July their two governments had reached agreement on the outlines of conditions under which trading might take place, Lloyd George said. "Unfortunately, this Polish episode intervened and threatened a very serious conflict between the two countries."[85]

"Episode" in this context is a meaningful word. The Red Army had nearly succeeded in bringing communism to Poland; its failure, however, made the effort itself merely an episode in an episodic history, as Kamenev's presence in England had been. "We therefore shall want to know from the Russian Government," Lloyd George told Kamenev—and Krasin—at the close of the interview, "whether they mean to abandon their policy of propaganda in this country. Upon that will depend the question of whether we will discuss with them the question of peace." This was more a rhetorical flourish than a dramatic ultimatum. For already during the course of the interview Lloyd George had implied that if the two governments could not discuss "peace" they could still talk about trade. Moreover, it is clear that his distinction between Kamenev and Krasin was also at least partly rhetorical, designed to satisfy his colleagues. No sooner had the "dishonorable" Kamenev got safely out of the country than the Admiralty intercepted what Henry Wilson described as "a scandalous wire" from Chicherin to Krasin, "advocating the most barefaced 'red' action over here."[86]

Wilson, of course, continued to rage—in his diary—against Lloyd George. The Field Marshal took Kamenev at his word: the Soviet delegation was "one unit," and should be treated as such: *all* its members should be expelled from England, a sentiment in which Wilson was joined by Curzon, Churchill, and Walter Long.[87] With Trenchard, Wilson continued to talk of resigning and exposing the government. But nothing came of these threats. Nor did anything come of Wilson's wish for a head-on collision with the Labour movement. "I am convinced we must have this fight & the sooner the better in such a good cause as the present," he wrote on 23 September in contemplation of a miners' strike. A week before he had

---

[85] *Ibid.*, p. 791.

[86] Wilson MS diary, entry for 13 September 1920. I have not found this telegram.

[87] See memoranda by Curzon and Churchill, 16 and 21 September 1920, each entitled "Krassin and Klishko," Cabinet papers C.P. 1897 and 1898, Cab. 24/111, and an untitled paper from Walter Long, 30 September, C.P. 1909, Cab. 24/112.

doubled the size of the arms caches he had formed at infantry depots around the country to arm "Loyalists" for civil warfare.[88] No such denouement occurred, however: the threat of a strike temporarily passed, and the Council of Action, although remaining in existence, subsided into memoranda-issuing middle age. Only Wilson's suspicions of Lloyd George remained unabated. The last words in his diary for 1920 were: "Is he a Bolshevist?"[89]

In the end, the government decided not to publish the intercepted telegrams. Instead, on 15 September the Cabinet agreed to release a statement refuting, point by point, a letter from Kamenev to a Liberal M.P. which appeared in the previous day's press denying Lloyd George's allegations against him. The statement asserted that "the Government have evidence which flatly contradicts" Kamenev's denials, but it did not indicate what the nature of that evidence might be.[90]

Such reticence did not, it should be noted, protect the Code and Cypher School. Lloyd George had virtually told Kamenev that the British government was reading the mission's telegraphic traffic. Moscow also had other warnings. On 19 December Mikhail V. Frunze, the commander of Soviet forces on the southern front, reported that Yamenko, the former chief of Wrangel's radio station in Sebastopol, had revealed that "all our codes, as a consequence of their simplicity, are deciphered by our enemies." Yamenko himself had "read the whole series of our most secret ciphers, both of a military-operational and of a diplomatic character." Frunze continued:

In particular the most secret correspondence of the Narkomindel with its representatives in Tashkent and in Europe is known word for word to the English, who have organized a network of stations designed particularly for listening to our radio. This accounts for the deciphering of more than one-hundred of our codes. The keys to those codes which have not submitted to reading are sent from London where a Russian subject, Feterliain, has been put at the head of cipher affairs having done such work before in Russia. The general conclusion is that all our enemies, in par-

[88] Wilson MS diary, entries for 13, 23, and 15 September 1920.
[89] *Ibid.*, entry for 31 December 1920.
[90] Minutes, Cabinet 51 (20), 15 September 1920, noon; Cab. 23/22. The text of the government's statement (appendix I to the minutes) appeared in *The Times* and other papers the following day. Kamenev's letter, to Lt. Cmdr. J. M. Kenworthy on 11 September, was published in *The Times* on the 14th.

ticular England, are *au courant* with all our internal military operations and diplomatic work. . . . I report the foregoing for the taking of appropriate measures.[91]

And a week later, 26 December, Chicherin instructed Krasin—in a message which, of course, was deciphered in London—that

We have ascertained that our actual cypher systems do not present sufficient power of resistance, and that our cypher correspondence is deciphered and becomes known to the governments of countries hostile to us. Having this in view, no really secret information, the discovery of which could compromise us and cause serious harm to the "Republic" or the "Party," should under any circumstances be sent by radio or by the telegraph of a foreign state. Such information should be sent by couriers, and anything particularly secret mentioning names and so on should, even in this event, be sent in cypher. The only more or less reliable cypher we consider to be the double-cypher key "KOKOS," which may be used in special circumstances until the establishment of new cypher systems.[92]

It could have come as no surprise, therefore, when Admiral Sinclair wrote to Hankey the following 22 March calling the attention of the Cabinet "to the remarkable drop which has occurred in the output of Russian telegrams from the Code and Cypher School, as although a large number of such telegrams are received daily, it is not possible at present to decypher them." Sinclair's memorandum continued:

There appears to be no doubt that this drop can be directly traced to the publication of certain telegrams concerning the "Daily Herald" and Kameneff in August-September, 1920. [*N.b.*: These were the intercepted *wireless* messages originally published on 19 August and then referred to in subsequent newspaper articles.] As a result of this, the Soviet Government realised the dangers of its methods of cyphering and has now succeeded in providing its agents abroad with a new series of cyphers.

It is the considered opinion of the experts in the Code and Cypher School that these new methods, while entailing a very considerable increase of work to the cypherers, render it impossible for the experts to guarantee any marked increase on the present output.

[91] Frunze to Lenin, Trotsky, Chicherin, military High Command, and Central Committee, telegram, 19 December 1920; Trotsky Archives, item T 628.
[92] Chicherin to Krasin (London), telegram 1252, 26 December 1920; intercept 005130, Lloyd George MSS, file F/203/1/11.

Sinclair concluded, in a statement of almost incredible audacity in view of the role he had played the previous autumn in urging full publication of the intercepts, no matter what the cost:

This state of affairs was forecasted by the Director of Naval Intelligence when the publication of the telegrams referred to was under consideration in August, 1920.

Rear-Admiral Sinclair begs to again point out that if this form of intelligence is employed for the purposes of publicity, there appears to be a grave danger that the fighting Services and the Government may lose it altogether.[93]

✧

Throughout September 1920, while these events involving the Soviet mission—and what might, potentially, have been a very severe threat to Lloyd George's Coalition government—took place in London, Piłsudski's armies continued their advance, pushing back Soviet forces on a wide front and solidifying their decisive victory of the previous month. Concurrently, the Soviet government turned its attentions to the campaign in the south against Wrangel. These two strands should quickly be traced to their ends before we return to the main thread of our account.

So far did Polish forces advance into borderlands with diminishing Polish populations that both the British and the French governments felt it necessary to caution Warsaw on the virtues of moderation.[94] These warnings were unnecessary, however. Although Piłsudski himself wanted once again to pursue the goals for which he had launched his spring offensive, his ambitions received no support from any important political sector. The Polish government was intent on reaching a satisfactory accord with Moscow. On 2 September the Polish and Soviet negotiators at Minsk agreed to

[93] Sinclair to Hankey, 22 March 1921. Hankey passed the memorandum to Lloyd George and scrawled upon it: "Prime Minister. You and I always feared that this would be the result." (Lloyd George MSS, file F/25/1/20.)

[94] See Rumbold (Warsaw) to Curzon, telegram 889, 3 October 1920; *British Documents*, vol. XI, no. 552. For the joint Anglo-French protest against Polish expansionist policies see Derby (Paris) to Curzon, telegram 1173, 7 October; *ibid.*, no. 556. Curzon's own (stronger) views are in his telegram 1074 to Derby, 7 October; *ibid.*, no. 560. On 9 October, despite previous disavowals of intention, the Poles occupied the disputed Lithuanian town of Vilna. For the British reaction see Curzon to Derby, telegram 1085, 11 October; *ibid.*, no. 564, and J. D. Gregory's note on his talk with the Polish Chargé d'Affaires in London, 11 October, *ibid.*, no. 566. For the indignant Polish rejection of these warnings, see Loraine (Warsaw) to Curzon, telegram 931, 14 October; *ibid.*, no. 576.

transfer their discussions to the more accessible (and neutral) locale of Riga, where talks were resumed on the 23rd. Naturally the earlier Soviet demands were forgotten. So also was the Curzon Line. The preliminary treaty of peace signed at Riga on 12 October gave to Poland a frontier some 200 kilometers further east. This line, incorporating into Poland some three million people of other than Polish nationality, mostly Byelorussians and Ukrainians, was to endure until the new partition which marked the beginning of the Second World War.[95]

Even before the signature of the Treaty of Riga the Soviet leadership, sensing that the Poles had no desire to continue the war, began to transfer forces southward to mount a final campaign against Wrangel, who appealed in vain to Warsaw for help. These Soviet reinforcements made Wrangel's defeat inevitable. Without them the Bolsheviks had nevertheless been able to repulse his efforts in mid-August to gain another mainland foothold by landing troops in the Kuban country east of the Sea of Azov. With them, during October, they recaptured those parts of the mainland which Wrangel had taken during his June offensive. Then, in a series of attacks extending from 7 through 11 November, Soviet forces broke through the heavily fortified White positions on the Isthmus of Perekop, the last natural barrier guarding the Crimea. Now all Wrangel's remaining troops lay exposed. Rather than continue to fight against hopeless odds, the Regent of South Russia (as he called himself) ordered his men to retreat to the Crimean ports, there to embark on whatever ships could be found.[96]

Among them were no British ships. Chicherin need not have bothered, as he did on 15 November, to send Curzon a warning that Moscow would regard as a hostile act the use of British vessels to evacuate Wrangel and his troops: the Cabinet decided on the 11th, with Winston Churchill and Walter Long registering dissents for the official record, not to give Wrangel assistance even in evacuating women and children, much less fighting forces.[97] Nor was an ap-

---

[95] See Wandycz, *Soviet-Polish Relations*, pp. 250-78. The text of the preliminary peace of 12 October 1920 is in *Dokumenty vneshnei politiki*, vol. III, pp. 245-56. The final treaty, signed at Riga on 18 March 1921, is on pp. 618-60.

[96] See Wrangel's memoirs in *Beloe delo*, vol. VI: for the Kuban expedition, pp. 137-77; for his efforts to persuade the Poles to continue fighting, pp. 178-201; for the battles in the isthmus and his decision to evacuate the Crimea, pp. 223-30.

[97] Minutes, Cabinet 60 (20), 11 November 1920, 12:15 P.M.; Cab. 23/23. In Churchill's view, the decision "might probably result in a massacre of the civilians

peal by the King of any avail.[98] So far as Lloyd George and the majority of the Cabinet were concerned, the British government's break with Wrangel, following the commencement of his offensive against British advice the preceding June, had been absolute. Curzon instructed Admiral de Robeck in Constantinople to point out to Wrangel that had he then accepted the British government's offer to mediate between himself and the Bolsheviks, the safety of his troops and of the civilian population would have been assured and evacuation made unnecessary. If Wrangel now wanted help, he must apply to the French government which had recognized his regime; to Paris would fall "sole responsibility for destination of refugees."[99]

Here was the final, bitter resolution of the Anglo-French dispute over the sudden French recognition of Wrangel. Although recognition had taken place in early August, the newly appointed French high commissioner, the Count de Martel, did not arrive with his staff of twenty officers until late October. At that late date his only accomplishment was the negotiation with Wrangel of an agreement whereby, in exchange for French "protection," the French would get possession of all Wrangel's ships, military and mercantile, to defray their expenses in rendering assistance.[100] In fact the French were able to give very little help in the evacuation itself. They woefully underestimated the magnitude of their task, expecting that only the White leadership and a few hundred followers would desire resettlement abroad. Instead, no fewer than 146,000 Russians elected to come out. They were transported largely on their own

---

in the Crimea." Long was not present at the meeting, but the minutes record him as later expressing the wish to join Churchill in dissenting.

[98] Stamfordham wrote Lloyd George from Balmoral on 14 November 1920 (Lloyd George MSS, file F/29/4/32), saying that although the King understood and appreciated the government's refusal to render further assistance to Wrangel, he nevertheless "appeals to you in hopes that his Government may yet be able to do something to save if possible the women & children from the terrible fate which will inevitably befall them at the hands of the victorious Bolshevist Army."

[99] For Chicherin's radioed message to Curzon, 15 November 1920, see *Dokumenty vneshnei politiki*, vol. III, p. 329; English version in *British Documents*, vol. XII, no. 815. For Curzon's telegram 1085 to de Robeck (Constantinople), 13 November, see *ibid.*, no. 809. De Robeck conveyed Wrangel's appeal for British help in his telegram 1191 to Curzon, 10 November; *ibid.*, no. 806.

[100] For the agreement between Wrangel and de Martel, 11 November 1920, see Wrangel's memoirs, *Beloe delo*, vol. VI, pp. 233-34. Admiral McCully, the American representative at Wrangel's headquarters, reported that de Martel's arrival on 19 October was followed by the arrival of three French vessels bearing aircraft, artillery, clothing, and other supplies; McCully (Constantinople) to Secretary of State, telegram 85, 25 October: U.S. National Archives, State Department file 861.00/7604.

ships—those which eventually fell to France. Wrangel did nothing to discourage such a mass exodus: his goal was to maintain his force intact and to work, as Chiang Kai-shek was later to work on Taiwan, toward the day when he could return to his homeland as a liberator.[101]

Although the French gave relatively little assistance in the evacuation, they manfully struggled to meet their obligation to "protect" the refugee masses. French funds helped them temporarily to settle in teeming camps around Constantinople and elsewhere in the Levant. These funds were supplemented by the American Red Cross and by voluntary contributions from British military and naval personnel stationed in the Straits and heartsick that their government would take no part in assisting such a wretched section of humanity. The French would have none of Wrangel's irredentist ambitions, however. They insisted that his men surrender all their arms, and they worked to disperse them to every part of the globe, thus breaking up potential military units and at the same time relieving themselves of the burden of support. The British government did not entirely abdicate from a similar role. It already had its share of White Russian refugees from previous evacuations. In the year 1920 these refugees cost the British taxpayer nearly one million pounds.[102]

✧

The departure of Wrangel's defeated forces from the Crimea followed by only a few days the third anniversary of the Bolshevik seizure of power. For the first time in its existence the Soviet regime had no cause to feel beleaguered. Isolated partisan leaders, like Nestor Makhno, remained as minor harassments, but Moscow faced no enemy of significance. Moreover, by any rights the campaigns against Wrangel and the Poles should—although they did not—at last have exorcised the specter of foreign intervention from the minds of the Bolshevik leaders. When Warsaw seemed most sorely menaced the Western Allies could spare only words, not battalions. And for Wrangel Britain, the Power most feared in Moscow, had not even words.

[101] See Hardinge's despatch 362 to Curzon from Paris, where he had succeeded Derby as Ambassador, 31 January 1921; *British Documents*, vol. XII, no. 832.

[102] *Idem.* See also the quoted excerpts from a Foreign Office paper of 22 January 1921, *idem*, n. 4, and despatch 2337/161 to the War Office, 3 December 1920, from General Sir Charles Harington (Constantinople), who had succeeded Milne as commander of British forces in the Straits, *ibid.*, no. 824.

In three years the Bolsheviks had learned much about the world. Although the same revolutionary slogans and manifestoes continued to come from their printing presses, the actual spread of the Revolution abroad, whether spontaneous or under the prodding of Red Army bayonets, seemed so remote a prospect by late 1920 as no longer to figure uppermost in the Kremlin's foreign policy. If the end of the Polish war and the civil war heralded a change in Moscow's approach to the world, the world also had to abandon any comforting notions about the early demise of communism in Russia. For some statesmen, such as those who governed France and the United States, this was no easy task. Others, such as Lloyd George in Great Britain and Nitti and Giolitti in Italy, had revised their views long before. Early in 1920 the British Prime Minister began to push not only for the restoration of commercial relations with Russia, but for a full peace settlement as well.

Thus the end of the Polish-Soviet war and the defeat of Wrangel imposed no new policy decisions on David Lloyd George. He had already determined to come to terms with the Bolsheviks. Although Kamenev had been expelled, Krasin remained in London. The "Polish episode," in particular, had placed an obstacle in the way of negotiations, but with its removal the Prime Minister could pursue his original course, faced with tactical problems but not with basic decisions. These tactical problems will form the subject of the final chapter in this book. But before we can turn to them we must give close attention to an important dimension of the Anglo-Soviet relationship not yet here considered—the renewal, in the very different circumstances of the postwar era, of the old Anglo-Russian rivalry in the Asian borderlands which lay between the two empires. During 1918 and 1919 the rivalry had been dormant. The hardpressed Soviet regime had been in no position to pursue it, and the British had extended their area of influence proportionally. But once the Bolsheviks had disposed of all their White opponents save Wrangel, they could turn their attention southward—towards Turkey, the Caucasus, Persia, and Afghanistan—as their Tsarist predecessors had done.

PART THREE

The Anglo-Russian Rivalry in the East

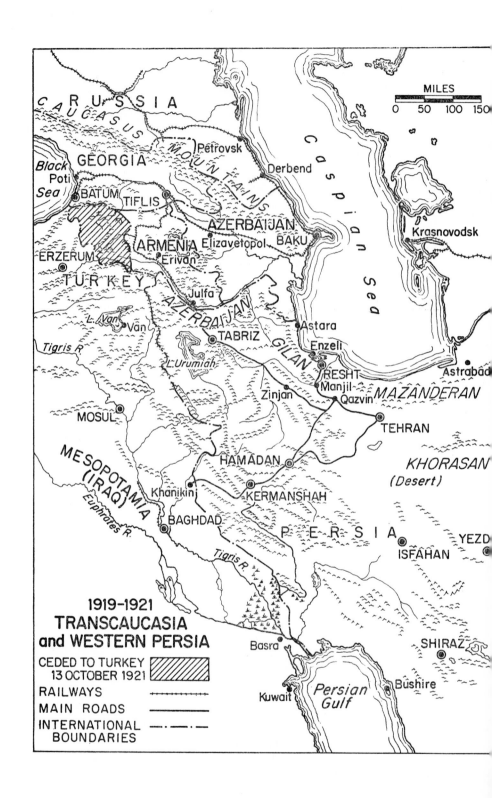

MILES

0   50   100   150

RUSSIA

C A U C A S U S

GEORGIA

Black
Poti
Sea

BATUM

TIFLIS

Petrovsk

Derbend

Caspian Sea

Krasnovodsk

ERZERUM

ARMENIA   Elizavetopol

Erivan

AZERBAIJAN   BAKU

TURKEY

Julfa

AZERBAIJAN

L. Van   Van

TABRIZ

L. Urumiah

Astara

Enzeli

GILAN

RESHT
Manjil
Zinjan   Qazvin

Astrabad

MAZANDERAN

Tigris R.

MOSUL

TEHRAN

HAMADAN

KHORASAN
(Desert)

MESOPOTAMIA
(IRAQ)

Khanikin

KERMANSHAH

Euphrates R.

BAGHDAD

P E R S I A

ISFAHAN

YEZD

Tigris R.

1919-1921
TRANSCAUCASIA
and WESTERN PERSIA

CEDED TO TURKEY
13 OCTOBER 1921

RAILWAYS

MAIN ROADS

INTERNATIONAL
BOUNDARIES

Basra

SHIRAZ

Kuwait

Persian
Gulf

Bushire

CHAPTER VIII

THE RIVALRY RENEWED

His Majesty's Government are not indifferent to fate of Georgia and are strongly in favour of her independence but other burdens are such that they cannot say what practical form their sympathy is likely to take.

We can therefore only express close sympathy.

—*Curzon, in a telegram to the British Chief Commissioner in Transcaucasia, 15 December 1920*[1]

DURING nearly the entire century preceding the First World War the international rivalry which had most vexed the British government was not the United Kingdom's relationship with Germany or even that with France (although there had been many vexing aspects to Anglo-French relations), but that with Russia. And Russia seemed most menacing to British interests not in Europe, where there were available multiple counterweights to the extension of Russian influence, but in Asia, where the frontiers of the two empires ran more or less parallel for thousands of miles, separated only by weak and insubstantial buffer states over which both London and St. Petersburg sought to extend control. This rivalry had been submerged only in the early years of the twentieth century by the greater danger which each began to fear emanating from Germany. It is therefore scarcely surprising that in the aftermath of the war which brought about Germany's defeat, the Anglo-Russian rivalry in the borderlands of Asia should be renewed—now, however, vastly exacerbated by the ideological transformation represented by the "Great October Revolution."

The symbol both of this renewed rivalry and of the ideological gulf which now divided the two nations was the opening call for a "holy war, to be directed first of all, against British imperialism," sounded by Zinoviev to the 1,981 delegates to the "First Congress of

[1] *British Documents*, vol. XII, no. 642.

the Peoples of the East" held in Baku during September 1920. Here was the Asian counterpart to the Second Congress of the Communist International which, meeting in Moscow two months before, had confidently cheered on the European Revolution which the Red Army was then carrying deep into Poland.[2] For anyone who cared to listen, pronouncements such as those from either of these gatherings seemed to furnish ample proof of the "aim of world wide revolution" (as one British Cabinet paper of December 1920 called it)[3] which motivated the Soviet regime. Obviously this aim aroused concern in London; the amount of time given to discussing the issue of "propaganda" (the shorthand term which increasingly came to stand for the whole complex of Soviet revolutionary activities against British interests, especially in Asia) is proof enough— although a cynic might add that Lloyd George, if not Curzon, was more anxious about the possible effect of Soviet propaganda on the Conservative members of the Coalition than on the farther reaches of the British empire.

Yet, paradoxically, there were few people in high places in London who listened with any real attention to the Bolshevik outpourings. In truth, there was not much they could listen to. The British national press scarcely noticed either the Moscow or Baku congresses, although Soviet propagandists strove to publicize them and the Baku meeting even featured such newsworthy merriments as the burning in effigy of Lloyd George, Millerand, and Woodrow Wilson. Official agencies did little better than the press. The Foreign Office was, of course, not represented at either congress, and was therefore dependent for its information on summaries broadcast by the Bolsheviks themselves, local press reports, and reports and materials furnished by the Secret Intelligence Service (the intelligence agency charged with espionage abroad—its military branch was M.I.6), military and naval intelligence officers, and the Government of India's Special Bureau of Information. Judging from their available reports, these agencies devoted more effort to deriding the congresses, particularly the one at Baku, than to making a serious

[2] Both of these congresses have been described in countless places. Carr's account is as good as any and better than most: *Bolshevik Revolution*, vol. III, pp. 187-209, 251-70.

[3] "Note on the Military Situation created by recent events in Russia, Caucasia, Turkey and Greece," War Office, 22 November 1920, Appendix E to Cabinet Paper C.P. 2274, 7 December, Cab. 24/116; printed in *British Documents*, vol. XIII, London, 1963, no. 181.

attempt to summarize and analyze their proceedings. Thus the Constantinople station of the Secret Intelligence Service noted in its weekly summary for 30 September: "The majority of the delegates [at Baku] seem to have been illiterate and to have taken far more interest in each other's weapons and in selling the produce, which they had brought with them from their native countries, than in the proceedings of the Conference. According to the Russian newspaper 'Communist' of Baku of September 3rd, scenes of a pantomime order occurred on the occasion of the unveiling of a statue erected to the memory of Karl Marx." This report concluded with a summary view that was identical with that expressed by all the other intelligence services:

The general impression is that the Congress has been a failure. From the point of view of those Muslims, who sincerely expected to further the cause of Islam, it is certainly a failure. If the so-called delegates were really selected by their own people, and there is reason to believe that a number of them were so chosen, very little good will have been done to the Bolshevik cause. If, on the other hand, the idea was merely to collect a number of Asiatic undesirables with a view to enlisting them as agents and agitators, the Bolsheviks may possibly have achieved a certain degree of success, but time alone will tell.[4]

These reports were duly furnished to the Foreign Office, which duly entered them in appropriate files. But this process of registration was accompanied by very little analysis. There were no Foreign Office memoranda about either congress. The jackets in which the reports were filed were for the most part unencumbered even by in-

---

[4] "Weekly Summary of Intelligence Reports Issued by S.I.S. (Constantinople Branch), for week ending 30. 9. 20."; file E 13451/262/44, F.O. 371/5171. Other S.I.S. reports on the Baku Congress were in the weekly summaries for 24 September and 14 and 28 October, files E 12803/—/—, F.O. 371/5171; and E 13846/—/— and E 14269/—/—, both in F.O. 371/5172. Military Intelligence reports on Baku are in G.H.Q. General Staff Intelligence, Constantinople, weekly report no. 88 for week ending 27 September 1920, no. 2737 "I"; file E 13552/—/—, F.O. 371/5171. Naval Intelligence's version is in Intelligence Summary no. 20, 13 October 1920, Commander in Chief, Mediterranean Station, to D.N.I.; file E 13903/—/—, F.O. 371/5172. Government of India Special Bureau of Information weekly intelligence summaries contained only scattered references to the Baku congress; file N —/179/97, F.O. 371/5382-83.

On the Second Congress of the Communist International there was even less: Basil Thomson's "Monthly Review of Revolutionary Movements in British Dominions Overseas and Foreign Countries," no. 21, July 1920, devoted one page to it; Cabinet paper C.P. 1804, Cab. 24/111. Thomson's office later wrote a Special Report (no. 19) on "The Second Congress of the Third International—July-August 1920," November 1929; Cabinet paper C.P. 2284 (circulated 13 December), Cab. 24/116.

formal minutes. The only Foreign Office minute written about the Baku congress read, in its entirety: "We have heard from other sources that the Baku Conference was a farce."[5]

It is with considerations such as these in mind that we should approach a discussion of the "Eastern question" as it figured in the making of British policies toward Russia during the year preceding the Anglo-Soviet Trade Agreement of March 1921. Both Moscow and London were agreed on one thing: that just as in the half-century before 1914, the most critical confrontation between Russia and Britain would take place not in Europe but in the borderlands stretching from the Straits to China. Yet there was no dialogue, or even argument, between the two sides. In the nineteenth century statesmen from both countries spoke in terms of military encroachments, spheres of interest, and concessions. For the British Empire these terms continued to hold their importance. The Soviet leadership, on the other hand, now agonized (as at Moscow and Baku) over the difference between "bourgeois-democratic national liberation movements" and liberation movements that were "revolutionary." Such distinctions were lost upon the "practical" men of Whitehall; that their Bolshevik opponents would actually take them into account in planning future actions was almost too absurd an idea to be countenanced. For this reason, although British politicians, officials, and national press showed great concern over the *fact* that Bolshevik propagandists were trying to rouse the peoples of Asia and the Middle East, they tended to disregard the actual *content* of the pronouncements that came from the Soviet government and the Comintern concerning conditions in these lands.[6]

❖

Miss Elizabeth Monroe has cogently observed that "the present generation is apt to underrate the enormous role played by India in the British scale of values before the Indian Independence Act of 1947."[7] As she and others have pointed out, the necessity to make

[5] The minute was dated 2 December 1920; file 3390/244/38, F.O. 371/5435. I was able to find *no* Foreign Office comment on the Comintern Congress.

[6] These events—the Second Congress of the Comintern in particular—naturally enough attracted more attention within the Labour Movement; the Second Congress took place at the time of a split in the ranks of Labour which culminated in the emergence of a separate Communist Party. See Graubard, *British Labour*, pp. 130-34, and Kendall, *Revolutionary Movement in Britain*, pp. 228-33.

[7] Elizabeth Monroe, *Britain's Moment in the Middle East 1914-1956*, London, 1963, p. 11.

secure the approaches to India, both by sea and by land, was the mainspring of Britain's "eastern" policy, and much of its African policy as well, throughout the imperialist phase of the nineteenth and well into the twentieth century.[8]

  These concerns were no less real or urgent in the aftermath of the World War, despite the vast difference in circumstances which the war had brought. Russia, whose expansionism had been looked upon as the chief threat to British India during so much of the earlier period, was still the primary source of anxiety.[9] Only now the danger seemed to come not so much from Russian arms as from Russian doctrines—supported, where possible, by Russian arms (the "propaganda aided by military pressure" of the War Office memorandum). Revolutionary doctrines propagated by Moscow found fertile soil throughout the Middle East among the nationalist movements to whose growth the war had given such impetus. During 1919 and the years which followed, the editorial columns of many a newspaper and the reports of many an Imperial administrator were filled with dire predictions about the effects of the combined forces of Bolshevism and Eastern nationalism.

  Within the British government and the Government of India there were many different views of the nature and the seriousness of the threat to the British Empire posed by Soviet Russia, and the means available to combat it. Before the war Britain had relied wherever possible upon buffer states to create a barrier between Russia and India. Afghanistan was the ideal buffer state—ideal because its territory was large and difficult to traverse and because British influence in Afghan affairs, slight though it had been, was nevertheless greater than Russian influence, a fact that had been recognized in the clause of the 1907 Anglo-Russian Convention acknowledging Britain's special interest in Afghanistan and requiring that all Russian relations of any sort with the Amir and his government should be conducted through British channels. A less ideal but still serviceable arrangement prevailed regarding Persia, itself long an object of active competition between its two powerful neighbors. In the

---

  [8] *Ibid.*, p. 18. See Max Beloff, *Britain's Liberal Empire 1897-1921* (Volume I of *Imperial Sunset*), London, 1969, *passim*, and Wm. Roger Louis, *Great Britain and Germany's Lost Colonies*, Oxford, 1967, *passim*.
  [9] For an excellent brief account of the pre-war Anglo-Russian rivalry see Firuz Kazemzadeh, "Russia and the Middle East," in Ivo J. Lederer, ed., *Russian Foreign Policy: Essays in Historical Perspective*, New Haven, Conn., 1962, pp. 489-521.

Persian case there was no possibility of Russia's opting out. Instead, the 1907 Convention divided the country into three zones, the large northern one becoming a Russian sphere of influence; a southeastern one, covering the entire length of the Persian-Indian and most of the Persian-Afghan borders, becoming a British sphere; the territory between them, including the Gulf (and, incidentally, all the oil that had yet been discovered), remaining neutral, with both London and St. Petersburg allowed to obtain concessions within it.[10]

These arrangements insured not only that there would be no common frontier between Russia and India, but also that the only foreign influence in the territories bordering upon India would be British.[11] Thus Russia was restrained in Asia. Of nearly equal importance for British interests was that she should also be restrained in Europe. For this purpose Britain had historically relied on the decaying Ottoman Empire; support of the Turks was often embarrassing and distasteful, particularly for liberals, but it was the most practical way of barring the Straits to Russia.

After the war, under the prodding of Curzon, the British government tried—although with some acknowledgment of the vast changes the war had brought—to recreate the pre-war system, including the reliance upon buffer states. This aim underlay the government's desire to perpetuate the old arrangements in Afghanistan, to extend the British sphere of influence in Persia to encompass the entire country, and to support the claims for independence of the three newly created republics of Transcaucasia. Only in the case of Turkey, which had already been chopped up and parcelled out for future delivery as a result of the web of secret treaties concluded during the war, was British policy—calling for a magnanimous peace that would still leave a strong Turkish counterweight to Russia—frustrated from the outset.[12]

Before the war Britain's eastern policies had been pursued with

[10] The negotiation of the Anglo-Russian Convention is described in Harold Nicolson, *Lord Carnock: A Study in the Old Diplomacy*, London, 1930, pp. 206-57; the Convention itself is summarized in an appendix, pp. 447-50.

[11] This included even those border regions which did not lie directly between Russian and Indian territory; thus the Convention recognized the suzerain rights of China over Tibet, and stated that Russia admitted that Great Britain had a special interest in the maintenance of Tibet's territorial integrity.

[12] For an account of Curzon's aims in the Turkish settlement, and a summary of the relevant secret treaties which made their implementation impossible, see Nicolson, *Curzon*, pp. 75-90.

scant regard for the wishes of the populations (or in some instances even of the governments)[13] involved. By 1919 the importance of giving weight to local preferences was not seriously disputed anywhere within the British government. Yet in practice it often seemed extremely difficult to frame policies which took into account the force of eastern nationalism and nevertheless still achieved the traditional objectives of safeguarding India and the Imperial lines of communication. In dealing with this dilemma there was considerable, often bitter, argument, in which at least three broad positions can be discerned. Not surprisingly, they may be identified with the three departments of state most directly involved: the Foreign Office, the War Office, and the India Office.

On Eastern questions the Foreign Office was, effectively, Lord Curzon. He had devoted his working lifetime to Eastern concerns, he held strong policy preferences, and in dealing with these questions he was willing to work tirelessly, with consummate attention to details. Few officials of his department would have dared put forward recommendations which conflicted with his preferences even if they had them—and it is by no means clear that they did. Moreover, he received strong support from Lord Hardinge, the Permanent Under-Secretary and, like Curzon himself, also a former Viceroy of India. Curzon and Hardinge disagreed on many things and their relationship was often uneasy; on Eastern matters, however, they were as one.

Readers of the second volume of the present work have already seen something of Curzon's views in his urgent (but futile) appeals during the summer of 1919 that British troops should remain in occupation of Transcaucasia rather than be withdrawn, and his insistence during the apparent crisis following Denikin's collapse in January 1920 that British military and naval forces should be reintroduced into the area to man the Batum-Baku line and once again to take over the Caspian flotilla.[14] During the rest of 1920 he and Hardinge were to protest repeatedly against further withdrawals of

[13] The Amir of Afghanistan resented the Convention and refused to indicate his concurrence with it; the Russian and British governments nevertheless considered operative those portions affecting Afghanistan despite the provision in the Convention that they should enter into force only when the consent of the Amir was obtained. See W. K. Fraser-Tytler, *Afghanistan: A Study of Political Developments in Central and Southern Asia*, 2nd ed., London, 1953, pp. 179-80.

[14] See Volume II, pp. 230-31, 331.

British forces, first from Batum, where a garrison had been left, then from Persia.

Both men predicted that these retractions of British armed strength would have the most dire consequences. Their arguments, which were echoed by officials of the Foreign Office both in London and in the field, were strikingly similar to the so-called "domino theory" of the effects of communist victories which has achieved currency in recent years regarding Southeast Asia—that the falling of one state to the communists would, like the toppling of one domino against its neighbor in a standing row, bring about in turn the downfall of all the others in a given geographical region, including some whose position at first sight seemed very sound. Just as the proponents of the domino theory argued that a commitment of Western support at any threatened point was essential to keep all of Southeast Asia from succumbing to communist military and political warfare, so Curzon, Hardinge, and their Foreign Office juniors insisted that to remove British garrisons from threatened points in the Middle East would initiate a chain reaction that might result even in the "loss" of India.[15]

All of the Foreign Office's arguments were displayed in a long minute written by Hardinge to Curzon on 20 May 1920 in reaction to War Office insistence that British forces should be withdrawn from garrisons at Batum and in North Persia.[16] Hardinge wished, he began, to point out "some of the consequences of these measures." He dealt with Batum first:

Once the Allied troops have left Batoum, Georgia will be deprived of further moral or material support, and there is little doubt that she will, in the course of a few weeks, throw in her lot with the Bolsheviks and blame us for having betrayed her. The reproach will be well deserved. As for Armenia, with the Bolsheviks in Azerbaijan,[17] the Turks in the south-west, and the Georgians in a hesitating frame of mind, there is little doubt that the Erivan Government, which is already accused of extreme tendencies, will in the end become Bolshevik. This will facilitate greatly the approach of the Bolshevik troops from Baku to Persia through Tiflis

[15] For expressions of these views during 1920 by subordinate Foreign Office officials see memoranda by E. W. Birse (6 January), L. Oliphant (14 June), and G. P. Churchill (20 January); *British Documents*, vol. XIII, nos. 364, 464, and 616. See also 483 from H. C. Norman, British Minister in Tehran, 13 July; *ibid.*, 511.

[16] Hardinge's minute is in file Confidential/General/363/19; F.O. 800/156. Excerpts are in *British Documents*, vol. XIII, no. 433, n. 4.

[17] Soviet forces occupied Azerbaijan in late April, 1920; see below.

and Erivan to the railhead at Tabriz. The whole of the Caucasus will then have become Bolshevik, and it is not unlikely that Mustapha Kemel [*sic*] will join hands with them with a view to driving the French out of Cilicia[18] and ourselves from Mosul. . . .[19]

Here, then, was the first consequence of a British evacuation—the destruction of the Allied position in Turkey. But this would be only the beginning; Hardinge continued:

Once the evacuation of Tabriz and Kasvin has been effected the fall of Teheran is inevitable. . . . The Anglo-Persian Agreement[20] will have become a scrap of paper, the Europeans of Teheran will be obliged to fly towards the South, and anarchy and destruction will prevail. If and when a large Bolshevik force is concentrated at Kasvin and Teheran, the flanks of both India and Mesopotamia will be exposed and the Bolsheviks will be in a position to choose whether to attack in the east or in the west. If they decide to attack in the east their task would be much facilitated by the landing of further troops on the shores of the Caspian in the vicinity of Astrabad, whence they could make a joint advance on Meshed accompanied by a simultaneous advance from the north from Askabad. Any such move on the part of the Bolsheviks towards Meshed and the Afghan frontier would probably mean an Afghan-Bolshevik alliance of a temporary kind, accompanied by war on India by Afghanistan. We know from intercepts that such an alliance is still in contemplation, though not yet concluded. . . .

I need hardly say that you know just as well as I do how disastrous the effect of our evacuation and betrayal of Persia will be on our subjects in India, both Mohommedan [*sic*] and Hindu, and the loss of prestige that we shall suffer throughout the whole of the East.

All these dire consequences, Hardinge concluded, would not have been in prospect had the War Office agreed to the request the Foreign Office had so urgently made the previous January for British forces to hold a line between Batum and Baku. Then the request

[18] Cilicia is the ancient name for the region of southern Turkey north and north-west of Syria. It had been promised to the French under the Sykes-Picot Agreement of 1916; after the war they insisted on taking it as a Mandate territory and established a military occupation over the region in January 1920. The French troops withdrew, after constant harassment by Kemalist forces, in October 1921 following the signature of the Treaty of Ankara between France and Kemal's government.
[19] Mosul, the northwestern district of Mesopotamia (Iraq), was occupied by British troops at the close of the war. London regarded the area as strategically essential to the Arab kingdom for which Britain would receive a Mandate. Its fate was ultimately decided by the League Council, who awarded it to Iraq in 1924.
[20] For this agreement, see below, chap. IX.

had been refused; Sir Henry Wilson had firmly maintained that the necessary three or more divisions simply were not available, and Churchill had insisted that if they were, they would have been better employed in support of Denikin in South Russia, or in an advance on Moscow through Poland.[21]

On matters such as these, Wilson's views, expressing the caution (perhaps the over-caution) of the professional soldier and not Churchill's more daring, and more wishful, thinking, dominated the War Office. At many points in the course of this study we have seen Wilson protest that British military commitments were too great. Weekly during 1920, sometimes almost nightly, he would commit to his diary his growing anxieties that garrisons such as the ones in Batum and North Persia were too weak to be useful against a serious attack and too isolated to be relieved before suffering "disaster" (a word he constantly used) in the form of unacceptable casualties, and that "our small army" was spread dangerously thin and should be concentrated at those points where British interests of the very greatest importance were threatened, such as Ireland, England itself (where Wilson feared working-class unrest), India, Mesopotamia (as Iraq was then called) and Egypt. (With the partial exception of India, it should be noted, all these were points where in Wilson's mind the danger to British interests came from *internal* dissolution rather than external aggression.)

The C.I.G.S.'s anxieties were encapsulated in long italicized passages of a paper he submitted through Churchill to the Cabinet on 9 June. *"Is it realized that at the present moment we have absolutely no reserves whatever (in formations) with which to reinforce our garrisons in any part of the world* where an emergency may at any moment develop without warning?" he asked. He could not, he said, emphasize too strongly "the danger, the extreme danger, of His Majesty's Army being spread all over the world, strong nowhere, *weak everywhere, and with no reserve to save a dangerous situation or to avert a coming danger."* Withdrawals and consolidations were imperative. British forces under the command of General Milne at Constantinople (the so-called Army of the Black Sea) should be cut by fifteen battalions, including the garrison at Batum, to only six. Most important, however, from Wilson's point of view, was the complete withdrawal of British forces from Persia. Here eleven

---

[21] See Volume II, pp. 324, 332-33.

battalions were involved. But the potential for a growing involvement seemed to Wilson greater in Persia than anywhere else: unless these troops were withdrawn "we shall *almost inevitably find ourselves committed to a process of gradual reinforcement which may entail unlimited liabilities.*" Always at the back of Wilson's mind was the example of North Russia which, he reminded the Cabinet, began with a landing of only 150 soldiers at Murmansk, but which "*in the absence of a definite policy absorbed nearly 20,000 British before it ended.*"[22]

Wilson was not an advocate of what was then called the "forward policy" for the defense of India, which insisted that there should be preponderant British influence, and preferably British military presence as well, in all of the lands bordering on India. His skepticism was shared by his senior colleagues on the General Staff, and also, it is worth noting, by the British officer who had had the widest experience in commanding troops against the Bolsheviks and who, after London's withdrawal of support from Wrangel during 1920, commanded the only British force which still saw combat against Soviet forces—Major General Sir Edmund Ironside, who commanded the inter-Allied North Russian expedition in 1918-19 and who led the North Persia Force during the period September 1920–February 1921. In the next chapter we shall look closely at Ironside's command in Persia. Here, however, we should note that he profoundly disapproved of the presence of British forces there. He gave vent to his disapproval in his diary. On 14 December 1920 he wrote: "India should be defended behind her own frontiers and not in advance of them." And he continued: "There is no doubt that the question of an invasion of India by Russia was always held up as a bogey, in order to ensure a proper Army in India, but bogey it was nevertheless. It is fantastic to think of Russian armies invading India. Gradual penetration of Persia and Afghanistan, certainly, but that is another thing to an invasion of India."[23] Here was the argument, on military grounds, that the virtually impassable nature of the terrain on India's frontiers made a "forward policy" unnecessary. In an earlier diary entry, on 26 November, Ironside had presented the case against such a policy in different terms:

[22] "British Military Liabilities," Cabinet paper C.O. 1467, circulated by Churchill on 15 June 1920; Cab. 24/107. Churchill appended an Air Staff Memorandum, 14 June, making the same points.
[23] Ironside MS diary, entry for 14 December 1920.

I personally cannot see that we shall gain very much from controlling Persia. . . . We do not want an extension of our military commitments but rather a reduction if possible. Even if we are controlling Persia the strategic position of our forces is impossible. We should have to withdraw if the Soviet went for us. Why deliberately make a common frontier with the Soviet? The defence of Persia isn't our job. We need defend only the Karun valley [far to the south near the Persian Gulf] and the Anglo-Persian oil. India isn't protected through our control of Persia. It merely means that Indian troops will be employed permanently outside India and that cannot go on long. . . . We must liquidate in the spring. No tax-payer can stand the racket any longer. We cannot take a forward policy like this. Surely this is not the way to fight the Bolsheviks? At the end of a very long line of communications. The menace will grow, but it will not be a military menace.[24]

Here were three distinct arguments: 1) Persia (and, therefore, by extension, Transcaucasia) was not a region of great strategic importance for the defense of India; 2) this being the case, the financial drain imposed by continued British military presence was intolerable; and 3) anyway, the menace of Bolshevism was political, not military, and military means would not eliminate it. The first of these arguments, of course, was strictly military, while the second was essentially economic and the third political. The first was entirely the province of the War Office; the latter two were particularly the property of the India Office and the Government of India, and were put forward with vehemence both by Edwin Montagu, the Secretary of State in London, and Lord Chelmsford, the Viceroy at Delhi.

Their views were well represented in a blunt note from Montagu to Curzon in January 1920. "The danger of the Bolsheviks to Persia and to India seems to me to be so largely the fault of the Home Government in their anti-Mohemmedan [*sic*] policy that I really don't know how far we shall be able to rely upon Indian troops to assist in any fighting in Persia," he wrote. "We could have made Pan-Islamism friendly to Great Britain. We are making it hostile."[25] Chelmsford elaborated upon this argument in telegrams to Montagu the following winter. The war, he said, had brought a curious reversal of roles between Britain and Russia. Before 1914 the British had been the "champions of Islam against the Russian Ogre."

[24] *Ibid.*, entry for 26 November 1920.
[25] Letter, Montagu to Curzon, 5 January 1920; Curzon MSS, box 65.

Peace, however, had brought the frankly punitive and annexationist Treaty of Sèvres between the Allies and Turkey and the Anglo-Persian Agreement of 1919 which was universally regarded by Persian nationalists as the means by which their country would be reduced to a semicolonial status. To Indian Moslems these two treaties appeared as an "example of Britain's crushing of Islam." In Russia, on the other hand, the end of the war had brought a government whose every public statement proclaimed the end of imperialism and the dawn of an era of self-determination.

To Chelmsford the contrast was obvious, if misleading: "Ostentatious abnegation of Czarist gains and ambitions" on the part of the Russians was "meant to throw Great Britain's general attitude and demands . . . into high relief, and thus foster anti-British propaganda. . . ." The "real defence" against the incursion of Bolshevism into India in the long run, the Viceroy felt, lay not in military cordons but in the growth throughout the East of a "nationalist spirit" hostile to the basic tenets of Bolshevism. In the changed circumstances of the postwar world, nationalism throughout the region would be a powerful force directed against all external enemies. Continued British "presence," whether military or merely economic, would blind nationalist leaders to the fact that for them the real danger came from Moscow, not from London.[26]

The India Office (and the government of India) and the Foreign Office thus took positions almost diametrically opposed on these important questions of Britain's Eastern policy. In considering their differences, two considerations should be kept in mind. First was that expenditures whose rationale was the defense of India and of the approaches to India (including, for example, the British force in Transcaspia during 1918-19, and British forces in northern and eastern Persia) were carried in large measure on the budget of the government of India. Thus Curzon and his officials at the Foreign Office were not confronted so directly with the financial implications of the policies they recommended. And thus the India Office was impelled to express with particular vehemence its contention that the defense of India began at home. The government of India was very short of funds, Montagu told a meeting of the Inter-Departmental Conference on Middle Eastern Affairs (the official name of

[26] Chelmsford to Montagu, telegrams 107 S and 1393 S, 22 January 1921 and 6 December 1920; *British Documents*, vol. XIII, nos. 662 and 624, n. 3.

the successor to the War Cabinet's Eastern Committee of 1918—still, however, universally referred to as the "Eastern Committee") gathered in April 1920 to consider the future of a British and Indian force based at Meshed in northeastern Persia. The £3 million that had been asked of Delhi to maintain the force (half the total cost, the other half being borne by London) would be better spent on the India side of the Afghan frontier. From a purely Indian point of view, Montagu said, it would be better to save the money now and risk the possibility of a Bolshevik advance through Persia, for such an attack could be satisfactorily met only on the Indian frontier itself.[27]

The second consideration to be borne in mind was the long-standing personal antipathy between Curzon and Montagu. Harold Nicolson referred to it as a controversy "between the new school of Oriental psychologists and the old"—between those who were committed, as Montagu and Chelmsford were in the Indian internal reforms which bore their joint names,[28] to the principle of genuine self-determination, and those still inclined towards the old ways of paternalistic imperialism. There was more, however: In 1920 Curzon was sixty-one, Montagu a full twenty years his junior. Curzon was a Conservative, the inheritor of English and Irish landed peerages, never really at ease in Lloyd George's cabinets of lapsed liberals and new-style businessmen. Montagu was a Liberal with better relations than most of his fellow Coalition Liberals with their former brethren who had not accepted (or been offered) the coupon. He admired and followed Lloyd George for his liberalism of old; he accepted only with reluctance the Prime Minister's new Tory colleagues. Like Curzon he was the son of a peer, but his father was a Jew and a City merchant-banker, only lately ennobled. Each had a first-rate mind. Each was an articulate advocate. Each felt for the other what may best be described as controlled contempt.[29]

[27] Inter-Departmental Conference on Middle Eastern Affairs, 37th Minutes, 13 April 1920, 5 P.M.; F.O. General/216.

[28] This is not to imply that Montagu and Chelmsford were personally close or were always in agreement on Indian policy. Eleven years Chelmsford's junior, Montagu thought the Viceroy too conservative and slow to react. See S. D. Waley, *Edwin Montagu: A Memoir and an Account of His Visits to India*, New York, 1964, esp. pp. 223 and 228.

[29] Nicolson, *Curzon*, pp. 99-103, 134. Waley, *Montagu*, passim. For a brilliant sketch of Montagu's personality, see John Maynard Keynes, *Essays in Biography*, London, 1933. The Montagu MSS at Trinity College, Cambridge, contain dozens of acrimonious letters exchanged between Montagu and Curzon during the period 1919-22.

The antipathy between the two secretaries of state inevitably affected the relationship between their departments. In January 1921 there arrived in the Foreign Office an information copy of a telegram from Lord Chelmsford in Delhi to Montagu. For Britain's Eastern dilemmas the Viceroy prescribed a drastic solution: to "cut ground from under Bolshevism by scrapping Anglo-Persian Agreement and repudiating Turkish Treaty [of peace]." Such measures would represent a realistic accommodation to the forces of nationalism in the Middle East. There were many elements in Persia and elsewhere, he said, "with whom mistrust of Russia is ingrained, to whom Bolshevik practice would be repugnant, and who, given a change of attitude on our part, would see through Bolshevik professions of friendship." However, he cautioned, without a change in British policy the necessary "revulsion against Bolshevism" might come too late.[30]

Curzon, of course, was the principal author of the policies which, in this and other telegrams, Chelmsford so roundly condemned. When this message reached him he vented his outrage in an angry minute. Considering that the government of India had refused to take any responsibility for British policy in Persia (the immediate subject of discussion), he wrote, "I regard the advice with which they so liberally regale us as an impertinence and would not pay it the compliment of a reply."[31]

These, then, were three broad approaches, each advanced by a different department of state, to the problem of protecting British interests in the East from the dangers posed by Soviet rule in Russia. Those of the War Office and the India Office, although based upon quite different premises, had similar policy implications: disengagement and future non-involvement. On the other hand, the Foreign Office's approach was vigorously activist and interventionist. Yet because of the opposition of the other two departments its approach could not hope for endorsement by the Cabinet, particularly a Cabinet bent on economizing. Curzon himself commented bitterly in a departmental minute on 29 April 1920: "as the W.O. always declare that no place which it is vital to hold on political grounds can ever

[30] From Chelmsford's telegram 107 S, 22 January 1921, cited above, n. 26.
[31] Curzon's minute, 29 January 1921, is in *British Documents*, vol. XIII, no. 662, n. 7.

be held by a less force than 2 divisions—I am placed at a great disadvantage."[32]

It was enough of a blow to Curzon's hopes that the General Staff was willing flatly to state that a commitment of British armed strength in Transcaucasia and Persia would expose intolerable weaknesses in other areas where British interests were greater. But an equally determining factor was the assertion by the India Office and the government of India that the Empire did not need the protection which Curzon wished to provide, and that indeed it was precisely the British "presence" he envisioned that would most effectively move local nationalists to embrace the communist standard. Given this sort of internal opposition to any activist role, it was inevitable that during 1920 and early 1921 the British government should assume the posture of a mere bystander to the Soviet thrust which overran the republics of the Caucasus and threatened to overrun Persia as well.

The story of the Soviet conquest of Transcaucasia has been well told.[33] Azerbaijan fell, virtually without resistance, at the end of April 1920. On the 27th local communists delivered an ultimatum to the Azerbaijani government insisting on a transfer of power within twelve hours. By the next day units of the Red Army were in Baku. There they did not stop simply with the establishment of the so-called Azerbaijani Socialist Soviet Republic, but instead immediately began to advance into Armenia and Georgia. These two republics were spared, however, by the fact that the Soviet invasion began just at the time of the Polish drive into the Ukraine: on 3 May an emergency order from Moscow directed that the offensive in the Caucasus should be called off.[34] But the halt was only temporary. On 29 November, the war with Poland settled, Soviet forces took advantage of a conflict between the Armenians and the Turks (just as they had taken advantage of a conflict between the Azerbaijanis and the Armenians) to move into Armenia. Now only Georgia was left. There the Red Army met stiffer resistance. The conquest, which began

---

[32] *Ibid.*, vol. XII, no. 546, n. 4.

[33] The two best accounts are Kazemzadeh, *Struggle for Transcaucasia*, pp. 276-328, and Richard Pipes, *The Formation of the Soviet Union: Communism and Nationalism 1917-1923*, 2nd ed., Cambridge, Mass., 1964, pp. 225-41. Pipes makes use of important Soviet material which was unavailable when Kazemzadeh's book, and the first edition of his own book (1954), were published.

[34] Pipes, *Formation of the Soviet Union*, p. 227.

with a thrust towards Tiflis on 17 February 1921, was not completed until Batum was occupied on 19 March, three days after the signature in London of the Anglo-Soviet Trade Agreement. The short-lived independence of Transcaucasia was finished.

In Britain these events were looked upon with sorrow. The plight of the Armenians had for years gripped popular sympathy, and during 1919 and 1920, Georgia had been widely applauded as a thriving anti-Bolshevik social democracy.[35] But (at least within the British government) the Soviet conquests were also viewed with resignation. In the War Office the whole of Transcaucasia was written off as early as mid-November 1920, and probably long before that.[36] Even Curzon was aware that, given the reluctance of his Cabinet colleagues to agree to the measures he considered necessary, there was little Britain could do to decide the fate of the three Transcaucasian republics. In April, when General Milne at Constantinople asked London for guidance as to British policy in the region Curzon directed the Foreign Office to reply: "It is not part of the policy of H.M.G. to prevent by force of arms the advance of the Bolsheviks into Georgia."[37]

This same statement went on, however, to say that Curzon nevertheless thought that Great Britain should continue to take responsibility for the defense of Batum. Over this polyglot Black Sea port, indeed, Curzon fought a rearguard action against his colleagues

[35] The massacre of Armenians by the Turks became an important *motif* of anti-Turkish war propaganda in Britain, just as it had been a liberal *cause célèbre* ever since the Congress of Berlin, when Great Britain was chiefly responsible for putting the bulk of the Armenians under Ottoman rule. The Georgian cause in Great Britain was promoted chiefly by the Labour Party, which was natural enough considering the important part played in the Second International Congress by Georgian leaders such as Tseretelli and Chkheidze. Typical of what Britons during 1920 were being told about Georgia was the following statement by Ethel Snowden on her return from an investigatory visit as a member of an official delegation of the Second International:
"The first thing I can quite definitely say is that the whole of Georgia is bitterly hostile to Bolshevism; peasants and townspeople alike. . . .
"The people of Georgia are great believers in a political democracy. That is another way of saying that they are hostile to the dictatorship of the minority." (*The Times*, 14 October 1920.)
[36] The War Office memorandum of 22 November 1920, cited above, n. 2, asserted that the completion of the Soviet conquest was only a matter of time. The prediction that the Transcaucasian republics would "go Bolshevik" appears in Sir Henry Wilson's diary as early as 12 January 1920 and it is clear from the rest of his diary that Wilson never saw need to modify this judgment.
[37] The Foreign Office reply was dated 14 April 1920; excerpts in *British Documents*, vol. XII, no. 529, n. 8.

throughout the spring of 1920. During the preceding summer, at the time of the Cabinet's decision to withdraw the two British divisions which since the winter of 1918-19 had been stationed along the railway and oil pipeline between Baku and Batum, he had succeeded in persuading them to leave a garrison temporarily at Batum. Its mission was to prevent the port from becoming an object of hostilities among the Georgians, the Armenians (who sought an outlet to the sea), and their more powerful Russian and Turkish neighbors. But Curzon was also moved by the hope that the fact of a British presence at Batum, like the *de facto* recognition of the governments of the three republics which he had secured from the inter-Allied conference at Paris in January 1920, would strengthen them in their resistance to Soviet power.[38]

To Henry Wilson, needless to say, the potential risk involved in leaving a two-battalion garrison force in so vulnerable a position was intolerable. On 3 February 1920, while Curzon was absent on a Riviera holiday, Wilson got the Cabinet's permission to withdraw it—a permission that Curzon succeeded in having rescinded at another Cabinet meeting, two weeks later. Cowed, perhaps, by Curzon's predictions of disaster, and in the absence, this time, of Lloyd George, who was more effective than any of his colleagues at puncturing Curzon's ponderous generalities, the Cabinet agreed on 18 February that the Batum garrison might remain at least until Curzon could try to persuade the French and Italian governments to share the burden, with the ultimate hope of converting the town and a

[38] The town and surrounding territory were constituted the British Military Province of Batum under the garrison commander as Military Governor. Authority for this occupation was derived from the Armistice with Turkey (Batum having been ceded to Turkey by Russia under the Treaty of Brest-Litovsk in 1918); the ultimate disposal of the province would be determined by the Allies as part of the Turkish peace settlement. For an account of the British occupation regime, see Sir Harry Luke, *Cities and Men*, London, 1953, vol. II, pp. 100-01 (during the period April-October 1920, while a naval officer on Admiral de Robeck's staff, Luke was Acting British High Commissioner in Transcaucasia), and Kazemzadeh, *Struggle for Transcaucasia*, pp. 200-02. Good contemporary pictures by Frenchmen, one a journalist and the other an academic, are Paul Gentizon, *La resurrection georgienne*, Paris, 1921, pp. 35-44, and Emile Leseueur, *Les Anglais en Perse*, Paris, [1922], pp. 27-29. See also Bechhofer, *Denikin's Russia*, pp. 3-38, and the final despatch by the Commander of the British Army of the Black Sea, General Sir G. F. Milne, 11 August 1920, printed as the 4th Supplement to the London Gazette of 4 January 1921. A Soviet view, alleging (with only a telegram from Chicherin as evidence) that the British used Batum as a base for continued large-scale assistance to Wrangel despite claims to the contrary, is in V. I. Adamiya, *Iz istorii angliiskoi interventsii v Gruzzi (1918-1921 gg.)*, (From the History of English Intervention in Georgia, 1918-1921), Sukhumi, 1961.

zone around it into a free port guaranteed by the League of Nations. "Such a solution," Curzon told his colleagues, "appears to be the only guarantee against Batoum becoming a cockpit, not only of fratricidal struggles between the Caucasian States, but of revived rivalry between larger and more dangerous powers, Turkey, Germany, Russia."[39]

For a while it seemed that Curzon might be successful. But by the time of the San Remo conference in late April, when Batum was discussed in the context of the Turkish peace treaty and of the final shape of the Armenian state, the earlier (and somewhat grudging) willingness of the French and the Italians cooled even more while units of the Red Army, under bombardment from British warships, pursued some 3,000 Cossacks, remnants of Denikin's forces, down the Black Sea littoral toward Batum, and it suddenly appeared as if the garrison force would have to do more than merely keep order in the town. The arguments advanced by Nitti, the Italian premier, in defense of his government's hesitation are worth summarizing: to send troops to Batum in the face of a threatened Soviet attack, he said, would in effect be to wage war against the Bolsheviks. But the few battalions for which Curzon asked would be far from sufficient to defend the port, and their presence—foreign troops on soil which many Russians (if not Georgians or Turks or Armenians) regarded as Russian—would only further the process whereby Bolshevism was becoming a Russian nationalist movement. The few Allied battalions would be driven into the sea, and then the Powers which furnished them would feel bound to fight. Thus events would determine policy. If war with Russia were desired, the Supreme Council should make a definite decision to that effect. But he himself, Nitti declared, could not and would not join in such a war.[40]

[39] See: (1) Conference of Ministers, 3 February 1920, 11:30 A.M.; minutes appended to those of Cabinet 10(20), Cab. 23/20. (2) Minutes, Cabinet 11(20), 18 February 1920, 5:30 P.M.; Cab. 23/20, and Wilson MS diary, entry for 18 February (excerpts in Callwell, *Wilson*, vol. II, p. 228). (3) Wilson to Milne, telegram 83558 CIGS, 3 February; W.O. 33/1000, no. 5665A. (4) Curzon's memorandum of 9 February, Cabinet paper C.P. 594, Cab. 24/97 (printed in *British Documents*, vol. XII, no. 497).

[40] Minutes, Supreme Council, 22 April 1920, 11 A.M.; San Remo; *British Documents*, vol. VIII, no. 10. For other discussions of Batum at San Remo, see nos. 6, 12, and 13. For reports of the Red Army's advance towards Batum, see *ibid.*, vol. XII, nos. 529, 532, n. 2, 542, and 546. The decision to take naval measures against the Soviet advance was made by Curzon and Admiral Earl Beatty, the First Sea Lord, on Beatty's initiative on 7 April. See Admiralty telegram 866Z, 8 April; *ibid.*, no. 532.

As it happened, the threat to the Batum garrison did not materialize; soon after the San Remo Conference the approaching Soviet forces ceased their advance. One of Moscow's responses to Poland's sudden invasion of the Ukraine, as we have seen, was abruptly to call off the Soviet offensive in the Caucasus (having already absorbed Azerbaijan) and to initiate peace negotiations with both Georgia and Armenia. Thus, when Curzon hinted on 24 April that Anglo-Soviet trade discussions would be postponed unless the hostilities over Batum ceased, Chicherin was able to reply—after a ten-day delay while his government was deciding upon a course of action—not only that military operations had been suspended and that peace negotiations with Georgia were about to begin, but also that Moscow was ready "to take into consideration and discuss the special interests of Great Britain in the Caucasus"; he added barbedly, "so far as these exist and so far as the British Government will amicably make them known."[41] These assurances, such as they were, were repeated by Krasin in his conversation with Lloyd George and Curzon in London on 7 June. The Soviet emissary also added a barb: not the Red Army but the British army, by occupying Batum, "fettered the free expression of the will of the population" of Georgia; the British government should therefore announce the date by when it was proposed that its forces would be withdrawn.[42]

Krasin need not have been concerned: Henry Wilson, with Churchill's support, had no intention of allowing the British garrison to remain at Batum, regardless of the slackened Soviet pressure. Accordingly, he interpreted an inconclusive discussion of Batum in a Cabinet on 21 May devoted to a general review of Eastern and Russian policy as giving him authority once again to instruct Milne to withdraw the garrison if he wished. Curzon, once again, was outraged. Wilson had not "fairly or faithfully" carried out the instructions of the Cabinet, he wrote to the Field Marshal. "You have gone beyond this and given Milne a direct tip to withdraw at once; and this telegram was sent off without reference to me or to anyone." The Foreign Secretary concluded with a complaint he would often make about both the War Office and the India Office—and they

---

[41] Curzon (San Remo) to Hardinge (London), telegram 25, 24 April 1920, for radio transmission to Chicherin; *ibid.*, no. 689. Chicherin (Moscow) to Curzon, 5 May; *ibid.*, no. 694 (Russian text in *Dokumenty vneshnei politiki*, vol. II, no. 336).
[42] The Anglo-Soviet conversations of 7 June 1920 are cited above, chap. III, n. 27.

about the Foreign Office: "I find it almost impossible to conduct any policy when the W.O. put their own views into telegrams which they send off without any consultation."[43]

Regardless of Curzon's anguish, on 11 June the Cabinet gave formal approval to what by then had become a *fait accompli*. Accompanying this decision was another for the despatch to Batum of a political officer who would work out the details for handing over the town of Georgia, including—pious hope—free access to the port and its connecting railway for the Armenians and the (now Soviet) Azerbaijanis.[44] The actual evacuation of the garrison, the last remaining organized British force on the territory of the former Russian Empire, took place on 9 July.

For the British government, handing Batum to the Georgians was a gesture of frustration and despair. The problem of Batum was the problem of Transcaucasia in microcosm: the Georgians, Armenians, and Azerbaijanis were unable to settle their differences no matter how urgent the external dangers menacing them all. There was virtually no time during the period between the emergence of the three republics to independence at the end of the war and the final Soviet conquest of Transcaucasia in March 1921 when some border dispute or more far-reaching territorial claim did not involve the armed forces of one against another—occasionally against both of the others.[45] In Transcaucasia these wasteful nationalistic struggles undoubtedly had an emotional basis which seemed real enough, but more remote Western statesmen, wishing for the creation of a confederation sufficiently strong to resist the incursions of both the Bolsheviks and the Turks, could view them only as criminally foolhardy. And it was scarcely possible to arouse great enthusiasm for shipping arms to the governments of the three republics—all of whom requested them—when it seemed as likely that they would employ them against one another as against a common Soviet enemy.

---

[43] Minutes, Cabinet 30(20), 21 May 1920, noon; Cab. 23/21. Curzon to Wilson, letter, 23 May; Curzon MSS, box 65. I have not been able to find a copy of Wilson's telegram 84828 to Milne, about which Curzon sharply complained.

[44] Minutes, Cabinet 35(20), 11 June 1920, noon; Cab. 23/21. Curzon to de Robeck (Constantinople), telegram 537, 11 June; *British Documents*, vol. XII, no. 577.

[45] See Zourab Avalishvili, *The Independence of Georgia in International Politics, 1918-1921*, London, 1940, pp. 147-258, and Kazemzadeh, *Struggle for Transcaucasia*, pp. 174-314. In many instances conflict among the states of Transcaucasia was prevented by the intervention of British military authorities. See General Sir G. P. Milne's despatch of 11 August 1920, cited above, n. 39.

The British government, on Curzon's urging, eventually did furnish arms to both the Georgians and the Armenians, but these were largely small-arms, and not in great quantities.[46] London's general attitude to the internecine feuding among the Caucasian peoples was reflected in Curzon's reaction to a report that the Armenians, seemingly threatened with imminent invasion by both the Turks and the Bolsheviks, had appealed to the Georgians for a deathbed alliance. Georgia, Curzon telegraphed to the British High Commissioner in Tiflis, could hardly be pressed to ally herself with a prostrate Armenia. And he added, almost as an epitaph: "We have always urged the importance of cooperation on both countries. They have not listened and have suffered accordingly."[47]

Moscow, of course, was quick to exploit the divisions among the Caucasian states. Thus the Red Army's move into Azerbaijan from the north in April 1920 took place at a time when nearly all the Azerbaijani regular troops were massed on the Armenian frontier in the southwest. During these events the Georgian government maintained a nervous neutrality, for which it was rewarded a few days later by the Soviet government's agreement to sign a treaty expressing unqualified recognition of Georgia's independence. The Soviet seizure of Armenia seven months later followed a long dispute between Armenia and Georgia over the district of Borchalo, which each claimed, and came immediately on the heels of a Turkish attack on Armenia aimed at overthrowing the Treaty of Sèvres. Here again the Georgians stayed neutral. But their turn was soon to come, despite their treaty with Moscow.[48]

Ironically, it came only a few days after Georgia had finally succeeded in gaining *de jure* recognition from the Great Powers. That this was merely legal recognition and entailed no concrete addition to Georgia's security was a fact underlined by the vote of the Assembly of the League of Nations the previous 16 December not to admit Georgia—or the three Baltic States, two of whom, Estonia and Latvia,

---

[46] For correspondence regarding the supply of arms to the republics of Transcaucasia, see *British Documents*, vol. XII, nos. 497, 517, 534, 535, 537, 557, 565, 567, 611, 612, 618, 632, 646, 650, 651.

[47] Curzon to Stokes (who succeeded Luke at Tiflis), telegram 360, 18 November 1920; *ibid.*, no. 620.

[48] Luke, *Cities and Men*, vol. II, p. 107. For the Russo-Georgian treaty of 7 May 1920 see Kazemzadeh, *Struggle for Transcaucasia*, pp. 297-300. In a secret supplement to the treaty the Georgian government pledged itself "to recognize the right of free existence and activity of the Communist party," a serious blow to Georgian internal security.

were also granted *de jure* recognition along with Georgia—and thus extend to them the guarantee of assistance against external aggression which each League member was obliged to extend to all others under Article 10 of the Covenant. None of the Great Powers, much as they might sympathize with the cause of Georgian independence, had the means to preserve it. Those votes in favor of Georgia's admission came entirely from small powers, confident that they themselves would not be called upon to provide assistance, and hoping to establish a precedent that, if necessary, might some day be invoked on their own behalf.[49]

❖

It took the Red Army precisely one month—from 17 February until 17 March 1921—to bring "self-determination" to Georgia. This military campaign coincided with a successful diplomatic campaign which saw, during the same month, the conclusion of agreements for the commencement of normal relations between the Soviet government and the three militantly nationalist regimes which had come to power in the aftermath of the World War in the ancient lands on Russia's south flank: Kemal's Turkey, Amanullah's Afghanistan, and Reza Khan's Persia. Together with the Anglo-Soviet trade agreement, as E. H. Carr has pointed out, these three agreements marked the denigration of the notion of Moscow as the center of the world revolution and deliverer of the oppressed masses of the East, and a new emphasis on the notion that Moscow, as the seat of the Soviet government, would have to make its way in the world of noncommunist states, and that its relations with that world would perforce have to be placed upon a governmental basis.[50]

[49] The Supreme Council, meeting in Paris on 26 January 1921, decided to extend *de jure* recognition to Estonia, Latvia, and Georgia, and the Powers did so on the following day. The recognition of Lithuania was postponed because her dispute with Poland over Vilna meant that neither her capital nor her boundaries were yet decided. See Lord Hardinge's telegram no. 62 to the Foreign Office (Hardinge had become Ambassador in Paris), 26 January, 8:10 P.M. (*British Documents*, vol. XI, no. 687), and Curzon's minute of 31 January (*ibid.*, no. 688, n. 2); also Avalishvili, *Independence of Georgia*, pp. 281-86.

The action by the League of Nations is described *ibid.*, pp. 269-80. For the debate in the Assembly, see League of Nations, *The Records of the First Assembly*, Geneva, 1920, pp. 615-34 (16 December 1920). For the British government's policy see the exchange of telegrams between Balfour in Geneva and Hankey in London, 4 and 10 December 1920, *British Documents*, vol. XII, nos. 637 and 640.

[50] Carr, *Bolshevik Revolution*, vol. III, pp. 289-90. See also Harish Kapur, *Soviet Russia and Asia, 1917-27: A Study of Soviet Policy Towards Turkey, Iran and Afghanistan*, London, 1966, pp. 46-52.

Thus it was no bar to the Turkish-Soviet agreement, concluded on 16 March, the same day as the Anglo-Soviet agreement, that a few weeks previous to its signature seventeen leading Turkish communists were discreetly murdered, presumably by Kemal's agents.[51] The agreement, concluded only after the armies of each side had effectively divided Armenia between them, assured Kemal of Soviet moral and material support in his war against the Greeks and their British protectors. Against this Soviet-Turkish liaison the British government could exert virtually no leverage so long as Lloyd George and Curzon refused to admit that the government of the Sultan at Constantinople was only a shabby façade, that the painstakingly drafted Treaty of Sèvres was moribund, that Greece was too weak a reed on which to stake the fortunes of the Allies in Asia Minor, and that Kemal had already demonstrated that he had emerged as the dominant force in Turkey.[52]

Both in London and in the Middle East there were British officials who urged that the surest way to prevent a Kemalist-Soviet combination would be radically to alter the premises of British policy and give active support to Kemal; the nationalism he symbolized, they said, would then assert itself in the form of a revived pan-Turanianism which would inevitably be anti-Soviet so long as large groups of Turkic people continued to live under Moscow's control.[53] This last premise was in fact accepted by Lloyd George. At an inter-Allied conference in early December 1920 he used it to quiet French anxieties regarding reports of a growing Soviet-Kemalist rapprochement.[54] Yet he did not go on himself to draw the conclusion, as the French and Italians soon did, that the whole direction of the Allied treatment of Turkish nationalism should be changed. For the Prime Minister, otherwise so adaptable in his conduct of foreign policy,

---

[51] Carr, *Bolshevik Revolution*, vol. III, p. 301. The text of the Turkish-Soviet agreement and an accompanying exchange of notes between the signatories is printed in *Dokumenty vneshnei politiki*, vol. III, pp. 597-607. The agreement is summarized in Arnold Toynbee, *Survey of International Affairs, 1920-1923*, London, 1925, pp. 371-73.

[52] For a discussion of British policy regarding Turkey, see Nicolson, *Curzon*, *passim*.

[53] See, for example, Stokes to Curzon, telegram 480, Tiflis, 6 November 1920, *British Documents*, vol. XIII, no. 171, and the War Office's "Note on the Military Situation created by recent events in Russia, Caucasia, Turkey and Greece," 22 November 1920, cited above, n. 2.

[54] "British Secretary's Notes of a Conference . . . between Representatives of the British, French, and Italian Governments . . . ," London, 3 December 1920, 11:30 A.M.; *British Documents*, vol. VIII, no. 98, esp. pp. 845-47.

this was a curious rigidity. Two years later, at the time of Chanak, it was to cost him his job.

Thus the British government remained a somewhat nervous but nevertheless passive bystander to the developing relationship between Moscow and Ankara.[55] The same was true regarding the Soviet courtship of Afghanistan. Under the Anglo-Russian Convention of 1907 Great Britain had been given effective control of Afghanistan's foreign relations. Although the Amir, Habibullah, never gave his formal assent to this arrangement as the Convention required him to do, he nevertheless felt constrained by subsidies and less tangible bonds of sentiment to adhere to it, and therefore, despite pan-Islamic agitation from Turkey, Afghanistan remained strictly neutral during the World War. Yet as in virtually every other Middle Eastern country, the war sharply quickened the pace of nationalism within Afghanistan. In early 1919 Habibullah was persuaded to demand from the Viceroy of India that the Peace Conference then sitting in Paris should recognize his country's complete independence and freedom of action.

Before the Viceroy could reply, however, Habibullah had been murdered, and his place taken by his twenty-eight-year-old third son, Amanullah, an ambitious nationalist. In order to cement his hold on the country Amanullah rashly launched a *jihad*, or holy war, against India, hoping to annex large tracts of Indian territory. In doing so he was moved by vastly exaggerated rumors of riots and unrest which led him to think that the British hold on the subcontinent might be shaken. He was badly mistaken. Begun in early May, the war lasted little more than three weeks and ended in the defeat of the Afghans. But the treaty of peace, signed at Rawalpindi, on 8 August, nevertheless formally gave to Afghanistan the complete independence for which Habibullah had asked and for which, as one of his principal objects, his son had gone to war. Keenly aware of the growing strength of Eastern nationalism and of the limits of British strength within India, the government of India, which had charge of the treaty negotiations, was not disposed to be vindictive. It did, however, discontinue the subsidy it had been paying the Amir.[56]

[55] For this nervousness, see the weekly summary of intelligence reports issued by the Constantinople station of the Secret Intelligence Service: file—/262/44, F.O. 371/5170-72 (in the series cited above, n. 4). These summaries contained many reports (and rumors) of Soviet aid to the Kemalists.

[56] Ludwig W. Adamec, *Afghanistan 1900-1923: A Diplomatic History*, Berkeley,

Amanullah used his new-found independence to enter into relations with Russia, the Power his predecessors had most feared. It has been alleged, although not conclusively, that the young Amir had received Soviet encouragement and support in his plans for war.[57] Whatever the truth of these allegations, there is no doubt that Moscow saw in feudal, backward Afghanistan a natural ally against British imperialism. Soviet-Afghan relations, begun with an exchange of emissaries at Amanullah's request in 1919, were made formal by an agreement between the two countries signed in Moscow on 28 February 1921. The following day, also in Moscow, Afghanistan and Kemalist Turkey signed a treaty of alliance—a gesture with little other than propagandistic impact. "What was significant in all of this," writes E. H. Carr, "was not the extension of propaganda for world revolution but the succession of Soviet Russia to the traditional Russian role as Britain's chief rival in central Asia."[58]

There was nothing the British government could do to preserve Afghanistan against Soviet penetration. Both London and Delhi were fearful that the consulates provided for under the Soviet-Afghan treaty would be used (in the words of a letter which Sir Robert Horne handed to Krasin on 16 March 1921 at the signing of the Anglo-Soviet trade agreement) "to secure facilities for attacks through Afghanistan against the peace of India."[59] Military pressure against the Afghans was out of the question. Kabul could be bombed from the air, as it was during the brief war in May 1919. But such measures would only serve to drive the Afghans completely into the arms of the Russians. Thus there remained only diplomacy—and the possibility of matching the promises of economic assistance contained in the Soviet-Afghan treaty, an early example of the sort of competition between the communist and non-communist worlds which, in subsequent decades, the Afghans (and others) learned so skilfully to encourage.

---

pp. 108-35; the text of the Treaty of Rawalpindi is on pp. 182-83. See also Toynbee, *Survey, 1920-1923*, pp. 376-84, and Fraser-Tytler, *Afghanistan*, pp. 194-200.

[57] L.V.S. Blacker, *On Secret Patrol in High Asia*, London, 1922, p. 186. Blacker was an Indian Army intelligence officer. See Chattar Singh Samar, *India and Anglo-Soviet Relations (1917-1947)*, London, 1959, pp. 39-41, and Carr, *Russian Revolution*, vol. III, p. 237.

[58] *Ibid.*, p. 292; for the Turkish-Afghan alliance see p. 291, n. 5. The text of the Soviet-Afghan agreement is printed in *Dokumenty vneshnei politiki*, vol. III, pp. 550-53. For a summary of its provisions, see Toynbee, *Survey, 1920-1923*, pp. 385-86.

[59] For this letter, see below, chap. X and the appendix to this volume.

This situation was only another indication of just how great had been the transformation from the world of 1914 to that of 1920. In 1914 Afghanistan had been virtually an appendage of Britain's Indian Empire; six years later the ability of London or Delhi to control events in Kabul was very drastically reduced. These changes were far more readily understood from the subcontinent than from the United Kingdom. Faced with ruling the largest Moslem population in the world in the aftermath of a treaty of peace which dismembered the Ottoman Empire and put large numbers of its former subjects under non-Moslem European powers, more aware than officials and politicians in London of the impossibility of keeping order in India in the event of large-scale disturbances, and aware at the same time of the degree to which the peoples on India's North-West Frontier were susceptible to agitation from Afghanistan across the border, the government of India was much more willing than the Foreign Office in London—and even than the India Office—to take measures which could be (and were) frankly described as "buying off" the Afghans.

Therefore, much to the distress of the King's government in London, a representative of his government in Delhi co-existed in Kabul during 1921 with a Soviet envoy. For Sir Henry R. C. Dobbs, the Foreign Secretary of the government of India, his mission had a minimizing objective: maintaining British access to Afghanistan and at least the relative neutrality of the Amir's government in the hope, as he put it in a telegram to his colleagues in Delhi, "that even if we were forced to admit Bolsheviks into political and economic competition with us in Afghanistan, such competition would be in the end innocuous, and we should be easy winners and ultimately with patience regain former influence."[60]

Dobbs's mission followed the first round of Afghan-Soviet negotiations which were to result in the treaty of 28 February 1921. British intelligence services had monitored these negotiations carefully, and reported that treaty drafts in the autumn of 1920, when the Amir invited the British to send a representative to Kabul, provided for a mutual pledge not to enter into arrangements with a third power hostile to the other, and for the establishment of consulates at desig-

---

[60] Dobbs's telegram 65 C, 9 March 1921, was repeated to London as telegram 399 S from Viceroy (Foreign and Political Department), 10 March; Cabinet paper C.P. 2713, Cab. 24/121.

nated locations on each other's territory. These provisions clearly were of more benefit to Moscow than to Kabul, and seemed directly aimed at British interests: it was unlikely that Russia would ever wish to combine with any other power against Afghanistan, and the consulates requested by Moscow were in eastern Afghanistan, all too near the Indian frontier peoples among whom it was feared that Bolshevik agitation would be effective. In exchange for these concessions, Moscow would provide the Afghan government with a financial subsidy (specified at one million gold rubles during the first year) and technical assistance. These provisions, in essence, constituted the treaty that was eventually concluded the following February. The British also suspected, but never confirmed, that a secret protocol provided for the supply to Afghanistan of Soviet arms.[61]

In London, these terms—coming at a time when Amanullah sought, as well, a treaty of friendship with the British government that would contain many of the same sorts of provisions—were viewed as outrageous. As Montagu cabled Chelmsford on 29 October 1920, the Cabinet agreed "that the mere existence of friendly relations between Afghans and Bolsheviks need not necessarily preclude our coming to terms with former, but no purpose is served by pretending to accept plea of Bolshevik help in developing Afghanistan when it is matter of common knowledge that Bolshevik policy is solely inspired by desire to damage us." If the Afghans were actually to sign such a treaty with Moscow, then Britain could not contemplate any agreement which would also involve British aid to Kabul: "To do so would be in effect to subsidise a movement openly aimed at destruction of British Empire."[62]

To Chelmsford, in Delhi, London's outrage seemed unjustified. Amanullah's attitude in seeking advantage from both of his great neighbors while assuming no obligations directed against either, the Viceroy telegraphed, was "not notably more indefensible" than the same attitude, before the war, on the part of the Persians. A "contest in Afghanistan between us and [the] Bolsheviks would doubtless be found inconvenient," but aside from going to war with the Afghans

[61] For these suspicions regarding Soviet arms, see, *e.g.*, Montagu's memorandum, "Treaty with Afghanistan," 9 May 1921, Cabinet paper C.P. 2922; Cab. 24/132. For the Soviet-Afghan treaty negotiations, see Adamec, *Afghanistan 1900-1923*, pp. 142-48; the text is on pp. 188-91.
[62] Montagu to Chelmsford (Delhi), telegram 2921, 29 October 1920; Cabinet paper C.P. 2031, Cab. 24/114.

to expel Soviet influence—a step that would probably lead to war with Moscow as well—Britain would have to choose between either total aloofness or "participation with Bolsheviks in financing Afghan Government and developing country." Chelmsford chose the latter:

Absolute aloofness would only lead ultimately to complete domination of Afghanistan by Bolshevik influence and abandonment of her neutrality, while our participation with Bolsheviks in her development should, owing to our superior economic strength and facilities, attract her gradually to our sphere and in any event weaken her internal forces of fanaticism.

We should doubtless greatly prefer exclusive domination of Afghanistan, but development of events has now made this impossible without war, and we consider that we must content ourselves with second best course indicated above and accept all its implications with our eyes open. . . . As things stand, so long as Afghanistan manages to maintain neutrality and fairly friendly relations with Bolsheviks without unfriendliness towards us, there is no danger of Bolshevik attack on her, and our frontier problem will be mainly exclusion of propaganda instead of military defence against attack on northern Afghan frontier.[63]

The gap between London and Delhi was, on this as on so many issues of Eastern policy, nearly unbridgeable. Throughout the next twelve months the almost acrimonious exchange of telegrams continued. At each stage, however, the Cabinet in London drew back and ultimately deferred to the Council in Delhi. Thus, in December 1920, when the Viceroy insisted that Dobbs should go to Kabul to negotiate a treaty of friendship with the Amir despite the fact that the Afghans were pressing ahead their dealings with Moscow, and would not give the British assurances that their interests were not being harmed, Montagu telegraphed that the Cabinet feared "misrepresentation and even humiliation" at the hands of the Afghans, but that the matter lay so much within the province of the government of India that it must use its own judgment and take full responsibility without further reference to London.[64]

Given this permission, Dobbs went. From January until November

---

[63] Chelmsford (Delhi) to Montagu, telegram 1214 S, 19 October 1920; Cabinet paper C.P. 1996, Cab. 24/112.
[64] Chelmsford (Delhi) to Montagu, telegram 1360 S, 25 November 1920; file N 3356/127/97, F.O. 371/5382. Montagu to Chelmsford, telegram 3880, 8 December; Cabinet paper C.P. 2272, Cab. 24/116. See the Cabinet's discussion: minutes, Cabinet 66(20), 6 December, 5 P.M.; Cab. 23/23.

1921 he engaged in gruelling negotiations with the Amir and his government. In March he (and Delhi) fought for, and won, London's agreement that he should put forward a draft treaty despite the signature of the Soviet-Afghan pact of only a few weeks before. On the 15th the Viceroy telegraphed: "We feel so strongly and unanimously on this vital matter that we deem it necessary to place our views in unmistakable plainness on official record. And fortified by success of policy we steadfastly pursued in the face of much criticism in India and outside in keeping Afghanistan out of the great war, we are assured that His Majesty's Government will not override our anxiously-considered and as anxiously reconsidered views on a matter so directly affecting India."[65]

By such pleading Delhi once again got the authority (and the responsibility) it wished, although the rhetoric in response from London was unchanging. Thus, on 11 May Montagu telegraphed: "That India should be paying a subsidy to the Amir whilst at the same time he had formed a treaty under which he was receiving money from the Bolsheviks, is a solution which we find difficult to justify and to which we could assent only with the most extreme reluctance. It opens up unlimited possibilities for the Amir to play us off against the Russians, and the Russians off against us; applying to each in turn for an increase in subsidy, and seeking every opportunity to profit by any dissensions between Russia and ourselves."[66]

In the end, no subsidy was paid. On 22 November 1921 Dobbs and Mahmud Tarzi, Amanullah's foreign minister (and father-in-law) signed what was termed a "neighborly" treaty, establishing diplomatic and trade relations between Afghanistan and Great Britain but, except for some small British gifts, providing for no economic or military assistance. The Amir's government had proved so mercurial during the immediately preceding months—at one moment holding out hopes that it might repudiate its treaty with the Russians and sign an exclusive treaty with Britain, at another suddenly introducing new demands—that Dobbs drew back the treaty of "friendship" (and the subsidy) he had once offered.[67]

---

[65] Viceroy (Foreign and Political Department) to Montagu, telegram 372 S, 15 March 1921; Cabinet paper C.P. 2738, Cab. 24/121.

[66] Montagu to Reading (Lord Reading had succeeded Chelmsford as Viceroy), telegram (no number indicated), 11 May 1921, circulated by Montagu as Cabinet paper C.P. 2928 with covering note stating that Lloyd George, Curzon, and Churchill had concurred in sending it; Cab. 24/123.

[67] Dobbs' negotiations are described in detail in Adamec, *Afghanistan 1900-1923*,

In getting without payment most of that for which they had been prepared to pay, Dobbs and the government of India were beneficiaries of the fact that Soviet-Afghan relations were not soon again as cordial as they seemed during 1920. Soviet interests in fomenting revolution in India quickly declined into the reality of state relations with Great Britain. Moreover, Soviet-Afghan relations were scarcely helped by Amanullah's expansionist ambitions, which ran northward as well as south: he saw himself as the future leader of a confederation of Central Asian states including Ferghana, Khiva, and Bukhara, ancient kingdoms then under uneasy, recently imposed Soviet control. In 1922 Afghan troops were on the brink of marching northward to support a revolt of the Basmachi of Ferghana and Bukhara. They were restrained by a stern Soviet *démarche*. This episode marked the nadir of Soviet-Afghan relations, but they never became so close as to give London real cause to fear for the safety of India.[68] Conditions *had* drastically changed since the Anglo-Russian Convention of 1907 which had made Afghanistan a British preserve. Afghanistan had opened to the world. Yet it still remained what the authors of the 1907 Convention had intended, a serviceable buffer between its great neighbors.

British interests in both pre-war and postwar Afghanistan were essentially negative and defensive—to keep others out, in order to preserve the security of India, not to secure economic benefits for themselves. Indeed, British economic interests in Afghanistan were virtually nonexistent. The same was true regarding British interests in Turkey. That the British government should be a bystander to the developing relationships between each of the two countries and Soviet Russia was inevitable, and was implicitly acknowledged as such by those responsible for the making of British foreign policy.

Persia, during these years, was also an object of Soviet courtship. A Soviet-Persian agreement was signed at the same time as those linking Moscow with Ankara and Kabul. In the eyes of the British government, however, the Persian case differed markedly from the other two. In Persia, principally in the oil fields around the Gulf, British firms and the British government itself had significant investments, supported by a military presence which during the World War had

---

pp. 136-42, 148-66; the text of the treaty of 22 November 1921 is on pp. 183-88. Adamec had access to India Office and Government of India papers.

[68] Fraser-Tytler, *Afghanistan*, pp. 202-03.

multiplied manyfold and spread throughout the country. In 1920 and 1921 these interests were directly challenged by a Soviet armed invasion. The British government could not remain a bystander to either the Soviet courtship or the Soviet invasion without acknowledging that its position in world politics had been altered in nature and reduced in scale. Yet ultimately it did so. In the following chapter we shall try to understand how and why.

CHAPTER IX

PERSIA

We do not want, we never have wanted, to make ourselves responsible for the government of Persia. But we do want to help Persia to stand on her own legs. If she were to fall into the hands of Russia, or to become a dependent ally of Russia, our whole position in the East would be gravely imperilled and the cost of maintaining it immeasurably increased.

—Lord Milner to his Cabinet colleagues,
24 May 1920[1]

ENZELI (now called Pahlavi), Persia's chief Caspian port, is a small town at the tip of a narrow peninsula some 200 miles down the coast from Baku. Before the World War it had been the center of the Russian caviar industry in the lower Caspian. After the war Russian influence in northern Persia had given way to that of Great Britain, and Enzeli was the seat of a small garrison of British and Indian forces. During the spring of 1920 this garrison stood watch over the eighteen remaining vessels of the Caspian fleet which the British had organized in 1918 and then, the following summer, had turned over to Denikin.[2] With the collapse of Denikin and the Soviet takeover of Azerbaijan, these ships had fled to Enzeli. There the Persian and British authorities had confined them to port pending some decision, somewhere, regarding their fate. Inevitably, however, they remained a prized commodity: their possessor would by that very fact be a major Caspian naval power.

At dawn on 18 May 1920 these vessels were suddenly seized in a surprise raid by Soviet forces. The seizure of the ships (and what remained of their anti-Bolshevik Russian crews) was the only ostensible object of the descent. But some of the troops who landed from the thirteen warships which appeared in Enzeli that day were not to leave the north Persian province of Gilan for over a year, and

[1] Cabinet paper C.P. 1337, Cab. 24/106.
[2] See Volume I, p. 320, and Volume II, pp. 331-32.

[349]

the humiliating defeat they inflicted on the small British garrison that morning in May was a shock whose spreading waves marked the ruin of British policy in Persia.

Persia (not until 1935 was it officially renamed Iran) had long been an object of Anglo-Russian rivalry. Traditionally, Britain had played the role of Persia's protector against Russian encroachments, a role which drastically changed in 1907 with the signing of the Anglo-Russian Convention dividing the country, as we have seen,[3] into spheres of influence. The Convention scarcely contributed to British popularity among the Persians; it indicated that the British government was prepared to use their country as a bargaining counter in the more deadly rivalry that was developing between London and Berlin.

Although the Persian government maintained a formal neutrality throughout the World War, the country nevertheless became a battle-ground for Turkish, Russian, and British armies. Russian forces from the Caucasus combined with British-Indian forces from Mesopotamia to form a front against the Turks in western Persia. This Anglo-Russian combination was dissolved by the revolutionary events within Russia during 1917. Even before the Bolshevik seizure of power in November, Russian troops in Persia had ceased to fight and were in the process of being withdrawn.[4] Russia's departure from the war left Britain the dominant power throughout Persia.

In Persia as elsewhere the infant Bolshevik regime made a virtue of its weakness. On 14 January 1918, in a note to the Persian government, the Soviet government formally repudiated the Anglo-Russian Convention and renounced all Russian rights that were contrary to Persian sovereignty. In addition, it promised to assist the Persians to expel all British and Turkish troops from their country. More specific was another Soviet note of 26 June 1919, announcing the annulment of all Persian debts to Tsarist Russia, the renunciation of all Russian public and private concessions in Persia, and the handing over to Persia of all Russian properties on Persian territory, including banks, railroads, port installations, and other enterprises.[5]

Shrewd propaganda though these notes might have been, they nevertheless represented a forced abdication of Russian power. For

---

[3] See above, chap. VIII.   [4] See Volume I, pp. 13-14.
[5] For texts of these notes, see *Dokumenty vneshnei politiki*, vol. I, pp. 91-92, and vol. II, pp. 198-200.

Curzon, always more concerned with Eastern than with European matters, this eclipse of Russia in Persia presented an opportunity for which he had yearned ever since the days when, as a young traveller, he had written a massive account of the land and its peoples.[6] He had regretted the "unfortunate" Anglo-Russian Convention from the outset.[7] Now it could be undone. Persia could be brought completely under British influence; she and the British Empire would prosper together, and a British protectorate over Persia would make the British Empire doubly secure. Curzon carried this vision to a meeting of the Cabinet's Eastern Committee on 30 December 1918. He found there a general opinion that British commitments in the Middle East should be reduced and Persia left to its own devices. Yet he persisted, and won his colleagues' reluctant consent for the Foreign Office to enter into the negotiations with Persia which eventually resulted in the Anglo-Persian Agreement of 9 August 1919.[8]

The agreement was the very embodiment of Curzon's ambitions. Despite a first article which proclaimed that the British government would continue "to respect absolutely the independence and integrity" of Persia, the essence of the agreement went far toward making Persia a British vassal state. British experts would advise the Persian treasury and supervise the collection of customs duties; British officers would construct a railway network; and the Persian government would pay for all these services out of a British loan of £2 million, secured against customs revenues and carrying an interest charge of 7 per cent.[9]

On the day on which the agreement was signed in Tehran, Curzon addressed to his Cabinet colleagues a memorandum in which he attempted to justify his persistence. Reflecting on the "most satisfactory result" of the negotiations, he wrote:

> If it be asked why we should undertake the task at all, and why Persia should not be left to herself and allowed to rot into picturesque decay, the answer is that her geographical position, the magnitude of our interests in the country, and the future safety of our Eastern Empire

[6] George N. Curzon, *Persia and the Persian Question*, London, 1892.

[7] The term is from a memorandum by Curzon for the Cabinet, 9 August 1919; *British Documents*, vol. IV, no. 710. See also Nicolson, *Curzon*, pp. 125-26.

[8] *Ibid.*, pp. 132-34.

[9] Cmd. 300 (1919). *Agreement between His Britannic Majesty's Government and the Persian Government.* Two items of the Agreement were not published and remained secret. See *British Documents*, vol. IV, no. 711, n. 1, and no. 734, n. 2 and enclosure 7.

render it impossible for us now—just as it would have been impossible for us at any time during the past fifty years—to disinterest ourselves from what happens in Persia. Moreover, now that we are about to assume the mandate for Mesopotamia, which will make us coterminous with the western frontiers of Persia, we cannot permit the existence, between the frontiers of our Indian Empire in Baluchistan and our new Protectorate, of a hotbed of misrule, enemy intrigue, financial chaos, and political disorder. Further, if Persia were to be left alone, there is every reason to fear that she would be overrun by Bolshevik influences from the north. Lastly, we possess in the south-western corner of Persia great assets in the shape of the oilfields, which are worked for the British Navy and which give us a commanding interest in that part of the world.[10]

The agreement was not in fact the iniquitous and one-sided instrument of exploitation that it was quickly made out to be, not only in Bolshevik propaganda but in the Persian press as well.[11] Persia was desperately poor; her affairs were miserably mismanaged; foreign technical assistance and foreign capital were both vitally necessary if she were ever to prosper. The agreement, however, did not simply provide for foreign assistance: it made certain that all technical assistance of any importance, and the bulk of the capital, would be British. British (and other) investors would therefore be assured that their funds would be well managed, and their interests protected.

This was not, in fact, an unreasonable arrangement, nor was it one which would not have brought benefit to Persia. Nevertheless, it was doomed from the start by the fact that to Persian nationalists it appeared to make their country a mere appendage of the British Empire. The very circumstances of its birth enforced this impression. The negotiations for the agreement were carried on in secret between the British Minister in Tehran, Sir Percy Cox, and the Persian Prime Minister, Vossuq-ed-Dowleh, and two colleagues. All three Persians were well-known as anglophiles. Vossuq was valued so much by the British that they paid the Shah (a weak, flaccid young man of

---

[10] Curzon's memorandum of 9 August 1919 is cited above, n. 7.

[11] Richard W. Cottam in *Nationalism in Iran*, Pittsburgh, 1964, pp. 183-84, notes that of twenty-six newspapers and other periodicals published in Tehran at the time, all but one denounced the agreement, most of them in strongly nationalistic language. See also Nasrollah Saifpur Fatemi, *Diplomatic History of Persia 1917-1923: Anglo-Russian Power Politics in Iran*, New York, 1952, pp. 73-77. In both the United States and France, of course, the agreement was regarded as merely another example of English perfidy (see *ibid.*, pp. 54-63).

twenty-four who was constantly afraid for his life) a monthly personal subsidy of some £2,600 (15,000 tomans) so long as he should retain him in office. Yet the three were not so anglophile as to be above demanding (and receiving) a payment of £131,000 from the British as the price of affixing their signatures to the agreement, a fact which was inadvertently hinted at in the House of Commons in November 1920 and immediately broadcast in Tehran as conclusive evidence that Vossuq and his cronies had sold their country to London.[12]

These circumstances made it impossible that the agreement should ever go into effect. The 1906 constitution (Persia's first) required that all treaties should be ratified by the Majlis, as the national legislative assembly was called. Had Vossuq sought ratification for the agreement immediately after its signature, he might conceivably have succeeded. But as time passed, opinion hardened, and unrepresentative though the Majlis was, it was nevertheless responsive enough to nationalist currents so that an affirmative vote became steadily more unlikely.[13] Curzon, meanwhile, refused to believe that the agreement could be looked upon as anything but the expression of disinterested British benevolence he believed it to be, and he therefore continued to insist that it should be ratified.[14]

Within the brief period June 1920–February 1921 Curzon's insistence was responsible, at least indirectly, for the downfall of three Persian prime ministers. None would even summon the Majlis to

[12] Statement by Cecil Harmsworth, Parliamentary Under Secretary at the Foreign Office, 9 November 1920; 134 *H.C. Deb.*, cols. 969-70. For reaction in Persia, see H. C. Norman (British Minister, Tehran) to Curzon, telegrams 751 and 766, 18 and 25 November 1920; *British Documents*, vol. XIII, nos. 582 and 588. The news reached Persia in part because of a lapse by Norman: one of the duties of the British Minister at Tehran at this time was censorship of incoming news telegrams. On this occasion, as Norman apologized to Curzon, the offending passage escaped his notice.

For details of the British subsidy to the Shah, see the memorandum by Lancelot Oliphant of the Foreign Office, 14 June 1920; *British Documents*, vol. XIII, no. 464, p. 518. Until publication of this volume in 1963, the fact that bribes had been paid to the three ministers had never been substantiated. That the transaction was known at the time can be seen from J. M. Balfour's contemporary account: *Recent Happenings in Persia*, London, 1922. See also Fatemi, *Diplomatic History*, pp. 25-26.

[13] See, *e.g.*, the analysis by H. C. Norman (Cox's successor in Tehran) in his telegram 562 to Curzon, 6 August 1920; *British Documents*, vol. XIII, no. 534.

[14] For examples of Curzon's insistence, see the following telegrams to Norman in Tehran: no. 382, 19 July 1920; no. 401, 31 July; no. 407, 5 August; no. 422, 13 August; no. 501, 12 October; no. 532, 5 November; no. 592, 9 December (*ibid.*, nos. 514, 531, 533, 540, 564, 576, 606).

meet, much less put the agreement before it. A fourth prime minister, Sayyed Zia al-Din, did summon the Majlis, but in order to denounce the agreement, not (despite his pro-British sentiments) to seek its ratification.[15] By the time of the *coup* which brought Sayyed Zia to power, however, Curzon had given up the ungrateful Persians in despair. During the previous summer he had acquiesced in the decision of the Treasury and the India Office to cease the monthly subsidy of some £70,000 (350,000 tomans) which they had jointly been paying the Persian government since the war years.[16] And on 16 February 1921, he telegraphed to H. C. Norman, Cox's successor at the Tehran Legation: "It remains for Persia, having rejected our assistance, to extricate herself in her own way."[17]

❖

One of the principal objectives of the Anglo-Persian Agreement had been the provision for Persia of a single uniformed national army, organized and led by British officers, to replace the medley of forces—some British, some Persian—which had previously existed. The creation of a national army was necessary because both the War Office and the government of India had long been determined that the British and Indian troops for whom they shared responsibility should be withdrawn from Persia as soon as possible, because of the vast expense of maintaining them there. In their absence, however, the country would be nearly defenseless against either a Soviet invasion or a Soviet-sponsored internal uprising—the dangers Curzon had in mind when he sent the message quoted above. In either event the result would be the extension of Soviet influence, or even control, over much, if not all, of the country. What Persian forces there were could not be relied upon: the danger was ever present that they might lapse into brigandage, and Persia into anarchy.

It must not be forgotten that Persia during the first two decades of the twentieth century was scarcely a nation in any meaningful

---

[15] Sayyed Zia came to power on 21 February 1921. For the circumstances, see below.

[16] For this suspension of payments see the Foreign Office memorandum of 14 June 1920 cited above, n. 12, and the correspondence cited there. Payments from the British and Indian governments actually stopped on 24 October 1920 (see Curzon to Norman, telegrams 501 and 508, 12 and 20 October; *British Documents*, vol. XIII, nos. 564 and 565), but the Persian government was able to secure funds for the following four and one-half months by the device of a lien on the Imperial Bank of Persia (see Curzon to Norman, telegram 544, 11 November; *ibid.*, no. 580).

[17] Curzon to Norman, telegram 81, 16 February 1921; *ibid.*, no. 678.

sense of the term. Its vast terrain was broken into several distinct geographical areas by high, nearly impassable mountain ranges. Its population, in turn, was divided among several racial and linguistic groups. Although Tehran and a few other large towns had something approaching an urban life, most of the population lived far from these centers in conditions of ignorance and extreme poverty, either in isolated villages or in migratory tribes. Violent conflict was not uncommon between rival provincial notables or rival tribes or, despite the fact that each tribal chief swore allegiance to the Shah, between a tribe and the central government. The central government itself was never strong enough to cope with the lawlessness of the tribes.[18] It was inevitable, therefore, that during the several decades preceding the World War the British and Russian governments should each have intervened to protect the interests which their subjects, or they themselves, had in Persia.

The principal instrument of Russian intervention was the so-called Persian Cossack Division, formed in 1879 as a bodyguard for the Shah and throughout its existence under his direct authority. It was organized along Russian Cossack lines, many of its officers (including its commander) and noncommissioned officers were Russians, and it was heavily subsidized from the Tsar's treasury. Stationed in the north, where Russian interests predominated, it was until the war the most efficient and powerful military force in the entire country.[19]

During the pre-war decades the British had no comparable force under their control. From time to time British forces from India would cross into Persia to deal with marauding tribes, but they did not remain. In 1911 the British government supported (and subsidized) the Persian government in its desire to create a national gendarmerie under Swedish officers. This force never became very effective. Moreover, its Swedish officers were blatantly pro-German in their sympathies. During the first years of the war, German agents moved throughout Persia trying to rouse the tribes against Britain and Russia. In 1916, therefore, the British incorporated the gendarmerie, minus its Swedes, into a Persian force under British and

[18] For a detailed discussion of these factors, see Cottam, *Nationalism in Iran*, especially pp. 23-59, 92-98.
[19] See Firuz Kazemzadeh, "The Origin and Early Development of the Persian Cossack Brigade," *American Slavic and East European Review*, vol. XV, no. 3, October 1956, pp. 351-63.

Indian leadership to keep order in the southern section of the country—the South Persia Rifles.[20]

Both the South Persia Rifles and the Cossack Division were Persian forces under foreign officers. The end of the war, however, also found two British (or, more accurately, British-Indian) forces on Persian territory, the East Persian Cordon Field Force and the North Persia Force. Both were formed as a consequence of the collapse of Imperial Russia. The East Persian Cordon was established in February 1918 in order to patrol the thousand-mile eastern border of Persia to prevent the infiltration of German and Turkish agents into India and Afghanistan. After the war it remained in order to combat a new danger, the spread of Bolshevism into Khorasan, the northeastern province of Persia.

The costs of maintaining the two battalions of infantry, regiment of cavalry, and battery of mountain artillery which made up the East Persian Cordon were shared by the War Office and the government of India. In the conditions of postwar stringency, however, each perceived more urgent uses for these resources. To the government of India, moreover, the Cordon force seemed more a provocation than a protection: it was too small to repel a serious Bolshevik attack, and based as it was at Meshed, near the confluence of the borders of Persia, Russia, and Afghanistan, it invited challenge. Its voluntary withdrawal, Delhi contended, would be far less damaging to British prestige than a forced withdrawal under fire. In London, the Secretary of State for India, Edwin Montagu, shared these views. "I cannot be a party to defending India from the far side of Afghanistan while Afghanistan is in its present condition," he wrote to Curzon on 5 January 1920. To Curzon, however, such contentions were absurd: in his view the Cordon force was a deterrent, not a provocation. It was a part of the "glacis of India" for which Delhi should be willing to pay. If too weak, it should be strengthened, not withdrawn. Decisions of such political moment should not be made on narrow budgetary grounds. These were, of course, the same arguments Curzon used in urging the retention of the British garrison at Batum and, indeed, virtually every such force in the Middle East. Each time the issue between budgetary constraints and Curzon's

---

[20] See Percy Sykes, *A History of Persia*, 3rd ed., London, 1930, vol. II, pp. 469-72, for the Swedish gendarmerie, and pp. 476-84, for the South Persia Rifles, of which Sykes had been commanding officer.

political conceptions was forced, Curzon lost. He lost the Meshed force at a Cabinet meeting on 5 May 1920.[21]

The second of the two British-Indian forces in Persia, the North Persia Force, is the more important for our narrative: from the time of the Soviet landing at Enzeli on 18 May 1920 until its own withdrawal in April of the following year it was actively engaged in military operations against Soviet and Persian rebel forces. "Norperforce," as it was called, was the successor to General Dunsterville's "Dunsterforce" which during the spring of 1918 had been sent to northern Persia to serve as a barrier against the Turks. Dunsterforce's stand against the Turks at Baku has been described in the first volume of the present work.[22] After its escape from Baku to Enzeli in September 1918 Dunsterville himself was recalled, but the force remained, strung out along the lines of communication from Baghdad to Tehran, a symbol of the assumption by Great Britain of the role in northwestern Persia which before the war had been played by Russia. Never was it a large force. In May 1920 it consisted of one British and three Indian infantry battalions, a squadron of Guides cavalry, a field battery and a mountain battery, and three or four aircraft. A British official serving in Tehran at the time wrote that when the number of troops necessary to guard and maintain the lines of communication was subtracted, Norperforce had a deployable fighting strength of fewer than 2,500 men, many of them scattered about at small outposts such as the one at Enzeli, where in May 1920 there were perhaps 500.[23] These were the troops which retreated before a larger Soviet force on 18 May.

The position of the garrison at Enzeli and, indeed, of Norperforce in general, had been the subject of confused, acrimonious, and ultimately inconsequential discussion in London over the preceding six

[21] Montagu to Curzon, 5 January 1920; Curzon MSS, box 65. Viceroy, Army Department (Delhi), to Montagu, telegram 3721, 19 March 1920; appendix to Cabinet paper C.P. 1200, Cab. 24/104. Inter-Departmental Conference on Middle Eastern Affairs, 37th Minutes, 13 April 1920, 5 P.M.; F.O. General/216. Minutes, Cabinet 24(20), 5 May 1920, noon; Cab. 23/20. See also Churchill's statement, 14 December 1920, in 136 *H.C. Deb.*, col. 220.

[22] Volume I, pp. 305-10.

[23] So reported at Cabinet 30(20), 21 May 1920, noon; Cab. 23/21. According to a War Office memorandum to the Foreign Office, 17 February 1921, total strength in North Persia was British Army (all ranks), 2,200; Indian Army (all ranks), 9,000. Most of this force was employed to guard the communication lines between Baghdad and the Caspian (file E 2213/2/34, F.O. 371/6401). See also Balfour, *Recent Happenings*, pp. 183 and 187.

months. One participant characterized these discussions as a tug-of-war between the Foreign Office's insistence on the retention of the scattered outlying garrisons in northwestern Persia and the Treasury's demand for cuts in military expenditures, with the War Office torn both ways in the middle.[24] In this instance, unlike the case of the East Persian Cordon, India was not involved. Norperforce (and its budget) was wholly a War Office concern. It guarded not the approaches to India but those to the mandate territory of Mesopotamia (Iraq), and it therefore was an extension of the British military command at Baghdad.

Behind the confusion and the acrimony—in the eyes of the War Office, at least—lay the fact that the British government had never made the policy decision of whether or not it would use its own forces to defend Persia against an armed attack. Churchill put this issue to his Cabinet colleagues: "Are we to defend Persia or not? If we do not, Persia will be demoralized by Russian Bolshevism and thereafter devoured by Russian Imperialism. If we do we shall, in all probability, find ourselves drawn into a very considerable and indefinite entanglement. It seems very easy to send a few hundred men to Teheran; we shall not find it so easy to take them away."[25] Churchill wrote these lines on 15 June, after the Soviet landing at Enzeli. But his own position had been clear throughout the spring: Norperforce should be withdrawn as soon as possible, and the £3.5 million a year required to keep it in the field should be put to better use.[26]

Within the higher reaches of the War Office, Churchill's position, consistently favoring withdrawal, was perhaps the most clearcut. It was in large measure shared by Henry Wilson and Percy Radcliffe who, as C.I.G.S. and Director of Military Operations respectively, were the senior military officers most directly concerned. Yet, perhaps because they (Radcliffe in particular) were reluctant to send forward written judgments that were clearly in the sphere of foreign, rather than military, policy, they tended to focus not on Norper-

[24] General Radcliffe, in the Inter-Departmental Conference on Middle Eastern Affairs, 38th Minutes, 17 May 1920, 3 P.M.; F.O. General/216.

[25] "British Military Liabilities," Cabinet paper C.P. 1467, 15 June 1920; Cab. 24/107.

[26] The figure is from Cabinet Finance Committee, 27th Minutes, 12 August 1920, 5 P.M.; appendix I to Cabinet 49 (20), Cab. 23/22.

force as a whole, but on its isolated garrisons—Enzeli, Resht, on the mainland only a few miles from Enzeli, and Tabriz, far to the northwest near the border of Soviet Azerbaijan. These outpost forces, they recommended, should be withdrawn, and Norperforce concentrated at its headquarters at Qazvin, much closer to Tehran. Even in this recommendation, however, Wilson and Radcliffe were slightly hesitant. Thus, on 13 May, five days before the Soviet landing at Enzeli, Wilson passed on to Churchill a General Staff memorandum, signed by Radcliffe, urging such a concentration of forces, with the following covering note of his own: "I feel it only right to point out that the withdrawal of the British advanced detachment from Enzeli will most probably be speedily followed by a corresponding advance on the part of the Russians who are obviously bent on reasserting their sway in N. Persia on pre-war lines, *but unless H.M.G. are prepared to go to war with Russia,* there is little chance of our being able to prevent them doing so."[27]

Perhaps because of the apparent gap between Churchill's outspoken desire during 1919 to commit British forces to an anti-Bolshevik crusade and his equally outspoken appeal during 1920 for a reduction in British military commitments—an inconsistency that called his judgment into question—or perhaps because of the reluctance with which Radcliffe, as the War Office representative on the Eastern Committee, put forward his views, Curzon was able effectively to disregard the War Office's position on Persia throughout the period preceding the Enzeli landing. Here was wishful thinking in the extreme. Curzon, and Sir Percy Cox in Tehran, sought during the winter of 1919-20 to reassert British naval presence in the Caspian by once again taking over Denikin's ships, as the most effective means of protecting Persia against a Soviet invasion. This, however, was out of the question. As Curzon telegraphed Cox on 7 February:

Position in Caspian is thoroughly understood and was exhaustively considered. We should have liked to replace British flotilla and personnel, and were prepared to run considerable risks for that object. But Admiralty were unable to sanction the venture unless War Office would guarantee

---

[27] Wilson's note, also dated 13 May 1920, was on "Situation in North West Persia, May 1920"; W.O. 106/961 (italics in original). See also Radcliffe's remarks at the Eastern Committee meeting of 17 May cited above, n. 24.

the security of Baku, and War Office would not do the latter unless two Allied divisions with a third in reserve could be provided to hold the Batoum-Baku line.

These were not forthcoming, and the scheme was reluctantly dropped.[28]

Four days later, on 11 February, Churchill sent to the Cabinet a General Staff memorandum recommending that, in the absence of a definite decision to defend Persia with British forces, the Enzeli garrison should be withdrawn "in order to escape the loss of prestige involved in a retirement in contact with the enemy."[29] Yet when the Cabinet met to consider the paper a week later, it rejected withdrawal and, obviously under Curzon's urging, decided on what came to be called the policy of the "bold front" at Enzeli. The detachment at Enzeli, with the aid of additional artillery and reinforcements available from the main body of Norperforce, was considered sufficient to deter Soviet forces from attempting a "serious landing." The minutes of the meeting stated that "the General Officer Commanding, Mesopotamia, was accordingly to make arrangements to offer a bold front to the Bolsheviks at Enzeli, but, as there was no intention of holding on to Enzeli if that place were seriously attacked, he was to provide for a safe withdrawal in the event of such attack." And to Baghdad went orders repeating these same phrases, adding that the Enzeli garrison should "endeavour by bluff to prevent [the Bolsheviks] seriously attacking."[30]

Given the recrimination which, as we shall see, followed the Enzeli landing, it seems almost incredible that Churchill and Henry Wilson allowed these orders to be sent, or that Curzon was able to leave a meeting of the Eastern Committee in mid-March, at which Radcliffe was present, with the impression, as he telegraphed to Cox, that "Military opinion here is . . . convinced that any attack in force by Bolsheviks against Persia is most improbable and may practically be discounted. Real danger lies in infiltration of Bolshevik individual agents or small parties and spread of insidious propaganda, which could not be prevented, even by largely augmented forces."[31]

[28] Curzon to Cox (Tehran) telegram 67, 7 February 1920; *British Documents*, vol. XIII, no. 373.

[29] Cabinet paper C.P. 647, 11 February 1920; Cab. 24/98.

[30] Minutes, Cabinet 11(20), 18 February 1920; 5:30 P.M.; Cab. 23/20. For the orders to General Haldane at Baghdad, see *British Documents*, vol. XIII, no. 374, no. 4.

[31] Curzon to Cox (Tehran), telegram 153, 22 March 1920; *ibid.*, no. 395. The

On 17 May, the day preceding the Soviet landing, Curzon called the Eastern Committee into session again, this time to consider Radcliffe's General Staff memorandum of the 13th recommending withdrawal from Enzeli and Tabriz to Qazvin. Since the March meeting the situation had changed considerably. Independent Azerbaijan had fallen to the Red Army, giving Soviet Russia not only another land frontier with Persia but also the important naval base of Baku, from which seaborne operations could be launched. And on 6 May a Soviet destroyer and torpedo boat had put in at Astara, in Persian Azerbaijan just across the border from Soviet Azerbaijan, in an effort to enlist the Persian Cossack detachment there in a forthcoming sea and land campaign against British forces in Persia.[32] All this was known in England. Yet Curzon was so convinced that any withdrawal would simply invite a Soviet descent that he could take Radcliffe's cautious admission that the "policy of bluff" had thus far seemed to have the desired effect and telegraph to Cox: "Position at Enzeli does not appear to be exposed to immediate danger either by land or sea." Therefore, unless Cox demurred, the orders governing the deployment of Norperforce would be unchanged.[33] By the time Cox received this message, Enzeli was in Soviet hands.

As it happened, Major General H. B. Champain, the commander of Norperforce, was himself at Enzeli on 18 May. He had come from Qazvin the previous day to witness the test-firing of newly installed shore batteries. But the only shells fired came from Soviet warships in the harbor. Under cover of a dawn barrage, Soviet troops landed on the neck of the peninsula, cutting off the British garrison in its encampment at the tip. Surprise was complete. Champain evidently concluded that the onset of firing meant the end of any attempt to bluff or maintain a "bold front," for he immediately ordered a retreat to the mainland. But his retreating troops ran up against Soviet forces already emplaced on the neck of the peninsula. A brief skirmish convinced him that his only recourse was negotiation, and he sent an emissary to the Soviet leader, F. F. Raskolnikov,

---

meeting was: Inter-Departmental Conference on Middle Eastern Affairs, 36th Minutes, 17 March 1920, 5 P.M.; F.O. General/216.

[32] Reported by Cox (Tehran) to Curzon, telegram 260, 9 May 1920; *British Documents*, vol. XIII, no. 422.

[33] Inter-Departmental Conference on Middle Eastern Affairs, 38th Minutes, 17 May 1920, 3 P.M.; F.O. General/216. Curzon to Cox (Tehran), telegram 268, 18 May 1920; *British Documents*, vol. XIII, no. 433.

Commander of the Caspian Red Fleet, who insisted that the British must surrender Denikin's ships and other military supplies. If these conditions were complied with, Raskolnikov said, the British troops would be allowed to retire to the mainland; the eventual future of Enzeli would be determined by direct Anglo-Soviet negotiations. Champain telegraphed the British mission at Tehran for instructions but received no reply. Apparently communications had been disrupted. Therefore he decided that in the circumstances, confronted by overwhelming force, he had no choice but to comply. His troops evacuated Enzeli that very evening, leaving behind all of Denikin's ships and also their own guns and large stores of munitions and other military implements.[34]

News of the events at Enzeli first reached London the following evening, 19 May. At the War Office Henry Wilson was outraged. That night he wrote in his diary: "We are at last at the opening phases of great and dangerous trials for the Empire." Nevertheless, he had no desire to meet the Soviet challenge at Enzeli. "For months," he wrote, "I have been begging the Cabinet to allow me to withdraw from Persia and from the Caucasus [British forces were still, at this time, at Batum]. Now perhaps they will." And to Curzon, the following day, he wrote: "Perhaps the 'regrettable incident' at Enzeli which has now occurred and which will be followed by others may lead you to change your mind and even trust, a little, in the advice of the responsible advisers."[35]

Churchill was less restrained. As soon as he had heard the news he went with Wilson to the House of Commons to seek out Bonar Law, who had been leading the government during Lloyd George's recovery from a brief illness, in order to request a Cabinet meeting. Bonar Law agreed, and promised to get Lloyd George up from the country for a meeting on the 21st.[36] On the 20th Churchill wrote

[34] For published accounts of the Soviet landing at Enzeli, see: Cox (Tehran) to Curzon, telegram 289, 18 May 1920, relaying Norperforce telegram from Kazvin dated 19 May, 1 A.M., *ibid.*, no. 434; Lord Derby (Paris) to Curzon, telegram 601, 20 May, relaying a Persian government report, *ibid.*, no. 437; Raskolnikov's own account in *Petrogradskaya Pravda*, 15 July, printed in Eudin and North, *Russia and the East*, pp. 178-80; Balfour, *Recent Happenings*, pp. 185-89; Georges Ducrocq, "La Politique du gouvernment des Soviets en Perse," *Revue du Monde Musulman*, vol. LII, December 1922; *The Times*, 20 May 1920. In War Office records, see General Haldane's telegrams X/8723, X/8753, and X/8893 from Baghdad, 19, 23, and 30 May; W.O. 95/4968.
[35] Wilson MS diary, entry for 19 May 1920. Wilson to Curzon, 20 May; Curzon MSS, box 65.
[36] Wilson MS diary, entry for 19 May 1920.

to Curzon to give him notice that he intended to ask the Cabinet not only to withdraw all British forces from Persia to defensible rail-heads in Mesopotamia but also to dissolve the Eastern Committee, which was, he implied, Curzon's captive instrument. He wished, he said, to review the events of the precedings ten days. Wilson had circulated the paper urging the evacuation of Enzeli, which the General Staff had long considered not only costly but increasingly dangerous. "As soon as this comes to the notice of the Foreign Office, a meeting of the Eastern Committee is held, to which neither the C.I.G.S. nor I were summoned and of which we were both in igno-rance, but a decision is taken against the evacuation of Enzeli on which telegrams and orders are sent."[37]

Here, of course, Churchill and Wilson were the victims of poor staff work: Radcliffe had, after all, been at the meeting. Churchill went on, however, to state a more substantive complaint that went to the very heart of his differences with his colleagues:

In consequence of this, our force has been first rounded up and then allowed to retire in circumstances of great humiliation to British arms. The same thing will happen at Kazvin and Batoum if we continue on the present lines. There is something to be said for making peace with the Bolsheviks. There is also something to be said for making war upon them. There is nothing to be said for a policy of doing all we can to help to strengthen them, to add to their influence and prestige, to weaken those who are fighting against them, and at the same time leaving weak British forces tethered in dangerous places where they can be easily and suddenly overwhelmed.

I do not see that anything we can do now within the present limits of our policy can possibly avert the complete loss of British influence throughout the Caucasus, Trans-Caspia, and Persia. If we are not able to resist the Bolsheviks in these areas, it is much better by timely with-drawals to keep out of harm's way and avoid disaster and the shameful incidents such as that which has just occurred.

I should have been only too ready to have helped you with a different policy which, properly supported, would ere now have ended this criminal regime in Russia. But in view of the decisions which were taken six and eight months ago [*i.e.*, to cease British support of Kolchak and Denikin], and in view of the uninstructed state of public opinion, I think that is impossible. It only remains to accept the consequences and withdraw our

[37] Churchill was exaggerating: telegrams, but not orders, were sent. There was no need for orders; existing orders remained in effect, as Curzon told Cox in the telegram cited above, n. 33.

forces everywhere to defensive positions in close proximity with their railheads, where they can be cheaply maintained and where they can operate effectively against an aggressive enemy. I must absolutely decline to continue to share responsibility for a policy of mere bluff.[38]

Churchill's concerns were echoed by a leading article in that same day's issue of *The Times*, which declared that "ministers still approach Middle Eastern matters with the habits of mind induced by the war." They practiced, it said, "Gallipoli methods," incurring "enormous responsibilities with light-hearted eagerness, without counting the cost, without reckoning up their resources, and without considering where they will be if something unexpected happens."[39] Here, of course, was an attack aimed primarily at Churchill, who in the popular mind bore most of the blame for the disaster at Gallipoli and who had been the most outspoken advocate of military measures—"adventures," his critics called them—in Russia. But now, unknown to *The Times*, such strictures matched Churchill's own.

Curzon undoubtedly felt them acutely, just as, at the Cabinet meeting lasting all afternoon on 21 May, he felt more acutely than usual his chronically painful back.[40] Under these baleful influences he began the meeting with what Henry Wilson described as a "violent attack" on him and the General Staff for not making clear at an earlier stage just how endangered the garrison at Enzeli was. Wilson countered by reciting the warnings that had been given, and reminding Curzon that with Denikin's downfall, the Soviet take-over in Azerbaijan, and the thawing of the Volga, where the Soviet fleet had wintered, the situation had in fact grown even more dangerous. Now, he said, there were only two choices: either concentrate all British forces at Qazvin and "*really* fight, which meant a large increase of force," or "clear out of Persia and go back to our rail-heads."[41] Wilson was supported by Churchill. Against them were Curzon and Milner who, as Secretary of State for the Colonies, bore principal responsibility for Mesopotamia.[42] They argued, ac-

---

[38] Churchill to Curzon, 20 May 1920; Curzon MSS, box 65.

[39] *The Times*, 20 May 1920.

[40] So Churchill noted in the letter cited below, n. 44.

[41] Wilson MS diary, entry for 21 May 1920.

[42] There are two sources for this meeting: Wilson's MS diary entry (which differs in some important respects from the version printed in Callwell, *Henry Wilson*, vol. II, p. 240) and the official minutes—Cabinet 30(20), 21 May 1920, noon, Cab. 23/21. The latter summarizes arguments in much more detail, but does not attribute views to individuals.

cording to the minutes, that withdrawal even from Batum, much less from Persia, would be

tantamount to an invitation to the Bolsheviks to enter and make themselves master of North Persia; the friendly Persian Government would then fall; there would be an end to the Anglo-Persian Agreement which . . . had been concluded with the object of establishing decent conditions and providing a barrier against Bolshevism; the hopes that the Anglo-Persian Agreement would serve as a model for the administration of Egypt and Mesopotamia would disappear; in time the Bolsheviks would either penetrate to the borders of Mesopotamia, or Persia, permeated by Bolshevism, would go rotten; our position in Mesopotamia could then only be secured by much larger forces than we were prepared to maintain there; the reaction to our abandonment of Persia would weaken our whole position in the East.

In predicting such dire consequences, Curzon and Milner did not, in fact, differ much from Churchill and Wilson; where they did differ was in their estimates of the British Empire's capability to forestall them. There was, however, another, altogether different, line of argument at the Cabinet meeting on 21 May. The minutes do not identify its proponents, nor does Wilson's diary. Almost certainly they included Lloyd George and H.A.L. Fisher, the President of the Board of Education. Possibly they included Edwin Montagu, Sir Robert Horne, and Bonar Law.[43] The minutes state:

. . . it was pointed out that there was no evidence that the Bolsheviks had designs on Persia. They had many prior commitments in re-organizing their own country, in driving out the Poles, and in establishing their boundaries. Their communications were notoriously deficient, and would probably not enable them to invade a country like Persia, where even we, with all our resources, found difficulty in maintaining a small force; Persia was not a rich country likely to attract them. Even if they entered Persia, it would be long before they could penetrate as far as the borders of Mesopotamia. It was more probable that they would seek their aims by means of propaganda, which our occupation would not prevent; or it was possible that their object might be to re-establish the position Russia had occupied in North Persia under the Anglo-Russian Agreement. The

---

[43] These persons were all present. Wilson's diary indicates that Lloyd George argued for withdrawal, but does not identify the arguments he used. Fisher would certainly have taken this line for good Liberal reasons, and Horne and Bonar Law, although Conservatives, generally went along with Lloyd George on such issues. Montagu, as we have seen, consistently opposed Curzon's notions regarding the utility of a British "presence" in southwest Asia.

British people would never embark on a difficult and costly war for the purpose of preventing the Bolsheviks from establishing this position, or even for preventing a Russian invasion of Persia.

Therefore, this strand of argument concluded, since the United Kingdom could not keep Soviet influence out of Persia by force of arms, it should encourage the Persians to reach their own arrangements with Moscow—precisely the reverse of existing policy. Here, of course, was yet another iteration of the basic arguments over the nature of the Soviet challenge and British capabilities for dealing with it which had divided the Lloyd George government ever since the Armistice of 11 November 1918. And in this instance, as always, a compromise was found that enabled the Cabinet to avoid committing itself on those basic arguments. The date, it will be remembered, was just before Krasin's arrival in London—his first conversation with Lloyd George would take place in little more than a week's time. "The Cabinet generally felt," the minutes stated, "that advantage should be taken of the forthcoming conversations with M. Krassin, if possible, as a condition of entering into trade relations, to effect an all-around settlement which would include the East as well as the delivery of British subjects still retained in Bolshevist hands, or, at any rate, to clear up the situation and to establish exactly how we stand with the Bolsheviks." In the meantime, the War Office could order Norperforce to withdraw from its advanced outposts and to concentrate at Qazvin. Decisions as to its eventual disposition would be postponed.

For Curzon, such an outcome meant that British forces would for the time being remain in Persia. Perhaps they might still be used to buttress his Anglo-Persian agreement. For Churchill, on the other hand, the Cabinet's action represented a start toward the total withdrawal he wanted to achieve. In a more mellow mood he again wrote a note to Curzon, commiserating with the Foreign Secretary for the physical pain he obviously had suffered at the meeting, and then observing: "It is a gt (*sic*) pity that we have not been able to develop any common policy between W.O. & F.O. I have to bear the abuse of F.O. policy & to put the money for it. Yet there is no effective cooperation or mutual support. You have willingly acquiesced in the destruction of the Volunteer armies, because of their friction with your Georgians & Azerbaijanis. Now you expect me with the very slender weak & raw forces at my disposal to carry out the military side of a policy which requires for its success strong friendly Russian armies."[44]

✧

Within a fortnight of this Cabinet meeting General Champain had withdrawn the British garrison at Resht and the handful of troops at Tabriz, concentrating his force at Qazvin and leaving only one outlying garrison—at Manjil, halfway between Resht and Qazvin, where a pass afforded a natural defense against attack from the north.[45] These retreats in the face of apparent Soviet pressure scarcely added to British prestige, in Persia or anywhere else. Two months before the Enzeli landing Curzon had reminded Sir Percy Cox that under the Anglo-Persian Agreement of 1919 the British government "undertook no obligation to defend the present frontiers of Persia against all attack"; rather, the agreement—which, in any case, had not yet been ratified by the Majlis—represented only "a moral obligation to do our best on Persia's behalf." Whether or not Cox used this language with the Tehran government is not clear, but Bonar Law was bluntly explicit when, in reply to a question in the House of Commons on 20 May, he stated that the British government was under no obligation to respond to the Soviet landing.[46] Meanwhile, in Paris, the French press lost little time in pointing up the irony that the Anglo-Persian Agreement had made Persia a British protectorate which the British were unable to protect.[47]

For a while after the Enzeli landing it appeared—in London, at least—that the Persians might not, after all, need protection. A Soviet note on 23 May, in response to a protest from the Persian government, declared that the landing had been carried out by the local Soviet naval commander on his own responsibility in order

[44] Churchill to Curzon, 22 May 1920; Curzon MSS, box 65.

[45] The War Office's orders (cited above, n. 30) called for a delaying action at the Manjil pass.

[46] 129 *H.C. Deb.*, col. 1602. Curzon's "reminder" to Cox was telegram 153, 22 March 1920; *British Documents*, vol. XIII, no. 395. The Government of India, it should be noted, disagreed. On 21 February the Foreign and Political Department telegraphed to London: "Although we recognize that Anglo-Persian agreement does not technically commit British Government to defence of present Persian *régime*, public opinion in the East almost certainly holds that His Majesty's Government are morally committed. . . . To withdraw all forces . . . may expose them to charges of breach of faith, and react on operations not only in Persia but in Afghanistan, making our relations with latter more difficult." (telegram 204 S.; Cabinet paper C.P. 795, Cab. 24/99)

[47] The French reaction is surveyed in Derby's despatch 1593 to Curzon, 25 May 1920; *British Documents*, vol. XIII, no. 444.

to seize Denikin's ships and thus make the Caspian safe for navigation; Soviet forces would leave Persian territory as soon as "military requirements" permitted.[48] Even before news of this note
reached him Curzon optimistically (and groundlessly) told the
Persian Foreign Minister, who was visiting London, that he did not
believe that the Bolsheviks contemplated a "serious" invasion of
Persia, and that he would not be surprised if they soon withdrew
their forces.[49]

Another Persian protest on 4 June brought similar, and lengthier,
Soviet reassurances.[50] Reassurances or none, however, Soviet forces
remained at Enzeli, and early in June they occupied Resht as well.
Having failed to get the support they wanted from the British
government, the Persians decided to seek help from the League of
Nations. The situation was, in fact, the first case of aggression
against a member state which had been brought to the League, and
enthusiasts of the international organization, such as Lord Robert
Cecil and the League of Nations Union, were anxious that it be
faced squarely.[51]

Moreover, Sir Eric Drummond, the League's Secretary General,
saw in the Persian appeal a means of bringing about international
recognition of the Soviet government, which would necessarily be
invited to send representatives to the League to discuss settlement
of the Soviet-Persian "dispute." In order to induce Moscow to
accept League intervention, the League would, under Drummond's
scheme, agree to arbitrate the Polish-Soviet dispute: the Polish
armies which had invaded Russia in late April were now deep
within Soviet territory, and League action offered one means of
getting them out. Drummond put this proposal privately to Philip
Kerr, who agreed that it offered, in one stroke, a means of bringing
peace to Eastern Europe, recognition to the Soviet regime, strength
to the League, and, incidentally, relief to the Persians.[52] For just

[48] Chicherin to Prince Firuz, 23 May 1920; *Dokumenty vneshnei politiki*, vol. II,
pp. 542-43. Reported to London in Cox (Tehran) to Curzon telegram 320, 28 May;
British Documents, vol. XIII, no. 446.
[49] Curzon to Cox (Tehran), telegram 283, 27 May 1920; *ibid.*, no. 445.
[50] The Persian protest and the Soviet reply, from Chicherin, are printed in
Dokumenty vneshnei politiki, vol. II, pp. 557-60.
[51] *The Times*, 9 June 1920.
[52] Drummond's memorandum of 26 May 1920 and Kerr's covering note the same
day for Lloyd George are in Lloyd George MSS, file F/90/1/9.

these reasons, however, Drummond's scheme was stillborn: his objectives were not shared by the French nor (so far as recognition of Moscow was concerned) by Curzon. The Foreign Secretary, indeed, found the Persian appeal very embarrassing, pointing up as it did Great Britain's apparent inability to protect its client, and he made a concerted but vain effort to prevent it from being aired.[53]

The League Council addressed the Persian situation at a special session in London on 16 June, with Curzon in the chair. Fortunately for him (if not for the Persians), none of the other Powers was anxious to involve itself in a possible conflict with Soviet Russia over Persia, and the Council decided that since "negotiations" between the Persian and Soviet governments were already in progress —they had exchanged notes and the Persian Foreign Minister had an appointment to see Krasin in London the following day—and since the Soviet government said that it had already ordered the evacuation of Persian territory and had declared its peaceful intentions towards Persia, the Persian government was to be commended for bringing the situation to the Council's attention, and was to keep the Council informed of future developments.[54] This was the League's only action, although Soviet forces were not to leave Persian territory for over a year. As a leader in *The Times* stated the following morning: "A few more sittings of the Council of the League of Nations like that over which Lord Curzon presided at St. James's Palace yesterday would go far to kill the very idea of a League."[55]

✧

On 4 June 1920 a minor Persian landowner and religious figure, Mirza Kuchek Khan, had led a band of his followers into Resht on the heels of the withdrawing British garrison and there proclaimed the establishment of the Persian Soviet Socialist Republic. Immediately he sent a message to Lenin requesting "help in liberating us and all weak and oppressed nations from the yoke of Persian and English oppressors." Another message, to the foreign legations in

[53] See Balfour's note to Lord Hardinge, 5 June 1920, *British Documents*, vol. XIII, no. 452; minutes on it by Hardinge and Curzon, 9 June, *idem*, n. 3; and Oliphant's memorandum of a conversation with Prince Firuz, 10 June, *ibid.*, no. 458.
[54] *League of Nations: Official Journal*, No. 5 (July-August 1920), pp. 214-18. See Fatemi, *Diplomatic History*, pp. 209-15.
[55] *The Times*, 17 June 1920.

Tehran, proclaimed the abolition of the Persian monarchy and requested recognition for the new "government."[56] News of these events reached London several days before the League's brief encounter with Persia's problems on 16 June; it should have been sufficient to dispel any optimism that the Soviet forces in Gilan might soon withdraw.

Kuchek Khan was well known to British civil and military officers in Persia. In 1915, at Tehran, he and a small group of others—mostly bourgeois liberal intellectuals like himself—began to hold regular discussions to draw up a program aimed at complete national independence, social reform, and Islamic unity. To him and his followers the government at Tehran had fallen so completely under Russian and British control that their only recourse was to organize a rival government and attempt to take power. They chose as their base the provinces of Gilan and Mazanderan along the Caspian Sea; because they often lived in the dense forests of this region cut off from the rest of Persia by high mountains they became known as "Jangalis," or jungle-dwellers.[57]

The Jangalis were able fighters, and for much of the time during the period 1917-19 they ruled their region, successfully resisting incursions by British, Russian, and Persian government forces. Such was their power that General Dunsterville was forced to conclude an agreement recognizing Jangali authority in Gilan in order to safeguard the lines of communication for his expedition to Baku during the summer of 1918.[58] Subsequently, however, the movement became seriously weakened by internal divisions, and it was dispersed by central government forces in mid-1919. From this time Kuchek Khan fell increasingly under the influence of his much more radical lieutenants, including some who were avowed communists. By the spring of 1920—with Persia seemingly reduced to the position of a British dependency by the Anglo-Persian Agreement—he had reluctantly become convinced that only through Soviet assistance could he achieve his reformist, nationalist goals. Thus the

---

[56] For Kuchek Khan's proclamation and note to Lenin, see Eudin and North, *Russia and the East*, pp. 96-97; for the note to the foreign legations in Tehran see Cox to Curzon, telegram 361, 10 June 1920, *British Documents*, vol. XIII, no. 457.

[57] For an account of Kuchek Khan's career previous to the establishment of the Gilan Soviet regime, see M. Martchenko, "Kutchuk Khan," *Revue du Monde Musulman*, vol. XL-XLI (1920), pp. 98-115.

[58] Major-General L. C. Dunsterville, *The Adventures of Dunsterforce*, London, 1920, pp. 14, 27-30, 155-74, 204-05.

Jangalis entered Resht in June 1920 behind Raskolnikov's Bolshevik forces, and the more radical Jangali leaders persuaded Kuchek Khan to proclaim the Persian Socialist Republic.[59]

Quickly the Jangalis managed to extend their control over all of Gilan and Mazanderan. Concurrently, in the same region, a Persian Communist Party was formed, its cadres coming from a party founded several years earlier among the many Persian workers employed in the Baku oil fields. These communists inevitably found themselves in important positions in Kuchek Khan's government. So ruthless were they in the imposition of measures for sovietization —drastic land reform, requisitions from the peasantry, and an antireligious campaign—that on 19 July Kuchek Khan himself, with some of his followers, withdrew once again into the forests. He remained aloof from the "soviet" regime until May 1921 when he returned to take part in a "united front" government whose forces were decisively defeated—with Kuchek Khan losing his life—by the revitalized Persian Cossack Division following the withdrawal of Soviet forces from Gilan in September.[60]

Throughout its brief life the insurgent regime was dependent on Moscow for its very existence, a fact which the Russian communist leaders found a source of considerable embarrassment in their efforts to reach a *détente* with the West. From the outset they denied any responsibility for events in Gilan. The initial landings at Enzeli, it will be recalled, they attributed to a decision made personally by the local naval commander. Later, in early June, they maintained that all *Russian* forces had been withdrawn from Persia, their mission of recovering Denikin's ships accomplished: any remaining communist troops were those of the Azerbaijan Soviet Republic, over which Moscow had no control. On 10 July 1920, in a note to the Persian government, Chicherin stated a position from which Soviet spokesmen did not deviate throughout the following years— that despite the "similarity in ideas between the government established at Resht and the Russian government" the Soviet attitude to-

---

[59] George Lenczowski, *Russia and the West in Iran, 1918-1948: A Study in Big-Power Rivalry*, Ithaca, New York, 1949, pp. 56-57.

[60] The most exhaustive treatment of the Gilan regime, based on a thorough survey especially of Soviet, but also of Persian and Western, materials is the long anonymous review article, "Persia," *Central Asian Review* (London), vol. IV, nos. 3 and 4, 1956; see pp. 303-16. See also Lenczowski, *Russia and the West in Iran*, pp. 57-60.

wards the Persian internal struggle was one of rigid nonintervention.[61] Later—presumably after it had become evident that the Gilan regime would not carry communism to the rest of Persia—the Soviet government stated that Azerbaijani troops were remaining in northern Persia only to shield their own country against British attacks, and that if the British agreed to withdraw their forces from Persia Moscow would use its influence to secure the withdrawal of the Azerbaijanis.[62]

The precise nature of the relationship between the Soviet regime in Moscow and the Jangalis is still unclear, as is the extent to which the Jangalis were supplemented in their military operations by Russian or Azerbaijani formations. Published accounts are generally vague on these points.[63] From contemporary observations by diplomatic and military officers, however, we can draw certain conclusions. First is that the great preponderance of troops at the disposal of the Gilan regime were Persians—many, no doubt, recruited from among the Persian oil-field workers at Baku and trained by Red Army instructors, but nonetheless Persians.[64] On the other hand these Persians were significantly augmented by Russians. Hassan Arfa, the Iranian soldier and diplomat, who in 1920 was a lieutenant commanding a platoon of the Gendarmerie, speaks in his memoirs of encountering a Soviet force of some 300 men, mostly Russians, but including some Azerbaijanis.[65] At several points in his diary Major General Edmund Ironside, who, as we shall see, commanded Norperforce during the period October 1920–February 1921 (the period which saw almost all its combat against the rebels), refers to the fact that his men had taken Russian prisoners including, on one occasion, an officer, and on another a Communist Party member. After one engagement Ironside noted that his Russian prisoners were nearly all conscripts, after another that of the twenty-seven prisoners

[61] Eudin and North, *Soviet Russia and the East*, pp. 97-98, citing *Soviet Russia*, New York, 14 August 1920, p. 174.

[62] See the note from Karakhan to the Persian emissary in Moscow, 22 January 1921, *Dokumenty vneshnei politiki*, vol. III, pp. 491-93.

[63] See *Central Asian Review*, vol. IV, pp. 303-16, for a survey of these accounts.

[64] Commander Luke, at Tiflis, noted in his diary on 21 June 1920 a report by a Persian diplomatic representative at Baku that the Persian Communist Party had created a large organization at Baku for the recruitment and training of Persian oilfield workers, and that by that date 4,000 of them had already been transported to Gilan. Luke, *Cities and Men*, vol. II, p. 156. See also Ducrocq, *Revue du Monde Musulman*, vol. LII, p. 87.

[65] General Hassan Arfa, *Under Five Shahs*, London, 1964, pp. 95-100.

his men had taken that day, one was a Georgian, another an Armenian, and all the rest Russians from the Red Army's 244th Regiment. On yet another occasion he recorded that his intelligence staff had intercepted radio messages from Russian headquarters at Enzeli bitterly complaining to Moscow about the inactivity and cowardice of the Jangalis. In January 1921 Ironside estimated that the "Bolshevik" troops in Gilan, which had come to call themselves the "Persian National Army," included some 400 Russians in their total strength of 6,000. And while he noted that his men captured some Turkomans and even an Afghan fighting against them, he never once mentioned the capture of any Azerbaijanis. On at least two occasions, the rebels were supported by bombing aircraft.[66] From these observations it seems clear that Soviet military support of the Gilan regime, despite Moscow's claims of non-intervention, was relatively extensive. Moreover, the presence of so many Russian soldiers seems to indicate that Moscow went to no great effort to make it appear that external support for the Persian communists was coming only from "independent" Soviet Azerbaijan, and not from Soviet Russia.

❖

If 400 Russians in north Persia were too many to make credible a claim of non-intervention, they were few enough to be easily withdrawn or disavowed. Soviet policy in Persia during 1920 and 1921, just as elsewhere in the East, was essentially opportunist. Its maximum goal was a Communist regime in Tehran; a minimal goal, and one far more likely of achievement, was the removal of British influence, not only from Persia but from the rest of the Middle East. Lenin and his colleagues were fully aware of just how thinly stretched were the military resources of the British Empire in the aftermath of the World War, and, therefore, of how truly indivisible the fabric of internal peace within the Empire had become. Even a low-keyed insurgency in north Persia would have much wider ramifications. Kamenev touched on these ramifications in a tele-

---

[66] Ironside MS diary, entries for 27 October, 10 and 23 November, 30 December 1920, 30 January, and 11 February 1921. Norman (Tehran) to Curzon, telegrams 41 and 74, 19 and 30 January 1921 (both conveying Ironside's views); file E 1009/— and 1449/2/34, F.O. 371/6399. The bombing—of Resht on 28 and 29 September 1920, when the town was in Persian Cossack hands—was reported in Government of India, Special Bureau of Information, Weekly Report no. 33 for 2 October 1920; file N 179/179/97, F.O. 371/5382.

gram to Chicherin just before his expulsion from England in September 1920, stating:

The insurrections in Mesopotamia have brought to the front the entire policy of the British Government in Central Asia. The British troops in Persia are operating from Bagdad. The evacuation of Mesopotamia which is being sought in some political circles [in England] must entail the evacuation of Persia; on the other hand, pressure on the British troops in North Persia will strengthen the position of the Mesopotamian insurgents. Britain has no troops to send to Mesopotamia except those which are in India and which she is afraid to move. A revolution along the line Enzeli-Hamadan-Bagdad threatens the most vital interests of the British Empire and breaks the status quo in Asia created by the Treaty of Versailles.[67]

The retreat of the British and the formation of the communist regime in Gilan and Mazanderan strongly reinforced the Persian government in its conviction, which had been growing throughout the spring, that it should deal directly with Moscow to work out a means of safeguarding Persia from Bolshevism; this conviction resulted, eventually, in the Soviet-Persian treaty of 26 February 1921. For Curzon, the prospect of direct Persian-Russian relations recalled the unhappy past which it had been the purpose of the Anglo-Persian Agreement to banish forever. Thus, when Prince Firuz, the Persian Foreign Minister, called on 8 April to propose that, since every other state bordering upon Russia seemed to be entering into negotiations with Moscow, perhaps Persia should too, Curzon indignantly replied that he could see no analogy between the position of Persia and that of Finland, the Baltic States, or the states of Transcaucasia—the British commitment to Persia, under the agreement, was much greater than that to any of the others. It was not his business, he said, to impose a veto on Persia's actions, but he could scarcely view with sympathy the "spectacle of Persia running around for other alliances and arrangements" at the moment "when she was beginning to reap [the] first fruits of the Anglo-Persian Agreement." In his opinion the cessation of "Bolshevik hostilities" in the East would be much more likely to result from the successful completion of the Anglo-Soviet commercial negotiations which were shortly to begin than from "sporadic treaties" between Russia and the various smaller

[67] Kamenev (London) to Chicherin, telegrams 481-82, 1 September 1920, intercept 04003; Davidson mss.

Eastern countries. Relating this interview to Cox in Tehran, Curzon noted a reason for objecting to Persian-Soviet negotiations which he had not put to Firuz: "You will realise, what I did not add, that under cover of a treaty Bolshevik agents and propaganda directed against Great Britain might easily find a secure foothold in the country.[68]

Even after the Enzeli landings and the establishment of the rebel regime in Gilan, Curzon continued to insist that the Persian government should place its faith in British diplomacy, and not enter into separate negotiations with Moscow. On 7 June, at the second meeting between the British and Krasin, Curzon protested strongly against Soviet "direct aggression against Persia," but his protest was blunted by Krasin's contention that the order for Soviet forces to leave Enzeli had "already been given."[69] If it had been given it was not implemented, and the British "ultimatum" to the Soviet government on 30 June laid down as "the fundamental condition," upon which the British government would insist if negotiations for a trade agreement were to continue, a promise by Moscow to refrain from "any attempt by military action or propaganda to encourage any of the peoples of Asia in any form of hostile action against British interests or the British Empire."[70] This condition, Curzon telegraphed H. C. Norman on 13 July, was "specially devised for protection of Persia;" its acceptance by the Soviet government (in Chicherin's note of 7 July)[71] would, he hoped, alleviate Persian fears regarding the "Bolshevik invasion" of Gilan and Mazanderan. Here, perhaps, was naive optimism on Curzon's part. Yet he added to his expression of faith in the continued efficacy of Britain's writ a curious disclaimer, which shows that he may, after all, have understood just how vain his hopes were: "Our difficulty arises from the fact that it is apparently difficult to discriminate between Russian Bolsheviks and Persian Bolsheviks."[72]

Whatever Curzon may have thought of the efficacy of Soviet promises, the Persian government concluded that in the absence of

[68] Curzon to Cox (Tehran), despatch 85, 10 April 1920, and telegram 182, 11 April; *British Documents*, vol. XIII, nos. 406 and 407.

[69] Minutes, *ibid.*, vol. VIII, no. 25, pp. 302-03.

[70] For the British note of 30 June 1920, see above, chap. III, n. 68.

[71] Chicherin's note is cited above, chap. IV, n. 18.

[72] Curzon (Spa) to Norman (Tehran), telegram 2, 13 July 1920, *British Documents*, vol. XIII, no. 510.

a solid British military commitment, the only way it might forestall an advance on Tehran, and perhaps even regain control over the Caspian provinces, was through direct negotiations with Moscow. Moshir ed-Dowleh, who succeeded Vossuq as Prime Minister in late June, told H. C. Norman that although he personally felt that little good could come of direct Persian-Soviet negotiations, "public opinion" insisted upon them. On 23 July Norman reported that the Persian ambassador at Constantinople had been sent to Moscow as a special envoy.[73]

Meanwhile, at the end of July an event occurred which still further shook Persian faith in the British: without warning, General Champain, the commander of Norperforce, suddenly decided to withdraw to Qazvin the garrison he had left astride the important pass at Manjil.[74] His orders did not require him to do so—the move was a matter of his own discretion. According to Ironside, who replaced Champain two months later, the British garrison had not been seriously menaced. Apparently Champain had panicked.[75] In Tehran, naturally enough, the Persian government took this latest withdrawal as a sign that the British were about to abandon Persia entirely to the mercies of the Russians and their Persian communist allies. From this point onward Curzon's continued sermonizing to the effect that the Persians had brought their dire situation on themselves and that in order to rectify it they needed only to ratify the Anglo-Persian Agreement, fell on deaf ears.[76]

At this time, August 1920, with British influence seemingly contracting along with the withdrawal of British military power, and with Persian-Soviet negotiations about to begin in Moscow, a new factor—the Persian Cossack Division—entered the complex pattern of events. From it, largely through the efforts of General Ironside,

[73] Norman (Tehran) to Curzon, telegrams 453 part 2, 465, and 519—3, 7, and 23 July 1920; *ibid.*, nos. 500, 503, and 521.
[74] Norman (Tehran) to Curzon, telegram 548, 31 July 1920; *ibid.*, no. 529. Haldane (Baghdad) to War Office, telegrams X/9638 and X/9560, 31 July and 1 August 1920; W.O. 95/4968.
[75] Ironside MS diary, entries for 3 and 11 October and 5 December 1920 and 24 March 1921.
[76] Norman (Tehran) to Curzon, telegram 553, 2 August 1920; *British Documents*, vol. XIII, no. 532. Balfour, *Recent Happenings*, p. 198, commented that the withdrawal from Manjil "did more than any foreign intrigue could possibly achieve to injure the British position" in Persia, and "had an even more disastrous effect than the Enzeli episode upon British prestige."

there was to come an unexpected solution to the dilemma of Persia's apparent weakness in the face of Soviet strength.

In 1920 the Cossack Division was composed of some 6,000 Persian soldiers and noncommissioned officers under 237 Persian officers, 56 Russian officers, and 66 Russian n.c.o.'s; in fact, it was closer in size to a brigade than a division.[77] Its commander was a Russian colonel named Starosselski. From its formation in 1879 until the upheavals of 1917 the force had received large Russian subsidies. Rather than have these payments lapse and the force dissolve at a crucial stage of the war when Persia was threatened with German and Turkish invasions, the British and Indian governments had jointly assumed the burden on an *ad hoc* basis. With the end of the war, however, there seemed little reason to continue this arrangement: it scarcely seemed to be in British interests to prolong the presence in Persia of those very Russian influences which the Anglo-Persian Agreement had been designed to eliminate. Starosselski, moreover, was alleged to share some of his monthly British subsidy with both the Shah and the Persian Minister of War, in order to assure himself of their continuing support; it was also rumored that he had provided himself with a liberal cushion in foreign bank accounts.[78] In December 1919, therefore, the India Office announced that it could no longer continue its share of the subsidy payments, and at the same time Curzon telegraphed Cox that the British government's own share would also cease at the end of the month.[79] Because of Cox's objections, the British share was temporarily continued: Cox had argued that it should not be cut off before the joint British-Persian military commission, then meeting in Tehran to plan the shape of the future Persian army, could submit its recommendations.[80]

The commission reported in mid-March 1920, and as was expected it advised that the Cossack Division, together with the South Persia

[77] Ducrocq, *Revue du Monde Musulman*, vol. LII, p. 96, and Ironside MS diary, entry for 10 October 1920.

[78] Ironside MS diary, entries for 7, 24, and 28 October 1920. Norman (Tehran) to Curzon, telegrams 703 and 710, 25 and 27 October 1920; *British Documents*, vol. XIII, nos. 566 and 570.

[79] Curzon to Cox (Tehran), telegram 662, 20 December 1919; *British Documents*, vol. IV, no. 873.

[80] Cox (Tehran) to Curzon, telegram 804, 27 December 1919; cited in *ibid.*, vol. XIII, no. 387.

Rifles and the gendarmerie, should be dissolved and their personnel transferred into the new Regular Army.[81] Here was a recommendation, but implementing it was another matter. When Starosselski was informed, he bluntly refused to comply. The status of the Cossack Division, he said, was regulated by Persian-Russian treaties which he regarded as still in force and to whose alteration he would not be a party. Moreover, he asserted, the Shah, to whose person— rather than the Persian State or government—the force owed its loyalty, had promised that he would not agree to its dissolution. To cooperate in any way with the proposed arrangements for bringing all Persia's armed forces effectively under British control, Starosselski said, would open himself to charges of "having traitorously sacrificed Russian interests."[82]

This last objection underscored one reason why the British in Persia, and also the government of Vossuq ed-Dowleh, considered the dissolution of the Cossack Division to be so urgent a matter: Starosselski and his fellow Russian officers were distrusted. Regardless of the ideological gulf which separated them from the new rulers of Russia, there was nevertheless a real possibility that they might decide that this gulf was transcended by the fact of common nationality and the long tradition of Anglo-Russian rivalry over Persia. It was then March; the Volga would shortly thaw enough for Soviet naval traffic, vastly increasing the risks of an invasion of Persia. In such an event the loyalties of the Cossack leaders would be sorely tried.[83]

The possibility of the Cossack Division's being enlisted by its Russian officers on the Soviet side was, perhaps, an argument for halting its subsidy, but one which cut two ways. It could hardly be dissolved against its wishes except by superior force—an extremely distasteful operation even if clearly superior force were available, and in Persia in 1920 there was no certainty that it was. Therefore, if the subsidy were ended, the Cossacks might *then* go over as a body to the Soviet side, or else operate independently within Persia as brigands living off the land. Thus for the British government the question of what to do with the Cossack Division was by no means easy.

[81] Cox (Tehran) to Curzon, telegram 126, 13 March 1920; *ibid.*, no. 387.
[82] Related in Cox's telegram 126, 13 March, cited above, n. 81.
[83] *Idem.*

It was made no easier by the vacillation of the young Shah. On 3 May, passing through Cairo on his return to Persia after a long sojourn in Europe, he told a British official that he intended to dismiss Starosselski and transfer the Cossacks to British control immediately upon reaching Tehran. He repeated these assurances in Tehran a month later both to the British Minister and to his own Prime Minister, Vossuq ed-Dowleh.[84] But apparently he could not bring himself to take action. Therefore Curzon telegraphed to Norman on 19 June that although the Shah would not dismiss Starosselski, the British government would nevertheless cut off its subsidy to the Cossacks. The Shah and his government would then have to find the necessary funds themselves.[85] That this was a decision impelled by the Treasury's drive for economy rather than by a definite conclusion regarding the risks involved in dealing with the Cossacks was shown by Curzon's subsequent agreement to Norman's proposal that the subsidies should be continued at least for two or three months by means of the postponement by the Imperial Bank of Persia (a London corporation) of the interest payments owed it by the Persian government.[86]

Ironically, at just the time of the British withdrawal from Manjil the Cossack Division began having apparent success against the rebels. After Ironside took command of Norperforce he noted in his diary: "I hear that as our men sulkily withdrew the Persian Cossacks going forward jeered at them. What a thing to happen. . . ."[87] Not only did the Cossacks drive the rebel forces back from Manjil, but in mid-August they occupied Resht as well. These successes, combined with the British withdrawal, made Starosselski—in the words of the British financial adviser to the Persian government, Sydney A. Armitage-Smith—"master of North Persia." If Starosselski did not go over to the enemy, Armitage-Smith observed in a report telegraphed by Norman to Curzon on 11 August, he would be able to pose as the "saviour of Persia," and he went on to note: "Dictatorship exercised by a Russian who regards destruction of work of British

[84] Norman (Cairo) to Curzon, as Allenby's telegram 449, 7 May 1920 (Norman, like the Shah, was also passing through Cairo on his way to Tehran); *ibid.*, no. 418. Norman (Tehran) to Curzon, telegrams 371 and 377, 11 and 13 June 1920; *ibid.*, no. 418, n. 3, and no. 461.
[85] Curzon to Norman (Tehran), telegram 327, 19 June 1920; *ibid.*, no. 471.
[86] Norman (Tehran) to Curzon, telegram 453 part 1, 3 July 1920, and Curzon to Norman, telegram 363, 7 July; *ibid.*, no. 499 and no. 506, n. 5.
[87] Ironside MS diary, entry for 11 October 1920.

Military Mission as only alternative to his own expulsion is not consistent with exercise by His Majesty's Government of a predominant influence in Persia."[88]

The Cossack successes, however, were short-lived. In the words of Armitage-Smith's deputy, their "meteoric advances" were followed by "even more meteoric retirements."[89] Attempting to take Enzeli late in August they were not only repulsed but driven from Resht as well. Resht again fell to them in October, but after only a few days they were once again driven out, scarcely firing a shot as they retreated in panic before a much smaller rebel force. Starosselski was discredited.[90] By this time Ironside had arrived and had taken command of Norperforce; in the Cossack Division's retreat he saw his opportunity once and for all to rid it of its Russian officers.

Ironside arrived in Persia during the first days of October. Passing through Baghdad on his way, he was told by General Sir A. L. Haldane, under whose Mesopotamian command Norperforce operated, that he had been picked for Norperforce because of his reputation as a resourceful leader of isolated, independent forces, and that —unlike his predecessor, Champain—he would be given a free hand.[91] It was a free hand, however, within the narrow limits imposed by the British government's refusal (or inability) to provide any additional troops to reinforce him in the event of a large-scale Soviet invasion of North Persia, and by the expectation that Norperforce would almost certainly be withdrawn in the spring of 1921. These limitations were made clear in a telegram from the War Office to Haldane on 6 October. But the telegram left the problem of coping with Starosselski entirely to Ironside, saying only that its solution would "depend chiefly on Ironside's own personality, tact, and firmness."[92]

Readers of the first two volumes of this study will need no introduction to the six-foot-four-inch, 275-pound Ironside, who command-ed Allied forces in North Russia until their withdrawal in Septem-

---

[88] Norman (Tehran) to Curzon, telegram 571, 11 August 1920; *British Documents*, vol. XIII, no. 539.

[89] Balfour, *Recent Happenings*, p. 201.

[90] Norman (Tehran) to Curzon, telegrams 600 and 703, 29 August and 25 October 1920; *British Documents*, vol. XIII, nos. 544 and 566.

[91] Ironside MS diary, entries for 28 and 29 September 1920.

[92] War Office to Haldane (Baghdad), telegram 86467, 6 October 1920; *British Documents*, vol. XIII, no. 561.

ber 1919. He was a blunt man, and he chose to deal bluntly with Starosselski. His actions are vividly described in his diary and in Norman's telegrams to Curzon. Shortly after his arrival he had been urged by Moshir ed-Dowleh, the Prime Minister, not to interfere with the Cossacks, on the ground that such an extension of British influence would provoke Soviet counteraction.[93] Accordingly he did not, but on 24 October, following the repetition of the Cossacks' frenzied retreat from Resht, he once more came to the capital from Norperforce headquarters at Qazvin. Of this interview with Moshir he wrote in his diary:

... I had gingered up Norman and an ultimatum was delivered by us both as to Staros[selski]. I insisted upon his being recalled, dismissed and called upon to render an account of the money he had spent in the so-called campaign. I told the [Prime] Minister that he had asked me not to interfere and I had refrained, but now the Persian Cossacks had collapsed and we could waste no more money on them.

The wretched man was up against it. He wriggled in his chair like an eel at the end of a line. He said that his head would be chopped off if he went to the Shah and asked for the dismissal of his own special favourite. He suggested other names. Anything to escape. I felt like a bulldog with a small dog cornered in front of me. I was told that to institute British control in the Persian Cossacks now would make the [Anglo-Persian] Agreement impossible. I told him he made no effort to make it possible and that I had no intention of instituting British control. I merely refused to have British money embezzled and wasted by the Russians. ...

The Prime Minister wept and wrung his hands, and short of kneeling at my feet he did everything to attempt [*sic*] me to change. I left him exhausted, but not too impolite to forget the departure coffee. Norman tells me that I frightened him thoroughly and that he will get Starosselski dismissed.[94]

Reporting the same interview to Curzon, Norman was not quite so optimistic, but he emphasized that in his opinion whether or not the Prime Minister would cooperate was no longer a crucial matter: even if Moshir were to resign over the British ultimatum, he said, other Persian politicians could be found who would both dismiss Starosselski and steer the Anglo-Persian Agreement through the

[93] Ironside MS diary, entry for 7 October 1920.
[94] *Ibid.*, entry for 24 October 1920.

Majlis.[95] Thus, when Moshir did in fact resign two days after Ironside's visit, on 26 October, Norman was unperturbed, and advised the Shah to send for Sipahdar-i-Azam, of whose willingness to carry out the British legation's wishes he had already made certain. Norman saw the Shah on both the 26th and 27th, and secured his reluctant agreement to dismiss Starosselski. He would do so against his better judgment, the Shah stated, in order to give proof of his sincere desire to further British policy. Now the British would be his sole support, and he pleaded that they should not abandon him.[96] Meanwhile, Ironside ordered a detachment of his force up into the Manjil Pass behind the withdrawing Cossacks in order to stop the pursuing rebel troops and demonstrate Norperforce's superiority.[97]

Ironside and Norman were anxious that the Shah dismiss Starosselski and order him to leave the country without coming to Tehran, fearing that if he did reach the capital he might cause the Shah to change his mind, and perhaps even to install a government sympathetic to the Russian colonel. Ironside had no means for preventing such a development once the Cossacks reached Tehran—Norperforce was forbidden by its orders from operating in or near the capital. He therefore took the precaution of intercepting the telegraphic communications between the various Cossack detachments. When one message came ordering the Cossacks to evade Norperforce and head for the capital Ironside had it relayed but with a changed place of rendezvous. By this means, on 29 October, the British force was able to meet, disarm, and bring to Qazvin important elements of the Cossack Division, leaving Starosselski, who had succeeded in making his way to Tehran, without effective military support.[98] As soon as he learned that Starosselski had reached the capital Norman sent a message to the Shah, requesting that the Shah should receive the colonel, "reprimand him severely for his disobedience, order him at once to hand over his command to a Persian officer designated to receive it, to return to his house and remain there without seeing anybody, and to leave again for Kasvin tomorrow with same Persian

[95] Norman (Tehran) to Curzon, telegram 703, 25 October 1920; *British Documents*, vol. XIII, no. 566.

[96] Norman (Tehran) to Curzon, telegrams 709 and 710, 26 and 27 October 1920; *ibid.*, nos. 569 and 570.

[97] Ironside MS diary, entry for 27 October 1920; also "situation report" from Ironside to War Office, 6 November (copy included in diary for that date).

[98] Ironside MS diary, entry for 29 October, 1920; also "situation report" of 6 November.

officer under pain of being sent back under arrest."[99] The Shah complied, and the climax was pure melodrama. On 31 October Starosselski strode into Ironside's headquarters in Qazvin. It was their first meeting. Starosselski bowed deeply, saying "I have no arms." And then he said: "I congratulate you, you have won."[100]

❖

Two days previous to this denouement, on 29 October, Curzon had telegraphed to Norman bitterly complaining that the British government had not the "slightest warning" of the events he and Ironside had initiated in Persia, and that they represented a "complete *volte-face*" in British policy. Until only a week before, Curzon said, Norman had asked the Foreign Office, despite its doubts, to believe that "success of British policy in Persia was inseparable from Premiership of Mushir-ud-Dowleh . . . and toleration and support of Starosselski." But now, Curzon continued, "all this is changed, and the leading actors are in course of voluntary or compulsory disappearance from the scene without any previous consultation with His Majesty's Government." And he warned Norman: "In deciding upon new policy in the manner which you have described, and in selection of agents to work it, you will doubtless recognize that General Ironside and yourself have assumed no slight responsibility, which will require the justification of success."[101]

Yet how was one to define "success" in a situation so complex as that of Persia in late 1920? For Curzon the definition was easy: "success" meant the quick ratification of the Anglo-Persian Agreement by the Majlis in order that the agreement—his agreement—might bear its unduly delayed fruits for both countries. Norman,

[99] Norman (Tehran) to Curzon, telegram 716, 29 October 1920; *British Documents*, vol. XIII, no. 574, n. 1.

[100] Ironside MS diary, entry for 31 October 1920. See also Norman (Tehran) to Curzon, telegram 718, 1 November; *British Documents*, vol. XIII, no. 574.

In reply to a question in the House of Commons on November 1920, Cecil Harmsworth, for the Foreign Office, denied that the dismissal of Starosselski was due to any other than Persian internal causes (134 *H.C. Deb.* col. 1519). Contemporary published accounts, however, showed that much was known about the British connection with these events. See Ducrocq, *Revue du Monde Musulman*, vol. LII, pp. 102-03; Balfour, *Recent Happenings*, 203-05; and Lesueur, *Les Anglais en Perse*, p. 67. These have been the basis for subsequent secondary accounts, including Soviet ones, of which the most elaborate is L. I. Miroshnikov, *Angliiskaya expansiya v Irane (1914-1920)* (English Expansion in Iran, 1914-1920), Moscow, 1961, pp. 189-90.

[101] Curzon to Norman (Tehran), telegram 521, 29 October 1920; *British Documents*, vol. XIII, no. 573.

caught between the clear demands of his chief and the murky facts of Persian politics, had a somewhat more complicated notion of "success": recognition that the agreement had by now become such an embarrassment to all concerned that it should probably be re-negotiated, and that in the meantime the British should act independently of the agreement to form the British-led Persian army which had been one of the agreement's principal goals. Such a move would require continued British military presence in Persia. In any case, if the British government held that a communist Persia was a menace to the Empire it would scarcely do to leave Persia defenseless, and thus invite a Soviet takeover, in retaliation for the failure of the Majlis to ratify the agreement.[102]

Yet a third definition of "success" was that of Ironside, who did not have to deal with Curzon. On 24 December 1920 he wrote in his diary:

The more I consider this show the more I think we ought to get out of it. The state of affairs which allows us to be opposed in a state of actual war to a greatly inferior Bolshevik Army, without being allowed to deal with it, is unsatisfactory [a reference to the fact that he was forbidden by the War Office, which feared a greater involvement that might make withdrawal more difficult, from launching an attack on the rebel forces north of Manjil]. The Bolshevik says that he is only helping the would-be Soviet element in Persia while we are helping the old corrupt capitalist system. We cannot complain about his backing Kuchik Khan if we back the Shah. We are both mixing up in the internal politics of Persia. We want a status quo ante and they want a revolution.[103]

"Success," for Ironside, would come from the withdrawal of both sides, Britain and Russia, to enable the Persians to work out their own destiny. But in the confused and anarchic state of Persian politics Ironside's version of success would include one additional element: a military dictatorship which would impose sufficient order on the Persian armed forces to prevent a Soviet invasion. Reflecting on such a prospect in a "situation report" to the War Office on 8 December, he noted: "That would solve many difficulties and enable us to depart in peace and honour."[104]

[102] See Norman (Tehran) to Curzon, telegrams 765, 793, 807, and 809—25 November and 7, 11, and 13 December; *ibid.*, nos. 586, 599, 609, and 611.
[103] Ironside MS diary, entry for 24 December 1920.
[104] A copy of Ironside's report of 8 December 1920 is in his MS diary for that date.

Ironside had a candidate in mind—a Persian colonel who, soon after Starosselski's dismissal, became commander of the Cossack Division. His name was Reza Khan. Later he would be known as Reza Shah Pahlavi. He was to supply the forceful leadership necessary to preserve Persia's independence and prevent any possibility of a Soviet take-over. In so doing he was also to do much to root out the last vestiges of the special role of British men and British money within Persia. It is idle to speculate upon whether or not he would eventually have come to power had Ironside not singled him out; but it is clear that Ironside and his British colleagues were largely instrumental in placing Reza Khan in a position to bring about the *coup d'état* of 21 February 1921 which put effective power into his hands.

For some time after the departure of Starosselski and the other Russians from the Cossack Division it was by no means certain that the force itself would stay in being. Both Ironside and Colonel W.E.R. Dickson, the head of the Anglo-Persian military commission which had sat at Tehran for many months, vainly awaiting the ratification by the Majlis of the Anglo-Persian Agreement in order to begin its planned reorganization of the Persian army, considered the Cossacks too undisciplined, and—with Norman—recommended that the division be disbanded and its Persian officers and men incorporated into the national army.[105] This proposal was ultimately dropped, largely because of London's reluctance to assume financial responsibility for so drastic a reorganization. During November and December both Curzon and Lloyd George made speeches in Parliament implying that since the Persians had not ratified the agreement, they would be left to fend for themselves as Britain disengaged.[106] Curzon made clear to Norman in Tehran that London would pay the costs of a few British officers briefly taking charge of the training and organization of the Cossacks, but of nothing more extensive.[107] Thus—almost by default—the division, minus its Russian cadres, remained in being.

[105] Norman (Tehran), to Curzon, telegram 765, 25 November 1920; *British Documents*, vol. XIII, no. 586.

[106] Curzon's speech was on 16 November 1920 (42 *H.L. Deb.* cols. 276-91); Lloyd George's was on 15 December (136 *H.C. Deb.* cols. 584-85).

[107] Curzon to Norman (Tehran), telegram 560, 19 November 1920; *British Documents*, vol. XIII, no. 584. Curzon reported Cabinet policy: minutes, Cabinet 62(20) 18 November 1920, 11:30 A.M.; Cab. 23/23.

The division was based at Agha Baba, some fifteen miles west of Norperforce headquarters at Qazvin. Thus Ironside was in a position to observe the progress his officers and those of Dickson's military commission were making with the Cossacks. From the outset, he was impressed by Reza Khan. He was not, at first, the division's commander: when Starosselski was dismissed the Shah appointed in his place the senior Persian officer, Sirdar Hamayun. At that time Reza Khan was in command of the Cossack squadron at Tabriz, and he had assumed effective civil leadership of the region as well. His resourcefulness and decisiveness had impressed British officers who knew him, and their favorable comments caused Ironside to single him out from a list of Persian officers on 2 November, before Starosselski and the Russians had even left the country.[108] He was brought to Agha Baba. By the time Ironside went to inspect the division on 14 January 1921 he found that although Hamayun was still nominally in command, Reza Khan (whom Ironside later described as "the most manly Persian" he had met)[109] was "the real life and soul of the show." The Cossacks themselves were being transformed from a ragged, undisciplined collection into an efficient fighting force. On this visit Ironside instructed the British liaison officer with the Cossacks to allow Hamayun to go off "to visit his estates," and to place Reza Khan in acting command. Hamayun was not unhappy to go; under the stringent controls instituted by the British the Cossack commander was no longer able to use his position, as Starosselski had done, for personal enrichment.[110]

By this time Ironside's views of the future role of Reza Khan and the Cossacks had crystallized. He knew that all British forces would be withdrawn from North Persia in April, perhaps even earlier. Although there would be little danger of a real Soviet invasion in force, he felt, the British departure might well be followed by an attempt at internal revolution, helped by an attack on Tehran by rebel forces from Gilan. Unless drastic measures were taken, such a revolution would be likely to succeed. These measures would necessarily include replacement of the "useless" ministers of the Tehran government with sterner men who could command sufficient force to put down rebellion from within and invasion from Gilan. Moreover, because of the unsettling effects such a transformation might have,

---

[108] Ironside MS diary, entry for 2 November 1920.
[109] *Ibid.*, entry for 31 January 1921.   [110] *Ibid.*, entry for 14 January 1921

it should take place while British troops were still in the country to offer a protective screen. They would be able to withdraw afterwards in the knowledge that they were not delivering up Persia to a communist revolution.[111]

Ironside was under no delusion that a military *coup d'état* would not in itself be revolutionary, but his diary makes clear that he viewed such a *coup* primarily as the replacement of one set of nondemocratic elites by another and more desirable set. Moreover he sought to guard against a transformation of Persian society that would be too extreme, and therefore unsettling. In his last conversation with Reza Khan, on 12 February 1921, he told him that Norperforce would not oppose any effort by him to seize power provided that the Shah was not deposed. Reza Khan promised that he would not be.[112]

The conversation on the 12th was the last between the two men because on the 14th Ironside received a telegram summoning him to Baghdad immediately. As he learned on arrival, Churchill had just moved from the War Office to the Colonial Office, and he had called together a conference at Cairo of British officers and officials from all over the Middle East to discuss the future of the Arab world. Ironside was among those summoned. Before leaving Persia he went to Tehran to try to persuade the Shah to bring Reza Khan to a position of power. The Shah refused.[113]

Ironside's talk with the Shah took place on 15 February. Six days later, before dawn on the 21st, Reza Khan entered Tehran at the head of a column of 3,000 Cossacks. Only one police post attempted to offer resistance. When it did so the Cossacks opened fire and killed seven of the defenders. Quickly the Cossacks established control of the capital and of all government ministries. Before their entry, while they were still outside the town, representatives of the Shah and the Cabinet had gone to meet them in order to ascertain their purposes and, if possible, to dissuade them from entering. Reza Khan's reply, telegraphed to Curzon by Norman, was one whose substance would be repeated on many continents as the twentieth century unfolded:

Riza Khan said that Cossacks who had had experience of Bolsheviks

[111] *Ibid.*, entries for 14 and 19 January 1921.
[112] *Ibid.*, entry for 12 February 1921.
[113] *Ibid.*, entries for 14 and 15 February 1921. The Cairo conference is the subject of Aaron S. Klieman, *Foundations of British Policy in the Arab World: The Cairo Conference of 1921*, Baltimore, 1970.

and knew what they were, were tired of seeing one inefficient Government succeed another at Tehran where apparently nobody was making any preparations to oppose Bolshevik advance which would follow withdrawal of British troops. They were therefore coming to Tehran to establish strong Government which would see to this matter. They professed loyalty and devotion to the Shah, but were determined to set aside the evil counsellors by whom he had been surrounded. They also professed goodwill to us and said that no foreigners had anything to fear.[114]

Ironside, of course, was scarcely surprised when news of the *coup* reached him in Baghdad just before his departure for Cairo. Entering the reports in his diary he commented, "So far so good." And he added: "I fancy that all the people think that I engineered the coup d'état. I suppose I did, strictly speaking."[115]

❖

Reza Khan—whom Norman described to Curzon on 3 March as "an honest and capable officer without political ambitions"[116]—did

[114] Norman (Tehran) to Curzon, telegram 121, 21 February 1921; *British Documents*, vol. XIII, no. 681. There is no indication in any of Norman's reports (published or in Foreign Office files) that he had any foreknowledge of Reza Khan's *coup d'état*. This is not surprising: repeated entries in Ironside's diary show that he had no high regard for Norman and, in particular, that he felt the British Legation in Tehran was dangerously lax in its security procedures.
Two Foreign Office minutes on the above telegram are worth quoting. Lancelot Oliphant remarked on 22 February that the news was "astounding," and added: "This large body of men cannot have passed through or near Kasvin without General Ironside having some inkling of their presence." To which, on the same day, Curzon added: "Mr. Norman has at last found a worthy rival in the art of creating Persian Governments and Prime Ministers." (file E 2386/2/34, F.O. 371/6401).
[115] Ironside MS diary, entry for 23 February 1921. There is no evidence in War Office files I have seen that Ironside ever, at least for the record, revealed his own involvement in the events bringing Reza Khan to power. On at least one occasion—passing through Baghdad immediately after the *coup*—he commented on its circumstances in a manner which gave no hint that he himself had had anything to do with them. (Haldane to War Office, telegram X/1577, 23 February 1921, W.O. 95/4969). After the Cairo conference Ironside did not return to Persia; because the departure of Norperforce, beginning in April, was so imminent, he was assigned instead to command British fighting units in Mesopotamia.
The present account is the first to treat specifically the degree of British involvement in Reza Khan's *coup d'état*. Previous accounts have been only vaguely circumstantial. See F.A.C. Forbes-Leith, *Checkmate: Fighting Tradition in Central Persia*, London, 1927, pp. 78-79; Lesueur, *Les Anglais en Perse*, pp. 148-59; Arfa, *Five Shahs*, pp. 106-13; Ducrocq, *Revue du Monde Musulman*, vol. LII, p. 107; and O. S. Melikov, *Ustanovleniye diktatury Reza-Shakha v Irane* (The Establishment of the Dictatorship of Reza Shah in Iran), Moscow, 1961, pp. 25-26.
[116] Norman (Tehran) to Curzon, despatch 29, 3 March 1921; cited in *British Documents*, vol. XIII, no. 681, n. 1.

not take the office of Prime Minister for himself. Ironside had exaggerated the strength of Reza Khan's position in early 1921. He had no political base, and his leadership of the Cossacks was an insufficient platform from which to seize titular control. Therefore he allied himself with Sayyed Zia al-Din Tabataba'i, the liberal, reformist editor of an influential Tehran newspaper. Sayyed Zia became Prime Minister following the *coup*, Reza Khan taking only the post of commander in chief of the armed forces.[117] It was quickly apparent, however, that Reza Khan retained a predominant power which steadily increased with the passage of time. The alliance with Sayyed Zia was short-lived. A new Prime Minister, this time Reza Khan's choice, took office in mid-May, Reza Khan having already made himself War Minister as well as commander in chief. In 1923 he took the premiership for himself, and two years later he overthrew the Shah and proclaimed himself successor. The journey he had begun at Agha Baba in November 1920 was complete. Ironside had misread only the timetable, not the destination.

All this lay in the future, in the sphere of Persian domestic politics. Our concern is with the effects of Reza Khan's *coup d'état* on the British-Persian-Soviet relationship at the time when Anglo-Soviet relations were fast approaching the watershed marked by the Trade Agreement of 16 March 1921—scarcely three weeks following the march of the Cossacks into Tehran. Immediately after coming into office the government of Sayyed Zia took two steps which indicated just how much the position of Persia in the context of the Anglo-Russian rivalry had changed: the Prime Minister issued a statement formally denouncing the Anglo-Persian Agreement of

---

[117] Melikov, *Ustanovleniye diktatury Reza-Shakha*, p. 25, citing a Persian source, contends that the British in Persia aimed at placing not Reza Khan but Sayyed Zia in power, because of Sayyed Zia's liberalism and pro-British sentiments, and that they viewed Reza Khan's coup only as a means to that end. Ironside's diary, which does not even mention Sayyed Zia, makes clear that for him at least this supposition is erroneous.

In the Foreign Office, interestingly enough, Sayyed Zia was *blamed* for the *coup*. Thus on 22 February 1921 C. P. Churchill, of the Eastern Department, minuted on the file cited above, n./114: "The whole thing is evidently the result of a plot and Sayyed Zia-ed-Din, the probable new Prime Minister, is no doubt at the bottom of it." And on 3 March, Norman urged London not to be hard on the new regime, stating: "New Prime Minister is the first who has ever seriously attempted to introduce reforms and thus put Persia in a position to help herself, and I trust fact that he has attained office by somewhat drastic methods will not prejudice His Majesty's Government against him." (telegram 135, file E 2883/2/34, F.O. 371/6401).

August 1919, and at the same time he directed the Persian diplomatic representative in Moscow to sign a treaty between the Persian and Soviet governments.[118]

Neither step was a new departure. Each simply gave formal status to an already existing state of affairs. That the Anglo-Persian Agreement had long been moribund was well known in London as well as in Tehran. By denouncing it, however, the Persian government gave notice that the old client relationship was not only no longer acceptable, but not even discussable. Similarly, it was well known that secret Persian-Soviet negotiations had been under way in Moscow since the preceding summer; the Foreign Office had intercepted the telegraphic traffic between the Persian negotiator and Tehran, and in late December the Persian Prime Minister even gave Norman a copy of the draft then under negotiation.[119] Thus the treaty's signature on 26 February 1921 by the new government of Sayyed Zia, only five days after it came to power, was no surprise. The importance to London of the Soviet-Persian treaty, like that of the denunciation of the Anglo-Persian Agreement, lay not in its terms but in its indication of the nationalistic, independent course that Persia would thenceforth pursue.

The Soviet-Persian treaty was a simple and straightforward document. Much of it was devoted to reiteration of various previous Soviet declarations renouncing every vestige of the special position in Persia that had been occupied by the Tsarist government and by private Russian citizens, with the understanding that the renounced concessions should remain the property of the Persian people and not be transferred to any foreign power. In addition there was a mutual pledge, by then customary in Soviet treaties, of non-interference in the internal affairs of the other party. Finally, in exchange for these Soviet renunciations, the Persians conceded one vital right: in the event that a third party should "attempt to carry out a policy of usurpation by means of armed intervention in Persia, or if such a Power should desire to use Persian territory as a base of operations

[118] Norman (Tehran) to Curzon, telegrams 125 and 132, 26 and 28 February 1921; *British Documents*, vol. XIII, nos. 683 and 686. The text of the Persian-Soviet treaty of 26 February 1921 is printed in *Dokumenty vneshnei politiki*, pp. 536-44; an English translation is in Fatemi, *Diplomatic History*, pp. 317-35.
[119] The texts of the Persian telegrams are in file E—/2/34, F.O. 371/6399-6402. For the draft given to Norman, see his telegram 833 to Curzon, 27 December 1920; *British Documents*, vol. XIII, no. 621.

against Russia," and if the Persians themselves were not strong enough to prevent it, then "Russia shall have the right to advance her troops into the Persian interior for the purpose of carrying out military operations necessary for its defense." These troops would be withdrawn as soon as the danger to Russia had been removed from Persia. This clause was, of course, aimed directly at Great Britain. Moreover it furnished a justification for the continued presence of Soviet forces in Gilan. Yet it was eventually to be formally invoked not against the British, but against Germany in the Second World War.

We have seen that during the summer of 1920 Curzon viewed the prospect of direct Persian-Soviet relations with strong dismay, despite the British government's evident lack of ability to dislodge the communist regime from Gilan. During the winter of 1920-21 he was scarcely more enthusiastic—on one occasion he instructed Norman to warn the Persians that London would not tolerate an agreement between Persia and any other country which would infringe upon British rights and interests[120]—but he did reluctantly concede that the negotiations between Tehran and Moscow just might forestall a Soviet invasion immediately on the heels of a British withdrawal. Yet even here he added: "But prospects of this must be so attractive to Russians that they could hardly be expected to forgo the occasion."[121] And he went on to suggest that the Shah and his government should perhaps consider the possibility of abandoning Tehran and northern Persia to the communists and establishing a rump state, consisting of the central and southern parts of the country, with its capital at Isfahan or Shiraz. Shiraz, near the Gulf, was the base of the British-led South Persia Rifles (to whose support, however the British government had, as a result of Persian failure to ratify the Anglo-Persian Agreement, decided to stop contributing);[122] the southern region, moreover, was the center of British

[120] Curzon to Norman (Tehran), telegram 586, 8 December 1920; *British Documents*, vol. XIII, no. 602.

[121] Curzon to Norman (Tehran), telegram 5, 3 January 1921; *ibid.*, no. 628.

[122] Curzon informed Norman on 19 November 1920 (telegram 560; *ibid.*, no. 584) that the necessity to reduce expenditures would mean that British support of the South Persia Rifles would have to cease by the end of the year unless the Majlis were to ratify the Anglo-Persian Agreement. Curzon eventually succeeded in getting the Cabinet to agree to an extension until 31 March 1921, but since the Persian government would not commit itself to taking on the burden of support after that date, the British government decided to withdraw its officers and n.c.o.'s

interests and investments in Persia, particularly the great petroleum fields.

These apprehensions—expressed by Curzon in January 1921, before Reza Khan's coup—were shared by Foreign Office officials who dealt with Persian affairs,[123] as well as by Norman in Tehran. So certain was he that a Soviet invasion would follow the withdrawal of British forces that in early January he called a meeting of European residents of the capital to discuss arrangements for the immediate evacuation of women and children. Norman's panic annoyed the European residents, frightened the timid Shah, and scarcely added to British prestige among the Persians. Even Curzon felt moved privately to telegraph his minister that he seemed to be acting a trifle precipitately.[124]

Within the councils of the British Empire the staunchest proponents of more optimistic views were those whose direct responsibility was the governing of India. We have already seen something of their views in the general discussion of British Eastern policies at the outset of the preceding chapter. Expressed in a series of telegrams from the Viceroy, Lord Chelmsford, to Edwin Montagu, the Secretary of State for India, during December 1920 and January 1921, they are worth elaboration here.[125] Their essence was that Great Britain should disengage and leave Persia "to work out her own salvation," providing at the very most only discreet financial advice. They were based upon the premise that "any policy involving direct financial or military assistance on our part must inevitably prevent growth of that nationalist spirit, which is, in the long run, our real defence against incursion of Bolshevism."

Thus the Government of India advised that London should renounce the Anglo-Persian Agreement before the Persians did so themselves. And despite the fact that Persia would not "be able, in our lifetime, to raise an Army fit to oppose an external enemy," the

then. (Curzon to Norman [Tehran], telegrams 44 and 67, 22 January and 8 February 1921; *ibid.*, nos. 661 and 671).

[123] See the memorandum by G. P. Churchill, 20 December 1920; *ibid.*, no. 616.

[124] Norman (Tehran) to Curzon, telegram 17, 8 January 1921; *ibid.*, no. 640. Curzon to Norman, unnumbered telegram, 21 January; *ibid.*, no. 660. See also Balfour, *Recent Happenings*, pp. 209-12, and Lesueur, *Les Anglais en Perse*, pp. 150-51.

[125] These telegrams from Chelmsford to Montagu included nos. 1393S (6 December 1920), 23 S (5 January 1921), and 107 S (22 January); *British Documents*, vol. XIII, nos. 624, n. 3 (full version: Cabinet paper C.P. 2263, Cab. 24/115), 634, and 662.

British government should nevertheless give up all responsibility for supporting or officering the Cossack Division and the South Persia Rifles. As soon as the Persians realized that they would have to defend their country themselves, they would "make shift" with their "own Oriental methods of diplomacy." Britain's "disappearance into the background" would "rob Bolshevism of her one valid excuse, and possibly remove temptation for open aggression."

In any case, to the Government of India open Soviet aggression against Persia seemed a remote prospect. There was no reason to think that the forthcoming signature of a treaty between Moscow and Tehran would be merely a prelude to a Bolshevik invasion. On the contrary, the treaty proposals put forward by the Russians seemed "peculiarly shrewd, devised to undermine our position, and to further their main end in Persia, viz., internal rupture under the influence of Bolshevik propaganda." For this purpose Moscow's "ostentatious abnegation" of Tsarist rights and privileges in Persia was designed to contrast with London's general attitude and specific demands under the Anglo-Persian Agreement: British policy in Persia could be portrayed throughout the Moslem world as "another example of Britain's crushing of Islam," thus providing Moscow with devastating propaganda which could be effectively countered only by a similar British renunciation. The Government of India was also strongly opposed to any scheme to remove the Shah's government from Tehran and establish it at Isfahan or Shiraz: such a move would not only make certain the sovietization of the whole of northern Persia, but it would also appear simply as a British-inspired effort to assure continued British domination of the south. Instead, the Persian government should be encouraged to remain in Tehran and "gamble on sincerity of Bolshevik assurance that they will not invade Persia in the event of our withdrawal."

This was the sort of advice Curzon did not want to hear, and he dismissed it by noting that the Government of India had opposed the Anglo-Persian Agreement from the outset.[126] Yet like it or not, the British government was driven by events along the course the Viceroy had recommended. Sayyed Zia's denunciation of the agreement finally disposed of that emotion-laden issue. The new Prime Minister was a warm friend of Great Britain, however, and for a while after his coming to power it appeared as if many of the arrangements prescribed under the agreement would come about even

---

[126] In a minute on 29 January 1921, cited in *ibid.*, no. 662, n. 7.

in its absence. British experts unobtrusively went to work in the Persian treasury, and a scheme was worked out for British officers retained by the Persian government to continue to lead the South Persia Rifles, the force itself being nominally incorporated into the gendarmerie in order to deprive the Russians of a pretext for complaining about British control of the Persian Army.[127] Sayyed Zia did not last long enough, however, to bring any of these plans to fruition. As we have seen, the government which followed his in May 1921 was firmly under the sway of Reza Khan, who had no love for Great Britain despite the role British officers had played in bringing him to power. By September the British civil and military officers who had been retained under Sayyed Zia had all been dismissed.[128]

Yet Reza Khan's *coup d'état* was the first step in the strengthening of just those forces of nationalism within Persia to which the government of India had looked as the only effective bulwark against a communist revolution. Reza Khan was to Persia what Kemal was to Turkey. His accession marked the beginning of a rapid decline of British influence in Persia, a decline which reached its nadir in 1951: Dr. Mussadiq only completed, in rather more precipitate a manner, a process Reza Shah had initiated three decades previously. Like Kemal, however, Reza was even more concerned about the danger posed by his Soviet neighbor to the north. In one of his telegrams to London during January 1921 Lord Chelmsford had warned that the combination of Bolshevik propaganda and British policy in Persia had done much to reverse the notion, traditional in Persia and throughout the Moslem world, that Britain was a friend and Russia an enemy.[129] For Reza Shah, however, Britain was merely untrustworthy, while Russia, because of proximity, was threatening. The policies he pursued in the course of his reign took this distinction into account. Although the Persia over which he ruled was far removed from the client state which Curzon had hoped to obtain under the agreement of 1919, Curzon's successors, eyeing their far-flung Middle Eastern responsibilities, more than once had reason to be grateful to him.

[127] These arrangements are described in the following telegrams: Norman (Tehran) to Curzon, nos. 130 (26 February 1921), 150 (10 March), 192 (31 March); Curzon to Norman, nos. 117 (14 March) and 123 (17 March); *ibid.*, nos. 685, 694, 696, 700.
[128] Balfour, *Recent Happenings*, pp. 254-80.
[129] No. 107 S of 22 January 1921, cited above, n. 125.

PART FOUR

The Anglo-Soviet Accord

CHAPTER X

THE TRADE AGREEMENT

Our purpose at present is to arrange a trade agreement with England and to start regular trade, so as to be able to purchase as soon as possible the machinery required . . . to reestablish our national economy. . . .

We do not for a moment believe in lasting trade relations with the imperialist powers; what we shall obtain will be simply a breathing space.

—Lenin at the Eighth Congress of Soviets of the R.S.F.S.R., December 1920.

We must boldly conclude an agreement and naturally be prepared for a further struggle, since no treaties will save us from a struggle until communism is victorious in the West.

—Krasin in a telegram to Chicherin, 30 December 1920[1]

There is a great change in Russia itself; there is a change from the wild extravagant Communism of a year or two ago, or even a few months ago . . . a complete change in the attitude of the Bolshevik Government to what is called capitalism, towards private enterprise, towards communal effort, towards nationalisation.

—Lloyd George to the House of Commons, 22 March 1921.

IN the Curzon papers, formerly at Kedleston, now at the India Office Library, is a sheaf of jottings in Curzon's own hand on Foreign Office notepaper, headed "List of LG interference with or going behind back of FO." The list is a long one, but written more forcibly and underlined with more strokes than any other entry is "R Trade Agreement." Another entry, inscribed with only slightly less vehemence, is "Krassin."[2]

[1] Telegrams 1871-72; intercept 005132, Lloyd George MSS, file F/203/1/11.
[2] Curzon MSS, Box Z.

There was justice in Curzon's complaint, but the grievance was one endemic to his job. Few of his successors (or predecessors) as Secretary of State for Foreign Affairs had quite so thin a skin, or quite so easily injured a sense of *amour propre*. But all of them, had they been so inclined, could have compiled a list of instances in which the Prime Minister they served "interfered with or went behind the back of" the Foreign Office. So could every American Secretary of State and—with even more justice—every Soviet Commissar for Foreign Affairs.

Yet prime ministers, presidents, and Soviet chairmen have their justified complaints, too. Lloyd George did not keep a list of instances when Curzon and the permanent officials of the Foreign Office tried to impede what he sought to accomplish. Had he done so, the Russian Trade Agreement would surely have been high upon it. It would have been high, as well, on a list of the Prime Minister's complaints against the War Office, the Admiralty, and the Treasury. Such lists, however, are the product of frustration, and therefore Lloyd George had no need for them: more often than not he got what he wanted, despite the opposition of senior bureaucrats and well-placed politicians. And he wanted, and got, the trade agreement with Moscow.

The trade agreement, and a consequent normalization of relations between London and Moscow, had been a principal purpose for the Prime Minister throughout 1920. The Polish-Soviet war had been an obstacle, as, indeed, had been Kamenev's duplicitous behavior during the tense August days. But September had brought the consolidation of Poland's victory and Kamenev's expulsion from the United Kingdom, the former to Lloyd George's undoubted relief, the latter to the gratification of his colleagues and perhaps also—the Prime Minister's outrage at his climactic 10 September meeting with Kamenev was surely unfeigned—of himself as well: a wrong now righted, a slate wiped (more or less) clean. Thus, on 10 September, even as he moved to expel Kamenev, the Soviet "political" representative, he sought to reassure Krasin, the "trade" representative, that now that the "Polish episode" was finished, negotiations between their two governments might be resumed.

With his own Cabinet Lloyd George could not be quite so direct. At least three of his principal colleagues—Curzon, Churchill, and Walter Long—were eager to expel not only Kamenev but all the rest of the Soviet mission in London, including Krasin, thus putting an end to the negotiations.[3] Since he could not get their approval, Lloyd George worked instead to limit the potential damage of their stated opposition. Thus he carefully kept the lines from being drawn in Cabinet meetings, but only at the cost of delay: on 30 September and again on 12 October the Cabinet agreed to postpone any decision on whether or not to proceed with the negotiation of a trade agreement.[4] Not until mid-November did the Prime Minister feel confident enough of his position to draw the issue to a head.

❖

It is worth recalling at this point that the discussions between Lloyd George and Krasin during May and June had already produced an agreed-upon basis for an Anglo-Soviet accord. This was contained in the British note of 30 June and Chicherin's answering telegram of 7 July. The note, summarized at length above,[5] listed four conditions which had to be fulfilled before trade could begin. They were, briefly: 1) a mutual undertaking to refrain from any interference in the internal affairs of the other, including, in particular, Soviet attempts to encourage the peoples of Asia in action hostile to the interests of the British Empire; 2) immediate exchange of all remaining prisoners; 3) recognition "in principle" by the Soviet government that it was "liable to pay compensation to private citizens who have supplied goods or services to Russia for which they have not been paid"—with, however, the determination of these liabilities, and the settlement of "other questions relating to debts or claims by Great Britain on Russia or by Russia on Great Britain" (including the amounts, much larger than British private claims, owed to the British government by previous Russian governments) left for a later formal peace conference; and 4) the mutual granting of trade facilities with the provision that each government could exclude agents of the other *non grata* to itself.

Chicherin's telegram of 7 July accepted these "principles" as the basis for an agreement between the two governments, the agreement

---

[3] So each of them wrote in memoranda to the Cabinet. See Curzon's "Krassin and Klishko," Cabinet paper C.P. 1897, 16 September 1920, Cab. 24/111; Churchill's "Krassin and Klishko," Cabinet paper C.P. 1898, 21 September, *idem*; and Long's untitled Cabinet paper C.P. 1909, 30 September, Cab. 24/112.

[4] Minutes, Cabinet 53(20), 30 September 1920, noon, and Cabinet 54(20), 12 October, 11:30 A.M.; Cab. 23/22.

[5] See above, chap. III, n. 68.

to be the subject of negotiations which, he insisted, were to begin without delay.[6] Of course, no immediate negotiations took place. This was one price which the Soviet regime had to pay for refusing to halt the Red Army's march on Warsaw. It was not a high price however: when the British Cabinet at its meeting on 30 September agreed to postpone any decision on whether or not to reopen trade negotiations, it also agreed that a stiff note, cast in the language of an ultimatum, should be sent to Moscow. But precisely because it was cast in such language, it held out the hope that compliance with its terms would lead to the renewal of negotiations.

Despatched to Chicherin the next day over Curzon's signature, the note referred to the Anglo-Soviet "agreement" of 30 June–7 July, and called particular attention to the British conditions regarding subversion and propaganda and the exchange of prisoners. "These conditions have been and are being flagrantly violated," it said. Not only had Kamenev, while in England, "engaged in almost open propaganda, and attempted to subsidise a campaign . . . against the British Constitution and British institutions," but the recent congresses at Moscow of the Communist International and at Baku of the Peoples of the East had given ample evidence of the anti-British purposes of the Soviet Communist Party, and therefore of the Soviet government. Furthermore, despite Soviet assurances, British subjects continued "to languish in Russian gaols," or were refused permission to leave the country. The British government still hoped to arrive at a commercial agreement with the Soviet government. However, it looked upon such an agreement as a first step not merely to commercial prosperity but also to a genuine normalization of relations. It therefore had to know whether or not the Russians were prepared to live up to their side of the understanding of 30 June–7 July. In any case, the note asserted, "the consistent violation of these conditions can no longer be permitted."[7]

The bulk of Curzon's note of 1 October was devoted not to Soviet subversion and propaganda, but to the continued detention on Soviet territory of British subjects—a matter on which the Cabinet could unite in outrage regardless of how other Russian issues divided it.

---

[6] Chicherin's telegram is cited above, chap. IV, n. 18.
[7] The text was published in the *Daily Herald*, 8 October 1920, and the *Daily Telegraph*, 11 October.

Until all such prisoners had been freed and allowed to leave, Curzon said, the British government could not sign a trade agreement. Indeed—and here was Lloyd George's concession to Curzon, Churchill, and their allies—it could not even carry on further negotiations for an agreement. During the next several weeks the diplomatic correspondence between London and Moscow was almost entirely taken up with the question of prisoners, and the other matters dividing the two governments were not seriously discussed again until it was disposed of. If we should digress here to examine this problem, it is because the participants in these events also did so.

The exchange of prisoners, with the exception of those guilty of "grave offenses," had been provided for, it will be recalled, by the O'Grady-Litvinov agreement signed in Copenhagen in February 1920.[8] Within the following few months 124 British prisoners of war and 727 civilians arrived in England from Russia, and all Russian prisoners actually in the United Kingdom, plus a good many more from various points in Western Europe—some several thousand in all—had been repatriated.[9] However, by the summer of 1920 there still remained 109 Russians, originally imprisoned by the Turks, at a camp in Egypt, and a few others in Canada, Turkey, and India, for whom the British government was in the process of making transportation arrangements.[10] These Russians were thus distinguished from a number of British subjects still on Soviet territory for whom, so it seemed in London, nothing was being done. Some fifteen members of a military railway mission captured in Siberia in January 1920 were known to be held in Moscow. An unknown number of civilians, thought to be at least one hundred (some classified as "grave offenders") were reportedly detained at Moscow, Petrograd,

---

[8] See Volume II, p. 343.

[9] So stated Curzon's note to Chicherin of 1 October 1920, cited above, n. 7. For the repatriation of Russian prisoners from Western Europe, see *British Documents*, vol. XII, no. 738, n. 4.

[10] Lord Allenby, British High Commissioner in Egypt, reported in telegram 570, 12 June 1920, that there were 109 Russians at El Qantara (*ibid.*, no. 791). In a note to Chicherin on 9 October (text in *The Times*, 11 October) Curzon placed this figure at 129 and said that there were fourteen Russian prisoners in Canada. And according to a statement by Churchill in Parliament on 15 June (130 *H.C. Deb.*, col. 1052) there were eleven Russians held by the British military authorities in Turkey. On the other hand, both Bonar Law and Lloyd George referred in Parliament (26 and 28 October 1920; 133 *H.C. Deb.*, cols. 1519 and 1965) to the forthcoming repatriation of 300 Russian prisoners who had been detained in Egypt and Constantinople. Possibly these 300 included some held by others than the British.

Vologda, and at other towns.[11] Overshadowing all these, however, were some sixty-two prisoners held at Baku. Curzon, in his note of 1 October, described their plight as "even more painful" than that of all the others, and in the eyes of both the British government and public the Baku captives came to stand for all the rest.

At the outset they numbered not sixty-two but thirty-two, five naval officers and twenty-seven ratings, who arrived on 28 April 1920 at the Baku railway station *en route* from Constantinople, via Batum, to the Persian port of Enzeli. The mission for which they had volunteered was to take charge of the remaining vessels of Denikin's Caspian fleet and to mount their naval guns ashore in order to defend Enzeli against a possible Soviet invasion—the invasion which in fact occurred only three weeks later. Their arrival in Baku coincided with that of the Red Army, then in the process of making Azerbaijan the first Soviet Republic in Transcaucasia. The coincidence was most unfortunate: wholly ignorant of the political transformation which had occurred, the British naval party stepped from their train into arrest and captivity.[12] During the next few days they were joined by twenty other British subjects—a military mission of three officers and eight other ranks who had been stationed in Baku, and nine civilians, including the vice-consul and one woman, the Russian wife of the orderly to one of the officers.

All of them were herded into one small, earthen-floored, verminous room of the Baku Central Prison—a building which had been designed for 800 inmates but which in the aftermath of the communist takeover contained nearly 6,000. As time passed additional

---

[11] Information regarding British prisoners remaining on Soviet territory was very difficult to obtain, due to Soviet professed inability—or reluctance—to furnish it. Curzon summarized what information there was in his note to Chicherin of 9 October 1920 (cited above, n. 10). The category of "grave offenders" was discussed by Curzon and Lloyd George with Krasin in their conversation of 7 June 1920 (*British Documents*, vol. VIII, no. 25, pp. 299-301). The conditions under which British—and other, including Russian—prisoners were held in Russia was the subject of a report by a special committee appointed by Curzon in May 1920 (see below, n. 97). The committee noted that "the terrible experiences of British subjects during imprisonment in Russia . . . were not, so far as we can discover, nearly so severe as those of the Russians themselves. They also appear to have undergone less privations than other foreigners." Cmd. 1041 (Miscellaneous No. 13 [1920]), *Interim Report of the Committee to Collect Information on Russia*, 4 November 1920, p. 2. Two of the British prisoners of war captured in Siberia have left memoirs: Francis McCullagh, *A Prisoner of the Reds: The Story of a British Officer Captured in Siberia*, London, 1921, and L. E. Vining, *Held by the Bolsheviks; the Diary of a British Officer in Siberia, 1919-20*, London, 1924.

[12] See Luke, *Cities and Men*, vol. II, pp. 104, 138-39, 184.

British subjects were placed with these fifty-two (for a few days even a hapless businessman and his wife and two children in transit from Persia) until at the time of their release they numbered sixty-two. During much of their internment they were given little food—for some periods none—and allowed no exercise or contact with the outside world. In August, after repeated representations from London, they were transferred from the Central Prison to a private house where conditions were not much better.[13] Finally they were freed in early November. All had survived, but their ordeal constituted a vexing chapter in the developing Anglo-Soviet relationship.

Of all the British subjects in Soviet hands, those at Baku received much the most notice by the British public. Vivid and, as it turned out, not grossly exaggerated accounts of the conditions under which they were held circulated both in the press and in Parliament, and the cell in which they were incarcerated quickly became known as the "Black Hole of Baku."[14] The fact of their continued confinement, despite a stream of protests from London, was repeatedly held up a symbol of the folly of attempting to reach an accord with the Bolshevik regime.[15] This public attention to the plight of the Baku captives had as a consequence a similar focus of concern on the part of the government. Temporarily, at least, the other British prisoners were thrust into the background: the whole issue became, in effect, that of the prisoners at Baku.

For Lloyd George, it was preposterous, and politically very awkward, that long after the signature of the O'Grady-Litvinov agree-

[13] For the conditions under which the captives were imprisoned, see *ibid.*, pp. 184-94, and a letter from one of them, Captain W. J. Cowen, who escaped, in *The Times*, 3 August 1920. See also Luke's telegram 277 to Curzon from Tiflis, 8 June 1920, reporting the account of Dr. Alshibaya, the Georgian diplomatic representative at Baku, in whose care Luke had entrusted British interests in Azerbaijan; *British Documents*, vol. XII, no. 575. And see the "Foreign Office Memorandum on British Prisoners at Baku," 27 July 1920; *ibid.*, no. 744. On 1, 2, and 3 December 1920, just after the prisoners had reached England, *The Times* carried long interviews with them about their captivity, and printed excerpts from the prison diary of one naval gunner.

[14] See, *e.g.*, headlines in the *Daily Mail*, 26 and 27 July 1920.

[15] It is an index of the extraordinary popular concern over the Baku prisoners that questions about them were asked on twenty-seven of the fifty-nine days on which the House of Commons sat between 13 May 1920, when the plight of the prisoners first became generally known, and 21 August, when the House rose for the long summer recess. A typical reaction was that of a retired Brigadier General (J. Wilfred-Stirling), a letter from whom, in *The Times* of 6 October 1920, asked: "Is England so effete, is the power of the Empire so feeble, that her citizens can with impunity be imprisoned in black holes, starved, and insulted without redress?"

ment and at a time when his government was entering into trade negotiations with Moscow, British subject should still be detained on Soviet soil. Thus, during his first talk with Krasin in London on 31 May the Prime Minister dismissed the question of prisoners as "really quite a small matter," but at the same time he made it clear that the issue was one on which the British press and public had very strong feelings; therefore, until all the British prisoners were repatriated his government could not enter into further negotiations.[16] Yet Lloyd George drew back from making this threat real. Just two months later, indeed, Curzon was to write to Bonar Law: "you ought to know . . . that on 2 occasions at least when I have taken or attempted to take stronger action to get these poor devils released I have been stopped by the PM for fear of imperilling his negotiations w[ith] Krassin."[17]

If the Baku prisoners were an embarrassment to Lloyd George, they seem to have been somewhat the same for the Soviet government. In a series of messages to London during July, Chicherin and Litvinov insisted that the prisoners were in Azerbaijani, not Russian, hands and that the matter was therefore one to be settled by direct negotiations between the governments of Great Britain and the Soviet Republic of Azerbaijan. The latter, they insisted, was a sovereign government, and they emphatically rejected the notion that international undertakings entered into by the R.S.F.S.R., such as the O'Grady-Litvinov Agreement, should be binding upon any other Soviet Republics. Neither was the government of the R.S.F.S.R. under any *obligation* to take steps to force the hands of the governments of the other Republics. Nevertheless, Chicherin said in messages on 19 and 28 July, if the British government would make a direct request of the Azerbaijani government, the Russian government would "pave the way" for it. And Litvinov—who, after all, had negotiated and signed the February agreement on prisoner exchange, and who therefore must surely have felt some kind of personal stake involved—similarly assured the British Chargé d'Affaires in Copenhagen that Moscow would support "any demand" London might make directly to the communist regime in Baku.[18]

[16] *British Documents*, vol. VIII, no. 24, pp. 287-88.
[17] Letter, Curzon to Bonar Law, 26 July 1920; Bonar Law MSS, file 99/3/22.
[18] These communications were the following: letter, Litvinov to British Chargé d'Affaires, Copenhagen, 14 July, summarized in the Foreign Office memorandum of 27 July cited above n. 12; telegram, Chicherin to Curzon, 19 July, summarized in

From Lloyd George's government there were three separate reactions to these contentions that Baku was independent of Moscow—one for the Russians, one for the British public, and one for the Azerbaijanis. For the Russians, the reaction was sharp rejection; as a note to Litvinov on 21 July stated, "the information in His Majesty's Government's possession" was "to the effect that all power in the Azerbaijan Republic was in the hands of the Commander of the 11th Army, subject to the Supreme Control of the Moscow Soviet, who are represented there by a Commissar."[19] And in a telegram to Chicherin a week later Curzon bluntly stated: "I am convinced that a word from Moscow Government is all that is required to set these persons free and I must urgently request that this be done without further delay. Public opinion in this country will not tolerate further procrastination."[20] To emphasize to Moscow this British concern, Curzon had previously suspended the repatriation of the Russians at the camp in Egypt, and he ordered the detention (and, for a brief period, the imprisonment) of six agitators, arrested in India as "Bolsheviks," who had arrived in England in the course of being deported to Russia.[21]

But to insure that British public opinion would, in fact, "tolerate further procrastination" and not react in such a manner as to make further negotiations with the Soviet regime politically impossible, Lloyd George publicly took quite a different line. On the very day on which Curzon sent the telegram quoted above, the Prime Minister rose in the House of Commons and, in response to questioners who contended that Baku was simply the puppet of Moscow, he asserted:

---

idem; telegram from Chicherin to Curzon, relayed by British consulate, Reval, 28 July, *British Documents*, vol. XII, no. 745; telegram, Chicherin to Curzon, 31 July, *ibid.*, no. 749; statement, Litvinov to British Chargé, Copenhagen, reported in latter's telegram 654, 31 July, *ibid.*, no. 753, n. 1.

[19] Foreign Office telegram 386 to Copenhagen, 21 July; from memorandum cited above, n. 12.

[20] Curzon to Chicherin, in telegram 218 to British consulate, Reval, 29 July 1920; *British Documents*, vol. XII, no. 747.

[21] Orders were sent to Lord Allenby in Cairo on 6 July 1920 to suspend repatriation of the Russians in Egypt; Chicherin was informed in a telegram the previous day (see *ibid.*, no. 738). The detention in London of the six deportees from India is noted in the Foreign Office memorandum of 27 July cited above, n. 13. The imprisonment of five (excluding one woman) was ordered because of the sentencing to death on charges of "speculation" of the British Vice-Consul at Baku; when his sentence was cancelled (he was returned to the rest of the British prisoners) the five in London were released, but they were kept under surveillance.

Baku is not in Russian territory, but belongs to the Azerbaijan Republic. There is no means of direct telegraphic communication with Baku . . . our information is that Baku is entirely under the control of the Azerbaijan Republic. In so far as we can bring any influence to bear upon them, we have done our best, and we have also brought pressure to bear in Moscow, in order to induce them to communicate with the Azerbaijan Republic. . . . I do not know the extent of the responsibility of Russia for the prisoners at Baku. I am not satisfied for the moment that they are directly responsible.[22]

Finally, to the Azerbaijanis themselves the British government sent direct overtures, implying (presumably in order to hasten the prisoners' release: there was no doubt that they were being cruelly treated) a certain degree of acceptance of the Azerbaijani claims to independence. Thus on 11 August, through Litvinov, who had offered his good offices, Curzon sent to Baku a formal request for the release of the prisoners, asserting that "As a state of hostility does not exist and never has existed between Great Britain and the Republic of Azerbaijan there can be no reason or justification for the continued detention of the British subjects within the territory of the Republic. . . ."[23]

The Azerbaijani reply to this appeal, when it finally reached London more than a fortnight later, brought dismay and exasperation: the prisoners would be released, said the Azerbaijani Commissar for Foreign Affairs, M. D. Huseinov, in a telegram to Litvinov on 28 August, provided the British released a group of Kemalist Turks they were holding on Malta.[24] Such a request had, in fact, been made when the British naval mission was first interned at Baku, but apparently it had not been regarded as a serious proposal.[25] Now,

---

[22] 132 *H.C. Deb.*, cols. 1621-23 (29 July 1920).

[23] Curzon to Grant Watson (for Litvinov), Copenhagen, telegram 411, 11 August 1920; *British Documents*, vol. XII, no. 756.

[24] The text of Huseinov's telegram to Litvinov is in Luke, *Cities and Men*, vol. II, p. 188. The Azerbaijani government also sent the proposal directly to the British Minister in Tehran, who relayed it to London in his telegram 599, 28 August 1920 (*British Documents*, vol. XII, no. 767, n. 2).

For the circumstances in which the Turkish prisoners came to be at Malta, see a Foreign Office memorandum on the subject, 21 July 1920, *ibid.*, vol. XIII, no. 100. Most of them had been arrested by the Turkish government. Some, however, had been arrested by the British, either as war criminals or for violations of the armistice agreements. Both classes were being held on Malta for the same reason: shortage of adequate prison facilities within Turkey.

[25] See Curzon's telegram to Derby in Paris, no. 535, 8 May 1920; *ibid.*, vol. XII, no. 555.

however, it was taken seriously—at least to the extent of being flatly rejected. But the implications of an alliance between Kemalist nationalism and Islamic (and now Soviet) Azerbaijan were not lost.[26]

That the notion of such a combination should have its appeals both in Baku and in Angora (Ankara) was scarcely surprising. Yet there is one aspect of Huseinov's proposal to exchange the British prisoners for the Turks which still is not clear. In mid-September in Tiflis, where he had come to negotiate with the Georgian government, Huseinov told a prominent British socialist visitor that the "suggestion" for the exchange had come from Litvinov.[27] There are two possible interpretations of this remark. The first is that it demonstrates, as the British government suspected, that the Baku regime was simply the agent of the Russian Soviet regime, and that decisions on the disposition of the British prisoners were made in Moscow. A contrary interpretation, however, is equally plausible: that in the first months after the Soviet takeover of Azerbaijan the Baku communist regime was relatively independent of Moscow in many areas—in the case of the British prisoners most embarrassingly so— and that Litvinov had suggested the Turkish prisoners on Malta as a *quid pro quo* because of a supposition that such a suggestion would surely have a great appeal among the Moslems of Azerbaijan. (In any event, there was nothing more concrete the Azerbaijanis could hope to obtain from the British by continuing to hold the prisoners.) Moscow could suggest, not dictate—and hope that the continued detention of the prisoners would not become so much a *cause célèbre* within Great Britain as to provide Curzon, Churchill, Henry Wilson, and others with an excuse to insist that the Lloyd George government should cease its flirtation with Russia.

[26] For the rejection of the Azerbaijani proposal, see Curzon's telegram 424 to Grant Watson in Copenhagen, 6 September 1920; *ibid.*, no. 767. For reflections on the possibilities of a Kemalist-Soviet alliance, see Colonel Stokes' telegram 480 to Curzon, Tiflis, 6 November 1920, *ibid.*, vol. XIII, no. 171; Admiral de Robeck's telegram 1190 to Curzon, Constantinople, 10 November 1920, *ibid.*, no. 174; and the War Office memorandum of 22 November 1920 cited above, chap. VIII, n. 2.

[27] The British socialist visitor was Ramsay MacDonald, who had come to Tiflis as a member of a fact-finding delegation sent to Russia and Georgia by the Second International. MacDonald saw Huseinov, and also Leonid Stark, the deputy chief of the Russian diplomatic mission in Georgia, at the request of Commander Luke, the Acting British High Commissioner in Transcaucasia, because of Luke's feeling that an intervention by a socialist of MacDonald's eminence might persuade the Azerbaijani Communists to release their British prisoners. See Luke, *Cities and Men*, vol. II, pp. 191-92.

If the precise extent of Moscow's direct control over the Baku regime in these early days is still a matter of conjecture, there can be no doubt about the extent of Moscow's influence.[28] By October 1920, in any case, the British government had clearly succeeded in impressing the Russian leadership with the fact that the continued detention of the Baku prisoners was seriously jeopardizing the prospects of an Anglo-Soviet accord. Constant badgering in Parliament had driven Lloyd George to state in public what he had previously only told Krasin in private—that until the prisoners were freed would there be not only no trade agreement, but also no further negotiations for a trade agreement.[29] The note from Curzon to Chicherin on 1 October threatened more than merely a break-off of negotiations. It stated: "We have given an undertaking, to which we have scrupulously adhered, that we shall not assist in any hostile action against the Soviet Government, but unless by October 10 we have definite evidence that the conditions laid down as to the release of British prisoners are being complied with, we shall take whatever action we consider necessary to secure their release."[30]

The Soviet leadership seems to have taken this warning seriously. "At the present moment," Chicherin wrote in a letter to Krasin on 5 October, "it must be recognized that all the elements hostile to us in Great Britain have become extraordinarily more insolent and are full of hope." Therefore, he said, the Soviet side should carefully appraise its statements and actions: there was no need to give those elements which sought a rupture a handle on which they could pull.[31] Chicherin was obviously worried. Yet he still would not, or could not, simply direct the Baku government to release its

[28] Just as the actual workings of the machinery for control and influence among present-day communist states are closely guarded secrets, so the actual (as opposed to theoretical) relationships which prevailed between Moscow and the "independent" Soviet Republics during the early years of communist rule are still areas where relatively little information is available. For a good discussion of the problem, see Carr, *Bolshevik Revolution*, vol. I, pp. 380-98.

[29] On 3 June 1920 Lloyd George—and on 8 July Bonar Law—stated in Parliament that the freeing of all British prisoners was a necessary preliminary to the resumption of *trade relations* with Russia (129 *H.C. Deb.*, cols. 2032-33; 131 *H.C. Deb.*, cols. 1643-44). On 2 and 5 August, however, the Prime Minister was driven to promise that the release of all prisoners would be a necessary preliminary even to continued *negotiations* for a trade agreement (132 *H.C. Deb.*, cols. 1993 and 2621).

[30] Curzon's note of 1 October 1920 is cited above, n. 7.

[31] Letter, Chicherin to Krasin, London, 5 October 1920; *Dokumenty vneshnei politiki*, vol. III, pp. 233-34.

prisoners. Thus, on 3 October he radioed to Litvinov that Curzon's note of the 1st "renders urgent the completion of the exchange of prisoners," and that therefore Moscow was sending a "special delegate" to Baku "to speed up negotiations with the Azerbaijan Government."[32] And in reply to the British note the Soviet government (in a note from Krasin) once again repeated its assertion that it could only offer its good offices for negotiations between the British and the Azerbaijanis. But this time it suggested that each party should send a special delegate to Tiflis, there to be joined by a Soviet delegate who would "give every assistance in the negotiations." If the British agreed to this procedure, the Soviet note continued, there was every reason to believe that they would be satisfied with the outcome.[33]

And so—ultimately, and after a fashion—they were. But the negotiating process dragged for yet another month. The British government assented to the Soviet suggestion of negotiations in Tiflis, and entrusted the assignment to Colonel Stokes, the British High Commissioner there. Stokes found, however, that although the Soviet delegate, Leonid Stark, was prepared, the Azerbaijani delegate had not received sufficiently precise instructions to enable him to enter into negotiations, and it was near the end of October before he was able to do so.[34] Finally, on 1 November, the three signed a simple agreement to the effect that all the British prisoners at Baku would be freed and sent to Tiflis and that Stokes was so to inform London in order that a steamship, ready to load at Constantinople with the Russian prisoners from Egypt and Turkey, could do so and make for Odessa with them.[35]

These arrangements were eventually completed, but not before the British Admiral commanding the Mediterranean fleet had wired London for permission to bombard Odessa from the sea and air if

[32] Chicherin's *en clair* radio message to Litvinov, then in Christiania (Oslo), was intercepted by the Admiralty and printed in its *Wireless News*, no. 596, 5 October; U.S. National Archives, State Department file 861.00/7563.

[33] Note from Krasin to Lloyd George, 6 October 1920; *Dokumenty vneshnei politiki*, vol. III, pp. 237-42. An English version appeared in the *Daily Herald* of 9 October and the *Daily Telegraph* of 11 October.

[34] So Stokes reported in his telegram 445 to Curzon, Tiflis, 21 October 1920; summarized in an admonitory telegram from Curzon to Chicherin on 27 October (no. 292 to Leslie in Reval; *British Documents*, vol. XII, no. 795).

[35] Text in *Dokumenty vneshnei politiki*, vol. III, p. 313.

there were signs that the Soviet side was not complying with the agreement (he was refused),[36] and British naval vessels in the Baltic had actually halted a Finnish steamship and removed from it the six Bolshevik detainees from India who had been allowed to sail from London on the assumption that the exchange would be effected without delay.[37] These minor alarms notwithstanding, the month of November 1920 saw the repatriation of all the Russian prisoners who had been in British hands, and of virtually all the British subjects who had been detained in Russia. With the exchange of the prisoners an important obstacle to the restoration of normal relations between Britain and Russia was removed. The difficulties, delays, and annoyances involved, however, did not augur well for the future of this "normal" relationship.[38]

[36] Commander in Chief, Mediterranean, to Admiralty, telegram 538 Z, 2 November 1920; *British Documents,* vol. XII, no. 801. The rejection of Admiral Webb's request came from Curzon, who felt that a threat of bombardment would serve "no useful purpose" (*idem,* n. 2). Walter Long had written to Curzon on 11 October also recommending bombardment of Odessa; Curzon MSS, box 65.

[37] The heavy-handed British handling of the incident created a minor crisis in Finnish-British relations. For relevant correspondence, see *British Documents,* vol. XII, nos. 797, 799, 800, 803, 804, 808, and 810.

[38] Although the British government was undoubtedly justified in its complaints about the dilatory manner in which the Soviet government handled the problem of the exchange of nationals, there seems never to have been any realization in London that the problem was by no means "symmetrical"—that is, that there were great differences between the difficulties it caused the two respective sides.

In the O'Grady-Litvinov agreement of February 1920 each government promised to assist subjects of the other who wished repatriation. For the British this was no problem. They held a certain number of Russian prisoners who wished to be returned, and eventually they were. On the other hand, there were living in the United Kingdom and throughout the Empire great numbers of persons who had some claim to Russian citizenship. Under the O'Grady-Litvinov agreement they also had a right to repatriation. Scarcely any, however, wished to leave the prosperous and stable societies in which they now lived to return to a war-ravaged and communist-ruled Russia. Those who did wish to be repatriated were easily accommodated by the British government.

Just the reverse was true for persons living in Russia who might have had some claim—often quite remote—to classification as British subjects. Confronted with revolution, civil war, and expropriation, many were only too eager to leave the country where (in the most extreme cases) they had been born, had spent all of their lives, and whose language they spoke before any other. To the Soviet government they presented great problems. First, scattered as they were over the huge expanses of Russia, they had to be informed of their right to leave (in a message to Chicherin on 11 September 1920 Curzon complained that outside Moscow and Petrograd the Soviet government was making no attempt to publicize the opportunity for repatriation; telegram 238 to Leslie in Reval, *British Documents,* vol. XII, no. 774). Then their claims for classification as British subjects had to be accepted. As Chicherin apologetically stated in a telegram to Curzon on 23 November 1920 (*ibid.,* no 819) all this, in the still disorganized state of Russian administration, was not easy.

The Trade Agreement

❖

While the question of prisoners was still outstanding negotiations in London between the Soviet trade mission and the British government were halted. So, too, did Curzon succeed in keeping the issue of the trade agreement from coming before the Cabinet, despite Lloyd George's expressed impatience.[39] But within the British government, at the official level, preparations and discussions continued. The vehicle for these processes was the so-called Inter-Departmental Russian Trade Committee. Composed of representatives of the Treasury, Board of Trade, Foreign Office, Department of Overseas Trade (a separate organization, although attached to the Foreign Office), War Office, Admiralty, Home Office, Post Office, and the Ministries of Munitions, Shipping, and Food, with E. F. Wise as its chairman, the committee's locus was the Prime Minister's office. It had been set up by Lloyd George the previous January, following the Allied decision to allow trade with the Russian cooperative societies, in order to coordinate action among the various concerned (and scarcely concerned) British departments. Its assignment, once discussions with Krasin began in May, was to consider "the terms to be included in a Trade Agreement if the Cabinet decides that such an Agreement is desirable." In late September, despite the Cabinet's decision to put off such a decision, Lloyd George granted to Sir Robert Horne, President of the Board of Trade, the power—subject to appeals from other ministers concerned—to resolve disputes arising within the committee.[40]

Such a role should have gone to Curzon—so he and the senior officials at the Foreign Office must have thought. Perhaps because of this slight, certainly because of his general opposition to concluding any agreement with Moscow before the Soviet government had ceased all activities hostile to British interests in the East, Curzon took an attitude of total aloofness to the process by which the terms of the agreement were worked out. He himself, for instance, would not communicate directly with Krasin, nor would he allow his sub-

[39] For Lloyd George's impatience and Curzon's refusal, see Hankey's letters to Curzon, 28 October 1920, Curzon MSS, box 65, and to Churchill, 9 November, file 18/E/194, Cab. 21/200.

[40] So Hankey informed the Cabinet on 24 September 1920; Cabinet paper C.P. 1880, Cab. 24/111. The origins and terms of reference of the committee are outlined in two Cabinet papers: C.P. 1349, 27 May 1920, Cab. 24/106, and C.P. 1778, 16 August, Cab. 24/110.

ordinates to do so.[41] To his Cabinet colleagues, he explained the Foreign Office's attitude: "In these circumstances the Foreign Office finds itself in a position of no small difficulty. It has no desire to oppose trading relations with Russia on their own merits. But, as things are at present, it sees itself expected to enter into relations with a State which makes no secret of its intentions to overthrow our institutions everywhere and to destroy our prestige and authority, particularly in Asia."[42]

To senior officials within the Foreign Office he was more blunt. "I desire to have nothing to do with the agreement myself," he commented in early December 1920 in response to a complaint by Sir Eyre Crowe (Hardinge's successor as Permanent Under Secretary) that the Foreign Office's files contained no indication as to who drafted the proposed British version of the trade agreement, or whether any Foreign Office draftsmen or legal advisers had been consulted even informally. In fact, Curzon seems to have laid down as a general policy, although almost certainly one that was not written down, that (in the words of a minute by J. D. Gregory on 11 November) the Foreign Office was "precluded from criticising or interfering in the elaboration of the Trade Agreement." A month later, when Crowe seemed inclined to ask that a word in the draft agreement should be changed, Gregory warned that by offering such advice "we abandon our position of assuming no responsibility either for it or its drafting." Crowe restrained himself.[43]

Such "restraint" was matched by officials of other departments. Thus, when Wise convened the interdepartmental committee on 14

---

[41] Krasin complained in a letter to Lloyd George, 1 December 1920, that his notes to the Foreign Office had been unanswered and unacknowledged. That same day Philip Kerr then wrote an explanatory memorandum to Lloyd George saying: "It is true that the Secretary of State does not communicate with Monsieur Krassin officially. The method employed is to answer direct to Monsieur Chicherin at Moscow when it is a case of a Note from Monsieur Krassin embodying a telegram from the Moscow Government; to communicate through Mr. Wise and occasionally even to telephone to Mr. Klishko on matters of minor importance. The only exception to this rule was on October 27th, when on the instructions of the Secretary of State, Monsieur Krassin was invited to call at the Foreign Office and told categorically that the obstruction being placed on the repatriation of British subjects from Baku must cease at once." (Lloyd George MSS, files F/58/2/14 and F/90/1/26).

[42] Curzon's memorandum, "Russian Trade Negotiations," was Cabinet paper C.P. 2099, 14 November 1920, Cab. 24/114.

[43] See: Curzon's minute, undated, on Crowe's minute of 2 December 1920 on file N 3804/207/38, F.O. 371/5434; Gregory's minute, 11 November 1920, on file N 2513/30/38, F.O. 371/5420; and Gregory's minute, 13 December 1920, on file N 3962/207/38, F.O. 371/5434. Gregory was head of the Northern Department.

August (when the fate of Warsaw was still very much in the balance) to consider the initial draft version of the trade agreement, the War Office, Admiralty, Treasury, and Home Office representatives each stated—in different terms, of course—that they were instructed to take no part in the discussion.[44] Previously, the War Office and the Admiralty had responded to a Cabinet request for an enumeration of "particular points" each wished to see incorporated into any settlement with Moscow by listing terms that, in effect, would have disarmed the Red Army and confined the Soviet fleet to its home ports—demands not surprising to anyone familiar with the political behavior of armed services.[45]

Nor it is surprising that the Admiralty, when given the opportunity, did more than merely put forward a list of obviously unacceptable demands: despite Cabinet policy to the contrary, it maintained a blockade of Soviet Black Sea ports throughout the late summer and autumn of 1920. On 24 September Hankey addressed a courteous "private and confidential" letter to Walter Long saying that he thought he ought to draw the First Lord's "personal attention" to the blockade "in case you think it worth while to take any action to insure that there is no divergence between Admiralty instructions and the Cabinet policy." Three days later an official memorandum from the Admiralty to the Foreign Office asserted that "their Lords Commissioners" did not know the Cabinet's policy, and added: "Their Lordships have never concurred in the resumption of trade relations with the Soviet Russia. . . . Their Lordships are not in agreement, also, with the proposals [*sic*] respecting the Black Sea." Not until six weeks later, and after a personal intervention by Bonar Law, did a telegram go out to the Admiral Commanding-in-Chief, Mediterranean, stating that government policy regarding commercial trade in the Black Sea was that no restrictions should be placed upon it.[46] Other officials, in other departments, did no better.

[44] Cabinet paper C.P. 1778, cited above, n. 39, contained a summary of the meeting.

[45] These responses were by Churchill and Admiral Lord Beatty, respectively—Cabinet papers C.P. 1451 and 1361, 11 June and 28 May 1920—Cab. 24/107 and 24/106.

[46] The Cabinet decided in June 1920, as a result of Wrangel's attack on the mainland from his Crimean stronghold, to withdraw all military and naval support from him, including the blockade; see above, chap. II. The Foreign Office reminded the Admiralty of this policy in a letter of 18 September. Hankey's letter of 24 September to Long is in file 18/E/194, Cab. 21/173. The Admiralty's memorandum to the Foreign Office, 27 September, together with the Foreign Office letter of the 18th and Bonar Law's personal letter to Sir James Craig, Permanent Under Secretary

A Board of Trade memorandum of 10 August stated that British shippers were free to export goods to Soviet Russia under license. This was in accord with Allied policy as decided by the San Remo conference in April. However, the memorandum blandly added: "in practice no licenses are granted."[47]

Such tactics are typical of the conservative behavior of bureaucracies. Many a head of many a government has been worn down by them, and many a policy has therefore been stillborn for lack of implementation. Lloyd George had to contend with even more than these efforts. He also had united against him most of the British financial community, including the Governor of the Bank of England and the chairmen of the largest banks and insurance companies, all protesting that no agreement should be signed unless the Soviet government recognized all, rather than only some, classes of debts contracted by themselves and by previous Russian governments.[48]

Lloyd George was undeterred, however. Once it became clear that the remaining British prisoners would be released, the only politically compelling argument against a Cabinet decision to go ahead with the negotiation of the trade agreement fell to the ground. The Prime

---

at the Admiralty, are either quoted or summarized in Cabinet paper C.P. 2093, 13 November, Cab. 24/114. The text of Admiralty telegram 409 Z to Admiral Commanding-in-Chief, Mediterranean, 11 November, was circulated as Cabinet paper C.P. 2088; Cab. 24/114.

[47] The memorandum, "Note on Possible Blockade Measures Against Russia," was circulated as Cabinet paper C.P. 1779, Cab. 24/110. For public statements on licensing policy, see 131 *H.C. Deb.*, cols. 27-28; 133 *H.C. Deb.*, cols. 1312-13; 135 *H.C. Deb.*, col. 66; and 139 *H.C. Deb.*, col. 539.

[48] For this opposition: Letter from Montagu Norman, Governor of the Bank of England, to Austen Chamberlain, 21 July 1920; circulated as Cabinet paper C.P. 1674, Cab. 24/109. Letter to Lloyd George from Norman, R. M. Holland Martin (chairman, Bankers Association), and F. Huth Jackson (chairman, Accepting Houses Committee), 27 September; Cabinet paper C.P. 1917, Cab. 24/112. Letter to Lloyd George from R. W. Hanna, acting secretary of British Chambers of Commerce, 6 October; Cabinet paper C.P. 1944, Cab. 24/112. Letter to Lloyd George from chairmen of eight large insurance companies "who are holders of Russian Government securities," 5 October; Cabinet paper C.P. 1954, Cab. 24/112. Letter to Balfour from Evelyn Hubbard, chairman of Guardian Assurance Co., Ltd., 6 October, file 18/E/194, Cab. 21/200, stating: "In a pretty long experience, I remember nothing that has aroused more indignation (tempered with incredulity) than the publication of the proposed Trade Agreement with Russia. I appeal to you as our member, to put your foot on it and *stop it*." File N—/30/38, F.O. 371/5420, contains dozens of similar protests addressed to the Foreign Office. See also *The Times*, 27 and 30 September and 7, 9, and 13 October, for reports of protests by various business and financial organizations.

Minister evidently determined that the other arguments—that negotiations should await Soviet cessation of all anti-British activity in the East, and also a general recognition of debts—were politically much less potent than the image of British servicemen and civilians languishing in verminous Russian prisons.

On the other hand, an equally potent image—unemployment in the United Kingdom—impelled him forward. As Hankey wrote to Curzon on 12 November, informing him that Lloyd George had placed the trade negotiations on the agenda for the next Cabinet meeting, the Prime Minister was convinced that there was "every prospect of continued unemployment on a serious scale."

He apprehends [Hankey continued] that in the very near future there will be an insistent demand from the labouring classes for the re-opening of trade with Russia. It may be true that Russia is not in a position to give orders for which she can pay, but unless the right to trade is sanctioned almost at once, it will, in the Prime Minister's view, unquestionably be alleged and widely believed, that one cause of unemployment is the refusal of the Government to complete the Trade Agreement.[49]

Here was one prudential argument—that the government could not afford not to seem to be taking every measure to combat unemployment, including, especially, tapping the hitherto untouched Soviet market. We shall refer to this argument again. So, also, will we examine a second prudential argument which imbued Lloyd George with a sense of urgency—that the quick conclusion of the trade agreement was necessary in order to keep moderates in the ascendancy within the Soviet government. Krasin himself put this argument to E. F. Wise on 11 November when he delivered the text of a virtual ultimatum from Chicherin complaining that more than four months had passed since the "formal agreement" of 30 June–1 July between the two governments, months in which the British had raised "entirely irrelevant political questions" as a "pretext" for delaying trade talks; "matters," Chicherin declared, "can no longer be allowed to drag on in the manner in which they have dragged on."[50] Although Krasin told Wise that he regretted the peremptory tone of Chicherin's note, he said (according to a memorandum Wise

[49] Letter, Hankey to Curzon, 12 November 1920; Curzon MSS, Box 65.
[50] The message Krasin delivered was a note from Chicherin to Curzon, 9 November 1920; text in *Dokumenty vneshnei politiki*, vol. III, pp. 320-24, English translation in *British Documents*, vol. XII, no. 807.

wrote afterward) that he himself felt that "the time had now come when either we must conclude an Agreement or the policy of trade must fail." Wise thus summarized Krasin's argument: "If, however, we could not quickly come to an agreement he would have to return to Moscow and it would be impossible to resist the argument of those who opposed him that the policy of moderation had failed and that only by recourse to other means could Russia force recognition from the Powers. He would himself regret this strongly. . . ."[51]

Lloyd George brought the issue to resolution at two climactic Cabinet meetings on the mornings of 17 and 18 November. On the 14th, in preparation for these sessions, Curzon had put to his colleagues a long paper summarizing the Anglo-Soviet relationship to date as he saw it. The essence of his argument came in the following sentences:

In these proceedings . . . it has been my duty, as Foreign Minister, to fight throughout for the full and honest fulfilment of the assurances on which alone in my opinion can an agreement with the Soviets either be justified or have a chance of success, conditions . . . which (except in respect of repatriation of prisoners, and there neither fully nor sincerely) no attempt has been made by the Russians to fulfil. For the sake of Russia herself and of employment in England during the winter, everyone of us would be glad to see commercial relations established. But I should be a poor guardian of the interests committed to me if, after this had been done and every trump card that we possess surrendered, I found that, owing to any negligence on my part, British interests or the British Empire were still exposed without mitigation to the ceaseless and deadly assaults on the part of the Bolshevik Government and its agents, which have for months been directed against them. . . .

It seems to me that we are certainly justified in demanding *as a preliminary* to trade relations very definite evidence that Bolshevik hostility shall cease *now*. We have given abundant evidence of our fidelity to our assurances in respect of Wrangel, Poland, and in other quarters. Can the Bolsheviks produce a single case of suspended hostility or countermanded propaganda in any part of the East? On the contrary I could, but for the fear of wearying the Cabinet, produce overwhelming evidence that the one objective at which the whole of their policy is and has been aimed is India, and I firmly believe that the renewed lease of life which the agreement if concluded will give them, will be consecrated to no purpose

[51] Wise's "Memorandum of Interview with M. Krassin," 11 November 1920, with a covering letter from Wise to Philip Kerr, 12 November, is in Lloyd George MSS, file F/48/3/27; copy also in file 18/E/194, Cab. 21/200.

more unswervingly than to the subversion and destruction of the British connection with the Indian Empire.[52]

Curzon's colleagues had heard these arguments from him often enough before. And they heard them again at the Cabinet meeting on 17 November.[53] Horne began with a long recitation of the economic benefits that might come from the restoration of trade with Russia. Curzon was thus allowed to play one of his favorite roles, the outraged defender of principle against profit. He did not, he said, "dispute the propositions of the Board of Trade." His criticism was directed not at the economics but at the conditions of the agreement, which the Russians had not fulfilled. "The Russian menace in the East is incomparably greater than anything else that has happened in my lifetime to the British Empire."

Yet Curzon could offer no remedies. Thus he left himself vulnerable to arguments such as Horne's "I feel strongly the only way we shall fight Bolshevism is by trade," or Lloyd George's contention that although the Soviet government had not lived up to the conditions agreed upon in the exchange of 30 June–7 July (indeed, Krasin had argued quite explicitly that the conditions would not be operative until the trade agreement was actually signed), neither had the British. The Prime Minister said: "We acted as though the agreement were not in operation or as if it were suspended. We unloaded rifles at Dantzig with our own troops. We organized a military mission to Poland and invited the French to co-operate. If this agreement were in operation we had no business to do these things. . . . The only way in which we can justify ourselves is that the agreement was not in force. . . ."

As happened so often, the case against Curzon was sealed by Bonar Law, the leader of his party. The tone and flavor of Bonar Law's rambling intervention comes through the verbatim record that was kept for this meeting. He said:

I agree with Horne: we have been playing with this Russian situation

---

[52] Curzon's memorandum is cited above, n. 42. (Italics in original.)

[53] Minutes, Cabinet 61(20), 17 November 1920, 11:30 A.M.; Cab. 23/23. This meeting and the one on the 18th were exceptional in that seemingly verbatim records, as transcribed by Thomas Jones of the Cabinet secretariat (who was skilled at shorthand), were preserved and typescripts appended to the Cabinet Office official file copies of the minutes. These typescripts—retained on file, probably, because of the highly controversial nature of the trade agreement—are an invaluable historical source.

too long. You cannot go on talking and not conclude an agreement. We are in for bad unemployment. There is some business to be got in this way. If we make no agreement the effect on the public mind of the imaginary volume of trade which would never take place, but which they *think* would take place if there were an agreement, would be very bad. As to propaganda—it is a small part of the danger. They are forming an alliance with Kemal—if that goes on the agreement will be broken. If we make no agreement we shall have no leverage against the political hostility of Russia. We should then be inviting them to carry on hostilities. We shall have power to stop the agreement. . . . We shall have far more chance of exercising pressure on Russia after an agreement. I agree with Horne that Bolshevism will come to an end under civilised conditions. There are conflicting elements within the Soviet Government and a party that loathes a trade agreement. It is our business to consider what is our interest. What is the use of our saying that we won't do trade because we cannot get the old debts paid? . . . We have been shilly-shallying for two years. We shall lose the chance of political influence and do it at the expense of losing some trade.

There remained only for Lloyd George to apply a price-tag. The Russians were prepared to place £10 million worth of orders in the United Kingdom once an agreement was signed, he said. Half would go for wages. "If we refuse it will leak out that we turned it down because of Persia and Tashkent and because we hate the Bolsheviks at a time when we are voting £4 or £5 millions for the unemployed." (Thomas Macnamara, the Minister of Labour, interjected that government spending for the Out-of-Work Donation was £5 million.) The Prime Minister then adjourned the meeting until the following day with a stinging attack upon Curzon and the bureaucracy:

As to propaganda, Curzon says we must have an undertaking that propaganda has ceased. Even with the best will in the world with Bolshevik outbreaks you will not be able to restrain it. As long as there is a pamphlet published in India our officials, who are violently anti-Bolshevik, will hold that the conditions have not been fulfilled. Our officials would have helped Wrangel if they had had their way. It is no use saying that if six months hence there is no propaganda you will enter into an agreement. By that time you will be in the depths of trade depression and you will be forced to make a trade agreement. . . . I hope you will allow Horne to negotiate on the basis of the draft agreement of July 1st. If we try to enlarge it we are departing from it. It was circulated at the time. If we make conditions *precedent* it will mean that we are not prepared to trade while there is a Soviet Government. I have heard predictions about the fall of the Soviet Government for the last two years. Denikin, Judenitch, Wrangel, all have collapsed, but I cannot see any immediate prospect of the collapse of the Soviet Government.

The meeting the next morning, 18 November, showed that Curzon had more supporters than Lloyd George may have thought.[54] Only Austen Chamberlain had taken his side on the 17th, and Chamberlain's interests in "precedent conditions" (as they came to be called) were less in those relating to propaganda than in those relating to debts. "I feel bound *ex officio* to call attention to my clientele, the financiers, the accepting houses," he explained on the 18th. "The great financial houses are wholly opposed to this agreement." On the 18th Curzon and Chamberlain were joined by Churchill, whose opposition to any accommodation with Bolshevism was taken for granted, and by Edwin Montagu, whose was not; Montagu was particularly exercised by the Soviet-Afghan agreement, and evidently wanted Moscow to annul it as a token of good faith, an action that was scarcely likely. Balfour, also, was clearly unhappy, but he stopped short of declaring himself when Lloyd George finally brought the issue to conclusion. The record reads:

The Prime Minister: May we take it that the principle of concluding a trading agreement is accepted?
Lord Birkenhead [the Lord Chancellor, formerly F. E. Smith]: Yes—with great difficulty, I agree.
Lord Curzon: I want conditions precedent.
Mr. Montagu: I agree with Curzon.
Mr. Churchill: I should like a discussion on the conditions. I have not accepted the P.M.'s ruling.
Lord Curzon: Long agrees with me. I have a letter from him.[55]

Lloyd George, of course, had the votes. He did not need, nor did he get, any explicit affirmations of support other than Birkenhead's. The minutes merely indicate that "a considerable majority" agreed that Horne should be authorized to conclude a trade agreement along the lines of the June-July exchange of notes. Hankey noted in his diary, however, that Churchill, Curzon, and Milner voted against

---

[54] Minutes, Cabinet 62(20), 18 November 1920, 11:30 A.M.; Cab. 23/23. Just as for the previous meeting, a verbatim typescript was appended.

[55] Long was unable to attend the meetings and wrote to offer Curzon his support. Letter, Long to Curzon, 17 November 1920; Curzon MSS, box 65.

continuing the negotiations. The minority were good losers, however. Only Churchill, who at the previous day's meeting had passed
Birkenhead a note saying that he might even resign from the government if the decision went against him and who, Hankey noted,
was quite pale and extremely upset at the moment of decision, felt
constrained to make clear his dissociation from the Cabinet's action.
He stated: "Signing this agreement in no way alters the general
position we have taken up as to the Bolsheviks, namely, that Ministers shall be free to point out the odious character of their regime.
It seems to me that you are on the high road to embrace Bolshevism.
I am going to keep off that and denounce them on all possible occasions."[56] Churchill's point was a serious one, and he was taken
seriously. The official "conclusions" of the meeting included the
statement that "It was generally understood that the conclusion of a
Trading Agreement on these lines would not be assumed to hamper
the discretion of Ministers in public statements regarding the Bolshevist system of Government."[57]

If the minority were good losers, Lloyd George was, as always, a
gracious winner. As in so many other instances when he got what
he wanted from a meeting, whether simply of his own Cabinet or of
allied governments, he made sure that his colleagues (or opponents)
did not depart with visibly empty hands. The "conclusions"—presumably drawn up after the meeting on the 18th by Lloyd George
and Hankey, perhaps with the assistance of Philip Kerr, who also
attended—also stated that either in the trade agreement itself or else
in an accompanying document the British government would draw
the attention of the Soviet government "to any specially important
respects in which, in accordance with the terms of the Agreement,
the Bolsheviks must alter their present procedure or policy, e.g. to
annul their Treaty with Afghanistan, to desist from co-operation
with Mustapha Kemal, and from hostilities or propaganda in Persia,
India, etc." And to "communicate with" Horne on these points, the
Prime Minister named a three-man committee—Curzon, Montagu,
and Churchill. But at the same time, through Hankey, he privately
instructed Horne not to allow Curzon and Churchill to be obstruc-

---

[56] From the verbatim transcript of the meeting of 18 November. Hankey's diary
entry for 18 November is in Roskill, *Hankey*, vol. II, pp. 172-73.
[57] From the Minutes of the 18 November meeting.

tive. He was, Hankey noted, "determined to put the agreement through."[58]

✧

Between August 1920 and March 1921 there were no less than four British drafts of the trade agreement, and at least one separate Soviet draft.[59] Although these several versions differed in form, their substance in fact remained the same from the initial draft to the final treaty. (The final version is printed as an appendix to this volume.) Each draft began with a preamble stating that the document constituted a preliminary agreement for the resumption of trade pending the conclusion of a formal treaty of peace (thus, it should be noted, implicitly acknowledging that the two governments had been at war) which would regulate their future economic and political relations. Then—depending on the draft—the preamble went on either simply to refer to the conditions laid down in the British note of 30 June and accepted by the Soviet note of 7 July, or, instead, to spell out at varying lengths what the most important of those conditions were: a mutual undertaking not to engage in hostile action against the other or to conduct, outside of its own borders, any propaganda against the other, and additional assurances regarding the exchange of citizens of the other who wanted repatriation.

A third condition, of course, concerned the problem of debts. The Soviet draft treaty dealt with debts in its preamble, referring to "the recognition in principle of the liability of the Russian Soviet Gov-

[58] *Idem*, and Hankey's diary entry for 19 November 1920 in Roskill, *Hankey*, vol. II, p. 173.
[59] The British drafts were: (1) 14 August 1920: appended to Cabinet paper C.P. 1778, cited above, n. 39. (2) 30 September: relatively minor revisions of (1) by Horne, circulated together with an alternative version of Article 8 (on debts) by Sir Hubert Llewellyn Smith, Joint Secretary of the Board of Trade, as Cabinet paper C.P. 2086, Cab. 24/114; this draft—but not the alternative Article 8—was leaked to *The Times*, which published it "through the courtesy of a correspondent" on 5 October. (3) 25 November: revised by Horne in light of Cabinet preferences, Cabinet paper C.P. 2166, Cab. 24/115; this version, handed to Krasin on the 29th, is printed in *British Documents*, vol. VIII, pp. 869-78. This was slightly amended in a version dated 14 December; the amendments are indicated in brackets in *idem*. (4) 5 January 1921: Cabinet paper C.P. 2431, Cab. 24/118. This version, handed to Krasin before his departure for Russia on 8 January, was printed in *The Times*, 25 January.
The only full Soviet draft, dated 14 December 1920, is in file N 4655/207/38, F.O. 371/5434. It is printed alongside the British draft of 25 November in *British Documents*, vol. VIII, pp. 869-78.
The final version is cited below, n. 116.

ernment to pay compensation to private citizens who have supplied goods or services to Russia for which they have not been paid."[60] This was scarcely lawyer's language. Early British drafts incorporated a similar but more elaborately worded statement in the body of the agreement and, for form's sake, made the obligation mutual. In the final version roughly the same statement was placed in a separate declaration following the body of the treaty. As we shall see, its placement and its vague wording represented a significant British concession.

With the exception of this article on debts in the earlier British drafts, the body of the agreement in all of the drafts dealt only with matters directly pertaining to facilities for trade. Each party would remove all obstacles to trade with, and in no way discriminate against the trade of, the other. Each would treat the other's ships, crews, and cargoes according to "the established practice of commercial nations" with regard to privileges, immunities, and the use of port facilities of every kind. Although all questions relating to patents and copyrights were to be left to the formal treaty of peace that was to follow, each party would immediately begin to treat passports, powers of attorney, and other documents issued or certified by the "competent authorities" of the other "as if they were issued or certified by a recognized foreign government." (This was the second inference, in early British drafts at least, that London was not according the Soviet regime *de jure* recognition. The first was a clause in the preamble, eliminated in the final version, that the trade agreement "shall not be deemed to affect the view which either party may hold as to the legal status of the other.")

Naturally, the agreement gave much attention to the problem of how each of the parties would be represented in the territory of the other. It provided that each could nominate as many of its nationals as would reasonably be necessary, given the conditions of trade in the other country, for service there as resident trade agents, shippers, and the like. They would have the ordinary privileges and immunities necessary to carry on their work, such as freedom from conscription, the right to make normal commercial use of posts, telegraphs, and wireless communications, and the right of egress from the country. In addition to these commercial agents, each party could also appoint a mutually agreed number of "official agents"

[60] *British Documents*, vol. VIII, p. 870.

who would have immunity from search and arrest and the right to send and receive couriers with sealed pouches; essentially, they would have diplomatic privileges. These rights accorded to both classes of agents were, of course, qualified by each party having the power to refuse to admit—or to require to withdraw—any citizens of the other *non grata* to itself.

Finally, the agreement contained an article—the subject, as we shall see, of some controversy during the negotiations—in which the British government declared that it would take no steps "to attach or to take possession of any gold, funds, securities, or commodities" exported from Russia in payment for imports or for credits. In other words, the British government would not seize these articles against Russian debts. But the article said nothing about the efforts of *private* claimants to attach Russian property. The agreement was to take effect immediately upon signature, and was to continue until six months after either party gave notice of a desire to terminate it. Immediate termination was permitted, however, in the event that either party were seriously to infringe the agreement—or in the event that the courts of the United Kingdom were to hold that British subjects could attach Soviet property in payment for Russian debts.

❖

Although the Cabinet decided on 18 November to resume formal negotiations for a trade agreement, not until nearly two weeks later, the 29th, was a draft treaty officially communicated to Krasin. Wise almost certainly had kept him informed about earlier drafts—one, in any case, was published in *The Times* on 5 October, as the result of a leak[61]—but until 29 November their contact had been wholly unofficial and informal. The draft given to Krasin contained some significant changes from earlier versions, amendments and additions which had been proposed by the three-man committee of Curzon, Montagu, and Churchill and for the most part accepted by Horne, who was in charge of the drafting process.[62] Presumably these changes were the cause of the eleven-day delay in the draft's pres-

[61] See above, n. 59.
[62] The three presented their report, together with suggested revised language for several parts of the agreement, as Cabinet paper C.P. 2138, 24 November 1920; Cab. 24/115. The following day Horne circulated a revised draft of the agreement with a note indicating the extent to which he had taken into account the committee's report; Cabinet paper C.P. 2166, *ibid.*

entation. For the most part they occurred in the preamble. Here were the stronger prohibitions against propaganda and subversion for which Curzon and his supporters had asked. Their inclusion was the price Lloyd George felt obliged to pay to mollify the dissidents in his government. In fact, it was a small price, for the changes were entirely of the sort that would now be termed "cosmetic." Instead of simply citing the Anglo-Soviet accord of 30 June–7 July, the new version spelled out (but added nothing of substance to) the prohibitions, laying down the following condition for British adherence to the agreement:

That each party refrains from hostile action or undertakings against the other and from conducting outside of their own borders any propaganda direct or indirect against the institutions of the other party and more particularly that the Soviet Government desists and refrains from undertaking or assisting any hostile action or propaganda in the United Kingdom or any part of the British Empire against the institutions of the British Empire and from any attempt by military, diplomatic action or propaganda to encourage any of the peoples of Asia in any form of hostile action against British interests or the British Empire, especially in the region of the Caucasus and Asia Minor, Persia, Afghanistan and India, and also restrains Russian citizens from any such action or propaganda.[63]

The only other important change in the new British draft was a tightening of the language concerning debts. As before, the Soviet government formally recognized its liability to pay compensation to private British subjects for goods or services rendered to Russian governments or Russian citizens in cases where payment had not been made owing "to the Russian Revolution or to any act of the Soviet Government" (as the draft of 29 November put it)—*i.e.*, nationalization or confiscation, as well as default on bonds and other government obligations. The new version added the qualification, important for domestic political purposes, that *all* claims of either party or of its nationals—*i.e.*, the British government as well as British private claimants—would be dealt with in the forthcoming formal treaty of peace, and that the trade agreement's stated declaration on debts to private persons in no way implied that they would receive preferential treatment when the final reckoning came.[64] This

[63] *British Documents*, vol. VIII, p. 870.
[64] *Ibid.*, p. 876. This revised language was essentially that proposed by Sir

was Lloyd George's reply to the complaints of his colleagues and the financial community that the much larger governmental debts had been forgotten. Once again, however, the change was declaratory, not substantive.

Perhaps the most important reason why the change was not substantive was resistance from the Soviet mission. Krasin reported to Chicherin on 12 November that "financial, diplomatic and other circles hostile to us are attempting to force the Cabinet to include in this draft conditions absolutely unacceptable for us—for example recognition of debts and so on." However, he went on, "both officially and privately we are rigorously pointing out to all without exception that the inclusion of such a paragraph will mean a rupture, and can only be made by the British Government with the provocative object of a rupture."[65]

While Krasin was making clear to the British government that any departure from the terms of the 30 June–7 July exchange would be unacceptable, he was likewise warning his own government. Chicherin wanted to restrict Moscow's acknowledgment of a liability to pay claims of British private citizens only to debts incurred by the Soviet regime, excluding previous obligations. Such a reservation, Krasin telegraphed, was "hardly defensible": the British note of 30 June referred, he said, to "goods delivered and services rendered to Russia without any reservations confining them to the period of Soviet rule." He himself, he reminded Chicherin, had the previous July proposed rejection of this point, but the Central Committee had accepted it, and the Soviet note of 7 July had expressed no reservations. "One cannot one day accept a point and the next day disclaim it," Krasin said.[66]

In the end, Chicherin capitulated. The Politburo, he telegraphed to Krasin on 7 December, had accepted his view and had decided "to

---

Hubert Llewellyn Smith in September in order to meet some of the complaints of the financial community; see above, n. 59.

[65] Krasin to Chicherin, 12 November 1920, on p. 21 of a compilation of intercepted telegrams entitled "Text of Draft Trade Agreement with Soviet Russia with comments and criticism by the Moscow Foreign Office and M. Krassin." Circulated "with the compliments of the Director of Intelligence, at the request of the Rt. Hon. Winston Churchill, M.P.," the compilation bears no date. Davidson MSS.

[66] Krasin to Chicherin, telegrams of 24 and 30 November 1920, in compilation cited above, pp. 22 and 7. (The message of 30 November is also in Lloyd George MSS, file F/203/1/11: telegrams 1478-82, intercept 004929, circulated 6 December.)

adhere literally to the July notes without any additions."[67] Krasin undoubtedly strengthened his case by his contention, put forward in
messages both before and after the Politburo's decision, that agreement to the British conditions of 30 June in fact committed Moscow
to very little. Recognition of liability had been "in principle" only;
actual settlement would await a peace conference in which the
Soviet government could "oppose to the claims of the capitalist
world our counterclaim for the destruction of the whole of Russia,
the murder of millions of peasants and workers and the three years
of blockade." Here, Krasin asserted, was Moscow's "greatest diplomatic victory . . . we have forced England and all Europe to agree
to our principle that the discussion of Soviet Russia's debts is possible only at such a conference as may terminate with the conclusion
of a general durable peace."[68] Krasin was in no hurry for such a
peace conference, however. "It is not at all in our interests to hasten
peace negotiations," he telegraphed to Chicherin. He explained:
"we must first draw England and other countries into commercial
and business intercourse with us; it is necessary that new commercial
concessional interests should become so firm, that our refusal at the
peace conference to pay old debts shall not result in a new blockade
or intervention."[69]

These telegrams, and presumably most (if not all) of the others
exchanged between Krasin in London and his colleagues in Moscow
were available to Lloyd George and to other senior members of the
British government. Later, as we have seen, this stream of Soviet
communications was to dry up when Moscow adopted new, less
easily broken ciphers, but during the period before Krasin's departure once again for Moscow in early January 1921 the possession of
these messages undoubtedly made easier the British task of negotiation. Thus, Lloyd George and (almost certainly) Horne, if not
officials like Wise, were aware that the Politburo had given Krasin
real negotiating flexibility only with regard to those clauses in the
trade agreement which actually governed the conditions of trade.
The Politburo distinguished between these "definitive clauses" and

[67] Chicherin to Krasin, telegram, 7 December 1920, p. 13 of compilation cited
above, n. 65.
[68] Krasin to Chicherin, telegrams, 24 November and 13 December 1920, pp. 22
and 23 in compilation cited above, n. 65.
[69] Krasin to Chicherin, telegrams 1793-95, 24 December 1920; intercept 005129,
circulated 4 January 1921, Lloyd George MSS, file F/203/1/11.

the "repetition of the July agreement," which was, with its references to debts and to the mutual cessation of hostile activities and propaganda, "merely a statement of principles" whose "final working out" would come at a future peace conference.[70] The Politburo was insistent that the British government should have real incentives to go through with the notion of a full-fledged political conference which would end in *de jure* recognition of the Soviet regime and a specific political settlement in the East. Chicherin therefore insisted that the trade agreement should not be allowed to serve as a substitute for such an accord. He telegraphed to Krasin:

. . . if the trade agreement should be signed now, this will not guarantee us in any way from further attacks and England's policy will remain as double-faced as it is now. You build too much hope on the interests of those trade groups which are interested in an agreement with us. On the other hand our Eastern policy will suffer a heavy blow. We can on no account agree to these enormous sacrifices without receiving similar compensation. At the same time it is quite possible that England will sign an agreement with us in order to make us quarrel with our Eastern friends. Having done this she will hasten to seize the first opportunity to break off the agreement, leaving us isolated. The inference to be drawn from this is not that the agreement must on no account be signed—on the contrary it is necessary to us—the inference is that we must not make ourselves cheap and must not capitulate without compensation, i.e. we must keep to the July basis. We can only agree to concrete concessions in the East at a political conference with England and on condition that we receive similar concessions from England also in the East. What these concessions are to consist of will be discussed when the time comes.[71]

Krasin put forward his government's position in a series of informal working sessions with Wise and a few with Sir Robert Horne during the first three weeks of December. At these meetings the details of the trading arrangements were worked out. On the 21st, however, Lloyd George was present.[72] The British side, and perhaps the Soviet delegates as well, had evidently decided that the

[70] Chicherin to Krasin, telegram, 14 December 1920, pp. 1-3 in "Supplement, 24th December, 1920, embodying texts dated 14th to 18th December, 1920," to compilation cited above, n. 65. Davidson MSS.
[71] Chicherin to Krasin, telegram, 15 December 1920, pp. 3-6 in "Supplement," cited above, n. 70.
[72] "Draft Secretary's Notes of a Conference of British Ministers with the Head of the Russian Trade Delegation . . . ," 21 December 1920, 6:45 P.M.; *British Documents*, vol. VIII, no. 102, pp. 879-92.

issues were sufficiently political to warrant his participation. The Prime Minister was accompanied by Bonar Law, Horne, Wise, Hankey, Kerr, and two senior civil servants from the Board of Trade. Opposite them were Krasin, Klishko, and Sir William Bull, a London solicitor whom the Soviet mission had engaged. Curzon was not present; in fact, the Foreign Office was not represented at all. The Foreign Secretary was present in spirit, however: Lloyd George explained to Krasin that the preamble in the British draft agreement conveyed to him on 29 November had singled out specific regions and countries where the Soviet government was "especially" to desist from hostile action or propaganda because otherwise it would be impossible to get the approval of those members of the British Cabinet—meaning principally Curzon—who were "specially interested in those particular countries."

Krasin's response was tactfully to point out that the new British preamble was logically absurd. In the exchange of 30 June–7 July, he said, the Soviet government had already given a general undertaking not to carry on propaganda, and it would do so again in the trade agreement. But it did not like listing particular countries since they were covered in any case by the general undertaking. Here, perhaps, was Soviet sensitivity. But here also, as Lloyd George must have been aware, was Moscow's refusal to be specific regarding obligations undertaken under the agreement's preamble. Krasin did, however, back away one step: if London insisted on listing particular countries, Moscow would compound the absurdity by inserting its own list of countries where the British were especially to desist from anti-Soviet activities. Lloyd George replied: "Certainly there is no objection to your naming every country in the world." His own government had listed "the Caucasus [which, it should be noted, was already largely Soviet territory, with only Georgia—whose conquest was not far off—remaining independent] and Asia Minor, Persia, Afghanistan and India" because "a good deal of hostile propaganda had been carried on in those particular areas against British interests." He did not challenge the right of the Soviet government to continue with the activities until the trade agreement came into operation, he said, but afterward they all must cease.

Krasin demurred that he was only a trade negotiator, and that he would have to refer such a political question to Moscow. His next objection, however, also pertained to propaganda: the stipulation in the British draft that the Soviet government would "restrain" Russian citizens from anti-British actions or propaganda. He had put the same objection to Horne at one of their working sessions five days previously. His government could not give such an undertaking, he had said; it would be contrary to the Soviet constitution, just as the British government could not restrain the anti-Soviet utterances of Winston Churchill. Horne had replied that the British government did not care what Soviet citizens did "against Britain" on Soviet territory; "it was when agents in Afghanistan, India, etc. sought to stir up sedition that a hostile act was committed."[73] At the meeting on 21 December Lloyd George was ready to delete the passage to which Krasin objected and to substitute language which accorded with Horne's explanation: "It is understood that the term 'conducting any official propaganda' includes the giving by either party of assistance or encouragement to any propaganda conducted outside its own territories. The parties undertake forthwith to give all necessary instructions to their nationals to conform to the stipulations undertaken above."[74] The British government, Lloyd George explained, "could not prevent individual Englishmen going out to conduct propaganda in any particular country." But it could undertake not to give them encouragement or assistance; the Soviet government, he said, could do the same.

Nothing more about "propaganda" was said at this session, the only meeting between Lloyd George and Krasin preceding the signature in March of the trade agreement. Indeed, the problem had scarcely been touched, nor was it ever seriously to be. Oddly enough, Lloyd George had not even mentioned the thorny problem of the Communist International, although the Cabinet, meeting on 26 November to approve the more stringent prohibitions regarding propaganda put forward by Curzon, Montagu, and Churchill, had explicitly stipulated: "That, in the case of the Agreement being concluded, it should be understood that the Russian Government would not be allowed to escape responsibility for hostile propaganda by sheltering itself behind the activities of the 'Third International.'"[75]

[73] Minutes, Sixth Meeting of Russia Committee with Soviet Delegation, 16 December 1920; file N 4715/207/38, F.O. 371/5434. I have been able to locate the minutes of only a few of these working sessions; many evidently did not make their way into the Foreign Office files.
[74] *British Documents*, vol. VIII, p. 883.
[75] Minutes, Cabinet 64(20), 26 November 1920, 12:15 P.M.; Cab. 23/23.

Horne had tried, with no effect, to raise the matter of the Comintern at his working session with Krasin on 16 December. According to his information, he had said, the Comintern was "subsidized" by the Soviet government; the two sides must reach some understanding about it. Krasin replied with a flat denial: "he did not know," the meeting's minutes record him as saying, "of a single act or order on the part of the Soviet Government that would indicate to him that the Soviet Government had given any funds in support of the Third International." On the other hand, he said, "the British Government has spent considerable funds in financing armies against Soviet Russia." His government would restrain its own agents, but the Comintern "was an international organisation and it was extremely unlikely that the Soviet Government would accept responsibility for it." He himself, Krasin said—in effect, dismissing the issue—looked forward to trade as a salutary influence on the propagandists of both sides.[76] There is no indication that Horne raised the topic with Krasin again; as we have seen, Lloyd George did not do so at their meeting on 21 December.

In that meeting, once Krasin's objections to the "propaganda" portions of the British draft treaty had been disposed of, the Russian delegate next raised the question of debts. Here he objected not merely to the new British draft, but to its predecessors as well, for holding the Soviet government liable not only for governmental debts to British private citizens, but also for the debts to them of private Russian citizens. Under such a formula, he said, Moscow could be held liable for the private debts of former aristocrats, even for those of Denikin or Wrangel! Horne replied that the British government had in mind only those private obligations whose payment was made impossible by, for example, Soviet nationalization of the debtor's property. The discussion was not a long one; the topic was quickly dropped. But Krasin eventually won his point. The "Declaration of Recognition of Claims" of the final trade agreement returned to the looser language of the British note of 30 June. It spoke simply of compensating those who "have supplied goods or services to *Russia*"—and left unanswered the question of just what was meant by "Russia." Presumably this question, like so many others, would be answered at the formal peace conference for which the trade agreement was only—ostensibly—a preliminary.

[76] The minutes of this session are cited above, n. 73.

Since the Soviet government's recognition of its obligations was only "in principle," it was scarcely likely that any payments would be made before then.

The other matters vexing Krasin that December evening were nearly all related to a fear that British citizens with unsatisfied Russian claims would be able to attach Soviet goods or gold imported into the United Kingdom. On that very day a High Court judge had awarded a load of recently imported Russian plywood to a claimant. But he declared that he had done so only because the British government did not recognize the Soviet regime as the *de facto* government of Russia, and therefore British courts could not recognize the Soviet government's nationalization and confiscation decrees.[77] On the other hand, as Lloyd George stated repeatedly to Krasin, the very act of signing a trade agreement with the Soviet government would signify British recognition of its *de facto* status. Perhaps Krasin did not understand; more probably he was merely being cautious. In any case he insistently asked Lloyd George to promise that in the event of an adverse court decision following the signature of the trade agreement the government would introduce into Parliament special legislation protecting Russian goods and gold against attachment. Not surprisingly, Lloyd George refused. The trade agreement itself would be unpopular enough with many of his government's supporters in the House of Commons. Special legislation in favor of Russian imports would carry too great a political cost.[78]

[77] Aksionairnoye Obschesttvo A. M. Luther (plaintiff) v. James Sagar and Co. (defendant) before Mr. Justice Roche, High Court of Justice, King's Bench Division, arguments heard 29 November 1920 (summarized in *The Times*'s Law Reports 30 November) and decision rendered 21 December (*The Times*, 22 December).

[78] Had the Soviet government wished to import gold into the United Kingdom, additional problems would have been involved. There were no restrictions on the import of gold. Once inside, however, it could only be melted down or re-exported by special license, such as that granted in the case of South African gold. In the circumstances it could be sold only to the Bank of England, which would pay an arbitrarily fixed mint price of 77s. 9d. per ounce instead of the world price, then around 116s. per ounce. Thus, assuming the Bank would be willing to buy gold, it would be sold at something like 33 percent discount. But in the case of Russian gold, the Bank asserted that it would not buy any in the absence of a guarantee of title from the British government—which the government was unwilling to give. See the Foreign Office memorandum of 14 July 1920, *British Documents*, vol. XII, no. 741; the memorandum from the British Ambassador in Washington (Geddes) to the Under Secretary of State, 26 November 1920, *Foreign Relations, 1920*, vol. III, pp. 723-24; and the Foreign Office memorandum of 30 December, *British Documents*, vol. VIII, pp. 866-69. These restrictions on gold export were provided under

The Anglo-Soviet Accord

❖

Political pulse-taking from the distance of half a century is scarcely possible with any degree of precision, but it is safe to say that among members of Parliament, and among that portion of the public which had any knowledge at all of the Anglo-Soviet negotiations, the detractors of the trade agreement were badly outnumbered. We have already noted who they were—the banking and financial community of the City of London, particularly those members of it, undoubtedly a large number, who either had Russian interests of their own or had clients with Russian interests. Among them were a not inconsiderable number of members of Parliament; most of the members who spoke out against the trade agreement also declared their personal interests as, for example, directors of companies with expropriated Russian holdings. Their views were echoed, and reinforced, on the financial pages and in the editorial columns of the conservative press.

Whatever their feelings regarding the rest of the trade agreement, the various elements of this opposition concentrated their attention on one aspect: the question of debts. Thus, memorials addressed to the Prime Minister from such bodies as the Governing Committee of the Stock Exchange, the chairmen of the major insurance companies, the Executive Council of the Association of the British Chambers of Commerce, the Federation of British Industries, and the Imperial Commercial Association, together with editorial after editorial in *The Times*, the *Morning Post*, and the *Daily Telegraph*, all insisted that the *sine qua non* of any trade agreement must be the complete recognition by the Soviet government of all Russian debts, national, municipal, and private, including the obligation to pay compensation to all foreigners whose properties in Russia had been expropriated.[79]

---

the Gold and Silver Export Control Act of 1920, a measure introduced in order to check the outflow of specie to the United States. (See *Board of Trade Journal and Commercial Gazette*, 10 February 1921, p. 166.) It should be noted that this situation of an enforced discount remained the same after the conclusion of the trade agreement; the British government would not make concessions for Russian gold that it was unwilling to make for other sources (save South Africa).

[79] These protests from the financial community are cited above, n. 48. It should be noted that the list of protesting bodies included some, such as the Federation of British Industries, ostensibly more representative of the world of manufacturing than of that of finance. Was this a case—not uncommon among business pressure groups—of a leadership and its staff not representing the majority of its members? For newspaper editorials, see *The Times*, 28 September, 1 and 5 October, 18 November, 22 and 24 December 1920, 6 and 25 January 1921, and 11 and 17 March,

The Trade Agreement

To these arguments the government had an easy response: it had not by any means forgotten about the debts. Indeed, it regarded them as of very great importance, and in the trade agreement it had secured Soviet recognition of one category of claims—those of private persons—and assurance that all other categories would be "equitably dealt with" in the forthcoming formal peace treaty. As Horne told the House of Commons on 22 December, the government was making its present arrangements without disavowing any of the debts, and without prejudicing future claims. And meanwhile, unless trade were started and the Russian economy thereby restored, there would be nothing for claimants to claim.[80]

Optimism of this sort was cheap, but the predictions of a future settlement were not on the face of it unreasonable, and they could scarcely be proved wrong in advance. The impression is left, however, that the "Russia traders" (as they were called) in the government—Lloyd George, Bonar Law, and Horne—did not worry overmuch about the domestic political price of their inability to secure an effective debt settlement. They were well aware that the business community was by no means united on the question, a fact admitted even by *The Times*, which deplored editorially that "a certain class" of businessmen cherished the delusion that it would be possible to sign a trade agreement with the Soviet government in the existing circumstances.[81] And they were also aware that for every member of Parliament who rose to demand that the government seek Soviet acknowledgment of all Russian debts, there were half a dozen others who spoke out to insist that the economic health of their constituencies depended on the early revival of Anglo-Russian trade.

Those for whom the word "depression" connotes the years 1929-36 tend to overlook the severe but shorter slump in the economies of many of the advanced industrialized states during the early 1920's. Of all those affected, none felt the decline more acutely than the United Kingdom. British prewar prosperity had been due in large measure to the combined circumstances of overseas markets, overseas investments, the predominant position of British shipping, and

---

and the *Daily Telegraph*, 19 November and 17 March. For simple venom, however, the *Morning Post* had no rival. See especially 11, 17, and 20 November 1920, and 7 and 17 March 1921.

[80] 136 *H.C. Deb.*, col. 1875.   [81] *The Times*, 22 December 1920.

the international role of sterling and the City, which had characterized much of the century preceding 1914. With the war came ir-
reversible changes in all of these circumstances: liquidation of many
foreign investments, loss of overseas markets to native industries and
to other foreign suppliers, similar shifts in shipping patterns, and the
growing importance of New York (and the dollar) as a rival to
London as the center of world banking and finance. For a period of
roughly one year, April 1919 through April 1920, Great Britain
shared in the world-wide "boom" brought about by the opportunity
to replenish stocks depleted by four years of war. But the early
summer of 1920 saw a peaking in the demand for British goods and
services, and by late summer a serious decline had set in.[82]

In October 1920 the Ministry of Labour initiated a "Special Weekly
Report on Unemployment" which was circulated to the Cabinet.
Its bleak figures gave Lloyd George ample justification for his instinctive judgment that the financial community's opposition to the
Russian trade agreement was politically of little importance. The
number of wholly unemployed workers who registered at labor
exchanges mounted at a virtually linear rate from 318,096 on 27
August 1920 to 2,077,722—something like twenty percent of the
industrial labor force—the following 20 May; it was estimated that
half again as many workers were working short-time, thus representing disguised unemployment not reflected in the figures. The
Ministry's report for 10 December 1920 stated:

> Unemployment is still increasing in London and in the industrial areas
> of the country generally. The position appears to be growing worse both
> in the cotton and woolen textile industries. Practically all woolen and
> worsted firms are now on short time. . . . The boot and shoe industry has
> reached a critical stage and work people hitherto on short time are now
> being dismissed and factories closed indefinitely. Depression continues in
> the hosiery, lace, and wholesale clothing industries. No improvement is
> reported in either the engineering or shipbuilding industries. . . . In the
> iron and steel trades the position is slightly worse. . . .[83]

[82] For a discussion of the 1919-20 "boom" and subsequent slump, and also of the
longer-range phenomena referred to here, see A. C. Pigou, *Aspects of British Economic History 1918-1925*, London, 1948, *passim*.

[83] "Special Weekly Report on Unemployment. No. 9. Week Ended December
10, 1920," Cabinet paper C.P. 2297; Cab. 24/116. Figures such as those given here
were reported weekly, with occasional compilations covering longer periods. The
August figure is from Report No. 9; the May figure, and the number on short-time
relief, is from Report No. 30, 27 May 1921, C.P. 2997; Cab. 24/123. For a discussion

With unemployment came unrest. Basil Thomson, in a report to the Cabinet at the same time, warned: "Unemployment hangs like a dark shadow over the community. It is far from having touched the bottom, and if we may judge by the present temper of the men, serious disturbances are only a matter of time. . . . As conditions become worse they listen more readily to the doctrines of class war and compare their lot with that of the employers."[84]

In this climate of hardship and anxiety, therefore, the government and especially the Labour movement and the Soviet trade delegation did very effective jobs of selling. In particular, the Soviet contribution to this British domestic process should not be underestimated. As soon as Krasin reached Western Europe—when he was in Scandinavia during the spring of 1920 waiting for permission to enter England—he began placing orders for manufactured goods.[85] He continued to do so after he arrived in the United Kingdom. During the late summer and early autumn, while Kamenev was occupied with (and the British government's attention was focussed on) the Polish crisis, Krasin went about the country conferring with businessmen and bankers, discussing future purchases of British manufactures and even going so far as to place several million pounds' worth of actual or provisional orders for textiles, shoes, and machinery of all sorts—the products of just those British industries which had been hardest hit by the depressed conditions of trade and employment.[86] (It should be noted, as a benchmark, that in

---

of the proportion of the total labor force represented by these figures, see Pigou, *Aspects*, pp. 9-41.

[84] "Report on Revolutionary Organisations in the United Kingdom," no. 84, 9 December 1920; Cabinet paper C.P. 2273, Cab. 24/116.

[85] See in particular the trading agreement signed in Copenhagen on 15 May 1920 between Krasin, representing Tsentrosoyuz, and a consortium of fourteen Swedish concerns, providing for Soviet purchase of manufactured goods in exchange for gold (text in *Dokumenty vneshnei politiki*, vol. II, pp. 516-23). On the same day, also in Copenhagen, Krasin signed a contract with the Swedish firm of Nordquist and Holm, for the purchase of 100 locomotives and an option to purchase 900 more (text in *ibid.*, pp. 523-28).

[86] Cabinet paper C.P. 1890, "Contracts for the Supply of Goods to Soviet Russia," by the Board of Trade, 27 September 1920, listed orders totalling £1,788,500. See reports in *The Times*, 10 and 17 September, the *Daily Herald*, 17 September 1920, and the *Manchester Guardian*, 1 February 1921. The War Office was much exercised that the cloth and shoes which made up a substantial proportion of the Soviet contracts to date would go to clothe the Red Army. The General Staff submitted a memorandum in early October 1920 (circulated by Churchill as Cabinet paper 1936; Cab. 24/112) urging that this trade be stopped but not suggesting how that might legally be accomplished. The matter was raised in Cabinet on 21 September,

1913 4.4 percent of British exports, worth £27,693,000, went to Russia, while 5.2 percent of the United Kingdom's imports, or £40,270,000, came from Russia; allowing for a more than threefold increase in prices since 1913, an equivalent volume at 1920 prices would have been something like £90 and £125 million, respectively.)

These discussions, and Krasin's placement of orders, continued throughout the period preceding the signature of the agreement. Amid the stagnation of postwar British industrial life, they had an energizing effect exceeding by many times the value of the sales involved. A manufacturer subjected to Krasin's blandishments and the prospects of a contract was not likely to join *The Times* in decrying the trade agreement as "infamous" and "dishonourable"— two words used with particular frequency. Nor were his competitors, who hoped for similar contracts, or manufacturers in other industries, who began to calculate the effects on their balance sheets of potential Soviet purchases. Liberal newspapers like the *Daily News* or, especially, the *Manchester Guardian*, with its intimate connections with the metal fabricating and textile industries of the North and the Midlands, were loud in urging the government to make haste in concluding the agreement.

The Labour movement was even more powerfully affected by these considerations. For Labour, Russian trade meant a promise of jobs for thousands of unemployed workers, and the promise of more work and higher pay for those who were employed. In addition, the trade agreement symbolized the coming to terms with the Soviet government for which Labour had worked so long. Therefore, during the autumn and winter of 1920-21, branch meeting of trades unions and the Labour Party throughout Great Britain passed resolutions welcoming the agreement and urging the government to conclude it speedily.[87] On 15 November, before Lloyd George had announced the Cabinet's decision to resume the trade negotiations, the *Daily Herald* warned: "If the negotiations are broken off by the pompous obstinacy of Lord Curzon, it is the British workers, already scourged by unemployment, who will be the chief sufferers." At the

---

but after some confusing discussion it was deferred, never to be brought back (minutes, Cabinet 52[20]; Cab. 23/22). Henry Wilson noted in his diary (entry for 29 September) his disquiet that these transactions seemed to meet with the tacit approval of Lloyd George and the Cabinet.

[87] The *Daily Herald* contained dozens of such resolutions.

same time, the Council of Action, unheard from since early September, called for its local councils to be ready in the event that the Government did not act.[88] In January a special joint conference on unemployment of the Labour Party and the Trades Union Congress resolved that unobstructed trade with Russia would be a principal solution to the nation's economic problems.[89] This unbridled optimism regarding the agreement, universal within the Labour movement, was encapsulated by James O'Grady, the M.P. and trade union leader who had negotiated the prisoner exchange with Litvinov, who flatly told the House of Commons: "I venture to assert that within four weeks from the time of signature it will set the wheels of industry going."[90] Even members of Labour's radical left, who viewed the illness of the British political and economic system as too fundamental to be much affected by enlarged foreign trading, found grounds for optimism. Thus, G.D.H. Cole, the political theorist, contributed an article to the *Herald* asking: "What more congenial employment can [British workers] have under Capitalism than to work, even as the wage-slaves of capitalist employers, in order to supply the needs of the world's only Socialist Republic?"[91]

The government, to its credit, did better than this. During the principal parliamentary debate on the agreement, on 22 December 1920, Sir Robert Horne, who as President of the Board of Trade was the government's spokesman, sharply criticized Labour statements promising an instant resurgence of Anglo-Russian trade to postwar proportions. "I beg the House to believe that it will be years and years before that can happen again," he said. Neither did Horne make claims such as Lloyd George and others had done earlier in the year regarding the Russian wheat, from "bulging corn-bins," that would flow to a hungry Europe. Indeed, he said, Russia had no commodities with which to trade, and could use only gold until its transportation system could be reconstructed. Those who touted the trade agreement as a panacea did a great disservice, Horne warned, and he added: "It is a great pity if any exaggerated account goes out to the country which will excite hopes which can only be falsified."[92]

---

[88] *Ibid.*, 16 November 1920.   [89] *Ibid.*, 28 January 1921.

[90] 136 *H.C. Deb.*, col. 1865 (22 December 1920). In the same vein, *The Observer*, on 21 November 1920, predicted: "In the first twelve months after the reopening of trade Russia would certainly place in this country orders for machinery and manufacture to the tune of at least £100,000,000."

[91] *Daily Herald*, 7 December 1920.   [92] 136 *H.C. Deb.*, col. 1869.

If the government did its best to dispel exaggerated notions concerning the potential economic effects of the trade agreement, it fell victim itself to an ungrounded optimism regarding the agreement's political effects. We have seen this optimism in Lloyd George's statements, early in 1920, regarding the "civilizing" effects on Bolshevism of commerce—of "fighting anarchy with abundance." He held to this theme, with variations, throughout the year. Thus, at his annual appearance at the Lord Mayor's Banquet in November, he maintained that Bolshevism was "such a ludicrous creed, such a crazy creed," that it was only a passing phase which could not survive. What would survive in Russia, however, would be anarchy. Only by bringing Russia back into the economic life of Europe could the effects of anarchy, within Russia and without, be minimized.[93] These arguments were echoed by Horne in the House of Commons on 22 December. For Bolshevism, he said, the British government had only loathing. "But you will not destroy it by isolating Russia. The only way in which you will succeed in killing Bolshevism will be by bringing Russia and the Russian people under the civilizing influence of the rest of the world, and you cannot do that in any better way than by beginning to enter into trade and commerce with them."[94] And again, on 9 March, in the final debate before the signature of the agreement, Horne asserted: "I am all for trading with Russia. I detest, as much as anyone, the crimes committed by the Soviet Government, but it is no good saying you can cut yourself off forever from a country which has gone through such experiences. If you wish to bring it back to civilisation the sooner you trade with it the better."[95]

A more elaborate statement of this argument came from the Foreign Office, in a paper by H.F.B. Maxse on "the political aspect of trading with Russia."[96] Formerly a naval officer attached to the British naval mission in Poland, Maxse had come to the Foreign Office's Northern Department (the renamed Russia Department, which now, however, had responsibility for the Baltic states and Scandinavia as well) in July 1920. He was the author of many— perhaps the majority—of the policy memoranda on Russia written

---

[93] *The Times*, 10 November 1920.
[94] 136 *H.C. Deb.*, col. 1876.   [95] 139 *H.C. Deb.*, col. 537.
[96] Maxse's memorandum, dated 22 November 1920, is in *British Documents*, vol. XII, no. 818.

in the year after his arrival. In the paper in question, dated 22 November, he argued for the conclusion of the trade agreement on the grounds that *whether or not* it produced the economic results that were optimistically expected of it, the British government could reap political benefits.

If it were an economic success, he said—if Anglo-Russian trade were to begin to flow—the political effects within Great Britain would be obvious. Reduced unemployment and a healthier domestic economy would "cut the ground from under the agitator's feet, for social and economic unrest is the best ally of the Soviets in their objective of world-revolution." This would be no small political gain. Within Russia, a successful trade agreement might temporarily strengthen the hand of the Soviet government by raising its prestige. However, Maxse continued, "it will be a very modified and much less dangerous Soviet that survives." Here, again, was the argument about trade's "civilizing role." Increased trade, bringing increased contact with the outside world, will greatly change the position of Soviet local authorities; "they will then have opportunities for local profit, and once they see which side their bread is buttered it is more than probable that the days of the Communist Government as such will be numbered." This was precisely what Lloyd George and Horne had been arguing.

Maxse himself, however, was not optimistic about the economic success of the trade agreement. There were many indications, he wrote, "that the trading agreement by itself will be quite insufficient to promote trade." Little was known definitely about Russia's exportable assets, but after the hardships which had beset the country for so long they could not be plentiful. Therefore trade would have to depend upon Soviet credit, which was virtually nonexistent. The trade agreement said nothing about credit. Maxse characterized it as "essentially permissive"; it would strip away the barriers to trade, but it would supply none of the lubrication necessary to start the machinery of trade moving. It was not improbable that very little trade would result from it. What, in that case, would be the political position?

To answer this question, he said, one must be mindful that Soviet policy sought "to upset the existing political and economic world order, in short world-revolution." For this purpose, the best weapon in the Soviet government's armory was the "cruel persecution" which it, the first proletarian government, suffered at the hands of capitalist governments. This persecution enabled the Bolshevik leaders to mobilize the latent patriotism of the Russian people, while abroad it gave them "a spurious claim on the sympathies of the downtrodden masses"—or those who liked to think of themselves as such. Maxse then came to the crux of his argument:

The permissive trading agreement blunts the edge of this weapon. Whether or not trade results, it will be no longer possible for the Soviet Government to excuse its own failures at home on the ground of capitalist blockade, or to claim sympathy abroad. Once the Soviet Government is robbed of its martyrs' halo it will have to stand or fall on its own merits. If then, no trade results we shall have weakened the Soviet position in Russia, and we shall have drawn the teeth of the most dangerous opponents of our institutions at home. One point however must be emphasized, it is only by absolutely open and honest dealing on our part that this result can be achieved; any restrictive measures on trade, any action which could be construed as a "capitalist boycott" would only strengthen the Soviet hands at home and add fuel to our internal troubles here.

This was an ingenious argument, but, in retrospect at least, it was not impressive: to argue that a scrupulously observed trade agreement would force the Soviet regime "to stand or fall on its own merits" was perhaps even more naive than to argue that trade would bring a transformation of the regime away from revolutionary Bolshevism. Each argument betrayed the Western liberal's failure to understand the forces which bound Soviet regime and society together, and to appreciate the degree to which the regime, even by 1920, could shape the Soviet citizen's perceptions of external reality. Another, somewhat similar, argument should also be noted: that within the Soviet government there was taking place a far-reaching struggle for power upon whose outcome would importantly depend the future evolution of the Soviet system, and the sort of role it would play in international affairs—a struggle which could significantly be influenced by the trade agreement.

Perhaps the most insistent proponent of this argument was E. F. Wise. This was not surprising: Wise was the civil servant most involved in the day-to-day negotiations with the Soviet mission and he had a correspondingly great stake in the successful conclusion of an agreement. Moreover, while engaged in these efforts he was directly attached to the Prime Minister's office, and Lloyd George, of all men, could have been expected to be responsive to arguments based upon the premise of a competition for political power and influence. Wise, in turn, was much influenced by L.G.M. Gall, formerly of the British embassy at Petrograd, then serving as secretary of a special committee charged by Curzon with inquiring into the nature and practices of the Soviet system. This committee—chaired by Lord Emmott, a retired politician and civil servant—did not issue its long final report until late March 1921; when the report did appear it served the immediate purposes of no one, the trade agreement having already been concluded, and it therefore sank into the archives almost without a trace.[97] Gall, however, was a keen observer of Soviet politics, and the analyses he produced as background for the Emmott committee were exactly what Wise needed.

We have already noted Wise's report, in November 1920, of his interview with Krasin in which the Russian warned that unless the trade agreement were quickly concluded, that faction within the Soviet government which opposed the "policy of moderation" would gain predominant influence. In early January he sent forward for the Prime Minister two memoranda by Gall, one on the recently concluded All-Russian Congress of Soviets, the other on the composition of the Presidium of the newly elected Central Executive Committee —early exercises in the now flourishing science of Kremlinology. In his own covering letters, Wise distinguished what he called "two tendencies, the one towards trade and economic development and the other towards propaganda in the East." Gall had divided the Presidium (which was not, after all, anything like as important a body as the Politburo of the Central Executive Committee of the Communist Party) into right, center, and left factions, but he did not

[97] Cmd. 1240 (Russia No. 1 [1921]), *Report (Political and Economic) of the Committee to Collect Information on Russia.* The report was dated 25 February 1921, but not published until late March. It consisted of 115 pages (with 52 pages of appendices) of informed and balanced comment on the Soviet system, clearly all written by Gall. The committee's original terms of reference, dated 17 May 1920, were "To enquire into conditions under which British subjects were recently imprisoned or detained in Russia and generally to obtain information in regard to the economic and political situation in that country." Its interim report on prisoners, issued in November 1920, is cited above, n. 11. It was formally established by Curzon; why, or how much he himself actually had to do with it, remains a mystery. Neither its final nor its interim report attracted more than passing notice from Parliament or the press.

draw specific policy conclusions from this breakdown.[98] Wise did. He wrote:

You may, I think, take it that the Right and Centre are in favour of a Trade Agreement even at the cost of undertaking to stop propaganda. The Right, of which Krassin is a distinguished member, will, I think, carry it out in the letter and in the spirit. The Centre will decide as to whether they carry it out by the course of events. They are genuinely anxious for the internal reconstruction and economic reorganisation of Russia and they realise, as was shown by Lenin's speech on foreign concessions, that they are absolutely dependent on foreign capital and initiative if they are to get a move on within a reasonable time. But they have an eye on the world revolution even if it is delayed for several years. The Left are the out and out Eastern propagandists, whose policy is based on the assumption that Europe is just waiting for them to lead the world revolution.

My impression . . . is that if we can get trade going on a substantial basis we need not worry much about propaganda from the Centre, because the facts of the European situation and the true information which will be brought out of Russia by traders and others as to the mess there . . . will provide a full and sufficient antidote for all the gas which the Left and others may emit.[99]

Wise's advice was that the agreement should be concluded as soon as possible. His own impression was that "the Moderates are still on the top but that they cannot expect to remain there unless they can bring off the Trade Agreement and really re-open trade very rapidly." Lenin, in Wise's estimation, was the "chief exponent" of an early trade agreement. In this instance Lenin had the support of Trotsky, who had his own reasons for giving it. But Lenin would "not be able to resist the Bukharin faction if he is unable to point to some tangible and useful results of his policy."[100]

It is easy to fault this sort of elementary Kremlinology—just, indeed, as it is often easy to fault the more sophisticated Kremlinology of recent years. Clearly the Soviet government was not a monolithic whole, and analyses which assumed that Soviet decisions and actions were the outcomes of a process of political competition were

---

[98] Gall incorporated such analyses into the Emmott committee's *Report*. See his categorization of the Presidium (p. 24), the Council of People's Commissars (p. 29), and the Central Committee of the Communist Party (p. 30).

[99] Wise to Philip Kerr, letter, 7 January 1921; Lloyd George MSS, file F/48/3/32.

[100] Wise to Kerr, letter, 5 January 1921; Lloyd George MSS, file F/48/3/30.

(and are) potentially more useful for policy-making purposes than are explanations of Soviet behavior in terms of decisions by a unitary, rational, purposive entity. Yet Wise and many of his successor Kremlinologists—lacking, in many instances, sufficient information accurately to define individual and organizational roles and goals—tended to endow two or three identifiable factions with the same monolithicism as others ascribed to the whole Soviet government. In the hands of a partisan like Wise, who was himself an advocate of the goals he ascribed to one of the factions, such analyses ran the danger of being seriously misleading, particularly when put forward as justifications for action.

❖

Writing in early January 1921, Wise had good reason to be optimistic that his plea for an early conclusion of the trade agreement would be heeded: Lloyd George himself predicted speed. Indeed, so confident did he feel that the domestic opposition to the agreement was not politically significant that on 23 December he told the House of Commons the government would regard the cordial reception the House had given to Horne's detailed exposition of the trade agreement the previous day as authorization to go ahead and conclude the agreement during the coming winter parliamentary recess.[101]

He was, as it turned out, too optimistic. When Parliament reconvened on 15 February the agreement was still unsigned. Krasin had gone to Moscow in early January with the latest British draft. He was not to return to London until early March. During his absence sporadic exchanges were carried on by telegram, concerning almost entirely, the "propaganda" clause of the preamble.

In his talk with Krasin on 21 December, it will be remembered, Lloyd George had agreed that the Soviet government could list the countries in which it was especially concerned that the other side should stop its hostile activities, just as could the British government. Chicherin did so in a long and disjointed telegram to Curzon on

[101] 136 *H.C. Deb.*, cols. 2118-19. It is noteworthy that on the previous day, despite an announcement by Bonar Law before the beginning of debate that the government had arranged a discussion of the trade agreement for the express purpose of learning whether or not the House approved of the general lines of its approach, only *one* member, Major R. W. Barnett, delivered himself of a speech (as opposed to scattered interjections) attacking the agreement. Barnett was the director of a company whose extensive oilfield properties at Baku had been confiscated by the Soviet government.

4 February.[102] Its bulk was a tedious retracing of the events of the past half year. There would be no need to summarize it here but for the fact that the British response revealed much about the attitudes with which London entered into its accord with Moscow.

Chicherin began by stating that he now agreed that mere reference to the Anglo-Soviet "agreement" of 30 June–7 July would be too vague, leaving too much room for misunderstanding. For illustration he turned to Curzon's notes to him of the previous autumn—"a glaring example" of "false conclusions and unfounded complaints." He listed specific allegations: it was not true, he said, that Soviet troops had been sent to Persia; once Denikin's fleet at Enzeli had been disposed of, "Russian military and naval forces were withdrawn from Persian territory." The Enzeli raid had been solely for the defense of Soviet Russia and could in no sense be regarded as threatening British territory or interests. Neither had Moscow established, as Curzon had alleged, a school at Tashkent to train the peoples of the East in anti-British revolutionary activities. Chicherin also denied any Soviet hand in bringing to power, during the autumn of 1920, a communist regime in Bukhara: "the liberation of the working masses of Bokhara was their own affair." Finally, Moscow had not "tried to conclude a treaty with Afghanistan aimed at stirring up rebellion among the tribes on the Indian frontier."

Here was Chicherin's defense. He now turned to the attack. In those very countries in which the Soviet government had been "falsely accused of hostile actions against Britain," he said, the British government itself was "carrying out a policy of irreconcilable hostility to Russia." In Persia, Asia Minor, the Caucasus, and Afghanistan British and other Allied agents were constantly conspiring against the security of Soviet Russia and Azerbaijan and seeking to undermine the cordial relations which existed between the Soviet government and nationalist elements everywhere. And the anti-Soviet campaigns of neither Piłsudski nor Wrangel would have been possible without the active support of the *Entente* governments; the number of British weapons captured in the Crimea showed just how extensive British support of Wrangel had been.

Therefore, Chicherin concluded, in order to prevent future "mis-

---

[102] Text in *Dokumenty vneshnei politiki*, vol. III, pp. 501-06. The only British newspaper to publish a translation of the entire text was the *Daily Herald*, 9 February 1921. A partial translation appears in Degras, *Soviet Documents*, vol. I, pp. 230-33.

understandings," the two governments should meet for "exhaustive discussion" and should "clearly and unambiguously define their mutual obligations and the scope of their respective interests, from infringing which both sides should refrain." The British draft preamble had stipulated that Moscow should especially respect British interests in "Asia Minor, Persia, Afghanistan and India" (the Caucasus had since been dropped from the British list—and, as we saw in Chapter VIII, written off in London); the Soviet government wished a similar British declaration of non-interference with Soviet interests in the same countries as well as in those states of the former Russian Empire which were now independent. In addition, the British government must promise to "refrain and desist from encouraging or supporting in any way hostile actions against Soviet Russia on the part of Japan, Germany, Poland, Rumania, Hungary, Czechoslovakia, Bulgaria, Greece, and Yugoslavia, and will not interfere in Soviet Russia's relations with other countries nor hamper these relations." Finally, both parties would reciprocally agree to "respect the independence and integrity of Persia, Afghanistan, and of the territory of the Turkish National Assembly"—the last being that controlled by Mustapha Kemal, with whom the British were virtually at war. On this basis, the Soviet government would be happy to conclude the trade agreement.

One consequence of Krasin's return to Moscow was the return of negotiations to the level of ministers of foreign affairs. Chicherin's long and tendentious proposal was addressed, of course, to Curzon rather than to Horne, and it was Curzon who—without consulting the Cabinet—chose not to reply to it at all. In a memorandum to the Cabinet he explained why:[103]

M. Chicherin's latest reply with the new draft preamble which M. Krassin is bringing back is even more impudent and mendacious than his previous performances. He actually declares that there are no Russian forces in Persia, although the Soviet treaty now being concluded with Persia (of which we have the text)[104] provides specifically for their withdrawal: he says that there is no propagandist organisation at Tashkent, although we know everything about it; he declares that the Russians had nothing to do with the revolution in Bokhara, although we have seen all

---

[103] Curzon's memorandum, undated but entered in the Foreign Office file on 14 February 1921, is in *British Documents*, vol. XII, no. 835.
[104] See above, chap. IX.

the telegrams from Moscow directing it; he protests that the Russians have not tried to conclude a treaty with Afghanistan, with a view to inciting trouble on the India frontier, although we are familiar with the exact terms in which this end is sought to be obtained; he denies all connection with the Third International, which is entirely under Muscovite control.

With so colossal and finished a liar it is useless to cope. Nor after my last reply, which I said would be the last of the series,[105] would I propose to do so. The fusilade might go on till the dark-haired among us become grey, the grey-haired white, and the white bald.

So much for Chicherin's prefatory contentions. As for the Soviet additions to the trade agreement's preamble, they were "ludicrous in their absurdity," and were "no doubt introduced as a prize illustration of Soviet humour." The pledges Moscow asked of London, Curzon said, were "incomparably wider and more precise" than those which London sought to obtain. The "brightest touch" was the inclusion of Kemal's territory. "This might be very good fooling," Curzon continued, "but it does not help us to a conclusion, and if we once begin to wrangle about this or that country and this or that phrase we may go on for ever." He proposed, instead, that Britain's specific pledge should be confined to the independent states of the former Russian Empire, and left at that. For the whole enterprise was, in any case, pointless: "We shall keep our undertaking," the Foreign Secretary said, "and the Soviet will not keep theirs; but the conviction has now been forced upon us that that is an inseparable feature of dealing with such people."

Curzon did not go on to ask the obvious question: why, then, deal with such people at all? Presumably he felt that this was a question about which he had already had his say and which the Cabinet had resolved against him, and that there was no use in reopening it. Nor did he go on to make the logical proposal of omitting the whole question of hostile activities and "propaganda" from the trade agreement, and—since trade was presumably judged to be desirable—confining the document simply to commercial matters, perhaps adding general expressions of good will if such embellishment were felt

[105] This "last reply" was a note to Chicherin, 6 January 1921 (text in *The Times*, 7 January), in answer to allegations by Chicherin in a telegram of 31 December (*Dokumenty vneshnei politiki*, vol. III, pp. 440-41; translation in *The Times*, 7 January) that the British government was entirely responsible for the delay in reaching the trade agreement; Curzon called for an end to "barren polemic" and for the speedy return of Krasin, empowered to sign the agreement.

to be necessary. Curzon would not, of course, have been the man to make such a proposition. More than anyone else in the Cabinet he was fearful for British interests in the East. And less than anyone else was he interested in the commercial aspects of the agreement. He closed his memorandum by reminding his colleagues that they had decided that if and when the trade agreement was signed Sir Robert Horne should simultaneously hand to Krasin a letter "indicating in greater detail our evidence as to the steps actually taken by the Soviet Government in propaganda and hostilities in the countries specifically referred to." Such a letter had long since been prepared and kept up to date. It would, he thought, "have a damping effect even upon the humour of M. Chicherin."

The letter in question—printed, along with the trade agreement, as an appendix to this volume—was another demonstration of the detailed knowledge which British intelligence agencies possessed of Soviet intrigues in Afghanistan and along the Indian frontier, a listing of specific activities which Moscow would be expected to stop now that London had made an honest woman of her. As such it was impressive. But as an instrument of British foreign policy it was less so. *The Times*'s comment upon it (it was printed, along with the agreement, on 17 March, the day after the agreement was signed) was apposite: "Excellent in itself, the covering letter seems scarcely to harmonise with the Agreement it covers."[106]

We can imagine that this opinion was shared by the Soviet government. Krasin is said to have telegraphed Moscow after signing the trade agreement that its fruits would depend upon "our prudence, our tact, our self-control."[107] This was precisely the lesson that Curzon hoped he would draw from the British *démarche*. But his colleagues, less interested than he in commerce and industry and more dedicated to revolutionary ends, could with justification draw a very different lesson: that London was more concerned with form than with substance, with a stern public warning to Moscow for the sake of the record rather than with insuring that the complained-of practices actually ceased before the commencement of trade. The Soviet leaders might well, as George Kennan has cogently observed, have regarded such behavior on the part of the British government

---

[106] *The Times*, 17 March 1921.
[107] Excerpts from Krasin's telegram to Moscow appear in his wife's biography of him (Lubov Krassin, *Krassin*, pp. 133-34). It is not among the "intercepts" I have found.

as "a particularly odious bit of Western cynicism and hypocrisy: as efforts to pull the wool over the eyes of the Western public in the hope of getting a greater cut of Soviet trade." Kennan goes on in this same passage to remark on the "shallowness of understanding" of Soviet ambitions and strategies revealed in the concern over "propaganda" which characterized Western—particularly British— negotiations with the Soviet government throughout the 1920's. The Soviet leaders were not just "making propaganda" for their views, Kennan notes, nor were they merely "exhorting people to adopt a different outlook on the ordering of society." They were, instead, systematically attempting to manipulate the political processes of other societies, and organizing groups within them to overthrow their own governments and seize dictatorial power. In emphasizing "propaganda" in their protests, Kennan concludes, "the Western governments were revealing how poorly they understood the nature of the force that was being brought to bear against them, how little they had analyzed it, and how inadequately prepared they were to deal with its methods and tactics."[108]

There is much to this judgment. But in the case of the British government it must be qualified a bit. There were few illusions either among the members of the Cabinet or within the Foreign Office as to Soviet aims and methods. The deadly seriousness with which the Bolshevik leaders pursued their revolutionary goals was amply appreciated in London, even if Soviet power, in the aftermath of civil war and foreign intervention, may have been underestimated. Unquestionably this was true for leading members of the Cabinet. Curzon, certainly, was aware of the dimensions of the Soviet challenge to Britain's imperial role, but he deprived himself of any real effectiveness within the Cabinet because he could propose no counter-measures save an ostrich-like policy of having no dealings with Moscow. Churchill was equally knowledgeable, but he too had deprived himself of effectiveness by preferring, for so long, a military solution which carried with it costs that made it politically unacceptable. Certainly Lloyd George, and probably Bonar Law and Horne, also knew that the Soviet threat was more than simply "propaganda." That the trade agreement and its accompanying letter emphasized

[108] George F. Kennan, *Russia and the West under Lenin and Stalin*, Boston, 1961, p. 199.

"propaganda" owed more to unimaginative draftsmanship than to faulty understanding.

Lloyd George, Bonar Law, Horne, and others in the government *can* be blamed, however, for their naive but apparently quite genuine faith that the processes of opening Soviet Russia to the world—to trade, foreign investment, and normal diplomatic and commercial intercourse—would soften and perhaps even fundamentally change the Bolshevik regime, and would cause it to abandon the revolutionary aims and methods that were so offensive to Western liberal sentiment. No statement better illustrates this attitude than Lloyd George's defense of the trade agreement before the House of Commons on 22 March, eight days after its signature. The Prime Minister called attention to Lenin's moderate speeches at the Tenth Party Congress, which had concluded in Moscow on the 16th, presaging the New Economic Policy, and he commented:

Some of my hon. Friends here have talked about this being a recognition of a Socialist Government, that we were shaking hands with murder, when all the time we are simply converting them. This is a gentlemanly process of instruction which has been going on. . . . The moment [the Soviet leaders] begin to realise they cannot run their country except upon the same principles which have brought prosperity to Russia is to put an end to their wild schemes. . . . From the first moment I have had dealings with them I knew I was dealing with men of great ability, and the only thing that proves they are able men is that they are giving up all these doctrines.[109]

Rather than replying point by point to Chicherin's tendentious telegram of 4 February, Curzon, after an interval of three weeks, sent the Foreign Commissar a brief message saying that "controversial discussion by telegram" could have no practical result: the British government would instead await Krasin's return to London.[110]

The Soviet delegate arrived on 4 March. Before leaving Moscow he told a *Daily Herald* correspondent that he would do his best to be accommodating. On one issue in particular, however, he could

[109] 139 *H.C. Deb.*, cols. 2511-12. For the Tenth Party Congress and the New Economic Policy, see Schapiro, *Communist Party*, pp. 207-09.

[110] Curzon to Chicherin, through Reval as telegram 20, 25 February 1921; *British Documents*, vol. XII, no. 837.

make no concessions: his government could not be held responsible for the activities of the Communist International. "We can't be responsible any more than your Government for the Primrose League, of which Lord Curzon is the head, and which may do us considerable damage," the *Herald* quoted Krasin as saying.[111] The analogy was singularly inappropriate, but Krasin's anxiety was misplaced. There is no evidence that the British side ever again, after Horne's ineffective effort the previous December, attempted to challenge the Soviet government's contention that the Comintern was simply an organization of private persons (some of them, admittedly, holders of high positions in the Soviet Party and government) whose actions in their private capacities were not subject to its control. The final trade agreement deleted altogether even the watered-down reference to private citizens which Lloyd George had proposed during his talk with Krasin on 21 December.[112]

Negotiations between the two sides resumed on Friday, 11 March, a week after Krasin's return. That same day Klishko passed word to Wise that Krasin "could sign anything which he himself approved within the next week." After that, Moscow would assume that difficulties had arisen and the delegation would have to refer matters there, which would raise "the possibility of mischievous intervention" by Chicherin.[113] Whether these fears were genuine or were put forward as part of his negotiating strategy, Krasin was able to sign the agreement well within his week of grace. There remained, in fact, little to be negotiated. Such talks as took place were conducted by Horne, not by the Prime Minister, who presumably felt that all the basic decisions had indeed been made. On Monday, 14 March, Horne got the Cabinet's final approval to go ahead and sign an agreement, warding off a last-minute attempt (presumably by Curzon—the minutes in this as in most instances do not attribute views

---

[111] *Daily Herald*, 17 February 1921.

[112] This deletion may have been the purpose of Krasin's insistence. The draft agreement handed him by the British at the end of November 1920 stipulated that the Soviet government would "restrain" its citizens from anti-British behavior; Krasin's objections caused Lloyd George, during their talk of 21 December, to weaken this to an obligation for both sides to "give all necessary instructions to their nationals" to conform to the agreement's stipulations concerning hostile activities (cited above, n. 74); the final agreement provided only that the two governments should give instructions to *agents* and all persons *under their authority*, presumably only governmental employees in their official capacities.

[113] Wise to Kerr, letter and memorandum, 11 March 1921; Lloyd George MSS, file F/48/3/34.

to persons) to reopen the whole issue of "precedent conditions." Horne's cause was helped by Krasin's having put forward a new version of the preamble which asked not only that Britain refrain from anti-Soviet activities, but that the British government should somehow take responsibility for curbing such activities on the part of Japan, Germany, Poland, Rumania, Hungary, Czechoslovakia, Bulgaria, Greece, and Yugoslavia. This request made it possible for the whole Cabinet, winners and losers alike, to unite in tough-minded indignation.[114]

As a result of this Cabinet meeting, and of another meeting between Horne and Krasin the following day, the list of countries in which each side was, in particular, to refrain from activities hostile to the other was whittled down. In the final version of the preamble the Soviet government declared that it would refrain from encouraging "the peoples of Asia" in actions contrary to British interests, "especially in India and in the Independent State of Afghanistan"; the British government gave a similar undertaking "in respect of the countries which formed part of the former Russian Empire and which have now become independent." This was precisely the formula Curzon had recommended.[115]

Horne and Krasin affixed their signatures to the completed trade agreement early on 16 March.[116] Only hours later, in the Gulf of Finland, Soviet forces launched a crushing attack against the rebellious sailors who had seized the fortress city of Kronstadt on 2 March in the name of a socialism less repressive than Bolshevism, and who had held it in the hope that their cause would gain adherents on the mainland. The coincidence of the two events is worth noting: the British government signed the trade agreement at a time when the future of the Kronstadt rebellion, and therefore of the Soviet regime,

---

[114] Minutes, Cabinet 13(21), 14 March 1921, noon; Cab. 23/24. The Cabinet had before it a memorandum by Horne, 11 March, Cabinet paper C.P. 2706 (Cab. 24/121), to which Krasin's new proposed amendments to the agreement were annexed. Curiously enough, this Cabinet meeting—including Curzon's attempt to reopen the issue of "precedent conditions"—was the subject of a detailed report in the *Daily Herald*, which also reported in detail on the final negotiations between Krasin and Horne. These leaks probably came from the Soviet delegation and (for the Cabinet meeting) from E. F. Wise. See *Daily Herald*, 12, 16, and 17 March 1921.

[115] In his memorandum of 14 February 1921, cited above, n. 103.

[116] *Daily Herald*, 17 March 1921. The next was published as Cmd. 1207, *Trade Agreement between His Britannic Majesty's Government and the Government of the Russian Socialist Federal Soviet Republic*. See appendix to this volume.

was still in some doubt. Within the Foreign Office, there was a strong disposition to delay the signing of the agreement until the outcome at Kronstadt was clear. J. D. Gregory put it in a minute written on 2 March, when first reports of the Kronstadt disturbances reached London: "Even the extreme advocates of the Agreement can hardly want to conclude it with a regime which may conceivably be tottering, while it is the best weapon we can put into the hands of the opposition, namely to hold up the agreement to conclude with them, if *they* prove more respectable than the present gang. To sign now might easily have the immediate effect of restoring the latter's shaken position and giving them a new lease on life."[117]

This view was put forward, and rejected, at the Cabinet meeting on 14 March. Meanwhile, London's official attitude toward the events at Kronstadt was expressed in a telegram on the 11th from Curzon to the British Minister in Helsingfors: "His Majesty's Government are not prepared themselves to intervene in any way to assist the revolutionaries," he said. But in a postscript, marked "very confidential," he added: "There is no reason, however, why you should advise the Finnish Government to take a similar course or to prevent any private societies or individuals from helping if they wish to do so."[118] By the 22nd, however, when the House of Commons met to discuss the agreement the government had signed, the revolt had been decisively crushed. Kronstadt was not mentioned in the debate, but Lloyd George may well have had it in mind when he asserted: "This is purely a trading agreement, recognising the Soviet Government as the *de facto* Government of Russia, which undoubtedly it is. . . . They have as complete control over that vast territory as any Government could possibly have under the present conditions, and therefore they have to be recognised as the de facto Government of that Empire."[119]

The legal significance of *de facto* recognition was soon apparent. On 12 May the Court of Appeals overturned the previous High Court decision awarding a load of Soviet plywood to a British claimant. Since the British government had recognized the Soviet

---

[117] Gregory's minute was on file N 2704/4/38; F.O. 371/6847. For the events at Kronstadt itself, see Paul Avrich, *Kronstadt 1921*, Princeton, 1970. As Avrich makes clear (pp. 118, 123, 212, 219) the anti-Bolshevik emigration viewed the Anglo-Soviet agreement as a "stab in the back."

[118] Curzon to Kidston Helsingfors), telegram 22, 11 March 1921; *British Documents*, vol. XI, no. 706.

[119] 138 *H.C. Deb.*, col. 2506.

government as that having actual authority in Russia, stated the judgment, then the acts of that government—such as confiscation or nationalization—"must be treated here with all the respect due to the acts of a duly recognised foreign sovereign State"; a British court "could not pretend to express an opinion upon the legality or otherwise of its acts."[120] Thus Soviet goods delivered to British purchasers were assured of protection. A subsequent High Court decision, on 13 July, assured similar protection to Soviet gold imported into the United Kingdom as payment for British goods.[121]

These decisions, combined with the British government's action, as soon as the trade agreement was signed, of ending the requirement of export licenses for shipments to Russia, meant that there were no further legal hindrances to Anglo-Soviet trade. Even more important was the symbolism involved. The Soviet mission in London became a permanent, rather than a transient presence. In August a British trade mission opened in Moscow—the first official representation of one of the Great Powers in the Soviet capital since 1918. Here, certainly, was evidence that the communist regime was a lasting force which must be reckoned with. Once the ice was broken, others plunged in: within little more than a year the Soviet government had concluded similar trade agreements with Germany, Italy, Sweden, Norway, Austria, and Czechoslovakia. Bolshevik Russia had taken its most important step toward full membership in the bourgeois community of states it so despised.

[120] Court of Appeals, Aksionairnoye Obschesttvo A. M. Luther v. James Sagar and Co., judgment by Lord Justice Bankes, 12 May 1921 (Law Report, *The Times*, 13 May). The crucial piece of evidence was a statement by the Foreign Office to the defendant's solicitors on 20 April: "I am directed by Lord Curzon of Kedleston . . . to inform you that His Majesty's Government recognises the Soviet Government as the *de facto* Government of Russia." Lord Justice Scrutton, concurring, said that at a time when the British government took so much in taxes and death duties the morality of Soviet confiscations could hardly be questioned!

[121] High Court of Justice, Chancery Division, A. G. Marshall v. Mary Grinbaum and Others (the Bank of England), judgment by Mr. Justice Peterson, 13 July 1921 (Law Report, *The Times*, 14 July). This was a carefully arranged test case (for the arrangements, see Horne's letter to Krasin, 11 January; *British Documents*, vol. XII, no. 828). The judgment was on a narrow issue—that under the laws of Tsarist Russia a holder of state bonds did not have a claim on the state gold reserve as backing for his bonds, and that therefore, assuming that the Soviet government had inherited the Tsarist gold reserves, he had no presently valid claims either—but the judge made clear that he could well have made a determination similar to the one in the Sagar case.

CHAPTER XI

RUSSIA, BOLSHEVISM, AND THE STATECRAFT OF DAVID LLOYD GEORGE

THE trade agreement marked the end of the phase of almost open hostility between the British and Soviet governments, but it ushered in no era of harmony and cooperation. Soviet "propaganda," directed by the Communist International against the institutions of the United Kingdom and the British Empire, did not appreciably slacken. The "formal general Peace Treaty" promised in the preamble to the trade agreement was never drafted. Nor did the Soviet government ever make a payment on the debts it had recognized "in principle." The trade agreement also resulted in precious little trade—only £108 million in the first five years, £282 million in the first decade.

These modest results should scarcely have been surprising, even to David Lloyd George. To many people in Great Britain, including some members of his Cabinet, the agreement was merely a provisional settlement with a provisional government. To Curzon and Churchill it was precisely that—and who can say that in the years following March 1921 they were any less considerable figures than Lloyd George in British politics or foreign policy? Curzon threatened to, and almost did, break off relations with Moscow in 1923; although the Soviet regime was recognized *de jure* by Ramsay MacDonald's short-lived Labour government in 1924, relations were broken off altogether in 1927 by the Conservatives, who once again counted Churchill among their number. Indeed, if the more die-hard Conservatives had had their way, relations would not readily have been restored, as they were when MacDonald returned to office in 1929.

The real significance of the trade agreement was not so much that it marked a coming to terms with the revolutionary regime in Moscow, although undoubtedly it did mean that. It was more important, however, as a part of the general policy of appeasement that marked British conduct of international affairs in the aftermath of the World War. On this touchstone of policy virtually all British politicians—in contrast with virtually all French politicians—could agree. Unlike the French in their relationship to the Germans, the British had no "enemies"; they had had, and would have again, rivals—indeed, in the circumstances which followed the end of the World War, Britain's greatest rival was France, followed closely by the United States. But it made no sense for British statesmen to pursue policies that would make rivals into enemies. Europe's breaches were to be healed. Germany was to be brought back into the community of nations—as was Russia, regardless of the regime which sat in Moscow. This was the vision of David Lloyd George. It was, as well, the vision of lesser men.

✧

It was remarked in the preface that this volume and each of its two predecessors constitute a study of British statecraft in a distinct "policy environment." Volume I, *Intervention and the War*, examined the origins of intervention in Russia as a part of the grand strategy of the war against the Central Powers. Involvement of Allied forces in Russia came about almost imperceptibly, by small increments, often from the execution of particular tasks assigned through military channels by officers acting with only the vaguest sort of political guidance. This absence of political direction was scarcely surprising given the demands of the war in the West—Russia, after all, was only a "side-show"—and given the exhaustion of politicians. Lloyd George, indeed, scarcely appears in Volume I, and when he does it is often in the role of spectator, or rallier of support for "decisions" already "taken" at lower levels. Winston Churchill does not appear at all.

So long as the war was in progress, the problem of Russia was seen as the military problem of trying to reconstitute the Eastern Front against Germany. For a considerable period, even after the signature of the treaty of Brest-Litovsk, it appeared that the Soviet government might give at least tacit cooperation to this effort, but Lenin and his colleagues clearly felt too vulnerable to retaliation from the Germans to allow cooperation for long. When a British force of battalion strength landed at Murmansk in May 1918 to prevent military supplies stored there from falling into the hands of the Germans, it did so with Soviet acquiescence; ten weeks later, when a similar force landed at Archangel for a similar purpose, it came ashore against Soviet opposition and with cooperation from local anti-Bolshevik elements who had scores of their own to settle. The pattern was repeated, in different ways and with different local configurations, across the territory of the former Russian Empire. In such a manner did the civil war, and foreign intervention in it, spring from common origins, the latter fueling the former.

Until the end of the war against Germany, the War Office necessarily had the leading role in the making of British policy towards Russia. The armistice of 11 November 1918 brought no diminution of this role, however. If the presence of British forces in North Russia, Siberia, and (shortly afterward) South Russia and the Caucasus would not have assured the continued predominance of "military" considerations, the coming to the War Office of Winston Churchill surely would have done so. Churchill had vast resources of energy and he threw most of them into the campaign against the Bolsheviks. For six months following the armistice he retained the initiative where Russia was concerned. Others within the government found themselves responding to War Office proposals. The Prime Minister was well aware that this was so and, as we have seen, he grew increasingly distressed by Churchill's role. He himself tried to take the initiative with the Prinkipo proposal and, later with Bullitt's mission. Both were failures, but during the spring of 1919 he got acceptance of the principle that future British contributions to the anti-Bolshevik effort would be sharply limited. Thus, when first Kolchak and then Denikin and Yudenich failed, the way was clear for Lloyd George to move to come to terms with the Soviet regime. That, of course, has been the subject of the present volume.

From June 1919 the dominant figure in Russian policy was Lloyd George. All initiatives flowed from him and from others who owed their positions, and hence their loyalties, predominantly to him— Philip Kerr, Sir Robert Horne, E. F. Wise. To them, and not to the professionals of the Foreign Office, Lloyd George turned at critical moments. The Prime Minister, indeed, had little use for the professionals of the Foreign Office. "Our officials would have helped Wrangel if they had had their way," he told the Cabinet on 17

November 1920 in justification of his having placed the negotiations of the trade agreement in other hands.[1] For Lloyd George the allegation was routine, but it was none the more true by virtue of its repetition. As it happened, the officials of the Foreign Office (or at least those who dealt regularly with Russian problems) would not have helped Wrangel; as we have seen, they strongly argued against any assistance to him. Nor did they differ much from Lloyd George in their assessment either of the "threat" of Bolshevism or of the desirability of coming to terms with the Soviet regime, although they were less sanguine than he over the possibilities and potential impact of trade. By and large, however, they were closer to him on these issues than they were to their own ministerial chief, Curzon. But since the Prime Minister got on so poorly with Curzon he could scarcely have felt much inclined to reach through the Foreign Secretary to employ his staff when there were other channels available. As a result the Foreign Office reacted, wrote analyses, and did battle with other ministries and ministers. But its effect on the overall direction of British policy toward Russia, and often even on the day-to-day details, was not great.

Lloyd George's coolness toward Curzon and (for different reasons) the professional diplomats is one explanation of the Foreign Office's relative lack of importance in making policy toward Russia. Another may be the fact that, like ministries for external affairs everywhere, the Foreign Office was best equipped to handle bilateral relationships of the usual sort, with a British embassy or legation in the other country and an accredited mission from the other country in London. It presided, of course, over the machinery for official bilateral communications. Clearly this system was susceptible to penetration and control by the Prime Minister and his Cabinet, but the very existence of diplomatic machinery, and the volume of day-to-day bilateral traffic it handled, provided sufficient insulation to place a particular bilateral relationship at just that much greater a remove. Anglo-Polish relations were of this sort, as were Anglo-French relations, or even British relations with the short-lived republics of the Caucasus. But there was no British mission in Moscow, and Krasin and Kamenev were highly irregular representatives in London. The Russia Department of the Foreign Office (later, the Northern Department) did not, during the period covered by these three volumes,

[1] See above, chap. X.

have a bilateral relationship to nurture. Thus, aside from their obviously special political importance, Anglo-Soviet relations were especially susceptible to being taken over, even in their day-to-day aspects, by the Prime Minister and his own staff. The eclipse of the War Office[2] and the inability of the Foreign Office to take a lead were accentuated, of course, by the Prime Minister's peculiar faith in the efficacy of trade as a means of both "civilizing" Bolshevism and bringing about the recovery of Europe, and also by the increasing symbolic importance in British politics of relations with Soviet Russia. For these reasons this volume, more than either of its predecessors, has been an account of the statecraft of David Lloyd George.

✧

The accord with the new men in Moscow was the doing of Lloyd George more—by far—than of anyone else. Could lesser men in Great Britain have accomplished the same result? The question is moot. The Conservatives could not. Red-baiting was long popular among back-bench members of the Tory party, and among the constituents responsible for sending them to Westminster—a relatively small proportion of the total British electorate. Conservative prime ministers have been and still are peculiarly sensitive to their imprecations. Labour, of course, saw things differently—but Ramsay MacDonald had things much easier in 1924 when he could portray himself merely as following in and broadening Lloyd George's footsteps. MacDonald, moreover, went out of his way to make plain his distaste for the Soviet regime while at the same time moving to normalize relations with it, just as Lloyd George had done.

It is a commonplace, and no less accurate for being so, that Lloyd George was one of the most calculatingly devious figures in the modern political life of Great Britain or, for that matter, of any other nation. His own defense of his style is often quoted: "I was never in favour of costly frontal attacks, either in politics or war,

---

[2] It should be noted that the War Office still retained substantial *negative* influence, in the sense that objections from Henry Wilson and the General Staff could effectively veto proposals involving the deployment of additional British troops. It was the refusal of the War Office to sanction the despatch of additional forces and, indeed, even the continuation of existing force commitments (such as the garrison at Baku or the North Persia Force), which made Curzon's policies unacceptable to the government.

if there were a way round." A.J.P. Taylor, in his 1961 Leslie Stephen lecture at Cambridge, which is perhaps the best summation of Lloyd George's strengths and weaknesses, remarked:

> He was the leader of a predominantly Right-wing coalition; yet his instincts were all to the Left. He did not browbeat his followers. Instead he led them with much blowing of trumpets in one direction until the moment when they discovered that he had brought them to an exactly opposite conclusion. Conciliation of Germany was prepared under a smoke-screen of "Hang the Kaiser" and "Make Germany Pay." The Soviet leaders were Bolshevik untouchables until the day when Lloyd George signed a trade agreement with them. The trade-union leaders were a challenge to civilisation at one moment; and were being offered whiskey and cigars at the next. Ireland was the supreme example. . . . The Unionists were told that Lloyd George had murder by the throat; and then found themselves called upon to surrender everything which they had defended for nearly forty years. Men do not like being cheated even for the most admirable cause.[3]

Was such subterfuge necessary? Here again the question is moot. Lloyd George was, as R. A. Butler reportedly said of Anthony Eden, "the best Prime Minister we've got." No other Liberal (as Lloyd George once was and again became) could have presided over the House of Commons elected in November 1918—although a fair rejoinder is that no other Liberal would have tried. Among the supporters of the government in Parliament opposition to dealings with the Bolsheviks, as we have seen in all three volumes of the present work, was at nearly all times overwhelming. The same was true, it should be noted, of the supporters of all the other governments on the side which fought the war against the Central Powers, with the exception, perhaps of the Italy of Nitti and Giolitti—and Italy, with its special demands and its special pleading for them could scarcely have taken the lead on an issue in whose outcome the Italian government was as little interested as it was in bringing Russia back into the European system. In appraising Lloyd George's handling of the Russian problem, it is important to keep in mind, therefore, that neither within his own government nor within those of its allies were there leaders who were willing to expend their political capital to achieve the same outcome. At home, those who

[3] A.J.P. Taylor, *Lloyd George: Rise and Fall*, Cambridge, 1961, p. 34.

shared his views came predominantly from the ranks of Labour and the Opposition Liberals, but in the circumstances Lloyd George could scarcely acknowledge the fact. Woodrow Wilson, who perhaps might have been expected to desire the same sorts of outcomes and who joined Lloyd George in pushing Prinkipo in January 1919, proved a weak reed over Bullitt's mission in March. By 1920 he was a broken reed.

Within the British government, there was no one else who would or could take the lead on Russia. Trial balloons, when they came, came largely from Lloyd George himself, as in the case of his Guildhall speech of November 1919. Bonar Law could and did use his enormous political weight to keep his Conservative followers in line, but he would not take the lead. His support was negative rather than positive, derived not from any optimism about future trade with Russia but from a wish to forestall "the effect on the public mind of the imaginary volume of trade which would never take place, but which they *think* would take place if there were an agreement"[4]— in other words, to deprive Labour of a handy stick with which to beat the government. In the circumstances, this role, of following rather than leading, was perhaps sufficient, and all Lloyd George could have asked. One thing is clear: had Bonar Law thrown his weight to the side of Basil Thomson, Henry Wilson, and the other service chiefs in August 1920 over the issue of the presence in England of Kamenev and Krasin (and, by extension, the whole issue of the evolving relationship with the Soviet regime), Lloyd George's government would have collapsed and what now looks like a conspiracy of paranoids would in the history books have the status of Chanak. Indeed, it would have a unique status—the only instance of a military cabal's having brought down a British Prime Minister.

Nor could Lloyd George have expected support from the other principal Conservatives. Chamberlain, Curzon, Long, and Milner were scarcely enthusiastic regarding dealings with the Bolsheviks— indeed, each actively opposed such a course for most, if not all, of the period covered by these volumes. Arthur Balfour, who retained a special interest in the Foreign Office after Curzon replaced him there in August 1919, was more receptive than most of his colleagues to Lloyd George's arguments, but he devoted more energy to rhetorical exchanges with the Bolshevik leadership than he did to

---

[4] See above, chap. X.

actively working toward the political outcomes sought by Lloyd George.[5]

This is not to say that Lloyd George was totally without allies. Robert Horne, able and resourceful and something of a force within the Conservative Party, seems to have shared Lloyd George's faith in the domestic economic effects of an accord with Moscow. To Horne as President of the Board of Trade, and not to Curzon as Foreign Secretary, went the day-to-day negotiation of the trade agreement. Horne was Lloyd George's only real supporter on Russia among Conservative ministers. Among the Liberals in the Coalition Government perhaps only H.A.L. Fisher was in unequivocal agreement, and Fisher's donnish background and position as President of the Board of Education did not give him much weight on such an issue, important though his role was on domestic matters. On some aspects of the Russian problem—those having to do with the British Empire's response to Bolshevik manipulation of Asian nationalism and with the alleged Soviet military threat to India— Lloyd George got important and valuable support from Edwin Montagu, but Montagu's support did not extend to trade relations: here he tended to side with the City banking circles from which his father had made the family's fortune.

The curious thing about the handling of the Russian problem within the British government during the period with which we have been concerned is just how little support—as contrasted with acquiescence—Lloyd George received from his ministerial colleagues. Acquiescence was the key, however. Bonar Law, Chamberlain, Balfour, and most of the other Conservative ministers did not want to end the Coalition—at least not yet. Had they wanted to, the controversy over the expulsion of Kamenev and Krasin in August 1920

[5] Balfour was Acting Foreign Secretary while Curzon was on holiday during late summer 1920. A note from Chicherin contended that since Soviet Russia was a true democracy, it was incapable of engaging in wars of conquest—meaning the Polish venture. Chicherin supported his contention with a detailed statistical argument concerning distribution of wealth within Soviet society. Balfour's reply, in which he subsequently took considerable pride, stated that he was not prepared to doubt, or even to discuss, Chicherin's statistical investigations. And he added: "But speaking for himself, he may perhaps be permitted to observe that he never for a moment questioned the complete efficacy of Soviet methods for making rich men poor; it is in the more difficult, and in Mr. Balfour's view, more important task of making poor men richer that failure is to be feared." (Chicherin to Balfour, 25 August; *Dokumenty vneshnei politiki*, vol. III, pp. 144-47; translation in *The Times*, 27 August. Balfour to Kamenev, for Chicherin, 1 September; *The Times*, 3 September.)

would have given them their chance. Moreover, Lloyd George's less than straightforward style made opposition to his Russian policy much more difficult than it otherwise might have been. At each decisive point he was able to confront his colleagues with arguments which Churchill, Curzon, Long, and the others who actively opposed his policy could not effectively counter, yet more often than not he managed to focus discussion on issues of tactics, leaving veiled his own long-range goals.

Perhaps equally important to Lloyd George's success was the fact that those who opposed his policies could not agree on alternative policies. The anti-Bolshevik crusade Churchill urged with such insistence from the Armistice until Denikin's collapse in the winter of 1919-20 attracted no support from those—and they included virtually the entire Cabinet—who sensed the depths of war-weariness among the working classes of the Western democracies, from whose number would perforce come the forces Churchill would have thrown against the Bolsheviks. On the other hand, Churchill, as Secretary of State at the War Office, would not support the ambitious proposals of Curzon, which would have involved leaving large British garrisons at many points along the eastern and southern peripheries of the Soviet state as a barrier to Bolshevik "expansion," military or doctrinal. And against both Churchill and Curzon the economizers—Chamberlain, Bonar Law, and of course Lloyd George himself, all of whom perforce had to focus their attention on domestic as well as foreign affairs—invariably prevailed.

The prevalence of the economizers against the proposals of Churchill and Curzon, each of which would in their separate ways have required the expenditure of substantial military resources, is one important explanation of why a policy of active anti-Bolshevism was never regarded as a workable possibility. Even more important was the realization—sensed, perhaps, most acutely by Lloyd George, but shared by nearly all his colleagues—that powerful as might be the anti-Bolshevik impulses among the Coalition's parliamentary and popular supporters, the impulse to avoid involving the United Kingdom in another war was stronger still. The Polish-Soviet crisis of July-August 1920 came, therefore, as a moment of truth. The nearer the brink of war appeared, the more forceful were the barriers which kept the British government from being swept over. It was a truth which throughout was plain to Lloyd George.

Yet if considerations such as these explain why military intervention in the Polish-Soviet war was never a serious possibility, even had
the Polish state collapsed, they by no means explain the British
government's active effort to come to terms with the Soviet regime
during 1920. Here we are driven back to Lloyd George's conception
of international affairs and the place of Great Britain within them.
This was essentially a commercial conception, with roots, perhaps,
in Lloyd George's modest origins as a Welsh solicitor. Nations, like
firms or even people, were markets for and suppliers of goods and
services. The imperatives of commerce were commanding upon
nations, just as they were upon individuals. When Lloyd George
spoke, as frequently he did, of the vast potential market of Russia
or the urgent need in the West for Russian wheat and raw materials,
he undoubtedly thought that he was not exaggerating, just as he undoubtedly believed that commerce would be a powerful force for
"civilizing" the Bolshevik leadership.

No nation, moreover, had more reason to play such a civilizing
role than Great Britain, the world's leading commercial and financial power. The epithet "nation of shopkeepers" must not have
seemed opprobrious to Lloyd George: undoubtedly to him it was
accurate, and a reason for others to be envious—so long as the shops
were prosperous. And prosperity would be severely impeded if the
world were to continue to be divided into hostile camps. Russia, and
Germany too, must be brought back into the community of nations,
for without them Europe's recovery would be much delayed. Their
continued isolation would only mean festering grievances—the
causes of future wars. Since the French, an emotional people, could
not (or would not) heal the wounds of Europe the task must fall
to Britain. Here was Lloyd George's notion of "appeasement," which
must have seemed to him a down-to-earth, "concrete" notion. By
contrast, traditional diplomatic concerns, such as rank, power, and
status, must have seemed pale abstractions. Curzon's imperial vision
was just such an abstraction. Curzon was to be humored for what
he represented as a force in British political life. His views, after
all, were shared by many who sat on the benches behind Lloyd
George, upon whom the Prime Minister ultimately depended for
office, but nonetheless Lloyd George must always have felt them
utterly strange.

❖

Curzon thought in abstractions. Lloyd George, when he thought of foreign affairs, thought less of "power" or "interest" or abstractions labelled "Labour," "France," "Poland," or "Bolshevism" than of living, breathing, manipulable persons. Millerand, Nitti, Patek, Grabski, Krasin, Kamenev, all of whom he had met and bargained with, but also Piłsudski, Wrangel, Chicherin, and Lenin—they and others like them constituted "international politics" for Lloyd George, just as Bonar Law, Curzon, Derby, Birkenhead, Churchill, Northcliffe, Asquith, Grey, Addison, Clynes, Hodges, Bevin, Smillie, Lansbury, and a hundred others constituted "domestic politics." Like almost all professional politicians who rise to the top in an open, competitive political system such as that of the United Kingdom or the United States in the twentieth century, Lloyd George looked upon "international politics" as politics abroad, or something like a replication (with, of course, appropriate but simplistic differences) of politics at home. Abroad, just as at home, he usually got what he wanted by a process of cajoling, persuasion, compromise, and concession, or else he adjusted his image of what he wanted to accord with what he found he could get by these means. (This process of adjustment—largely subconscious—gives rise, incidentally, to the not infrequent situation wherein a politician sees no inconsistency in actions and images perceived by others as blatantly inconsistent.)

Undoubtedly Lloyd George's instincts told him that in order to get what he wanted, or in some cases *needed*, for political survival, he had to discover what the other party to a bargaining situation wanted or needed for *his* political survival. This suggests another meaning of his statement that he was "never in favour of costly frontal attacks . . . if there were a way round": every man has his price; one may in the end decide it is too high to pay, but the essence of professionalism in politics is an instinctive disposition to work to discover what that price actually is. Less skilful politicians often do not bother. Their political lives are seldom as long, nor usually do they climb as high.

In principle, this is as powerful a precept when applied to politics abroad as it is to politics at home. But in practice it rarely is. Home politics constantly throw up landmines to threaten a politician's survival, but foreign politics do so only sometimes. When they do, he will give them his full attention. But attention spans are finite in high places as in low, and "out of sight, out of mind" is as true a maxim in politics as in any other pastime. Millerand, Piłsudski, even Lenin, were often out of Lloyd George's mind; Bonar Law, Asquith, Northcliffe, and Clynes were seldom out of his sight. The Prime Minister worried very much about giving Bonar Law what he needed to assure his political survival: that was the best way to assure his own. On far fewer occasions did he need to worry about doing the same for Millerand or Krasin. But he knew that if he pushed Millerand to the wall of the Chamber of Deputies the French premier would not hesitate to strike back in such a way as to endanger his own hold on the House of Commons. And he knew that Krasin was his closest ally within the Soviet government; failure to give him sufficient concessions to sell the trade agreement to his more skeptical colleagues would severely jeopardize the agreement, and Lloyd George had invested enough of his own political capital in bringing about an agreement that failure would have hurt him with the Liberals (both Coalition and Opposition) and with the entire Labour movement while doing nothing to help him on the Right.

For Krasin, and for Anglo-Soviet relations, relatively short spans of attention on the part of the Prime Minister were perhaps sufficient: the two societies intersected, or intermeshed, at only very few points. By contrast, Anglo-French relations were immensely rich, variegated, and complex. During 1920 they were severely stretched over German reparations; they were strained even further over Poland, Wrangel, and the issue of whether or not there should be any contact at all between the Allies and the Soviet government. At each of these crisis-points Lloyd George and Millerand would hurriedly arrange to meet. Their meetings resulted in patched-up solutions—often mere rhetorical bridges that scarcely spanned the intervening chasm. In these alliance politics, as Richard E. Neustadt has shown in another context, the "quick fix" is seldom sufficient.[6] Yet quick fixes were all too inevitably the product of the hurried consultations between the British and French premiers. "Don't overload his politics"; in such words, nearly half a century later, did an adviser caution an American president before a crucial meeting with the head of a major allied government.[7] The advice has wide ap-

[6] Richard E. Neustadt, *Alliance Politics*, New York, 1970, *passim*.
[7] The advisor was Francis M. Bator; the visitor (in August 1967) was Kurt Georg Kiesinger, Chancellor of the Federal Republic of Germany.

plication. But reminders are not enough. Politicians who are justifiably mindful of the play of politics in their own societies, where their own stakes lie, are seldom able to concentrate sufficiently on another politician's stakes in another society to avoid overloading his politics. More often than not, as Lloyd George and Millerand must surely have seen in their relations with one another, the result was to jeopardize the position of each in his own political arena and to make more difficult the achievement of what each sought.

Thus Lloyd George's policy of appeasement was ultimately unsuccessful. In his so-called Fontainebleau memorandum, written at the Paris Peace Conference, he had attempted to outline the basis of a non-punitive peace for Europe.[8] Due to the intransigence of his Allies in Paris and of the Coalition back benches at home, he succeeded only in weakening the enforcement provisions of a basically punitive treaty—perhaps the worst possible outcome. And during the following three years he managed neither to dissociate his government from the main thrust of the French reparations policy nor to blunt its worst excesses, much less to turn that policy around.

His handling of the problem of Russia was not notably more successful. During 1919 and early 1920 he succeeded in extricating the United Kingdom from its disastrous military intervention in support of the Whites in the Civil War. But during 1918 and early 1919, almost certainly against his better judgment, he had allowed colleagues like Milner and Churchill to go forward with that intervention, while at the same time denying them the resources which were its only hope of success. Once he had ended intervention, he moved by means of trade negotiations to reach what was, in effect, a political settlement with the Bolshevik regime. But neither the Bolsheviks nor the Conservative members of his own government viewed the settlement as such. There was a trade agreement, but little trade. And hostility between the two societies, nurtured by the unsuccessful intervention, continued without much abatement and with—at the hands of Lloyd George's successors—even some exacerbation. Long after Lloyd George had left office, these two strands of failure, if they can be called such, came together. In 1939 the British and Soviet governments had it in their power to combine so as to

---

[8] Cmd. 1614, *Memorandum Circulated by the Prime Minister on March 25, 1919* ("Some Considerations for the Peace Conference Before They Finally Draft Their Terms"), 1922.

forestall the outbreak in Europe of a war whose roots were nurtured by the processes of peacemaking twenty years before. They did not. Their mutual distrust was too great.

To point to this subsequent history is not, however, to suggest that Lloyd George should not have pursued the policies he did. Those who sought a more punitive peace with Germany or abstinence from any relations with the Soviet regime in Russia surely would not, if unopposed by "appeasers" such as Lloyd George, have been notably more successful in forestalling the future outbreak of large-scale warfare in Europe. Nor can we easily imagine that had Lloyd George somehow been more forthright in his methods and more candid about his goals the ends he sought would have been more solidly achieved: the forces working against them, both within the Alliance and within his own Coalition, were simply too powerful. About this situation the word "tragic" is not inaptly used.

✧

Of all the statesmen on the world scene during the period covered in the present volume and its two predecessors, Lloyd George had the broadest vision. Those who doubt this should only reread his Fontainebleau memorandum of March 1919 and compare it with the utterances on international affairs of any other political leader of the time. This is not to say, however, that Lloyd George's vision was particularly profound. He could appreciate, and warn against, the dangers inherent in a vengeful peace. But he never adequately appreciated the sources of the French thirst for vengeance. He could see that under the circumstances of 1919 neither Great Britain nor her allies could bring sufficient resources to bear to intervene effectively on the side of the Whites in the Russian Civil War. But he never seemed to comprehend the fundamental gulf which lay between the new rulers of Russia and the rest of the world.

Bolshevism, to Lloyd George, was a collection of "wild theories" by men with their "heads in the clouds." The Bolsheviks themselves were "barbarians." But like other barbarians they could be civilized, and would be if the rest of the world did not permit them to remain in their harmful isolation. The wild theories would be displaced by sensible business methods without which commerce would be impossible. Clearly some of the changes Bolshevism had wrought upon Russian society would remain. But moderation would ultimately prevail, or else the new men would fail and be replaced by men no more palatable to liberal British sensibilities—men like Denikin or Wrangel.

Bolshevism was thus an aberration, but not a permanent one. Its adherents were susceptible to the same sort of influence, even manipulation, as were those of any other wild theory—such as Sinn Fein or the more doctrinaire forms of socialism at home. Henry Wilson noted with horror that Lloyd George behaved as if he were "with *friends*" when he met with Kamenev and Krasin,[9] but the Prime Minister was simply practicing the magic that had worked so many times at home, or within the Councils of the Allies. By 1920 there were few who had not succumbed to it—not for nothing did Keynes call him a "syren" and an "enchantress"[10]—at least until they had a chance to think better of it.

The Bolshevisk representatives in London were among the few who did not succumb. So, of course, were their colleagues in Moscow. Lloyd George paid the Soviet leaders the supreme insult of not taking them seriously. Their hostility to the United Kingdom and the British Empire and their desire to foment revolution throughout its reaches were lumped under the innocuous and misleading heading of "propaganda" and scarcely touched upon in the tough bargaining sessions with Krasin during the winter of 1920-21 before the signature of the trade agreement. Their insistence that Soviet citizens had been deeply harmed by the British and other foreign intervention in the Civil War, and that, therefore, if the Allies pressed claims for the debts of previous Russian governments they would press equally large counter-claims, was never even mentioned in all the Cabinet discussions that paralleled the Anglo-Soviet negotiations. Clearly the possibility of counter-claims was viewed in London simply as a Soviet bargaining measure. Perhaps it was merely that. But the scars left by foreign intervention upon Russian bodies and Bolshevik psyches were all too genuine.

Others within the British government took Soviet hostility and Soviet threats more seriously. Curzon did, as did Churchill, Milner, and Long—the four ministers who dissociated themselves from the Cabinet vote in favor of the trade agreement—not to mention the

---

[9] Cited above, chap. VII, n. 25.
[10] John Maynard Keynes, *Essays in Biography*, New York, 1933, p. 36.

senior officers of the fighting services. Indeed, like so many who came after them, they took the "Soviet threat" too seriously, exaggerating Moscow's capability to bid others, from different nations and with different interests, to do its will. But fearful though they were of Communist revolution both in the Empire and at home, these men offered no program of their own more comprehensive than forswearing contacts with the Bolshevik regime until some undefined future date—if ever—when it would cease its interference in other peoples' politics. Lloyd George viewed their opposition with skepticism, and rightly so. For it subsumed within it opposition to, and in some cases fear of, the Communist and non-Communist Left at home. Maurice Cowling, in his interesting book on *The Impact of Labour 1920-1924,* writes: "From one point of view the history of the Lloyd George Coalition from 1919 until the end of 1922 is the history of serious, powerful and determined attempts at a high level of competence to resolve the major problems which the war had left and the Peace Treaties created." These were, he says, questions "of immense significance" in the context of world politics. But he continues: "In the British context their significance was very different. In British politics they became detached from the world context to which they belonged to become the battle-cries of conflicting groups whose objects were to gain, or keep, political power more even than to settle Europe's problems or to improve Britain's place in it." In the domestic context, Cowling observes, "it was a question not just of the preservation of particular parties but of the implied threat to the social order."[11]

If Lloyd George differed from Curzon, Churchill, Milner, Long, and others in his government in taking less seriously than they the threat seemingly posed by the Bolsheviks, he differed from them also in not taking Labour—and the threat to the social order contained in some Labour rhetoric—very seriously either. The Council of Action offended him not because it seemed an embryo Soviet (as it did to some of his colleagues) but because its principal *raison d'être* was to prevent what he himself had no intention of allowing: British military intervention in the Polish-Soviet war. As he told the House of Commons at the height of the Polish crisis, the Council

---

[11] Maurice Cowling, *The Impact of Labour 1920-1924: The Beginnings of Modern British Politics,* Cambridge, 1971, pp. 108-09.

was "swinging . . . a sledge hammer against an open door . . . merely for purposes of display."[12] Here was contempt, not fear.

Others did not remain so cool. It is no coincidence that at the same time that Field Marshal Sir Henry Wilson was stockpiling weapons in depots across the country for use against the Council and other Labour "extremists" he was also confiding to his diary his suspicion that Lloyd George might be "deliberately shepherding England into chaos and destruction."[13] In this view, of course, Wilson himself was extreme. So were the other officers who seemed to share his nightmare vision. But there were many civilians—mostly Conservative back-benchers, but ministers as well—who deeply feared Bolshevism, who identified Labour's militant and not-so-militant Left with the Bolshevik cause, and who were not a little uneasy that the Prime Minister was so unperturbed. They did not go so far as to break with him over the issue, however. Just as he depended on them for his office, so they also depended upon him. He was their link to the Left that they feared. The Coalition forged by the coupons of November 1918 was based precisely upon the supposition that Lloyd George would attract Labour votes. The supposition was correct. No one within their own ranks could have rendered the Conservatives such a service, just as no Conservative could (as Lloyd George did) resolve the thorny and intractable problem of Ireland. By 1922, however, partly because his contempt for the Left was so apparent, Lloyd George had burnt his bridges to Labour. Then the Conservatives burnt theirs to him.

It was a fate not undeserved. The balancing act had gone on too long, and had become almost an end in itself. For years Lloyd George had held things together. First, in the grimmest months of the war, when the institutions of British government seemed overwhelmed, it was British society itself: as no one else could, Lloyd George bridged the deepening class divisions and secured Labour's continued cooperation (cooperation, some would say, in an enterprise from which Labour stood only to lose). Next it was the combination of military forces, under Foch as generalissimo (a role urged upon him by Lloyd George), which finally broke German

---

[12] Cited above, chap. VI, n. 32.   [13] See above, p. 276.

resistance. Later it was the alliance of governments, each with its different fears and different goals, which made the peace settlements. And throughout it was the uneasy Coalition, to which he owed the premiership. Yet the striking thing about his years as Prime Minister was how little *beyond* holding things together Lloyd George was able to accomplish. In wartime this was accomplishment enough. But in peace it was not. He was premier for four years following the armistice of 11 November 1918. During that time his government was responsible for no program even remotely as significant as his great reforming budgets of the prewar years when he was Chancellor of the Exchequer.

To hold up such a standard is perhaps unfair. The times were too turbulent, and resources too scarce, for great domestic programs. For much of the period 1918-22, Lloyd George's energies were necessarily concentrated on foreign affairs and issues of internal order (Ireland was both). Yet, as we have seen, with the exception of the Irish treaty, his diplomatic accomplishments were not lasting, admirable though the instincts and motivations which underlay them might be. Appeasement was a noble conception. But it could not succeed when others sought vengeance and reparation. There is no evidence that Lloyd George really gave any thought to the long-range consequences of the vastly different approaches to international politics of Britain and France. Nor is there evidence that he appreciated the enormous changes, accelerated by the War, in the international position of Great Britain.

Policy toward Russia was an obvious reflection of the changing nature of Britain's world role. During 1919 and 1920 the British government decided not only to liquidate military intervention in support of the Whites against the Bolsheviks, but also not to take on new commitments in the wake of the White collapse. Finland, the three Baltic republics, the three republics of Transcaucasia, and later Poland and Persia—all either sought British protection against Soviet Russia or else (like Persia) loomed large in the plans of Curzon and others who viewed them as barriers to the spread of Bolshevism into the lands of the British Empire. In none of these cases, however, did the British government take on new commitments. The decisions not to do so amounted to recognition that the United Kingdom (or, for that matter, the British Empire) could do little, if anything, to stem the expansion of Soviet influence and even Soviet control into the surrounding borderlands, much as the peoples of those lands might want to resist it.

If Lloyd George did not seem to appreciate the significance of these decisions, few around him did either. Nor, during the period with which we have been concerned, at least, did others come forward with clear conceptions of Britain's role and the efficacy of British power and influence. If Edwin Montagu and the government of India had a vision of Asian international relationships which relied upon indigenous forces of nationalism, rather than British garrisons, as guarantors against the spread of Soviet influence into the Indian and Arab lands of the Empire, their vision was articulated (and assimilated) only by themselves. The stated rationale for British withdrawal from Transcaucasia and Persia and acquiescence in a Soviet role in Afghanistan as great as Britain's was the budgetary one of scarce resources; if there was a dominating unstated rationale it was Lloyd George's political calculation that the domestic economizers on the one hand, and the Labour movement on the other, were more potent forces to reckon with than were Curzon, Milner, and the other prophets of Britain's imperial role.

All these signs of a drawing down in the East did not, however, imply a realignment of British priorities to emphasize, for instance, a European role. Far from it. Throughout the period between the two world wars—especially, indeed, as Hitler's Germany grew in power and in the force of its demands—there were influential British voices insisting that the United Kingdom's role was oceanic and imperial rather than European. There were others, of course, who urged just the opposite. Not surprisingly, there was no one of any importance in British political life during the period covered by these three volumes—save, perhaps, for Winston Churchill—who grasped both the inevitability and the significance of the choices which eventually would have to be made. The United Kingdom and its Empire together constituted a world power of the first rank. In July 1921, when Lloyd George began the negotiations with Eamon De Valera which eventually gave rise to the Irish treaty, he ordered a big map of the British Empire, "with its big blotches of red all over it,"[14] to be hung on the wall of the room where they

[14] The phrase is from Frances Stevenson's diary entry for 14 July 1921; *Lloyd George: A Diary*, p. 227.

met. We do not know whether the map impressed De Valera as Lloyd George intended it to do, but it clearly impressed the Prime Minister. Not for nearly half a century did the last of those blotches finally fade, and Lloyd George's successors make a clear and unambiguous choice for Europe, but by 1919 and 1920 the fading had imperceptibly started.

The meaning of the incremental decisions of those years was not understood until much later. Indeed, it was the essence of Lloyd George's style of leadership that they should not be understood, and he himself was not much inclined to reflect much upon them. He had more immediate objectives: for instance, holding the Coalition —and also British society—together. Being more immediate, they were more important. All of us like to eat our cake as well as have it. We should not complain when our political leaders do the same. Nor should we downgrade the statecraft of David Lloyd George because he did not succeed in laying the foundation for the international order of compromise and appeasement which he instinctively sought. Despite his flaws, he was the best of his contemporaries. We cannot rightfully ask for more.

APPENDIX

FACSIMILE

16 March 1921

TRADE AGREEMENT BETWEEN HIS BRITANNIC MAJESTY'S GOVERNMENT AND THE GOVERNMENT OF THE RUSSIAN SOCIALIST FEDERAL SOVIET REPUBLIC.

WHEREAS it is desirable in the interests both of Russia and of the United Kingdom that peaceful trade and commerce should be resumed forthwith between these countries, and whereas for this purpose it is necessary pending the conclusion of a formal general Peace Treaty between the Governments of these countries by which their economic and political relations shall be regulated in the future that a preliminary Agreement should be arrived at between the Government of the United Kingdom and the Government of the Russian Socialist Federal Soviet Republic, hereinafter referred to as the Russian Soviet Government.

The aforesaid parties have accordingly entered into the present Agreement for the resumption of trade and commerce between the countries.

The present Agreement is subject to the fulfilment of the following conditions, namely :—

(a) That each party refrains from hostile action or undertakings against the other and from conducting outside of its own borders any official propaganda direct or indirect against the institutions of the British Empire or the Russian Soviet Republic respectively, and more particularly that the Russian Soviet Government refrains from any attempt by military or diplomatic or any other form of action or propaganda to encourage any of the peoples of Asia in any form of hostile action against British interests or the British Empire, especially in India and in the Independent State of Afghanistan. The British Government gives a similar particular undertaking to the Russian Soviet Government in respect of the countries which formed part of the former Russian Empire and which have now become independent.

(b) That all British subjects in Russia are immediately permitted to return home, and that all Russian citizens in Great Britain or other parts of the British Empire who desire to return to Russia are similarly released.

It is understood that the term " conducting any official propaganda " includes the giving by either party of assistance or encouragement to any propaganda conducted outside its own borders.

The parties undertake to give forthwith all necessary instructions to their agents and to all persons under their authority to conform to the stipulations undertaken above.

I.

Both parties agree not to impose or maintain any form of blockade against each other and to remove forthwith all obstacles hitherto placed in the way of the resumption of trade between the United Kingdom and Russia in any commodities which may be legally exported from or imported into their respective territories to or from any other foreign country, and not to exercise any discrimination against such trade, as compared with that carried on with any other foreign country or to place any impediments in the way of banking, credit and financial operations for the purpose of such trade, but subject always to legislation generally applicable in the respective countries. It is understood that nothing in this Article shall prevent either party from regulating the trade in arms and ammunition under general provisions of law which are applicable to the import of arms and ammunition from, or their export to foreign countries.

Nothing in this Article shall be construed as overriding the provisions of any general International Convention which is binding on either party by which the trade in any particular article is or may be regulated (as for example, the Opium Convention).

II.

British and Russian ships, their masters, crews and cargoes shall, in ports of Russia and the United Kingdom respectively, receive in all respects the treatment, privileges, facilities, immunities and protections which are usually accorded by the established practice of commercial nations to foreign merchant ships, their masters, crews and cargoes, visiting their ports including the facilities usually accorded in respect of coal and water pilotage, berthing, dry docks, cranes, repairs, warehouses and generally all services, appliances and premises connected with merchant shipping.

Moreover, the British Government undertakes not to take part in, or to support, any measures restricting or hindering, or tending to restrict or hinder, Russian ships from exercising the rights of free navigation of the high seas, straits and navigable waterways, which are enjoyed by ships of other nationalities.

Provided that nothing in this Article thall impair the right of either party to take such precautions as are authorised by their respective laws with regard to the admission of aliens into their territories.

III.

The British and other Governments having already undertaken the clearance of the seas adjacent to their own coasts and also certain parts of the Baltic from mines for the benefit of all nations, the Russian Soviet Government on their part undertake to clear the sea passages to their own ports.

The British Government will give the Russian Soviet Government any information in their power as to the position of mines which will assist them in clearing passages to the ports and shores of Russia.

The Russian Government, like other nations, will give all information to the International Mine Clearance Committee about the areas they have swept and also what areas still remain dangerous. They will also give all information in their possession about the minefields laid down by the late Russian Governments since the outbreak of war in 1914 outside Russian territorial waters, in order to assist in their clearance.

Provided that nothing in this section shall be understood to prevent the Russian Government from taking or require them to disclose any measures they may consider necessary for the protection of their ports.

IV.

Each party may nominate such number of its nationals as may be agreed from time to time as being reasonably necessary to enable proper effect to be given to this Agreement, having regard to the conditions under which trade is carried on in its territories, and the other party shall permit such persons to enter its territories, and to sojourn and carry on trade there, provided that either party may restrict the admittance of any such persons into any specified areas, and may refuse admittance to or sojourn in its territories to any individual who is *persona non grata* to itself, or who does not comply with this Agreement or with the conditions precedent thereto.

Persons admitted in pursuance of this Article into the territories of either party shall, while sojourning therein for purposes of trade, be exempted from all compulsory services whatsoever, whether civil, naval, military or other, and from any contributions whether pecuniary or in kind imposed as an equivalent for personal service and shall have right of egress.

They shall be at liberty to communicate freely by post, telegraph and wireless telegraphy, and to use telegraph codes under the conditions and subject to the regulations laid down in the International Telegraph Convention of St. Petersburg, 1875 (Lisbon Revision of 1908).

Each party undertakes to account for and to pay all balances due to the other in respect of terminal and transit telegrams and in respect of transit letter mails in accordance with the provisions of the International Telegraph Convention and Regulations and of the Convention and Regulations of the Universal Postal Union respectively. The above balances when due shall be paid in the currency of either party at the option of the receiving party.

Persons admitted into Russia under this Agreement shall be permitted freely to import commodities (except commodities, such as alcoholic liquors, of which both the importation and the manufacture are or may be prohibited in Russia), destined solely for their household use or consumption to an amount reasonably required for such purposes.

V.

Either party may appoint one or more official agents to a number to be mutually agreed upon, to reside and exercise their functions in the territories of the other, who shall personally enjoy all the rights and immunities set forth in the preceding Article and also immunity from arrest and search provided that either party may refuse to admit any individual as an official agent who is *persona non grata* to itself or may require the other party to withdraw him should it find it necessary to do so on grounds of public interest or security. Such agents shall have access to the authorities of the country in which they reside for the purpose of facilitating the carrying out of this Agreement and of protecting the interests of their nationals.

Official agents shall be at liberty to communicate freely with their own Government and with other official representatives of their Government in other countries by post, by telegraph and wireless telegraphy in cypher and to receive and despatch couriers with sealed bags subject to a limitation of 3 kilograms per week which shall be exempt from examination.

Telegrams and radiotelegrams of official agents shall enjoy any right of priority over private messages that may be generally accorded to messages of the official representatives of foreign Governments in the United Kingdom and Russia respectively.

Russian official agents in the United Kingdom shall enjoy the same privileges in respect of exemption from taxation, central or local, as are accorded to the official representatives of other foreign Governments. British official agents in Russia shall enjoy equivalent privileges, which, moreover, shall in no case be less than those accorded to the official agents of any other country.

The official agents shall be the competent authorities to visa the passports of persons seeking admission in pursuance of the preceding Article into the territories of the parties.

VI.

Each party undertakes generally to ensure that persons admitted into its territories under the two preceding Articles shall enjoy all protection, rights and facilities which are necessary to enable them to carry on trade, but subject always to any legislation generally applicable in the respective countries.

VII.

Both contracting parties agree simultaneously with the conclusion of the present Trade Agreement to renew exchange of private postal and telegraphic correspondence between both countries as well as despatch and acceptance of wireless messages and parcels by post in accordance with the rules and regulations which were in existence up to 1914.

VIII.

Passports, documents of identity, Powers of Attorney and similar documents issued or certified by the competent authorities in either country for the purpose of enabling trade to be carried on in pursuance of this Agreement shall be treated in the other country as if they were issued or certified by the authorities of a recognised foreign Government.

IX.

The British Government declares that it will not initiate any steps with a view to attach or to take possession of any gold, funds, securities or commodities not being articles identifiable as the property of the British Government which may be exported from Russia in payment for imports or as securities for such payment, or of any movable or immovable property which may be acquired by the Russian Soviet Government within the United Kingdom.

Appendix

It will not take steps to obtain any special legislation not applicable to other countries against the importation into the United Kingdom of precious metals from Russia whether specie (other than British or Allied) or bullion or manufactures or the storing, analysing, refining, melting, mortgaging or disposing thereof in the United Kingdom, and will not requisition such metals.

X.

The Russian Soviet Government undertakes to make no claim to dispose in any way of the funds or other property of the late Imperial and Provisional Russian Governments in the United Kingdom. The British Government gives a corresponding undertaking as regards British Government funds and property in Russia. This Article is not to prejudice the inclusion in the general Treaty referred to in the Preamble of any provision dealing with the subject matter of this Article.

Both parties agree to protect and not to transfer to any claimants pending the conclusion of the aforesaid Treaty any of the above funds or property which may be subject to their control.

XI.

Merchandise the produce or manufacture of one country imported into the other in pursuance of this Agreement shall not be subjected therein to compulsory requisition on the part of the Government or of any local authority.

XII.

It is agreed that all questions relating to the rights and claims of nationals of either party in respect of Patents, Trade Marks, Designs and Copyrights in the territory of the other party shall be equitably dealt with in the Treaty referred to in the Preamble.

XIII.

The present Agreement shall come into force immediately and both parties shall at once take all necessary measures to give effect to it. It shall continue in force unless and until replaced by the Treaty contemplated in the Preamble so long as the conditions laid down both in the Articles of the Agreement and in the Preamble are observed by both sides. Provided that at any time after the expiration of twelve months from the date on which the Agreement comes into force either party may give notice to terminate the provisions of the preceding Articles, and on the expiration of six months from the date of such notice those Articles shall terminate accordingly.

Provided also that if as the result of any action in the Courts of the United Kingdom dealing with the attachment or arrest of any gold, funds, securities, property or commodities not being dentifiable as the exclusive property of a British subject, consigned to the United Kingdom by the Russian Soviet Government or its representatives judgment is delivered by the Court under which such gold, funds, securities, property or commodities are held to be validly attached on account of obligations incurred by the Russian Soviet Government or by any previous Russian Government before the date of the signature of this Agreement, the Russian Soviet Government shall have the right to terminate the Agreement forthwith.

Provided also that in the event of the infringement by either party at any time of any of the provisions of this Agreement or of the conditions referred to in the Preamble, the other party shall immediately be free from the obligations of the Agreement. Nevertheless it is agreed that before taking any action inconsistent with the Agreement the aggrieved party shall give the other party a reasonable opportunity of furnishing an explanation or remedying the default.

It is mutually agreed that in any of the events contemplated in the above provisos, the parties will afford all necessary facilities for the winding up in accordance with the principles of the Agreement of any transactions already entered into thereunder, and for the withdrawal and egress from their territories of the nationals of the other party and for the withdrawal of their movable property.

As from the date when six months' notice of termination shall have been given under this Article, the only new transactions which shall be entered into under the Agreement shall be those which can be completed within the six months. In all other respects the provisions of the Agreement will remain fully in force up to the date of termination.

Appendix

XIV.

This Agreement is drawn up and signed in the English language. But it is agreed that as soon as may be a translation shall be made into the Russian language and agreed between the Parties. Both texts shall then be considered authentic for all purposes.

Signed at London, this sixteenth day of March, nineteen hundred and twenty-one.

R. S. HORNE.

L. KRASSIN.

DECLARATION OF RECOGNITION OF CLAIMS.

At the moment of signature of the preceding Trade Agreement both parties declare that all claims of either party or of its nationals against the other party in respect of property or rights or in respect of obligations incurred by the existing or former Governments of either country shall be equitably dealt with in the formal general Peace Treaty referred to in the Preamble.

In the meantime and without prejudice to the generality of the above stipulation the Russian Soviet Government declares that it recognises in principle that it is liable to pay compensation to private persons who have supplied goods or services to Russia for which they have not been paid. The detailed mode of discharging this liability shall be regulated by the Treaty referred to in the Preamble.

The British Government hereby makes a corresponding declaration.

It is clearly understood that the above declarations in no way imply that the claims referred to therein will have preferential treatment in the aforesaid Treaty as compared with any other classes of claims which are to be dealt with in that Treaty.

Signed at London, this sixteenth day of March, nineteen hundred and twenty-one.

R. S. HORNE.

L. KRASSIN.

Letter presented to L. B. Krasin by Sir Robert Horne
simultaneously with their signature of the
Anglo-Soviet Trade Agreement on 16 March 1921.

Sir,

In handing over the Trading Agreement between the British Government and the Russian Soviet Government, signed of this date, I am instructed on behalf of his Majesty's Government to bring to the notice of the Soviet Government facts within their knowledge which disclose activities on the part of the Soviet Government in the regions of India and Afghanistan, which are inconsistent with the stipulations in the Agreement, and which therefore must at once be brought to an end if the good faith of the Agreement is to be observed.

The Soviet Government have made no secret, in their public statements and in their official Press, that the main object of their recent policy is the overthrow of British rule in India; and his Majesty's Government have for a long time past been aware of the intrigues in which the Soviet Government, with their agents, subordinates, and associates, have been engaged, by various means and from different directions, for the furtherance of that object.

One channel of approach, to which attention has been particularly drawn as the result of recent negotiations, is that through Afghanistan. His Majesty's Government have the strongest reasons for believing that one of the main objects, on the part of the Soviet Government, of the negotiations that have been proceeding between that Government and the Government of Afghanistan, has been to secure facilities for attacks through Afghanistan against the peace of India.

The Russian envoy at Kabul, Suritz, has made a point, in his negotiations with the Afghan Government, of assistance to be rendered by the Soviet Government to the tribes on the North-West Frontier of India. Throughout the negotiations he has maintained as one of the principal demands to be conceded by the Afghans a guarantee of safe transport throughout Afghanistan without delay of a large number of rifles and large quantities of ammunition for the frontier tribes on the British side of the border. This, as he and his Government cannot fail to be aware, is an act of direct hostility to India; the grant of the guarantee and the grant of facilities by the Afghanistan Government would, as the Afghans know, not be tolerated by the Indian Government; and to instigate the Afghan Government into taking such a step is no less a direct act of hostility. The arrival of arms and ammunition would by itself, as the Soviet Government well know, be almost sufficient to incite the tribes into turbulence and aggression on Indian territory. Not content with this probability, but determined to make sure of the result, the Soviet representative has established communication with the more consistently anti-British of the tribal leaders, and in so doing he has been careful to implicate leading Afghans, notably Nadir Khan, the commander-in-chief, with whom Suritz had a confidential interview when certain tribal *Maliks* had been summoned by the former to Kabul. Nor has Suritz alone been indulging in these intrigues.

Jamal Pasha whose mission to Afghanistan was undertaken with the approval of Moscow as it was felt, no doubt, that his presence would appeal to the religious as well as national sentiment of the Afghans, has been in touch with the tribal leaders and, having been assured that the necessary funds would be supplied by the Soviet Government, has furnished them even larger quantities of munitions than Suritz did. Mahendra Partap, an Indian renegade, who was a German agent during the war, and who accompanied Suritz to Kabul, has been similarly active among the tribes within, as well as without, British limits in a more northerly direction, along the Chitral frontier, Wakhan and on the Pamirs.

Mahendra Partap is but one of the band of notorious Indian sedition-ists, most of whom were German agents, and who have for many years used every means of attacking the British Government in the East. A number of these are now employed under Bolshevist auspices and maintained by Bolshevist funds in disseminating disloyalty in India and fomenting an anti-British feeling in countries contiguous to India, principally in Afghanistan. Among these it is sufficient to name Barkatallah, who accompanied the first Bolshevist envoy, Bravin, to Kabul, and is again there, having accompanied Jamal Pasha; Acharigah and Abbur Rab, who accompanied Suritz to Kabul; Mookerjee, who is with the Central Government in Moscow, and Marabindra Natu Rey, now at Tashkent in Turkestan.

Were nothing known of the present activities of these self-convicted traitors, the fact of their employment by the Russian Government would be enough to cast the gravest suspicion on the good faith of the Soviet Government towards Great Britain in the East. But it is well known that such of these persons as are or have been in Kabul, have been there for the purpose of establishing touch with disloyal elements in India. Rey's presence in Tashkent is due to a more elaborate undertaking of the same nature. At Tashkent is established the advanced base for Indian work, with a political department and a military technical centre; here is provided instruction in revolutionary tactics for all Indians arriving in Turkestan from whatever direction. From this group already emissaries have been dispatched into India through Afghanistan.

If it is contended that a revolutionary base situated so far from the

Indian frontier as Tashkent can threaten no serious danger to India, the reply is furnished by the opinion pronounced by Suritz that Tashkent is only a *pis-aller*; he has declared his conviction that the base will have to be removed to Kabul as soon as circumstances permit; that unless close contact was established by the base with India itself and with the tribes on the India frontier, good work is beyond the power of the base; at Kabul only can its object be achieved.

The intention of the Soviet Government in the matter is disclosed beyond possibility of concealment; it is a point on which Jamal Pasha has received instructions precisely similar to those Suritz is endeavouring to carry out.

Similarly, to facilitate the spread of revolutionary teaching in India, Suritz endeavoured to secure from the Afghans facilities, under treaty rights, for the establishment of printing presses in Kabul, and it is beyond dispute that propaganda in India would be a permanent function of the consulates which he aims at establishing at Kandahar, Ghazni, and Jalalabad. Though in deference to Afghan representations the consummation of these objects also may have been postponed for the present, the intention is plain.

But though Soviet representatives may be unwilling to press the Afghan Government too much on these points at the moment, they have stated that they have already sent emissaries into India to investigate the possibilities of revolutionary work, whether in the Army, among the agrarian or industrial population, or by organizing the Extremist political classes on lines favourable to Bolshevist and revolutionary projects, and that they have received a report from one of these agents to the effect that it only remains for the Central Government at Moscow to sanction the energetic prosecution of activities so incompatible with the generally accepted functions of a diplomatic representative.

Reference has already been made to the recent negotiations for the conclusion of a treaty between the Soviet Government and the Afghan Government; and some of the proposals put forward. It is desirable to summarize briefly the principal grounds for complaint, apart from those already mentioned, which his Majesty's Government find in these proceedings.

The British Government take no objection to the conclusion between the Afghan and Soviet Governments of treaty engagements providing in the usual way for neighbourly relations and commercial intercourse, although they must point out that even the Imperial Russian Government recognized that Afghanistan lay outside its sphere of influence. But the arrangements aimed at by the Soviet Government in recent negotiations provide among other things for gifts of money, munitions, and aeroplanes to the Afghan Government, and for the establishment of Soviet consulates on the eastern borders of Afghanistan.

Whatever view they might in other circumstances possibly have taken of such provisions, his Majesty's Government are compelled in the present instance, bearing in mind the avowed desire of the Soviet Government to overthrow British rule in India, and the fact that Russia has no possible commercial or other interests in eastern Afghanistan, to regard these proposals on the part of the Soviet Government as anti-British measures pure and simple.

Evidence is also not wanting of recent operations even more immediately hostile on the part of the Soviet Government. It is known that Indian revolutionaries have urged the formation of a military centre on the Chitral-Pamir frontier. An Army Order issued by the Soviet authorities has announced the unfurling of the Red Flag on the Pamirs as an indication to the people of India that their deliverance is at hand; and there is reason to believe that a project for action in these regions is now under consideration.

Enough has been said to indicate the general nature of the activities of the Soviet Government upon the cessation of which his Majesty's Government must insist as an essential corollary of the conclusion of any agreement between the two Governments.

(This version, from *The Times*, 17 March 1921, bore no signature)

SELECTED BIBLIOGRAPHY

UNPUBLISHED DOCUMENTS AND PRIVATE PAPERS

The most important unpublished materials used in the preparation of this volume were:

The Records of the Cabinet Office, the Foreign Office, and the War Office in the Public Record Office, London.

The Lloyd George Papers in the Beaverbrook Library, London.

The Curzon Papers, formerly at Kedleston, now in the India Office Library.

The Diary of Field Marshal Sir Henry Wilson in the possession of Major Cyril J. Wilson.

The Papers of Viscount Davidson of Little Gaddesden, now in the Beaverbrook Library.

The Diary of Field Marshal Lord Ironside of Archangel in the possession of Lady Ironside.

The Trotsky Archive in the Library of Harvard University.

Other unpublished materials used were:

The Records of the Department of State in the National Archives of the United States, Washington.

The Bonar Law Papers in the Beaverbrook Library.

The Austen Chamberlain Papers in the Library of the University of Birmingham.

The Hankey Papers in the Library of Churchill College, Cambridge.

The Papers of Edwin S. Montagu in the Library of Trinity College, Cambridge.

The Papers of J. Pierrepont Moffat in the Library of Harvard University.

PUBLISHED DIPLOMATIC PAPERS

Documents on British Foreign Policy 1919-1939, First Series, Vols. I-IV (E. L. Woodward and Rohan Butler, eds.), 1947-52, and Vols. VIII-XIII (Rohan Butler and J.P.T. Bury, eds.), 1958-63, London: H. M. Stationery Office.

Bibliography

Dokumenty i materialy do historii stosunków polsko-radzieckich (Documents and Materials on the History of Polish-Soviet Relations), Vol. III, Warsaw: Polska Akademia Nauk i Akademia Nauk ZSRR, 1964.

Dokumenty vneshnei politiki SSSR (Documents on the Foreign Policy of the U.S.S.R.), Vols. II and III, Moscow: Ministry of Foreign Affairs, 1958 and 1959.

Papers Relating to the Foreign Relations of the United States: 1920, Vol. III, Washington: Department of State, 1936.

PARLIAMENTARY PAPERS

Official Report, Parliamentary Debates: House of Commons.

Official Report, Parliamentary Debates: House of Lords.

Cmd. 300 (1919). *Agreement between His Britannic Majesty's Government and the Persian Government,* 9 August 1919.

Cmd. 587 (Russia No. 1 [1920]), *Agreement Between His Majesty's Government and the Soviet Government of Russia for the Exchange of Prisoners,* 12 February 1920.

Cmd. 1041 (Miscellaneous No. 13 [1920]), *Interim Report of the Committee to Collect Information on Russia,* 4 November 1920.

Cmd. 1240 (Russia No. 1 [1921]), *Report (Political and Economic) of the Committee to Collect Information on Russia,* 25 February 1921.

Cmd. 1207 (1921), *Trade Agreement between His Britannic Majesty's Government and the Government of the Russian Socialist Federal Soviet Republic,* 16 March 1921.

Journal officiel, Chambre des Députés, Paris, 1920.

League of Nations, *The Records of the First Assembly,* Geneva 1920.

League of Nations, *Official Journal,* Geneva, 1920.

BOOKS AND ARTICLES

V. I. Adamiya, *Iz istorii angliiskoi interventsii v Gruzzi (1918-1921 gg.)* (From the History of English Intervention in Georgia, 1918-1921), Sukhumi: Abgosizdat, 1961.

Hassan Arfa, *Under Five Shahs,* London: John Murray, 1964.

Captain Marion Aten and Arthur Orrmont, *Last Train Over Rostov Bridge,* New York: Messner, 1961.

Bibliography

Zourab Avalishvili, *The Independence of Georgia in International Politics, 1918-1921*, London: privately printed, n.d. (*circa* 1941).

Paul Avrich, *Kronstadt 1921*, Princeton University Press, 1970.

James Moncreiff Balfour, *Recent Happenings in Persia*, London: Blackwood, 1922.

Carl Erich Bechofer Roberts, *In Denikin's Russia and the Caucasus, 1919-1920*, London: Collins, 1921.

Max Beloff, *Imperial Sunset*, Volume I: *Britain's Liberal Empire, 1897-1921*, London: Methuen, 1969.

George A. Brinkley, *The Volunteer Army and the Allied Intervention in South Russia, 1917-1921*, South Bend, Indiana: Notre Dame University Press, 1966.

Alan Bullock, *The Life and Times of Ernest Bevin*, Vol. I, *Trade Union Leader 1881-1940*, London: Heinemann, 1960.

Major General Sir C. E. Callwell, *Field-Marshal Sir Henry Wilson, Bart., G.C.B., D.S.O., His Life and Diaries* (2 vols.), London: Cassell, 1927.

Edward Hallett Carr, *A History of Soviet Russia: The Bolshevik Revolution, 1917-1923* (3 vols.), London: Macmillan, 1950-53.

Eber Malcolm Carroll, *Soviet Communism and Western Opinion, 1919-1921*, Chapel Hill: University of North Carolina Press, 1964.

Lt. General Sir Adrian Carton de Wiart, *Happy Odyssey*, London: Jonathan Cape, 1950.

W. P. and Zelda K. Coates, *A History of Anglo-Soviet Relations*, London: Lawrence & Wishart, 1943.

Winston S. Churchill, *The World Crisis: The Aftermath*, London: Thornton Butterworth, 1929.

Margaret I. Cole, ed., *Beatrice Webb's Diaries, 1912-1924*, London: Longmans, 1952.

Richard W. Cottam, *Nationalism in Iran*, University of Pittsburgh Press, 1964.

Council of Action, *Report of the Special Conference on Labour and the Russian-Polish War*, London, 1920.

Maurice Cowling, *The Impact of Labour 1920-1924: The Beginnings of Modern British Politics*, Cambridge University Press, 1971.

Norman Davies, "Lloyd George and Poland," *Journal of Contemporary History*, vol. 6, no. 3, 1971, pp. 132-55.

Viscount D'Abernon, *The Eighteenth Decisive Battle of the World*, Warsaw, 1920, London: Hodder and Stoughton, 1931.

Bibliography

Richard Deacon, *A History of the British Secret Service*, London: Frederick Muller, 1969.

Jane Degras, ed., *Soviet Documents on Foreign Policy*, Vol. I: *1917-1924*, London: Oxford University Press for Royal Institute of International Affairs, 1951.

General A. I. Denikin, *Ocherki russkoi smuty* (Sketches of the Russian Turmoil), Vols. IV and V, Paris, 1924-26.

I. Deutscher, *The Prophet Armed: Trotsky, 1879-1921*, London: Oxford University Press, 1954.

Georges Ducrocq, "La Politique du gouvernement des Soviets en Perse," *Revue du Monde Musulman*, Paris, Vol. 52, 1922, pp. 84-180.

M. K. Dziewanowski, "Piłsudski's Federal Policy, 1919-1921," *Journal of Central European Affairs*, Part I: Vol. X, No. 2, July, 1950, pp. 113-28; Part II: Vol. X, No. 3, October, 1950, pp. 270-87.

Xenia Joukoff Eudin and R. C. North, *Soviet Russia and the East, 1920-1927: A Documentary Survey*, Stanford University Press, 1957.

Nasrollah S. Fatemi, *Diplomatic History of Persia, 1917-1923: Anglo-Russian Power Politics in Iran*, New York: Moore, 1952.

Louis Fischer, *The Soviets in World Affairs: A History of the Relations Between the Soviet Union and the Rest of the World 1917-1929* (2 vols.), London: Jonathan Cape, 1930 (reissued, Princeton University Press, 1951).

F.A.C. Forbes-Leith, *Checkmate, Fighting Tradition in Central Persia*, New York: R. M. McBride & Co., 1927.

W. K. Fraser-Tytler, *Afghanistan; A Study of Political Developments in Central Asia*, 2nd ed., London: Oxford University Press for Royal Institute of International Affairs, 1953.

Paul Gentizon, *La résurrection géorgienne*, Paris: Leroux, 1921.

André Géraud ("Pertinax"), "British Policy as Seen by a Frenchman," *Journal of the Royal Institute of International Affairs*, Vol. IX, No. 2, March, 1930, pp. 154-79.

M. V. Glenny, "The Anglo-Soviet Trade Agreement, March 1921," *Journal of Contemporary History*, Vol. V, No. 2, April, 1970, pp. 63-82.

Stephen R. Graubard, *British Labour and the Russian Revolution, 1917-1924*, Harvard University Press, 1956.

Bibliography

James W. Hulse, *The Forming of the Communist International*, Stanford University Press, 1964.

Harish Kapur, *Soviet Russia and Asia, 1917-27: A Study of Soviet Policy Towards Turkey, Iran and Afghanistan*, London: Michael Joseph, 1966.

Rosa Federovna Karpovna, *L. B. Krasin, sovetskii diplomat*, Moscow: Izd. sotsialno-ekonom. lit., 1962.

Firuz Kazemzadeh, "The Origin and Early Development of the Persian Cossack Brigade," *American Slavic and East European Review*, Vol. XV, No. 3, October, 1956, pp. 351-63.

Firuz Kazemzadeh, "Russia and the Middle East," in Ivo J. Lederer, ed., *Russian Foreign Policy: Essays in Historical Perspective*, Yale University Press, 1962, pp. 489-530.

Firuz Kazemzadeh, *The Struggle for Transcaucasia (1917-1921)*, Oxford: George Ronald, 1951.

George F. Kennan, *Russia and the West under Lenin and Stalin*, Boston: Little, Brown, 1961.

Walter Kendall, *The Revolutionary Movement in Great Britain, 1900-1921*, London: Weidenfeld & Nicolson, 1969.

Aubrey Leo Kennedy, *Old Diplomacy and New (1876-1922)*, London: John Murray, 1922.

John Maynard Keynes, *Essays in Biography*, New York: Harcourt Brace, 1933.

Titus Komarnicki, *The Rebirth of the Polish Republic*, London: Heinemann, 1957.

Joseph Korbel, *Poland Between East and West: Soviet and German Diplomacy toward Poland, 1919-1933*, Princeton University Press, 1963.

Lubov Krassin, *Leonid Krassin: His Life and Work, by His Wife*, London: Skeffington, n.d. (1929).

Marjan Kukiel, "The Polish-Soviet Campaign of 1920," *Slavonic Review*, Vol. VII, No. 22, London, June, 1929, pp. 48-65.

Labour Party, *Report of the Twentieth Annual Conference*, London, 1920.

Labour Party and Trades Union Congress, *The Report of the British Labour Delegation to Russia*, London, 1920.

Edgar Lansbury, *George Lansbury, My Father*, London: S. Low, Marston & Co., 1934.

Bibliography

George Lansbury, *The Miracle of Fleet Street, The Story of the Daily Herald*, London: The Victoria House Printing Co., 1925.

George Lenczowski, *Russia and the West in Iran, 1918-1948*, Ithaca: Cornell University Press, 1949.

Vladimir Ilich Lenin, *Sochineniya* (Works), 3rd ed., 30 vols., Moscow: Gosizdat, 1935-37.

———, *Sochineniya*, 4th ed., 38 vols., Moscow, 1942-50.

———, *Polnoe sobranie sochinenii* (Full Collected Works), 5th ed., Moscow, 1958-.

Émile Lesueuer, *Les Anglais en Perse*, Paris: La Renaissance du Livre, n.d. (1922).

Sir Harry Luke, *Cities and Men. An Autobiography* (3 vols.), Vol. II, *Aegean, Cyprus, Turkey, Transcaucasia, and Palestine (1914-1924)*, London: Geoffrey Bles, 1953.

I. M. Maiskii, "Anglo-sovetskoe torgovoe soglashenie 1921 goda" (The Anglo-Soviet Trade Agreement of 1921), *Voprosy Istorii* (Problems of History), Moscow, May, 1957, No. 5, pp. 60-77.

John Brown Mason, *The Danzig Dilemma: A Study in Peacemaking by Compromise*, Stanford University Press, 1946.

M. Martchenko, "Kutchuk-Khan," *Revue du Monde Musulman*, Paris, Vol. 40-41, September-December, 1920, pp. 98-115.

O. S. Melikov, *Ustanovleniye diktatury Reza-Shakha v irane* (The Origins of the Dictatorship of Reza Shah in Iran), Moscow: Akademiya Nauk SSSR, Institut Narodov Azii, 1961.

William Mellor, *Direct Action*, London: Leonard Parsons, 1920.

Sir Francis Meynell, *My Life*, London: Bodley Head, 1971.

A. M. Mikhelson, P. N. Apostol, and M. W. Bernatsky, *Russian Public Finance during the War*, Yale University Press for the Carnegie Endowment, 1928.

L. I. Miroshnikov, *Angliiskaya expansiya v Irane (1914-1920)* (English Expansion in Iran, 1914-1920), Moscow: Izd. vostochnoii lit., 1961.

B. L. Mogilevskii, *Nikitich* (*Leonid Borisovich Krasin*), Moscow: Gospolitizdat, 1963.

Elizabeth Monroe, *Britain's Moment in the Middle East, 1914-1956*, London: Chatto & Windus, 1963.

Charles Loch Mowat, *Britain Between the Wars, 1918-1940*, London: Methuen, 1955.

Bibliography

Harold Nicolson, *Curzon: The Last Phase, 1919-1925,* London: Constable, 1934.

P. V. Ol, *Inostrannye kapitaly v Rossii* (Foreign Capital in Russia), Petrograd: NFK, 1923.

Leo Pasvolsky and Harold G. Moulton, *Russian Debts and Russian Reconstruction: A Study of the Relation of Russia's Foreign Debts to Her Economic Recovery,* New York: McGraw-Hill, 1924.

"Persia," *Central Asia Review,* Vol. IV, Nos. 3 and 4, London, 1956, pp. 303-16.

Josef Piłsudski, *Erinnerungen und Dokumente* (4 vols., J. P. d'Ardeschah, trans.), Essen: Essener Verlagsanstalt; Vol. II, *Das Jahr 1920,* 1935; Vol. IV, *Reden und Armeebefehle, 1936.*

Richard Pipes, *The Formation of the Soviet Union: Communism and Nationalism 1917-1923,* 2nd ed., Harvard University Press, 1964.

Harry Pollitt, *Serving My Time: an Apprenticeship to Politics,* London: Lawrence & Wishart, 1940.

A. C. Pigou, *Aspects of British Economic History 1918-1925,* London: Macmillan, 1948.

Raymond Postgate, *The Life of George Lansbury,* London: Longmans, 1951.

G. N. Rakovskii, *V stane belykh* (*ot Orla do Novorossiiska*) (In the Camp of the Whites, from Orel to Novorosiisk), Constantinople: "Pressa," 1920.

John S. Reshetar, Jr., *The Ukrainian Revolution, 1917-1920: A Study in Nationalism,* Princeton University Press, 1952.

Lord Riddell, *Lord Riddell's Intimate Diary of the Peace Conference and After, 1918-1923,* London: Gollancz, 1933.

Günter Rosenfeld, *Sowjetrussland und Deutschland 1917-1922,* Berlin: Akademie-Verlag, 1960.

Stephen Roskill, *Hankey: Man of Secrets,* Vol. II: *1919-1931,* London: Collins, 1972.

Chattar Singh Samra, *India and Anglo-Soviet Relations, 1917-1947,* Bombay-London: Asia Publishing House, 1959.

Leonard Schapiro, *The Communist Party of the Soviet Union,* New York: Random House, 1960.

Alfred Erich Senn, *The Emergence of Modern Lithuania,* Columbia University Press, 1959.

Bibliography

J. V. Stalin, *Sochineniya* (Works), Moscow: Gospolizdat, 1947, Vol. IV.

Frances Stevenson (Countess Lloyd George), *Lloyd George: A Diary*, ed. by A.J.P. Taylor, London: Hutchinson, 1971.

———, *The Years that are Past*, London: Hutchinson, 1967.

George Stewart, *The White Armies of Russia: A Chronicle of Counter-Revolution and Allied Intervention*, New York: Macmillan, 1933.

Witold Sworakowski, "An Error Regarding Eastern Galicia in Curzon's Note to the Soviet Government," *Journal of Central European Affairs*, Vol. IV, No. 1, April, 1944, pp. 1-26.

Sir Percy Sykes, *A History of Persia*, 3rd ed., London: Macmillan, 1930, Vol. II.

A.J.P. Taylor, *English History, 1914-1945*, Oxford University Press, 1965.

———, *Lloyd George: Rise and Fall*, The Leslie Stephen Lecture, 1961, Cambridge University Press.

———, ed., *Lloyd George: Twelve Essays*, London: Hamish Hamilton, 1971.

———, *The Trouble Makers: Dissent over Foreign Policy, 1792-1939*, London: Hamish Hamilton, 1957.

Arnold Toynbee, *Survey of International Affairs, 1920-1923*, London: Oxford University Press for Royal Institute of International Affairs, 1925.

Lev D. Trotsky, *Sochineniya* (Works), Vol. XVII: *Sovetskaya respublika i kapitalisticheskii mir* (The Soviet Republic and the Capitalist World), Part II: *Grazhdanskaya voina* (The Civil War), Moscow-Leningrad: Gosizdat, 1926.

Piotr S. Wandycz, *France and her Eastern Allies 1919-1925: French-Czechoslovak-Polish Relations from the Paris Peace Conference to Locarno*, Minneapolis: University of Minnesota Press, 1962.

———, *Soviet-Polish Relations, 1917-1921*, Harvard University Press, 1969.

———, "Secret Soviet-Polish Peace Talks in 1919," *Slavic Review*, Vol. XXIV, No. 3, September, 1965, pp. 425-49.

Général Maxime Weygand, *Mémoires* (3 vols.), Vol. II: *Mirages et réalité*, Paris: Flammarion, 1957.

Trevor Wilson, *The Downfall of the Liberal Party 1914-1935*, London: Collins, 1966.

Bibliography

Arnold Wolfers, *Britain and France between Two Wars*, New York: Harcourt, Brace, 1940.

General Baron Peter Nikolaevich Wrangel, "Zapiski (Noyabr 1916 g.-Noyabr 1920 g.)" (Notes, November 1916-November 1920), *Beloe delo* (The White Cause), Nos. V and VI, Berlin, 1928.

Index

Index

Berkenheim, A. M. (Russian cooperative representative), 39 n. 64

Berliner Tageblatt: cited, 261

Bernstorff, Count Johann von (German Ambassador in U.S. 1908-17): on British code-breaking, 290

Berthelot, Philippe (Quai d'Orsay official): policy re Russia, 29; drafts Lympne declaration re Poland, 217; 147, 152, 210

Bevin, Ernest (dockers' leader): *Jolly George* incident, 51; justifies "direct action," 52; leads delegation to Lloyd George re Polish crisis, 222-24

Birkenhead, Lord (Lord Chancellor): reluctance re trade agreement, 419

Black Sea: British naval forces in, 16, 77, 82, 109, 215, 413

blockade of Russia: end of, 11-12, 98; issue of restoration, 215, 216; Navy continues contra Cabinet policy, 413-14

Bogdanov, A. A. (Bolshevik leader), 89 n. 2

Brest-Litovsk, Treaty of, 34, 90, 455.

Briggs, Lt. General Sir Charles J. (chief, military mission, South Russia), 23

British Empire: effects on of World War, 4; nationalism in, 4-5, 321; in communist ideology, 5; threatened by revolutionary propaganda, 19; assessments of nature of Soviet "threat" to, 100, 321, 461; indivisibility of internal stability, 373; and "propaganda" clause of Anglo-Soviet trade agreement, 375, 424

British Socialist Party, 123

Brock, Vice Admiral Sir Osmond de B. (deputy chief, Naval Staff): and controversy re "intercepts," 280

Browning, Admiral Sir Montague (Second Sea Lord): and controversy re "intercepts," 280

Budenny, General Semen: leads cavalry against Denikin, 66; in Polish campaign, 78, 135, 142

Bukhara: Soviet intentions re, 163, 444; Afghan ambitions re, 347

Bukharin, Nikolai: alleged opposition to Anglo-Soviet trade agreement, 442; 162

Bull, Sir William: represents Soviet trade delegation, 428

Bullitt, William C.: mission to Russia, 11; and Lloyd George's policies, 456, 460

Butler, R. A., 459

Cambon, Jules: and Polish borders, 20

Cambon, Paul (French Ambassador, London), 95, 96

Campbell Krook, Major A. D., 47 n. 88

Carr, E. H.: report re Polish policy, 137-38; on Kamenev, 194-95; on Soviet role in Asia, 339, 342

Carton de Wiart, Brig. General Adrian (chief, British military mission, Warsaw), 27, 28

Caspian Sea: British naval force in, 349;

Soviet naval force in, 349-50; Curzon seeks new presence in, 359-60; 100, 109

Caucasus: *see* Transcaucasian republics

Cecil, Lord Robert (Conserv. M.P. & Chmn., League of Nations Union): urges League action to stop Polish offensive, 56-58; on policy re Polish-Soviet crisis, 178, 179; and League action re Soviet occupation of Gilan, 368

Centre Party: Churchill's plan for, 282

Chaikovsky, N. V., 65 n. 11

Chamberlain, Austen (Chancellor of Exchequer): role in Coalition, 7-8; and policy re Russia, 8, 460; limits aid to Denikin, 11; and Anglo-Soviet negotiations, 100, 101, 102, 105; and controversy re expulsion Kamenev and Krasin, 281, 283; Lloyd George on, 300; opposes trade agreement, 419

Champain, Major General H. B. (commander North Persia Force): and rout of Enzeli garrison, 361-62; 367, 376, 380

Chanak, 460

Chelmsford, Lord (Viceroy of India): opposes Curzon's policies as anti-Islam, 328-29, 394; would rely on nationalism as force hostile to communism, 329, 393; urges competition with Moscow for influence in Afghanistan, 344-46; optimistic re consequences for Persia of British withdrawal, 392-93; on Soviet-Persian treaty, 393

Chicherin, Georgi V. (Soviet Commissar for Foreign Affairs): urges Polish-Soviet negotiations; agrees to British terms re Wrangel, 77; seeks British aid re Bela Kun, 77; on British policy, 117, 118, 120, 121, 124, 162, 163-65, 408, 427; on French policy, 117, 121; on Japan in Siberia, 121; on British vulnerability in Asia, 117, 122; on "trade" vs. "peace" negotiations, 122, 124; agrees to 30 June 1920 British conditions, 144, 148, 399-400; agrees to London conference re Poland, 187, 188-89; urges sending Kamenev to London, 193 n. 18; and Soviet-Polish peace terms, 170, 212-13; and deception re "civic militia" clause, 253, 254, 259, 261; and return of Kamenev, 301; and *Daily Herald*, 271, 284; warns Krasin that ciphers penetrated, 309; warns Curzon against aiding Wrangel's evacuation, 311; on British interests in Transcaucasia, 336; denies responsibility for "Persian Socialist Republic," 371-72; and British prisoners at Baku, 408-09; and final negotiations for trade agreement, 415, 426, 427; replies to Curzon's "propaganda" charges, 443-44; details British anti-Soviet activities, 444-45; statistical defense of Soviet system, 461, n. 5

Chinda, Viscount (Japanese Ambassador, London), 147, 150

Index

Index

Index

Index

Index

Books written Under the Auspices of the Center of International Studies
Princeton University

Gabriel A. Almond, *The Appeals of Communism* (Princeton University Press 1954)

William W. Kaufmann, ed., *Military Policy and National Security* (Princeton University Press 1956)

Klaus Knorr, *The War Potential of Nations* (Princeton University Press 1956)

Lucian W. Pye, *Guerrilla Communism in Malaya* (Princeton University Press 1956)

Charles De Visscher, *Theory and Reality in Public International Law*, trans. by P. E. Corbett (Princeton University Press 1957; rev. ed. 1968)

Bernard C. Cohen, *The Political Process and Foreign Policy: The Making of the Japanese Peace Settlement* (Princeton University Press 1959)

Myron Weiner, *Party Politics in India: The Development of a Multi-Party System* (Princeton University Press 1957)

Percy E. Corbett, *Law in Diplomacy* (Princeton University Press 1959)

Rolf Sannwald and Jacques Stohler, *Economic Integration: Theoretical Assumptions and Consequences of European Unification*, trans. by Herman Karreman (Princeton University Press 1959)

Klaus Knorr, ed., *NATO and American Security* (Princeton University Press 1959)

Gabriel A. Almond and James S. Coleman, eds., *The Politics of the Developing Areas* (Princeton University Press 1960)

Herman Kahn, *On Thermonuclear War* (Princeton University Press 1960)

Sidney Verba, *Small Groups and Political Behavior: A Study of Leadership* (Princeton University Press 1961)

Robert J. C. Butow, *Tojo and the Coming of the War* (Princeton University Press 1961)

Glenn H. Snyder, *Deterrence and Defense: Toward a Theory of National Security* (Princeton University Press 1961)

Klaus Knorr and Sidney Verba, eds., *The International System: Theoretical Essays* (Princeton University Press 1961)

Peter Paret and John W. Shy, *Guerrillas in the 1960's* (Praeger 1962)

George Modelski, *A Theory of Foreign Policy* (Praeger 1962)

Klaus Knorr and Thornton Read, eds., *Limited Strategic War* (Praeger 1963)

Frederick S. Dunn, *Peace-Making and the Settlement with Japan* (Princeton University Press 1963)

Arthur L. Burns and Nina Heathcote, *Peace-Keeping by United Nations Forces* (Praeger 1963)

Richard A. Falk, *Law, Morality, and War in the Contemporary World* (Praeger 1963)

James N. Rosenau, *National Leadership and Foreign Policy: A Case Study in the Mobilization of Public Support* (Princeton University Press 1963)

Gabriel A. Almond and Sidney Verba, *The Civic Culture: Political Attitudes and Democracy in Five Nations* (Princeton University Press 1963)

Bernard C. Cohen, *The Press and Foreign Policy* (Princeton University Press 1963)

Richard L. Sklar, *Nigerian Political Parties: Power in an Emergent African Nation* (Princeton University Press 1963)

Peter Paret, *French Revolutionary Warfare from Indochina to Algeria: The Analysis of a Political and Military Doctrine* (Praeger 1964)

Harry Eckstein, ed., *Internal War: Problems and Approaches* (Free Press 1964)

Cyril E. Black and Thomas P. Thornton, eds., *Communism and Revolution: The Strategic Uses of Political Violence* (Princeton University Press 1964)

Miriam Camps, *Britain and the European Community 1955-1963* (Princeton University Press 1964)

Thomas P. Thornton, ed., *The Third World in Soviet Perspective: Studies by Soviet Writers on the Developing Areas* (Princeton Universiy Press 1964)

James N. Rosenau, ed., *International Aspects of Civil Strife* (Princeton University Press 1964)

Sidney I. Ploss, *Conflict and Decision-Making in Soviet Russia: A Case Study of Agricultural Policy, 1953-1963* (Princeton Universiy Press 1965)

Richard A. Falk and Richard J. Barnet, eds., *Security in Disarmament* (Princeton University Press 1965)

Karl von Vorys, *Political Development in Pakistan* (Princeton University Press 1965)

Harold and Margaret Sprout, *The Ecological Perspective on Human Affairs, With Special Reference to International Politics* (Princeton University Press 1965)

Klaus Knorr, *On the Uses of Military Power in the Nuclear Age* (Princeton University Press 1966)

Harry Eckstein, *Division and Cohesion in Democracy: A Study of Norway* (Princeton University Press 1966)

Cyril E. Black, *The Dynamics of Modernization: A Study in Comparative History* (Harper and Row 1966)

Peter Kunstadter, ed., *Southeast Asian Tribes, Minorities, and Nations* (Princeton University Press 1967)

E. Victor Wolfenstein, *The Revolutionary Personality: Lenin, Trotsky, Gandhi* (Princeton University Press 1967)

Leon Gordenker, *The UN Secretary-General and the Maintenance of Peace* (Columbia University Press 1967)

Oran R. Young, *The Intermediaries: Third Parties in International Crises* (Princeton University Press 1967)

James N. Rosenau, ed., *Domestic Sources of Foreign Policy* (Free Press 1967)

Richard F. Hamilton, *Affluence and the French Worker in the Fourth Republic* (Princeton University Press 1967)

Linda B. Miller, *World Order and Local Disorder: The United Nations and Internal Conflicts* (Princeton University Press 1967)

Wolfram F. Hanrieder, *West German Foreign Policy, 1949-1963: International Pressures and Domestic Response* (Stanford University Press 1967)

Richard H. Ullman, *Britain and the Russian Civil War: November 1918-February 1920* (Princeton University Press 1968)

Robert Gilpin, *France in the Age of the Scientific State* (Princeton University Press 1968)

William B. Bader, *The United States and the Spread of Nuclear Weapons* (Pegasus 1968)

Richard A. Falk, *Legal Order in a Violent World* (Princeton University Press 1968)

Cyril E. Black, Richard A. Falk, Klaus Knorr, and Oran R. Young, *Neutralization and World Politics* (Princeton University Press 1968)

Oran R. Young, *The Politics of Force: Bargaining During International Crises* (Princeton University Press 1969)

Klaus Knorr and James N. Rosenau, eds., *Contending Approaches to International Politics* (Princeton University Press 1969)

James N. Rosenau, ed., *Linkage Politics: Essays on the Convergence of National and International Systems* (Free Press 1969)

John T. McAlister, Jr., *Viet Nam: The Origins of Revolution* (Knopf 1969)

Jean Edward Smith, *Germany Beyond the Wall: People, Politics and Prosperity* (Little, Brown 1969)

James Barros, *Betrayal from Within: Joseph Avenol, Secretary-General of the League of Nations, 1933-1940* (Yale University Press 1969)

Charles Hermann, *Crises in Foreign Policy: A Simulation Analysis* (Bobbs-Merrill 1969)

Robert C. Tucker, *The Marxian Revolutionary Idea: Essays on Marxist Thought and Its Impact on Radical Movements* (W. W. Norton 1969)

Harvey Waterman, *Political Change in Contemporary France: The Politics of an Industrial Democracy* (Charles E. Merrill 1969)

Richard A. Falk and Cyril E. Black, eds., *The Future of the International Legal Order*, Vol. I, *Trends and Patterns* (Princeton University Press 1969)

Ted Robert Gurr, *Why Men Rebel* (Princeton University Press 1969)

C. S. Whitaker, Jr., *The Politics of Tradition: Continuity and Change in Northern Nigeria, 1946-1966* (Princeton University Press 1970)

Richard A. Falk, *The Status of Law in International Society* (Princeton University Press 1970)

Henry Bienen, *Tanzania: Party Transformation and Economic Development* (Princeton University Press 1967, rev. edn. 1970)

Klaus Knorr, *Military Power and Potential* (D. C. Heath 1970)

Richard A. Falk and Cyril E. Black, eds., *The Future of the International Legal Order*, Vol. II, *Wealth and Resources* (Princeton University Press 1970)

Leon Gordenker, ed., *The United Nations and International Politics* (Princeton University Press 1971)

Cyril E. Black and Richard A. Falk, eds., *The Future of the International Legal Order*, Vol. III, *Conflict Management* (Princeton University Press 1971)

Harold and Margaret Sprout, *Toward a Politics of the Planet Earth* (Van Nostrand Reinhold Co. 1971)

Francine R. Frankel, *India's Green Revolution: Economic Gains and Political Cost* (Princeton University Press 1971)